SOFT LOGIC

The Epistemic Role of Aesthetic Criteria

D1522258

Joseph Grünfeld

University Press of America,® Inc.
Lanham • New York • Oxford

Copyright © 2000 by
University Press of America,® Inc.
4720 Boston Way
Lanham, Maryland 20706

12 Hid's Copse Rd.
Cumnor Hill, Oxford OX2 9JJ

Library of Congress Cataloging-in-Publication Data

Grünfeld, Joseph.
Soft logic : the epistemic role of aesthetic criteria / Joseph Grünfeld.
p.   cm.
Includes bibliographical references and index.
1. Knowledge, Theory of—Miscellanea. 2. Logic, Modern—20th century—Miscellanea.
3. Aesthetics, Modern—20th century—Miscellanea. I. Title.
BD161.G78 1999   121—dc21   99—051871 CIP

ISBN 0-7618-1577-5 (pbk: alk. ppr.)

Contents

Philosophy

Acknowledgments

I wish to express my gratitude for permission to reprint: "Fuzzy Logic," "Gadamer's Hermeneutics," "Feyerabend's Flight from Reason," "Kittay's Theory of Metaphor," "Derrida's Deconstruction," "Prerational Power Play," "Art and Alienation," and "Rorty's Pragmatism" appeared in *Science et Esprit*. "Postmodernist Disclosures" appeared in *Iyyun*, and "Acquiring Taste" appeared in *Cybernetica*. "The Philosophical Disenfranchisement of Art" and "Iconology" appeared in *Art and Artists*.

J.G.

Introduction

You don't see something until you have the right metaphor to let you perceive it, Robert Shaw said, echoing Thomas S. Kuhn.[1] Whereas for the critics of Newton gravity was some sort of magical force operating at a distance, Einstein was guided by the metaphor "field of gravity" to develop his theory of relativity. Similarly, unlike Aristotle, Darwin perceived nature as a process and assumed that in order for something to be real, it has to opt for survival. While all such analogical reasoning remains inconclusive, it provides an impulse for further exploration. Aesthetic criteria play a crucial role in all such thinking. Mathematicians are guided by a feeling for fit, order, symmetry and simplicity. You cannot derive such norms from the facts, but they must be relevant, and what is relevant depends at least partly on the circumstances and the intentions of the speaker. That is why philosophers have had a hard time resisting the transition from talking about how things are to how they ought to be. Since there is usually more than just one way to describe a situation, what governs such discourse is rarely recognized as logic at all. As in a game or an artwork, what constitutes a problem in science remains open-ended. Since we are dealing in all such cases with strands of overlapping similarities that make only for family resemblances, standard Aristotelian logic and its principle of noncontradiction do not apply in the usual manner. Whether something constitutes a problem, or whether it is real, cannot be settled without reference to context. A "problem situation" is not something "seen" literally; rather it is a manner of speaking, a metaphor. Tomas Kulka points out that the oddity of metaphor is shown to derive from the fact that metaphorical truth has no counterpart in metaphorical falsehood.[2] Instead of a universal system of valid rules, we get merely limited and contextual similarities. There may be no wrong answer to the question of what is going on in a painting or picture. Aesthetic judgments are based on such partial analogies, which render their conclusions nontransitive. We assimilate a new style by analogy with what we are already familiar, as we do in translation.

What renders language a means of communication is indeed logic but this does not amount to a system of universally valid rules. Rather it is a network of specific conventions that change with context and time. Thus denouncing logocentrism, Derrida does not give up logic altogether. What he questions rather is the existence of a universally binding body of valid rules. Unlike Kratylus who denied the very possibility of telling the truth because you cannot step even once into the same river, Derrida goes on talking, or rather writing. Yet, what is conveyed by such writing is open to endless and conflicting interpretation, and is therefore devoid of precise decidable meaning. We retain the capacity to communicate, but there is no overarching metadiscourse to pinpoint the truth. Since many of the key terms in philosophical discourse, such as time, reality, change, and knowledge, do not attain closure, arguments involving them remain inconclusive. Importantly what is lost in such reasoning is the transitivity of inference. If A merely resembles B, and B resembles C, it does *not* follow that C will always resemble A. And judging by resemblance is much more common than has generally been realized. There is no universal logic anymore than there is one uniform reality to which everything can be reduced. The positist quest for a unified science reflects a craving for simplicity and uniformity that largely ignores the analogical nature of all actual reasoning. Symbolic and metaphorical modes of thinking, which are largely analogical, play a significant role in the interpretation of formal systems. Deductive consistency and precision are due to abstraction from specific content, as are all concepts to some degree. Thus, whether something is true or real can only be decided in context. The more open the concept, the more restricted its relevance. When we follow Wittgenstein's advice to look and see what the word *game* means, we discover that is has diverse uses. As we actually apply such words as *art* or *science*, they are not merely descriptive but evaluative. There is no definite set of criteria separating art from nonart or science from mere opinion. A theory of art or of science as the true statement of their necessary and sufficient properties, their essence or their common denominator is not merely difficult to formulate, it is altogether impossible, since it attempts to state definite criteria of a concept whose very use depends on there being no such set. The concept of science, as its use reveals, is open to diverse contextual and historical interpretations; it reflects the organization of the new, which remains unpredictable. When the role of conceptual innovation was recognized in science, it was also realized that what passes for scientific method changes over time. While Aristotle considered physical motion in the sublunar world to be erratic and unpredictable, for Descartes and Newton it became subject to precise mathematical calculation and measurement.

Scientists believe in binary logic and linear mathematics because they work. They enable us to calculate and reason much more accurately and efficiently than is possible by means of ordinary language. Scientists have learned to trust their mathematics more than their intuition as they discovered that truth in science is not infrequently counterintuitive. Thus, there need be no similarity of structure between the neat world of mathematics and the messy world of facts. Logic is normative: it does not tell us how the world is but how we ought to reason and calculate. Kosko's strategy to legitimize inconsistencies by means of fuzzy logic reduces the effectiveness of such reasoning rather than increasing it. But for binary logic there would be no defuzzification, for fuzzy things are not anymore real than are well-defined precise things. How accurately we define our entities depends on the purpose at hand as well as on our conventions. The language, however, in which we define and interpret any formal system is always a natural language – that is to say, a collection of fuzzy sets that is nonlinear to boot. In such an aggregate, the subsets behave quite differently from the global set, and as a consequence we do not usually know how to solve the nonlinear equations that define the parameters. This also explains why a verbal text permits more than just one interpretation. Stressing the inadequacy of standard mathematics to do justice to the complexities of our world, Kosko proposes a nonlinear version and a fuzzy logic that presumably yields a better fit. But to make a convincing case, he must show how to solve these nonlinear equations. Rejecting the randomness with which probability theory allegedly has filled the world, he substitutes fuzziness. But by ignoring the normative character of logic, he in effect equates fuzzy logic with fuzzy thinking. While he realizes that fuzzy logic won't help us in ethics, he somehow assumes that it is the key to how we ought to reason.

A painting resembles its object but there is no precise point at which this ceases to be the case. Analogy gives us only partial consistency as does metaphor, yet they are also instrumental in changing our intuitions. Resemblance is no less a matter of degree than is relevance, and both are not simply discovered; rather they are established by a particular speaker on a specific occasion. There need not be a similarity of structure between facts and norms, but there must be relevance for an argument to be possible, and what is seen to be relevant on one occasion changes with perspective. Metaphorical truth has no counterpart in metaphorical falsity because metaphors, like analogies, permit us to be inconsistent. The logic of a situation is not something we derive from the facts – it is a norm relevant to the facts, and what is relevant depends on how we view the situation. What we consider to be literal truth on one occasion may become subject to diverging interpretations. Our attempts to settle such ambiguities and inconsistencies lead us to further distinctions in our terminology or notation, and in this manner increase their accuracy. Language is "in order" as long as we take the relevance of our own logic for granted, and novel insights have the potential to modify what we take to be rational or logical. With the invention of non-Aristotelian logics in the twentieth century, our understanding of what constitutes logic has undergone significant change. We have come to realize that *all* logic is potentially metaphorical and analogical, and that what passes for standard logic is only a special case in a vastly more extensive field of analogical and metaphorical reasoning. Being altogether counter-intuitive, Cantor sets or the Heisenberg uncertainty principle can no longer be treated as clear and distinct ideas in the Cartesian manner. One major way of being innovative is to establish relevance by means of analogy and metaphor, and in this manner artists, no less than scientists and mathematicians, invite their respective audiences to notice and take interest in new objects, situations or problems for either aesthetic enjoyment or further research.

Reasonableness

Gelernter argues that the conventional cognitive science view of thought – that thought is merely mental modeling, that it centers on analysis, abstraction, logic, reasoning and problem solving – is dramatically incomplete. The spectrum idea puts emotion at the center of the cognitive universe by making it a glue of thought, the force that engenders creativity. If we add simulated emotion to a computer program, we might arrive at a very close approximation of human thought. Kosko claims that the neat world of binary logic and mathematics does not fit the messy world to which it refers. Scientific claims and statements are inexact because they depend on simplifying assumptions, on a particular choice of words, or on "all things being equal." But logic is normative and there need not be a similarity of structure between the language or mathematical notation we use and the world to which they refer. Logic tells us about how we *ought* to reason, not about how the world is. By the time a scientist masters his way of thinking, becoming comfortable with the hard practice of calculus, he is likely to have lost sight of the fact that most differential equations cannot be solved at all. With computers, trial and error geometry becomes possible, a finer grid giving a sharper picture at the expense of longer computation. The traditional models are betrayed by their linear bias. Amsterdamski emphasized that our idea of rationality is not purely epistemological and descriptive but that it is historically relative and evaluative. The more we know about the world, about ourselves, and about how we come to know anything, the more difficult it is to believe that our knowledge is independent of our biological makeup, the specific functioning of our brains, the language we use, the culture we inherit, and the social institutions in which we live.

We are not in charge of language, Gadamer and Derrida agree. Gadamer, however, conceives the original phenomenon of language as dialogue, whereas Derrida questions Gadamer's claim that hermeneutics is independent of metaphysics. He calls attention to something Gadamer takes for granted, namely the willingness of each partner to be open to what the other has to say. Indeed both Gadamer and Derrida stick to their own language. Derrida's position amounts to a rejection of the very possibility of dialogue, but what he would put in place of Gadamer's "good will" to be understood is never made clear. In rendering what we say intelligible, we must make it accord with some of our beliefs for only through them can we understand at all. Gadamer criticizes traditional hermeneutics for fixing arbitrarily the horizon by which we understand a text. His own horizon metaphor, by contrast, seeks to do justice to the largely unconscious character of all hermeneutical understanding. The problem is that such unconscious behavior does not provide us with any detailed explanations in semantics, history, or hermeneutics. Thus, his "fusion of horizons" is merely a metaphor for denying our ability to understand a text literally. While he emphasizes the metaphorical character of language use, this inevitably remains parasitic on literal meaning. Hermeneutic thinkers can be characterized by their common concern to resist the idea of the human intellect as a wordless and timeless source of insight. They insist that language and history are always both conditions and limits of understanding. But this is not to say that our reflective understanding can never break through a specific linguistic tradition and criticizes it incisively. In rejecting coherence theories of truth, hermeneutical thinkers undermine our ability to render such criticism conclusive. Neither translation across different cultures nor interpretation of ancient texts would be possible at all were it not for a species-specific human nature. While we cannot subject all our beliefs to critical examination at the same time, we do not thereby have reason to discard the ideal of objectivity as one worth pursuing.

Ricoeur denies that there is a general hermeneutics, and holds that each hermeneutic description is only valid in its particular domain. But there can be no conflict of interpretations unless all these domains are subject to the same logic. Quine's empiricism is "soft" because he can never reliably identify the stimulus that prompts assent or dissent by direct observation or in an inductive manner. Responsible beliefs grade off into irresponsible ones, and Quine's empirical checks are unable to draw the line between them. Science and philosophy are artforms, argues Feyerabend, much like painting and literature. All scientists produce works of art, he states, the difference being that their material is thought, not paint, or melodious sound. But while claiming that arguments in favor of a certain world view depend on assumptions that are accepted or rejected for subjective reasons, he himself tries to convince us by argument that a pluralistic and tolerant attitude would be more reasonable. Polanyi's analysis of tacit knowing provides examples of an extension of logic into the informal and contextual. All logical reasoning contains informal elements by means of which it establishes coherence and provides genuine explanations of what is accepted perceptually as well as conceptually. Goodman and Elgin's contention that there are many worlds, is prompted by the discovery of separately adequate but irreconcilable descriptions and depictions. For them, a "world" is an intended manner of speaking or depicting, and what holds such a world together is conceptual relevance. The "rightness" of a world version is a species of soft logic, but beyond calculable fuzzy logic we lose our ability to delineate such constructions. Their relevance is no less metaphorical than is the "given" world that Goodman and Elgin reject.

Metaphor

Metaphor could be defined as figurative language, which has the effect of drawing our attention to non-encoded similarities. Since there is a simultaneous awareness of both the language and what it represents, metaphor enables us to conceive more than we can currently say. The subsidiary subject "organizes" one's thought about the principal subject in a new way, and this operation makes metaphor irreducible to any one literal formulation. We need metaphor because in some cases it is the only way of saying what we mean. Lakoff and Johnson argue that our ordinary conceptual system, in terms of which we both think and act, is fundamentally metaphorical. Metaphors play a crucial role in the construction of our social and political reality, yet they are typically viewed within philosophy as matters of mere language. Metaphor is one of our most important tools for understanding partially what cannot be understood totally: our feelings, aesthetic experiences, moral practices, and spiritual awareness. Truth does not form a conceptual system but emerges from more or less local coherences. Kittay's perspective interpretation of metaphor does not permit her to decide which terms are to be understood metaphorically and which are to be taken literally. She speaks of the "furniture of our mind" to illustrate the weakly cohesive set to which such relations belong. But she admits that the various relations she describes cannot be regarded as definite, and this makes her theory of metaphor inoperative. It amounts to taking metaphorical understanding as the model for scientific knowledge. The problem with Kittay's metaphorical theory of language and of metaphor in general is that they are literally false and logically inconsistent. Hausman believes that appropriateness in metaphors cannot be justified by mere acceptability of further linguistic data or perspectives. Given the strong sense of "creativity" on which he insists, his realism is designed to explain the continuity of reference through time. But while he focuses on the conditions of intelligibility that render future growth possible, this can only be realized by hindsight. Creativity remains relative to a historical tradition, and all that metaphors finally accomplish is a modification, however radical, of some discourse or style.

Deconstruction

By deconstructing the either/or logic of noncontradiction that dominates the Western tradition, Derrida attempts to elaborate the "other" logic. Debunking the old traditions, however, he becomes victim of the restrictive binary logic he likes to belittle. Thus, deconstruction's inability to monitor the quality of criticism turns out to be a serious omission. Ashmore argues that a deconstruction of deconstruction does not just cancel things out but throws doubt upon the notion of an objective world. Experimentation with self-referential techniques has been a staple of twentieth-century avant-gardes in literature, painting, drama, and film. His concern is to deconstruct the theory and practice of level separation, emphasizing the fundamental uncertainty of discourse. He prefers to cultivate this limitlessness as a new pragmatic pluralism: a pluralism that recognizes itself. Derrida questions the tradition of philosophy as an autonomous discipline, the pursuit of a timeless self-validating truth. But attempting to deconstruct the rationalist philosophical tradition, he wants at the same time to retain its critical authority. Since deconstruction does not amount to a method, he is incapable of preferring one reading of the text to another. When deconstruction sets itself up as the antithesis of philosophical reason, it becomes self-destructive and pointless. Although displacement is not explicitly discussed in Derrida's writings, it is central to his de-centering mode of critique. Displacement is above all about women, the unconscious and Jewishness, for these are all exemplary instances of the marginal. His own writing proceeds by means of contamination, a discontinuous model of innovation and change, as happens when the analogy is weak. Lines of binary logic that had been associated with writing are loosened up by the vagueness of style. Since all communication is necessarily modeled in the decoder's way, Derrida's theory of deconstruction makes no sense unless some network of difference is already in place. The problem then becomes to demonstrate that any one established scheme for analyzing or interpreting familiar phenomena is more adequate than another. While opposing the pretensions of totalizing any system of differences imposed on the ever-changing human experiences, he fails to show that such a difference makes a difference.

Postmodernism

Spariosu claims that a proper understanding of the concepts of power and play reflects the polarized character of Western mentality, which since its origin in ancient Greece has altered between a prerational and a rational meaning. Prerational thought conceives of play as a manifestation of power in its innocent form, with its sheer delight in emotional release and raw arbitrary violence. The prerational mentality does not disappear with the emergence of the rational one but becomes submerged and repressed. Spariosu admits, however, that society has a vested interest in rational thought because it assures order, stability, predictability, and facility of communication. Megill shows how, under modern conditions, Nietzsche's will to power becomes self-defeating. His approach to Nietzsche, Heidegger, and Foucault is a product of his reading of Derrida. Nietzsche and his followers call certainty into question, and return us to a situation where there is no longer one, single, literal truth, that is, one privileged meaning. We ought to look with suspicion at the notion of a single, privileged truth and the corresponding distinction between possessors of such truth – the chosen – and those who are not chosen. Such exclusion becomes unbearable when each community has the power to destroy the other as increasingly is becoming the case. Cahoone argues that modernity is eroding its own foundations, and he identifies this self-negating strain with subjectivism, which he believes we must overcome. Preferring the Aristotelian tradition, according to which the knower and the known exhibit an internal relation, he realizes that subjectivism cleared the way for modern science by separating science from religion, and by making possible their simultaneous retention. What he seems to forget, however, is that

Aristotelianism was defeated by modern science – and by the subject-ivism that made it possible – for good reasons. Postmodernism implies a contradiction of the modern without any transcendence of it. In such contexts everything becomes surface, and objectivity and authority are lost: even grammar falls apart. Fashion is now an overriding subjective code. It provides the dream images of the objective, albeit in the repressed and distorted form available in a commodity society. The televised and the untelevised are inseparable, and filming becomes a postmodern displacement of metaphysics. Decentered, allegorical, schizophrenic – however we choose to diagnose its symptoms – post-modernism is usually treated, by its protagonists and antagonists alike, as a crisis in Western European institutions. Symptoms of our loss of mastery are apparent everywhere in cultural activity today, and nowhere more than in the visual arts. Collage's heterogeneity produces a signification that can be neither univocal nor stable; each cited element breaks the continuity or the hierarchy of discourse. This leads to a double meaning: That of fragment perceived in relation to its text of origin, and that of the same fragment as incorporated into a new whole, a different totality. The increase in fragmentation and privat-ization of modern literature – its disintegration into a host of distinct styles and mannerisms – foreshadows deeper and more general tendencies in social life.

Aesthetics

Gadamer is concerned with the sense we might speak of as "truth" in a work of art. Art is encountered in a form that resists pure concept-ualization; the ambiguity of art answers to the ambiguity of human life as a whole, and therein lies its unique value. The experience of art should not be viewed in epistemological terms. It is related, rather to the broader category of the imagination, it its "free" play and product-ivity. By means of art, we are able to look at the productivity of the imagination and its interplay with understanding. The world apart from value is a theoretical construct devised for political purposes as much as for scientific ones, and obviously not only the really real world. The language of aesthetics is designed to shield the initiated, disarm the critics, and exclude the vulgar, but internalized canons of taste are necessarily unstable. Even if a painting cannot depict perception, it can allude to or intimate facts about perception in a metaphorical fashion. Taste judgments are not merely capricious and idiosyncratic, and giving reasons for them is legitimate. There is a way to be found to speak of errors and lapses of taste. In failing to make the proper response, one is not so much wrong as different, and it is a difference that leaves one outside a vital community. We are dealing here with a species of "soft" logic. To reduce art to its presumed biological foundations, as Scharfstein does, fails to do justice to either the complexity of art or its diversity. Human art presupposes a specific cultural context – a web of associations and memories, that provides it with its unique meaning.

Art

The word "art" has a complicated variety of uses that reflects a complex logic: unforseeable novel conditions are always forthcoming or envisageable. Whether something is art is not a factual but a decision-related problem, where the verdict turns on whether or not we enlarge our set of conditions for applying the concept. The object becomes a work of art by resembling sufficiently an established artwork. Art is not a natural kind, it is a cultural kind, and a feature of our cultural conventions is that they exhibit arbitrariness. Roberts argues that the radical impulse of modernism and its critical dominance had to succumb to its own contradictions. The predicament of contingency in modern art signals the need for a change of paradigm. But where there is no depth, there can be no signifying surface either, and such nihilism means the collapse of all criteria for judging an artwork. We have learned that meaning is unstable and that the reign of enlightenment was ephemeral. McEvilley rejects the modernist belief in progress, the idea that all past ages were essentially aspiring to become what we are now. But this involves the difficult ideal of letting things be what they are before being appropriated into categories not their own. He himself admits that multiculturealism cannot be the end of history as it contains countless unsolved themes and issues. While agreeing with the subjectivists, that feeling is natural in the arts, Best insists that aesthetic appreciation is not unreasoned, a matter of irrational or non-rational feelings and attitudes. One can disagree only if there is something to disagree about, and if we can recognize contradictory reasons *as* reasons. But even if we grant Best the view that not everything goes in art, this does not provide us with valid criteria for judging specific responses in the arts as appropriate. The assumption that the object to be interpreted has, or could have, a single meaning in relation to which the interpretation is correct or incorrect, no longer holds firm in the context of art. It is regarded as a merit, not a deficit, in a work of art, if it is replete with an abundance of meanings that are only gradually discovered. The arts bring back into life the richness and variety that scientific understanding has abstracted from the world.

Berleant emphasizes that artists have altered our very ability to identify what art is and our capacities for experiencing it. The developments of the past century are part of a transformation in perception and understanding that compels us toward a different aesthetic. Interpretation is ubiquitous, and this is as true of the social and cultural areas, of fact and perception, as it is of texts. Artistic problems are hard to state and most of them are dealt with intuitively. The aesthetic merit of a thing depends on the degree to which it satisfies our desire to make sense of the world perceptually and conceptually in a form that is appropriate to our cognitive faculties. Art can bring unknown or half-known areas of experience home to us, but it has only a weak link with the observable facts. Danto adopts the Hegelian view that regards history as the drive to break through to the consciousness of itself. But while Hegel believed this to have been attained in his own philosophy, Danto does not accept that the history of philosophy came to a final end with Hegel. He does, however, adopt an eschatological view of art. Viewing the history of art from his New York vantage point during the last two decades, Danto concludes that further breakthroughs are unthinkable. Yet breakthroughs come always as a surprise, and the notion of history coming to an end is not one with which he himself is comfortable. Contrary to Wittgenstein, Mitchell concludes that it is futile to attempt to purge the world of images. Our ideas of what vision is and what is worth looking at are all deeply embedded in social and cultural history.

Philosophy

Rorty's pragmatism is unable to account for the success of astrophysics and the failure of astrology. Any pragmatism that renounces prediction and control will have a hard time distinguishing between what works and what doesn't. What he calls pragmatism is largely a disinclination to deal with certain traditional philosophical problems. He is a philosopher who claims a novelist's privileges, yet isn't content to offer his own pragmatism as mere fiction. Wood emphasizes that what cannot be said in one language-game may well be expressible in another, since there are no a priori limits to what can be said. In philosophy the claim of truth is underpinned by a whole system of concepts and values, not just a single concept of truth in the abstract. The product is a philosophy that contests its own possibility, while at the same time never quite destroying it. The breakthrough to a philosophical "beyond" is a mirage. Nielsen rejects coherence as a weaker form of foundationalism, but on his own terms he cannot know that epistemology is not a viable enterprise, or that there is no point in metaphysical inquiry. Ignoring the historical impact of the philosophical tradition in science, art, morality, and politics in Western civilization, Rorty and Nielsen nevertheless remain part of it.

Notes

[1] James Gleick, *Chaos, Making a New Science,* New York, NY: Penguin Books, 1987, p. 262.
[2] *Iyyun* 42, July 1993, p. 456.

Section 1

Reasonableness

Chapter One

Smart Machines

Gelernter argues that, up to a point, reasoning is understood by philosophers and psychologists, and computers can fake it. But there is one big piece of practice that goes by many names – creativity, intuition, insight, metaphoric or holistic thinking – that all boils down to drawing analogies for which we are unable to provide a convincing model.[1] Inventing a new analogy – hitching two thoughts together, sometimes two superficially unrelated thoughts – brings about a new metaphor and, it is generally agreed, drives creativity as well. Studies and intuition suggest that creativity hinges on seeing an old problem in a new way. How such analogical thinking works is the great unsolved problem. The way in which a person happens to be thinking at a given moment depends on a characteristic "mental focus." At the high end, thought is analytic and penetrating; it deals in abstractions and displays a demythologizing intelligence, and it is dominated by linked facts. Almost all attempts to simulate thought on a computer have dealt exclusively with this narrow, high-focus brand at the top of the spectrum. As we set off down the spectrum, thinking becomes less penetrating and more diffuse, consciousness gradually spreads out, and emotion starts to replace logical problem solving as the glue of thought. The unexpected transitions from a thought A to a seemingly unrelated thought B are precisely the occasions on which analogies are discovered and metaphors emerge. Affect linking is responsible for bringing these leaps about; they are not random but come about when two recollections engender the same emotion, and they only happen towards the low-focus end of the spectrum.[2] Thought processes tinged with the hallucinatory are also associated with ancient man. In more ways than one, dream thought traffics in associations, in unexpected connections, and it is remarkable that childhood thought does too. A common characteristic of young preschool children's conversation is *chaining* – that is, free-associating,[3] and a series of studies have shown young children to be startlingly good at metaphor. Metaphor brings on meaningful but nonobvious connections.[4] Logic and analysis are not childhood specialties, and children tend to be poor at manipulating abstractions. But adults can also be conspicuously incompetent at logic, analysis and abstraction, for example, when they are sleepy. Adults are bad at logical *thought* when they are asleep. A certain amount of problem solving can occur in a dream, but dream thought is notably not logical and not analytical, nor is it abstract. Logic, analysis, and abstraction are nonspecialties of ancient man as well.

In modern psychology, an "analytic" or "rational" or "convergent" style is contrasted with something called "divergent" or "productive" or "lateral" or "metaphoric" thought. Sometimes "left brain" thinking is contrasted with "right brain" in a broadly similar way. What these dichotomies miss, in the opinion of Gelernter, is the crux of the matter: that these two styles are connected. Lower mental focus causes all these latter processes to occur.[5] The mainstream sees thought as reasoning, problem solving, analysis, and mental modeling, with an occasional dash of common sense, but thinking is vastly richer than that. As focus falls, attention becomes more diffuse, and creativity centers, according to a fairly solid consensus, on restructuring:[6] on finding unexpected analogies that allow a person to see old problems in a new light. We say that inspiration "hits us," that is, happens unsought, and creative states presumably do not happen to everybody. The conventional philosopher's and computer scientist's view of thought as a keen docile instrument is a mere reflection of our rational bias. But the conventional cognitive science view of thought – that thought is merely "mental modeling," that it centers on analysis, abstraction, logic, reasoning, and problem solving – is dramatically incomplete. An abstraction is defined by a few traits shared by many substances; it is merely a branch of related memories examined as a single bundle. As they mature, children move their cognitive grounds inexorably up the spectrum – and gradually language becomes possible. Memories formed at high focus are easily recalled, whereas the breadth and inclusiveness of memories formed at low focus make them slippery. What emerges isn't detail but ambiance; childhood memories are hard to recall as are dreams. As the gravity of logic slackens, the objects dissolve into disconnected floating images. Thinking is primarily and overwhelmingly remembering; mental models are created in order to solve problems, but direct problems disappear as focus diminishes. The "restructuring" to which creativity is attributed centers on metaphorical linking. Affections are the key; "happy" and "sad," "angry" and "scared" are emotions, yet it is crucial that the list not stop there but that it also encompass what are sometimes called the "aesthetic" emotions. It is hard to understand precisely such mental states – what a person might feel on an unexpectedly warm spring morning, or an empty beach in winter, or driving past a childhood home, or hearing a clock ticking loudly in the silence. Such occasions might evoke an emotional response, even though they are a far cry from "happy" or "sad." They are subtle and idiosyncratic, blended for a particular occasion, and they have no names.[7] For the affect link to work, the thinker must "re-experience," *feel* his memories, because as focus sinks, logic starts to dissolve, and we start to feel our recollections. Sloppy thinkers are especially prone to draw conclusions from stereotyped examples. A low-focus train of thought is not logical and tolerates contradictions; it has no concept of contradiction. It has no direction, no premises, no goals, no conclusions. Yet low-focus trains are not random; they are thematic, and these themes are emotional themes. The theme is latent and plays no role in the manifest content of the thinker's recollections. Ancient texts like the Bible and *Iliad* were routinely produced at lower settings of the focal dial than we are used to, and dreams have something of the same character.

Gelernter wants to study mind as if it were art. Thought science centers mainly on learning and problem solving, while emotion, "alternate" thought styles, and the cognitive past are of no great concern. But what is more puzzling about the higher cognitive mind is its creativity, its holism, and its passion for the analogical.[8] Thought is usually confused within reasoning, and rationality (that is, logical cogency) is accepted as the touchstone of good thinking. The field recognizes the existence of "nonrational" thought styles; you can be a good divergent thinker but not too smart (as intelligence tests define "smart") and vice versa. Thought scientists tend to be obsessed with computers, since they are their chief source of mind metaphors and their models for human thought, and aspects of the mind that don't fit the computer model are (unintentionally) lopped off. An unsurprising result is the tendency to downplay or wholly ignore the role of emotion in cognition.[9] Our culture wrongly teaches us that thoughts and feelings lie in almost separate worlds.[10] Emotion itself is a form of cognition,[11] but artificial intelligence researchers and cognitive scientists have generally tended to avoid the subject of emotion. Creativity can only emerge, Gelernter believes, as a byproduct of affect linking in low-focus thought, and no existing computer program has ever grappled with low-focus thought.[12] Emotions are fundamental to thought; when you get hold of a bunch of memories, similarities reinforce each other, and aspects that aren't shared fade quietly into the background.[13] The overlay model accounts for an interesting fact that emerges from Wittgenstein's observation; we may have a clear idea of some concept without being able to point to even one paradigm example.[14] Your mental focus governs your relationship not merely to your thoughts but also to your perceptions.[15] Only at high focus does the thinker control his thought stream and his perceptions; when he sees something interesting, he proceeds to investigate. Low-focus thinking, on the other hand, is accompanied by an unraveling of control and the onset of an all-inclusive passivity. Everyone is capable of a wide range of focus settings, but thinkers with a relatively high-focus gait approach the world on radically different terms from low-focus thinkers. As focus declines, you might not understand the input of phrases exactly, you might forget the precise context, and you tend merely to skim the text. At the lower focus, you are paying no attention to the text at all. We expect children who are good readers to show a decently developed capacity for high-focus thought, but there is a role for low-focus reading in poetry, for example. You have far more experience stored in your memory than you will ever see at high-focus.[16] The observer perceives more than he knows.

Sustained high-focus thought makes possible logic, analysis, rationality – science, mathematics, engineering, and all rigorous cogent scholarship. These are the achievements that define the modern mind.[17] Sustained high-focus thought becomes a settled habit as rigorous analytic thinking yields reliable benefits that are far more tangible and useful than the vague and elusive results that low-focus thinking offers. A world of exclusively low-focus thought would be a world without abstractions. It would presumably have no concept of, but would have a feeling for, "truth." True things would have some characteristic emotional tone, There is a lot more to the complex process we call "reasoning" than merely formulating and applying syllogisms. But the manipulating of these rules is the heart of logic, the basis for reasoning. Grasping word meanings and thinking deductively are two names for the same phenomenon, and that phenomenon is high-focus thought.[18] Empiricist science is, at base, a high-focus approach to the world. Approaching the world of your thoughts at high focus means that you fasten on details and probe deeper, picking out the shared particulars and operating by abstractions. The likeness principle tends to be obscured when we think of remembering in terms of "associations," but any computer can behave *as if* attraction existed between the data items it stores internally, if you program it to do so. There is a gradual and continuos transition of knowledge from episodic to semantic,[19] but as you accumulate similar memories, you tend to confuse them. Focusing has the side effect of causing you to disregard context and ambiance: making high-focus thought the norm, setting it at the center of your cognitive universe, is the supreme and defining achievement of the modern mind.[20]

The affect link allows us to associate two memories that seemingly share nothing. The ability to think metaphorically or in analogies – to recognize that one entity is, in some way, like a superficially very different other – is a supremely valuable accomplishment. Restructuring the problem clearly has to do with finding analogies. If the solution to a hard problem eludes you, inspiration takes the form of an analogy that allows you to see the problem in a new light. The creative thinker comes up with useful combinations of ideas that are already in his repertoire but which have not been previously brought together.[21] Restructuring and analogy finding are crucial to creativity, but they remain mysterious. The more obvious the analogy, the more likely you are to discover it, yet it is precisely the *less* obvious analogies that interest us if we care about insight and creativity. Today, the logical or analytical component of modern thought is understood, at least to some extent, whereas analogy finding is understood much less. Emotion is a content transcending abstraction, and hence emotion can link memories whose content are completely different.[22] The affect link isn't sufficient but it is necessary to understand creativity and obviously some people are better at low-focus thought or affect linking than others. They have grater emotional acuity. The essence of spirituality might be a sense of connectedness, a sensation that "all life is linked," and this in turn motivates sustained low-focus thought. But any attempt to give it a definite positive content in ordinary language is bound to fail because ordinary language can deal only with ordinary life, while the transcendent is precisely what stands out of the ordinary.[23] Not every affect link reveals a fact of scientific value, or of practical use, but every affect link indicates a truth. The emergence of childhood and of mankind both revolve about the emergence of language, and an ever more acute self-consciousness seems to accompany the emergence of the modern mind.

Gelernter concludes that ancient man must not only have lived but have thought differently from us. Hallucinations were more common in former times, even thought the transition from ancient thought styles to modern ones lasted many centuries and may even today not be complete. Hallucination and illogic are both characteristic of low-focus thought. Infancy and childhood entail sharp limits on the capacity for logic and reasoning, i.e. on the ability to manage abstractions.[24] You see connections and resemblances, but at minimum focus you make no choices: you are powerless to decide. Something may occur that you know perfectly well stands for or really means something else, for there may be separate images linked together by shared emotional content. Dream thought isn't logically constructed and abstract, but emotionally produced and concrete; it is outside your control, not merely vivid but hallucinatory. As your mental focus sharpens, you become adept at new thought techniques. But simultaneously you have grown accustomed to experiencing the world in low-focus terms, terms under which the world is full of strange, deep, unexpected connections. As human knowledge deepens and narrows, modern minds and habits of thought are simply unable to see what ancient man saw.[25] A software metaphor of the mind underlies and reinforces the field's most basic and damaging bias: to be aware only of the highest-focus sliver of the cognitive spectrum, and to mistake the abstract, logical, analytical sliver for the whole of thought. The mind is an abstraction that can be described without reference to its implementation, without reference to the human physiology. But in order to think, you must have emotions, and in order to have emotions, you must have a body. The body, of course, is not mere information processing machine; it is a complex assemblage of sensors, transducers and moving parts. In order to respond directly to the real world, software isn't enough. You have to stimulate not only the body but its environment, and the amount of information obtainable in short order by an inquisitive human being is staggeringly large.

A real memory has relevance and it has structure. A memory isn't merely a bag of features; the elements relate to each other, often in the sense of the features of an image relating to each other. And a real memory is "multimedia." It may involve sights, sounds, and smells, and crucially emotions. In the spectrum view, logic isn't a matter of abstract rules, it grows out of memory sandwiching at high-focus. Thus, the probe *blue* brings blue-related memories to mind, and blueness is the characteristic they share. This sort of reasoning is informal; it is provided not by rules and principles but directly by memories. The FGP computer program Gelernter has developed works not by deploying abstract rules but by using memory sandwiches as if they were rules. The result is a system that is capable of venturing some opinions, potentially interesting ones, on the diagnosis of a medical case, or a law case or the prognosis of a business situation.[26] Lots of such "expert systems" have been developed, but most of them work not on the basis of "memories," but on the basis of abstract rules. These rules generally take the form of assertions like "if conditions A, B, C prevail, then draw the conclusions X, Y, Z with the degree of certainty P." The FGP program, on the other hand, reflects its "memories" and develops as they collectively evolve. Whenever you describe a new case in the program, it retains that case as a "memory." When you enter a new inquiry, the program might respond, in effect,

> This new set of facts reminds me of a patient who was described to me three weeks ago. I didn't know the diagnosis then, but it now occurs to me that perhaps the right answer should have been x.

As the number and variety of its memories grow, the program's behavior becomes more nuanced and sophisticated. Eventually it may be in a position to comment intelligently on rare or peculiar cases on the basis of its own "experience" along the lines of "I don't know what the diagnosis is, but I did see something once that may be relevant."[27] Whenever the program reaches a conclusion, it is in a position to cite specific cases to support that conclusion, and as a result, it can explain and defend its behavior not merely by stating "that's what the rule says" but by citing specific cases. The program even makes intermediate judgments on the data as they are presented.

The program's behavior is limited by the quality of its memories. These descriptions are invariably somewhat vague and will never be perfectly consistent, but over the course of thousands of such descriptions, consistent patterns should emerge. The computer is now in a position to explain to its human users what it is "feeling." The human trainer needs to impart to the computer, roughly speaking, which emotions are best and which are worst. We cannot expect human-like thinking if the computer has no tendency to prefer happy thoughts to sad ones.[28] If the user is looking for insights by operating the machine at low-focus, as certain degree of drifting concentration and free association is inevitable. When we have added emotion, then and only then will our computer be capable of surprising us with an occasional genuine insight. It will be capable of citing a medical or legal or financial precedent that seems, at first sight, to come out of left field, but proves upon inspection to have deep relevance to the case at hand. Such feats aren't likely to occur often, but the computer, compared to a human expert, for all the crudity of its simulated emotions, has the interesting advantage of having a perfect memory, and that memory is vast.[29] A sophisticated "emotional" computer would largely control its own focus settings. The spectrum idea puts emotion at the center of the cognitive universe; it makes emotion the glue of thought, the force that engenders creativity. In the course of normal conversation, a person is entitled to lots of slack, for humans say things all the time that are meaningful only against the background of the fact they *are* humans. Normal human conversation doesn't probe for these assumptions because normal conversation takes place only among humans. The question is no longer, as in the Turing test, whether a computer can pass itself off as a person. The question is whether there are grounds for intelligent communication with a computer despite the fact that it *is* a computer. The question *is the computer intelligent?* reduces itself to the question *is it like us?* To simulate intelligence is to simulate humanness.[30] French notes that analogy finding is considered by many to be the *sine qua non* of intelligent behavior.[31] Thinking and having a mind translate into the practical skill of understanding. You believe that some other entity understands some utterance (gesture, and so forth) exactly to the extent that you believe the utterance arouses in this other entity the same emotions that it arouses in you. Under the right circumstances, we can be convinced that an infant understands us, or for that matter, that a dog does. I am convinced that you have grasped the import of my statements just insofar as I believe that your emotional reaction is like mine. That if I am horrified, surprised, amazed, amused, so too, at least to some extent, are you. A perception of shared emotion is what convinces me that communication has succeeded. Where sympathy exists, no purely "intellectual" test is needed or matters, and where it doesn't, no strictly intellectual test will convince you that you are in the presence of understanding. To *see* you mean *understand*, but we also say *that idea has touched me*, it *smells wrong*, or *doesn't sound right*. Consciousness doesn't happen at any particular point (there is no theater and no stage): it consists instead of a bunch of separate discontinuous events. Simple brained creatures are likely to experience the world as fragmentary and they are not bothered by the illusion of an observer-self. If we add simulated emotion to a computer, we might arrive, Gelernter argues, at a very close approximation of human thought. Such a computer might seem to us as if it understands – as if it has a mind.

Ancient pieces of literature capture a particular kind of thinking. The ancient narrator perceives the real world as ordered, sometimes by what we would call dream logic; he is a lower-focus thinker than we are apt to be. If what he says doesn't fit logically, it fits emotionally, and such low-focus thought trains have a quality that makes them strange to the modern mind. These themes are not to be understood, they are to be felt, and once you feel the theme, the thinking begins to cohere. The mind of these ancient times is quite capable of logic and reasoning, and orderly coherent narrative. But it remains comfortable too in cognitive neighborhoods where we no longer go, except in our dreams. Modern minds ask constantly, "given these circumstances, what follows logically?" – but never "given these circumstances, what follows emotionally?" The brain hasn't changed but our cognitive habits have and what ties the pieces together isn't logic but emotion and shared imagery. Stories that share no relationship in substance – they are not about the same thing at all – may well include the same image, for one reason or another. But that shared image may reveal emotional linkage; the imagery of passages isn't identical, it merely has the same feel. An underlying emotion can generate a whole series of dream-stories that share little or no manifest content; that merely represent successive embodiments of the same emotional theme. It is not a logical sequence of stories but an echo-chamber, a mirror image, a resonating system. We don't understand certain characteristics of ancient thought, and laid out flat, ancient texts are deceptively intelligible, merely doltish. But if we walk away satisfied on that basis, we have no hope of grasping this literature in its real beauty and depth.[32] Scolnic's discussion of a well-known obscure passage in Exodus (was Moses "horned?")[33] emphasizes the impossibility of pinning down the biblical text as if it were a modern logical narrative. These are the honestly bewildered judgments of high-focus man on the low-focus worlds of antiquity and childhood and his own dreams.[34] We ought not to be surprised that young children use metaphor *before* they have mastered abstract thought – before they are able to explain what they are doing. Children's thought streams will typically be richer than adult's in low-focus thought.[35]

Notes

[1] David Gelernter, "The Muse in the Machine," *Computerizing the Poetry of Human Thought,* New York, NY: The Free Press, Macmillan, 1994, p. 3.

[2] *Ibid.,* p. 7.

[3] J. Garbarino, F. M. Stott, and the faculty of Erikson Institute, "What Children Tell Us: Eliciting, Interpreting, and Evaluating Information from Children," San Fransicso, CA: Jossey-Bass, 1989.

[4] Gelernter, "The Muse in the Machine," p. 12.

[5] *Ibid.,* p. 14.

[6] K. J. Holyoak, "Problem Solving," *Thinking: An Invitation to Cognitive Science,* vol. 3, eds. D. N. Osherson and E. E. Smith, Cambridge, Mass: MIT Press, 1990.

[7] Gelernter, "The Muse in the Machine," p. 28.

[8] J. A. Fodor, "Precis of the Modularity of Mind," *The Behavioral and Brain Sciences* 8 (1), p. 4.

[9] Gelernter, "The Muse in the Machine," p. 42.

[10] M. Minsky, *The Society of Mind,* New York, NY: Simon & Schuster, 1986.

[11] H. Leventhal, "The Integration of Emotion and Cognition: A View from the Perceptual-Motor Theory of Emotion," eds. M. S. Clarke and S. Fiske, *Affect and Cognition: The Seventeenth Annual Carnegie Symposium on Cognition,* Hillsdale, NJ: Lawrence Erlbaum Associates, 1982.

[12] Gelernter, "The Muse in the Machine," p. 46.

[13] *Ibid.,* p. 50.

[14] L. Wittgenstein, *Philosophical Investigations,* Oxford: Basil Blackwell 1953, p. 32.

[15] Gerlernter, "The Muse in the Machine," p. 53.

[16] *Ibid.*, p. 63.

[17] *Ibid.*, p. 65.

[18] *Ibid.*, p. 72.

[19] *Ibid.*, p. 75.

[20] *Ibid.*, p. 76.

[21] K. J. Gilhooly, *Thinking, Directed, Undirected, and Creative,* New York, NY: Academic Press, 1988, p. 86.

[22] Gelernter, "The Muse in the Machine," p. 87.

[23] L. Dupre, *The Other Dimension,* Garden City, NY: Doubleday, 1972, p. 16.

[24] Gelernter, "The Muse in the Machine," p. 107.

[25] *Ibid.*, p. 112.

[26] *Ibid.*, p. 137.

[27] *Ibid.*, p. 138.

[28] *Ibid.*, p. 144.

[29] *Ibid.*, p. 146.

[30] *Ibid.*, p. 155.

[31] R. M. French, "Subcognition and the Limits of the Turing Test," *Mind* 99 (393), 1990, p. 64.

[32] Gelernter, "The Muse in the Machine," p. 187.

[33] B. E. Scolnic, "Moses and the Horns of Power," *Judaism* 40 (4), 1991, pp. 569-579.

[34] Gelernter, "The Muse in the Machine," p. 188.

[35] *Ibid.*, p. 191.

Chapter Two

Fuzzy Logic

Kosko emphasizes that all facts are matters of degree: the facts are always fuzzy or vague or inexact to some degree. Only mathematics is black and white, and it is just an artificial system of rules and symbols. Science treats the gray and fuzzy facts as if they were black and white facts of mathematics. The rapid spread of fuzzy ideas in the Far East and the opposition to them in the West show that the opposition to them is a philosophically and culturally conditioned world view. We can put black and white labels on these things but the labels will pass from accurate to inaccurate as the things change. More precision does not take the gray out of things. Yet in much of our science, mathematics, logic and culture we have assumed a world of black and whites that does not change. The digital computer, with its high-speed binary strings of 1s and 0s stands as the emblem of black and white logic and its triumph. This faith in *bivalence* reaches back in the West to the ancient Greeks. Aristotle's binary logic comes down to one law: A or not-A; the sky is blue or it is not blue; it can't be both. Aristotle's "law" defined what was philosophically correct for over two thousand years, even though binary truth has always faced doubt. Thus, the Buddha lived in India almost two centuries before Aristotle, and the first step in his belief system was to break through the black and white world of words, pierce the bivalent veil, and see the world as it is, see it filled with "contradictions," with things and nothings, with A *and* not-A.[1] You find this fuzzy and gray theme in Eastern belief systems from Lao Tzu's Taoism to Zen Buddhism in Japan. More recently, in the West, Werner Heisenberg showed physicists that not all scientific statements are true or false; many, if not most, statements are indeterminate, uncertain, gray – fuzzy. The world of mathematics does not fit the world it describes, for the two worlds differ. One neat and the other messy, it takes faith in language, a dose of make-believe to make the two worlds match.[2] Statements of fact are not all true or all false; they are imprecise and vague. While in theory philosophers could tell matters of logic from matters of fact, in practice they ignored the split and treated the messy matters of fact as if they were neat matters of logic.

Probability does not solve this mismatch problem, for it fills the world with the phantom of "randomness," a concept mathematicians for years have tried to define.[3] Probability has turned modern science into a truth casino. It has proved a powerful tool for social prediction and control but, in the opinion of Kosko, this does not soften the mismatch between logic and fact.[4] He points out that most people, at the same time, are both satisfied and dissatisfied with their jobs. Scientists believe in bivalent logic and mathematics because they work; yet they work, of course, only to some degree. So fuzzy logic says that logic itself is a matter of degree, and in the fuzziest case the thing equals its opposite: the glass of water is both half-empty and half-full. Whether it is one or the other depends on how we look at it, our values, and whether we are optimists or pessimists. Scientists beg the question of bivalence, but any criticism of it must fail without a working alternative, and Kosko proposes fuzzy logic as such an alternative. He argues that while Western scientists and engineers ignored or attacked fuzzy logic, their Eastern counterparts largely applied it and launched the long-awaited era of commercial machine intelligence. No human brain works with Aristotle's syllogisms or with computer precision: it is messier than that. Some things, of course, are not fuzzy, no matter how closely you look at them. These things tend to come from the world of mathematics, but when you move out of this artificial world, fuzziness reigns. Fuzziness means multivalence. It means there is more than one option, perhaps an infinite spectrum of them. It means analog instead of binary procedures, infinite shades of gray between black and white. Logicians in the 1920s and 1930s first worked out multivalued logic to deal with Heisenberg's uncertainty principle in quantum mechanics. The principle suggests that we really deal with three-valued logic: statements that are true, false, or indeterminate. Bivalence trades accuracy for simplicity, for it requires some force of fitting and rounding off, as when you state whether you are for or against a politician or satisfied with your job.[5]

The Information Age presupposes bivalence because it rests on the "digital revolution" in signal processing and microprocessor computer chips. Such digitalization imposes a grid on the curve, and then the system discards reality and keeps only the digitized numbers (the black dots on the grid). If the computer answered "more or less," we would not think that the computer meant it, that it spoke the truth. We expect every "well-formed" statement to be true or false, not true more or less, or false somewhat. The villain of bivalence is logical contradiction" A *and* not-A,[6] for in bivalent logic contradiction implies everything, it allows you to prove and disprove any statement. But so far no one has proved that the axioms of modern mathematics do not lead to statements that contradict one another. Still there is little tolerance for views that admit contradictions or overlap between things and nothings. Fuzzy logic confronts this intolerance head on, influenced perhaps by Eastern mysticism. Fuzziness or multivalence holds everywhere in between the corners of the number line or cube. But you can work with fuzzy units just as you can work with binary units, and you don't have to round off.[7] The fuzzier the answer, the more A and not-A look alike, and at the midpoint you cannot tell a thing from its opposite, just as you cannot tell a half-empty glass of water from a half-full one. As we gain more information, we get a clearer, more accurate picture of the world: we get a better view of the facts. But this does not take the fuzziness out of the facts, and the question *Where do we draw the line?* haunts black-and-white reasoning in a world of grays. The split between thing and nothing grows still more complicated when the thing is reactive. Objects and behavior are, to some degree, art and nonart depending on tastes, tradition and whim. Beauty is both fuzzy and reactive; it depends on the speaker and on the culture. Beauty lies not solely in the eye of the beholder; it lies there only to some degree.[8] Legal decisions are also fuzzy and relative; courts convict persons who commit crimes with enough intent and acquit those who commit them with enough diminished capacity. Judges, legal scholars, and the rest of us search for borders between personal freedom and government control, between man and state, choice and command. Jokes shade into insults or slander or harassment. Legal concepts vary among cultures and with them. The great increases in information in the twentieth century have not helped us draw lines between justice and injustice, fairness and unfairness, right and wrong. In many ways the future looks fuzzy.[9]

Kosko claims that fuzziness has reduced the ancient and undefined concepts of "randomness" and "probability" that hold between the sets. Fuzzy logic has added to machine intelligence by showing us how to make machines reason more as we do, with common sense learned from experience.[10] But common sense is something we take for granted, not something we know explicitly how to define. Most scientists still attack fuzzy logic as being against the bivalent faith, and only the commercial success of fuzzy products has made it an issue. At root fuzzy logic or multivalence is a world view or ideology, but so, of course, is bivalence, and we often use probability talk when we are not sure of something. Randomness is everywhere but we find only the footprints of it; we never catch probability in the act.[11] We "tend" to observe the most probable event, and we expect the most probable outcomes to occur, even though we silently buy a lottery ticket or play the slot machine or smoke a cigarette. Science plays the percentages too; it holds the maximum likelihood view as the grand organizing principle of the scientific world view. Kosko concludes that we need a gray or fuzzy science in order to model our gray world better.[12] But logic is normative and neither our mathematical symbols nor the natural language we use need to have the same structure as the world they refer to. Probability attempts to make the bivalent package reasonable, but it has its psychological roots in our gambling hunches, and so far it has no logical justification. Probability is a psychological side effect of forward-looking creatures, just as free will is, and that really means that probability is built into our minds, that it is part of science's infrastructure. We see probability everywhere because it lies in our glasses.[13] Kosko regards probability or randomness as a psychic construct or a Jungian archetype or a mental trend that helps us to organize our perceptions and memories, and most of all our expectations. Probability gives structure to our competing casual predictions about how the future will unfold. It ranks or weights future alternatives and has its powerful psychological reality rooted in our neural microstructure.[14] The widespread gambling and games of chance in primitive as well as modern cultures suggest that probability reasoning may be a cultural constant like hero worship, fertility rituals, or incest and adultery taboos. It allows us to bet before we act and to improve the outcome of acting, and natural selection favors a brain mechanism that helps the organism make its next move in a changing and dangerous world.

Kosko concludes that the universe, if gray, is not random but determinate – all things are a matter of degree. Russell's logic and Heisenberg's quantum mechanics shook science and forced scientists to rethink mathematics and science. Aristotle's logic and scientific bent have shaped much of the modern Western mind and defined its range of parameters, its boundary, its list of the correct and incorrect. To a large degree, Aristotle still defines what is *philosophically* correct in logic and reasoning. The Buddha, on the other hand, refused to get caught up in words: he tolerated A *and* not-A. He seems the first major thinker to reject the black-white world of bivalence. That alone took great insight and detachment and tenacity in an age with no formal analysis. The Buddha refused to let words get in the way of what matters to a living and dying organism. The bivalence of science denies gray truth, and that tactic leads to paradoxes and self-contradictions. The fuzzy view emphasizes that almost all truth is gray, partial, and fractional; it lets mathematical truths remain black and white as extreme cases of gray.[15] Bivalent science denies that truths are gray and maintains they are tentative, while fuzzy logic agrees that scientific truths are tentative but still claims they are gray. The focus on statements has reduced the analysis of truth to the study of language. Fuzzy theorists have done the same but they allow more scores; they allow an infinite continuum of gray scores between 0 and 1. Philosophers distinguish logical truth from factual truth. Logical truth comes from symbols and their formal relationships; it does not depend on how the world is.[16] They follow Aristotle in calling factual truth *contingent* and logical truth *necessary*; a logically true statement is a statement true in all possible worlds. In this view, the way we add and multiply numbers should work in all possible worlds. Mathematics is a formal system, since we can manipulate mathematical symbols and not understand what they mean. We can just apply the syntax rules as a computer does when it adds up numbers or proves a theorem. The computer shows the truth of the theorem but it does not "understand" its meaning.[17] All formal systems work that way; you don't have to interpret to apply them. Fuzzy logic views truth as accuracy, and accuracy is clearly a matter of degree. The precise but artificial statements of mathematics are always 100-percent accurate or 0-percent accurate, whereas statements about the world have accuracy scores between these two extremes. You can prove only mathematical and logical coherent statements in an arbitrary formal system of made-up rules. You cannot guarantee what you can test, and you cannot test what you can guarantee; the logical and the factual do not meet.

Ironic as it sounds, inaccuracy is the central assumption of science. Only the "empty" tautologies of mathematics and logic enjoy the status of accuracy. Scientific claims and statements are inexact and provisional; they depend on simplifying assumptions or on a particular choice of words, on "all things being equal." When you speak, you simplify, and when you simplify, you lie.[18] Scientists are trying to find the mathematics that best fits the world, and while they work in mathematics and test in mathematical formulations of their experiments, they never achieve the logical certainty of mathematics. Scientists tend to believe they do mathematics when they do science, and this holds particularly in advanced science like physics or at the theoretical frontier of any science whose claims come as mathematical claims. What was inaccurate or fuzzy truth all along gets presented in the all-or-none status of binary logic. Positivist philosophers and scientists make all statements certain by giving factual statements the status of logical statements, and, in effect, they try to make fact fit their binary mathematics. And they cover up or cloud the whole issue with probability disclaimers that all such black-white talk holds only with "some probability." Rounding off lies at the heart of working with symbols and speech, for it compresses information. It simplifies matters by reducing the many to the few, the complex to the manageable. Bivalence or rounding off trades accuracy for simplicity, but if your round off too much, you pay the penalty of bivalent self-contradiction and land in paradox: then the water glass is both half empty and half full. Heisenberg's quantum uncertainty principle ended, or at least dented, our blind faith in the certainty of science and factual truth. This faith had grown since the days of Isaac Newton to the status of religious dogma. But up close it could provide only partial, uncertain and fuzzy truths. It took the new mathematics of Russell and the new quantum mechanics of Heisenberg to make us first really doubt the logic that we inherited from Aristotle.

Paradoxes of self-reference have the same form; they both assert and deny themselves. They have the logical form of a contradiction, A *and* not-A, and they vex mathematicians and Western philosophers. At the same time many mathematicians dismiss the paradoxes as word play and few mathematicians lose sleep over Russell's paradoxes even though every branch of mathematics depends on set theory. The set or collection or class is the fundamental structure in mathematics, since nothing, too, is a set; the empty set.[19] No one wanted to give up consistency altogether for this is essential for rational communication. So the fuzzy view maintains that paradoxes of self-reference are half-truths, fuzzy contradictions. The truth lies in the middle; you cannot round off the midpoint to any one corner. Paradoxes are the rule and not the exception; rather pure black and white is the exception. Paradoxes also show how bivalence costs; you trade accuracy for simplicity. Heisenberg demonstrates that even in physics the truth of statements is a matter of degree; he made people question bivalent logic by showing that in quantum mechanics there are some things we can never know. The more you pin down the velocity of an electron, the less you can pin down its position, and vice versa. In a nonlinear theory the parts do not add up to the whole, and groups do not behave as their members do. But scientists try to make things simple, and that is in good part why they stuck with bivalence. Their first instinct is to fit the linear model to a nonlinear world. We know much more linear mathematics than nonlinear mathematics, but the nonlinear theory fits the facts better, and that is why we revert to ordinary language in explaining what the mathematical notation means. A nonlinear quantum mechanics may not lead to an uncertainty principle, for wherever you have linear theories you will have uncertainty relations; you cannot pin down a signal completely in time and frequency. We inherited from the Pythagoreans a belief in absolutes and pure forms, in the white and black, and the true and the false.[20] But most of our words stands for fuzzy sets, while most of modern science stands against the logic of fuzzy sets.[21] Everything is vague to a degree you do not realize till you have tried to make it precise.[22] In all such borderline cases "doubtful objects" are easily found about which we are unable to say either that the class name does or does not apply.[23] The noun *house* stands for a fuzzy set of houses, since some structures are more "a house" than others. *Old House* stands for a smaller set of houses, but how old is old? It is a matter of degree. We think in fuzzy sets and we each define our fuzzy boundaries in different ways and with different examples. Thought is set play, and fuzzy logic is reasoning with fuzzy sets.[24] Numbers are fuzzy too; there are numbers close to zero or nearly zero; there are numbers, like big numbers, or very small numbers which are fuzzy numbers. The closer a small number is to zero, the more it belongs to the fuzzy set of small numbers. We might draw the fuzzy number zero as a bell curve centered on the exact number 0.[25] Mathematics, as we know, it is but a special case of fuzzy mathematics, a special limiting case – the degenerate case of black and white extremes in the mathematical world of grays. We can draw the fuzzy number of zero in infinitely many ways.

In practice fuzzy logic means making computers reason with fuzzy numbers in the form of if-then statements or rules of thumb. Every traffic is heavy to some degree, and every green light stays on long to some degree. The knowledge or intelligence comes from associating these two events. Fuzzy sets arise when borders blur, when thing overlaps nothing, when A overlaps not-A. But this state of overlap or contradiction cannot hold in bivalent logic. A set is fuzzy when elements belong to it to some degree; only an arbitrary line can be drawn between happy and not-happy, honest and dishonest, young and not-young. A fuzzy logic does not draw hard lines between opposites, and we live with a mix of happiness and unhappiness, honesty and dishonesty. Fuzzy sets exist outside of mathematics; to some degree, we all belong to every grouping and belief system, fad, cult, or trend. We all subscribe, to some degree, to every political party, every sexual orientation, every lifestyle, every side of the argument. We grow and learn as we age, and that just means that our fuzzy units change as we move from belief to disbelief and back again. Fights break out when some person, group, or government tries to round us off their way, tries to make us all A or not-A, to turn our fuzzy units into binary units and squash our fuzziness. In this sense voting asks for trouble.[26] Everything reduces to subsethood but the part contains the whole only to some degree; a "concept" is not only its luminous center but also the surrounding sphere of meaning and influence to some degree. The hard and abrupt contours of our ordinary conceptual system does not apply to reality. The world is thus a bivalent abstraction constituted of entities that are discontinuous with nothing between them. And in order to bring relations into the scrap heap of disconnected entities, the mind has to conjure up spirits, forces and whatnot from the vast deep of its own imagination. All this is due to the initial mistake of enclosing things or ideas or persons (or sets) in hard contours that are purely artificial, and not in accordance with the natural shading of continuities that are or should be well known to science and philosophy alike.[27]

Critics demanded that Lofti Zadeh, who coined the term "fuzzy logic," show that fuzziness was not probability in disguise. Zadeh did not bother with the fight, for he saw that as the system gets more complex, precise statements had less meaning. There are those who feel that the gap between precise mathematical language and a messy world reflects the fundamental inadequacy of conventional mathematics – the mathematics of precisely defined points, fractions, sets and probability measures. For coping with the analysis of, say, biological systems, and for dealing effectively with systems that are generally orders of magnitude more complex than man-made systems, we need a radically different mathematics, a mathematics of fuzzy or cloudy qualities that are not describable in terms of probability distributions. Indeed the need for such mathematics is becoming increasingly apparent even in the realm of inanimate systems, for in most practical cases the a priori data, as well as the criteria by which the performance of man-made systems is judged, are far from being precisely specified or having accurately known probability distributions.[28] The notation, however, is what we lack, and the verdict of mere feeling is liable to fluctuate. Zadeh used the fuzzy set as a chunk of common sense; the old view of *tall* was bivalent but tallness, like most properties of the world, is a matter of degree. He chose the word "fuzzy" because of its ties with common sense. As the complexity of a system increases, our ability to make precise and significant statements about its behavior diminishes until a threshold is reached beyond which precision and significance (or bivalence) become almost mutually exclusive. The closer one looks at a real-world problem, the fuzzier becomes its solution; indeed, precision increases fuzziness.[29] Most of the critics dismissed fuzziness as randomness in disguise, whereas Zadeh focused on the expressive power of fuzzy sets, and how well it fits with our words. For Zadeh to be right or even plausible, Aristotle had to be wrong, and that meant things did not have to be black and white. Kosko regards bivalent truths just to be conditioned reflexes but he fails to explain why bivalent logic and mathematics work after all. Bivalent logic not only runs computers but has served us well for thousands of years; it may come with some costs but it is simple and it works. Quine champions that claim; he thinks you can live with a floating boundary. He also suggests that everything is convention – so why argue? But Kosko points out that scientists work in narrow specialties, and that they fear the whole of science, too. And bivalence is one of the deepest key ideas of science; it is so deep that we take it for granted in our attempts at scientific reasoning. What we largely ignore is that words stand for sets of things, and that these things are fuzzy; the things belong to words to some degree, and this is how a group of sentences gives a fuzzy system.

Japanese fuzzy-system researchers expect that fuzzy logic will enable development of computer science that adjust to people rather than the reverse. Fuzzy logic is capable of expressing linguistic terms such as "maybe false" or "sort of true." In general, fuzzy logic, when applied to analog computers, allows them to evaluate the human reasoning process, quantify imprecise information, make decisions based on vague and incomplete data, yet – by applying a "defuzzification" process – arrive at definite conclusions.[30] The problem of teaching computers "common sense" is that what we take to be common sense is taken for granted; it is by definition something we do not know how to define or make precise. A fuzzy system can model or approximate any system. It is just a branch of fuzzy if-then rules, and all such rules define patches that try to cover some wiggly curve. The better the patches cover the curve, the smarter the system, and the more uncertain the rules, the bigger the patches. If the rules are so precise they are not fuzzy, then the patches collapse to points and they don't cover much of anything.[31] Leibniz dreamed of symbolic logic and *ars combinatoria* or computer language that could put all our rules in symbols and reason from them to reach mathematical truths and daily facts. Today computer scientists have created the field of artificial intelligence, or AI, based on belief that knowledge is rules, and that you can write down rules in the black and white language of computers and symbolic logic. But after 30 years of research and billions of dollars in funding, Artificial Intelligence has so far not produced smart machines or smart products. The AI fans claim this is only because they can't yet put enough rules in computers. But fuzzy researchers have build hundreds of smart machines and think they know why the AI engineers have failed. While you need rules, you don't need a lot of rules for many tasks; you need fuzzy rules.[32] A fuzzy rule relates fuzzy sets. Sense is common only to some degree, even if we see and hear and taste and touch the same things. The world hits us with signals and we sense them through the unique eyes and ears and tongue and skin that our DNA gives us. The world hits each of us with a unique set of signals, and that is why each word stands for different fuzzy sets of things to each of us. A child's idea of *large* or *slow* or *fair* changes as she grows older.[33] The fuzzy view was just common sense. It was considered daring and novel at the time because you first had to get your university degrees in the old black and white school, and then doubt that school and rediscover what any layman could have told you about common sense; that it is vague and fuzzy and hard to pin down in words and numbers.[34] But that still does not persuade scientists, and you have to show them the mathematics before they will accept such an idea.

The fuzzy system Kosko proposes is nonlinear but it approaches a linear system, as you can always cover a curve with a finite number of fuzzy patches. The less you know about a problem, the sloppier your rules as you use fewer fuzzy sets to stand for more things and cases. The fuzzy sets lose their fuzziness as the triangle widths by which we define them shrink, and along the way they lose their common-sense meaning. Such fuzzy orders can also model dynamic systems that change with time. But in practice no one knows how to write down the equations for most systems because they are too nonlinear. Fuzzy systems guess at the equations for you; they let you express what you know in a nonmathematical language. The main advantages of this approach are in implementing "rules of thumb" experiences, intuitions, hunches, and the fact that it does not need a model of the process.[35] You find good mathematical models only in textbooks and classrooms; they are toy answers to toy problems, and the real world pays no attention to most of them. Scientists often respect mathematics more than truth, and they do not mention that a mathematical guess is no less a guess than a guess in everyday language. A mathematical guess has more dignity the less mathematics you know. Fuzzy systems let us model systems in words, and you can use them in physics or communications or neuroscience. You can use fuzzy systems any place we today use brains, and you can use them in places where even brains don't work. In fuzzy system rules "fire" all the time; they fire in parallel, and all rules fire to some degree. They fire partially, and that is how associative memory works. The result is a fuzzy weighted average. You defuzzify a set when you replace it with a number or a centroid.[36] You add up a lot of things and weigh each thing to some degree; you do it by feel, and this picks answers but it does not explain them.[37] Each reason you give is a matter of degree, each has a fuzzy or gray weight. No one reason throws the decision; rather they all add up to a decision and your choice depends on complex and nonlinear processings in your brain. What really counts with fuzzy systems is the tie between words and sets, for unlike rules, principles are vague and abstract and full of exceptions. They change slowly with time as culture evolves.

Real problems are unique and sloppy and hard to pin down in exact mathematical terms. Thus, fuzzy theory has emerged as a means suited to represent uncertainty contained in the meaning of each word. Fuzzy artificial intelligence as an application of this theory is expected to play an important role in the future establishment of an intimate relationship between men and computers. We seek a system that learns fuzzy rules from experience, that turns expert behavior into fuzzy rules. You don't find violinists, woodcarvers, or aerobic teachers who can explain how they do what they do. We learn a new idea or pattern only if it resonates with what we expect to see or hear or think.[38] Since fuzzy rules are patches, with enough data the fuzzy system can *learn* any system,[39] and real data clusters need not fall neatly into the patch cells defined by the fuzzy set triangles. You quantify when you round off or when you pick an example. At first adaptive quantifier points do not spread out well, and that gives a small number of bad rules. Then with more training data, the adaptive quantifier points spread out and track the facts. That gives more and better rules, and at this point we can drop the expert and just work with fuzzy rules. In practice, we then polish these rules by playing with the size and position of the fuzzy sets or by letting a "supervised" neural set tune in. A fuzzy cognitive map draws a casual picture; it ties facts and processes to values and policies and objectives, and it lets you predict how complex events interact and play out.[40] A fuzzy cognitive map lets everyone pack her own wisdom and nonsense into a mathematical picture of some place in the world. But once packed in, the fuzzy cognitive maps predict outcomes, and we can compare these with data to test them. The outcome of large fuzzy cognitive maps may surprise you, for the best most of us can do is argue about single arrows, and we do less well when we try to reason with the large set of connected concepts. Fuzzy cognitive images help us to see the big picture and do something with it. They thrive on feedback and they show global patterns, but as the fuzzy cognitive maps grow more complex, the hidden patterns become harder to see. They lay bare our beliefs and biases and our grasp of the world. Thus, the fuzzy cognitive map gives us a new way to represent knowledge.

Philosophically interesting terms such as *life* invariably are fuzzy, as they shade smoothly into not-life or death. The either-or choice lies at the heart of the abortion debate. We can just as well call growth death and say that *death* begins at conception. Some humans end up in comas, and their family, friends, physicians, and insurers have to think about where to draw the death line. Life is fuzzy, and the lines we draw will be arbitrary.[41] Life is a matter of degree, and so is death, but such fuzzy curves have considerable problems too: there are infinitely more curves and each person can draw her own curve and no two curves may ever be the same. Still, such a curve helps us to argue, even if it does not give us a line, and does not lead to either-or action. There is no hard line when a cell dies, for all our cells are living or dying to some degree.[42] A million forces in our brains, bodies and genes shape our thoughts, choices and behavior. Each day it gets harder to call one thing, event, or act good or bad or call it right or wrong. The truth can be a matter of degree yet that does not help ethics.[43] But neither, of course, does it help logic, for logic, too, is normative. Logical truth is empty, and in the end it is just symbol pushing, but scientists believe in binary logic and mathematics because they work. They enable us to calculate and infer much more effectively than is possible by means of ordinary language. Every day scientists make their favorite claim that "the data suggests such and such," and they do not, or maybe cannot, explain this suggestion. If the words tie to blobs, the claim is true to some degree, and the tighter the tie the truer the claim. Most of us think the universe is not fuzzy, but a set of things may belong to a universe merely to some degree. An electron or electron cloud belong to a region of space-time only to some degree, and what this suggests to Kosko is that logic does not differ from fact, His alleged mismatch problem assumes that there need to be a similarity of structure between the mathematics we use and the world it refers to. Logic, however, is normative; it does not refer to the world but to the manner we *ought* to reason and calculate.

Notes

[1] Bart Kosko, *Fuzzy Thinking, The New Science of Fuzzy Logic*, New York, NY: Hyperion, 1993, p. 6.
[2] *Ibid.*, p. 8.
[3] *Ibid.*, p. 11.
[4] *Ibid.*, p. 12.
[5] *Ibid.*, p. 21.
[6] *Ibid.*, p. 23.
[7] *Ibid.*, p. 25.

[8] *Ibid.*, p. 36.
[9] *Ibid.*, p. 38.
[10] *Ibid.*, p. 41.
[11] *Ibid.*, p. 47.
[12] *Ibid.*, p. 49.
[13] *Ibid.*, p. 53.
[14] *Ibid.*, p. 54.
[15] *Ibid.*, p. 80.
[16] *Ibid.*, p. 82.
[17] *Ibid.*, p. 84.
[18] *Ibid.*, p. 86.
[19] *Ibid.*, p. 99.
[20] *Ibid.*, p. 115.
[21] *Ibid.*, p. 119.
[22] Bertrand Russell, *The Philosophy of Logical Atomism,* La Salle, Il: Open Court, 1985.
[23] Max Black, "Vagueness: An Exercies in Logical Analysis," *Philosophy of Science*, vol. 4,(1937), pp. 427-55.
[24] Kosko, *Fuzzy Thinking*, p. 123.
[25] *Ibid.,* p. 124.
[26] *Ibid.*, p. 127.
[27] viz. Jan Christiann Smuts, *Holism and Evolution,* London: Macmillan, 1928.
[28] Lofti Zadeh, "From Circuit Theory to System Theory," *Proceedings of the IRE*, 1962.
[29] Kosko, *Fuzzy Thinking*, p. 148.
[30] *Fuzzy Logic: A Key Technology for Future Competitiveness*, U.S. Department of Commerce, November 1991.
[31] Kosko, *Fuzzy Thinking*, p. 158.
[32] *Ibid.,* p. 159.
[33] *Ibid.*, p. 160.
[34] *Ibid.*, p. 161.
[35] Ebrahim Mamdani, "Application of Fuzzy Logic to Approximate Reasoning Using Linguistic Synthesis," *IEEE Transactions of Computer C-26*, December 1977, pp. 1182-91.
[36] Kosko, *Fuzzy Thinking*, p. 172.
[37] *Ibid.*, p. 176.
[38] Stephen Grossberg, *Studies in Mind and Brain,* Reidel, 1982.
[39] Kosko, *Fuzzy Thinking*, p. 215.
[40] *Ibid.*, p. 222.
[41] *Ibid.*, p. 246.
[42] *Ibid.,* p. 250.

[43] *Ibid.*, p. 256.

Chapter Three

Chaos

Gleick argues that clouds represent a side of nature that the mainstream of physics had passed by, a side that was at once fuzzy and detailed, structured and unpredictable. For as long as the world has had physicists inquiring into the laws of nature, it has suffered a special ignorance about disorder in the atmosphere, in the turbulent sea, in the fluctuations of wildlife populations, in the oscillations of the heart and the brain. The irregular side of nature, the discontinuous and erratic side – these have been puzzles to some, or worse, monstrosities.[1] But in the 1970s, a few scientists in the United States and Europe began to find a way through disorder. They were mathematicians, physicists, biologists, chemists – all seeking connections between different kinds of irregularity. Physiologists found a surprising order in the chaos that develops in the human heart, the prime cause of sudden unexpected death. Ecologists explored the rise and fall of gypsy moth populations; economists dug out old stock price data and tried a new kind of analysis. The insights that emerged led directly into the natural world – the shapes of clouds, the patterns of lightning, the microscopic interweaving of blood vessels, the galactic clustering of stars.[2] When Mitchell Feigenbaum began thinking about chaos, he was one of a handful of scattered scientists, mostly unknown to one another. A decade later, chaos had become a shorthand name for a fast-growing movement that is reshaping the fabric of the scientific establishment. At every major university and corporate research center some theorists ally themselves first with chaos and only second with their nominal specialties. Now that science is looking, chaos seems to be everywhere; it appears in the behavior of the weather, in airplane flight, in oil flowing in under-ground pipes. That realization has begun to change the way business executives make decisions about insurance, the way astronomers look at the solar system, the way political theorists talk about the stresses leading to armed conflict.[3] Chaos breaks across the lines that separate scientific disciplines because it is a science of the global nature of systems. It has brought together thinkers from fields that had been widely separated. Chaos poses problems that defy accepted ways of working in science, as it makes strong claims about the universal behavior of complexity.

The first chaos theorists, the scientists who set the discussion in motion, shared certain sensibilities. They had an eye for pattern, especially patterns that appeared in different scales at the same time. They had a taste for randomness and complexity, for jagged edges and sudden bumps. Believers in chaos speculate about determinism and free will, about evolution, about the nature of conscious intelligence. They feel that they are turning back a trend in science towards reductionism. Like relativity and quantum mechanics, chaos cuts away at the truth of Newton's physics. Relativity eliminated the Newtonian illusion of absolute space and time; quantum theory eliminated the Newtonian claim of a controllable measurement process; and chaos eliminates the Laplacian fancy of determinate predictability. The simplest systems are now seen to create extraordinarily difficult problems of predictability. Traditionally, when physicists saw complex results, they looked for complex causes. The modern study of chaos began with the creeping realization in the 1960s that quite simple mathematical equations could model systems every bit as violent as a waterfall. Tiny differences in input could quickly become overwhelming differences in output. Weather had a flavor that could not be explained by talking about averages. In theory, a computer could let meteorologists do what astronomers had been able to do with pencil and slide rule; reckon the future of their enterprise from the initial condition and the physical laws that guide its evolution. But it turned out that the weather was vastly more complicated. There was always one small compromise, so small that working scientists usually forgot it was there: measurements could never be perfect. The basic idea of Western science is that the small differences can be neglected, and there is a belief in convergence in the way things work. Economic forecasters rely on this assumption, though their success is less apparent. Edward Lorenz saw that there must be a link between the unwillingness of the weather to repeat itself and the inability of the forecaster to predict it. In science, as in life, it was well-known that a chain of events can have a point of crisis that would magnify small changes. But chaos meant that such points were everywhere. Nonlinear relationships are not strictly proportional, and nonlinear systems generally cannot be solved and cannot be added together. In fluid and mechanical systems, the nonlinear terms tend to be the features (such as friction) that people want to leave out when they try to get good, simple understanding. Nonlinearity means that the act of playing the game has a way of changing the rules.

Thomas Kuhn deflated the views of science as an orderly process of asking questions and finding their answers. He emphasized a contrast between the bulk of what scientists do – working on legitimate, well-understood problems within their disciplines – and the exceptional, unorthodox work that leads to revolutions. Not by accident he made scientists seem less than perfect rationalists.[4] Central to Kuhn's ideas is the vision of normal science as solving problems, the kind of problems that students learn the first time they open their textbooks. Such problems define an accepted style of achievement that carries most scientists through graduate school, through their theses work, and through the writing of journal articles that make up the body of academic careers. Under normal conditions, the research scientist is not an innovator but a solver of puzzles, and the puzzles upon which he concentrates are those that he believes can be both stated and solved within the existing scientific tradition. Then there are revolutions; a new science arises out of one that has reached a dead end. Often a revolution has an interdisciplinary character. Its central discoveries often come from people straying outside the normal bounds of their specialties. The problems that obsess these theorists are not recognized as legitimate lines of inquiry. Shallow ideas can be assimilated, but ideas that require people to reorganize their picture of the world provoke hostility. To chaos researchers, mathematics has become an experimental science, with the computer replacing laboratories full of test tubes and microscopes. Graphic images are the key. Thus, physical motion for Aristotle was not a quantity or a force but rather a kind of change, just as a person's growth is a kind of change. When Galileo looked at the pendulum, on the other hand, he saw a regularity that could be measured. To explain it required a revolutionary way of understanding objects in motion. Galileo's advantage over the ancient Greeks was not that he had better data; rather he saw the regularity because he already had a theory that predicted it. He understood what Aristotle could not; that a moving object tends to keep moving, that a change in speed or direction could only be explained by some external force, like friction. But the regularity Galileo saw is only an approximation. Small nonlinearities were easy to disregard; people who conduct experiments learn quickly that they live in an imperfect world. In the centuries since Galileo and Newton, the search for regularity in experiment has been fundamental. An experimentalist looks for quantities that remain the same, or quantities that are zero, and that means disregarding bits of messiness that interfere with the neat picture. The story of Galileo dropping balls off the Tower of Pisa is a piece of myth inventing an ideal scientific world where regularities can be separated from the disorder of experience.[5] Students learned that nonlinear systems were usually unsolvable, which is true, and that they tend to be exceptions, which is not true. Traditionally, a dynamist would believe that to write down a system's equations is to understand the system. But because of the little bits of nonlinearity in these equations, a dynamist would find himself helpless to answer the easiest practical questions about the future of the system. The tiny imprecisions built into each observation or calculation rapidly takes over because this is a system with a sensitive dependence on initial conditions. Physicists assumed that any behavior they could actually observe regularly would have to be stable, whereas some systems are locally unpredictable yet globally stable. Real dynamical systems play by a more complicated set of rules than anyone had imagined; a complex system can give rise to turbulence and coherence at the same time. If regular equations could produce irregular behavior, to an ecologist that rang certain bells. Indeed the complexity of the real phenomena studies in the life sciences outstripped anything to be found in a physicist's laboratory. Biologists' mathematical models tended to be caricatures of reality, as did the models of economists, demographers, psychologists and urban planners. The standards are different but none of the early ecologists had the inclination or the strength to keep churning out numbers that refused to settle down. The stable solutions were the interesting ones, and the whole point of oversimplifying was to model regularity.

James Yorke had given the science of chaos its name; he felt that physicists had learned not to see chaos. In daily life, the (Lorenzian) quality of sensitive dependence on initial conditions lurks everywhere.

Small perturbances in one's daily trajectory can have large consequences. But it is no exaggeration to say that the vast enterprise of calculus made possible most of the practical triumphs of post-medieval science. So by the time a scientist masters this way of thinking about nature, becoming comfortable with the theory and the hard practice, he is likely to have lost sight of the fact that most differential equations cannot be solved at all.[6] If you can write down the solution of the differential equation, Yorke said, then necessarily it is not chaotic because to write it down, you must find regular invariants – things that are conserved, like angular momentum. But this is exactly the way to eliminate the possibility of chaos. The solvable systems are the ones shown in textbooks, and confronted with a nonlinear system, scientists would have to substitute linear approximations or some other backdoor approach. Textbooks show students only the rare nonlinear systems that would yield to such techniques, and do not display sensitive dependence on initial conditions. Nonlinear systems with real chaos were rarely taught or learned, and only a few were able to remember that the solvable, orderly, linear systems were the aberrations. Only a few, that is, understood how nonlinear nature really is. Yorke understood that the first message is that there is disorder, whereas physicists and mathematicians want to discover regularities. Beyond a certain point, periodicity gives way to chaos, i.e., to fluctuations that never settle at all. Yet in the middle of this complexity, stable cycles suddenly return. In the real world, an observer would see just the vertical scale corresponding to one parameter at a time. He would only see one kind of behavior – possibly a steady state, possibly a seven-year cycle, possibly apparent randomness. He would have no way of knowing that the same system, with some slight change in some parameter, would display patterns of a completely different kind.[7] Yorke had offered more than a mathematical result; he had shown that chaos is ubiquitous, stable, and structured. Biologists have overlooked bifurcations on the way to chaos because they usually lacked mathematical sophistication, and because they lacked motivation to explore disorderly behavior. Mathematicians had seen bifurcations but had moved on. Robert May, a man with one foot in each discipline, came to realize that here was a domain that was both astonishing and profound. May knew that the simple equations were just metaphors, and so he wondered how widely the metaphors would apply. Simple deterministic models would produce what looked like random behavior. As May looked at more biological systems through the prism of simple chaotic models, he continued to see results that violated the standard intuitions of practitioners. In epidemiology, for example, it was well-known that epidemics tend to come in cycles, regular or irregular. Measles, polio, rubella – all rise and fall in frequency. May realized that the oscillations could be reproduced by a nonlinear model, and he wondered what would happen if such a system received a sudden kick – a perturbation of the kind that might correspond to a program of inoculation. Naive intuition suggests that the system will change smoothly in the desired direction, but actually, May discovered, high oscillations are likely to begin. Even if the long-term trend was turned solidly downward, the path to new equilibrium would be interrupted by surprising peaks. In data from real programs, such as a campaign to wipe out rubella in Britain, doctors had seen oscillations just like these predicted by May's model. Yet any heath official, seeing a short-term rise in rubella or gonorrhea, would assume the inoculation program had failed.[8]

Each discipline considered its particular branch of chaos to be special to itself. But May realized that the astonishing structures he had hardly began to explore had no intrinsic connection to biology. No matter how elaborate linear mathematics would get, with its Fourier transformations, its orthogonal functions, its regression techniques, May argued that it inevitably misled scientists about their over-whelming nonlinear world. The mathematical intuition so developed ill equips the student to approach the bizarre behavior exhibited by the simplest of discrete nonlinear systems. Not only in research but also in the everyday world of politics and economics, we would all be better off if more people realized that simple nonlinear systems do not necessarily possess simple dynamic properties.[9] Economists generally assumed that the price of a commodity like cotton changed in two different ways, one orderly and one random. Over the long run, prices would be driven steadily by real forces of the economy – the rise and fall of the New England textile industry, or the opening of inter-national trade routes – while over the short term, prices would bounce around more or less randomly. But Hendrick Houthakker's data failed to match these expectations. Most changes were small, of course, but the rate of small changes to large ones was not as high as he had expected. The standard model for plotting variations is the bell-shaped curve. In the middle, where the bump of the bell rises, most data cluster around average, and on the sides, the high and the low extremes fall off rapidly. The bell-shaped curve represents the standard, so-called Gaussian distribution of things or the normal distribution. It makes a statement about the nature of randomness, but as a means of finding patterns of the economic data, the standard notions left something to be desired. No matter how he plotted them, Houtakker could not make the changes in cotton prices fit the bell-shaped model. Benoit Mandelbrot was beginning to see a similarity in surprisingly disparate places. Unlike most mathematicians, he confronted problems by depending on his intuitions about patterns and shapes. He already had the idea that other laws, with different behavior, govern random, stochastic phenomena. Economists already shared a conviction that small transient changes in price had nothing in common with large, long-term changes. But Mandelbrot was looking for patterns not at one scale or another, but across every scale. The numbers that were aberrations from the point of view of normal distribution produced symmetry from the point of view of scaling. Each particular price change was random and unpredictable but the sequence of changes was independent of scale; curves for daily price changes and monthly price changes matched perfectly. Incredibly, analyzed Mandelbrot's way, the degree of variation in prices has remained constant over a tumultuous sixty-year period that saw two world wars and a depression.

Within the most disorderly reams of data lived an unexpected kind of order. Scaling seemed to be a quality with a life of its own – a signature.[10] Mandelbrot argued, contrary to intuition, that in the electronic transmission of signals you never find a time during which errors were scattered continuously. Within any burst of errors, no matter how short, there would always be periods of completely error-free transmission. He was duplicating an abstract construction known as a Cantor set: a strange "dust" of parts, infinitely many yet infinitely sparse. Mandelbrot was thinking of transmission errors as a Cantor set arranged in time. It meant that, instead of trying to increase signal strength to drown out more and more noise, engineers should settle for a modest signal, accept the inevitability of errors and use a strategy of redundancy to catch and restrict them. Mandelbrot's scaling patterns suggested that the noise could never be explained on the basis of specific local events.[11] Prices can change in instantaneous jumps as swiftly as a piece of news can flash across a teletype wire and a thousand brokers can change their minds. A stock market strategy was doomed to fail, Mandelbrot argued, if it assumed that a stock would have to sell for $50 at some point in its way down from $60 to $10.[12]

Discontinuity, bursts of noise, Cantor dust – phenomena like these had no place in the geometries of the past two thousand years. The shapes of classical geometry are lines and planes, circles and spheres, triangles and cones. They represent a powerful abstraction of reality, and they inspired a powerful tradition of Platonic harmony. Euclid made of them a geometry that lasted two thousand years, artists found an ideal beauty in them; Ptolemaic astronomers built a theory of the universe out of them. But for understanding complexity, they turn out to be the wrong kind of abstraction.[13] Clouds are not spheres Mandelbrot is fond of saying; mountains are not cones. The new geometry mirrors a universe that is rough, not rounded, scabrous, not smooth. The understanding of nature's complexity brought a realization that the entanglements were not just random, not just an accident. It inspired a belief that the interesting feature of a lightning bolt's path was not its direction, but rather the distribution of zigs and zags. Mandelbrot's work made a claim about the world, and the claim was that such odd shapes carry meaning.

Wondering about coastlines and wiggly national borders, Lewis Richardson checked encyclopedias in Spain and Portugal, Belgium and the Netherlands, and discovered discrepancies of twenty percent in the estimated lengths of their common frontiers. In fact, Mandelbrot argues, any coastline is, in a sense, infinitely long. In another sense, the answer depends on the length of your measuring unit. Dividers skip over twists and turns smaller than, say, one yard, but the surveyor writes down the number anyway. Then he sets the dividers to a smaller length – say, one foot – and repeats the process. He arrives at a somewhat greater length because the dividers will capture more of the detail. He writes this new number down, sets the dividers at four inches, and starts again. This mental experiment, using imaginary dividers, is a way of quantifying the effect of observing an object from different distances, at different scales. Common sense suggests that these estimates should converge, and in fact, if the coastline were some Euclidean shape, such as a circle, this method of summing finer and finer straight line distances would indeed converge. But Mandelbrot found that as the scale of measurement becomes smaller, the measured length of the coastline rises without limit, bays and peninsulas revealing ever smaller subbays and subpeninsulas.[14] Since Euclidean measurements of length, depth, and thickness failed to capture the substance of irregular shapes, Mandelbrot turned to the idea of dimension. The process of abstraction that allowed Euclid to conceive of one- or two-dimensional objects spills over easily into our use of everyday things. Effectively, a road map remains two-dimensional even if it is folded up. In the same way, a thread is effectively one-dimensional and a particle has effectively no dimensions at all.[15] The dimension of a ball of twine, Mandelbrot says, depends on our point of view. From a great distance, the ball is no more than a point, with zero dimensions. From closer, the ball is seen to fill spherical space, taking up three dimensions. From closer still, the twine comes into view, and the object becomes effectively one-dimensional, though the one dimension is certainly tangled up around itself in a way that makes use of three-dimensional space. The notion of how many numbers it takes to specify a point remains useful. In macroscopic perspectives, twine turns into three-dimensional columns, and the columns resolve themselves into one-dimensional fibers; the solid material dissolves into zero-dimensional points. The effective dimension of an object turns out to be different from its mundane three dimensions. Factual dimensions become a way of measuring quantities that otherwise have no clear definition: the degree of roughness or brokenness or irregularity of an object. The claim was that the degree of irregularity remains constant over different scales. A Koch loop in which two sides of a triangle are infinitely broken to form new triangles remains continuos, never intersecting itself because the new triangles on each side are always small enough to avoid bumping into each other. If you draw a circle around the original triangle, the Koch curve would never extend beyond it,[16] yet the curve itself is infinitely long. This paradoxical result – infinite length in a fractal space – is contrary to all reasonable intuitions about shapes. A simple, Euclidean, one-dimensional line fills no space at all, but the outline of a Koch curve, with infinite length crowding into a finite area, does fill space. It is more than a line, but less than a plane. Mandelbrot could characterize the fractal dimension precisely: for the Koch curve, the infinitely extended multiplication of four thirds gives a dimension of 1.2618.[17]

Intuition as it was trained by the hand, the pencil, and the ruler, found these shapes quite monstrous and pathological. Intuition is not something that is given once and for all. Mandelbrot says that he has trained himself to accept as obvious shapes that were initially rejected as absurd, and he believes that anyone can do the same. Above all, fractal meant self-similar, and self-similarity is symmetry across scale; it implies recursion, patterns inside patterns. The Koch curve displays self-similarity, for it looks exactly the same even under high magnification. The same transformation is repeated under smaller and smaller scales. The unifying idea of fractal geometry brought together scientists who thought their own observations were idiosyncratic, and who had no systematic way of understanding them. The insights of fractal geometry helped scientists who study the way things meld together, the way they break apart, or the way they shatter. It is a way of looking at materials – the microscopically jagged surfaces, the tiny holes and channels of porous oil bearing rock, the fragmental landscapes of an earthquake zone.[18] Christopher Scholz found that fractal geometry provided a powerful way of describing the particular bumpiness of the earth's surface, and metallurgists discovered the same for the surfaces of different kinds of steel. The fractal dimension of a metal's surface often provides information that corresponds to the metal's strength. Fractal descriptions found immediate applications in a series of problems connected to the properties of surfaces in contact with one another. The contact between tire threads and concrete is such a problem, and so is contact in machine joints, or electrical contact. Contacts between surfaces have properties that turn out to depend on the fractal quality of the bumps upon bumps upon bumps. One simple but powerful consequence of the fractal geometry of surfaces is that surfaces in contact do not touch everywhere. Even in a rock under enormous pressure, at some sufficiently small scale it becomes clear that gaps remain, allowing fluid to flow. It is why two pieces of a broken teacup can never be rejoined, even though they appear to fit together at some gross scale.

Size and duration, qualities that depend on scale, are qualities that can help describe an object or classify it. A large earthquake is just a scaled-up version of a small earthquake. That distinguishes earthquakes from animals. A ten-inch animal must be structured quite differently from a one-inch animal, and a one hundred-inch animal needs a different structure still, if its bones are not to snap under the increased mass. It is hard to break the habit of thinking of things in terms of how big they are and how long they last. It happens that the equations of fluid flow are in many contexts dimensionless, meaning that they apply without regard to scale. Blood vessels, from aorta to capillaries, form another kind of continuum, and the nature of their branching if fractal. Just as the Koch curve squeezes a line of infinite length into a small area, the circulatory system must organize a large surface area into a limited volume. The fractal structure nature has devised works so efficiently that, in most tissue, no cell is ever more than three or four cells away from a blood vessel. Yet the vessels and blood take up little space, no more than about five percent of the body. Typical human lungs pack in a surface bigger than a tennis court, but anatomists are trained to look at one scale at a time, and thus the language of anatomy tends to obscure the unity across scales. For some purposes categories prove useful, while for others they mislead. A decade after Mandelbrot published his physiological speculations, some theoretical biologists began to find fractal organizations controlling structures all through the body. The urinary collection system proved fractal, as did the network of special fibers in the heart that carry pulses of electrical current to the controlling muscles. Mandelbrot's point is that the complications exist only in the context of traditional Euclidean geometry. DNA surely cannot specify the vast number of bronchi, bronchioles, and alveoli, or the particular spatial structure of the resulting tree, but it can specify a repeating process of bifurcation and their development. Theoretical biologists argued that understanding how such patterns were encoded and processed had become a major challenge to biology.[19]

Mathematics is full of channels and byways that seem to lead nowhere in one era and become major areas of study in another. The potential application of a piece of pure thought can never be predicted, and that is why mathematicians value work in an artistic way, seeking elegance and beauty as artists do. The term fractal came to stand for a way of describing, calculating, and thinking about shapes that are irregular and fragmented, jagged and broken up – shapes from the crystalline curves of snowflakes to the discontinuous dust of galaxies. Mandelbrot found his most enthusiastic acceptance among applied scientists working with oil or rocks or metals, particularly in corporate research centers. The structures that provided the key to nonlinear dynamics proved to be fractal. The early sense of self-similarity as the organizing principle came from the limitations on the human experience of scale. How else to imagine the very great and the very small, the very fast and the very slow, but as an extension of the known?[20] This myth died hard even as the human vision was extended by telescopes and microscopes. The first discoveries were realizations that each new change in scale brought new phenomena and new kinds of behavior, and scientists were beginning to talk in terms of theories that used hierarchies of scales. In evolutionary biology it became clear that a full theory would have to recognize patterns of development in genes, in individual organisms, in species, and in families of species

all at once. By the late twentieth century, in ways never before
conceivable, ranges of the incomprehensibly small and the unimaginably large became part of everyone's experience. As the culture
became familiar with photographs of galaxies and atoms, new kinds of
comparisons between large and small were inevitable – and some of
these were productive.[21] Often the scientists drawn to fractal geometry
felt emotional parallels between their new mathematical aesthetic and
the changes in the arts during the second half of the twentieth century.
Architects no longer cared to build blockish skyscrapers like the
Seagram Building in New York, once much hailed and copied. To
Mandelbrot and his followers the reason was clear; simple shapes are
inhuman. They fail to resonate with the way nature organizes itself or
with the way human perception sees the world. Our feeling of beauty is
inspired by the harmonious arrangement of order and disorder as it
occurs in natural objects – in clouds, trees, mountain ranges or snow
crystals. To Mandelbrot, art that satisfied lacks scale, in the sense that
it contains important elements at all sizes. A Beaux-Arts paragon like
the Paris Opera has no scale because it has every scale, and an
observer seeing the building from any distance finds some detail that
draws the eye. The composition changes as one approaches and new
elements of the structure come into view.[22] In terms of aesthetic
values, the new mathematics of fractal geometry brought bland science
in tune with the peculiarly modern feeling for untamed, uncivilized,
undomesticated nature. A new-romantic trend was perceived not only
in the arts but also in science.

For most physicists, turbulence seemed almost unknowable.
Engineers have reliable techniques for calculated flow, as long as it
remains calm. The practical interest is usually one-sided; make
turbulence go away. When flow is smooth or laminar, small disturbances die out, but past the onset of turbulence, disturbances grow cata-
strophically. This onset – this transition – became a critical problem in
science. The onset of turbulence can even be seen and measured in
laboratory experiments but its nature remains obscure. Even
supercomputers are close to helpless in the face of irregular fluid
motion.[23] At each scale, as you look closer at a turbulent eddy, new
regions of calm come into view; thus, the convention of homogeneity
gives way to the assumption of intermittency. The intermittent picture,
when idealized somewhat, looks largely fractal, with intermixed
regions of roughness and smoothness ranging down from the large to
the small. The paradigm for how turbulence starts comes from Lev D.

Landau's fluid dynamics. As new energy comes into the system, he conjectured, new frequencies begin one at a time, each incompatible with the last. Physicists accepted that picture, but no one had any idea how to predict when an increase in energy would create a new frequency, or what the new frequency would be. There is no natural deep theory for turbulence, and it is easy to see why turbulence resisted analysis. The equations of fluid flow are nonlinear partial differential equations, unsolvable except in special cases. Yet David Ruelle worked out an abstract alternative to Landau's picture couched in the terminology of Stephen Smale, with images of space as a pliable material to be squeezed, stretched, and folded into shapes like horseshoes. One advantage of thinking of states as points in space is that it makes change easier to catch. A system where variables change continuously up or down becomes a moving point, like a fly moving around in a room. If some combinations of variables never occur, then the scientist can simply imagine that part of the room is out of bounds; the fly never goes there. Spaces of four, five or more dimensions tax the visual imagination of even the most agile biologist. Yet complex systems have many independent variables, and at higher levels of energy simulation the picture becomes quite dramatic; evidence of complete disorder mixed with clear components of order, forming shapes that suggest "islands" to the astronomers. Disorder was channeled, it seemed, into patterns with some underlying common theme.[24]

The idea of underlying unity and common form in nature had an intrinsic appeal, but it had an also unfortunate history of inspiring pseudoscientists and cranks. Much mathematical analysis and much experience with real systems was needed to establish the power of the scaling idea. There was a kind of relativity in which the position of the observer, near or far, on the beach or in a satellite, affected the measurement. As Mandelbrot had seen, the variation across scales was not arbitrary; it followed rules. Information is stored in a plastic way, allowing unexpected juxtapositions and leaps of the imagination. It is possible that a system like the weather may never converge to an average. Edward Lorenz recognized that the average too fluctuated constantly, for when a parameter value was changed ever so slightly, the average might change dramatically. The earth climate might never readily settle into an equilibrium with average long-term behavior.[25] An observer might see one kind of behavior over a very long time, yet a completely different kind of behavior could be just as natural for the system. When order emerged, it suddenly seemed to have forgotten what the original equation was. Something about these functions, Feigenbaum realized, must be recursive, self-referential – the behavior of the one guided by the behavior of another hidden inside it. Such universality meant that different systems would behave identically. Feigenbaum was studying simple numerical functions but he believed that his theory expressed a natural law about systems at the point of transition between orderly and turbulent. The physical implication was that real-world systems behave in some recognizable way, and furthermore, that it would be recognizably the same. As nonlinear science arose in odd corners of different disciplines, the flow of ideas failed to follow the standard logic of historians. The emergence of chaos as an autonomous entity was a story not only of new theories and new discoveries but also of the belated understanding of old ideas. Scientists were biased by the customs of their disciplines or by the accidental paths of their own educations. But Feigenbaum had discovered the universality of fractal structures and created a theory to explain it. This met with surprise, disbelief and excitement. In the end, in order to understand, you have to change gears; it requires a different way of thinking about the problem.[26] One has to look for different ways of how the big issues relate to the small details. In one sense, art is a theory about the way the world looks to human beings. What artists have accomplished is realizing that there is only a small amount of stuff that is important, and then managed to say what it is.

Nonlinearity can stabilize a system no less than destabilize it. Nonlinear feedback regulates motion, making it more robust. In the presence of nonlinearity, a perturbation can feed on itself until it dies away, and the system returns automatically to a stable state. Albert Libchaber believed that biological systems use their nonlinearity as a defense against disturbances such as noise. Flow was a Platonic idea, assuming that change in systems reflected some reality independent of the particular instant. Libchaber adopted Plato's sense that hidden forms fill the universe. You can think of flow in many ways; flow in economics or in history. First it may be laminal, then bifucatory to a more complicated state, perhaps with oscillations; then it may be chaotic.[27] The universality of shapes, the similarity across scales, the recursive power of flows within flows – all were just beyond reach of the standard differential calculus approach to equations of change. But that was not easy to see, for scientific problems are expressed in the available scientific language. Libchaber and some other experimenters were convinced that dynamical shapes like leaves borrowed their form from a not yet considered weaving of forces. Even when the flow itself is past or invisible, the evidence of flow remains. As Theoder Schwenk saw it, the rolling of eddies, the unfolding of organic forms, the patterns of mountain ranges or of animal organs, all followed one path. He argued by analogy, and his case finally came down to a display of similarities. Apart form D'Arcy Thompson, not many biologists had pursued the undeniable unity of living organisms (as anticipated in Goethe's *On the Transformation of Plants*). Reductionism triumphed in nonlinear biology and everywhere else as well, from evolution to medicine. How else to understand cells but to study membranes and nuclei, ultimately proteins, enzymes, and chromosomes? When astronomy and physics emerged as secular sciences, no small part of the pain came from discarding arguments by design – forward looking teleology. In biology, however, Darwin firmly established teleology as the central mode of thinking about cause. An adaptive explanation for the shape of an organism or the function of an organ always looks not to its physical cause but to its final cause. D'Arcy Thompson asked that biology remember physical cause as well, mechanism and teleology together. Leaves come in just a few shapes, and the shape of a leaf is not dictated by its function.[28] He emphasized that neither accident nor purpose could explain the striking universality of forms. Theorists adopted Feigenbaum's techniques and found other mathematical routes to chaos, variants of period doublings, such patterns as intermittancy and quasiperiodicity. These two proved universal in theory and experiment. The experimenters' discoveries set in motion the era of computer exploration; physicists discovered that computers produced the same qualitative pictures as real experiments, and produced them millions of times faster and more reliably. In 1980, a European group provided a convincing mathematical explanation: dissipation deprives a complex system of many conflicting notions, dramatically bringing the behavior of many dimensions down to one.[29] A computer model is just a set of arbitrary rules chosen by programmers, whereas a real-world fluid, even in a stripped-down millimeter cell, has the undeniable potential for all the free, untrammeled motion of natural disorder. It has the potential for surprise.[30] It is hard to remember how easily nature can confound an experimenter, and whenever a good physicist examines a situation, he must wonder which bit of reality was left out, which potential surprise was sidestepped.

Many problems of abstract mathematics and real-world physics turn out to create boundaries that are almost unimaginably complex; magnified segments reveal a fractal structure, repeating the basic pattern on smaller and smaller scales.[31] The Mandelbrot set became a kind of public emblem for chaos, appearing on the glossy covers of conference brochures and engineering quarterlies, forming the centerpiece of an exhibit of computer art that traveled internationally in 1985 and 1986. Mandelbrot saw a seemingly smooth boundary resolve itself into a chain of spirals like the tails of sea horses. The activity of repeating a process indefinitely and asking whether the result is infinite resembles feedback problems in the everyday world. Unlike the traditional shapes of geometry, circles, ellipses and parabolas, the Mandelbrot set allows no shortcut. The only way to see what kind of shape goes with a particular equation is by trial and error, and the trial and error style brought the explorers of this new terrain closer in spirit to Magellan than to Euclid. New geometries always begin when someone changes a fundamental rule. Suppose a space can be curved instead of flat, a geometer says, and the result is a weird parody of Euclid that provides precisely the right framework for Einstein's relativity theory. Suppose space can have four dimensions, or five, or six. Suppose the number expressing *dimension* can be a fraction. Suppose shapes can be twisted, stretched, knotted. Or now, suppose shapes can be defined, not by solving an equation once, but by iterating it in a feedback loop.[32] Standard geometry takes an equation and asks for the set of numbers that *satisfy* it. But when a geometer iterates an equation instead of solving it, the equation becomes a process instead of a description, dynamic instead of static. A point is plotted not when it satisfies an equation but when it produces a certain kind of behavior; one behavior might be a steady state, another might be a convergence to a periodic repetition of states. Another might be an out-of-control case of infinity.[33] With computers, trial and error geometry becomes possible; a finer grid gives a sharper picture at the expense of longer computation. Each foray deeper into the Mandelbrot set brought new surprises, for no point of the set exactly resembles any other part at *any* magnification.[34]

For H. O. Peitgen and P. Richter the Mandelbrot set held a universe of ideas; a modern philosophy of art, a justification of the new role of experimentation in mathematics, a way of bringing complex systems before a large public. The subject is unstructured. In a structured subject, it is known what is known and what is unknown, what people have already tried and doesn't lead anywhere. You have to work on a problem that is known to be a problem, but a problem that is known to be a problem must be hard, otherwise it would already have been solved.[35] Computer exploration was giving mathematics the freedom to take a more natural path, Peitgen believed, the numerical power of computation and the visual cues to intuition would suggest promising avenues and spare mathematicians blind alleys. The people who looked at such pictures saw that all the scales have similar patterns, yet every scale was different. The study of fractal basin boundaries was the study of systems that would reach one of several nonchaotic final states, raising the question of how to predict which. The boundary proves to be a fractal set, not necessarily self-similar, but infinitely detailed. For some starting conditions, the outcome is quite predictable, but near the boundary, prediction becomes impossible.[36] Scientists studying fractal basin boundaries showed that the border between calm and catastrophe could be far more complex than anyone had dreamed. The system is determinate, but you can't say what it's going to do next. The process of mixing – ubiquitous in nature and industry, yet still poorly understood – proved ultimately bound up with the mathematics of chaos. Some systems would create disorder in one direction while remaining firm and methodical in another. It was as if the system had orderly impulse and a disorderly one together, and they were decoupling.[37] Information theory became a handle for grasping how noise in the form of random errors intertwined with the flow of bits. It gave a way of predicting the necessary capacity of communication lines or compact disks or any technology that encoded language, sounds or images. It put teeth in the crucial notion of "redundancy." In terms of Shannon's information theory, ordinary language contains greater than fifty percent redundancy in the form of sounds or letters that are not strictly necessary for carrying the message. Redundancy is a predictable departure from the random. Part of the redundancy in ordinary language lies in its meaning, and that part is hard to quantify, depending as it does on people's shared knowledge of their language and the world. Entropy is the name for the quality of systems that increase under the Second Law of thermodynamics: mixing, disorder, randomness. The concept is easier to grasp intuitively than to measure in any real-life situation. Order intrudes in ways that defy any straightforward counting algorithm. In the development of a person's mind from childhood, information is clearly not just accumulated but also generated – created from connections that were not there before. An alternative approach would be to forget about the physics and look only at the data, as though it were coming out of a black box. These methods became critical to the application of chaos to real world problems.[38] Tiny random data remain spread out in an undefined mass, but chaos – determinate and patterned – pulls the data into visible shapes. Of all the possible patterns of disorder, nature favors just a few.[39]

You can make your model more complex and more faithful to reality, or you can make it simper and easier to handle. To generalize and abstract, mapmakers highlight such features as their clients choose. Whatever their purpose, maps and models must simplify as much as they mimic the world. In the 1980s, chaos brought to life a new kind of physiology, built on the idea that mathematical tools could help scientists understand global complex systems independent of local detail. They studied chaos in respiratory disorders and psychiatrists explored the multidimensional approach to the prescription of antidepressant drugs. The normal cardiac regimen is periodic, but there are many nonperiodic pathologies (like ventricular fibrillation) that lead to the steady state of death. Researchers, using the tool of chaos, began to discover that traditional cardiology was making the wrong generalizations about irregular heart-beats, inadvertently using superficial classifications to obscure deep causes.[40] Trial and error has governed the design of artificial heart valves, and by changing the patterns of fluid flow in the heart, artificial valves create areas of turbulence and areas of stagnation. When blood stagnates, it forms clots, and when clots break off and travel to the brain, they cause strokes. Such clotting was the fatal barrier to making artificial hearts. Instead of flowing over a rigid surface, like air over an airplane wing, blood changes the heart's surface dynamically and nonlinearly.[41] In many cases, the onset of fibrillation remains mysterious; instead of contracting and relaxing in a repetitive, periodic way, the heart's muscle writhes uncoordinated, helpless to pump blood. Individual muscle cells respond properly; the parts of the fibrillating heart seem to be working as they should, yet the whole goes fatally awry. Fibrillation is a disorder in a complex system, just as mental disorders – whether or not they have chemical roots. It appears that defibrillators can be radically redesigned to improve their efficiency many times over. Dynamical things were generally counter-intuitive, and the heart is no exception, but physiologists have also begun to see chaos as health. It has long been understood that nonlinearity in feedback processes serves to regulate and control, whereas a locking into a single model can be enslavement, preventing a system from adapting to change. When you reach equilibrium in biology, you are dead. A physicist theory of *ideas* as regions with fuzzy boundaries, separate yet overlapping, pulling like magnets, yet letting go, would naturally turn to the image of a phase space with bases of attraction. Such models seemed to have the right features of stability with instability, and regions with changeable boundaries. The fractal structure offered the kind of self-reflective quality that seems central to the mind's functioning. Life and mind suck order from the sea of disorder.

It is generally assumed that complex behavior implies complex causes. It was also taken for granted that different systems behave differently. But now all that has changed; physicists, mathematicians, biologists, and astronomers have created an alternative set of ideas. Simple systems give rise to complex behavior, and complex systems result in simple behavior. Most importantly, the laws of complexity hold universally. More and more scientists realized that chaos offered a fresh way to proceed with the old data. The general picture of nonlinearity got a lot of people's attention – slowly at first, but increasingly nevertheless. The translation from mathematical terminology is: behavior that produces information amplifies small uncertainties but is not utterly unpredictable.[42] Whatever their field, scientists' task was to understand complexity itself. The Second Law of thermodynamics is a rule from which there seems no appeal, but this law has a life of its own in areas far removed from science. It has been taking the blame for the disintegration of societies, economic decline, the breakdown of manners, and other variants of the decadent theme. The secondary, metaphorical incarnations of the Second Law now seem especially misguided. In our world, complexity flourishes; somehow as the universe ebbs towards its final equilibrium in the featureless heat bath of maximum entropy, it manages to create interesting structures. Thoughtful physicists concerned with the workings of thermodynamics realize how disturbing is the question of a purposeless flow of energy producing life and consciousness. Compounding the trouble is the slippery notion of entropy, reasonably well-defined by thermodynamical purposes in terms of heat and temperature, but devilishly hard to pin down as a measure of disorder. Nature forms patters; some are orderly in space but disorderly in time, others orderly in time but disorderly in space. Some patterns are fractal, exhibiting structures self-similar in scale; others give rise to steady states or oscillating ones. The essence of chaos is a delicate balance between forces of stability and forces of instability. The finest scales proved crucial in the formation of snowflakes, for example, but the laws of pattern formation are universal. Evolution is chaos with feedback, Joseph Ford says; the universe is randomness and dissipation, but randomness with direction can produce surprising complexity. And as E. Lorenz discovered, dissipation is an agent of order.[43] Ecology based on a sense of equilibrium seems doomed to fail. The traditional models are betrayed by their linear bias. Although the attractor is chaotic, some predictability becomes possible in light of the deterministic nature of the model. The study of chaos reveals that it is not featureless but structured in patterns of infinite complexity.

Notes

[1] James Gleick, *Chaos, Making a New Science*, New York, NY: Penguin Books, 1987, p. 3.
[2] *Ibid.*, p. 4.
[3] *Ibid.*, p. 5.
[4] *Ibid.*, p. 36.
[5] *Ibid.*, p. 41.
[6] *Ibid.*, p. 67.
[7] *Ibid.*, p. 73.
[8] *Ibid.*, p. 79.
[9] *Ibid.*, p. 80.
[10] *Ibid.*, p. 86.
[11] *Ibid.*, p. 92.
[12] *Ibid.*, p. 93.
[13] *Ibid.*, p. 94.
[14] *Ibid.*, p. 96.
[15] *Ibid.*, p. 97.
[16] *Ibid.*, p. 99
[17] *Ibid.*, p. 102.
[18] *Ibid.*, p. 104.
[19] *Ibid.*, p. 110.
[20] *Ibid.*, p. 115.
[21] *Ibid.*, p. 116.
[22] *Ibid.*, p. 117.

[23] *Ibid.*, p. 123.
[24] *Ibid.*, p. 152.
[25] *Ibid.*, p. 169.
[26] *Ibid.*, p. 185.
[27] *Ibid.*, p. 195.
[28] *Ibid.*, p. 202.
[29] *Ibid.*, p. 209.
[30] *Ibid.*, p. 210.
[31] *Ibid.*, p. 220.
[32] *Ibid.*, p. 226.
[33] *Ibid.*, p. 227.
[34] *Ibid.*, p. 228.
[35] *Ibid.*, p. 230.
[36] *Ibid.*, p. 235.
[37] *Ibid.*, p. 255.
[38] *Ibid.*, p. 264.
[39] *Ibid.*, p. 267.
[40] *Ibid.*, p. 281.
[41] *Ibid.*, p. 283.
[42] *Ibid.*, p. 306.
[43] *Ibid.*, p. 311.

Chapter Four

The Rationality of Science

Amsterdamski points out that, in recent years, the landscape of historical and philosophical interpretation of the evolution of scientific knowledge has changed. Sociologists of knowledge analyze how knowledge is produced within specific social settings, and the local character of these studies raises the question of whether they can ever produce generalizable epistemological claims. But there is some theoretical, historically changing "background consensus," i.e., an *ideal of science*, within which scientific research is done.[1] There is a significant connection between the debates about the rationality of science and those about the role of science in modern culture. The question about the rationality of science and its development is not one with which scientists engaged in the specific disciplines are concerned. They know the "rules of the game," and rationality becomes problematic only when scientists begin to reflect about the goals and methods of these activities, and about their social functions. In the methodology of science, its rationality is usually treated as unproblematic; indeed science has, as a rule, been seen as the embodiment of human rationality. It is, of course, true that philosophers have long argued about the nature of this method (in philosophical discourse the descriptive and the normative usually appear together), but no one questioned the rationality of science. Even the romantics, who were opposed to rationalism accepted science as the bastion of rationality. Today, however, this has changed and the question of the rationality of science and its development has become one of the most controversial topics in the philosophical reflection on science.[2] For the first time we are no longer certain that progress in scientific knowledge and the technological progress linked with it are indeed always beneficial. Technology's capacity to threaten the continued existence of our species raises fundamental, moral, and political questions. As Robert Oppenheimer said after the Congressional hearings, "Physicists have now learned about sin." They have ceased to occupy a privileged position in the world. The prevailing accepted rules are themselves among the things that change and require an explanation, and to explain them one has to appeal to external, i.e. sociological, historical, and psychological factors. Kuhn points out that no methodology can provide criteria of choice among competing theories.[3] A thesis of the rationality of science in this sense does not allow for changes in the ideal of science, and plays an ideological role in defending the status quo. That is why the notion of the rationality of science has itself become problematic.

Amsterdamski argues that the concept of rationality is not purely epistemological and descriptive, but that it is historically relative and evaluative. What we today consider to be science is rooted in types of knowledge inherited from the past. There is no way to pinpoint when, where, and how science began, and not because we lack sufficient historical information. Rather, the root of the difficulty is that an answer to this question always depends on an ideal of knowledge that we accept. Those who treat science as a disinterested search for universally valid rules will see its origins in the cosmological and philosophical investigations of the ancient Greeks. Those who see it primarily as the ability to manipulate objects efficiently, may note its similarity with magic and technology. Thus, whether we locate the beginnings of science in the mathematical achievements of the Babylonians, the philosophical and cosmological speculations of the Greeks, or the mathematical and experimental models of Galileo – we are always choosing a tradition. An accepted ideal of science determines the answer to the question of where and how science started, and decides what types of knowledge are to be considered scientific. Such a classification is always normative, although every such tradition usually wrongly assumes that its own ideal of science is something obvious, unproblematic, and the only one possible. Thus, despite the repeated attempts of methodologists searching for universally valid criteria of demarcation, science can be distinguished from other types of knowledge in a historically adequate manner only conventionally and normatively. Not everything that has ever been, or might in the future be, considered science can be accommodated by such controversial definitions. An implicit assumption of some normative idea of science is a necessary condition for the formulation of all descriptive methodology. The question of whether other cultures also have science depends on our acceptance of a given ideal of scientific knowledge. Amsterdamski questions Kuhn's assumption that the developed scientific models are at any given time governed by only a single paradigm. The scientific revolution of the sixteenth and seventeenth centuries consisted not only of a number of discoveries that radically modified the paradigms of astronomy (Copernicus, Kepler, and Galileo), mechanics (Galileo and Newton), or chemistry (Boyle and Lavoisier), but rather in the formation and institutionalization of an altogether new scientific ideal, which made these particular discoveries possible and which was fundamentally different from the ideals that had guided research in antiquity and the Middle Ages.

For Kuhn, science does not constitute a whole, but rather a collection of various disciplines each defined by its own paradigm.[4] But Amsterdamski emphasizes that if modifications of disciplinary paradigms can occur without bringing about changes in the ideal of science (as for example, the rejection of Cartesian in favor of Newtonian physics), then the disruption of historical continuity in science or the total collapse of consensus within a discipline occurs far less frequently than Kuhn, and especially Feyerabend, suggest. One is no longer justified in maintaining that a scientific revolution completely destroys all possibilities of communication among those scientists who accept the old paradigm and those who accept the new one. The transition from one to the other is more in the nature of a conversion to a new faith than the result of persuasion by rational argument. The accepted ideal of science constitutes precisely this consensus, which makes possible the conduct of rational discussion while a transition from one paradigm to another is taking place.[5] It is important to realize that while changes from one descriptive paradigm to another (local revolutions) are fairly frequent in science, changes in the ideal of science (global revolutions) are rare. If one ignores the fact that the development of knowledge is codetermined by socially accepted and changing ideals, the history of science is presented as completely autonomous and rational, and is explained in terms of an ahistorical "logic of development" or "rational method," or as the development of an autonomous world of ideas and problems – "world three," as Popper has it.[6] Whatever fails to comply with this logic is then considered the result of extra-rational deviance or pathology. And as a result, there is no common ground between the philosophy and the sociology of science. But if the logic of science is a historic phenomenon rather than a "necessity of reason," it explains why certain rules for justifying claims will be considered rational, while others will not. These rules cannot serve to demarcate science from non-science once and for all, for they are accepted only on the basis of a conceptual ideal of science. Both the received ideal of science and the rules for pursuing science according to this ideal may become subject to philosophical critique. Disputes among supporters of such different systems are generally due to disagreements about basic cultural values, which science is expected to realize. The ideal determines which knowledge is considered scientific. The ancient Greek ideal of science as certain knowledge (*episteme*) implied that technological knowledge was not considered scientific, being neither exact nor certain. As Alexandre Koyré convincingly argues, the ancients did not have mathematical physics because they did not consider it possible; they did not admit that precision applies to terrestrial matter.[7] To create mathematical physics, it is necessary to believe that the book of nature is written in the language of straight lines, circles, and triangles (Galileo), or that knowledge of the sublunar world can be given the same constancy and precision as knowledge of the heavens. The use of measuring instruments in scientific investigations brought about a fundamental change in the accepted image of the world.

The accepted ideal of scientific knowledge constitutes a filter that determines what research will be considered worthwhile, interesting, and important. The range of questions formulated is always relative to a given state of knowledge. Thus, Amsterdamski rejects Popper's "world three," the world of ideas and problems. The logic of a problem situation specifies only the range of questions that can be posed, and delineates the number of possible directions for the further direction of knowledge. If methodological rules are not historically invariant but instead depend on an accepted ideal of science, then no methodology can constitute a supra-historical means of distinguishing science from other intellectual endeavors. Methodological rules turn out to be inadequate because they do not cover everything that historically has been considered science or that possibly might be considered science. Popper's intuition about the goal of investigation or any socially accepted ideal of science is neither eternal nor the only one possible. He does not admit that the logic of scientific discovery may be historically changing, or that it may be the result of a particular state of culture; instead he presents it as a logical necessity. But under changed social conditions science may well lose its autonomy. Whether a given explanation will be considered adequate depends on the accepted ideal of scientific knowledge. An explanatory method that appears adequate and rational in view of one ideal may be judged unsatisfactory or even irrational from a different perspective. One condition for resolving methodological disputes is a general consensus that reflects a shared ideal of scientific knowledge. The development of science from about 1700 to the 1870s was the realization of a specific ideal, which turned out to be considerably different from that of ancient or medieval science. The new science, as Bacon had said, would equip man with new inventions, allowing him to control nature and its forces. Such a science could overcome the ancient opposition between *episteme* and *techne*, and incorporate both.[8]

But one need not assume that this advent of modern science was inevitable. Amsterdamski rejects the view that the emergence of modern science was due to an abandoning of philosophical speculation. For while it paid lip service to radical empiricism, it was practicing something quite different, as Feyerabend emphasizes.[9] By introducing such strange concepts as "momentary action at a distance," and by differentiating absolute time and space from relative time and space that were only apparent, as well as by endowing the whole of matter with characteristics such as gravitation, Newton was not so much reporting on the experiments he had performed as constructing a conceptual apparatus by means of which physical experiments were henceforth to be interpreted. Newton's polemics with the Cartesians and with Leibniz were no disagreements between an empirical physicist and metaphysicians; rather they were a debate between opposing philosophers of nature. What actually changed was the very concept of experience by which scientists were attempting to check their theoretical constructions with the facts, and it was this change that allowed for the emergence of a new ideal of scientific knowledge.[10] Phenomena are no longer explained by means of everyday direct sensory experience, to what is visible, but by experiments, sometimes even thought experiments, which are used to investigate nature. This would be impossible without a questioning of the credibility of common sense, for which everyday experience is always the final authority. Instruments made it possible to study empirically objects that previously could not have been observed. Measuring instruments led to a separation of scientific knowledge from common-sense knowledge, and this eliminated from science all considerations of value and purpose. Instead of a world of objects presented to the senses, science was dealing with abstract bodies moving in abstract geometrical space according to universal laws. The world of sensual qualities accessible to direct perception was replaced by signs and relations, open only to measurement. To hold that the earth moves around the sun, common-sense experience had to be disregarded, and it became necessary to accept that reality is not necessary identical with what appears to our senses. In this matter science was changing the idea of human rationality and its criteria.[11] The previous views now seem nonsensical as long as we remain unaware of how our vision of the world and the ideal of science associated with it differ from those of earlier visions we now reject. The epistemological assumption that it is possible to engage in cognition totally isolated from all external factors, and the related notion of the autonomy of science as a social institution, reflected for a time the actual historical situation of science in society. It eliminated from science introspection, anthropomorphism and all ideas related to value and purpose. It assumed a knowing subject who was capable gradually to learn the truth that would be always and everywhere valid, and science came to be regarded as precisely this kind of knowledge.[12] It also brought about a strict separation between the realms of facts and that of values, which science could neither explain in its own categories nor altogether ignore.

Scientific investigators became professionals only in the twentieth century, reflecting a basic change in the role of science in society. Up to that time science did not have an institutional patron, and governments did not have a "science policy." Only in the last decades of the nineteenth century did the demand for new theoretical knowledge extend beyond the scientific community. The situation where one wrote exclusively for one's peers began to change, as new and powerful clients for such knowledge appeared on the scene. Scientists increasingly became dependent on external support, and the conviction that science has always a beneficial impact on social life began also to be questioned. Science is no longer a source of disinterested information and becomes the provider of goods and services. The scientist becomes an expert whose function is not to choose goals but to advise those in power how to achieve goals that have already been chosen. It is realized that the biological features of the knowing subject, the language he uses in articulating knowledge and reporting on reality, the historical conditions under which science is practiced, the culture of which it is a part, all play significant roles that should not be ignored. If Popper treats science as a means of biological adaptation, it cannot be said to be either true or false. As various non-Euclidean geometries were discovered in the nineteenth century, the Kantian notion that mathematics constitutes synthetic a priori knowledge had to be abandoned, i.e., that only one such syntax is possible. We can no longer say that in doing mathematics we are reading the book of nature as it was written.[13] But if all changes in our knowledge can be presented as changes in the language used to describe the world, everything that experience puts into question can be saved by an appropriate linguistic interpretation. Such a view is common to all versions of radical empiricism in science. Ontologically the subject belongs to the world he is investigating, while as a knowing subject he treats himself as if he were an external observer limited by no physical constraints and completely separate from the world he is investigating. However, modern physics questions the assumption of an autonomous subject; the theory of relativity postulates a temporal horizon beyond which the investigator cannot get information, since all transfer of information takes time. These possibilities are further restricted by Heisenberg's indeterminacy principle; we always pay a price for obtaining information, as we disturb the state of the system we are investigating. The subject's knowledge is not independent of his physical characteristics, and neither are his cognitive possibilities.

The theory of evolution and modern genetics likewise reveal a biological basis to all human intellectual capacities. Sociology of knowledge and anthropology have revealed the Eurocentric conventions of nineteenth-century culture; and as a consequence this culture can no longer be treated as the only possible or rational one. The quite specific historical situation in which scientists lived and worked until the last decades of the nineteenth century seemed to them the only possible one. It made them believe that science is the only disinterested search for truth rendered possible by a single methodology. As long as progress in knowledge and technology were treated as an unquestionable good, their ideal of science seemed unproblematic. Thus, the victory of the Copernican theory was seen as the triumph of the application of the rational method of investigation, not as a revision of accepted criteria of rationality. It was believed that Copernicus defended his theory by means of rational arguments whereas, as a matter of fact, rational arguments tended to support his opponents.[14] Thus, arguments against Copernicus, which appear irrational to us today, were implicitly rational according to an ideal of knowledge accepted at the time. It shows that the relevant ideal of science is regarded as unproblematic since we are unaware of its historical character. Thus, Popper *in The Logic of Scientific Discovery* was convinced that modern science is the manifestation of human rationality. By eliminating the knowing subject, he removes the possibility that extra-rational, genetic, historical, or social conditions have an impact on the development of scientific knowledge.[15] Revolutions in science bring about the replacement of one theory by another, but these changes are always the result of the application of the same rules by which choices are made among competing theories.[16] The view that the criteria of rationality are relative might be taken to mean that the development of knowledge cannot be treated as a continuos process, and that there is no rational reconstruction of this process even as an approximation. It was argued that the task of philosophy is to study only the context of justification, and to disregard all questions concerning the so-called context of discovery. Popper defends the rationality of scientific development without getting involved in the issue of to what extent the investigating subject can be independent of all extralogical factors, and thus is able to formulate statements that are valid always and everywhere. He claims that although they are human products, the objects of the "third world" are independent of man; they live their own life and evolve. Existing theories give rise to new problems that are not intended or even expected by their creators. And in this sense the third world transcends its creators; it is at the same time a super-human world.[17]

Amsterdamski points out, however, that in spite of some important differences, Popper's claim of the ontological status of the third world is remarkably similar to Plato's world of ideas and Hegel's Objective Spirit.[18] To grant that culture affects physical reality through us is not necessarily to assume the real existence of the world of concepts and problems. The knowledge of the subject, as Popper now admits, can never be free of various irrational and extra-rational constraints. The rational character of the development of science can only be maintained by means of a complete elimination of the investigating subject from epistemology. This permits Popper to argue that the development of the third world can be fully rational despite the fact that the knowing subjects are not fully rational as their subjective knowledge is always affected by extra-rational factors. By means of the distinction between the second (psychological) and the third (logical) world, Popper separates the realm of biology from that of logic. The way the third world functions is seen as a filter through which the "natural selection" of ideas takes place. A rational development of the third world is guaranteed by scientific criticism, which is the cultural extension of the biological medium of natural selection by trial and error. Objective knowledge is thus an improved means of human adaption.[19] Such criticism is rational because it allows for the elimination of errors and false beliefs without eliminating the humans who hold them or make them. Error in the animal world is usually fatal, whereas a human can correct his opinions and survive. Rationality is thus ultimately grounded in biological survival as scientific criticism is seen by Popper a cultural extension of biological development. Such grounding of human rationality in biology is also typical of the work of Piaget, Monod, Konrad Lorenz, and Noam Chomsky, as well as in many attempts to oppose historical relativism. Truth is made relative to species, and scientific knowledge is seen as a tool facilitating the adaption of the species to its environment. More recent studies prevented Popper to hold the idea of a rational subject he had maintained in *The Logic of Scientific Discovery*, and the source of these difficulties lies in the ahistorial treatment of the concept of rationality. Even though Amsterdamski finds Popper's ethics appealing, he does not believe that it is possible to legitimize it by means of scientific theory, or that the development of science provides such an unchanging model of rational attitude.[20] Amsterdamski emphasizes that philosophical problems cannot always be solved.

He rejects radical empiricism because no empirical fact can be recognized independently of some prior theoretical views. The problem of choosing criteria for competing theories is identical with the question of whether crucial experiments are possible in science. Popper emphasized that conclusive verification is impossible but he still believed in conclusive falsification. The logical asymmetry between verification and falsification was the starting point for his doctrine of falsification in science. Subjecting a theory to the most severe empirical tests constitutes the rationale of a scientific method that becomes progressive by the elimination of error. This method also serves as the basis for a historical reconstruction of the process by which we replace old theories by new ones. However, as Duhem points out, testing an isolated hypotheses is impossible because there are always some background assumptions that cannot be identified, and that is why crucial experiments are impossible.[21] It turns out that falsification, as it actually takes place, is no more conclusive than verification.[22] Duhem's thesis was radicalized by Quine who points out that a hypothesis can always be protected from falsification by the introduction of different background assumptions and the modification of background knowledge, and that these modifications might even concern rules of reasoning. If we have to accept that there are no rational rules for choosing among theories, then the development of knowledge in this sense is not a rational process. Arguments that at some point were considered conclusive later came to be regarded as inconclusive, either because certain background assumptions were not taken into account or because some possibilities of modifying the theory had not been considered. Our knowledge is not transparent to us, as some of our assumptions are taken to be obvious facts. Quine holds that no statement in science is immune to revision; indeed revision, even of the logical law of the excluded middle, has been proposed as a means to simplify quantum mechanics.[23] Our natural tendency to disturb the total system as little as possible leads us to focus our revisions upon specific statements. They seem to have a sharper empirical reference than highly theoretical statements of physics, or logic, or ontology, and the latter statements may be thought of as relatively centrally located within the total network. Amsterdamski concludes that since it is impossible to formulate conditions for nontriviality, Quine's thesis remains undecided.[24]

Lakatos's methodology of research programs undermines, in effect, the Popperian demarcation of science from nonscience.[25] The essential change from Popper's falsificationism comes with the idea that as long as there is no theory that meets the condition of "progressiveness," the previous theory is not to be considered falsified even if many empirical facts that do not agree with it are known. In cases of conflict between experience and theory, Lakatos offers theory time to prove its mettle, and treats as rational all attempts to save the theory in conformity with the basic assumptions of the program. There is no way to establish how many unsuccessful attempts to save a degenerating program are necessary before it becomes advisable to abandon it. Even when there is already a competing research program, there is always the possibility that the attempt to save the old program will finally succeed, while the competing program faces degeneration. Thus it turns out that the process of scientific development is not altogether rational. According to this view, the methodology does not specify specific selection criteria for choosing between competing theories but merely indicates rational criteria for the investment of resources in situations of risk. Discussions concerning the choice of research programs will, in practice, be subject to quite different criteria of rationality than those that are supported by methodology. They are subject to criteria of rationality of the institutions making these decisions.[26] This is precisely what seems to be happening in contemporary science where claims concerning the choice of research programs are subject to the rational criteria of "common sense" as interpreted by the sponsoring institutions. It is no longer possible to avoid sociological issues as science becomes part of these institutions and their way of functioning. Scientists choosing between alternative theories are guided by additional criteria such as theoretical simplicity, precision, internal consistency, coherence with other accepted theories, geniality, fruitfulness, and operational and practical utility. But it is very doubtful whether any of these additional criteria can be formulated unequivocally. It is certainly not possible to do so with criteria such as simplicity, generality, or theoretical fruitfulness.[27] It is equally impossible to rely on all these criteria together, as they may come into conflict with one another. The choice of the simplest theory, even if it were possible to formulate unambiguous criteria for simplicity, need not necessarily mean the choice of the most fruitful or the most general theory. We would still have to choose some criteria over others, and no methodology would be able to justify any such hierarchy of criteria.[28]

Amsterdamski agrees with Kuhn that in choosing among theories scientists rely on certain values rather than on unequivocal methodological criteria, and that these values can conflict with one another.[29] A demand for precision is characteristic only of some areas in modern science, and it does not apply equally to all disciplines. It is wrongly assumed that the development of scientific knowledge must either take place according to unchangeable methodological rules or that we have to admit, with Feyerabend, that "science is an essentially anarchistic enterprise."[30] Science is seen by Feyerabend as a kind of ideology, and since the methodological norms change historically, it is perhaps an illusion to believe in scientific progress. A critique of theories in the light of accepted facts is not sufficient because these facts are already fashioned by accepted theories that might require revision. Radical empiricism wrongly assumes the existence of an observation language that is neutral with respect to all theories. No fragment of our knowledge can be conclusively tested in isolation, and we are unable to account for all the assumptions that are in fact part of the testing procedure. Feyerabend emphasizes that we need a means of criticizing the accepted theory that goes *beyond* the criteria provided by the comparison of that theory with the facts.[31] An alternative theory might provide such a means, for it is not the experiment alone but theories alternative to the accepted ones – together with alternative ontological assumptions implicit in the accepted observational language – which can and should constitute the real basis for criticism. A good empiricist must be a critical and inventive metaphysician.[32] In cases where we do not take such alternative points of view into account, the success of a theory, just as the success of a myth, is simply the construct of its adherents.[33]

But Amsterdamski points out that no individual can consistently and exhaustively implement the norms of theoretical pluralism. Feyerabend believes that all individuals should at least strive to such a position, for what the individual alone cannot accomplish, can be attained by the scientific community. Moreover, the new theory may be unable to explain everything that its predecessor explained. Such partially or entirely incommensurable theories speak untranslatable (or not fully translatable) languages, and there is consequently no final criterion on the basis of which it would be possible to say that the empirical content of the new theory is richer. If the conditions of the invariance of meaning are not met, then we cannot say that development of knowledge takes place according to any set of methodological rules. In this case, there is no formal criterion for theory choice; science becomes no better than myth, and the replacement of one theory by another incommensurable with it is the result of persuasion and propaganda rather than rational argument.[34] When a new theory that is supposed to solve the emergent difficulties of the old theory is being formulated for the first time, it is usually unable to deal even with the empirical facts that its predecessor explained quite well. But Amsterdamski argues against Feyerabend that at least one *negative* criterion always functions in science: the accomplishments of preceding theories cannot simply be thrown out or invalidated for no reason. The development of science is not a continuous process, but a new theory must nevertheless somehow assimilate the accomplishments of its predecessors. Lack of accumulative growth is a break with all tradition: a process that is discontinuous in one respect may be continuos in another. No revolution, not even the most radical one, either in science or in social life, can ever remake the world from scratch, as it were. But for this, the history of science would be a series of completely independent episodes. Thus, every new theory faces the problem of interpretation and of assimilation of results achieved in a given discipline by its predecessors. Some "facts" can be disqualified, but until this has happened, they remain facts. There is no development in science without some inheritance of tradition, even if such a tradition is treated selectively.[35] Feyerabend's conclusion that anything goes in science follows only from a rejection of the principle of correspondence even in its weaker sense. But although he denied that the process of scientific development is not rational in the way in which his opponents believed it to be, he agrees with them that increasing the empirical content of science is something we should strive for, and that science, unlike mythology, ideology, or magic, is able to realize this. Yet he rejects a philosophy that treats technological progress as the highest value.

Amsterdamski points out that a radical pluralism as advocated by Feyerabend would destroy the consensus that renders a tolerant society possible. Even if science is only one thread in our culture, and not the dominant one, the question of its rationality addresses the issue of the kind of science we need today, and not the question of whether or not we need science at all.[36] There is a difference between science and politics, although there is no privileged position in which we do not have to deal with disturbing factors. From Bacon to Descartes, to Carnap and Popper, the notion of the knowing subject has produced a belief in scientific method that was supposed to be universally valid. It also served as the philosophical justification for the authority of science, its autonomy from philosophy, religion, and politics, as well as its institutional independence. But society became increasingly interested in the development of science as a result of its growing importance in practical matters. In both the natural and the social sciences, the knowing subject could no longer be treated as residing outside the world he is investigating. Thus, his autonomy is effectively

Soft Logic

questioned not only in physics, biology, and neurophysiology, but also in linguistics, cultural anthropology, sociology of knowledge and the history of science and, of course, philosophy. The great achievements of contemporary science – Einstein's theory of relativity, Heisenberg's principle of indeterminacy, the Gödel theorems – all seem to show that the more we know about ourselves and about how we come to know anything, the more difficult it is to believe that our knowledge is independent of our biological makeup, the specific functions of our brains, the language we use, the culture we inherit, and the social institutions in which we live.[37] The background consensus in science is not a manifestation of incremental human rationality since it is not historically stable, but it does reflect our human interest to find the truth.

Notes

[1] Stefan Amsterdamski, *Between History and Method, Disputes about the Rationality of Science,* Dordrecht/Boston/London: Kluwer Academic Publishers, 1992, p. viii.

[2] *Ibid.,* p. 3.

[3] Thomas S. Kuhn, *The Structure of Scientific Revolutions*, Chicago, IL: University of Chicago Press, 1970.

[4] Thomas S. Kuhn, *The Essential Tension*, Chicago, IL: University of Chicago Presss, 1977.

[5] Amsterdamski, *Between History and Method*, p. 16.

[6] Karl, R. Popper, *Objective Knowledge*, Oxford: Claredon Press, 1972.

[7] Alexandre Koyré, *Études d'histoire de la pensée philosophique*, Paris: Colin, 1961, pp. 312-13.

[8] Amsterdamski, *Between History and Method*, p., 47.

[9] Paul K. Feyerabend, "Problems of Empiricism," Part I, in R. G. Colodny (ed.), *Beyond the Edge of Certainty*, Englewood Cliffs, NJ: Princeton Hall, 1956, p. 154.

[10] Amsterdamski, *Between History and Method*, p. 47.

[11] *Ibid.*, p. 50.

[12] *Ibid.*, p. 56.

[13] *Ibid.*, p. 87.

[14] Alexandre Koyré, *Études Galiléenes*, Paris: Hermann, 1940, pp. 166-171.

[15] Karl R. Popper, *Objective Knowledge*; also, his *Unended Quest*, La Salle, Il: Open Court, 1976.

[16] Amsterdamski, *Between History and Method*, p. 107.

[17] Popper, *Objective Knowledge*, p. 159.

[18] Amsterdamski, *Between History and Method*, p. 113.

[19] *Ibid.*, p. 111.

[20] *Ibid.*, p. 121.

[21] Pierre Duhem, *The Aim and Structure of Physical Theory*, Princeton, NJ: Princeton University Press, 1954, p. 187.

[22] Amsterdamski, *Between History and Method*, p. 126.

[23] W. V. Quine, *From a Logical Point of View*, New York, NY: Harper & Row, 1961, p. 43.

[24] Amsterdamski, *Between History and Method*, p. 138.

[25] Imre Lakatos, "Falsification and the Methodology of Scientific Research Programmes," in *The Methodology of Scientific Research Programmes. Philosophical Papers*, vol. 1, Cambridge, MA: Cambridge University Press, 1978, p. 93.

[26] Amsterdamski, *Between History and Method*, p. 150.

[27] *Ibid.*, p. 154.

[28] *Ibid.*

[29] Kuhn, *The Essential Tension*, ch. 13.

[30] Paul K. Feyerabend, *Agianst Method: Outline of an Anarchistic Theory of Method*, London: NLB, 1975, p. 10.

[31] Paul K. Feyerabend, "How to be a Good Empiricist: A Plea for Tolerance in Matters Epistemological," *Philosphy of Science, The Delaware Seminar*, vol. 2, New York, NY: Wiley, Interscience, 1963, p. 8.

[32] *Ibid.*, p. 37.

[33] Amsterdamski, *Between History and Method*, p. 159.

[34] Paul K. Feyerabend, "Consolation for a Specialist, " *Problems of Empiricism*, vol. 2, Cambridge, MA: Cambridge University Press, 1981; see also his "In Defense of Aristotle: Comments on the Conditions of Content Increase," in *Progress and Rationality in Science*, eds. Gerard Radnitzky and Gunnar Anderson, Dordrecht: Reidel, 1978.

[35] Amsterdamski, *Between History and Method*, p. 170.

[36] *Ibid.*, p. 176.

[37] *Ibid.*, 183.

Chapter Five

Limits of Language

Following Heidegger's lead, both Gadamer and Derrida deny the possibility of a transcendental language-free standpoint for human understanding. And both, like Heidegger, regard the relationship to language as the primary philosophical issue, seeing language as the sense of our finitude, the place where we encounter the limits of our understanding.[1] However, their respective development of Heidegger's position is fundamentally different. For Gadamer, language is living speech in the medium of dialogue, whereas Derrida claims that the meanings generated by language always exceed our intentions. Language is presumed by him to be already writing, and the spoken word an already interpreted sign, infiltrated by nonsense, whose otherness lurks within meaning. Thus, for any particular concept, there may not be the possibility of deciding from among the competing meanings one that is true and authoritative.[2] In Gadamer, this leads to an emphasis on the authority and truth of texts. In Derrida, on the other hand, there is an underscoring of the irreducible equivocation and undecidability of meaning, even apparently toward questioning the concept of meaning itself.[3] On this basis, hermeneutics and deconstruction seem to offer us extremely different views of language. But in spite of their differences, they also have a common ground: both Gadamer's philosophical hermeneutics and Derrida's deconstruction present a significant challenge to the metaphysics of modernity whose assumptions continue to dominate not only a good deal of thinking within philosophy, but also within other interpreting disciplines such

as literary criticism, theology, and the social sciences. We are not the
ones "in charge" of language, Gadamer and Derrida agree. Gadamer,
however, conceives the original phenomenon of language as dialogue,
and this entails a hermeneutical reorientation of dialectics. Derrida, on
his part, questions Gadamer's claim that hermeneutics is independent
of metaphysics; he calls attention to something that Gadamer takes for
granted, namely the willingness of each partner in a conversation to be
open to what the other has to say. He claims that even the later
Heidegger has not really broken through the logocentrism of
metaphysics, for insofar as Heidegger asks about the essence of truth
or the meaning of Being, he still speaks the language of metaphysics
that looks upon meaning as something out there to be discovered.
When Gadamer wrote "Being which can be understood is language,"[4]
what really was implied is that it can never be completely understood.

The ideal of scientific knowledge that modern science follows
originated in a model of nature mathematically ordered (a model that
was first developed by Galileo in his mechanics). In this way natural
language lost its primacy, even though it did retain its own manner of
speaking. A consequence of this was that in modern logic and the
theory of science the model of language was replaced by a model of
universal notation. Both the Continental and the Anglo-American
tradition demonstrate the inevitability of the linguistic medium for
understanding, and as a consequence, the ideal of an ultimate
grounding over which apriorism and empiricism fought, loses its
credibility. Language is a domain that we cannot circumvent and in
which all consciousness and all knowledge articulates itself. This is
how the concept of interpretation has become crucial, and starting
with Nietzsche, how it became a challenge to all positivism. It was he
who raised the radical question whether what we take as given is not
after all merely the result of interpretation. The faith in agreed-upon
observation-statements did not last long even in the Vienna Circle,
because it turned out that in the natural sciences knowledge cannot
avoid the heuristic implications, that the so-called given cannot be
separated from interpretation.[5] Gadamer emphasizes that only in the
light of interpretation does something become a "fact," and that only
as part of the process of interpretation can we legitimately even speak
of observation.[6] Only when the process of understanding is disrupted,
that is, when understanding does not succeed, are questions asked
about the wording of the text. Whereas in living conversation one tries
to reach understanding through the give-and-take of discussion and

accompanies it with information and gesture, in writing, the openness that is implied in seeking the words cannot be communicated. Gadamer nevertheless maintains that the hermeneutical problem is basically the same for oral and written discourse. Interpretation of a text is no longer merely a means of getting back to an original expression of something. The multiplicity of meanings found in word-plays represents the deepest form in which speculative thinking comes to appearance, a thinking that explores judgments that oppose each other. Relations of meaning are recognized, even if vague and fragmentary, which sets limits to all discourse about rules and prescriptions when one is dealing with actual speaking.

In his reply to Derrida, Gadamer denies that the effect of understanding has anything to do with metaphysics or with the Kantian concept of a good will. He insists that whoever opens his mouth wants to be understood, otherwise he would neither speak nor write. Derrida, however, questions this assumed total commitment to consensus when we are trying to understand something. We never have the experience of being perfectly understood since the absence of a common language prevents a dialogue in Gadamer's sense from taking place. Indeed both Gadamer and Derrida stick to their own language. The issue of philosophical thinking for Derrida is not something that language can put into words. Thus, he would agree with Gadamer that hermeneutics and deconstruction do not stand for opposing positions, not because they have so much in common but because they develop in different directions. There cannot be a "ground" for deconstruction, since it is not a set of ideas forming a philosophical position to begin with.[7] Derrida's non-engagement with Gadamer could thus be a refusal to affirm the possibility not of dialogue itself but rather what Gadamer perceives as the necessary condition for dialogue: speaking only one common language. Dallmayr points out that interpretation has emerged as a far-from-straightforward or unilinear enterprise. In large measure the opposition between hermeneutics and deconstruction has tended to amount to little more than coexistence without contact or mutual agreement.[8] Whereas Gadamer's *Truth and Method* may be said to integrate hermeneutics with existential analysis (as outlined by Heidegger's *Being and Time*), Derrida pursues themes in Heidegger's later work, where notions like "meaning" or "being" are already problematic (though hardly abandoned). Behind these seemingly esoteric questions of textual reading and exegesis, broader issues of a practical political sort can be seen to emerge. Among other things, the

Gadamer-Derrida exchange concerns political communication and interaction appropriate to our "global city" or emerging cosmopolis.

Dallmayr points out that if there is a central focus or target to Derrida's deconstruction, it is the notion of an unfolding meaning or continuity of understanding. This target furnishes the critical impulse in all of Derrida's writings and, in particular, his assessment of Nietzsche. *Spurs*, subtitled *Nietzsche's Styles*, is an attack on the search for continuous meaning, or what Derrida calls "onto-hermeneutics." Contrary to an essentialist ontology, and to a hermeneutics wedded to stable meanings, there is for Derrida no such thing as the essence of something (e.g., the essence of "woman"), and that is why he questions Heidegger's exegesis, his attempt to find a meaning or the meaning of Nietzsche's writings. What surely has surfaced in his view, is the multidimesionality of the issues at stake. Both in the Paris exchange between Gadamer and Derrida, and in *Truth and Method*, a crucial ambivalence concerns the role of "rupture" or transformative change, and the relationship between continuity and discontinuity. In contrast to the gradual transformation leading from one point to the next, the transformation occurring in artworks is said to imply that something turns suddenly and as a whole into something else. Comments of this kind nevertheless do not prevent Gadamer in the end from reaffirming what he takes to be the inevitable primacy of understanding or "hermeneutical consciousness." The question clearly affects the status and range of hermeneutics for, needless to say, hermeneutics cannot supply the scope and possible limits of understanding. In *Truth and Method*, Gadamer admits that we do not have a standpoint that would allow us to see what limits and conditions us. Deconstruction, by contrast, pinpoints the limits of an intentional or existential hermeneutics – limits not externally imposed but endemic to the endeavor of understanding itself. Dallmayr criticizes a certain aloofness or nonengagement in Derrida's thought, his tendency not to engage in traditional philosophy or divergent views, but rather to circumvent and elude them. However, as he himself realized in one of his earlier writings, the step "beyond" or "outside" philosophy is much more difficult to take than is usually imagined.[9] There is no such thing as truth *per se* since truth is plural, but even variegated truth is truth of some sort, and equally difficult is the escape form "being." Contrary to Heidegger, Derrida discovers a varied and refracted character in Nietzsche's elements. In seeking to escape metaphysics, *Spurs* presents all traditional categories as basically exchangeable or undecideable – including truth and non-truth, meaning and non-meaning, being and nothingness – and by implication, good and evil. It is here that Derrida's key notion of *différance* converts into indifference, non-engagement and indecision. By stressing rupture and radical otherness, Derrida seeks to dislodge and uproot the inquirer's comfortable self-identity, while his insistence on incommensurability and non-understanding encourages mutual disengagement

Gadamer shares with Derrida the conviction that a text is no longer dependent on the author's intentions. He, too, holds that understanding is always understanding differently (*Andersverstehen*). What is pushed aside or dislocated when my word reaches another person, and especially when a text reaches its reader, can never be fixed in a rigid identity. For Gadamer, understanding means that one is capable of stepping into the place of the other in order to say what one has understood. Derrida, on the other hand, takes these to be logocentric illusions, which even Heidegger failed to escape, as his Nietzsche interpretation reveals. Derrida's misgivings about Gadamer's hermeneutics are that for all his efforts to recognize otherness, Gadamer still concedes too much to reciprocal under-standing and mutual agreement. Language, for Gadamer is always what we speak to others, even though we are all familiar with how difficult it is to have a conversation with someone when each speaks his own language, and both only to some degree understand the language of the other.[10] Gadamer is convinced that it is our historical fate in the West to speak the language of concepts, and he reminds us that this separation of poetry from thinking is what has made science possible. He simply cannot see how – for either Nietzsche or Derrida – deconstruction can mean the repudiation of this heritage.[11] Gadamer notices that Heidegger's breakthrough was achieved at almost the same time the "linguistic turn" got under way in Anglo-American philosophy. Before that, the role of language in philosophy had been largely ignored. But Heidegger continued to wrestle with metaphysics because if one gets back to the beginning, one becomes aware that from the start one could have gone into a different direction, as Eastern thought has done. This might well have been due to the circumstance that no grammatical construction of subject and predicate was available to lead Eastern thought into the metaphysics of substance and accident. It is consequently not surprising to find in Heidegger's going back to the beginning of philosophy a fascination with Eastern thought. But language, and especially the basic structure common to all languages in one's culture, are not easily circumvented. What we mean by the language of metaphysics is that certain conceptual formulation have imposed themselves on every language of present-day speech communities. In scientific and philosophical discourse we call this the role of terminology, even though in philosophy there are no generally accessible, that is to say, verifiable, realms of experience, designated by prearranged terminology. In philosophy, such concept words are never completely separate from the semantic field in which they attain their full meaning. There is no "language of metaphysics," there is only a metaphysical coinage of concepts that have been lifted from common speech. Such coinage of concepts may, as in the case of Aristotelian logic and ontology, establish a fixed conceptual tradition, and in this manner lead to alienation from living language. According to Gadamer, the logic of question and answer opens up a dimension of communicative understanding that goes beyond linguistically fixed assertion, and so also beyond any all-encompassing synthesis. His philosophical hermeneutics, therefore, pays particular attention to the speculative unity between the said and the unsaid. Contrary to Derrida, Gadamer is convinced that the principle of deconstruction involves something quite similar to what he himself is doing, since in carrying out what he calls *écriture*, Derrida, too, is trying to supersede the metaphysical realm of meaning that governs words. Like Heidegger, Derrida immerses himself in the mysterious multiplicity lodged in the word and in the diversity of its meanings; in the indeterminate potential of its differentiation of meaning. Gadamer, however, emphasizes that whoever wants to take deconstruction seriously and insist on difference, stands at the beginning of conversation, not at its end.[12]

Gadamer rejects the accusation that either Heidegger or his own philosophical hermeneutics can be accused of logocentrism in the sense found in Derrida's critique of Husserl.[13] From the very beginning, Heidegger sought to understand himself in terms of his positive attitude to Christian faith, and this religious impulse led him to criticize the Greek concept of being from the standpoint of temporality. Futurity, not presence, characterizes the being of *Dasein*. Like Kierkegaard, Heidegger insists that one must free oneself from understanding only "at a distance," and this is how Gadamer made dialogue central to understanding. Conversation defines itself precisely by the fact that the essence of understanding and agreement are not to be found in intended meaning. But in Gadamer's view, this does not require any return to *"écriture"* or writing, for writing is always intended to be read. Gadamer maintains that one cannot read what is written without understanding it,[14] even though one can, of course, recite Latin or Hebrew text in prayer without understanding the language. Thus, Gadamer's hermeneutics is really the art of grasping what someone has intended to say. He seeks to show that when it comes to poetry or other literary arts, not the word, nor the sentence, nor the discourse refers back to the intention of the author. Just as conversation gets its illumination from the conversational situation, so too, such a situative moment holds for all thinking. Even assertion must be understood as the answer to a question, if it is to be understood at all. The encounter between Gadamer and Derrida is not just a matter of exposing arguments because, for any confrontation to take place, one needs to have at one's disposal a fairly well-defined common ground. Whereas Gadamer defends a unitary concept of understanding, Derrida considers such limits as *"philosophèmes,"* themselves susceptible to deconstruction. Under such conditions, all that remains is to observe how the hermeneutical "good will" actually functions, and the Paris encounter between Gadamer and Derrida can serve as an opportunity to do this. Gadamer bestows an ontological dignity on prejudice, and that is how the prejudices of the individual, rather than his judgments, constitute the historical reality of his being.[15] But this also implies that prejudices should be dealt with on the basis of a distinction between what is "legitimate" and "illegitimate," and that ultimately some law can operate like a sieve to separate one from the other.[16] Frank also emphasizes that disputants must relate themselves to some issue, for otherwise they are not disputing with each other but just expressing a variety of judgments. The epistemological subject is no longer autonomous but acquires his self-understanding in a semiotic context. Essentially deconstruction and hermeneutics are philosophies of language; they realize that conversation cannot be controlled and that the meanings on which we agree need not be identical.

Until the mid-eighteenth century, exegesis (*Auslegung*) did not play any role in relating forms of knowledge to language. It was taken for granted that language rendered truth present as a logical form or as a synthetic judgment related directly to facts. Thus, rational speech (which by its nature is universal, true, and enlightening) was considered inherent in factual speech, and the problem of reaching agreement simply did not arise. Being a preestablished harmony, grammatically correct speech became an immediate and reliable representation of logically and correctly combined "ideas" (*Vorstellungen*). All this changed with the Romantic age, for now a narrowed-down community of thought turned into an idealized abstraction. As a consequence, language was seen as no more than a changeable situation in the conversation of individuals communicating with each other. There is no language as such, only the concreteness of real conversation, and such interactive speaking not only confers validity on language as a social fact but also imposes limits on it. What has been called the "linguistic turn" in philosophy, seeks to replace the world interpreted by the concept of reason (as it is represented in universal grammar for the purpose of communication) by the model of a linguistic "code" (of grammar, of language game, of language system, of structure, of evolutionary act, of consciousness formed by tradition, etc.). As a consequence, individual occurrences of structured speech are treated as special cases of a general rule. Scientific linguistics presupposes that language events are subject to laws that apply to systems of convention or tradition. Gadamer, by contrast, holds that conversation is not a representation of "truth" subsiding above or beyond itself, but that the realization of truth resides in the process of fusing two horizons – that of truth and that of tradition. Meaning arises in the reciprocity of an agreement in understanding that cannot be anticipated. Gadamer thus shares with Derrida the view that self-consciousness presupposes an articulated world reflected in tradition or symbolic order.

Derrida, however, questions John Searle's view that in a functioning grammar every representation of a sign is necessarily the repetition of the self-same (*Selbigen*). There is, says Derrida, no preestablished self-presence; indeed strictly speaking, the author is never co-present with what he writes. Derrida speaks of the "re-mark," that is, of the constant possibility of the speaker/author/reader/ interpreter placing a new emphasis on the meaning of a word, a sentence, a text, or a culture.[17] The sign that is repeated cannot guarantee its identity, and the identity of a term can only be assumed through a condition of closure and the invariability of the system. Conversations are always transformations of other and earlier conversations, just as signs are always transformations of other and earlier signs. This is why Derrida draws back from Gadamer's eagerness for conversation. Gadamer emphasizes that we are accustomed to understand and to claim understanding; we are always presupposing that there is something understandable. On the other hand, for Derrida, following Nietzsche, understanding is the transition to what is akin to one's own self; understanding appropriates. Gadamer identifies "being" with what can be understood as language, and implicit in this is also that which can never be completely understood.[18] What we find happening in language is not a mere reification (*Fixierung*) of intended meaning, but an endeavor that routinely transforms itself, or rather a continually recurring temptation to engage oneself in something or to become involved with someone.[19] Derrida agrees with Gadamer in interpreting Nietzsche's "will to power" as the impossibility of communicating and, therefore, of true understanding, for it wills only to annex and appropriate the other. Gadamer's ostensible "good will" to reach a commensurate understanding is, in Derrida's view, only a delusion. Understanding is invariably imagining the other into one's own world-picture whose coherence has been disturbed by the other. The presupposition of a common understanding is, on this view, a means of making one's own understanding prevail. That there remains something to be understood constitutes, on the view of Derrida, a metaphysical interpretation of the process of understanding.

Thus, Derrida interprets Gadamer quite differently from the way he wants to be understood. Gadamer implicitly suggests that understanding is a progressive linear process leading to intelligibility. Now, logically Derrida cannot wish to contest Gadamer because real understanding is considered by him to be impossible anyway. He holds that when using general concepts, one is always clearly following a certain scheme of understanding, and this means that one incorporates or assimilates the other to oneself.[20] It was Nietzsche who first recognized that metaphysics resides in language, and not primarily in what one thinks and says in language. This is the deeper reason why metaphysics resists "overcoming" in the manner of Heidegger. Language does not permit anything to be either thought or said that, as Gadamer alleges, has nothing to do with metaphysics. The real injustice towards the other, according to Nietzsche, does not reside in the fact that one does not wish to understand him, but rather in the fact that one must understand him in the only way one can. That is, one invariably thinks about the other in concepts that occur to oneself, no matter how fair one is trying to be the other. And this is something that cannot be otherwise, for even Gadamer says that he "cannot imagine" that Derrida really means what he says.[21] So Derrida concludes that "good will" to understand the other not only is useless, but that speaking about it hides the fact that by using the concept of "will" one is already assuming something that in reality is not there, not given (*was es nicht gibt*): namely a will common to all. The issue between Gadamer and Derrida is whether even with good will there can be true understanding. The presupposition here is that there exists an objective truth unknown to us, so that it is precisely good will that holds us together to seek it. But in some cases one refuses to take part in certain discourses, and that means that under these circumstances one does not want to be understood. The concept of interpretation is restricted to situations about which a clear set of goals and a rationality that corresponds to them are already agreed upon. Derrida's deconstruction does not deem to be a position as such; it merely directs our attention to what is unavoidably positional and metaphysical. That is how he identifies the logocentrism of Gadamer who presupposes an already existing community as an essential condition of understanding. Derrida emphasizes that whether such conditions really are given must always first be shown. However, in the very drawing of a boundary between what is comprehensible and incomprehensible, Derrida, too, elicits the distinction between what is "essential" and what is "inessential."

"Truth and Method" and "Text and Interpretation" are precisely what hermeneutics and deconstruction have in common. For deconstruction, the text is everything and there is nothing outside the text. But the concept of "text" is no longer simple and unproblematic once the search for principles that would allow one to grasp the real meaning of the text has been given up. The text is always open to multiplicity since it is nothing but a system of arbitrary signs. *Différance* invades the sign.[22] Neither word nor concept, *différance* is a paradoxical structure that plays its double meaning of difference and deferral. It refers to the undecidable relation between the event and the structure of language. Since nothing is simply present or absent, there is no master text that stands given and the conclusion remains deferred. For Gadamer the essential relationship is the event of understanding itself, which is the mediation of difference lacking an ultimate terminus within a historical horizon. The question that arises in the exchange – the question that is stated by Gadamer but never expressly stated by Derrida – is whether the interweaving of text and interpretation in philosophical hermeneutics is merely one more instance of logocentric metaphysics. This question inevitably comes up in any hermeneutics that considers meaning as something to be discovered. Gadamer's hermeneutics certainly accounts for interpretation as a search for meaning, even if he does admit meaning to be problematic. His own work is discussed by Gadamer as a "way back from dialectic to dialogue and conversation." The fact that a potential of otherness remains, suggests that for Gadamer the text is plural – and not because of the ambiguity of its content, but by virtue of the structure of interpretation itself.[23] Gadamer is convinced that without the projection of good will one enters a circle of having only one's own prejudices confirmed, and he emphasizes that interpretation always fails as a will to master. In order to understand at all, the reader presupposes that the subject matter of a text has a presumed unity of meaning. Naturally the text could be otherwise, but a text could not say whatever the reader wanted it to say. Granted, however, that Gadamer is not after meaning as such, i.e., that hermeneutics is not deconstruction, it can nevertheless be said to be logocentric insofar as Gadamer posits coherence and agreement in dialogue or conversation. This is pointed out by Derrida who denies that dialogue is capable to say one and the same thing under any condition, and who consequently concludes that agreement between partners is always an illusion. For Gadamer, understanding is always a form of dialogue, a coming to agreement within a structure of openness. Conversation is not a talking of something that is already there, but has the structure of an event that remains unfinished. Every reading that attempts to understand is only a first step and never comes to an end. We consequently need a continuing effort to find the common ground, and Gadamer's *logos* remains in principle always unfinished.

Whereas Gadamer takes language to be a "bridge" allowing for communication, Derrida has sought to convince us that language is precisely that which indefinitely defers meaningful understanding.[24] However, Derrida's position is one that can neither be consistently argued for nor deconstructed, and he, of course, is fully aware of this fact. Philosophically his position is altogether impossible because a philosophical argument or deconstruction is one that, by definition, seeks by means of various argumentative procedures to persuade; it is always one that seeks to arrive at a mutual understanding. Accordingly, Derrida abandons the usual philosophical procedures and adopts what might be called an *artistic* approach. If the "truth" of his position is one that cannot be argued for, cannot be *said*, it can perhaps nevertheless be *shown* or *demonstrated*, i.e., concretely instanced, made manifest and pointed out (*de-constrare*) precisely by means of a particular usage of language. The best way to show by means of language that understanding is not possible is to demonstrate that, in effect, we do not understand; to show how all attempts at dialogue inevitably result in failure to arrive at a meaningful mutual accord. It is evident that Derrida is not seeking to engage in a normal philosophical discussion. What he seems to be trying to say instead is that one can, with good will, come to mutual agreement. But such agreements are, in fact, forced by the concrete situation in which they happen to occur. The conversational situation is one that is characterized by inequality of position and power, such as the relationship between teacher and student, physician and patient, employer and employee, elderly well-established philosopher and younger contesting anti-philosopher. In cases such as these, the notion of an open dialogue in which the interlocutors share an equal status and seek to arrive at a pure disinterested agreement determined by good will alone is altogether unrealistic. Thus, the appeal to good will is a diversion, a mask, a cover for the exercise of power, although perhaps of an unconscious and non-deliberate sort.[25] But Madison makes the crucial point that what Derrida would put forward in place of Gadamer's good will is never made clear.

One possibility of how to define the limits of dialogue is pragmatically, and from this perspective Shusterman claims, Gadamer and Derrida have actually a great deal in common. Shusterman emphasizes that the issue of context is crucial to both Gadamer and Derrida since both regard meaning as in some way context-dependent and fluid. If understanding always depends on changing context, as Gadamer maintains,[26] how can we talk of such understanding as being opposed to misunderstanding? Even two interlocutors in the same concrete dialogical situation bring with them different contents or horizons of understanding. For Gadamer, tradition prestructures and thus unites the different understandings of its participants who are both shaped by it and who, at the same time, extend and reshape it. But since tradition is open-ended, this understanding is always a relative and uncompleted movement.[27] It raises serious doubts about the universal scope that Gadamer accords to heuristic understanding. This seems to be behind Derrida's question of whether "enlargement of context" is simply a continual expression or a discontinuous restructuring.[28] Shusterman makes the interesting point that the coherence necessary to speak of a common unifying tradition can be one that embraces conflict and debate, even about the nature of that tradition itself. Gadamer should have realized that the unity of tradition in which we live is far from being complete and never guaranteed. Tradition is more a motley patchwork of diverse practices and divergent games with which we continually have to struggle to consolidate and hold together, rather than Gadamer's unified and all-embracing great tapestry that securely supports us.[29] On the other hand, Derrida ought to acknowledge that, despite the obvious discontinuities and pluralities in our tradition, there are also some unities, some agreement and coherence of practice, without which effective communication and social interaction on which we all depend would be impossible. Derrida is right that there is never one maximally proper (completely comprehensive and unified) context for interpretation, for what counts as the "proper" interpretative context or "game" will itself obviously depend on the particular access of understanding that the interpreter brings with him. These aims and games are largely tradition influenced, and Gadamer may appeal to Derrida's argument that we can make no sense of something being intelligibly different without being able to map that difference on some common background of coordinates. To try to understand the other, or even recognize it as other, we must in some sense understand it on our own terms. In making it at all intelligible, we must make it accord with some of our beliefs, for only through them can we understand it al all. Schusterman suggests that it might therefore, seem more convincing to take mutual agreement not as a foundational source of understanding but as its desired end. Tradition has only succeeded in preserving and extending understanding because of its internal debates, whose factions it struggles to hold together in a partial unity or coherence. Even if Gadamer is right that we always wish to be understood (discounting that large area of the evasive and duplicious), it clearly does not follow that we always seek people to agree with us. Shusterman concludes that both Gadamer and Derrida concur that understanding implies both difference and consensus, rupture and continuity.

Derrida has frequently tried to disown the word "deconstruction" and, particularly, the extension it has undergone in other hands. But given the role he accords to the author's intentions, he knows as well as anyone that such protestations carry little weight.[30] Because Derrida was particularly sensitive to the self-defeating nature of any simple opposition to previous history and philosophy, he was also largely aware of the negative connotation of the French (and English) word "deconstruction." It seems that misunderstandings plague the encounter between Gadamer and Derrida, so that, at least on the basis of their written words, the proper verdict would have to be that the confrontation never took place.[31] But Bernasconi rightly raises the question of what a meaningful encounter would amount to in such a context. A challenge of this sort would, from the start, have to be designed to conform to Gadamer's belief in dialogue. It also seems that Gadamer does not show himself to be particularly conversant with Derrida's thinking. For Gadamer, Derrida was originally a proper name representing a position of critique of logocentrism. He attributes to Derrida the argument that it is sufficient for someone to have used certain key words for that person to stand accused of being metaphysical. Having identified Derrida in this way, it is not surprising that Gadamer seems to make metaphysical language the issue between them. But Derrida's translation of the language of philosophy resists the temptation to fix the meaning of words. Derrida can never let himself be identified with a particular reading, whereas, for Gadamer, agreement is crucially concerned with the maintenance of a common language. The difficulty is that in practice Gadamer, like Hegel, tends to enclose otherness in the circle of self-recognition and only rarely is otherness allowed to remain in its otherness.[32]

Bernasconi concludes that the hermeneutical notion of dialogue opens the way to a reading of texts which goes beyond what is expressly said in them. The first reading will frequently be characterized as "metaphysical" while also presenting itself as "beyond" metaphysics. It is therefore the task of the second reading to draw it back within metaphysics, and the text is ultimately undecidable between the two readings.[33] The distinction between metaphysics and what is beyond it cannot be accorded a definite status. That is why Heidegger concludes that a regard for metaphysics still prevails, even in the intent to overcome metaphysics itself.[34] Derrida's notion of the end of philosophy faces a similar dilemma; it turns out to be self-destructive, a notion that, as it were, interrupts its own discourse. Derrida's readers go astray when they identify one of the readings as Derrida's own because in doing so they upset the logic that questions such a procedure. From a historian's perspective, Derrida may appear simply to have added one more reading to the catalogue of readings that constitute the history of the text. But this would be to miss the strategy by which Derrida brings the text to the so-called edge of metaphysics (undecidable between inside and outside). There is not, as it were, a single truth to each text, nor is there a single correct reading, so that all others must be false and must, therefore, be rejected.[35] For Gadamer, this might well be an untenable heuristic conclusion,[36] since he seeks the truth encountered in the text, whereas Derrida draws attention to the history of the text. The text is not a meaning hidden behind the words that can by a strenuous effort be encountered. Every text has a history constituted by its various persuasive and powerful or influential readings. Before Gadamer is ready to take deconstruction seriously, there must first be an agreement to continue the dialogue, but agreement is not necessarily a goal or a precondition. It can also be an illusion. Encounters are not limited to what the participants intend, and much may be due only to accident. Indeed, if we focus on the truth claims of Gadamer and Derrida, and set ourselves the task of differentiating their standpoints, we will have to conclude that a true encounter never really occurred.

Sallis, consequently, questions Gadamer's model of dialogue. It is not, after all, an account of some natural understanding, and what is often produced is hostility and confusion rather than openness and agreement.[37] John Caputo also presents Gadamer as a "closet" essentialist, and detects two contradictory languages in his hermeneutics: one for "deep" truths that are above all time, the other for a model of interpretation rooted in our existential, historical, and finite existence. Breaking with Hegelian theology, Gadamer still seeks "deep truth" in texts. His traditionalism holds that, while there are indeed foundations for knowledge, they cannot be directly identified. Gadamer claims that our foundations lie deeper than we can say, and that we are primordially rooted in our traditions. Whereas foundationalism demands a reasoned account, tradition is so deeply lodged in our bones that it can only show up on the level of prejudgement (*Vorurteil*). The best we can do is unfold, lay-out (*auslegen*) the ground upon which we stand. We will have to admit that all questions are the issue of a will to power, and that is why in his debate with Derrida, Gadamer keeps coming back to Nietzsche. Gadamer has given up on the Hegelian notion of a definite historical form of *Geist*, i.e., of a pure form of reflective consciousness. He puts in its place a pluralized, historicized, non-hierarchical multiplication of historical forms and a concretely situated subject. He thinks of multiple, different – not better – unfoldings of the tradition, and his only canon is the longevity and vitality of the tradition itself. On the other hand, the more radical, more critical side of Heidegger's philosophy is just what Derrida wants to keep going. Ultimately Heidegger's thinking is concerned not with meaning or the truth of being, but with the giving or granting of meaning or truth. There is only the manifold. Thus Gadamer's hermeneutics and Derrida's deconstruction operate on different levels of meaning. Derrida's deconstruction has taken the step into that which grants meaning and delimits it. Deconstruction poses disturbing questions rather than trusting what is handed down. Derrida holds that languages, traditions, meanings, truth, and Being are only more or less static unities, effects that are held together in part by violence, in part by coercion, and in part by their usefulness for life.[38] By insisting on the impossibility of circumventing language in the process of understanding, Gadamer fails to draw the inevitable conclusion. He may idolize language, but Derrida suspects that deep truths are purchased by excluding what contaminates the system of truth, and by repressing what disturbs its unity. The unity of a tradition is in no small part due to the fact that educational systems keep spinning out the same yarn, while no one is around to tell the other side of the story. Deconstruction reveals that the deep unutterable truth of tradition is the result of the fact that the traces of the dissenters have been erased by the guardians of the truth, creating the illusion that we are dealing with ageless essences.[39]

Derrida does not enter the discourse of Gadamer; he puts himself outside its presuppositions, its conceptual frame, even though his own thinking overlaps many of the same concerns. Gadamer believes in truth that imposes itself on the mind as the immanent unity of meaning in a text or the self-presentation of a work of art. By contrast, Derrida's "writing," which acknowledges undecidability, voids the notion normally considered necessary to any philosophical dialogue. But while Derrida seems to disallow the conditions necessary for dialogue that lead inevitably to metaphysics, he does acknowledge that no one can stand outside his own epoch. He seems thus to put himself in a position of mastery – at least by assuming the privilege of deciding what is and what is not metaphysical. Refusing to take up a privileged position, such discourse could be characterized by the absence of some fundamental source of authority given to the speaker alone. Such a model stands in radical contrast to Gadamer's paradigm of dialogical understanding as the very overcoming of otherness and as the way of reaching agreement in understanding. Derrida, however, does inevitably assume authority to speak but, whereas Gadamer's goal is shared understanding, in Derrida language appears as a territory whose ownership is in constant dispute, and where, furthermore, there are no essential contents of understanding to be shared.[40] Eisenstein plausibly argues that Gadamer and Derrida need not be taken as debaters whose case is to be resolved, or between whom we must choose sides. Although their roles are antagonistic, we need not suppose that one is right and the other wrong. If Derrida could be taken seriously, he would eliminate all authority in language, every instance of true thinking and the very phenomenon of truth itself. But his point may well be that democracy, for example, is not just the internal ordering of equal voices or interpretive contents bounded by a single interpretive interest; it is rather the dynamic balancing among unequal voices, not only disagreeing but often talking across one another and aiming at different, occasionally overlapping goals. What is said is often incommensurable, and the whole linguistic field is, therefore, not subject to scientific or purely structural analysis. What Derrida has identified as belonging to property, signature, etc. (i.e., all that is unique and privileged in meaning) can provide lessons in what may be called the dynamics of incommensurability – getting used to viewing language not as a homogeneous dialogical space but as heterogeneous narrative. Rather than attempting a dialectical resolution of authority and openness, or necessity and freedom, we might look instead for a suitable interweaving of roles. Even the privileged authority of any interpretive game should not suppress the awareness of the incompleteness of all narrative.

Notes

[1] Diane P. Michelfelder and Richard E. Palmer, *Dialogue and Deconstruction, The Gadamer-Derrida Encounter*, Albany, NY: State University of the New York Press, 1989, p. 1.
[2] viz. Derrida, "Plato's Pharmacy," *La dissémination,* Paris, Éditions du Seuil, 1972, pp. 69-167; trans. by Barbara Johnson under the title *Dissemination* (Chicago, IL: University of Chicago Press, 1981), pp. 63-171;

and "The Ends of Man," *Marges de la philosophie*, Édition de Minuit, 1972, pp. 129-164, trans. with notes by Alan Bass under the title *Margins of Philosophy*, Chicago, IL: University of Chicago Press, 1982, pp. 109-136.

[3] Michelfelder & Palmer, *Dialogue and Deconstruction*, p. 2.

[4] Hans-Georg Gadamer, *Wahrheit und Methode: Grundzüge einer philosophischen Hermeneutik*, 2nd ed., Tubingen, J.C.B. Mohr, 1965, p. 450; trans. by Ed Garrett Barden and John Cumming under the title *Truth and Method*, New York, NY: The Seabury Press, 1975, p. 432.

[5] Hans-Georg Gadamer, *Text und Interpretation*, ed. Philippe Forget, Munich: Wilhelm Fink Verlag, 1984, p. 30.

[6] *Ibid.*, p. 32.

[7] Michelfelder & Palmer, *Dialogue and Deconstruction*, p. 9.

[8] Fred Dallmayr, "Hermeneutics and Deconstructoin: Gadamer and Derrida in Dialogue," in *Dialogue and Deconstruction*, Michelfelder & Palmer, p. 76.

[9] J. Derrida, *L'Écriture et la différance*, Paris: Seuil, 1967, p. 416, trans. by A. Bass under the title *Writing and Difference*, Chicago, IL: Univeristy of Chicago Press, 1978, p. 284.

[10] Hans-Georg Gadamer, "Letter to Dallmayr" (1985) in *Dialogue and Deconstruction*, Michelfelder & Palmer, p. 98.

[11] *Ibid.*, p. 101.

[12] Hans-Georg Gadamer, "Destruction and Deconstruction," in *Dialogue and Deconstruction*, Michelfelder & Palmer, p. 113.

[13] Hans-Georg Gadamer, "Hermeneutics and Logocentrism," in *Dialogue and Deconstruction*, Michelfelder & Palmer, p. 115.

[14] *Ibid.*, p. 118.

[15] Gadamer, *Wahrheit und Methode*, p. 261.

[16] Phillippe Forget, "Argument(s)," in *Dialogue and Deconstruction*, Michelfelder & Palmer, p. 137.

[17] Manfred Frank, "Limits of the Human Control of Language: Dialogue as the Place of Difference between Neocronstructionalism and Hermeneutics," in *Dialogue and Deconstruction*, Michelfelder & Palmer, p. 159.

[18] Gadamer, *Text and Interpretation*, p. 25.

[19] *Ibid.*, p. 26.

[20] Josef Simon, "Good Will to Understand and the Will to Power: Remarks on an Improbable Debate," in *Dialogue and Deconstruction*, Michelfelder & Palmer, p. 168.

[21] *Ibid.*

[22] James Risser, "The Two Faces of Socrates: Gadamer/Derrida," in *Dialogue and Deconstruction*, Michelfelder & Palmer, p. 177.

[23] *Ibid.*, p. 180.

[24] G. B. Madison, "Gadamer/Derrida: The Hermeneutics of Irony and Power," in *Dialogue and Deconstruction*, Michelfelder & Palmer, p. 193.

[25] *Ibid.*, p. 197.

[26] Gadamer, *Text and Interpretation*, p. 41; Hans-Georg Gadamer, "Reply to Jaques Derrida," in in *Dialogue and Deconstruction*, Michelfelder & Palmer.

[27] Gadamer, *Wahrheit und Methode*, p. 446. English trans., p. 428.

[28] Gadamer, "Reply to Jaques Derrida."

[29] Gadamer, *Wahrheit und Methode*, p. 321. English trans., p. 302.

[30] Robert Bernasconi, "Seeing Double: Destruction and Deconstruction," in *Dialogue and Deconstruction*, Michelfelder & Palmer, p. 234.

[31] John Searle, "Reiterating the Differences: A Reply to Derrida," *Glymph I*, Baltimore, MD: The John Hopkins University Press, 1977, p. 198.

[32] Bernasconi, "Seeing Double," p. 245.

[33] *Ibid.*

[34] M. Heidegger, *Zur Sache des Denkens*, Tübingen: Niemeryer, 1969, p. 25, trans. by J. Stambaugh under the title *On Time and Being*, New York, NY: Harper & Row, 1972, p. 24.

[35] Bernasconi, "Seeing Double," p. 247.

[36] Gadamer, *Wahrheit und Methode*, p. 90. English trans., p. 85.

[37] John Sallis, "Interruptions," in *Dialogue and Deconstruction*, Michelfelder & Palmer, p. 254.

[38] John D. Caputo, "Gadamer's Closet Essentialism: A Derridean Critique," in *Dialogue and Deconstruction*, Michelfelder & Palmer, p. 263.

[39] *Ibid.*, p. 264.

[40] Gabe Eisenstein, "The Privilege of Sharing: Dead Ends and the Life of Language," in *Dialogue and Deconstruction*, Michelfelder & Palmer, p. 270.

Chapter Six

Gadamer's Hermeneutics

Gadamer proposes to expand our prevailing views on scientific method to cover the kind of knowledge we gain from hermeneutical experience. He criticizes Kant for modeling scientific knowledge on the natural sciences and wants to augment it by both historical awareness and the insights we gain from literature and art. Some of this is in the tradition of Shaftesbury and Hume who emphasized that moral and aesthetic judgments do not obey reason but have the character of sentiment and taste. While such judgments do not enable us to decide particulars under universal rules, they do make it possible for us to know what is important and to see things from right and proper points of view. Taste is thus considered by Gadamer as a mode of knowing that cannot, however, be separated from its immediate situation, and cannot be reduced to rules and concepts.[1] Taste is concerned with the surface of things, and it is testimony to the changeability of all human judgments, as well as the relativity of all human values.[2] Gadamer emphasizes, however, that aesthetic experience reflects something fundamental in all human knowledge. The ambiguity of meaning that we encounter in a work of art extends to most symbolic expressions as well, and that is why one way of understanding a text may be as legitimate as another. Gadamer rejects this as an untenable hermeneutical relativism, and argues that we should adopt a broader Hegelian concept of aesthetic experience, i.e., a history of truth as it is seen in the mirror of art. The concept of world-view acquires its proper significance only in aesthetics; for it is the multiplicity of possible world views that has given this term its familiar meaning. Indeed the history of art is the chief example of a historical multiplicity that lacks the criterion of progress because it does not converge upon one true model of art. Gadamer insists that the only way to do justice to the notion of truth in art is to treat it historically.

To accomplish this, it becomes necessary to free art from the subjective connotations it has in Kant and Schiller and which have since dominated aesthetics. Gadamer argues that art, like play, has an objective reality in which it becomes meaningless to distinguish between literal and metaphorical images.[3] Whereas Kant denies that taste is a form of knowledge, Gadamer claims that aesthetic awareness is more than it explicitly knows of itself. Even the supposedly free and spontaneous inventions of a writer or artist appeal to a common tradition that they share with their public. They address an audience that must be prepared to appreciate their work and speak their language. They choose what they expect to have an impact on people, even though they may not be aware of doing this deliberately, and they, of course, cannot know what, if any, historical influence their work is going to have. It is quite inevitable that subsequent readers of a text appreciate it differently than what the author intended. Literature is a tradition of intellectual presentation and, as such brings with it its implicit history. But traditional hermeneutics was largely unaware of this when it claimed to reveal the original meaning of a text in both humanist literature and the Bible. Such literal meaning is not readily available because it is the whole of the canon that is supposed to guide the reader in his understanding of an individual passage. Once this unity was being questioned, such interpretation becomes impossible. It was Schleiermacher who first introduced the method of psychological interpretation, and who claimed that our object is to understand the author better than he is able to understand himself, and this view has indeed dominated much of subsequent hermeneutics. The artist is not necessarily the best interpreter of his own work, and has no special priority in this respect over the art critic or historian.

But it certainly makes a difference whether one is trying to understand a text as a literary work in terms of its composition and intention, or whether one sees it merely as a document in the investigation of a larger historical context. Gadamer treats all historical reality as if it were a text, and he takes hermeneutics to be the foundation of history.[4] In the study of history, subsequent events decide the importance of those preceding them, and success or failure causes a whole series of actions or events to have or lack meaning. No such sequential order applies to the interpretation of a text, on the other hand. Details of historical understanding are decided by a largely unconscious teleology that automatically disregards everything it considers insignificant. Of course, the final goal towards which the restless activity of mankind is directed cannot be discovered by means of historical thinking. All we can discover is confined by our horizon; yet a horizon is not a rigid frontier but something that moves with one and invites one to move further. Gadamer criticizes traditional hermeneutics for arbitrarily fixing the horizon by which we understand a text. By contrast, his own horizon metaphor seeks to do justice to the largely unconscious character of our understanding of how language works. He thus explains the taken-for-granted role of language in semantics as due to a submerged, prescientific categorization in our terminology. The problem is that such unconscious behavior does not provide us with much of an explanation in either history, semantics, or hermeneutics. On the other hand, he stresses the fluid variety of all possible meaning, and at the same time he insists that such categorization is not arbitrary after all. He seeks to explain how, in the immense variety of what the reader can find to have meaning and hence expect to discover, not everything has meaning. What is said by Gadamer to limit this almost infinite diversity in possible interpretation is the "prejudgment" (*Vorurteil*) imposed by largely unconscious language categorization. But this inevitably conflicts with the prevailing Cartesian ideal of knowledge, which demands that we reject everything that can in any way be doubted. Thus Gadamer's theory of interpretation falls short of the Cartesian demands for valid knowledge and, since he is also unable to provide us with explicit decision procedures in his hermeneutics, we remain unable to settle differences in interpretation.

Gadamer claims that there are always legitimate prejudices,[5] but it is one thing to admit that this is to some extent unavoidable, and quite another to accept any such particular prejudice as legitimate. If, as he maintains, all tradition is beyond reason, no real progress in hermeneutics is possible either. All understanding for him is merely a play within tradition, and it becomes a game that we cannot win. When we try to understand a text, we do not attempt to recapture the author's attitude of mind, but to regain the perspective within which he has formed his view – yet Gadamer fails to show that this is any more feasible in any literal sense. He argues that the anticipations of meaning that govern our understanding of a text are not subjective but proceed from our participation in a tradition. What belongs, however, to a tradition is by no means easy to settle, and this is, of course, the major cause for conflicting interpretations. That anyone who seeks to understand a text must be related to the language and tradition to which it belongs does not refute what Gadamer labels as hermeneutical nihilism. Only when we fail to accept what the text says do we try to "understand" it either psychologically or historically, but this does not provide Gadamer with any real comprehension as long as he denies that there is such a thing as a literal understanding of the text. He emphasizes that every age has to understand the transmitted text in its own fashion since the meaning of the text always goes beyond what the author intends. It is not just that the discovery of the true meaning of the text is a task that can never be completed, but that there is no such thing as a literal meaning of the text. What questions to ask is part of our historical perspective, but there is no "method" for asking questions either. Gadamer points out that the concept of "situation" inevitably limits our possibilities of vision and literal understanding, and this is what makes a metaphorical interpretation inevitable. An essential part of any situation is its "horizon," which is the range of vision or understanding that can be taken in from any particular standpoint. He thus attempts to elicit literal meaning from such metaphors as "narrowness of horizon," "expansion of horizon," "possible opening up of new horizons," and the like. He concludes that a person who has no horizon is one who does not see far enough and hence overrates what is nearest to him. Similarly, someone who has a horizon presumably knows the relative significance of what is within it. The problem is that Gadamer wants such visual figures of speech also to cover historical, i.e., temporal processes and events. The person who thinks historically comes to understand the true meaning of what has been handed down, without necessarily agreeing with it or seeing himself in it.[6] But the text that is understood historically abandons its claim of expressing something that is literally true.

Using the metaphor of "horizon" to emphasize the limits of all historical knowledge, Gadamer concludes that it can never be expressed by any one standpoint, or have a truly closed horizon. Horizons change for the person who is moving, and hence the horizon

of the past that exists in the form of tradition is also always in motion,
To acquire a horizon means for Gadamer that one learns to look
beyond what is at hand – not in order to look away from it, but to see it
better within the larger whole and in more accurate proportions. But
by the same token, there is for him no longer any isolated horizon of
the present or separate historical horizons – all understanding is a
fusion of horizons.[7] This, however, is itself a mixed metaphor that
attempts to explain our inability to understand anything literally.
Gadamer likens the way in which the interpreter belongs to the text to
the manner in which the vanishing point belongs to perspective. What
he wants to say is that the interpreter does not choose his point of view
arbitrarily, but finds it already given, but Gadamer finds it difficult to
explain in this fashion why a philosophical text or a poem requires
special effort on the part of the reader and interpreter. One problem is
that we are not only supposed to adopt a historical distance towards
the text, but at the same time literally to reconcile this with what we
conceive to be its true meaning. This is something that Gadamer's
hermeneutics does not really know how to do. He merely requires that
every text should be appreciated from a perspective that is appropriate
to it, yet fails to specify which point of view is the appropriate one for
any given occasion. The historian, for example, may examine the text
to find something that it is not itself seeking to provide. What the text
expresses historically is not merely what is intended by it, but what it
"betrays," and there are no identifiable limits to what a text can reveal
in this manner. In coming to realize that future generations are going
to understand the text differently than the way we do, Gadamer
implicitly denies that there can be anything like a true meaning of the
text.

Gadamer's fusion of horizons is thus really a metaphor
describing our *inability* to understand any text literally. Historical
relativity is taken by him as being equivalent to mere metaphorical
meaning and, in this manner, historical knowledge does not find its
fulfillment in any definite understanding either, but is taken to be mere
"openness to experience."[8] Such experience is identified by him as
what runs counter to our expectations; it is thus not something we can
claim to know literally but is, strictly speaking, something we do not
know. While the nature of this experience reveals itself to us by means
of questioning, he insists that there can be no procedure of learning to
ask such questions – and that is why there is no "method" to his
hermeneutics. Why any particular question arises and presses itself

upon us remains a mystery. Gadamer considers it more than a metaphor to describe the work of hermeneutics as a "conversation with the text,"[9] but such feedback is merely imagined and cannot, in any case, go beyond the predetermined language categories. From his plausible thesis that all interpretation is to some extent metaphorical, it does not follow that there can be no such thing as a literal meaning of a text. Since "to acquire the horizon of a question" is not something we can literally do, Gadamer's theory of interpretation turns itself into a metaphor. His vision of horizons does not provide us with any identifiable criteria for literal interpretation or conceptual relevance. He claims that we can understand a text only when we have understood the question to which it is the answer, yet he cannot tell us in any particular case what would be the right question to ask. To understand the logic of question and answer is merely to see that there are no isolated problems like there are stars in the sky.

The problem is that when there is a fusion of horizons, we may be left without any genuine questions to ask. Whether people understand each other can be discovered by inspection from their subsequent behavior. On the other hand, whether they speak the same language or whether a text has been understood cannot be settled in this manner. One problem is that Gadamer rejects categorically any possibility of nonverbal understanding,[10] yet it would seem that this forms the inevitable background for language learning on the part of the infant and for the general formation of new concepts. Contrary to Gadamer, we are able to make our understanding explicit not only in words, but also by means of musical and visual works of art. Indeed words significantly fail to express how we feel, and that is why our understanding frequently goes beyond any statement we can make. That our experience is more than we can say is something for which Gadamer's hermeneutics fails to account, and yet this is why our experience requires interpretation to begin with. He emphasizes the metaphorical character of language use, while this inevitably remains parasitic on literal meaning. To show that our available methods of analysis fall short of doing justice to the complexities of actual language use is not to demonstrate that logic is alien to language, or method to truth. It is only because he regards the metaphorical use of language as its real one[11] that Gadamer takes the fusion of horizons in interpretation as paradigmatic. But as all such understanding becomes inconclusive, no convincing hermeneutical arguments can be made. To say, as he does, that the world is linguistic in nature means to conflate the process of understanding with what is to be understood. What we accept as factual is not merely relative to the language we speak, but is also due to the way the world is. The limits of possible experience and the precise way the world is can never be fully expressed in language, and neither can aesthetic or hermeneutic insights. For Gadamer, all understanding is fundamentally translation, yet what makes such translation adequate cannot be fully verbalized. That is why theological, legal, philological, archeological, literary, and aesthetic interpretations are so different from one another.

Notes

[1] Hans-Georg Gadamer, *Truth and Method*, trans. by Sheed and Ward, New York, NY: Crossroad, 1985, p. 36.

[2] *Ibid.*, p. 53.

[3] *Ibid.*, p. 94.

[4] *Ibid.*, p. 175.

[5] *Ibid.*, p. 239.

[6] *Ibid.*, p. 270.

[7] *Ibid.*, p. 273.

[8] *Ibid.*, p. 319.

[9] *Ibid.*, p. 331.

[10] *Ibid.*, p. 345.

[11] *Ibid.*, p. 389.

Chapter Seven

Hermeneutical Understanding

Hermeneutical thinkers can be characterized by their common desire to resist the idea of the human intellect as a wordless and timeless source of insight. What is distinctive about human understanding is that it always exists in terms of some evolving linguistic framework that has been worked out in terms of some historically conditioned set of concerns and practices. Hermeneutic thinkers argue that language and history are always both conditions and limits of understanding; hermeneutics does not seek the conditions of intelligibility as such, as if understanding were always and everywhere the same.[1] Although new knowledge claims may evolve internally from previous knowledge claims, they do not consistently move toward a better and better ahistorical appreciation of reality. Instead we must rely on something like an emerging consensus of scientists regarding the validity, fruitfulness and cogency of new developments. That this is an inherently fallible and historically mediated process has been shown repeatedly by postempiricist philosophers of science like Kuhn, Feyerabend, Polanyi, Lakatos, and others. By acquiring our native tongue or by learning a specialized language of some field of study, we inherit with it a past we have not shaped. The language in which we participate unconsciously long before we begin to realize any of its limitations, fashions our own attempts to understand in a variety of ways. Language, so to speak, goes out ahead of our reflective understanding and shapes our grasp of the subject matter. We are always already biased in our thinking and knowing in our linguistic interpretation of the world. But this is not to say that our reflective understanding can never break through a specific linguistic tradition and criticize it incisively. It does mean that when we go beyond the limitations of any one mode of speaking, we never abandon the fundamentally linguistic character of our understanding. Even our most penetrating and radical critiques remain engaged in a language that has limitations and blind spots, and awaits its critique. Exchanging one language for another more critical and refined language never implies that we have somehow transcended our inextricable belonging to language in general. It does imply that our grasp of anything can never be final, exhaustive, or otherwise unlimited. We always understand in terms of some historically shaped language, for we always first understand by learning to get around in a certain speech community. The test for such an understanding is not whether we have learned how to associate certain words with certain "inner" experiences, but rather whether we can successfully "do things with words" in the communities in which we share the language. Understanding is not shared in a private sphere before the "eye of the mind," but is realized in the public sphere of discourse.

Yet, some understanding seems to be acquired by nonverbal skills like swimming or drawing that appear a function of our human physiology rather than our language and history. Understanding something is not just being able to talk about it, but is a skillful performance that is nonlinguistic, no less than verbal. Since we grasp linguistic and cultural meanings only within a given context, hermeneutics rejects foundationalist epistemologies. Foundationalism fails because we cannot make good its claim to have discovered a set of fully self-evident truths; rather the validity of any truth claim depends on an implicit context of meaning that is taken for granted. The attempt to form a propositionless philosophy of science fails because all meaningful statements have a deep linguistic history that makes their interpretation an endless task. There is no bedrock of first truths to discover, and the result is always just more interpretation or more talk. What foundationalism amounts to is the idea that we can develop a set of criteria, rules and categories that are sufficient to determine, unequivocally and for all times and places, the difference between meaningful and meaningless statements, valid and invalid inter-pretations, and true or false knowledge claims. These rules would lead, if we believe Descartes, to an indubitable knowledge of reality, or if we follow Kant, to an apodictic science of appearances, a sure and final knowledge of our moral responsibilities, and a definite grasp of the reasons for taste.[2] Even in our own century, this Cartesian/Kantian tradition of looking for the eternal noncontingent rules of all thought remained strong, particularly among the followers of Husserl's phenomenology and the logical positivists. Hermeneutics, by contrast, understands itself as a critique of this notion of a noncontingent autonomous intellect. According to Heidegger and Gadamer, the actual historical circumstances provide a set of tacit preunderstandings and concerns, in terms of which any act of understanding is ultimately made possible. This implies that understanding is never merely a function of what goes on in consciousness. When we understand, there is always an unconscious element we take for granted, and this means that understanding can never be exhaustively analyzed in terms of a priori rules, which the intellect formulates autonomously and then simply follows. Understanding always depends in part on social standards that evolve historically, and which the individual neither produces nor controls.

Hegel was the first to insist that "the true is the whole," and to suggest that the meaning of anything is inescapably contextual. Reason cannot be understood apart from the past or in isolation from the historically mediated language it speaks. But *The Phenomenology of Spirit* is also an attempt to show that history has its own logic: it is not by means of introspection but only through history that we come to know ourselves. According to Heidegger, likewise, it is not a set of ahistorical rules and categories that makes understanding possible. Rather, it is by means of different interests and practices, different concerns and commitments that we experience reality and make it intelligible. As these concerns and commitments change historically, so does our apprehension of reality. Talk of an ahistorical *cogito* or a transcendental ego obscures the way in which human beings are always deeply rooted in their historical circumstances. We forever find ourselves in a set of circumstances that are not of our own making and that we cannot abandon at will. We cannot evade the fundamental finitude and contingency of our lives, and even nature we come to understand only through a historical matrix. Our understanding does not rest on a priori rules or inherited structures of consciousness in terms of which all knowledge can be organized. It is a continually changing process that lacks an underlying identity, and only a gradual modification of this process is possible. This is to say that the role of preunderstanding is never accidental or in any way optional for us, since we have inherited ways of looking at things long before we begin to modify our ways of seeing and understanding. Our lives are defined by our preunderstandings, for all new understanding depends on our ability to relate new phenomena to our already existing set of understandings and concerns, which we take for granted. But such preunderstandings are not clear and well-defined claims that we have already established; rather they are claims that we take for granted and treat *in practice* as being beyond the need for justification. All understanding and explanation terminate in the taken-for-granted preunderstandings of the context. Reality is not hiding behind our historically mediated understanding but instead reality shows itself through our preunderstanding.[3] Heidegger translated Husserl's thesis that "consciousness is always consciousness of..." into the claim that we are always in the world with others and with things.[4] Reality does not mean whatever I take it to mean; it does not permit us to avoid the hard impersonal work of learning how things really are. Meaning is neither arbitrarily imposed from without nor discovered as a brute fact; rather it is worked out in a dialectical fashion in a finite historical context. According to Heidegger, a very important source of these preunderstandings is language, for it is language that makes possible rationality by giving us the ability to understand things as some sort or type of thing. Language allows us to grasp things in both their complex similarity and their distinctiveness from other things.

Gadamer emphasizes that language is not like a tool we can pick up and put down at will. We may choose a word or a phrase, but we do not choose either to use or not to use language. Since all thought is in language, we do not have pure wordless thought that is then accidentally expressed in language. Rather, in "finding the right words," we have the thought (and hence an understanding of the object) for the first time.[5] It is only by articulating a thought in some language that the thought itself becomes distinct and understandable. Our consciousness of the world is a linguistic consciousness that we can never leave behind.[6] Yet while there is no thought that is altogether beyond language, there are nonverbal skills, there is "knowing how" (e.g. to ride a bicycle) no less than "knowing that" (verbal statements). Gadamer insists that "all that can be understood is language,"[7] but to that extent, at least, he is still a Cartesian. Of course, all human understanding is limited and finite, whether linguistic or nonverbal, and every linguistic account is bound to be selective both in what it emphasizes and in its clarity and suggestiveness. But having a complex and nuanced language is a necessary condition for understanding what something is and how it is related to other realities. Indeed Gadamer's "preunderstanding" is essentially nonverbal, and only when it becomes formulated in language does it turn into part of our explicit verbal knowledge. Our understanding of some phenomenon will vary in sophistication and depth in proportion to the number of different ways we have of speaking of it. Yet our ability to relate these various ways of speaking to one another is itself extralinguistic, as Gadamer admits.[8] He seems to say that it is only through language that we have a world, whereas we live in the same world as infants even before we acquire language, and we remain always capable of translating any human language into our own. Indeed it is our nonlinguistic prejudgements as infants that make language learning possible in the first place. Definite ways of speaking (e.g. in science), on the other hand, change historically, and that is why deep adequate views cannot in the strict sense be guaranteed at all.

Even practitioners of the same method have need of a genuine exchange of viewpoints if they are to secure a firm grasp of the subject matter. Gadamer emphasizes that there is no one method on which all our research can be modeled. The linguistic account always carries with it unspoken meanings, and possibilities of understanding and critique to be explored and articulated. Indeed language becomes a theme of inquiry only when linguistic understanding breaks down or becomes otherwise problematic. We tend to overlook the role of language as such and focus our attention instead on realities it makes manifest. Gadamer points out that language itself has a way of carrying the participants along in a dialogue that exceeds their subjective awareness. We never understand in a disinterested fashion, for reason and judgment cannot function without making a type of value assessment about the significance and importance of a knowledge claim for the present circumstances. We are, therefore, not asymptotically approaching the same body of universal truth, and conflicts arise repeatedly because we are always confronted with a variety of contradicting linguistic accounts that contain innumerable nonverbal (i.e. "practical") possibilities. Gadamer refers to the Aristotelian term *phronesis* to characterize this situation, that is, a fallible, historically informed judgment of what is "best" now. The way such disputes are settled is never by applying a set of ahistorical criteria, but by trial and error as reached in a sustained dialogue. That may be why Gadamer's *Truth and Method* never discusses truth in any direct and systematic fashion. His hermeneutics concerns itself with modes of experience that lie outside natural science – i.e. with the experience of art, history, and philosophy. These are all modes of experience in which a truth is communicated that cannot be verified by methodological means proper to science.[9] His position entails a rejection of coherence theories of truth in these disciplines, but this in turn undermines his own ability to criticize opposing views conclusively. When everyday speech and ordinary language are the sources from which our understanding flows, this source cannot be effectively criticized once coherence has been repudiated. Dialogue picks up a topic always in the middle, that is, with a shared pre-understanding, yet such preunderstanding is not in turn open to effective criticism. The "logic" of conversation contains possibilities that emerge only through converting prejudgements into reasoned arguments. Gadamer owes a great deal to Heidegger's account of human being as *Dasein*, that is, as a being emerging from historically contingent possibilities and an open future. Since there are no external verities about *Dasein*, this leaves us not only without method but also without identifiable truth.

Gadamer follows Hegel in opposing the Cartesian strategy of claiming a paradigmatic privilege for mathematics and the mathematico-experimental sciences.[10] Gadamer does not propose that the sciences give up their Cartesian heritage, but he does want them to become aware of their estrangement from natural consciousness and of a necessary return to the larger context in which they are but one of the language games played.[11] Everything is under the strict governance of method except the choice of question to be asked; thus, what is established by statistics seems to be a language of facts, whereas what questions these facts answer, and what facts would begin to speak if other questions were asked, are hermeneutical questions.[12] Statistics are easily used for propaganda purposes because they seem to let facts speak, and hence pretend to an objectivity that really depends on the legitimacy of the questions asked.[13] There is no such thing as a method of learning to ask questions.[14] Gadamer speaks of the logic of question and answer as the key to hermeneutics, yet the nature and status of such a logic remain obscure. Westphal rightly suggests that Gadamer's reference to a "tacit dimension" indicates that more attention needs to be given to the relation of Gadamer and Polanyi.[15]

Understanding the text leads to a historical formulation of the relationship between its time and the time of the investigator. The historian may forget this in his drive for "objectivity," and his quest to know "how things really happened." But such preunderstandings do not provide answers of an already determined content in the sense of a prejudgement. In a successful conversation, the partners understand one another without being obliged to articulate explicitly the comprehensive horizon within which their understanding takes place. Thus, talk about the "question" the text poses can only be metaphorical.

Habermas points out that general linguistics immerses itself in the prevalence of language games without being able to justify the language game of analysis itself. Apparently every ordinary language grammar furnishes the possibility of transcending the language it determines, that is, of translating it into other languages. Since Humboldt, the sciences of language have been out to demonstrate a close connection between linguistic forms and world-view. But since we are never locked into a single grammar, Habermas concludes that the relativism of linguistic world-views and the monadology of language games are equally illusory. The concept of translation is itself dialectical; it expresses in language a state of affairs that cannot be literally expressed in it but can nevertheless be recalled "in other words." Gadamer calls this the hermeneutic experience, and emphasizes that translation is necessary only when understanding is disturbed. The role of the discussion partner includes virtually the role of the interpreter, that is, of someone who can not only converse in one language but can bring about an understanding between different languages. Wittgenstein believed that learning a foreign language has the same structure as growing up in one's own mother tongue because he lacked a dialectical concept of translation. For Gadamer, on the other hand, horizons are open and they shift; we enter into them and they in turn move with us. The life-worlds that determine the grammar of language games are not closed forms of life, as Wittgenstein's monadological conception suggests.[16] Wittgenstein showed how the rules of linguistic communication are, at the same time, rules for the instructional practice through which they can be internalized. But he failed to appreciate that the same rules also include the conditions of possibility of their interpretation. The limits of the world that a language defines are not irrevocable, and translation is the medium in which these revisions take place. Learning his mother tongue, the infant acquires not only conditions of possible consensus but also conditions of possible interpretation. The pluralism of language games constitute additional dimensions of interpretation, yet Wittgenstein saw only invariant linkages between symbols and activities. He failed thus to appreciate that the application of rules includes their interpretation and further development. To be sure, Wittgenstein has made us aware – contrary to the positivist bias – that the application of grammatical rules cannot in turn be defined at the symbolic level according to general rules; it can be inculcated only as a complex of language and practice, and internalized as a part of a life-form. But he remained enough of a positivist to conceive of this practice as the reproduction of fixed patterns.[17] Actually, however, language games are not monadically sealed off; they are porous to both translation and interpretation. The grammar of a language does not contain a rigid design for its application, and whoever has learned to apply its rules has not only acquired the ability to express himself but also to interpret experiences in the language. Along with their possible application, grammatical rules simultaneously imply the need for interpretation, but Wittgenstein failed to see this, and as a consequence he conceived the practice of language games unhistorically. While giving up on the notion of an ideal language, the concept of a language game remains indebted to an unacknowledged model of formalized languages. The ambiguity of ordinary language and the imprecision of its rules are for Wittgenstein only apparent; every language game is completely ordered, and the language analyst can rely on this as a standard for critique. Even though ordinary language cannot be reconstructed in formal language, its grammar is still no less precise and unequivocal than that of a calculus.

Gadamer uses the image of a horizon to capture the basic heuristic character of every concrete natural language. Far from having a closed boundary, each such language can in principle incorporate what is linguistically foreign and at first incomprehensible. We are always occupied with what is closest to us; thus, we have continually to curb a too hasty assimilation of the past to our own expectations of meaning. Historical events are constructed within the reference system of a story; they cannot be presented without relation to other, later events. The predicates with which a historical event is invariably presented require the appearance of later events in the light of which the event in question appears as a historical event. Consequently the historical description of events becomes in the course of time richer than is the empirical observation at the moment of their happening.[18] The language in which the historian presents events does not primarily express observations but the interrelations of a series of interpretations. The historian is no mere chronicler restricted to observation; he is engaged in communicative experiences, for just to do history is to employ some over-arching conception that goes beyond what is given. A series of events acquires the unity of a story only from a point of view that cannot be taken from these events themselves. As long as new points of view arise, the same events can enter into other stories and acquire new meanings. Translation aims at making what is alien our own; thus, hermeneutics is not to be viewed as a mere subordinate discipline within the humanities (*Geisteswissenschaften*).[19] The historical experience is prior to all method because it is the matrix out of which arise the questions that it then directs to science. Language is not simply a mirror; it is a game of interpretation in which we are engaged. Even the language games of the natural sciences remain related to the metalanguage presented in the mother tongue. Gadamer argues that history precedes me and my reflection, for I belong to history before I belong to myself. He concludes that an exhaustive critique of prejudice and of ideology is impossible because there is no zero point from which to proceed.[20] For Gadamer, prejudice is not the opposite of reason; it is a component of understanding linked to the finite historical character of the human being. It is a mistake to believe that there are only unfounded prejudices, and the project of a science free from prejudice is impossible. The accord that does support us is the understanding reached in dialogue, the question and answer relation.

There is the technical or instrumental interest that governs the empirical-analytical sciences and that constitutes the modern ideology. The humanities, by contrast, are essentially disciplines of culture and tradition. For Habermas, the principal flaw of Gadamer's account is to have ontologized hermeneutics. He insists that this experience cannot be canonized, and that the gesture of hermeneutics is one of acknowledging the historical conditions to which all human understanding is subject. The interpretation of a text cannot be treated as an extension of the dialogical situation. Gadamer accepted Heidegger's extension of the concept of hermeneutical understanding to cover and define human existence, and this made him go beyond method and include in hermeneutics not only science but history as well. No conceptual language constitutes a final constraint on thought as long as the thinker engages in dialogue. When Gadamer wrote that "Being which can be understood is language," it was implied that anything real can never be completely understood. What we find happening in speaking is not a mere reification of intended meaning, but an endeavor that continually modifies itself. Language is considered a bridge rather than a barrier, and interpretation is more than a technique of dealing with texts. In the twentieth century, both *text* and *interpretation* have acquired a new importance, and the shift is connected with the role that the phenomenon of language has come to play in our thought. The ideal of scientific knowledge that modern science follows came out of the model of nature as mathematically ordered (a model that was first developed by Galileo in his mechanics). In this way, ordinary language lost its primacy for science, while still retaining its dominance outside the natural sciences. In modern logic and scientific method, language was replaced by mathematical notation, but more recently interest in ordinary language has reemerged. Neither the neo-Kantians nor the early phenomenologists were interested in language, which came to play a pivotal role in the philosophy of Ernst Cassirer and Martin Heidegger. From Nietzsche we learned to doubt the grounding of truth in self-certainty and self-consciousness, and Freud acquainted us with the complexities of the unconscious. All this contributed to the discovery of the priority of language, and worked against the apparent evidence of self-consciousness and the positivist acceptance of "facts." The validity of protocol-sentences as the foundation of knowledge was abandoned even by the members of the Vienna Circle because it was realized that the so-called given can never be separated from interpretation. Thus, interpretation is not an additional superimposed procedure of knowing but constitutes the original structure of "Being-in-the-world."[21] Indeed, what makes something a text shows itself only by means of interpretation: preunderstanding, anticipation of meaning, and, thereby, a great many circumstances that do not appear in the text play a crucial role in the reading of the text. Every translation, even the so-called literal translation, is a sort of interpretation,[22] for it is generally taken for granted that the text must be interpreted not only literally.

Since Kant, epistemology has been taken as a foundationalist enterprise – one that separates knowledge from other forms of belief. Hermeneutics, on the other hand, rejects the idea that the primary task of philosophy is to supply foundations and guarantee certainty. It proclaims knowledge to be pragmatically relative to contexts of understanding, and makes the interpretation of texts a paradigm of the phenomenon of understanding in general. Epistemology and hermeneutics have thus evolved into competing views about what philosophical theories must do. Hermeneutics maintains that understanding is always interpretive, that there is no uniquely privileged standpoint, that reading rather than seeing is the paradigm case, and that science, understanding, and interpretation require periodical reexaminations. Both Derrida's grammatology and Gadamer's hermeneutics are theories of understanding on the model of reading. Instead of "interpretation," the grammtological investigation is characterized as "deconstruction" or "dissemination," and there is nothing like a hidden meaning that the heuristic interpretation must uncover. Signs refer only to other signs, and the text, like all language, is inherently discontinuous. Gadamer and Derrida de-emphasize the biological factors in human understanding, but while what we see is doubtless influenced by what we claim to know, human beings do grow up to see basically similar things across different languages, cultures, and historical epochs. Neither translation nor interpretation would be possible but for a species specific human nature. Indeed, Gadamer's preunderstanding is essentially pre-linguistic, for only *after* it has been formulated in language does it become historically or culturally relative; history, after all, is based on the interpretation of written texts. Many have come to suspect that the unity linking historical events into causal chains is really more a tradition of the historian's narrative than an observable empirical event.[23] Tied to the assumption that a tradition is essentially continuous is the belief that it consists of entities that can be circumscribed in a communicative discourse, no matter how diverse these entities are. But there must be *some* shared belief, if there is to be understanding at all, and that shared belief is represented in the assumption of a common human nature.

Derrida's view seems to be that we cannot say what we mean because intention is never fully presented to itself, and it is not transparent even to the intender. Reality is for Derrida only a textual activity because there is no "natural attachment" to the real referent even for proper names. Hoy rightly points out, however, that the historian and the philosopher, unlike the novelist, seem to write with the commitment to the actual existence of real events and definite truths.[24] The more adequate response seems to be not to deny that there are real objects but to point out that no event is ever captured in a description. Gadamer frequently reiterates that the historical problem is not a problem of method at all. He points out that it has been the obsession with *Method* and with thinking, i.e., that the primary task of hermeneutics is to specify a distinctive method for the humanities rivaling that of the natural sciences, that has plagued and distorted nineteenth-century hermeneutics. This led to a view of understanding as a primarily psychologic and subjective activity, involving some sort of empathy that enables us to identify with the intentions of the author of a text or of a historical personality. Hermeneutical understanding is what Gadamer takes to be characteristic of our relations with works of art, texts, and history. Contrary to Descartes and Hegel, Gadamer sees this as a task that can never achieve finality or closure. The meaning of what we seek to understand is not self-contained and does not exist in isolation; to understand is always to understand *differently*. The historical movement of human life consists in its never being entirely bound to any one standpoint and hence, it can never have a truly closed horizon.[25] The primary intention of *Truth and Method* is to defend and elucidate the legitimacy of speaking about the truth of works of art, texts, and traditions. Gadamer tells us that it was his intention to show that there is a different kind of knowledge and truth that is not covered by the method of the natural sciences, and that is only available to us through historical and hermeneutical under-standing. At the same time, he rejects what Hegel took to be ground for his conception of truth revealed in *Wissenschaft*, that "truth is the whole," the absolute knowledge that completes and overcomes experience.[26] Bernstein points out, however, that Gadamer himself is employing a concept of truth that he never fully makes explicit. His typical phrasing is to speak of a "claim to truth" that works of art, texts, and traditions make open to us. There is no objective or ahistorical perspective from which we can evaluate such competing claims to truth. There is no method that guarantees truth, but if there are no methods or criteria, there is no truth either, for it means that we can never verify what we claim to be true. When questions are asked about the validity of standards or criteria that are to serve as the basis for criticism, Gadamer tells us that they, too, are handed down to us and need to be recovered from tradition. But Bernstein points out that this response is not adequate because Gadamer does not fully realize that we are living in a time when the very conditions required for the exercise of *phronesis* – the shared acceptance and stability of universal principles and laws – are themselves breaking down. Many critics of

Gadamer stress the conservative implications of his philosophical hermeneutics.

A primary concern of modern philosophy that has persisted from Descartes until the present has been to turn philosophy into a "rigorous science," and to overcome a situation where philosophy appears to be the endless battleground among competing opinions. It presupposes that there are problems to be solved once and for all, and that there is a systematic methodology for doing this. More recently postmodernist writers like Rorty, Feyerabend, and Derrida have come to question this. There is no Archimedian point, no fundamental position, no theoretical perspective that lies outside our own historicity. There is no absolute knowledge or final understanding, and the point of philosophical hermeneutics is that it corrects the peculiar falsehood of modernity, the idolatry of scientific method and technology. It is all too frequently taken for granted that if we cannot come up with universally fixed criteria to measure the plausibility of competing interpretations, then this means that we have no rational basis for distinguishing better from worse interpretations. Kuhn, Lakatos, Feyerabend, Toulmin, among others, have demonstrated the essential openness and indeterminacy of criteria in choosing among rival theories, paradigms, and research programs. All of them would agree with Kuhn's claim that there is no neutral algorithm for theory choice, no systematic decision procedure that, properly applied, must lead each individual scientist to the same conclusion.[27] Kuhn himself realizes that many claims he has been making bear a close affinity with those that have been central to contemporary hermeneutics.[28] Gadamer rejects the thesis that Popper calls "The Myth of the Framework" – that we are prisoners caught in the framework of our theories, our expectations, and that there is no possibility of discovering these limitations.[29] We should not fool ourselves into thinking that there are any a priori limitations or any hidden constraints on the invention of new vocabularies and forms of discourse. Gadamer concludes that it is really philosophical hermeneutics rather than epistemology, "Method," or science that can achieve what philosophy has always promised us: some profound access to "truth." He, too, wants the comforts of consensus, even if it is only the consensus of the community of interpreters.[30] Thus, science is more like hermeneutical understanding than Gadamer realizes, and disputes about rival hermeneutical interpretations are more like "Method" than Gadamer acknowledges.[31]

Bernstein rightly points out that techniques of deconstruction can be turned against themselves. When decoded, such relativism is more honestly acknowledged by Feyerabend who tells us that, objectively, there is not much choice between antisemitism and humanitarianism.[32] The real issue is between those who think our culture, purposes, and institutions cannot be supported except conversationally, and those who still hope for other sorts of support.[33] Whereas Gadamer is a representative of modernity – at least insofar as he believes that philosophy (when properly reconstructed) still holds out the promise of knowledge and truth, even when all necessary concessions have been made – philosophers like Feyerabend, Rorty, and Derrida are postmodernist thinkers who seek to root out the last vestiges of a "metaphysics of presence." One of the deepest aspirations since Hegel – including Kierkegaard, Nietzsche, Marx, Freud, Heidegger, Wittgenstein, Foucault, and Derrida – has been to "end" philosophy. It is Heidegger who gave the idea of hermeneutics its maximal extension by characterizing hermeneutic understanding a necessary feature of all human experience. It is this all-encompassing sense of hermeneutics we find elaborated in Gadamer's *Truth and Method*.[34] Larmore points out that one reaction to this conceptual inflation may be to suspect that the term "hermeneutics" has lost any specific sense and has become a mere slogan. This expansion of the hermeneutical perspective to include all forms of knowledge and experience stems from the realization that, epistemologically, the interpretation of texts does not differ from the kinds of knowledge the natural sciences give us. Larmore argues that although the "historicity" of all knowledge claims does undermine certain important epistemological views, it does *not* imply, either in textual interpretation or elsewhere, the historical relativism that Gadamer in fact embraces. He has a "contextualist" view of justification of belief: we are never able to expose all our beliefs to scrutiny at the same time. The critical examination of some beliefs must always take place against the backdrop of other beliefs that, at least for the purpose at hand, are held constant and immune to revision.[35] Following Popper, Larmore emphasizes that critical reflection proceeding in a piecemeal fashion can attain at least relative objectivity. While we cannot subject all our beliefs to critical examination, we do not thereby have reason to discard that ideal as one worth pursuing as far as possible.

Even if the natural sciences are historically relative, there is progress in an instrumental and technological sense that is hard to explain away. The positions that Gadamer attacks are ones that most of us are naturally inclined to hold. They are that textual interpretation is concerned with determining the meaning, and not the truth, of what has been said or written; that it has as its object what the author intended to say; and that it attempts to reconstruct the author's meaning as it actually was, without confusing it with our own views about the subject matter. What a text means need not, it is true, coincide with everything the author had in mind. But if what the author meant in the act of composing the text is altogether irrelevant to what the text itself means, we would have no good reason to evoke the known beliefs of the author to ascertain the meaning of this text. Furthermore, if textual meaning did not coincide with what the author meant to say, we would have no right to presume that one part of the text illuminates the meaning of another part of the *same* text either. To be sure, nothing guarantees that an author will prove to be the best interpreter of his work, for it may contain meanings of which he is unaware. But this only implies that in the writing of texts, as in our other actions, we do not have an immediate and foolproof access to the full range of our intentions. Our intentions are shaped in a large measure by our beliefs, some of which remain beyond our critical control. It is undeniable that the interpretation we give reflects our historical and cultural situation, but it does not follow that objectivity and history form antithetical forms of knowledge.

Notes

[1] Brice R. Wachterhauser, "History and Language in Understanding," *Hermeneutics and Modern Philosophy*, Albany, NY: State University of New York Press, 1986, p. 6.

[2] *Ibid.*, p. 16.

[3] *Ibid.*, p. 26.

[4] Martin Heidegger, *Sein und Zeit*, Tübingen: Max Wiemeyer Verlag, 1977, p. 62; trans. by J. Macquarrie and C. Robinson under the title *Being and Time*, New York, NY: Harper & Row, 1962, p. 89.

[5] Hans-Georg Gadamer, *Wahrheit und Methode*, Tübingen: J.C.B. Mohr (Paul Siebeck), 1960, p. 394, trans. under the title *Truth and Method*, New York, NY: Barden and Cumming, 1975, p. 377.

[6] Wachterhauser, "History and Language," p. 31.

[7] Gadamer, *Wahrheit und Methode*, p. 450, *Truth and Method*, p. 432.

[8] Wachterhauser, "History and Language," p. 31.

[9] Gadamer, *Truth and Method*, p. xii.

[10] Merold Westphal, "Hegel and Gadamer," in *Hermeneutics and Modern Philoisophy,* Wachterhauser, p. 72.

[11] Hans-Georg Gadamer, *Philosophical Hermeneutics*, trans. David E. Linge, Berkleley, CA: 1976, p. 30; *Truth and Method*, p. 407.

[12] Gadamer, *Philosophical Hermeneutics*, p. 11.

[13] *Truth and Method*, p. 268.

[14] *Ibid.,* p. 329.

[15] Westphal, "Hegel and Gadamer," p. 86 n77.

[16] Jürgen Habermas, "A Review of Gadamer's Truth and Method," in *Hermeneutics and Modern Philosophy*, Wachterhauser, p. 247.

[17] *Ibid.,* p. 249.

[18] *Ibid.,* p. 256.

[19] Hans-Georg Gadamer, "On the Scope and Function of Hermeneutical Reflection," in *Hermeneutics and Modern Philosophy*, Wachterhauser, p. 278.

[20] Paul Ricoeur, "Hermeneutics and Critique of Ideology," in *Hermeneutics and Modern Philosophy*, Wachterhauser, p. 308.

[21] Hans-Georg Gadamer, "Text and Interpretation," in *Hermeneutics and Modern Philosophy*, Wachterhauser, p. 388.

[22] *Ibid.,* p. 391.

[23] Joseph Grünfeld, "On the Relations of Hume's Philosophical and Historial Writings," Ph.D. Thesis, The Hebrew University, Jeruselem, 1959.

[24] David Couzens Hoy, "Must We Say What We Mean? The Grammatological Critique of Hermeneutics," in *Hermeneutics and Modern Philosophy*, Wachterhauser, p. 412.

[25] Gadamer, *Wahrheit und Methode*, p. 288, *Truth and Method*, p. 271.

[26] Gadamer, *Wahrheit und Methode*, p. 337, *Truth and Method*, p. 318.

[27] Thomas Kuhn, *The Structure of Scientific Revolutions* (Chicago, IL: Chicago Univesity Press, 1970), p. 200.

[28] Thomas Kuhn, *The Essential Tension* (Chicago, IL: Chicago University Press, 1977), Preface.

[29] Karl Popper, "Normal Science and Its Dangers," in *Criticism and the Growth of Knowledge*, eds. Imre Lakatos and Alan Musgrave, Cambridge: Cambridge University Press, 1970, p. 56.

[30] Richard J. Bernstein, "What is the Difference that Makes a Difference? Gadamer, Habermas and Rorty," in *Hermeneutics and Modern Philosophy*, Wachterhauser, p. 362.

[31] *Ibid.,* p. 363.

[32] Paul Feyerabend, *Science in a Free Society,* London: 1978, pp. 8-9.

[33] Richard Rorty, "Pragmatism, Relativism, and Irrationalism," *Proceedings of the American Philosophical Association*, 1980, pp. 727-28.

[33] Richard Rorty, "Pragmatism, Relativism, and Irrationalism," *Proceedings of the American Philosophical Association*, 1980, pp. 727-28.
[34] Charles Larmore, "Tradition, Objectivity, and Hermeneutics," in *Hermeneutics and Modern Philosophy*, Wachterhauser, p. 147.
[35] Gadamer, *Wahrheit und Methode*, pp. 4263ff.

Chapter Eight

Ricoeur's Conflict of Interpretations

Some Anglo-American philosophers of language have tended to treat language as if it were a self-generating computing machine working without the intervention of the human speaker.[1] Ricoeur, on the other hand, is suspicious of formalistic approaches to language; instead he proposes a hermeneutics that focuses on words that have a certain type of multiple sense, a symbolic significance and a metaphorical structure. The hermeneutic task is to decipher this multiple significance, rejecting the quest for some pure and simple "given." Ricoeur attempts to ground hermeneutics in phenomenology not by the short route taken by Heideggar's ontology of understanding, but by means of successive investigations into semantics and reflection. Heidegger wanted to subordinate historical knowledge to ontological understanding, but he gives us no sense in what way historical knowledge is derived from this primordial understanding. Ricoeur's approach is based on the semantic elucidation of the concept of interpretation common to all heuristic disciplines; it is organized around the central theme of multiple meaning or what he calls symbolic sense. Exegesis has already accustomed us to the idea that a text has several meanings and that these meanings have a tendency to overlap. Interpretation for Ricoeur consists in deciphering the hidden meaning in the apparent meaning, in unfolding the levels of meaning implied in the literal meaning. There is interpretation wherever there is literal meaning, and it is in interpretation that the plurality of meaning is made manifest. Interpretation itself is composed of many different methods, but we have learned from exegetic disciplines (such as psychoanalysis) that the so-called immediate consciousness is a "false" consciousness. Thus, the logic of Ricoeur's hermeneutics is no longer a formal logic but a transcendental one; he remains convinced that a separate ontology is beyond our grasp because it is only through the process of interpretation that we perceive the being we interpret. For him, rival interpretations are not mere "language games," all equally valid. Interpretation does not spring from nowhere; rather one interprets in order to make explicit, to extend, and so to keep alive, the tradition within which one always remains.

The symbol invites us to think, calls for an interpretation, precisely because it means more than it says. An understanding of structures is a necessary condition between symbolic naiveté and heuristic interpretation.[2] In each heuristic discipline, interpretation is at the borderline between language and lived experience, and what can be symbolized is always found in nonlinguistic reality. Thus, multiple meaning is a means of detecting a condition of being,[3] and the philosophical interest of symbolism is that it reveals by its structure and meaning the equivocalness of being. Wilbur Urban has pointed out that what makes language an instrument of knowledge is precisely the fact that a sign can indicate one thing without ceasing to indicate another.[4] It is here that we grasp the effect of context, for when I speak, I realize only part of the potentiality signified, while the rest of the semantic possibilities continue to hover in the background. Since polysemy and symbolism are part of all language, words have a mode of presence other than the mode of existence of their structures. The possibility of symbolism is rooted in the universal function of language, namely the ability of lexemes to develop contextual variations. The mystery of language is that it says something about being. Speaker and hearer understand this relation immediately because for them language aims at something; it has the double function of saying something (meaning), and of saying something about something (reference). It was Frege who showed that, besides meaning (*Sinn*), it is reference (*Bedeutung*) that roots our sentences in reality. It is only at the level of the sentence that language says something, and short of this, it says nothing at all. The Chomskian school of linguistics concerns itself with the nature and the problem posed by the production of new sentences. Normal mastery of language involves not only the ability to understand immediately an indefinite number of entirely new sentences, but also the ability to interpret them. It is clear that a theory of language that neglects this "creative" aspect of language can be only of marginal interest.[5] The sentence is an event, since it is transitory, passing, ephemeral, whereas the word survives the sentence as a displaceable entity that holds itself available for new uses. Words have more than one meaning, yet they do not have infinity of meanings.[6] The univocity or plurivocity of our discourse is not due to our words but to the context in which they are uttered. In univocal discourse, that is, discourse that permits only one meaning, it is the context that expresses the semantic richness of the words by establishing a frame of reference, a theme, or an identical topic for all the words in the sentence. If the context tolerates or even preserves several meanings at the same time, we deal with symbolic language, which in saying one thing, says something else. More than one interpretation is justified by the structure of the discourse because the essential function of language is to be sought beyond the closure of signs.

What Freud, Nietzsche, and Marx put in question is something that appears to a phenomenologist as the origin of all meaning, namely consciousness itself. Whereas immediate consciousness does involve a kind of certainty, this certainty is not self-knowledge. Self-counsiousness in the strong sense comes not at the beginning of our investigation but at its end. It was Hegel who demonstrated that an individual consciousness cannot be equated with its own content. It belongs to the essence of consciousness never to be entirely explicit and, through this failure, consciousness discovers that its immediate self-certainty is mere presumption. The conscious is relative to the system by which it is interpreted, i.e., it is relative to its hermeneutics. Consciousness is not a given but a task; we might say that whereas consciousness is history, the unconscious is fate. Ricoeur rejects the easy eclecticism in which the conscious and the unconscious are vaguely complementary. We cannot simply add up Hegel and Freud, and give to each one half of man because the two readings cover exactly the same territory, and everything that can be said of the one can also be said of the other. Freud teaches us that men are not gentle creatures eager to be loved, but that they are essentially aggressive. Religion gets its conflicting force from the most tenacious as well as the most unrealistic of all desires – the desire for security. But Freud never considered the limits of his interpretation, and it remains unclear how psychoanalysis is to be coordinated with the sciences or with interpretations other than itself. Psychoanalysis has no means of resolving the problem of what Leibniz called "the radical origin of things;" all it can do is unmask the infantile and archaic representations that constitute this problem. While no one has done as much as Freud to break the tyranny of supposed facts, he holds on to a positivism that transcribes meanings into a language of mental hydraulics.

First there was Copernicus, who destroyed the narcissistic illusion by which the home of man was believed to be at rest at the center of the universe. Then there was Darwin, who put an end to man's illusion of being unconnected to the animal kingdom. And finally there was Freud, who discovered that man is not even master over his own psyche. All these discoveries met with resistance by a primitive and persistent narcissism. Freud made it clear that conflict is inescapable in human life, since in addition to the problem of becoming adult, there is the difficulty of attaining self-knowledge. Between satisfaction and suppression there does indeed open up the possibility of sublimation, but this is not enough to eliminate man's delusions and dreams. It is, therefore, not by chance that Freud – the materialist, determinist, scientist, and heir to the Enlightenment – finally turns to the language of tragic myth to say the essential. Ricoeur dwells on the ambivalent character of Freud's discourse who discusses meaning (i.e. the meaning of dreams, symptoms, etc.) together with force (repressions, conflicts, etc.). Freud can be read just as philosophers read Plato, Descartes, and Kant, for Freud's writings address themselves not just to professional psychiatrists but to the public at large. However, besides a speculative doctrine, psychoanalysis involves a method of manipulating desire. Such analysis is "work" because it is a struggle against resistances. The "facts" with which psychoanalysis deals are not verifiable by multiple independent observers; it is unlike a theory in physics or biology since the "work" involved is entirely within language. The result is that psychoanalytic method is much closer to the historical sciences than to the natural sciences. Ricoeur joins those logicians, semanticists, and methodologists who deny the scientific status of psychoanalysis. He emphasizes that psychoanalysis is limited by the very thing that justifies it, namely its decision to discuss all cultural phenomena entirely in terms of desire and resistance. Freud teaches that merely to know something will not make any real difference so long as the underlying desire has not been altered.

There is no real conflict of interpretation in Ricoeur between psychoanalytical and religious discourse. He considers the concept of original sin to be false knowledge, but maintains that this false knowledge is at the same time also a true symbol. Each of us discovers evil, finds it already in himself, and in tracing back the origin of evil to a distant ancestor, the myth discovers the situation of every man: evil has already taken place. But Ricoeur denies the legitimacy of all attempts to speculate about the concept of original sin as if it had proper consistency. Unlike technical signs, which are perfectly transparent, such symbolic signs remain partly opaque; what must thus be scrutinized in the concept of original sin is not its false clarity but its analogical richness. Its force lies in referring back to what is most radical in the confession of sin, namely the fact that evil precedes awareness. The only cognitive access to the experience of evil is through symbolic expression, yet there does not exist a general hermeneutics, only various separate domains. Since one of the essential characteristics of the symbol is that it is not arbitrary, Ricoeur emphasizes that each hermeneutics remains legitimate in its own context. But it should be noticed that there can be no conflict of interpretations if they are not subject to the same logic. Indeed, neither Hegel nor Freud would have admitted that they are in conflict with each other. All they share is a denial that consciousness knows itself completely, for after Hegel and Freud, consciousness is not immediate but mediate; it is not a source but a task; the task of becoming conscious. Ricoeur's reflection introduces a reductive and deconstructive interpretation because he agrees with Freud and Hegel that consciousness is originally false consciousness. At the same time, the symbols that teach us the nature of evil are said by Ricoeur to be resistant not only to factual knowledge but also to philosophical understanding.[7] Indeed both psychoanalysis and religion remain ultimately beyond Ricoeur's reflection; mere understanding remains powerless against desire, and the nature of evil is finally never understood. Even punishment defies his rational analysis because, if it is taken for granted that the criminal is entitled to punishment proportional to his crime, we can no longer accept original sin as something in which humanity is collectively implicated. Evil shows itself in false and violent synthesis, i.e. in political and ecclesiastic institutions. That evil may work toward the advancement of the Kingdom of Heaven is something the philosopher can never know. The God whom he is seeking does not exist as a source of moral obligation, as the author of the commandments. Ricoeur himself admits that, as a philosopher, he has no answer to these questions.

Notes

[1] Paul Ricoeur, *The Conflict of Interpretations*, ed. Don Ihde, Evanston: Northwestern University Press, 1974, p. x.

[2] *Ibid.*, p. 61.

[3] *Ibid.*, p. 66.

[4] Stephen Ullman, *The Principles of Semantics,* New York, NY: Philosophical Library, 1957, p. 117.

[5] Noam Chomsky, *Current Issues in Linguistic Theory,* New York, NY: Humanities Press, 1964, pp. 7-8.

[6] Ricoeur, *The Conflicts of Interpretations*, p. 93.

[7] *Ibid.,* p. 332.

Chapter Nine

Quine's Soft Empiricism

In science it is common usage to say that what we predict are observations. Theories are couched in sentences, and it is logic that connects sentences to sentences, but what we need as critical links in those connective chains are some sentences that are directly and firmly associated with our stimulations. Unlike a report or a feeling, the sentence must command the same verdict from all linguistically competent witnesses of the occasion. Quine points out, however, that such observability is vague at the edges, and that we fancy perspicuity only by fancying boundaries.[1] The observation sentence is the means of verbalizing the expectations that check on theory and the requirement of intersubjectivity is what makes science objective. Observation sentences are thus the vehicles of scientific evidence, but they are also the entering wedge in the learning of language. For Quine, observation sentences are the link between language, scientific or not, and the real world that language is all about.[2] It has now become fashionable to question observation terms, and to claim that the purportedly observable is theory-laden in varying degrees. Quine admits that the notion of observation is relative to one or another limited speech community. He claims, however, that since mathematics infiltrates all branches of our system, we shelter mathematical truth by exercising our freedom to reject other beliefs. Even though he denies that prediction is the ultimate purpose of science, his objective is as much to choose the revision as it is to maximize further success in prediction. Stimulation meanings have fuzzy boundaries, and in many cases no marshaling of tacit premises can quite define the observation category because of its vagueness. But it would nevertheless seem that Quine's broadest scientific categories escape empirical evidence altogether. He remains occupied with what has been central to traditional epistemology, namely the relation of science to sensory data, and the normative aspects of his epistemology get naturalized into a chapter of engineering. The most notable norm of Quine's naturalized epistemology coincides with Locke's saying that there is nothing in the mind that has not been in the senses. This is a prime specimen of naturalized epistemology, for it is the finding of natural science itself, however fallible, that our information comes only through impacts on our sensory receptors. Quine's point is normative because it warns us against telepaths and soothsayers.

In a technical view, normative naturalized epistemology tangles with margins of error, random deviation, and whatever else goes into the applied mathematics of statistics.[3] But Quine does not consider predictions as checkpoints of science to be normative; rather he sees them as defining the particular language-game of science, in contrast to other good language-games such as fiction and poetry. Prediction is not the main purpose of the science-game; it is what decides the game. It is only occasionally the purpose, and in early times it gave primitive science its survival value. But nowadays, the overwhelming purposes of the science-game are technology and understanding.[4] Quine is within the pragmatist tradition, for he too rejects the notion of "deep" truth and is content to "save the phenomena," not to postulate hidden or deep entities within or behind them. With our progressive systematization of science, we have gone on to reify liquids and invisible air, and we have integrated these things with bodies too small to be detected. Abstract bodies have long since proved indispensable to natural science – thus number, function, classes.[5] At this point the question arises of what to count as reification, and what to count as just a useful but ontologically noncommittal turn of phrase. For the idea that seemed to favor the reification of bodies, namely persistence between exposures, makes no sense for abstract bodies. Quine argues that the most decisive general mark of reification in our language and kindred ones are pronouns. When a language is regimented in the logical notation of a predicate calculus, the role of such pronouns is played by bound variables. So he concludes that to be is to be the value of a variable. Against Quine, it has been objected that what there is is a question of fact and not of language. It has also been objected that the logical notation of quantification is an arbitrary and parochial standard to adopt for ontological commitment.

Quine thinks of reference as relating names and other singular terms to their objects, but he realizes that singular terms may fail to refer to anything. Set theory also teaches that there are bound to be individually unspecifiable objects – unspecifiable irrational numbers notably – no matter how rich our notation and how cumbersome our expressions. He believes that the question of ontological commitment is parochial, though within a much broader range than is admitted by symbolic logic. What particular there may be is, therefore, indifferent to the truth of observation sentences. Once we have appropriately regimented our system of the world or part of it, we can so interpret it as to get by with only the slender ontology of whole numbers. Two ontologies, if explicitly correlated one-to-one, are considered by Quine to be empirically on a par, and there is no empirical ground for choosing the one rather than the other. As wholes they are empirically indistinguishable, but when we move beyond sensible bodies and proceed to posit atoms, electrons, quarks, numbers, classes, and relations, our imagination is bolstered by analogies in varying degrees. Light waves, for example, rest on a tenuous analogy, for unlike water waves, they are not waves on or in anything. It would seem then not only that the elementary particles are unlike bodies, but that there are no such entities to begin with. Theories can threaten not only the cherished analogy of elementary particles but the very sense of Quine's ontological question. On one reading, these deviations take the form of probabilistic predictions whereas, on an alternative reading, they call for basic departures from the logic of truth functions.

Quine's notion of radical translation, according to which the linguist tries to relate the native's behavior to his language from scratch, as it were, turns out to be merely a thought experiment. Critics have rightly argued that the thesis is a consequence of his behaviorism, and some have claimed that it amounts to *a reductio ad absurdum* of behaviorism.[6] But Quine insists that a behaviorist approach to linguistics is mandatory. Whereas in psychology we may or may not be behaviorists, in linguistics we have no choice because each of us learns his language by observing other people's behavior, and having his own faltering behavior observed and reinforced.[7] What is crucial, however, in every case, is how such situations are interpreted, and Quine admittedly has no theory of interpretation. The correctness of one's language in a philosophical discussion of this sort is certainly not subject to external checkpoints that can be applied to particular expressions. Quine insists that science is one language-game, and poetry and fiction quite another, yet his own philosophical language-game participates in both without further discussion. What should count as a shared situation is by no means obvious, and our mental life in particular is largely a function of the language in which we describe and discuss it. Quine's indeterminacy of translation demonstrates that there is more to linguistic behavior than what is to be gleaned from overt behavior in observable circumstances. Usually the concurrent, publicly observable situation does not enable us to predict what a speaker even of our own language is going to say, for utterances commonly bear little relevance to the circumstances outwardly observable at the time. Behaviorism is, therefore, not the only possible theory in linguistics as Chomsky and the Cartesian linguistic tradition demonstrate. There are always ongoing projects and unshared past experiences, and there are no sentences that hinge strictly on the concurrent publicly observable situation. Greetings, commands, and questions play no less a role in a child's acquisition of language than do declarative sentences. The radical translator can never be sure that the native's utterance is linked to any specific situation, and this can, therefore, not be settled conclusively by offering some sentences to the native's assent or dissent. Reference becomes inscrutable to the degree that there is more than one way of guessing the meaning of signs, yet Quine insists that empiricism must be taken as the key operative in language acquisition and in our interpretation of language generally. Once it is realized, however, that there is no one situation to which the native's observation sentence and the linguist's translation of it are empirically linked, Quine's adoption of Locke's saying that there is nothing in the mind that has not been in the senses becomes largely metaphorical. He himself realizes that the notion of "satisfaction" is far too vague to serve such a purpose, for what the relevant stimulus meanings are is a function of our interpretation, and Quine has no theory of interpretation. His empiricism is "soft" because we can never reliably identify the stimulations that prompt assent or dissent by direct observation or in an inductive fashion.

What either the linguist or the native "means" in radical translation is not subject to direct empirical verification, for Quine does not know which stimulations are sufficiently similar to count as the same response. Such a content does not exist even for the same speaker on different occasions, let alone for speakers of alien languages and cultures. Quine defines a sentence as observational for a whole community when it is observational for each member, but in radical translation this, of course, never happens. A situation is not a sense stimulus; rather it is a context taken for granted, and any two individuals cannot be said to be in the same situation without further ado. Quine assumes that they can do without intersubjective likeness of stimulation by means of mere empathy, for he believes that empathy dominates the learning of language both of the child and the field linguist.[8] Empathy, however, is something assumed; it is not open to direct behavioral inspection. We are said by Quine to have an "uncanny knack" for empathizing another's perceptual situation, and this is how we learn to speak the same language. But being ignorant of the relevant physiological and optical mechanisms, this does not amount to an empirical explanation in the required sense. Quine compares this "knack" to our ability to recognize faces without being able to describe them,[9] and by means of such an intuition he attempts to bridge the gap linking nerve endings to verbal behavior, or what comes to the same thing, link the object with the meaning we give the object. Success in communication is judged by smoothness in conversation, by frequent predictability of verbal and nonverbal reaction, and by the coherence and plausibility of native testimony. At the same time Quine admits that empathy is unable to bridge the gap between rival manuals of radical translation. While the fluency of conversation is said to be factual, the "facts" referred to turn out to be psychological and introspective. To account for communication, Quine theorizes that we are dissimilar machines similarly programmed,[10] yet we couldn't be similarly programmed unless we were birds of a feather. Quine locates the stimulations at the subject's surface, as it were, but postulates a preestablished harmony between behavior and language by means of empathy.

Unlike observation sentences, utterances resist direct correlations with concurrent stimulations. There is guesswork here, but revision sets in, determining tentative translation of a potential infinity of sentences. The routine of query and assent that had been the linguist's standby in construing observation sentences continues to be available at the higher and conjectural levels.[11] Linguists can usually avoid radical translation by finding someone who can interpret the language, however tentatively, into a somewhat familiar one. But it is only radical translation that exposes the poverty of data for the individuation of meanings.[12] Successive utterances may be expected to have some bearings on one another, but the translator depends on psychological conjectures as to what the native is likely to believe. The native's mind, failing evidence to the contrary, is presumed to be pretty much like that of the translator's. What Quine calls "practical psychology" proceeds on the assumption that one takes one's own language and culture pretty much for granted. There are no rules for deciding how much grotesqueness we may allow, and we cannot, therefore, expect that two radical translators, working independently, will come up with the same translation manual. Their manuals might be indistinguishable in terms of the native's behavior that the two translators have reason to expect, and yet each manual might prescribe some translation that the other translator would reject. Quine directs his indeterminacy thesis on a radically exotic language for the sake of plausibility, but the principle applies equally to the translator's own language. What the indeterminacy thesis is meant to bring out is that the radical translator is bound to impose as much as he discovers.[13]

The importance of analycity lapses in the light of Quine's holism. Dictionaries are occupied with explaining the meaning of words, and the work is neither myth nor capriciousness. Quine points out that it is not directed at cognitive equivalencies nor at synonymy of terms, and that it presupposes no particular notion of meaning. The lexicographer wants to improve his reader's chances at successful communication. Often a dictionary entry neither paraphrases the word nor labels its objects, but rather describes the use of the word in sentences. In practice we credit someone with understanding a sentence if we are not surprised by the circumstances of his uttering it or by his reaction to hearing it. We suspect that he does not understand a sentence if the event is dramatically at variance with these conditions. So no boundary is evident, no general criterion, for deciding whether he actually misunderstands the sentence or merely holds some universal theory regarding the subject matter.[14] Understanding, behavioristically viewed, is a statistical effect; it resides in multiplicities. Lexicography has no need for synonymy nor for sharp distinctions between under-standing and misunderstanding. The lexicographer does what he can to adjust the reader's verbal behavior to that of the community as a whole or some preferred part of it. This adjustment is a matter of degree and a vague one; a matter of fluency and effectiveness in dialogue.

Quine nevertheless insists that observation sentences, learned ostensibly, are where our command of language begins because our learning them from our elders depends heavily on their ability to guess that we are getting appropriate perceptions. For Quine, learning a language in the field and teaching it in the nursery are much the same at the level of observation sentences: a matter of perceiving that the subject perceives that p.[15] But such ascription of perception always calls for background knowledge and conjecture on the part of the ascriber as we move away from observation sentences. Even though a belief can have many believers, perceptions are tested as veridical, whereas beliefs are not. Manifestations of belief vary extravagantly with the belief and the circumstances of the believer, and ascriptions of belief run more tenuous as the supporting evidence becomes more diffuse. By contrast, the construction "perceives that p" is essential to the propagation of language, and at the empirical level it is only partly under control by the empirical evidence. This is because, by extrapolation and analogy, it has spawned a boundless and lawless ascription of beliefs. Responsible ones grade off into irresponsible ones, and Quine's empirical checks turn out to be incapable of drawing a line between the two.[16] Responsible belief is what can be checked, and the checking is done by us, but there is no consensus on how to draw a line between science on the one hand, and religion and magic on the other. Empathy is a product of culture, and it is the base, not only of belief, but also of "perceives that p" because the allowable departures from direct quotation depend on what the ascriber deems the quoted subject to have in mind. Bretano's notion of intentional discourse, which Quine adopts, is not subject to the kind of empirical checks on which Quine insists. There is consequently a lack of standards in the evaluation of beliefs. Quine retains intentional discourse because he believes that it is vital to communication and harbors indispensable lore about human activity and motivation. While he has no substitute for it, he does not consider it to be part of the scientific language-game. What Quine is out to preserve is the transparency and efficiently of classical predicate logic. He retains the intentional mode of discourse even though he considers its mentalistic strain archaic, a preference for final cause over efficient cause as a mode of explanation. Purpose is one of the mentalistic notions drawn from introspection, as are dispositions of capability. Quine realizes that the idea of efficient cause, that is the root of science, is also mentalistic in origin, since it is a projection of the subjective sense of effort. It did, however, gain the upper hand over final cause with the rise of physics in the Renaissance, as matter displaced mind in successful prediction.

What is true or false, it will be widely agreed, are propositions, yet the notion of proposition itself is ambiguous. Some understand the word as referring to sentences meeting certain specifications, while others understand it as referring rather to the meaning of such sentences. A weakness of this second position is the tenuousness of the notion of sentence meaning, and this tenuousness reaches the breaking point if one accepts Quine's thesis on the indeterminacy of translation. Ambiguity or vagueness of terms can cause the truth value of a sentence to depend on the speaker's intentions. To ascribe truth value to a sentence is to ascribe whiteness to snow. Ascription of truth just cancels the quotation marks: truth for Quine, following Tarski, is disquotation.[17] It seems paradoxical that the truth predicate, for all its transparency, should prove useful to the point of indispensability, but truth is notoriously enmeshed in paradox. The lesson of the antinomy is that if a language has at its disposal the innocent notations of quoting and appending, and also the notations of elementary logic, then it cannot contain also the truth predicate that disquotes its own eternal sentences – on the pain of inconsistency. Its truth predicate, or its best approximation to one, must be implicitly disquotational, and specifically must not disquote all the sentences that contain it. Quine concludes that the definition of satisfaction is inductive rather than direct; the two-place predicate "satisfies" becomes well-defined in its inductive way, but the grasp of the predicate and how to use it carries no assurance of the existence of a corresponding distinct object. Satisfaction, and truth along with it, retain the status that truth already enjoyed under the disquotation account: clear intelligibility without full eliminability.[18] It would seem, however, that the assumed contrast between object language and metalanguage in ordinary discourse is not fully intelligible either.

Quine's solution of the truth problem thus involves interlocked hierarchies. The paradoxes of set theory – Russell's, Burali-Forti's, Cantor's – have overruled the common-sense notion that clear membership conditions assure the existence of a class or a set. The class at each level admits members freely from all and only lower levels. We get a self-contained language with a hierarchy of better and better truth predicates, but no best truth predicate. Whereas it is quite in order for a truth value of a sentence to remain an open question, it is inconvenient to leave the very meaningfulness of a sentence forever unsettled.[19] One might accordingly relinquish the law of the excluded middle, and opt rather for a three-valued logic recognizing a limbo between truth and falsity as a third value rather than meaningfulness. A price is paid in the cumbersomeness of the three-valued logic, for when we move out of the two-valued truth functions (conjunction, alteration, and their derivatives), proliferation runs amok. It can still be handled, but there is an evident premium on our simple streamlined two-valued logic.[20] Quine realizes that those who ask what truth is, seek something deeper than disquotation, and that this is the valid residue of the correspondence theory of truth. His holism does not settle which sentences should be retained as eligible for truth and falsity, and while he insists that truth is one thing and warranted belief another, his behaviorist linguistics renders such a distinction unwarranted.

Those parts of mathematics that share no empirical meaning because they never get applied in natural science, i.e. the higher reaches of set theory, are still seen as meaningful by Quine because they are covered by the same grammar and vocabulary that generate the applied parts of mathematics. We are just sparing ourselves the unnatural gerrymandering of grammar that would be needed to exclude them. On Quine's two-valued approach they qualify as true or false, albeit inscrutably.[21] They are not wholly inscrutable, however, because the axioms of set theory are generalities already in the applicable part of the domain. Quine defines empirical content only for testable theories, and emphasizes that much solid experimental science fails testabitly in the defined sense. This can happen because of vague and uncalibrated probabilities in the backlog of theory; it also happens in more complex ways not clearly understood. But while he has no definition of empirical content to offer for such theories, he does believe that it makes sense to speak of empirical equivalence among them. Thus what it means for a theory to vary in ontology is not at all obvious. If this is just a question of words, as he maintains,[22] then, in the relevant sense, his whole pursuit of truth is just a question of words. He believes that theories or theory formulations can be logically incompatible and still be empirically equivalent. In this manner he imagines a global system empirically equivalent to our own, but on alien terms. As a staunch empiricist he wants to reckon both theories true while realizing that this line is unattractive if the alien culture is less "simple" or "natural" than our own. But there is no limit to how grotesquely cumbersome a theory might be and still be empirically equivalent to an elegant one. He decides in such a case to bar the alien terms from our language as meaningless since they do not add to what our own theory can predict. Yet Quine has no solid empirical reasons for consigning all contexts of such alien terms to the limbo of nonentities. What he takes to be "simplicity" and "naturalness" do not vindicate the difference between truth and warrantabilty on which he insists. Since he cannot know that the theories in question are empirically equivalent, his account of truth is merely sectarian, as he himself realizes. But then irresolubly rival systems of the world are a fantasy beyond linguistic usage. Limited to our human terms and devices, we grasp the world variously, and its "unity" or "identity" are forever beyond our grasp.

There is an evident parallel between the empirical under determination of global science and the indeterminacy of translation. In both cases the totality of possible evidence is insufficient to sustain the system uniquely, yet Quine insists that indeterminacy of translation has nothing to do with inaccessible facts and human limitations since dispositions to observable behavior are all there is for semantics to be right or wrong about. Only in the case of systems of the world is he prepared to admit that reality exceeds the scope of the human apparatus in unspecifiable ways.[23] What, therefore, the empirical underdetermination of the global science shows is that there are various defensible ways of conceiving the world.[24] What the indeterminacy of translation shows is likewise that the notion of propositions as sentence meanings is untenable. Quine's sectarian truth theory is unable to tell us why the understanding technology provides is preferable to other alien systems.

Notes

[1] W. V. Quine, *Pursuit of Truth,* Cambridge, London: Harvard University Press, 1990, p. 3.

[2] *Ibid.,* p. 5.

[3] *Ibid.,* p. 20.

[4] *Ibid.*

[5] *Ibid.,* p. 25.

[6] Joseph Grünfeld, *Changing Rational Standards,* Lanham, NY: University Press of America, 1985, pp. 100-121.

[7] Quine, *Pursuit of Truth*, p. 38.
[8] *Ibid.*, p. 42.
[9] *Ibid.*, p. 43.
[10] *Ibid.*, p. 44.
[11] *Ibid.*, p. 45.
[12] *Ibid.*, p. 46.
[13] *Ibid.*, p. 49.
[14] *Ibid.*, p. 58.
[15] *Ibid.*, p. 63.
[16] *Ibid.*, p. 67.
[17] *Ibid.*, p. 80.
[18] *Ibid.*, p. 88.
[19] *Ibid.*, p. 92.
[20] *Ibid.*
[21] *Ibid.*, p. 94.
[22] *Ibid.*, p. 96.
[23] *Ibid.*, p. 101.
[24] *Ibid.*, p. 102.

Chapter Ten

Feyerabend's Flight From Reason

Feyerabend rejects reason in favor of diversity; he is convinced that the uniformity imposed by reason reduces our joys, and our intellectual and material resources.[1] He believes that the quarrels of professors and the contortions of Western art shrink into insignificance when compared with the steady expansions of Western "progress" and the spreading of Western business, science, and technology. What is being imposed is a collection of uniform views and practices, which have the intellectual and political support of powerful groups and institutions. Cultural differences disappear as indigenous crafts, customs, and institutions are being replaced by Western objects, customs, and organizations. He argues that all this has been lost to the claims of objectivity. To say that a procedure or a point of view is objectively true is to argue that it is valid irrespective of human expectations, ideas, attitudes, and wishes. This, of course, is the fundamental claim today's scientists and intellectuals make about their work. Feyerabend points out, however, that while formal procedures make sense in some worlds, they become silly in others. Popper's demand to look for refutations and to take them seriously leads to an orderly development only in a world where refuting instances are rare. But this becomes impossible if theories are surrounded by an ocean of anomalies, as is the case in many social situations. The problem is that notions of scientific objectivity were used not only in creating knowledge but also to legitimize existing information. Feyerabend denies that there is just one right way of living, or universally valid and binding standards of knowledge. Reason has been a great success only among philosophers who dislike complexity and politicians who use it to justify their claims for hegemony.

Feyerabend concludes that to make sense of cultural variety we have to adopt relativism.[2] Efficiency has become the dominate value in Western civilization to such an extent that all moral objections to it seem naive and "unscientific." He insists that not values nor facts nor methods support the claim that science and science-based technology (IQ tests, science-based medicine and agriculture, and the like) over-rule all other enterprises.[3] It is to be expected that actions that seem perfectly normal in one culture are rejected and condemned in another. Our debates about abortion, euthanasia, gene manipulation, artificial insemination, and the intellectual, political, economic, and military exchanges between different cultures illustrate the way in which values change opinions, attitudes, and actions. The tensions that remain are between values, not between reason and irrationality. According to Feyerabend, it is not really possible to separate facts, values, and rationality in any strict manner because facts are constituted by procedures that contain values, and values change under the impact of facts. All principles of reasoning assume a certain world order, and the law of noncontradition does not apply in an absurd world.[4] Indeed, non-scientific cultures may have a clearer idea of the dangers lurking in radically new knowledge, the destructive forces inherent in information that is separated from its specific circumstances, and the repercussions likely to arise from changes in the course of nature. It would be shortsighted to assume that only the champions of progress now possess the key for survival. All we get, in the opinion of Feyerabend, is a monolithic monster "science" that is said to follow a single path and speak with a single voice.[5] He considers knowledge a local commodity designed to satisfy specific needs and solve restricted regional problems. Orthodox science accordingly is merely one institu-tion among many. Criteria of acceptance and of success may change from case to case in accordance with the values of those interested in a particular area of knowledge.[6] Decisions concerning the value and use of science are not scientific decisions; they are moral or existential choices to live, think, feel, and believe in a certain way. Feyerabend emphasizes that since many once utterly ridiculous views are now regarded a solid part of our knowledge, it makes sense to preserve faulty points of view for possible future use. The history of ideas, methods, and prejudices is an integral part of the ongoing practice of science, and this practice can change direction in surprising ways.[7] There are, therefore, plausible arguments in favor of a plurality of ideas, unscientific nonsense and allegedly refuted facts included. Science is to be treated as one tradition among many, not as a standard for what is and what cannot be accepted.[8] While the objectivist illegitimately separates theory from practice, thought, and emotion, and nature from society, all we really have, according to Feyerabend, is a variety of approaches based on different models and successful in restricted domains.[9]

Since natural societies grow without much conscious planning, experts are likely to be just as confused over fundamental issues as are the rest of us. Feyerabend wants the citizens at large rather than special groups to have the last word in deciding what is true or false, useful or useless, for their society.[10] Different societies look at the world in dissimilar ways and regard diverse things as acceptable. The attempt to enforce one unique truth has led to social disaster, and to empty formalizations and unfulfilled promises in the natural sciences.[11] Feyerabend insists that global distinctions between what is real and what is not are much too simplistic to captivate the complexities of our world. Each society behaves in an intricate characteristic way which, though conforming to pattern, continually reveals new and surprising features that cannot be captured in a formula. "Problems of realty" arise when ingredients of complex worlds are subsumed under abstract concepts; they appear because delicate matters are compared with crude ideas.[12] It was discovered that statements composed of concepts lacking in detail could be used to tell a new kind of story called "proof," whose truth "followed" from their inner structure and needed no support from traditional authority. The discovery was interpreted as showing that knowledge could be detached from tradition and made "objective." It seemed all one had to do was to accept what one had proved and reject the rest – and truth would appear in a culture-independent way.[13] But the fact that simple ideas can be connected in simple ways gives the resulting propositions special authority only if everything can be shown to consist of simple things – which was precisely the point on which disagreements arose. The discovery of proof procedures increased cultural variety; it did not replace it by a simple and true story.

Feyerabend, therefore, rejects the notion that tradition-independent points of view can overrule traditions. There exist many different ways of being and of knowing. Scientific theories branch out in different directions, use different and sometimes incommensurable concepts and evaluate events in diverse ways. What counts as evidence, or as an important result, or a "sound" scientific procedure depends on attitudes and judgments that change with time, profession, and even from one research group to the next. Nature can be approached in many ways, and for every statement, theory or point of view believed to be true with good reason, there exist conflicting arguments.[14] Feyerabend repudiates the widespread philosophical conviction that arguments must lead to unique conclusions. Since we are dealing with feelings, faith, empathy, and not merely intellectual matters, there is more than just one single medium of discourse. While rationalist philosophers tend to define relations in their own intellectual way, problems arise when different cultures or individuals with different habits collide. What the early Western rationalists invented was not argument as such but a special and standardized form of arguing that disregarded and explicitly rejected all personal elements. Thus, they claimed that they could offer procedures that were valid independently of human wishes and concerns.[15] The human element, however, was not eliminated; it was merely concealed, and the evaluation of success or failure remained relative to cultural and subjective factors. Even what is considered a law of nature depends crucially on metaphysical assumptions, language, mathematical notation, and the like. The discovery and development of a particular form of knowledge is a highly specialized and unpredictable process. For if we replace some concepts by others, even only slightly different ones, we become unable to state these results or to comprehend them. We obtain different data and conflicting evidence at different stages in the history of science. We take it for granted that our scientific laws are real and that the Homeric gods are not, but this merely reflects our own cultural bias in the opinion of Feyerabend. There is no comprehensive theory that is valid beyond the mere enumeration of detail, and that philosophers were traditionally seeking to grasp and to express. The regional character of natural phenomena, no less than social ones, was never overcome by either science or philosophy. Uniformity was always imposed by violence, not shown to be superior by argument.[16]

The problem is that Feyerabend's own thesis of incommensurabilty may not permit any such rational justification. We have to realize that a unified view of the physical world simply does not exist in his opinion. He agrees with Foucault that what passes as truth in science is basically an issue of institutional power, and that this is why science cannot afford to be tolerant of divergent opinion. It is the same attitude that now destroys non-Western cultures under the guise of "development." Feyerabend wants us to realize that not everybody lives in the same world. The worlds in which cultures unfold not only contain different events, they also contain them in different ways.[17] A dancer has knowledge of her limbs, an experimenter in his hands and eyes, a singer in the tongue, throat, and diaphragm. Knowledge resides in the ways we speak, and in the very flexibility inherent in linguistic behavior. Such language skills are not stable; they contain ambiguities and patterns of analogical reasoning. Language and perception interact, and the process of fitting description to situation often modifies the situation as well. Features lacking in a description tend to recede into the background, while those prominent in the language or culture become more distinct. The apparent familiarity of everyday "facts" is the result of habituation and training. Events are arranged in the special ways that have gained in popularity and have become routine. It is the routine that provides them with a foundation and decides what is real. Feyerabend rejects our educational system in which knowledge comes to be identified with what can be extracted from the written page. Such an approach mistakenly assumes that the history of a particular piece of information has no relevance for the understanding of its content. It goes without saying that he opposes the positivist distinction between the context of discovery and the context of justification. Even the most "objectively" written representation is comprehended by virtue of a process of instruction that conditions us to interpret standard phrases in standard ways. There is, therefore, no escape from either personal contact or history. Knowledge orders events, and different kinds of knowledge engender different ordering schemes that may create incommensurable problems. Concepts introduced in this manner remain adapted to the specific circumstances under which they were originally introduced. Indeed, Feyerabend believes that stories are the only form adapted to the complexities of human thought and action[18] but this is to ignore the power and precision that mathematical formulas have exerted in science and technology.

Feyerabend thinks that rationalist philosophers simply refused to accept the diversity of details at face value. They, therefore, came to distinguish between the world of appearances and the real world, which supposedly was simple, uniform, subject to stable universal laws and the same for all. To describe such a world, different concepts were required and new disciplines (epistemology and later the philosophy of science) arose in the attempt to explain how it was related to experience. An inferior sort of knowledge by acquaintance was attributed to "the many," that is, the common people and unphilosophical artisans. Statements like "this is red" or "that moves," which play such an important role in the lives or ordinary people were summarily excluded from the domain of truth.[19] Intellectuals claimed to possess insights unattainable to ordinary people and praised "oneness," i.e. monotony. In this manner, rationalists led a battle against traditional, undefined, and fairly irregular ways of thinking, speaking, acting, and arranging public and private lives.[20] By contrast, stonemasons, metalworkers, painters, architects, and engineers left buildings and artworks of all kinds, which shows that their knowledge of space and materials was more progressive, fruitful, and vastly more detailed than anything that emerged from the speculations of the philosophers. Followers of the theoretical traditions identify knowledge with universality, regard theories as bearers of information, and tend to reason in the standardized "logical" way. The members of the historical tradition, on the other hand, focus on what is particular. They rely on lists, stories, and asides. They reason from example, analogy, and free association, and use logical rules only when it suites their purpose. Feyerabend emphasizes the diversity and history-dependence of such logical standards.[21] He argues that rationalists did not introduce order and wisdom where before there was chaos and ignorance; rather they imposed a special kind of order that was different from the procedures of the historical tradition. But the theoretical approach ran into difficulties when it attempted to transform the historical traditions implicit in the crafts. While most scientists believe that science and science alone establishes the truth capable of surpassing all traditions, Feyerabend insists that all statements are human products and that they reflect the peculiarities of individuals, groups, and cultures. Science and its philosophical predecessors are part of special social traditions, not entities that transcend all history.[22] The "reality" science allegedly defines and uses to assimilate the more disorderly ingredients of our world is constantly being redefined to make it fit the fashion of the day. It is, of course, true that the validity of Maxwell's equations is independent of what people think about electrification. But it is not independent of the culture that contains them, for it needs only a minor modification of our technologies, ways of thinking, or mathematics, and we can no longer reason as we used to.

Feyerabend's flight from reason not surprisingly causes him to denounce realism as well. *Mimesis* underlies the idea, widespread in antiquity and still popular today, that the task of science is to "save the phenomena," i.e. to present them as correctly as possible using the available stereotypes. This theory of imitation survives in the popular image of the unprejudiced scientist who avoids speculation and concentrates on telling it as it is. The variety, however, of these ideas and their complexity suggest that it may well be impossible to reduce our ways of being in the world to a few simple, context, and observer-independent "objective" notions. Only philosophers who prefer simple, clear, and easily definable ideas to complex, unclear, and undecidable ones pretended by hindsight that there was essentially only one concept of knowledge and of being. Such fictions are still believed because of our cultural bias and, once introduced, they are not easily dislocated by argument. But there is no monolithic entity "science," and scientists themselves have come to criticize the view that there exists an "objective world" and a subjective domain, and that it is imperative to keep them separate. One of our most advanced sciences, elementary particle physics, has forced us to realize that it is impossible to draw a sharp boundary between the observer and the object observed. The role of qualitative ideas in the sciences and of progress is often concealed by a concern with quantitative detail. Feyerabend emphasizes that, in all such major scientific issues, qualitative assumptions play a decisive though often unnoticed role.[23] Even in ordinary counting we have first to decide what constitutes a unit, and this may be quite different for different purposes. There is more than just one answer to the question of how many constellations there are in the sky. Only the positivist confusion of constant numbers that seem clearly separable from each other and numbers of objects that depend on qualitative circumstances could have induced us to believe that numerical judgments are more "objective" than judgments of quality, structure, and value.[24] Feyerabend shows that the history of art presents us with a variety of techniques and means of representation employed for a variety of reasons and adapted to different purposes. The attempt to identify progress across all such reasons or purposes is an illusion. Thought receives content only by being connected with the thinker, and that is why all thought is essentially subjective and incapable of producing universal and unchanging results.

Philosophy is regarded as an art form like painting or literature by Feyerabend, who emphasizes that different forms of life produce different philosophies. Since such qualitative preferences have no compelling order, the philosopher has not been successful in overcoming relativism anymore than the artist. It does not make sense to arrange philosophies on a single progressive line.[25] The combination of quality and quantity, which allegedly characterizes the sciences, is itself qualitative and, therefore, subjective. A transition from one theory to another sometimes also involves a change in what are taken to be the facts and, if this happens, it becomes impossible to compare the facts of one theory with those of another. Qualitative elements in the sciences, or what comes to the same thing – fundamental ideas of a branch of knowledge, are never uniquely determined by the facts. That is why the battle between alternative quantitative points of view, being redefined whenever new ideas and instruments (experimental procedures, mathematical techniques) are introduced, never comes to an end. Feyerabend denounces the neopositvist tendency to reduce historical complexity to logical alternatives. Historical traditions like the humanities and the arts produce knowledge that is restricted either explicitly or by use to certain regions, and depends upon conditions specific to those regions. They produce regional or relative knowledge of what is good or bad, true or false, beautiful or ugly, and the rest. There are different regions each characterized by its own special "climate," yet all such views, Feyerabend insists, are nevertheless worth considering since all such regions are fluid and overlapping. Theoretical traditions, by contrast, seek to establish knowledge that no longer depends on or is relative to these special conditions, and which, therefore, is "objective." By now, many intellectuals regard theoretical or objective knowledge as the only kind worth considering. But Feyerabend emphasizes that the relativity of phenomena has never been overcome by either philosophy or the sciences. All we have are modest successes in narrow domains that may be incommensurable with other regions. He denies that there exists a world independent of us that we can explain in a critical way.

Yet the decision as to what is to be regarded as real is one of the most important decisions we make. Feyerabend insists that there is no idea so foolish that it may not some day lead to something of interest. Darwin showed that life is unreasonable and wasteful, for it produces an immense variety of species and individuals, and leaves it for the particular stage it has reached and the material surroundings to define and eliminate failures. From this Mach, Boltzmann, and other followers of Darwin inferred that the development of knowledge is also not a well-planned and smoothly running process. Feyerabend likewise concludes that scientists forge ahead and constantly redefine science, knowledge, and logic in their work.[26] He, therefore, considers history an important part of scientific research, as it is in the humanities and the arts, while neopositivism misused the name of science to propagate a rigid, narrow-minded, and unrealistic point of view. For Feyerabend, science is a process of adapting ideas to facts and to each other, and, as Mach has shown, in this process the results are not unique.[27] Like Mach, Feyerabend believes that common-sense perceptions that arose in this manner are organically older and better founded than is conceptual thought.[28] A rational account explains an idea by showing its logical connection with other uncontested views without taking into account how these views arose or why they should be accepted. This is why Planck talks about the irrational and metaphysical character of the basic scientific principles, and why Einstein discusses the religious dimensions of the scientific effort. While a carefully conducted experiment provides us with many details, the final secure support for the sciences comes form being related to the crude experiences of instinctive practices. Such intuitive knowledge, having been tested by a great variety of qualitatively different experiences, overrules specific experiments based on narrow assumptions in a restricted domain. There are thus many constraints beyond those allegedly imposed by "logic."

Feyerabend regards the conflict between Galileo and the Church as a clash between different traditions. He agrees with Cardinal Bellarmino that questions of fact and reality are ultimately value judgments. Accepting some phenomena as real and rejecting others as deceptive means choosing one tradition over another. Feyerabend points out that reality is a value-laden term, and that questions of reality are closely connected with human concerns.[29] He argues that scientific knowledge its too specialized and connected with too narrow a vision of the world to be taken over by society without further ado. It must be examined and judged from a wider perspective that includes human concerns and values. He wants to temper the totalitarian and dehumanizing tendencies of modern scientific objectivism by elements taken directly from human life and to that extent "subjective."[30] He dismisses the idea of a free and independent reason as a chimera, and warns that a democracy cannot simply bow to the assertions of scientists and philosophers. It must examine them carefully, especially when they touch upon such fundamental matters as what is reasonable and what is real. We have no universal language governed by reason but we can learn any specific idiom from scratch, as when a child learns it without previous translation. We also can change our native tongue so that it becomes capable of expressing hitherto alien notions, and thus the criteria by which we identify any natural language are subject to change. Every philologist, anthropologist, or sociologist who presents an archaic (primitive, exotic, etc.) world view, and every popular science writer who wants to explain scientific ideas in ordinary English knows how to construct out of English words an English-sounding model of the pattern of usage he needs for his novel purposes. The English with which we start is not the English with which we conclude our explanations.[31] Concepts no less than percepts obey figure – ground relations and are, therefore, liable to change. But such an extrapolation does not void speech of meaning as long as there exist analogies for what we are trying to express.

If we take the unchanged traditional concept of motion, we are forced to say that Zeno's Achilles paradox is nonsense. Feyerabend, on the other hand, emphasizes that measures of sense are not rigid and unambiguous, and their changes are not so unfamiliar as to prevent listeners from grasping what Zeno has in mind. Speaking a language and explaining a situation means both *following* rules and *changing* them. Theoretical physicists not infrequently play around with formulas that do not yet make sense to them until a lucky combination makes everything fall into place. These examples show, in the opinion of Feyerabend, how it is possible to assert without becoming incoherent that the Galilean notions are "incommensurable" with our own, and then go on to describe them in length.[32] It is essential, however, that such incommensurability be a rare event. It occurs only when the conditions for meaningfulness of the descriptive terms of one language (theory, point of view) do not permit the use of the descriptive terms of another (theory, point of view). While not every difference of meaning leads to incommensurability, incommensurable languages (theories, points of view) are not completely unconnected either. There exists a subtle and interesting relation between these conditions and meaningfulness. He believes that incommensurability is a difficulty for philosophers but not for scientists, because philosophers insist on stability of meaning through an argument. Scientists, on the other hand, being aware that speaking a language or explaining a situation means both following rules and changing them, are experts in the art of arguing across lines that philosophers regard as insurmountable boundaries of discourse.

Different cultures frequently establish some kind of contact but it is not the case that in doing so they create or assume a common metadiscourse or a common cultural bond. The connections may be temporary, ad hoc, and quite superficial. One must not confound a culture with its written manifestations (as, for example, Derrida does) or with the products of its artists and thinkers. Feyerabend rejects the view that the events and results that constitute the sciences have a common structure or that there must be elements that occur in every scientific investigation. Procedures that paid off in the past may crate a lot of trouble when imposed on the future. Successful research does not obey general standards; it relies now upon one theory, now upon another. A theory of science that devises standards and structural elements for all scientific activities, and authorizes them with reference to some rationality theory may impress outsiders – but it is much too crude an instrument for the people on the spot, that is, for scientists facing some concrete research problem. It is thus not quite clear what Feyerabend's own philosophy of science is supposed to accomplish. He thinks that only neopositivism still clings to the ancient idea that philosophy must provide formal standards for knowledge and action. The very search for new theories is thus not a reasonable undertaking[33] because some essential part of the knowledge we need to understand and to advance the sciences can come only from participation. Since such knowledge cannot be generalized, the very possibility of both science and philosophy is questioned by Feyerabend. At no time, of course, can scientists be sure that they already have the correct research methods, but they nevertheless proceed on the assumption that some ways of doing science are more adequate than others. Even if the logic of scientific research does not yield unique results, this does not seem to interfere with the pragmatic success of science. What we come to know as the history of science is the record of what has been considered successful, and the same is true of the arts. But for Feyerabend, all this is merely a matter of fashion. On the one hand, he maintains that apparently empirical facts are theoretical through and through[34] and, on the other, that the very search for such theories is futile. Since change of theory or of interpretation is not something that admits rational explanation, there is nothing that can be identified as progress in science. He admits that there are axiomatic foundations and that some scientific ideas have been defined in a precise way, but he emphasizes that they are nevertheless often *used* in a loose manner. He believes that even logic has now reached a stage when formalizations are being used in a freewheeling manner.[35]

Altogether the scientific enterprise seems to be much closer to the arts than the older logicians and philosophers of science once thought. Feyerabend concludes that all scientists produce are works of art, the difference being that their material is thought, not paint or marble or melodious sound.[36] Yet while stressing the similarities between science and art, Feyerabend seems to miss some crucial differences. That science and technology have become prevailing forces in contemporary life is more than just a matter of fashion. Neither the languages of modern sciences nor those of the arts are learned by simple immersion, in the manner a child acquires his native tongue without previous translation. Quantification and proof procedures established standards of precision and scope unmatched by any previous historical tradition, and those turned Western science and technology into a dominant force. The contention that "science works" does not remove Feyerabend's misgivings largely because, like Foucault, he regards science as a manifestation of institutional power and impersonal politics. Since, like Mach, he views the growth of knowledge in Darwinian terms, the fact that Western science and technology prevailed because they produced superior weapons should not upset Feyerabend. But it does, of course, and that is why he asks for arguments establishing their qualitative superiority, even though he also maintains that such arguments are impossible because of incommensurability. Moreover, if there are no objective reasons for preferring science and Western rationalism, this applies no less to his own brand of pluralism and tolerance.

Feyerabend holds science responsible for destroying the spiritual values that give meaning to life and for poisoning the environment. He realizes, however, that it is impossible for us to go back to a primitive and innocent culture because these are not matters of conscious control or of rational deliberation. Denouncing reason, Feyerabend nevertheless wants to convince us by argument that a more pluralistic and tolerant attitude would be more reasonable. Making scientists responsible for what he dislikes in modern culture, he fails to give them credit for prolonging our lives and raising our standard of living.

He identifies the claim for objectivity with a drive to get rid of all human elements and, hence, with becoming inhuman. But this flight from reason makes him ambivalent towards argument in general, for it means that there is no argument that will work with everyone. Arguments in favor of a certain world view (including his own) depend on assumptions that are accepted or rejected on subjective grounds and that lack general validity. What constitutes a problem is likewise due to local circumstances and is consequently culturally relative. All solutions allow for many ways of living outside the sciences, as is demonstrated by our artists and even by the wide spectrum covered by apparently "objective" concepts such as health. Nor does convergence of expert opinion establish an objective authority, since we have many different authorities to choose from. Thus, rationalists claiming for objectivity and universality are just trying to sell another tribal creed. The means of refutation (experimental equipment, the theories used for interpretation of results obtained) constantly change, and with them the nature of the arguments. The ways in which scientific problems are attacked and solved depend on the specific circumstances under which they arose; the formal, experimental, and ideological means available, and the wishes of those dealing with them. Feyerabend denies that either science or society conform to conditions that can be determined independently of personal wishes or cultural bias. A merely intellectual approach is, therefore, inadequate for understanding either science or society. His main objection is that while such an approach starts from a restricted context, it claims universal validity, and then feels justified to impose itself on everybody. He rejects such sweeping generalizations based on an alleged human nature in favor of personal contact, and his "politics" is purely subjective.[37] It would seem however that such objectivity is a matter of degree, and that even in the social sciences not everything goes. He is convinced that we cannot trust our experts, philosophers, healers, and educators – yet what he himself offers is, after all, a philosophical program. The realization that there are no objective solutions or progress, he hopes, should make us tolerant. For he is convinced that most of the misery in our world, the destruction of minds and bodies, the endless butcheries, are caused by people who have objectified their personal wishes and inclinations and thus have made them inhuman.[38] He is impatient with people who, though lacking experience with the complexities of scientific research, nevertheless claim that they know what it is all about and how it could be improved.

But there remains the question of why Feyerabend is afraid of reason. His real problem is with the validity of argument and the status of his own philosophical convictions, for in arguing against reason he makes more than just local and subjective claims. The philosopher, of course, need not be a rationalist, but he relies on argument to make his case even when he denounces reason. He may not be successful in convincing other people, but he goes on arguing as long as he is doing philosophy. Feyerabend wants to be a philosopher of science and a Dadaist at the same time. He fails to explain on what grounds we should accept his own philosophical claims, for he is not just telling us a story that demands only a willing suspension of disbelief. In criticizing science he takes his inspiration from the arts, yet contemporary science is much more of a success story than is modern art, and why science has prevailed remains a mystery for Feyerabend. His attempt to substitute the tacit reasoning in the arts for the precise calculations of science can, at best, serve only as a correction. There is no escape from reason for Feyerabend.

Notes

[1] Paul Feyerabend, *Farewell to Reason,* London, England and New York, NY: Verso, 1987, p. 1.
[2] *Ibid.,* p. 19.
[3] *Ibid.,* p. 24.
[4] *Ibid.,* p. 25-26.
[5] *Ibid.,* p. 27.
[6] *Ibid.,* p. 29.
[7] *Ibid.,* p. 33.
[8] *Ibid.,* p. 39.
[9] *Ibid.,* p. 53.
[10] *Ibid.,* p. 59.
[11] *Ibid.,* p. 61.
[12] *Ibid.,* p. 64.
[13] *Ibid.,* p. 67.
[14] *Ibid.,* p. 76.

[15] *Ibid.*, p. 87.
[16] *Ibid.*, p. 100.
[17] *Ibid.*, p. 105.
[18] *Ibid.*, p. 115.
[19] *Ibid.*, p. 116n21.
[20] *Ibid.*, p. 116.
[21] *Ibid.*, p. 118.
[22] *Ibid.*, p. 121.
[23] *Ibid.*, p. 146.
[24] *Ibid.*, p. 148.
[25] *Ibid.*, p. 155.
[26] *Ibid.*, p. 188.
[27] Ernst Mach, *Erkenntnis und Irrtum*, Leipzig, 1917, p. 175.
[28] *Ibid.*, p. 151.
[29] Feyerabend, *Farewell to Reason*, p. 254.
[30] *Ibid.*, p. 259.
[31] *Ibid.*, p. 268.
[32] *Ibid.*, p. 271.
[33] *Ibid.*, p. 284.
[34] *Ibid.*, p. 290.
[35] Joseph Grünfeld, "Quasi-Empirical Mathematics," in *Conceptual Relevance*, Amsterdam: Grüner, 1989, pp. 15-33.
[36] Feyerabend, *Farewell to Reason*, p. 294.
[37] *Ibid.*, p. 306.
[38] *Ibid.*, p. 311.

Chapter Eleven

Polanyi's Tacit Knowledge

Polanyi had long been critical of the extreme positivist view of science. The popular view seemed to imply that only scientific theories are capable of verification, and that moral, political, religious, and artistic ideas and principles are essentially unprovable, mere matters of emotional preference. No one seemed to see the extent to which the existence of this presumably verifiable science itself rested upon freely held beliefs, ideas, and purposes that not only could not be proved, but that could not even be made explicit. No one seemed to realize that the unprovability of these beliefs did not render them intellectually unacceptable or unworthy of being held. It was, therefore, necessary to show people, philosophers included, why and how this was so.[1] The recognition that science and fruitful, formal thought function by quite different principles than modern man's penchant for precise statements seemed to allow, came to be the central interest in Polanyi's philosophy. The early scientists, from Bacon to Newton, all agreed that knowledge must be based on observations and experiment, and that none of the traditional views should be accepted without critical scrutiny. Thus, the ideal of a complete and perfect objectivism emerged, which has prevailed down to our own day as the model of science. All personal subjective elements came to be regarded as obstacles to the attainment of such complete objectivity. Objectivism in science holds that something is the case independently of our minds, yet which is our business to come to know. The final arbiter of scientific theory is taken to be the crucial test in which all relevant factors are carefully controlled and which can, therefore, subject our theory to conclusive verification. Proponents of scientific objectivism, as a rule, disregard the fact that scientists were not actually conforming to such procedures, since they insisted that logic was logic, whether anyone followed it or not. Logical positivists denied to those inquiries and beliefs that could not be established in a detached manner the status of "knowledge." The notion that what counts as knowledge must be true and detached objectively seems to be still the basic creed of epistemologists and philosophers of science.

Hardly anyone today supposes that values are objective, and thus they are quite generally rejected as possible objects of knowledge. The replacement of moral ideas by philosophically less vulnerable because more basically vital objectives were carried out in all seriousness. Since it was assumed that the more elemental interests of men, such as their economic and power needs, would always exist, action based upon such interests came to be thought the only kind of realistic action. It was clear to Polanyi that scientists actually were *not* detached and perfectly objective, no matter what any of them or their apologists might say. He was not aware, at the time he was working on his ideas for *Personal Knowledge*, that some of the continental phenomenologists were developing ideas similar in many respects to his own. The basic term of his new epistemology was "tacit knowing," and his notion of tacit knowing was based on the views originally brought forward by the gestalt psychologists. They pointed out that in perception we perform an action: we accomplish a tacit integration of sensations and feelings into a perceived object that then gives meaning to these sensations and feelings, which they had not previously possessed. Seeing objects is the result of mastering a skill, of learning how to attain a meaningful (but inexplicit) integration of sensory clues and, therefore, is neither a matter of formal inference from sense data nor one of direct and immediate perception of objects.[2] What we see in a meaningful way is also influenced by what we have become used to seeing in the past; so not only what is at the corner of our eyes but also what is at the back of our minds functions as the background in perception. Previous integrations of clues – previously achieved meanings – seep into the back of our minds and function there as part of the subsidiary clues forming the background for new integrations of clues with objects.[3] We truly do, therefore, know more than we can tell.[4] If perception and knowledge were not intentional acts, truth could not be understood to be an ideal toward which we aspire.

"Truth" must then become a word we apply to whatever we are caused or conditioned to think.

Part of the background operative in perception is due to something other than simple physiologically built-in mechanisms. Some of it is provided by what we think we know of the world, and so is entangled with our intellectual and vital intentions. In a presentational painting, brush strokes are meaningless except as they enter into the appearance of the painting. It is the painting that is their meaning.[5] Meaning in these senses is something that must be grasped or seen or created by a mind. For Polanyi, meaning is never devoid of intention to find or achieve a comprehensive and intelligible integration. "Meaning" is, therefore, a triadic term, in that, in addition to the functionally different proximal and distal factors, there also must always be a person, a user, an interpreter involved.[6] A face does not exist without its features, and its features are meaningless without their being upon a face, even though neither can be reduced to the other. Meaning, says Polanyi, is always lost, sometimes for good, when in order to inspect the clues focally, attempts are made to withdraw ourselves from these feelings or perceptions and turn them into explicit existential objects. Brush strokes lose their meaning when studied focally, as do words when looked at or listened to too long in terms of their mere sound or shape. What is perceptually given is not restricted entirely by our basic perceptual mechanisms; it is partly the result of conceptual interpretation of which, however, we are aware only in a subsidiary way, not focally. Assumptions guiding scientific discoveries are, in the minds of their discoverers, fundamental guesses concerning the nature of things,[7] no mere summarizations of objective correlations between bits of phenomena. Scientific propositions do not refer definitely to observable facts, and there are no explicit rules by which a scientific proposition can be obtained from observable data. The operations of science have to be understood basically as skills since there are always unspecifiable clues. Once a species is established, it is defined by the presence of certain distinctive features that may be variable in shape. Maxims cannot be understood, still less applied by anyone not already possessing a good practical knowledge of the art or discipline. And so what our concept bears upon – what it really means – is indeterminate and much richer than any formal structure we could give it. Taxonomy is based on connoissership, and C.F.A. Pantin rightly considers this intuitive mode of identification, what he calls "aesthetic recognition," in contrast to the more systematic sort based on key features, to be the predominant mode of recognition in field work.[8]

Yet the exercises of such skills today is not highly regarded by scientific opinion. Both the knowledge and the subject matter established by such skills are disparaged by being regarded as the result of "merely subjective imaginings." Knowledge that we hold to be true and also vital is made light of because we cannot account for its acceptance in terms of a critical philosophy. We then feel entitled to continue using this knowledge even while flatly disparaging it. Instruments do not read themselves, but can only be read by connoisseurs, and the quantitative results of such instruments are meaningful only in terms of the particular theories and general notions about the world that function as subsidiary clues in the mind of the scientists who makes use of these results. Exact, quantitative, even machine-recorded observations without mentalistic interpreters could not operate either to substantiate or to refute any given hypothesis – let alone to generate one. It is the theory that decides what can be observed.[9] Science shows itself to be guided throughout by acts of personal judgment, as it establishes hitherto unknown coherences in nature. Our recognition of these coherences is largely based, as perception is, on clues of which we are not focally aware and that are indeed often unidentifiable. From the recognition of a problem to the ultimate decision of rejecting still conceivable doubts, factors of plausibility are ever in our mind. Polanyi's analysis of the process of discovery becomes the core of his philosophy of science. Copernicus, he reminds us, was not trying to find a logically simpler way of describing the heavenly phenomena; he understood that his discovery amounted to a new and truer version of reality. Kepler, Galileo, Dalton, Newton, the whole line of eminent scientists down to Bohr, Planck, Heisenberg, and Einstein, were all endeavoring to discover various aspects of reality, not simply more elegant logical correlations of phenomenal data.[10]

Polanyi considered the problem of discovery as the central problem in the philosophy of science long before Kuhn and Hanson began to call into question the strict formalizations of the scientific method.[11] To see the problem is to see something that is hidden; it is to have an intimation of the coherence of hitherto not comprehended particulars. Knowing a problem must be the kind of tacit knowledge we have of a face or a class, a knowledge of which we cannot give a fully explicit account, but which nevertheless is real. The intimations we have of a problem are akin to those we have of the fruitfulness of a discovery we come to accept as the solution of a problem. Somehow we are able to appreciate the wealth of its yet undiscovered consequences. We cannot know these explicitly, of course, but we have an anticipatory grasp of them. Facts do not force themselves on us since what we call a "fact" always involves our judgment. No problem is seriously taken up unless we feel that its possible solution would be worth the effort and time. These perceptive anticipations of feasibility are neither the result of strict rules nor of chance. Theories of scientific method that ignore this whole fluid mechanism of tacit knowledge deny the existence of a passionate personal commitment to one's surmises, which characterizes the creative scientist as it does the artist. That is why the scientist always attempts to prove his theories – never to disprove them. There is no scientific method or recipe for making good discoveries or good scientists. The power of such dynamic intuitions, Polanyi maintained, is due to the feeling of a "deepening coherence" we have all along the way to a discovery. That is also why we can sometimes pursue scientific discovery without knowing explicitly what we are looking for. It is a skill for guessing right, which can be improved by schooling,[12] but to know in this intuitive, tacit, and unspecifable manner what to look for does not give us the power to find it.

Basic agreement about the general shape of things in nature and about the way in which nature operates is essential to the existence of a community of cooperating scientists. What it is that has resulted from an experiment cannot be known without interpretation. New types of solution become acceptable because deepening coherence enables us to see somewhat beyond where we are, to transcend somewhat our present limitations, and we see that something makes sense before we can make out just what it does. Science can never be more than the affirmation of certain things we believe in. Whether a particular instance contradicts a theory, or is to be thought of as due merely to error, requires personal judgment. No event, until it has been given meaning by a mind, is a contradiction of anything. Even apparent agreement may leave some doubt, and the scientist must decide whether or not he believes such doubt to be reasonable. Contradiction to theories may often be explained away as due to experimental error, or simply accepted and endured as an unaccountable anomaly.[13] Personal judgment must decide what weight to attach to any particular sort of evidence, and the real sanction of

discovery lies in the detection of a coherence that we accept. It is
neither explicit theories, nor predictability, nor even manipulatability
that we seek in science – it is understanding and explanation.[14]
Polanyi's analysis of tacit knowing and of the relation between levels
of existence are examples of an extension of logic.[15] This logic proves
to be an informal one, but Polanyi insists that we call it logic rather
than psychology, for he calls "logic" the rules for reaching valid
conclusions from premises assumed to be true. Currently logic seems
to be defined as the rules for reaching strict conclusions from strict
premises, and he emphasizes that we should reject this definition since
no strict rules can exist for establishing empirical knowledge.[16] Even
formal logic must appeal to informalized supplements which, the
operator of the system takes for granted. Symbols must be identified
and their meaning known; axioms must be understood to assert
something; proofs must be acknowledged to demonstrate something;
and this identifying, knowing, understanding, acknowledging, etc., are
informal operations upon which the working of the formal system
depends. All formal systems in the end contain informal elements, for
only thus can they provide genuine explanations establishing logical
coherence in what is seen perceptually and conceptually.[17]

To the objection that our system of naturalistic science is proven
(or at least rendered plausible) by the objective fact that it works – as
against magical systems that do not – Polanyi tells us that the studies
of Evans-Pritchard with the Zande show that their beliefs become just
as stable as our scientific beliefs. Their belief system does this by
denying to any rival system the grounds on which it could take root.
Each instance that might possibly refute the old system is explained by
some part of the old system as a nonrefuting instance. Such devices as
calling any exceptions to our theories "anomalies," or dismissing them
as due to possible experimental error are some of the features that
enable our own scientific beliefs to possess the great stability they have
and to continue to be thought to work.[18] Yet Polanyi clearly accepted
scientific beliefs as true and rejected magic as false, while at the same
time holding that two alternative systems such as these cannot really
be argued, since they share no fundamental perceptions between them.
Refutation can only take place when there is a commitment to some
common principle to which disputants can appeal. So even if our
commitment to naturalistic explanations of science as opposed to
magical or theological ones is evident, we have no guarantee of their
truth. We can, therefore, ground ourselves on nothing but our beliefs

resting upon our capacities to notice coherences by means of our imagination. And, of course, there are no better justifications for our philosophical views: Polanyi is quite aware that in the last resort his statements affirm his own personal beliefs. What we affirm as real, however, is always richer in its capacities to manifest itself in the future than we have grasped it to be in our explicit thought. World views are imaginary projections; they are not products of scientific investigation.

To realize that there is a problem and to understand its solution is to see a range of potentialities for meaning that appear to be accessible. A mind strives to apprehend that which it believes to be comprehensible, but which it does not yet understand. Its choices are hazardous. They might succeed or fail, yet they are not taken at random, since they are controlled by our intentions. Such intentions do not occur spontaneously either, for they are due to the actualization of hidden potentialities. All knowing is a sort of doing and creating; perception, ordinary as well as scientific knowledge, poetry, and religion are all of this kind. There is no way to establish their truth or reality in a thoroughly detached, impersonal, objective way. All our integrations are believed to be realities, i.e. to have existence not fully determinate in our present grasp, and which we, therefore, expect to become manifest in further, as yet indeterminate ways. We believe a hydrogen atom is real, not merely a conceptual constraint, because we expect it to display qualities in the future that we cannot predict from our present grasp of it. We are supposing that the object of our concept has some nature of its own into which we may penetrate further.[19] Science in the modern age has tended, at least tacitly, to claim to have a monopoly on achieving knowledge of reality. This often unspoken claim has led to our tendency to assign a honorific status to tangible realities, since science appears to deal with them, and to regard all other sorts of possible entities or meanings to be illusory. Polanyi makes the startling counter-claim that a stone is, if anything, less real than a mind or a problem because we expect a far narrower range of indeterminateness in nature from a stone than we do from a mind. At some point it was man's mind that created (tacitly at first) the principles of truth, beauty, and morality as norms that should guide his behavior. Once brought into being, they have a structure and a thrust of their own, and we find ourselves subject to their intrinsic standards, just as we are in mathematics.[20] Polanyi seemed to think that the function of these realities is to create obligations binding upon us and, in this manner, to our direct lives. We in the modern world have adopted, because of the advent of positivist science, a strange view of the world and of our place in it that leads us to doubt the reality of these obligatory realities created by man, and to attempt to undercut them by reducing them to complex effects produced by the lower level drives for profit and power.[21] It seemed to be his hope that new insight into epistemology, and into an ontology correlated with it, would lay the foundation for the rebirth of faith in the reality of these "spiritual entities," as he sometimes called them.

Polanyi made a case for our personal participation even in the formal sciences of mathematics and symbolic logic. The acceptance of a mark on paper as a symbol implies that we believe that we can identify the mark in various instances of it, and that we know its proper symbolic use. We expect to recognize things that satisfy a formula as distinct from other things that fail to do so. Logical symbols must tacitly be held to represent states of affairs, or logic can have no application. We dwell in logical manipulation, projecting ourselves through it to the concept for which it stands. The tacit component of a formalized process is thus broadly analogous to that of a denotation. Taking in such a logical sequence is grasping it as a whole, a gestalt, of which the parts are seen in a subsidiary way rather than in a focal way. There are no proofs for solving problems; only more or less vague maxims, and this tacit ability to anticipate a hidden potentiality is essential both just to see the problem, and then to set out to solve it.[22] Polanyi generalized this recognition as the basis of all discovery;[23] he pointed out that the reductionisms currently in vogue in biology, neurology, and psychological behaviorism are all logically related to the basic assumption of a single-level universe of atoms which alone are believed to possess true reality. Contrary to this, he emphasizes that our understanding of a living animal choosing food or alertly listening, watching and reacting to what it notices, is an act of personal knowing similar to the animal's own personal act that our knowing appraises. It is achieved not by detached observation, but by participation in what we observe, in our dwelling in it. Our knowledge of such an active perceptive animal would altogether dissolve if we entirely replaced it by our focal knowledge of its several manifestations.

Behaviorists teach that in observing an animal we must refrain, above all, from trying to imagine what we would do if placed in the animal's position. Polanyi suggests, on the contrary, that nothing at all could be known about the animal that would be of the slightest interest to physiology, let alone psychology, except by identifying ourselves with the center of action in the animal and criticizing its performance according to standards set up for it by ourselves.[24] The behaviorist describes learning in objectivist terms such as "stimulus," "control," and "response," but these can be shown to apply to the process of learning only because their meanings are understood tacitly, smuggling into them their bearing on mental events involved in learning, which are all along kept covertly in mind. By dwelling on their behavior and so understanding what orients its particulars, we observe that animals are puzzled, that they try ways to solve their problems, that they are seeking food or a mate, that they fear, and, in higher animals, that they dream. We would be hard put to set out their behavior into significant patterns even for the purpose of behaviorist correlation, if we could not use our capacity for indwelling. The feeling by which we appreciate the achievements of beings lower than ourselves involves an extension of ourselves by which we participate in their achievements. Modern biological thinking, attempting to confine itself to physical and chemical forms and modes of operation, is left with nothing but chance as the originator of any particular structure of the DNA molecule. But the probability that these molecules have acquired their meaningful structure by mere chance is exceedingly small. Polanyi, therefore, concludes that DNA and every organism structured by it are meaningful organizations of essentially meaningless matter. Evolutionary history demonstrates that the overall direction in which evolutionary development has proceeded is that of attaining ever greater meaningfulness in terms of both structure and capacity to attain significance. There is a striking progress from the one-celled plants, capable of little more than sustaining themselves and of reproducing their kind, through animals sensitive as individuals to their surroundings, to more and more complex (and meaningful) animals, to mammals, and finally to man, whose capacity for achieving meaning seems still to stretch limitlessly before us. Pure chance mutations and natural structure would not appear to be able to account for the direction that evolution has actually taken.[25]

Polanyi thought that belief in values and obligations are true commitments, even if their truth cannot be objectively demonstrated. A person must be "carried away" by a poem, a painting, or even a religious ritual or object, even just to understand it. The semantic process by which a clear and forceful metaphorical meaning is established is similar to that by which a flag is made to symbolize a country. A poem is not a communication of facts, and we do not respond to a stage murder as if were real. Art, even representational art, has not been interested in creating the illusion that the objects it represents are real. If we make the canvas, the brush strokes, into focal objects, we lose the meaning of the painting, for we then do not see the story. Polanyi emphasizes that there is no scientific reason for rejecting the religious hypothesis that the world is meaningful. Developing an epistemology that is adequate to human thought, he rejects the reductionist tendencies in psychology, sociology, and biology in favor of an ontology of evolutionary achievement. But toward the end of his life, Polanyi himself considered his work a failure, for his purpose had been to restore the human mind to a healthy confidence in its powers. Positivism, he believed, left the sciences with nothing but arbitrary bases rather than commitment to reason and truth. Most of the disputes with Polanyi's views proceeded from a denial of his key contention that subsidiary-focal operations are involved in every interpretation or recognition of meaning.[26] Thus, Harré argues that what is subsidiary in perception should not properly be called "knowledge."[27] Harré seems to argue that we know only what we can tell;[28] he does not accept as logical anything that is not a case of explicit logic – logic is always explicit or it is not logic.

Polanyi, however, took issue with this prevalent view, and emphasized that there was a logic of tacit coherence. It was not an explicit logic, rather it was the way in which the mind dwells in subsidiary clues to reach across explicitly logical gaps. One does this in perception which, because the elements are not propositional, Harré does not consider logical to begin with. Polanyi, on the other hand, insists that we also do this in our scientific discoveries and in the justification of them. While we can give a logically explicit definition of what we mean by "meaning conditions," we cannot render explicit our understanding of when these conditions have been met. We do know – if we are a trained scientist – to make such judgments, but we cannot reduce our judgment to a finite list of criteria. We never make our judgments in this explicit manner – not in the dynamics of discovery nor in our justifications and criticisms. Yet we do not reach our judgments illogically or merely subjectively, since we are able to justify them by argument at least up to a point. We acquire a tacit awareness of rules (much as we do when we learn to ride a bicycle), an awareness that becomes more adequate as we become familiar with the context. The application of explicit logical rules always rest on indeterminate, subsidiary elements in which we simply dwell. Thus, what is involved in seeing an analogy is not merely noticing that two things are the same, which might be done by an electronic device that scanned each of the two cases point by point. Rather, it is determining that two different things have a significant similarity – that they are alike in respect to something. One has to come to any analogy with something in mind, since what is to count as an analogy depends on many tacit notions and clues. One could show Polanyi wrong only if one could point to some knowledge that is wholly explicit – like what comes out of a computer. But it seems patently obvious that this is in no sense "knowledge" until it has been interpreted as such by a mind with reference to some purpose.

All our observations are theory laden. Every scientific theory, Polanyi held, is fed by a vision of how things are, with the understanding that the manifestation of things might prove the vision wrong. The projection of entities into what exists beyond our grasp of them is a most important part of Polanyi's thought, for without it all things have only the reality of the meaning's focal integration we happen to achieve. There is, however, no way to decide with logical rigor that a given ontology about the world is true, since there is no objective way to match the two. Thus, we do or we do not commit ourselves to beliefs in certain existences. In art and religion we find we are "carried away" by the object, and it is this capacity of the object of our focal attention to carry us away, to move us deeply, that constitutes our meaningful integration of it into a focal object valid for us. Marjorie Grene believes that one of the chief values of Polanyi's epistemology is the way in which it bridges the gap between scientific and humanistic concerns by showing that all meaning or knowledge requires subsidiary-focal poles, and so demands our personal participation in it. Polanyi has shown that the insidious distinction our epoch has made between "science" and any other nonscientific activity or discipline has no reasonable justification. No meanings are wholly objective or wholly subjective; rather all are personal.[29] But the binary logic of natural science dealing with facts of experience is much more specific than that of mathematics, religion, or the arts. It is, therefore, legitimate to speak of verification in science in a sense which does not apply to other articulate systems. The two kinds of findings, the religious and the natural, Polyani held, bypass each other. Ronald L. Hall argues that the distinction made by Polanyi and by Prosch in

Meaning between science and art hides a deep affinity between them, namely that science is like the arts governed by aesthetic criteria and norms.[30] The scientist is not a robot; he is, just like the artist, passionately and personally involved in making novel and imaginative integrations. We argue as fully as we can for the positions we hold, but since these arguments always have a tacit dimension embedded in subsidiary clues, we can never demonstrate this. As Kant put it, we cannot have rules for applying rules ad infinitum; somehow we must simply see that what is present before us does satisfy our rule and is true. Thus, we know more about our mathematical and logical systems than is apparent from their notations; indeed more than we can ever explicitly tell. The rules of logic that function as norms of our systems of knowledge are due to assumptions that can never be fully demonstrated. Polanyi's tacit knowledge proceeds by means of a "soft" logic, i.e. one that is contextually relative and, therefore, only partially consistent. There are no rules for making discoveries, merely a context with which we can become familiar and in which solutions are tacitly judged. But attempts to go beyond a given context play a crucial role not only in the arts but also in science and philosophy. What we consider possible may, therefore, undergo radical transformation. The "other" logic may not provide us with altogether conclusive arguments, yet in extending the range of the arguable, it makes conceptual breakthroughs possible and becomes thus a necessary condition for future knowledge.

Notes

[1] Harry Prosch, *Michael Polanyi, A Critical Exposition,* New York, NY: State University of New York Press, 1986, p. 5.

[2] *Ibid.,* p. 54.

[3] Michael Polanyi, *Personal Knowlege,* Chicago, IL: The University of Chicago Press, 1958, p. 97.

[4] Michael Polanyi, *The Tacit Dimension,* Garden City, NY: Doubleday, 1966, p. 4.

[5] Michael Polanyi, "What is Painting?" *British Journal of Aesthetics*, 10 July 1970, pp. 227-31; Michael Polanyi and Harry Prosch, *Meaning*, Chicago, IL: The University of Chicago Press, 1975, pp. 86-92.

[6] Michael Polanyi, "Logic and Psychology" in *Knowing and Being*, Essays by Michael Polanyi, ed. Margorie Grene, Chicago, IL: The University of Chicago Press, 1969, pp. 30-31; "Knowing and Being" in *Knowing and Being*, pp. 181-2, 185-6.

[7] Michael Polanyi, *Science, Faith and Society*, London: Oxford University Press, 1946, pp. 42-5.

[8] C. F. A. Pantin, "The Recognition of Species," *Science Progress*, 1954, p. 587.

[9] Michael Polanyi, "Genius in Science," *Encounter* 38, January 1972, p. 48.

[10] Michael Polanyi, "Science and Reality," *Knowing and Being*, pp. 189-96.

[11] Prosch, *Michael Polanyi*, p. 95.

[12] *Ibid.*, p. 102.

[13] Polanyi, *Science, Faith and Society*, p. 31; *Personal Knowledge*, pp. 292-3.

[14] Polanyi, "Logic and Psychology," p. 37.

[15] "Science, Tacit and Explicit," Paper presented at the International Congress for the Philosophy of Science, Jerusalem, August 1964, (unpublished).

[16] "Polanyi, "Logic and Psychology," p. 42.

[17] Prosch, *Michael Polanyi*, p. 113.

[18] Polanyi, *Personal Knowlege*, pp. 287-94.

[19] *Ibid.*, pp. viii, 64, 117, 147, 189, 396.

[20] Prosch, *Michael Polanyi*, p. 139.

[21] Polanyi, *Personal Knowledge*, p. 364.

[22] *Ibid.*, pp. 127-8.

[23] Prosch, *Michael Polanyi*, p. 143.

[24] Polanyi, *Personal Knowledge*, p. 364.

[25] *Ibid.*, pp. 38, 384-6, 389, 400, 402.

[26] Prosch, *Michael Polanyi*, p. 208.

[27] Rom Harre, "The Structure of Tacit Knowledge," *Journal of the British Society for Phenomenology* 8, October 1977, pp. 174-5.

[28] Prosch, *Michael Polanyi*, p. 213.

[29] *Ibid.*, p. 238.

[30] Ronald L. Hall, "Some Critical Reflection on *Meaning*," *Zygon* 17, 1982, p. 15.

Chapter Twelve

Goodman's World Pluralism

Epistemology, as Goodman and Elgin conceive it, comprehends understanding or cognition in all its modes – including perception, depiction, and emotion – as well as description.[1] Our expectations and beliefs about our situation affect the character of our experiences concerning it; they guide our investigations and structure our perceptual field. What attracts our attention is most often what defeats or fulfills a hope or a fear, for what is routine often goes unnoticed. To characterize what is perceived requires a good deal of background knowledge of one sort or another, and the range of available alternatives is a function of the conceptual systems we have constructed and mastered. Things do not present themselves to us in any privileged vocabulary or system of categories; we have and use a variety of vocabularies and system of categories that yield different ways in which things can be faithfully represented or described. The alternatives of which such a scheme consists need not be mutually exclusive. A scheme typically orders a domain in terms of implicit alternatives, and such schemes do not provide different labels of the same collection of objects, but rather sort the objects into different collections or "worlds." What counts as being the same thing varies from one sort of object to another, since under different interpretations the realm consists of quiet different elements. Such systems are not identified by Goodman and Elgin with languages because not all systems are linguistic. Among familiar nonlinguistic systems are notations, interpretations, or pictorial schemes. But just what symbols make up a picture, or just what items constitute its reference is never completely settled.

Goodman and Elgin emphasize that symbol systems are artifacts; their syntactic or semantic features are not dictated by the domain, but result from decisions we make about how the domain is to be organized. The systems we construct determine the similarities and differences we can recognize, the levels of precision we can produce, and the degrees of determinateness we can achieve. Consistency is one obvious constraint on the adequacy of the system, for no acceptable system can permit the joint application of mutually inconsistent labels to a single object, yet such consistency cannot be achieved by fiat. In system building, we never start from scratch; inevitably we begin with some conception of the objects in the domain and with some convictions about them, and these guide our constructions. Since our presystematic judgments constitute our best guesses about the subject in question, they serve as touchstones against which to evaluate our constructions. The presumption in favor of entrenched predicates lasts only so long as their projection is inductively successful, for the bias in favor of entrenched categories does not preclude conceptual innovations. Different systems of categories serve different interests; in fantasy, for example, employment of unentrenched predicates is an effective literary device. Rightness, in this case, is a matter of providing a novel organization of a (real or fictive) realm – an organization that highlights hitherto unnoticed and often overlooked realms. Sometimes this forces us to reconsider the appropriateness and adequacy of the categories we are accustomed to use.[2] In metaphor, a familiar scheme is implicitly applied to a new realm or to its old realm in a new way. Typically the result is a novel organization of the realm, for the metaphorical scheme classifies together objects in the realm that are not classified together in the literal scheme. If, as seems likely, the metaphor has no exact literal paraphrase, it captures a resemblance that no literal predicate does. A metaphorical use of the term effects a likening of objects in its literal and metaphorical extensions, enabling us to recognize affinities across realms. Rightness of metaphorical categorization depends on whether the order achieved by the metaphorical application of a scheme is useful, enlightening, and informative. It also depends on whether the affinities it highlights between the metaphorical and literal referents of its terms are interesting, important, and otherwise apt.[3]

Systems are subject to multiple standards of rightness. If inconsistencies emerge, the system we construct must deviate from our antecedent convictions, or it may modify the boundaries of our original classifications. The goals and interests we want a system to realize may conflict as well, for other alternative resolutions are equally reasonable[4] and pluralism results. We trade cumbersome truth for serviceable approximations, that is, exchange utility for truth, and the choice depends heavily on what we want the system to accomplish. In spite of their world pluralism, Goodman and Elgin are convinced that the various systems complement each other, i.e. constitute something like a world of worlds that yields a deeper understanding of the subject than any single system alone provides. Conflicting, equally correct accounts are possible, and physics alternates between incompatible wave and particle theories. A variety of symbol systems can thus be constructed that are neither reducible to, nor justifiable in, terms of a single preferred base. These systems are subject to different standards, and there is no neutral vocabulary from which they all can be evaluated. But it does not follow that we can formulate statements in any way we please, or so construct a system that any claim we like turns out to be true.[5] World-versions can be right or wrong, and they are not arbitrary. Considerations of consistency, fidelity, and antecedent practice, satisfaction of our goals in systematizing, and adequacy for purpose at hand admit different specifications, receive different weightings, and are realized in different ways in the construction of different symbol systems. The admission that there are many right systems, and many standards of rightness thus does not collapse the distinction between right and wrong.

Goodman and Elgin reject all notions of pure givenness, unconditional necessity, a single correct perspective, or system of categories.[6] To deny that there is any such thing as *the* world is not to deny that there are worlds. Although "the earth is in motion" and "the earth is at rest" apparently contradict each other, both are true. Goodman and Elgin argue that such conflicting statements, if true, are true of different worlds. A world in which the earth is in motion is not a world in which the earth is at rest, for such worlds are heavily dependent on our accounts. The mistake is to talk of such systems as devices for representing an antecedent reality, because no sense can be made of motion (or anything else) except relative to one or another frame of reference.[7] The apparent conflict between true descriptions shows that they are not descriptions of the same thing. There are many worlds if any; Goodman and Elgin's talk of worlds amounts really to talk about true or right world versions. For philosophers like Rorty, Kuhn, and Feyerabend, loss of the world results in a skepticism that despairs of distinguishing between what is true and what is false. It, in effect, reduces science and inquiry to idle conversation. Once we become aware, however, that a "world" is an artifact, we come to notice the significant but often overlooked affinity among art, science, perception, and the fashioning of our everyday worlds. Goodman and Elgin's conclusion that there are many worlds, if any, is prompted by the discovery of separately adequate bur irreconcilable descriptions and representations. These grounds for world pluralism do not extend to a like-minded pluralism about works of art and literature. Goodman and Elgin emphasize that however such works are identified, the various interpretations in question are interpretations of a single text. This text can be identified significantly without appealing to any of the semantic and literary interpretations it bears, whereas there is no way to identify a world except by means of version, hence no way to identify a human subject to which such conflicting versions refer. A world dissolves under conflicting accounts, while a text persists under conflicting accounts. The identity of a text is a matter pertaining to the syntax of a language – to the permissible configurations of letters, spaces, and punctuation marks – quite apart from what the text says or otherwise refers to.[8] For Goodman and Elgin, figurative denotation is no less genuine than is literal denotation. We can significantly talk about mental images even though there are none,[9] and while there are no centaurs, there are descriptions, stories, and pictures of centaurs. Centaur descriptions or Don Quixote pictures may be right or wrong, and that indeed is all we have for discourse about natural objects as well. Questions about Don Quixote's life are as open to verification as are questions about Napoleon.

Goodman and Elgin argue that all that can be done to comply with the demand for "facts" is to say that the versions are versions of, that is, to give another version, even if the several versions remain at odds with one another. For them, a "world" is an entrenched manner of speaking or depicting, and what holds such a world together is conceptual relevance.[10] The "rightness" of a world-version is a species of soft logic, but there is a loss of simplicity in dealing with the rightness of a world version as compared with its truth because each fit becomes virtually unique. Beyond calculable fuzzy logic,[11] we rapidly lose our ability to identify world versions as a whole. The relevance that holds together such a world version is no less metaphorical than the "given" world that they reject. To say that we live in different worlds is literally inconsistent, for a world is supposed to be a totality. Metaphors, unlike literal statements, do not have to be consistent; thus, whether a given metaphor is inappropriate or irrelevant is often undecidable. But Goodman and Elgin convincingly argue against the mutual indifference of linguistics and art theory. The linguistic account does not explain our understanding of figurative language or of locutions in which grammatical rules are deliberately violated. For a literary work may achieve its effects not in spite of but because of its odd ungrammatical constructions, and to force a grammatical reading on such a text is to miss the point. Typically, the objects a term applies to metaphorically are not in the term's literal extensions. It will not do for the linguist to dismiss such cases as deviant – to contend that metaphorical sentences are strictly false or that stream-of-consciousness locutions are strictly ill-founded.

Goodman and Elgin consider it crucial that whether we characterize these sequences as true or false, we understand them as words and sentences. Metaphors are ubiquitous, so the failure of linguistic theory to explain our understanding of sentences containing metaphors is a failure to explain a considerable proportion of its subject matter.[12] What remains is an impoverished notion of linguistic competence, in particular since the linguist model cannot be extended to pictorial comprehension. Pictorial symbols belong to systems that are syntactically dense, since there is no way to determine what symbol a particular mark belongs to, or whether two marks constitute the same symbol. Any difference between pictorial marks might, therefore, be syntactically significant. Resemblance is often held to be that connection, and in the opinion of Goodman and Elgin such resemblance is discernible even to the uneducated eye.[13] But recognizing resemblance is no less problematic than comprehending meaning, and Goodman is famous for insisting that there is no innocent eye in interpreting a picture. We cannot tell what a picture represents just by looking, for anything looks many ways. Understanding a picture often involves knowing what the symbols represent, figuratively as well as literally, and such knowledge is not a native endowment but a complex constellation of acquired abilities. In different pictorial systems, different devices are being used and some learning is required to identify what even the most ordinary photograph represents. Such pictorial learning involves acquiring a wide range of perceptual and conceptual skills as well as developing a sensitivity regarding their exercise. The process is so automatic that we are apt to forget that interpretation occurs. Moreover, interpretation of a symbol depends on its place in the various symbol systems to which it belongs: a symbol system is a scheme of implicit alternatives to sort collectively the objects in a realm. But the same symbol can belong to several systems and so participate in a variety of sorting.

Goodman and Elgin admit that the resulting richness and complexity is hard to square with our ordinary unsophisticated comprehensions of pictures and sentences.[14] Understanding a symbol is not a all-or-nothing affair, and a symbol need not have a single, uniquely correct interpretation. The greater our store of relevant knowledge, the better our resources for (and, hence, prospects of) understanding what the symbol represents. Growth of understanding involves the recognition of several admissible alternative interpretations, and this occasions a reconsideration of some we have already accepted. Likeness varies with the comparative importance among the common properties, and thus with interest, context, and custom. Degrees of resemblance and realism are transient properties that fluctuate with practice.[15] What matters is not merely whether differentiation is theoretically possible, but whether it can be accomplished by the means available and approximate to the use of a given scheme. Thus, buildings are not texts or pictures, and usually do not describe or depict. Goodman argues that exemplification is one of the major ways in which architectural works mean. The ascription in such cases is largely metaphorical, and he believes that metaphorical truth is as distinct from metaphorical falsity, as is literal truth from literal falsity.[16] Strictly speaking, however, metaphors are not false, merely inappropriate or irrelevant. Stripping off or ripping out all construals (i.e. all interpretation and construction) does not leave a work cleansed from all encrustation but demolishes it.[17] Goodman realizes that the resolute deconstructionist will not flinch at this, for he dismisses unconstrued works as will-o-the-wisps, and treats interpretation as mere story telling. He is thus released from the hampering and hopeless search for a single right interpretation. But such freedom is bought at the price of inconsequence. That is why Goodman and Elgin take deconstruction as a prelude to reconstruction, insisting that among the many construals of a work some are right while others are wrong. Their problem is that a work may be right or wrong in many, sometimes radically different ways. Not only is the quest for a ready and inclusive test for rightness (i.e. for a key to all knowledge) patently absurd, but even a pat and satisfying definition can hardly be expected.[18] Thus, Goodman and Elgin declare themselves incapable to tell us what rightness finally is. Judgments of rightness are often said to be in terms of some fit, but whether it is a fit of parts together, or of the whole to context and background, remains obscure. In any case, it is not something that will tell us how to proceed.

Such rightness or fit are not cognitive categories, for Goodman proclaims an unwitting bias in favor of stupidity to be characteristic of both internalist and externalist theories of knowledge.[19] Apparently, any true belief can be constituted as knowledge by suitably configuring the range of relevant alternatives. As we refine our conceptual schemes, we increase our chances of error, and Goodman's epistemology lacks the resources to discriminate between significant and insignificant beliefs. His justification appeals mainly to community standards, for he believes that a person's epistemic prospects are best if his doxactic system includes no more than is necessary to justify his beliefs. The blunt man of solid inspired common sense, being untroubled by sublimities, may know what's what, while the more sensitive, finely tuned intelligence is distracted by nuances. In this manner, Goodman and Elgin conclude that knowledge, as contemporary theories conceive it, is not and ought not to be our overriding cognitive objective. For to treat it as such is to disvalue cognitive excellence such as conceptual and perceptual sensitivity, logical acumen, breath and depth of understanding, and the capacity to distinguish important from trivial truth. All hope of arriving at justified and certain truth vanishes largely because defeat and conclusion are built into the notions of truth, certainty, and knowledge from the beginning. Truth is conceived by Goodman and Elgin as an excessively narrow notion, for its range is restricted to the verbal, and within the verbal, to statements. Moreover, it pertains only to what the statement *says*, taking no account of what it may refer to in other ways such as exemplification, expression, or allusion.[20] And even within its own narrow province, truth is not the only, and often not the overriding consideration, for truth matters little in a statement not to the point. Simple summaries and smooth curves become the facts and laws by which we work and live.

By contrast, "right" and "wrong" are said by Goodman and Elgin to apply to symbols of all kinds, nonverbal no less than verbal. Rightness, unlike truth, is multidimensional; it is not only more complicated but also more volatile than truth. In this manner, truth becomes one among the many factors – along with relevance, effect, and usability – that enter into the rightness of what is being said or depicted. Truth is considered to be no more than an occasional ingredient of rightness;[21] the different applications and procedures of rightness are restricted to effecting a positive-negative dichotomy or a grading on a preferential scale – not a specific and direct application or reference. Rightness is said to be a matter of fitting and working, but what fits or works may be quite different in each particular case. Rightness is a fitting into a context or discourse or complex of other symbols, but such fitting is not taken as coherence because other factors such as seniority also count. Fitting is neither passive nor one-way but an active process; the fit has to be made and the making may involve minor and major adjustments to what is being fitted *into*, or what is being fitted *in*, or both.[22] The fitting is being tested by the workings, and while the resultant work may be of any kind, Goodman and Elgin are primarily concerned with cognitive work. Thus, while their talk of working may echo pragmatism, they make a point not to reduce rightness to practicality. For they emphasize that we can adopt strategies, vocabularies, and styles no less than statements. To adopt a symbol is to incorporate it into the apparatus in use, the fabric being woven, the work in progress.

In some notable instances, a category or predicate or hypothesis gains presence over others through entrenchment – the result of continued or repeated use. Entrenchment does not derive from rightness; rather conversely, entrenchment is what, along with further fitting and working, makes for rightness.[23] Making the fit may indeed call for altering the background, even though the background yields less readily than new proposals. Statements can be understood regardless of their truth and regardless of belief in them; thus, we understand requests and queries and works of art though they are neither true nor false, neither believed nor disbelieved, and subject to neither demonstration nor refutation. Much as rightness is broader in scope than truth, and adaption is broader in scope than certainty, understanding is broader in scope than knowledge.[24] The process goes on and on, for understanding remains always partial, and advancement of understanding consists in the improvement of the relevant skills, or in applying them to expand or refute what is understood. Understanding is what the cognitive process achieves, though what is understood is not always believed or established as true.[25] Goodman and Elgin concur with the skeptical conclusion that transcendent truth or certainty, i.e. knowledge as traditionally defined, are unattainable. The advancement of understanding starts from what happens to be currently accepted and proceeds to integrate and organize – to construct something that works cognitively, that fits together and handles new cases, and that may implement further inquiry and invention. The test is whether the candidates for new adoption can be made to fit and work, and what works at one time is not expected to work forever and everywhere, nor is even a successful construction taken to preclude further alternatives. This is why when truth and rightness are at odds, Goodman and Elgin choose rightness.

Notes

[1] Nelson Goodman and Catherine Z. Elgin, *Reconceptions in Philosophy and Other Arts and Sciences,* Indianapolis/Cambridge: Hackett Publishing Co., 1988, p. 5.

[2] *Ibid.,* p. 16.
[3] *Ibid.,* p. 17.
[4] *Ibid.,* p. 24.
[5] *Ibid.,* p. 26.
[6] *Ibid.,* p. 49.
[7] *Ibid.,* p. 51.
[8] *Ibid.,* p. 58.
[9] *Ibid.,* p. 85.
[10] Joseph Grünfeld, *Conceptual Relevence,* Amsterdam: B.R. Grüner Publishing Co., 1989.
[11] George J. Klir and Tina A. Folger, *Fuzzy Sets, Uncertainty and Information,* Englewood Cliffs, NJ: Prentice-Hall, 1988.
[12] Goodman and Elgin, *Reconceptions in Philosophy,* p. 109.
[13] *Ibid.,* p. 111.
[14] *Ibid.,* p. 119.
[15] *Ibid.,* p. 122.
[16] *Ibid.,* p. 40.
[17] *Ibid.,* p. 45.
[18] *Ibid.,* p. 46.
[19] *Ibid.,* p. 135.
[20] *Ibid.,* p. 154.
[21] *Ibid.,* p. 157.

[22] *Ibid.*, p. 158.
[23] *Ibid.*, p. 160.
[24] *Ibid.*, p. 161.
[25] *Ibid.*, p. 162.

Metaphor

Chapter Thirteen

The Logic of Metaphor

I. A. Richards was the first to enunciate clearly what has become known as the interactive view of metaphor, thus opening up the view of metaphor as tension. He further reminded us that metaphor can convey abstract ideas as well as pictorial, taking metaphor beyond the domain of a purely ornamental or image-presenting entity. This, in effect, is the preference of the cognitive over the semantic approach to metaphor, the view that words obtain meaning only from their connection with other words in a discourse. There is thus no standard or scientific meaning for any word: sentences are not built up out of fixed atomic units of meaning, and this makes metaphor a borrowing between contexts.[1] The standard view takes its stand on a distinction between literal and figurative usage of language, in which literal usage is to consist of the fixed meanings that Richards criticizes. The standard view is also questioned by F. Moore for depending on a notion of metaphor as a deviation from some supposed literal sense. There are many different levels of usage in language, not just two, and figures of speech, including metaphor, will have to be regarded as part of usage, not as deviations from it. Today's metaphor is tomorrow's literal sense.[2] The error is in the assumption that usage is, as it were, one-dimensional. There is a temptation to say that rhetorical questions are not questions at all, and that they are, therefore, deviant. But the rhetorical question is really a higher order employment of the conventions that enable us to ask questions to find out things we do not know. The question does not cease to be a question; rather, because it is a question where there should be none, we set out to consider why the speaker produced it.[3] The argument is that if someone does not mean to say what his utterance means, then he must mean to say something else. But his intention may be to *do* something, namely to produce a certain effect upon the hearer. Knowing the meaning of words is at the base of our use of language, but it is this very capacity that then makes possible the evocative use of language. Figures of speech can be employed (among their various functions) to direct our attention to a range of discovered, created, or creatable similarity and associations that are, as it were, merely optional relative to a given language (taken synchronically).[4] Metaphor could be defined as figurative language, which has the effect of drawing our attention to non-encoded similarities; it is not so much a change of meaning as an evocative exploitation of given meanings. By this evocative technique, the audience is made to think of, to explore, to recreate, a range of similarities not encoded in our ordinary first-order language, not given in the meaning of what is now said.

There is no semantic criterion that alone can determine a metaphor's reading. Even as familiar a metaphor as Plautus' "man is a wolf" doesn't permit the direct transfer of our beliefs about wolves to men. We are quite flexible in how we categorize things; a "heated debate" isn't hot in the ordinary sense. The most common explanation is that we recognize a metaphor when some sort of anomaly occurs. Depending on how the metaphor juxtaposes the two systems, a literal reading can be impossible, silly, irrelevant, or incomplete. Almost any two subjects have *something* in common, but not any two subjects can join to make a metaphor. Even a characteristic as abstract as rapacity means one thing when it refers to wolves, and quite another when it refers to men. We may reject the metaphor's picture of men, while still being capable of interpreting it. Almost any subject can be seen from more than one angle and the angle chosen influences the reading of the metaphor. Beliefs come in packages, and the packaging is partly determined by the domains we see as relevant. We see the attributes of "hunting for food" and "seeking advantage" as similar because we have constructed an abstract structure of what they share.[5] As Aristotle observes, a metaphor can go astray in at least two ways – it can be dull or it can be incomprehensible. A novel metaphor can be innovative in several ways; it may be phrased in an original way; it may offer an original view of its subjects; or it may make us see the relations between two domains in a new way.[6] The speaker need not use metaphor to characterize or set connections, but simply to present an image, and this creative freedom enjoyed by the speaker is most clearly visible in literary metaphors. For literal works are the natural environment of figurative speech.[7] Rhetoric features like economy, epigrammatic memorableness, and sensuousness are in competition with, and may be less important than, cognitive content. This is the positivist assumption that underlies the British empiricist attitude towards metaphor. There is, in principle, no limit to the number of different descriptions that can be given to any one object; nor is there any limit to the range of attitudes a description can express. The description under which a speaker conceives an object is not a once and for all construction made by the speaker. The speaker can entertain different conceptions of the same object at the same time, and on different occasions. The assumption of aesthetic purpose guides the construction of an analogy[8] because some metaphors characterize only in a weak sense.

The tendency has been to consider cognitive conflict or tension as unpleasant and dysfunctional, to be resolved as soon as possible. But increased cognitive activity or highlighted sensitivity might be appreciated for their own sake. Metaphor is usually treated either narrowly or as a type of literary device, or more generally (in the context of structuralism and semiology) as an aspect of the way in which people give meaning to the world and their place in it. Meaning derives from "opposition," for to understand what something is, one must also understand what it is not. Sometimes mutually exclusive properties are expressed simultaneously in relation to the same identity. Logically, of course, this is an impossibility, but phenomenologically self-contradiction of this kind actually occurs. The toy, for example, has two meanings, both of which are essential; it is a piece of plastic and also a horse. The "image" that such toys have derives from the fact that the two identities are conceptually made to overlap. The toy both is and is not what it purports to be, and both of these aspects apply at the same time. Similarly, a representational work of art derives its meaning as a work of art of this type and its special fascination from the fact that it both is, and is not, what it represents. In all these cases, as with toys, there is no real logical connection involved, since the "superimposed" identity is only implied or imagined. In the common definition of metaphor, one thing is treated as if it were another: the state is spoken of as if it were a ship, a woman as if she were a rose, a weapon as if it were a musical instrument.

Awareness of the language itself in poetry will tend to alternate between foreground and background.[9] I. A. Richards and Philip Wheelwright have argued that language itself is inherently metaphorical, since it involves reference to some kind of reality by means of another. Since language is based on the bringing together of opposites (the medium and the message, the words and what the words stand for), in just the same way as a figurative painting does, it would seem that language itself is essentially synergic. However, language is normally "transparent": one typically "sees through it" rather than being aware of it, and in this respect it tends to be unlike figurative painting or sculpture. Language only becomes part of a synergy when one is conscious of the language itself, so that there is a simultaneous awareness of both the language and what it represents. For this to occur, language must become "opaque" in some way, and this is one of the functions of poetry: to draw attention to the message itself as well as to the content of the message. An effective synergy will retain some element of the unusual and, therefore, unexpected, and much psychological and physiological research has demonstrated a relationship between unexpected events and arousal level. This process of bringing different identities together in the same "conceptual space" may be involved in creative thinking of all kinds.[10] This is the state of mind in which people generally do such things as going to the theater, watching sports events, or reading novels and poetry. Usually the physical setting of a work of art (such as an art gallery or theater) helps to induce the secure playful state of mind, and the nature of the work of art itself may also help to maintain this state. But if this state cannot be induced or maintained, then the serious-minded state will prevail and the synergies involved in the work of art will be felt as irritating or upsetting. It may even elicit anger, and this is more likely if the work of art is particularly unusual, so that it cannot be assimilated to the individual's expectations (he cannot "make sense" of it). Hence the anxiety and anger that new styles of art have tended to evoke in some kinds of people in recent history.

Nietzsche's writings offer a fascinating example of a uniquely metaphorical style, which seems to hover on the borderline of philosophy and poetry. As in many other areas, Nietzsche can be viewed as anticipating a major shift in twentieth-century thinking about metaphor, the breaking down of the clear distinction between literal and figurative language. No such thing as unrhetorical "natural" language exists that could be used as a point of reference; language is itself the result of purely rhetorical tricks and devices. Tropes are not something that can be added or abstracted from language at will; they are its truest nature.[11] Nietzsche points out that our common ways of speaking about things inevitably involve transpositions and distortions, and that the full nature of things is never grasped. There is no "real" expression and no real knowing apart from metaphor. But deception on this point remains: the most accustomed metaphors, the usual ones, pass for truths, and as standards for measuring rarer ones. The only intrinsic difference here is the difference between custom and novelty, frequency and variety. Knowing is nothing but working with the favorite metaphors, an imitation that is no longer felt to be an imitation.[12] Instead of regarding literal and figurative language as two distinct categories, Nietzsche views them as ideal poles of a continuum. Our notion of literal meaning reflects the power of creative artists to revive the energy of language by using words in novel ways and contexts. All language is a mixture of the literal and the figurative, since every figurative utterance has some element of the customary in it, and some element of the novel. For Nietzsche, *literal* and *figurative* do not refer to two different kinds of language but to opposed tendencies in all languages.[13] Man becomes man only through a process of metaphor. We misread ancient texts by trying to find a metaphorical depth beneath their surface meaning. What is regarded as literal at one moment may become figurative at another, and vice versa.

Nietzsche's purpose of undermining our naive faith in opposite values – the belief that good is good, and evil is evil, is well served by his principle of the continuity of the literal and figurative meanings. In Nietzsche's view, all meaning is a making meaningful; there is no meaning apart from interpretation, the more or less willful forcing of ideas into systems, that define their relations, and thus their significance. One's choice of master metaphor will determine what one regards as literal and what as figurative. What is figurative from one perspective is literal from another. Meanings struggle with one another for ascendancy because in Nietzsche's view, there is no natural hierarchy of meanings. The centrality of the principle of metaphor in Nietzsche's philosophy thus reflects his conviction that all meaning is ultimately poetic, that is, all meaning is the result of human making. By working to subvert the literal/figurative dichotomy, Nietzsche more basically undermines the distinction between natural speech and poetry, and hence, more generally, the distinction between nature and convention. For Nietzsche, to maintain that "there is no real knowing apart form metaphor" is ultimately to claim that all truth is human creation.[14] Nietzsche's *Genealogy of Morals* dwells on how man becomes man by moving from the literal to the figurative. At the same time, the tragedy of Nietzsche's account of the creative spirit in man is the way the symbolic messages of great artists and teachers are taken literally by their followers and hence distorted. Nietzsche sees Christianity as arising from a misreading of Christ's teaching, a taking literally of what Christ meant only figuratively. Once one understands that an expression like "kingdom of heaven" is a metaphor, one realizes that it is not a literal place to be reached or entered sometime in the future, but a spiritual state available right here and now.[15] With every diffusion of Christianity to still broader, still cruder masses of people, it becomes necessary to vulgarize it, to barbarize Christianity.[16] In the hands of the Church, Christ's spiritual teaching was progressively reinterpreted in material terms, and thus degenerated into dogma.

Nietzsche was acutely aware of how easily metaphors lose their vitality, of how quickly they pass from the realm of vivid novelty to that of dull familiarity. More than in the case of any other philosopher, Nietzsche's metaphors are no rhetorical embellishment of his prose. On the contrary, his metaphors are often the heart and the substance of his thought. What is distinctive, then, about Nietzsche's style is that one is never quite sure whether to take his language literally or metaphorically. The kaleidoscopic shifting between literal and figurative uses has the effect of undermining the reader's naive faith that he knows precisely what is real and what is symbolic. But by leaving the metaphoric status of his expressions unclear, Nietzsche exposes himself to the possibility of gross misinterpretations. In particular, he makes it very easy to take the "wrong" metaphors in his prose literally. Perhaps the most dangerous of Nietzsche's ambiguous figures of speech is his use of the term *war*, which has made him seem the intellectual ancestor of many forms of violence in the twentieth century. Nietzsche certainly would have been repelled by the uses to which his ideas have been put, but the fact remains that he often does get carried away by his own military metaphors. His rejection of any rigid formulation of his ideas has led him to express them in language that hovers in a twilight between literal and figurative meaning.

Metaphor has been important not only in literature and philosophy but also in science, where it performs an important role in the development of new theories. Janet Martin and Rom Harré argue that in science there is a need to make assertions about features of the world that lie beneath any possible direct experience. Metaphor offers us a terminology for such assertions that is both meaningful and able to present novel meaning; it enables us to "conceive more than we can currently say." If metaphor is just comparison, then the content of scientific assertions involving metaphor will be confined to realities of actual and possible experience. But it is basic to the position of the gestalt theory of metaphor that what is expressed by metaphor can be expressed in no other way. Black's contention is that each metaphor has two distinct subjects, and that the principal subject acquires new meaning through its involvement with the subordinary one. The subsidiary subject "organizes" one's thought about the principal subject in a new way, and this operation makes metaphor irreducible to any one literal formulation. Richards also emphasizes that metaphor is an intercourse of thoughts, as opposed to a mere shifting of words or crude substitution as suggested by the ornamental view of traditional rhetoric. It is thoughts (associated commonplaces) and not words that interact; the contribution of metaphor is not that this is a new description of a previously describable human condition, but that this subject, this particular mental state, and these particular connotations are revealed as such only through this metaphor. Thus, metaphor is not an adornment to what one already knows, but a vehicle for a new insight made available by this interaction of terms, leading to an enrichment of the literal description. We need metaphor because in some cases it is the only way to say what we mean.

The theoretical sciences experience crises in vocabulary owing to the fact that they refer to as yet only partially understood natural phenomena, and are capable of further refinement and disambiguation as a consequence of new discoveries. Normally, we introduce terminology to presumed kinds of natural phenomena long before our study of them has progressed to the point where we can specify for them the sort of defining conditions that the positivist account of language would require. The introduction of theoretical terms does require, however, some tentative or preliminary indication of the properties of the presumed kinds in question.[17] One must ask under what conditions such terms can be introduced into a language so that they may be intelligible. Thus, meaning theories that are essentially ostensive in character are excluded from a role in giving an account of that kind of metaphor in which new meaning is created, and at most they could explain how old meaning is reshuffled. In order to understand metaphor, we shall have to turn to a different way of conceiving meaning from whatever a term refers to. Simile, a simple "same saying," cannot reveal the richer and more complex alternative meaning of metaphor. If one does not wish to contemplate an infinitely complex world, and does not wish to treat science realistically, we must introduce some other form of predicate. The metaphorical employment of a term brings about a reordering of its semantic field, so generating intentional contents, most of which are yet to be explored. Metaphoric thinking can foster vagueness, but even primarily incorrect analogies can lead to useful research. Complex metaphors and analogies are treated as structure mappings between domains. Typically, the target system to be understood is new and abstract, and the base system in terms of which the target is classified is familiar and visualizable. Overlap in relations is necessary for the perception of similarity between two domains. A further complication is that literal similarity versus metaphorical relatedness is a continuum, not a dichotomy. An example of a complex analogy is Rutherfords' solar system model of the hydrogen atom. The analogy conveys that the two domains, though composed of different objects, share much of their relational structure.[18] In the atom/solar system analogy we do not attempt to map the relation between the temperature of the sun and that of the planet because it is considered irrelevant.

Before we check validity, we make implicit decisions concerning what set of relationships is important. The better analyzed the base, the clearer the candidate set of importable relations will be, and this is one reason that the base is usually a familiar domain. However, familiarity is no guarantee of specificity and it is possible to construct a poor analogy using a well-specified base. The clarity of an analogy refers to the precision with which the object mappings are defined, that is, exactly how the base modes are mapped on the target modes, and which set of predicates gets carried across. The richness of an analogy is its predicate diversity, but the richness of an analogy, like its clarity, can be defined before assuming its validity.[19] In the expressive analogy, there may be greater value in richness – in the sheer number and diversity of relationships conveyed – than in assuming that all the mappings are clear and consistent. Expressive analogies can fulfill their function without being clear and systematic, whereas explanatory analogies cannot.[20] Good science analogies are rated high on clarity and low on richness, bad science analogies, low on clarity and high on richness. In contrast, good literary metaphors are rated high in richness, and poor literary metaphors low in richness. The analogies of Paracelsus and Freud are far richer than those of Galileo and Rutherford; their lack of clarity and systematicity, though it prevents making strict predictions, does not necessarily diminish the aesthetic appeal of those analogies. Indeed, the presence of conflicting interests can contribute to a feeling of challenging paradox.[21] Such a metaphor can be a good artistic metaphor, capable of reverberating in interesting ways, of suggesting new associations, and of being called forth in many different situations. It may well lead to new understandings, but what it will not do is make the kind of strong new predictions of a well-clarified analogy. When predictions are derived from fuzzy analogies, they are often in remarkable close accord with a priori intuitions. Only a well-clarified analogy possesses a firm enough predicate structure to force a truly new and surprising prediction. The journals of scientists like Kepler, Maxwell, Poincaré, and Feynman make it clear that they entertained initially unruly analogies. It may well be that it is precisely in the process of focusing an initially vague, rich, multipurpose feeling of analogy into a well-defined model that much of the creative process in science takes place.[22]

Already Cicero, seeking to explain why a metaphorical term might be preferred even when a proper one exists, points to the delight of having one's thoughts led to something "other" without actually going astray.[23] In a theological context, however, the deviance or wandering of metaphor makes it the emblem of the errancy of all language. In the often repeated Pauline and Augustinian terms, metaphor, like all "figures," is the sign of exile from God into a "region of unlikeness."[24] The conception of the "mists" or "Painted Glass" of metaphor and the project of eliminating its "error" united Puritan theology and Baconian science, and gave to both their apocalyptic drive. The older parousial or paradisal impulse has its reflection in modern versions of the desire to purge language of its error, to regain the purity, which may be simply that of the object. Metaphor, which for the seventeenth century writers was a sign of paradise lost, is described by Northrup Frye as the instrument of analogy or "return." The multiplicity of plots contained within metaphor – transference, transgression, alienation, impropriety, identity – suggest why metaphor can be at work in so many genres, not just as figure of speech or rhetorical errant, but as a structural principle. So far, metaphor has not been mastered by any single translation.

Notes

[1] I. A. Richards, *The Philosophy of Rhetoric,* New York, NY: 1936, p. 94.

[2] F. C. T. Moore, "On Taking Metaphor Literally," in *Metaphor: Problems and Perspectives,* ed. David S. Miall, Sussex, NY: The Harvester Press, 1982 and New York, NY: The Humanities Press, 1982, p. 3.

[3] *Ibid.,* p. 5.

[4] *Ibid.,* p. 9.

[5] Roger Tourangeau, "Metaphor and Cognitive Structure," in *Metaphor: Problems and Perspectives,* p. 26.

[6] *Ibid.,* p. 32.

[7] Stein Haugom Olsen, "Understanding Literary Metaphors," in *Metaphor: Problems and Perspectives,* p. 38.

[8] *Ibid.,* p. 50.

[9] Michael Apter, "Metaphor as Synergy," in *Metaphor: Problems and Perspectives,* p. 63.

[10] Ibid., p. 70 n18.

[11] Frederich Nietzsche, *Ges mmelte Werke,* vol. V, Munich, 1922, pp. 297-300, trans. by Paul de Man under the title *Allegories of Reading,* New Haven and London, 1979, p. 105.

[12] *The Philosopher* (*The Philosophenbuch of 1872*), trans. and ed. by D. Braezeale under the title *Philosophy and Truth, Selection from Nietzsche's Notebooks of the Early 1870s,* Sussex and New Jersey, 1979, pp. 50-51.

[13] Paul Cantor, "Friedrich Nietzsche: The Use and Abuse of Metaphor," in *Metaphor: Problems and Perspectives,* p. 87 n5.

[14] *Ibid.,* p. 78.

[15] *Ibid.,* p. 79.

[16] Friedrich Nietzsche, "Antichrist," in *The Portable Nietzsche,* trans. W. Kaufmann, New York, NY: 1954, p. 610.

[17] J. Martin and R. Harré, "Metaphor in Science," *in Metaphor: Problems and Perspectives,* p. 105 n8.

[18] Dedre Gentner, "Are Scientific Analogies Metaphors?" in *Metaphor: Problems and Perspectives,* p. 113.

[19] *Ibid.,* p. 114.

[20] *Ibid.*, pp. 131 n21.
[21] *Ibid.*, p. 127.
[22] *Ibid.*, p. 129.
[23] *De Oratore* III x1, 160.
[24] *Confessions* VII x; XII xiii; 1 Cor 12.

Chapter Fourteen

Truth in Metaphor

Most traditional philosophical views permit metaphor little, if any, role in understanding our world and ourselves. But linguistic evidence shows that metaphor is pervasive in everyday language and thought. Metaphor is for most people a device of the poetic imagination and the rhetorical flourish – a matter of extraordinary rather than ordinary language. It is characteristically viewed as a matter of language alone, a matter of words rather than thought and action. George Lakoff and Mark Johnson, on the other hand, emphasize that our ordinary conceptual system, in terms of which we both think and act, is fundamentally metaphorical. The way we think, what we experience, and what we do every day is very much a matter of metaphor.[1] They point out that our conceptual system is not something of which we are normally aware. Thus, we don't talk about argument in terms of war, even though we actually win and lose arguments. We see the person with whom we are arguing as an opponent; we attack his position and we defend our own; we gain and lose ground; and we plan and use strategies in argument. The essence of metaphor is understanding and experiencing one kind of thing in terms of another. Thus, time in our culture is a valuable commodity; it is taken as a limited resource that we use to accomplish our goals. Because of the way the concept of work has developed in modern Western culture, where work is typically associated with the time it takes, and time is precisely quantified, it has become customary to pay people by the hour, week, or year. These practices are relatively new in the history of the human race, and by no means do they exist in all cultures. They have arisen in the industrialized societies and structure our basic everyday activities in a profound way. That is how we understand and experience time as the kind of thing that can be spent, wasted, budgeted, invested wisely of foolishly, saved or squandered.[2]

In allowing us to focus on one aspect of a concept (e.g. the battling aspects of argument), a metaphorical concept can keep us from focusing on other aspects of the concept that are inconsistent with that metaphor. In this way metaphor permits us partly inconsistent reasoning. Time isn't really money, but metaphorical concepts can be extended beyond the range of ordinary literal ways of thinking and talking into the range of what is called figurative, poetic, colorful, or fanciful thought and language. So when we say that a concept is structured by a metaphor, we mean that it is partially structured, and that it can be extended in some ways but not in others. Though the polar opposites, up-down, in-out, etc. are physical in nature, the orientational metaphors based on them vary from culture to culture. Our values form a coherent, though not a consistent, system as do our metaphors. There are indeed often conflicts among these values, and hence contention among the metaphors associated with them. What values are given priority is partly a matter of the subculture one lives in, and partly a matter of personal predilection, but there are cultures where balance and passivity are valued more than in our culture. Human purposes typically require us to impose artificial boundaries that make physical phenomena discrete. Metaphors like these are so natural and pervasive in our thought that they are usually taken as self-evident, direct descriptions of mental phenomena. The fact that they are metaphorical never occurs to most of us, and we take statements like "He cracked under pressure" as being directly true or false. We think of inflation as an adversity that can attack us, hurt us, steal from us, even destroy us, and the "inflation is the adversary" metaphor, therefore, gives rise and justifies political and economic actions on the part of our government. What all these metaphors have in common is that they allow us to make sense of phenomena in the world in human terms – terms that we can understand on the basis of our own motivations, goals, actions, and characteristics.

What part we pick out determines what aspects of the whole we are focusing on, but it is easy to find apparent incoherence in everyday metaphorical expressions. Time, in English, is structured in terms of the "Time is a moving object" metaphor, with the future moving towards us. The connections between metaphors are more likely to involve coherence than consistency.[3] If you say "The odds are against us" or "We'll have to take our chances," you would not be viewed as speaking metaphorically but as using normal everyday language appropriate to the situation. Nevertheless, your way of talking about, conceiving, and expressing your situation would be metaphorically structured.[4] Expressions like "wasting time," "attacking positions," "going our separate ways" are reflections of systematic metaphorical concepts that structure our actions and thoughts. The structure of our spatial concepts emerges from our constant spatial experience, that is, our interaction with the physical environment. But even what we call "direct physical experience" is never merely a matter of having a body of a certain sort; rather every experience takes place within a comprehensive background of cultural presuppositions. It can be misleading, therefore, to speak of direct physical experience, as though there were some core of immediate experience that we can then "interpret" in terms of our conceptual system. Cultural assumptions, values, and attitudes are not a conceptual overlay that we may or may not place upon experience as we choose. It would be more correct to say that all experience is cultural through and through, and, therefore, that we experience our "world" in such a way that our culture is already present in the very experience itself.[5] We experience ourselves as entities, separate from the rest of the world and, when things have no distinct boundaries, we often project boundaries upon them. We typically conceptualize the nonphysical in terms of the more physical – that is, we conceptualize the less clearly delineated in terms of the more delineated.

When we live by metaphors like "labor is a resource" and "time is a resource," as we do in our culture, we tend *not* to see them as metaphors at all. These two substance metaphors present labor and time as entities to be quantified – that is, measured, conceived as being progressively "used up," and assigned monetary values. In viewing labor as a kind of activity, the metaphor assumes that labor can be clearly identified and distinguished from activities that are not labor. It is assumed that we can tell work from play, and productive activity from nonproductive activity. The view of labor as merely a *kind* of activity independent of who performs it, how we experience it, and what it means, hides the issues of whether the work is personally meaningful, satisfying, and humane.[6] The quantification of labor in terms of time induces a notion of "leisure time" parallel to "labor time," In a society like ours, where inactivity is not considered a purposeful endeavor, a whole industry devoted to leisure activity has arisen. As a result, "leisure time" has become a resource, too – to be spent productively, used wisely, saved up, budgeted, wasted, lost, etc. What is hidden by the "resource" metaphors for labor and time is the way they turn our concept of "leisure" into something remarkably like "labor." The "resource" metaphors for labor and time hide the idea prevalent in other cultures and some subcultures of our own society that work can be play, that inactivity can be productive, and that much of what we classify as "labor" serves either no clear purpose or no worthwhile purpose. It is by means of conceptualizing our experiences in this manner that we pick out the "important" aspects of an experience. While not any one metaphor is sufficient to give us a complete construct and comprehensive understanding of all aspects, together they do the job of giving us a coherent understanding of what a rational argument is. There is no single image that completely fits all metaphors. Instead of consistency, we get partial coherencies and a partial satisfaction of our purposes.

We construct arguments when we need to show the connections between things that we take for granted and other things that are not obvious. There is no consistent image possible with any of the "argument" metaphors, but though consistency is not possible, there is metaphorical coherence.[7] Metaphor pervades our normal conceptual system. Because so many of the concepts that are important to us are either abstract or not clearly delineated in our experience (the emotions, ideas, time), we need to get a grasp on them by means of other concepts that we understand in clearer terms, such as spatial orientations and objects. It suggests that understanding takes place in terms of entire domains of experience and not in terms of isolated concepts. They are the product of our bodies, our interactions with our physical environment, and with other people within our culture. Even some natural kinds of experience are partly metaphorical; thus, the existence of time is a natural kind of experience that is understood almost entirely in metaphorical terms (by means of the spatialization of time, "time is a moving object," "time is money" metaphors). The standard view seeks to be objective, assuming that experiences and objects have inherent properties, and that human beings understand them solely in terms of true propositions. Against this, Lakoff and

Johnson argue that we comprehend, for example, *love* only partly in terms of such inherent properties as fondness, attraction, sexual desire, and the like. For the most part, our comprehension of love is metaphorical. There must be no fixed core of properties, and categories can be systematically extended in various directions for different purposes. Categories are open-ended, yet categorization is not random. Concepts are not defined solely in terms of inherent properties; instead they are defined primarily in terms of interactional properties. Since we speak in linear order, we constantly have to choose which words to put first. Syntax is not independent of meaning, especially metaphorical aspects of meaning. The "logic" of a language is based on the coherence between the spatialized forms of the language and the conceptual systems, especially the metaphorical aspects of the conceptual system.[8]

Metaphors are appropriate because they sanction actions, justify inferences, and help us to set goals; the meaning a metaphor will have for one will be partly culturally determined and partly tied to one's past experiences. The metaphor has the power to create reality rather than merely give us a way to conceptualize a preexisting reality, but it is by no means an easy matter to change the metaphors we live by. Many of our activities (arguing, solving problems, budgeting time) are metaphorical in nature, and the metaphorical concepts that characterize these activities structure our present reality.[9] Much cultural change arises from the introduction of new metaphorical concepts and the loss of old ones. Yet the idea that metaphors can create realities goes against most traditional views of metaphor. Metaphor has traditionally been viewed as a matter of mere language rather than a means of structuring our conceptual system and the kinds of everyday activities we perform. But changes in our conceptual system do modify what is real for us, and reflect how we perceive the world and act upon these perceptions.[10] The view that metaphor is just a matter of language and can at best describe reality stems from the idea that what is real is wholly external to, and independent of, how human beings conceptualize the world – as if the study of reality were exclusively the study of the external world. Such a view of reality – so-called objective reality – leaves out the real perceptions, conceptualizations, motivations, and actions that constitute most of what we experience. That is why different cultures have different conceptual systems, even though each culture provides a more or less successful way of dealing with its environment, both adapting to it and changing it. Not surprisingly, the social reality defined by culture affects its conception of physical reality. What is real for one individual as a member of a culture is a product both of his social reality and the way in which that reality shapes his experience of the physical world. Since much of our social reality is understood in metaphorical terms, and since our conception of the physical world is partly metaphorical, metaphor plays a very significant role in determining what is real for us.

Many of the similarities that we perceive are the result of conventional metaphors that are part of our conceptual system. New metaphors are mostly structural and by virtue of their entailment pick out a range of experiences by highlighting, downplaying, and hiding aspects of reality. The primary function of metaphor is to provide a partial understanding of one kind of experience in terms of another kind of experience. This may involve preexisting isolated similarities or the creation of new similarities. To an objectivist, it would make no sense to speak of metaphors as "creating similarities," since that would require metaphors to be able to change the nature of the external world, bringing into existence objective similarities that did not previously exist.[11] Lakoff and Johnson argue that things in the world do play a role in constraining our conceptual system, but they point out that things play that role only through our experience of them. Our experiences will differ from culture to culture and may depend on our understanding of one kind of experience in terms of another; that is, our experience may be metaphorical in nature. Properties and similarities, they maintain, can be expressed only relatively to a conceptual system. Metaphors have entailments through which they highlight and make coherent certain aspects of our experience. Metaphors may create reality for us, especially social reality; a metaphor may thus be a guide for future action, and people in power get to impose their metaphors. New metaphors, like conventional metaphors, can have the power to define reality, they do this through a coherent network of entailments that highlight some features of reality and hide others. The acceptance of the metaphor, which forces us to focus only on those aspects of our experience that it highlights, leads us to view the entailments of the metaphor as being *true*. Though questions of truth do arise for new metaphors, the more important questions are those of appropriate action. In most cases, what is at issue is not the truth or falsity of a metaphor but the perceptions and inferences that follow from it and the actions that are sanctioned by it.

In all aspects of life, not just in politics and love, we define our reality in terms of metaphors, and then proceed to act on the basis of these metaphors. We draw inferences, set goals, make commitments, and execute plans, all on the basis of how we in part structure our experience, consciously and unconsciously, by means of metaphor.[12]

Metaphors play a central role in the construction of social and political reality, yet they are typically viewed within philosophy as matters of "mere language." Philosophical discussions of metaphor have not focused on their conceptual nature, their contribution to understanding, or their function in cultural reality. The typical philosophical conclusion is that metaphors cannot directly state truths and that, if they can state truth at all, it is only indirectly, via some nonmetaphorical "literal" paraphrase.[13] Truth is always relative to a conceptual system that is defined in large part by metaphor. Most of our metaphors have evolved in our culture over a long period, while others are imposed upon us by people in power: political leaders, religious leaders, business leaders, advertisers, the media. We base our actions, both physical and social, on what we take to be true. Truth matters to us because it has survival value and allows us to function in our world. Most of the truths we accumulate – about our bodies, the people we interact with, and our immediate physical and social environments – play a role in daily functioning; they are so obvious that it takes a conscious effort to become aware of them. Thus, a front-back orientation is not an inherent property of objects like rocks, but rather an orientation that we project into them, and the way we do this varies from culture to culture. We perceive various things in the natural world as entities, often projecting boundaries and surfaces on them where no clear-cut boundaries or surfaces exist naturally. As is typically the case in our daily lives, truth is relative to understanding. In order to understand the world and function in it, we have to categorize it in ways that make sense to us in terms of the things and experiences that we encounter. Some of our categories emerge directly from our experience, from the way our bodies are, and the nature of our interactions with other people and with our physical and social environments. A categorization is a natural way of identifying one kind of object or experience by highlighting certain properties, downplaying others, and hiding still others. To highlight certain properties is necessarily to downplay or hide others, since focusing on one set of properties shifts our attention away from others.

In making a statement, we make a choice of categories because we have some reason for focusing on certain properties and downplaying others. True statements made in terms of human categories typically do not predicate properties of objects in themselves, but rather in interactional properties that make sense only relative to human functioning.[14] In making a true statement, we have to choose categories of description, and that choice involves our perceptions and our purposes in the given situation. What counts as an instance of a property depends on our purpose in using the category. Such categories are not fixed but may be narrowed, expanded, or adjusted relative to our purposes and other contextual factors. "Light consists of particles" seems to contradict "light consists of waves," yet both are taken as true by physicists relative to which aspects of light are picked out by different experiments. Understanding always involves human categorization, which is a function of interactional (rather than inherent) properties and dimensions that emerge from our experience.[15] Categories are neither fixed nor uniform; they are defined by prototypes, and are adjustable in context, given various purposes. Whether a statement is true depends on whether the category employed in the statement fits, and this in turn varies with human purposes and other aspects of context.[16] To understand a sentence as being true, we must first understand it. Thus, understanding that "the fog is in front of the mountain" is true is not merely a matter of picking out preexisting and well-defined entities in the world (the fog and the mountain), and seeing whether some inherent relation (independent of the human observer) holds between the well-defined entities. Instead, it is a matter of human projection and human judgment relative to certain purposes. The sentence is virtually never understood on its own terms without the evolution of some large gestalt that specifies the normal range of natural dimensions (e.g. purpose, stages, etc.). Whatever gestalt is evolved, we understand much more than is given directly in the sentence. We understand the sentence in terms of the way these gestalts fit together, and only relative to such understandings do issues of truth arise.

Getting a "normal" understanding of the sentence in terms of its categories is defined by prototype.[17] Our understanding of an argument situation will involve viewing it simultaneously in terms of both of the "conversation" gestalt and the "war" gestalt. In both the metaphorical and the nonmetaphorical cases, our account of how we understand truth depends on our account of how we understand situations.

Understanding life in terms of a story involves highlighting certain participants and episodes while ignoring and hiding others. As the circumstances of our lives change, we constantly revise our life stories, seeking new coherence.[18] Most of this background structure will never be noted, since it is presupposed in so many of our daily activities and experiences. Most of our indirect understanding involves understanding one kind of entity or experience in terms of another kind – that is, understanding by way of metaphor. Since any such understanding is always partial, we have no access to "the whole truth" or to any definite account of reality;[19] thus truth will always depend partly on coherence. Classical realism focuses on physical reality rather than cultural or personal reality, but Lakoff and Johnson emphasize that social, political, economic, and religions institutions, and the human beings who function within them are no less real than trees, tables, or rocks. Human concepts do not correspond to inherent properties of things but only to interactional properties; meaning is always meaning to someone. According to the objectivist approach, myths and metaphors cannot be taken seriously because they are not objectively true. Metaphors and other kinds of poetic, fanciful, rhetorical, or figurative language can always be avoided in speaking objectively, and they should be avoided since their meanings are not clear and precise and do not fit reality in any obvious way. The myth of subjectivism, on the other hand, holds that when important issues arise, regardless of what others may say, our own senses and intuitions are our best guides. The most important things in our lives are our feelings, aesthetic sensibilities, moral practices, and spiritual awareness, and these are taken to be purely subjective. Art and poetry transcend rationality and objectivity, and put us in touch with the more important reality of our feelings and intuitions. We gain this awareness through our imagination rather than reason. The language of imagination, especially metaphor, is necessary for expressing the unique and most personally significant aspects of our experience. In matters of personal understanding, the ordinary agreed-upon meanings that words have will not do.[20] There are no objective and rational means for getting at our feelings, our aesthetic sensibilities, and religious intuitions.

The portions of our lives governed by objectivism and subjectivism vary greatly from person to person and from culture to culture. In Western culture, objectivism is by far the greater factor, claiming to govern, at least nominally, science, law, government, morality, business, economics, and scholarship. But objectivism is a myth.[21] Since the time of the Greeks, there has been in Western culture a tension between truth, on the one hand, and art, on the other – art being viewed as illusion and rhetorical make-believe. Although Aristotle's theory of how metaphor works[22] is the classic view, his claim that metaphor is able to induce insight has never been carried over into modern philosophical thought. The fear of metaphor and rhetoric in the empiricist tradition is a fear of subjectivism – a fear of emotion and the imagination. Words are viewed as having "proper meaning" in terms of which truths can be expressed. To use words metaphorically is taken by the objectivist tradition as using them in an improper sense, to stir up the imagination and, thereby, the emotions, and thus to lead us away from truth and toward illusion. The Romantic tradition, by embracing subjectivism, reinforced the dichotomy between truth and reason on the one hand, and imagination on the other. By giving up on rationality, the Romantics played into the hands of the myth of objectivism, whose power has continued to increase ever since. Lakoff and Johnson show how metaphor combines reason with imagination. In one of its aspects, imagination involves seeing one kind of thing in terms of another – as it happens in metaphorical thought, and metaphor is taken by them as imaginative understanding. Since the categories of our everyday thought are largely metaphorical, and since our everyday reasoning involves metaphorical entailment and inferences, ordinary rationality is imaginative by its very nature. Metaphor is one of our most important tools for trying to understand partially what cannot be understood totally; our feelings, aesthetic experiences, moral practices, and spiritual awareness.

Truth is relative to understanding, which means that there is no neutral standpoint from which to obtain absolute objective truth about anything. But this does not mean that there are no truths; rather it means only that truth is relative to our conceptual framework. The system is grounded on, and constantly tested by, our experiences and those of other members of our culture in their daily interactions with other people, and with our physical and cultural environments.[23] What the myths of objectivism and subjectivism miss is the way we understand the world through our interactions with it. What objectivism misses is the fact that understanding, and therefore truth, is necessarily relative to our conceptual frameworks, and that it cannot be treated in any absolute or neutral conceptual system. Objectivism also misses the fact that conceptual systems are metaphorical in nature and involve an imaginative understanding of one kind of things in terms of another. Truth does not form a comprehensive system but emerges from more or less local coherences. What subjectivism specifically misses is that our understanding, even our most imaginative understanding, is given in terms of a conceptual framework that is grounded in our successful functioning in our physical and cultural environments. It also misses the fact that metaphorical understanding involves metaphorical entailment, which is an imaginative form of rationality.[24]

The myth of objectivism has dominated Western culture, and in particular Western philosophy, from the Presocratics to the present day. The view that we have access to absolute and unconditional truth about the world is the cornerstone of the Western philosophical tradition. This myth of objectivity has flourished in both the rationalist and empiricist traditions, which in this respect differ only in their accounts of how we arrive at such absolute truth. By contrast, Lakoff and Johnson declare metaphor as essential to human understanding, and as a mechanism for creating new meaning and new realities in our lives. It puts them at odds with most of the Western philosophical traditions, which has regarded metaphor as an agent of subjectivism and as subversive to the quest for absolute truth. They conclude that the meaning of a sentence cannot be obtained from the meanings of its parts and the structure of the sentence. Rather, the meaning of a sentence is given in terms of a conceptual structure, and most of the conceptual structures of a natural language are metaphorical in nature. According to the objectivist account of meaning, a person comprehends the objective meaning of a sentence if he understands the conditions under which it could be true or false.[25] The objectivist tradition views semantics as the study of how linguistic expressions can fit the world directly, without the intervention of human understanding. This technique uses definition of truth in terms of "fitting the world," which is technically defined by conditions of satisfaction in a mathematical model, as it were. The objectivist approach to truth requires that meaning, too, be objective, that it exclude all subjective elements, i.e. anything peculiar to a particular context, culture, or mode of understanding. Meaning is thus taken as independent of use, for according to the objectivist myth, the world is made up of objects that have well-defined inherent properties, independent of any being who experiences them, and that there are fixed relations holding among them at any given time. These views support a building block theory of meaning. Logical positivists, like Carnap, attempted to carry out an objectivist program by trying to construct a universally applicable formal, logical, language that had all the building-block properties. Quine, reacting to such universalist claims, argued that each language has its own ontology built into it, and what counts as an object, property, or relation may vary from language to language. It is possible to maintain such a thesis of ontological relativity within the confines of the objectivist program without having any recourse to human understanding or cultural differences. This relativistic position gives up on the possibility of constructing a single, universally applicable, logical language into which all natural languages can be translated adequately. It clams, instead, that each natural language carves up what is in the world in different ways – always picking out objects and properties that are really there. But since different languages may have different ontologies built into them, there is no guarantee that any two languages will be commensurable.[26]

The study of the building-block structure, the inherent properties of the parts, and the relationships among them has traditionally been called grammar.[27] It follows from this view of linguistic expression as objects that grammar can be studied independently of meaning or human understanding.[28] This tradition is epitomized by the linguistics of Noam Chomsky, who has steadfastly maintained that grammar is a matter of pure form, independent of meaning or human understanding. On this account it is possible objectively to say what you mean, and communication failures are matters of subjective errors. Objectivists recognize, however, that a person may understand a sentence in a given context as meaning something other than its literal objective significance, and objectivists typically admit that any full account of understanding will have to account for these cases, too.[29] Exaggeration, understatement, hints, irony, and all figurative language, in particular, are understood as cases where a speaker says one thing and means something else. Lakoff and Johnson argue in the Kantian manner that an adequate account of our experience, our thought, and our language, requires viewing objects only as entities relative to our interactions with the world and our projections on it.[30] They view issues having to do with meaning in natural language, and with the way people understand both their language and their experience as empirical rather than matters of a priori philosophical assumption and argumentation. In the objectivist tradition, metaphor is seen as only marginally relevant to an account of truth,[31] yet we have found that metaphor is pervasive, not merely in our language, but in our conceptual system as well. Metaphor is one of the most basic mechanisms we have for understanding our experience.

Lakoff and Johnson realize that a lot of competent mathematicians, logicians, linguists, psychologists, and computer scientists have designed objectivist models for use in the human sciences. But they point out that what is left out in those accounts are the experimental bases of metaphors and, in particular, what these metaphors hide. The natural question, to ask then, is whether people actually think and act in terms of consistent sets of metaphors, although a special case where they do is in the formulation of scientific theories. It is, moreover, comforting to have a consistent view of the world, a clear set of expectations, and no conflict about what you should do. Having a basis for expectation and action is important for survival, but it is one thing to impose a single objectivist model on some restricted situation and to function in terms of that model; it is quite another to conclude that the model is an accurate reflection of reality. The reason that our conceptual systems have inconsistent metaphors for the same concepts is that there is no one metaphor that will do. Each metaphor gives us some understanding of one or another aspect of the concepts, but in doing so hides others. Thus, to operate only in terms of a consistent set of metaphors is to suppress many aspects of reality. Successful functioning in our daily lives, therefore, requires a constant shifting of metaphors. Current formal techniques in computer science show promise of providing representations of *inconsistent* sets of metaphors. This could lead to an understanding of the way people reason and function in terms of coherent but inconsistent metaphorical concepts. The objectivist program is incapable of giving a satisfying account of human understanding, the nature of human rationality, human language and communication, the human sciences, moral and aesthetic values, scientific understanding, and the way in which the foundations of mathematics have a basis in human understanding. Interactional properties, experimental gestalts, and metaphorical concepts seem to be necessary for the adequate treatment of these issues.[32]

Subjectivist positions maintain that meaning is private, that experience is altogether holistic, that meanings and contexts have no natural structure, and that they cannot, therefore, be adequately represented. Against this, objectivism's focus on truth and factual knowledge is based on the importance of such knowledge for successful functioning in our physical and cultural environment. Lakoff and Johnson conclude that truth is always relative to understanding and based on a nonuniversal conceptual framework. Where objectivity is reasonable, it does not require an absolute, universally valid point of view, for being objective is always relative to a conceptual system and a set of cultural values. Reasonable objectivity might be impossible when there are conflicting conceptual systems or conflicting cultural values, and it is important to be able to admit this and to recognize when it occurs. According to the experimentalist myth, scientific knowledge is still possible, and the result would be a more reasonable assessment of what scientific knowledge is and what its limitations are.[33] What legitimately motivates subjectivism is the awareness that meaning is always meaning to someone, and that what is significant to one person depends not on rational knowledge alone, but on past experiences, values, feelings, and intuitive insights. Meaning is not cut and dried, it is a matter of the imagination and coherence. Experimentalism diverges from subjectivism in its rejection of the Romantic idea that imaginative understanding is completely unconstrained.[34] The experimentalist myth views interaction with the environment as involving mutual change. When people who are talking to each other do not share the same culture, knowledge, values, and assumptions, mutual understanding can be especially difficult. But such understanding is still possible through the negotiation of meaning. To negotiate meaning with someone, you have to become aware of and respect both the differences in your backgrounds and where these differences are important. Such metaphorical imagination is a crucial skill in creating rapport and in communicating the nature of unshared experience. This skill consists in large measure in the ability to bend your world view and adjust the way you categorize your experience. Problems of mutual understanding are not exotic; they arise in all extended conversations where understanding is important.[35] Where it really counts, meaning is almost never communicated according to the "conduit" metaphor, that is, where one person transmits a fixed, clear proposition to another by means of expressions in a common language, where both parties have all the relevant common knowledge, assumptions, values, etc. In all interesting cases, meaning is negotiated; you gradually figure out what you have in common, what is safe to talk about, how you can communicate unshared experience or create a shared vision. With enough flexibility in bending your world view, and with luck, skill, and charity, you may achieve some mutual understanding.[36]

Notes

[1] George Lakoff and Mark Johnson, *Metaphors We Live By,* Chicago, IL: The University of Chicago Press, 1980, p. 3.

[2] *Ibid.,* p. 8.

[3] *Ibid.,* p. 44.

[4] *Ibid.,* p. 51.

[5] *Ibid.,* p. 57.

[6] *Ibid.,* p. 67.

[7] *Ibid.,* p. 101.

[8] *Ibid.,* p. 138.

[9] *Ibid.,* p. 145.

[10] *Ibid.,* p. 146.

[11] *Ibid.,* p. 154.

[12] *Ibid.,* p. 158.

[13] *Ibid.,* p. 159.

[14] *Ibid.,* p. 164.

[15] *Ibid.,* p. 165.

[16] *Ibid.,* p. 166.

[17] *Ibid.,* p. 169.

[18] *Ibid.,* p. 175.

[19] *Ibid.,* p. 180.

[20] *Ibid.,* p. 188.

[21] *Ibid.,* p. 189.

[22] Rhetoric 1410 b.

[23] Lakoff and Johnson, *Metaphors We Live By,* p. 194.

[24] *Ibid.*

[25] *Ibid.,* p. 198.

[26] *Ibid.,* p. 203.

[27] *Ibid.,* p. 204.

[28] *Ibid.,* p. 205.

[29] cf H. P. Grice, "Meaning," *Philosophical Review,* 66 (1957), pp. 377-88.

[30] Lakoff and Johnson, *Metaphors We Live By,* p. 210.

[31] *Ibid.*

[32] *Ibid.,* p. 222.

[33] *Ibid.*, p. 227.
[34] *Ibid.*, p. 228.
[35] *Ibid.*, p. 231.
[36] *Ibid.*, p. 232.

Chapter Fifteen

Kittay's Theory of Metaphor

Kittay shows how philosophy has, in turn, rejected and embraced metaphor. Plato's disapproval prevailed in the more strictly philosophical texts, and Locke's denunciation of figurative language set the tone for the philosophical disregard for metaphor – a position in which rationalists and empiricists were united. Only the philosophers associated with the Romantic tradition realized its importance.[1] To its distracters it was mere embellishment, the swaying of passions, while to its champions its lack of utility, its sheer capacity for delight, was reason for its privileged place in language. Today, metaphor is experiencing a revitalized interest within philosophy, especially among analytic philosophers, who value metaphor not mainly for its affective and rhetorical efficiency but for its cognitive contributions. This tradition goes back to Aristotle who stressed the cognitive importance of metaphor, in particular metaphor based on analogy. Metaphor provides us with a way of learning something new about the world and about how the world may be perceived and understood. He and the scholastic tradition relied on the coincidence of language and reality. Distinctions in language were seen as captivating ontological distinctions,[2] and discovering analogical uses of language can help us to discover analogical states of reality. Kittay emphasizes the indispensability of analogical thinking for diverse areas of cognition and its relation to metaphorical thinking. Various hypotheses are at once generated analogically and metaphorically from current conceptualizations of the world, and metaphors result in placing one object in two perspectives simultaneously. The view of language and thought according to which metaphor appears as

ornament or comparison presupposes the conception of mind as a
passive receptacle of perceptions. These perceptions, when brought
together through proper rules of inference and logical deduction, result
in knowledge only when not adulterated by the imperfect but
indispensable vehicle of language. Instead, we need to understand
language as an expressive medium that allows us to say what we think
in language, just as the artist expresses himself in paint.[3] Still, it is the
view of language as conduit for our thought that has largely prevailed
in the dominant philosophical tradition.

Thus, the conception of thought and language necessary to move
beyond a restricted view of metaphor requires an understanding of
mind as active and creatively engaged in the forming of percepts and
concepts, as well as in unifying the diversity of the given. Metaphor is
the linguistic realization of this variety, since it does not record
preexisting similarities in things; rather, it is the linguistic process by
which we bring together diverse thoughts and thereby reform our
perception of the world. In turning away from logical positivism,
analytic philosophers have become impressed with the importance of
metaphor. Models in science must be understood as extended
metaphors – not literally true but useful representations of phenomena,
which often lead to fruitful theoretic conceptions and new empirical
discoveries. Hesse[4] showed that models are crucial for providing
theories with productive power, and that they figured not only
incidentally in the context of discovery but cognitively in the context
of justification. Models play a cognitive role in science, and yet they,
like the metaphors of our language, are obviously false and
unverifiable.[5] Kittay stresses the bearing of metaphor on creativity in
language and science, on paradigm shifts in the history of science, and
on change in meaning. Thus, the very criteria by which metaphor was
dismissed as meaningless or non-cognitive are now considered
questionable. There is the recognition of prima facie meaningfulness
of metaphorical language and of the evident importance of models in
science. Once it is realized that science is a human activity rather than
the repository of ultimate truths, and that cognition is shaping our
conceptions of the world, the creative play of metaphor is seen as
characteristic not only of poetry but also of science. When we come to
realize that language is a chief element in world-making, metaphor
illuminates the creative contribution of the mind to knowledge, and its
study forces basic revisions on our views on language and thought.
Kittay stresses that since metaphors do have meaning, they call for a

semantic account. but she admits that such a semantic account does not give us a complete comprehension of the ways in which we understand metaphor, and that this must, therefore, be supplemented by pragmatic considerations. Since all language is understood contextually, there is no room for a rigid distinction between the semantic and the pragmatic in our understanding of metaphor.

Kittay's theory of metaphor is perspectival: a language speaker uses one linguistically articulate domain to gain an understanding of another experimental or conceptual domain.[6] The problem is that gaining such a "perspective understanding" is itself a metaphorical, i.e. non-literal, notion that becomes self defeating in a scientific theory. Unless language is structured in specifiable ways, metaphor would have no cognitive meaning. Concepts are not free-floating;[7] they emerge from the articulation of contrasts and affinities in the expressive medium. The key to Kittay's holding metaphor cognitive is her contention that, in metaphor, two concepts are operative simultaneously. Black[8] has demonstrated that a metaphor is not an isolated term, but a sentence, and that it involves not only two subjects but a system of associated commonplaces. Kittay follows Saussure and Black in holding all language contextually and systematically related. Literal comparison takes place within fixed common or given categories, whereas comparisons in metaphor and simile cross categorical boundaries. An expression is not metaphorical in an absolute sense, but only relative to a set of beliefs and linguistic usages that may change through place and time; it is relative to a given linguistic community.[9] Since in metaphor a new perspective is being achieved, it is only in a sentence that we can tell whether a given word is used literally or metaphorically. It is a unit of discourse in which some conceptual or conversational incongruity emerges. Metaphors involve some sort of rule breaking that takes place not arbitrarily, but only in a certain specifiable fashion. Yet Kittay's perspectivism remains analogical and often does not permit her to decide what terms are to be understood metaphorically and which are to be taken literally.[10] This is also why her notion of metaphor is said to have a referent only anaphorically, i.e. in an indirect fashion.

Kittay emphasizes that her understanding of metaphor requires that a label functions not in isolation, but as belonging to a family. She defines this set of alternatives in terms of a semantic field; a word's meaning (e.g. "green") is partly determined by its position in the semantic field. But no one statement will capture the full meaning of metaphor and, while we may give an exposition of metaphor, we cannot paraphrase it completely. Metaphor is the primary way in which we accommodate new experience, and it is at the source of our capacity to learn and at the center of our creative thinking. Kittay argues that how we identify metaphor has not been adequately dealt with because writers have not correctly identified the unit of discourse that constitutes a metaphor. This unit is not merely an isolated sentence but a whole text, yet what constitutes such a text is, in turn, problematic. To view metaphors as deviant is to condemn a substantial part of both ordinary and specialized discourse as deviant. Speakers are hardly aware of making default assumptions, and they become conscious of them only when something occurs that jars them, such as the use of "she" rather than "he" when the context does not indicate the gender of the subject. Since variations of such default assumptions are continuous, when physicists today speak of the atom, they do not mean atom in the sense understood by Democritus. Considerations such as these brings to the fore questions of analicity in language, and the validity of the distinction between a dictionary and an encyclopedia. A given utterance is not simply composed by one part that is to be understood metaphorically, while the remainder terms are taken literally. Kittay stresses that even literal statements are highly context-dependent, and that for any given literal interpretation of an utterance we make implicit or explicit use of context. Thus, in fairy tales, we have to suspend disbelief and accept a world picture substantially different from our usual one. A metaphorical interpretation involves a more radical shift in the language use than when we merely revise or suspend our empirical beliefs with some concomitant semantic change. The reorganization that the conceptual oddity forces may also, in the end, direct us to a new conception of the world – either to new theories of the natural world or to a new vision of the world as reflected in a poem or novel.

Davidson[11] claims that both the idea of metaphorical meaning and the concomitant belief that metaphors possess a special cognitive content are mistaken. His argument is that meaning is context free and that aspects of language that are not context free are pragmatic, not semantic. Metaphorical interpretation is context-bound, and there is no meaning of metaphorical utterance beyond the literal meaning of the terms employed. Kittay, however, points out that speech act theory has taught us that contextual considerations can be systematic and, hence rule governed. Virtually any word, phrase, sentence, or group of sentences could reveal metaphorical meaning under right circumstances and in the right context. The set of background assumptions to which even the most evidently literal statements are relative, are just those plain matters that escape our notice, but which nonetheless are operative in our understanding of language.[12] It is not the case that the literal meaning is always the preferred one, since for most words in the language the number of possible meanings is indefinitely large, and much of our language is polysemiotic, as even a cursory examination of a good dictionary will reveal. Any context-free meaning is no more than an abstraction which, at most, can have only methodical significance. By investigating metaphor we learn that not only does a word have meaning in the context of a sentence, but that a sentence, too, lacks definite meaning outside its linguistic and situation context.[13] Kittay believes metaphor to be primary and considers literal language, with its referential and logical impetus, to be a pruning of this expressive medium, just as conscious thought is a constraint and a pruning of the rich resources of the unconscious.[14] It seems, however, that were it not for man's being conscious, it would make no sense to ascribe to him unconsciousness, and that lacking literal meaning, there would be no metaphor either. When a term is read metaphorically, a new sense is generated, but this would be pointless without the original literal meaning. Kittay takes the primary function of language to be not merely referential and communicative, but expressive, delineative, and articulative. Metaphor is the means available within natural language to extend such expressive capacity in often radical ways. We use metaphor when the resources of literal language are inadequate to articulate significant distinctions or unities.[15]

A sentence can carry information only if it is understood relative to the hearer's knowledge of our general, background, default assumptions. Until words combine, they are only partly "digitized" (in Dretske's[16] terminology), and such information is left in analogical form. But digitalization can take place in indefinitely many ways, and that some information remains in analogical form is the source of multiple ambiguities. This is a major reason why metaphor will not do in the formation of scientific theories, including the theory of language and of metaphor as proposed by Kittay. Contextual considerations remain secondary to language meaning, to meaning differentiation and even to the expressive capacities of language. When words combine, their informative content is selectively pruned so that the resulting image is coherent and appropriately informative. But ultimately the context cannot provide a term with contrasts and affinities not already provided by the language. What counts as a shift in the specification of meaning, and what as a transference, depends primarily on semantic, and only secondarily on pragmatic, considerations. Since metaphor involves systems and not just isolated ideas, the first step in interpreting a metaphor requires us to recognize that the background assumptions presumed by the context of an utterance is in conflict with such first-order interpretation. But to say that metaphorical meaning is a second-order meaning is to leave much of the first order meaning intact.

Kittay's strategy is to expand the sway of metaphor, for what is required to constitute second-order discourse is not a single, sufficient condition but a set of alternative conditions. Often, we will use metaphor when there is no distinct form or even a distinctly articulated semantic field for the topic. Kittay realizes that metaphorical analogies are asymmetric for the reason that one side of the analogy has a privileged status relative to the other. Yet she denies the primacy of literal meaning, claiming that first-order meaning need not necessarily be literal since it ultimately never is. It is language's adaptability in applying to fictive instances that is exploited in its accommodation to changing circumstances. The default assumptions are altered and there is a suspension of disbelief. Some metaphors, particularly poetic ones, leave the domain of the topic somewhat indeterminate, since we have here a figure operating on a figure. The metaphor may reveal more than was intended by its author, for while he may have intended one contrast, the hearer or reader may restore as many as will result in interesting relations. The cognitive rewards of making metaphors lie primarily in the spinning out of metaphorical implications made possible by the conceptual connections effected within semantic fields.[17] Kittay concludes that metaphor may violate certain linguistic rules without forfeiting the goal of mutual understanding. The use of metaphor exhibits the kind of creativity that consists in discovering the possibilities implicit in our linguistic system not yet discovered and known. Creativity in metaphor consists in the use of existing structure to forge new ones. She claims that metaphorical use of language is sometimes more valid than is literal use. The violation of conceptual constraints brings about a new conceptualization, a new way of conceiving some content domain. Indeed, most interesting metaphors involve a great deal of strain in language and thought. While not all judgments of similarity exhibit asymmetry, metaphor and simile always do, and often there is only a thin line between a metaphor and the creation of a fictional entity. That is why the temptation to regard metaphor as semantically deviant is strong and persistent. There is no apparent limit to possible innovative metaphorical uses.

Kittay emphasizes that, just as we require a relational theory of word meaning, we require a relational theory of sentence meaning. The language speakers share an understanding of what counts as a salient differentiation within the conceptual frame of language.[18] Natural language depends on signs that are types and not merely tokens. Without its relation to other specifically linguistic entities, the term cannot function in a signifying fashion as a relation to the nonlinguistic entity. The poet who attempts to express and communicate a unique, perceptual experience, an imaginative vision, charts out a new content domain. Likewise, when the new sciences of electricity, magnetism, genetics, and nuclear biology emerged, they were exploring previously inarticulated content domains. We identify a phenomenon as distinct prior to gaining an understanding of it. Using Dretske's terminology, we can say that a domain not articulated can at best provide us with analogic information. Or using epistemic concepts, we may conclude that we have *knowledge of* without yet having *knowledge that*, i.e. we have knowledge of *x* without realizing that *y* may be predicated of *x*. To acquire digitized information or prepositional knowledge, we require that the domain be articulated. The notion of a content domain may also be formulated as a related set of beliefs, both actual and possible, attainable to a given language community.[19] A. Lehrer[20] suggests that, rather than regarding semantic fields as mosaics, we should see them as composed of terms whose application to a content domain centers on certain foci. In such a model, gaps and overlaps are to be expected and, while each concept or term has a clear focus, it may, nevertheless, have indeterminate boundaries. Kittay shows that no matter how far-fetched the examples might be, it will always be possible to conjure up some content in which we suspend our usual default assumptions to allow what otherwise would seem incongruous and anomalous contrasts.[21]

For linguist philosophers who take the central questions of semantics to be questions of truth conditions, synonymy plays a central role in the theory of meaning. But if the sense of a term is a function of the way in which that term relates to other conceptually related terms, then questions of sense are not reducible to questions of truth conditions, and meaning is simply that which fixes reference. Instead of holding that the meaning of a sentence is dependent on its truth conditions, the truth conditions are dependent on how the meanings of the terms are established. They are due to contrastive relations with other terms, and among these various relations synonymy plays only a minor role. Kittay emphasizes that synonymy is always relative to a given context and, following Lyons, she adopts a broad and encompassing notion of context. This involves the tacit acceptance by both speaker and listener of all the relevant connections, beliefs, and presuppositions taken for granted by members of a speech community.[22] Kittay's default assumptions deny the possibility of absolute synonymy and replace it with partial synonymy. She speaks of the "furniture of our mind" to illustrate the weakly cohesive set to which such relations belong, yet, at the same time, she admits that the various relations she discusses cannot be regarded as definite.[23] This renders her theory of metaphor inoperative as a theory – by turning it into a metaphor. It amounts to taking metaphorical understanding as the model for scientific knowledge because considered as a theory, her analysis of metaphor is literally false and logically inconsistent.

Notes

[1] Eva Feder Kittay, *Metaphor, Its Cognitive Force and Linguistic Structure,* Oxford: Claredon Press, 1987, p. 1.

[2] J. F. Ross, *Portraying Analogy,* Cambridge: Cambridge University Press, 1981.

[3] *Ibid.*

[4] M. B. Hesse, *Models and Metaphors in Science,* Notre Dame: Notre Dame University Press, 1966, pp. 157-177.

[5] Kittay, *Metaphor,* p. 8.

[6] *Ibid.,* p. 14.

[7] Joseph Grünfeld, *Conceptual Relevance,* Amsterdam: B. R. Grüner Publishing Co., 1989.

[8] M. Black, *Models and Metaphors,* Ithaca, NY: Cornell University Press, 1962.

[9] Kittay, *Metaphor,* p. 20.

[10] *Ibid.,* p. 25.

[11] D. Davidson, "What Metaphors Mean," in *Inquiries into Truth and Interpretation,* Oxford: Oxford University Press, 1984.

[12] Kittay, *Metaphor*, p. 106.

[13] *Ibid.*, p. 115.

[14] *Ibid.*, p. 120.

[15] *Ibid.*, p. 125

[16] F. I. Dretske, *Knowledge and the Flow of Information*, Cambridge, Mass.: MIT Press, 1983.

[17] Kittay, *Metaphor*, p. 172.

[18] *Ibid.*, p. 216.

[19] *Ibid.*, p. 228 n10.

[20] A. Lehrer, *Semantic Fields and Lexical Structure*, Amsterdam, North-Holland, 1974.

[21] Kittay, Metaphor, p. 234.

[22] J. Lyons, *Introduction into Theoretical Linguistics*, London: Cambridge University Press, 1968.

[23] Kittay, *Metaphor*, p. 247.

Chapter Sixteen

Hausman's Metaphorical Realism

Hausman holds that the use of metaphor reflects a strong sense of innovation or creativity.[1] The importance of metaphor extends beyond literary criticism to the understanding and interpretation of nonverbal arts as well. He considers metaphors to be integral not only to visual art and music, but also to philosophical discourse and scientific theorizing.[2] But, in this manner, the very distinction between literal and metaphorical use of language is blurred. The metaphorical structure of nonverbal arts is illustrated by Hausman in paintings that show us obvious distortions of conventional perspectives. He realizes, however, that the paradox of creativity is not amenable to ready resolution; indeed, he believes that the paradox of metaphorical discourse cannot be resolved in principle.[3] Still, he insists that there are no substitute expressions for metaphor, for whereas analogies are based on comparison, metaphor introduces new significance into the world. While the distinction between literal and metaphorical expressions may not be hard and fast, we need to acknowledge that the function of some expressions can be distinguished as figurative from others that are not figurative. Some metaphors create unique insights, and these are irreducible with respect to the antecedents in their context. Hausman's claim is that this amounts to regarding them as creative constituents of the world.[4] Metaphors, and more generally, works of art, cannot be expressed without loss of significance in paraphrase or analysis. The metaphor depends not only on similarities but also on dissimilarities, and it is the role of disparities that extends the significance of metaphors. If creativity is merely making explicit what is already implicit, there would be no generating in Hausman's strong anti-Aristotelian sense.

Searle has challenged the suggestion that some metaphors create new similarities.[5] Hausman, on the other hand, holds that Searle's notion of plausibility is based on a rationalism requiring explanations to relate to something that is already antecedent and familiar. Hausman argues that if such an assumption governs what is plausible, then no view that advocates created newness has a chance. What is new, he maintains, is a gestalt-like family resemblance in which the outcome is more than a mere perspective.[6] But when we say that some expression or artwork is creative, we thereby indicate that we are unable adequately to explain it, and Hausman's "realism" is designed to account for this. He likens new creations to children who have personalities of their own, and whose particular combination of characteristics is unique.[7] What renders a person unique, however, is that *we* take interest in him as a person, that is, that we consider not only what makes him similar to other people, but also what makes him different from them. Hausman cannot explain how autonomous intelligibility is supposed to work because the future system or the subsequent changes in the aesthetic tradition are never known in advance; they are only discoverable by hindsight. A metaphor's intelligibility is related to its components as something like a family resemblance, and Hausman's realism turns out to be not much more than that. He emphasizes that metaphors express meaning through a tension, that is, some form of opposition, strain, or conflict of meaning within themselves or their context. As used here, such tension does not specifically refer to a psychological but to a structural condition. A metaphor brings together different kinds of meaning units, and they may cover expressions that are literally false. While the expressions may join incompatible and even inconsistent standard meanings, they nevertheless interact to say something not otherwise said under standard interpretation.[8] Part of what is needed in generating novel meaning is the tension in which it is seen as something that is strange, remote, or out of its category. But since the metaphor does not present sheer nonsense, it is at once standard and nonstandard.

It is crucial to Hausman's conception of metaphor to avoid understanding consequent meanings as paraphrases that could have been possible to formulate prior to the metaphorical statement. He argues that our inability to find a property common to all members of a family does not necessarily mean that there is no identity or coherence that enables us to recognize the family. A metaphor is comparable to the overall character that identifies a family.[9] As a linguistic item, a metaphor does not refer to a class of things already recognizable as a cluster of resemblances. Rather, it posits an intelligible cluster of clashing meanings, and that is how the new significance of a metaphor becomes unique. At the same time he emphasizes the paradoxical nature of metaphors and the difficulty of understanding what is radically new. Because understanding is tracing things to their antecedents, such knowledge and what is really new seems incompatible. The various theories either explicitly or implicitly treat metaphorical meaning or sense in terms of other, antecedent meanings or senses. Created metaphors are regarded by Hausman as naming or reference-fixing expressions that "give birth" to the reference they fix. In this manner, he is convinced, metaphors constitute reality, for they can be correct or faithful, and in terms of such expectations they can "convey" or "generate" insights, as Black[10] has pointed out. But Hausman goes beyond Black in insisting on conditions for metaphor other than the cognitive framework itself. He denies that appropriateness can be ultimately justified by mere acceptability of further linguistic data or perspectives to provide the larger system with the needed objectivity. He believes that creative metaphors take a fundamental responsibility for language as a whole, making language responsive to something independent of itself. But from the fact that creative metaphors bring about changes in the conventions of accepted language,[11] it does not follow that they are literally part of the world. His referents are said to be unique events, moments, or centers of relevance but this does not establish their extraconceptual or extralinguistic nature. The individuals Hausman assumes to exists are not determinably characterizable objects but merely foci of constraints on the meanings of intentional objects. He wants the conditions at issue to function independently of thought itself while using them as instruments for creation and discovery, yet the experimental encounter need not signify more than a cultural consensus that proves some metaphors as faithful and others as less faithful or appropriate.

Hausman admits that apart from the network of meanings, a metaphor would have neither the sense nor the reference it, in fact, does have.[12] Given the strong sense of "creativity" on which he insists, his realism is designed to explain why there is a continuity of reference through time. He argues that such novel referents enter the world as new children enter their families. Each takes on character-istics from his or her family and, in turn, contributes to its context. He takes seriously Peirce's suggestion that individuals are determinate without necessarily being spatial entities. He identifies new creative metaphors as centers of relevance for qualities, but realizes that the idea of relevance to extralinguistic conditions fails to ascribe truth value to metaphor. It merely implies that creative metaphors are performative instances of meaning, and thus they are said to have a force of generating or bringing something into being.[13] However, to name something as unique is not to bring it literally into existence. Metaphors may invite us to view the primary object in a different way, but the changes do not occur in the object itself, only in the viewing of it. While he realizes that a metaphor's reference-fixing is not itself true of false, he makes much of its being relevant or irrelevant and his realism is designed to account for this. What the metaphor designates as a matter of relevance constitutes the inclusion and exclusion of senses. These, however, are not future attributions, as Hausman claims,[14] since they are invariably made by hindsight. While he considers them conditions of intelligibility that render future growth possible, all this is never realized in advance. In the domain of art, likewise, what comes to be accepted as masterpieces and thus standards for future development, is invariably a product of historical judgment. Creativity can never be recognized *per se*, as Hausman has it, but only relative to a tradition, and all that metaphors finally accomplish is a modification, however radical, of discourse or style.

Discussing nonverbal metaphors, Hausman admits that we cannot say what their particular constraints are because we have no ready-made language for this purpose. We have to discuss them in a medium to which they do not belong.[15] But what he defines as visual or musical metaphors presupposes language. Criticism, likewise, can accomplish its task only by being at least more literal than its subject matter. He focuses on the metaphorical character of all interpretation, and while he admits the epistemological dependence of a work of art on the observer, he wants to preserve its ontological autonomy. Works of art, however, do not impose themselves on us; they have to be appreciated, and if they fail to be appreciated, they cease to be works of art. The constraints encountered are due to language and tradition, they are historical in character, and known only by hindsight. We can learn whether a metaphor is creative only by its consequences which may be long in coming. A metaphor or work of art can surprise us, but what surprises us is relative to what we have come to expect. In spite of his "realism," Hausman admits that, in the arts, significance is the outcome of an interplay of attention.[16] He identifies objective reality as what is independent (at least in part) of interpretation and, therefore, public and common to all. But metaphor and art do not refer to the world in this straightforward fashion in terms of standard conventional contexts. On the contrary, meanings are brought together that appear strange in relation to the literally understood. Hausman is unable to spell out the nature of this controlling focus; he considers relevance to be like a gravitational pull that remains open to changes that may occur in the future,[17] yet he fails to recognize its historical character.

He points out that the aesthetic and nonaesthetic functions of art are not distinct; because what is said crucially depends on how it is said. The "truth," however, that art or metaphor convey is not literal, for it is neither a correspondence to fact nor a full adherence to established language or style. "Truth" is thus given by Hausman the same weak, metaphorical sense that he ascribes to reality. Since neither is in principle subject to verification, they remain undecidable and subjective. This is the price he has to pay for his strong sense of creativity. A unique object cannot be exhaustively described because this is what we mean by being unique, yet if we adopt Hausman's strong sense of originality, the wonder is that we are able to identify it at all. He demands that identity be more than mere internal coherence but is unable to specify the additional constraints. The metaphorical structure he ascribes to reality lacks a discernible consistency to render it adequately coherent. He wants to make referents at least partly independent of thought, but what he calls "real" has to be created and discovered at the same time.[18] He admits that he cannot justify the validity of such constraints, but he believes that his own weak realism coheres better with everyday experiences. Yet he realizes, at the same time, the paradoxical character of individuals that are said to be created and discovered. Such are the consequences of his strong sense of creation *ex nihilo*. A novel style or a striking metaphor are creative only relative to a given medium or language, and neither do works of genius transcend their specific culture. Originality in writing, painting, or composing is always relative to a tradition, and its constraints are due to social convention. When an insight provided by a metaphor or work of art is said to be relevant to the world, it is really a social reality shaped by specific historical conventions we are talking about. What is interpreted, therefore, crucially depends on who is doing the interpreting and when. Nonverbal metaphors are relative not only to their own artistic traditions, but also to the language into which they are being translated and in which they are being discussed. They do not literally form part of the world, but are merely a mode in which the world is being perceived and represented. They are only a manner of speaking and of depicting reality, and while they may contribute to evolving intelligibility and advance novel understanding, they remain tradition-bound, and that is how they are not arbitrary. Creativity in the arts is not ex nihilo; the artist does not literally create a new world, but only a manner of speaking, depicting, or composing. Metaphors are a primary way of identifying and describing novelty, yet it does not follow from this that the world is literally a metaphor or a work of art.

Notes

[1] Carl R. Hausman, *Metaphor and Art,* Cambridge: Cambridge University Press, 1989, p. ix.

[2] *Ibid.*, p. 8.

[3] *Ibid.*, p. 10.

[4] *Ibid.*, p. 24.

[5] John Searle, "Metaphor," in *Expression and Meaning,* Cambridge: Cambridge University Press, 1979, pp. 76-116.

[6] Hausman, *Metaphor and Art*, p. 45.

[7] *Ibid.*, p. 107.

[8] *Ibid.*, p. 65

[9] *Ibid.*, p. 79.

[10] Max Black, "More about Metaphors," in *Models and Metaphors: Studies in Language and Philosophy,* Ithaca, NY: Cornell University Press, 1962, p. 41.

[11] Hausman, *Metaphor and Art.*, p. 89.

[12] *Ibid.*, p. 104.

[13] *Ibid.*, p. 114.

[14] *Ibid.*, p. 115.

[15] *Ibid.*, p. 119.

[16] *Ibid.*, p. 137.

[17] *Ibid.*, p. 144.

[18] *Ibid.*, p. 185.

DECONSTRUCTION

Chapter Seventeen

Deconstructing Deconstruction

Ellis points out that the very language of criticism has been influenced by deconstruction: talk of privileged ideas and of demystification is no longer restricted to deconstructionists.[1] But deconstructionists have generally reacted with hostility and even outrage to any serious criticism of deconstruction, and thus to any possibility of an exchange with their intellectual opponents. Given that kind of reaction, it is almost inevitable that any response is aimed not at the argument that has been made, but at the credentials and motives of opponents. Scholars who have discussed deconstruction in a critical way have generally elicited the response from its advocates that what they discuss is not, in fact, deconstruction, because any statement or logical analysis of what deconstruction is sins against its nature: it cannot be described and stated as other positions can. It is claimed that deconstruction cannot be discussed using tools of reason and logical analysis because it functions in a different way, both embodying and requiring a different logic, a kind of alternative or "other" logic. At first sight, to say that a different kind of logic has been established is to make a large and potentially very exciting claim. Its advocates, nevertheless, seem more content to use it than to present it explicitly, and reference to their new logic occurs mostly when deconstructive writings are objected to as incoherent or illogical. Yet a logic must work in some way, and it must be possible to describe that operation. By deconstructing the either/or logic of noncontradiction that dominates the Western tradition, Derrida's writings attempt to elaborate an "other" logic. But if *all* the positions concerned are equally uninteresting or mistaken, what is gained is not genuine sophistication but instead only an appearance of complexity. Binary logic is needed to characterize deconstructive logic, and when it is claimed that Derrida must be judged and evaluated by different logical standards, standards uniquely appropriate to him, there is no explanation of just what these standards are and how they are to be justified. If this were allowed to stand, neither debate nor evaluation of different viewpoints would be at all possible. This claim, moreover, regularly breaks down as advocates abandon it in order to discuss Derrida in relation to other thinkers, and use terms and procedures to discuss him that drop the claim for a separate linguistic and logical world.[2]

The assumption inevitably seems to be that rational analysis is inherently an inappropriate and unfair means of approaching deconstruction. This no longer is an attempt to demonstrate a specific alternative logic for deconstruction but, instead, a general attack on clear systematic argument. The positions seem to borrow the traditional attitudes of mysticism and other forms of irrationalism, yet it should be noted that most other aspects of what deconstructionists do and say are quite consistent with the traditional positions. Advocates see no problem in characterizing deconstruction correctly in opposition to an incorrect account by opponents, and all of this tends to throw doubt on the claim that deconstruction is a position that cannot be stated, or that any attempt to state it must, of necessity, be reductive and distorting. And so the claim that deconstruction is a special case, not to be judged or discussed by rational argument or ordinary logic, is a claim that is neither explained nor really consistently believed and acted upon by those who make it. Derrida observes that the Western tradition has regarded writing as inferior to speech and as mere representation of speech that was one stage removed from the essence of language. He argues that the reverse should be the case[3] and that, far from being a system advanced to record the already existing phenomena of language, writing is more critical to language than speech itself. Ellis points out, however, that traditional emphasis on written texts inevitably invokes a limited ethnocentric perspective, since it restricts study to those cultures and languages with a long written tradition like our own. Indeed, it is easier to see in Derrida's position not a correction of ethnocentrism but instead a determined reassertion of it that Saussure sought to correct and overcome. Speech quite clearly existed long before the invention of writing, and there still exist languages that are spoken but not written, whereas there are no natural languages that are written without being spoken. Children everywhere, of course, learn to speak before they are able to write.

What Derrida's argument really is concerned with is a much more familiar issue: the relation of words to things, signs to references, or, in its most traditional formulation, language to reality. Logocentrism, as Derrida calls the error he wants to eradicate and overcome; is not about the priority of speech over writing but about the relationship of words to their referents.[4] Since his intention is to demonstrate the shortcomings of logocentrism rather than to develop an alternative, Derrida is effectively prevented from focusing on the choice between many possible alternatives to logocentrism. The first thing that is likely to be said is that the error of logocentrism consists in subscribing to a belief in the "metaphysics of presence." As portrayed by Derrida, the logocentric system always assigns the origin of truth to the logos – to the spoken word, to the voice of reason the voice of God.[5] There is a strong tendency for Derrida's advocates to object that a demand for clarity begs the question at issue and violates the spirit of the deconstructive enterprise. Logocentrism here turns out to be much the same as the more familiar *essentialism*, the belief that words simply label real categories of meaning existing independently of language. A belief in immutable categories of meaning involves a fixation on the words of the particular language spoken by the believer, which he mistakes for the categories of the "real" world. We can only wonder what a "natural" and direct relationship between speech and meaning would be, for it is obvious enough that the actual phonemic shape of speech is arbitrary and conventional. The logocentric error is the illusion that reality and its ultimate categories are directly present to the mind passed on by language without being shaped or altered by it in any way whatsoever. It allows the terms of a given language to become so prominent in one's thinking that one can neither conceive of any alternative to them nor of any analysis that might question their coherence and sufficiency. One will inevitably come to believe that the words of that language reflect the meaning structure of the world.

Ellis points out that if the logocentric error were stated in any clear way, it would be far too obviously an unoriginal discovery. The belief of deconstructonists that they are attacking a superstition that still beguiles everyone seems quite out of touch with the reality of twentieth century debate in the theory of language. Deconstruction must find a prevalent unthinking belief to explode, for if it cannot, the special character of what it aspires to is rendered impossible.[6] He emphasizes that to pronounce something "problematic" is not a conclusion nor is it an intellectual achievement, for when we have done so, all we have accomplished is to point the way to a need for more thought and analysis of the issues involved. Derrida's approach does not permit investigating alternatives to his own rejection of logocentrism. Wittgenstein, for one, has shown that we decide that a mark is meaningless *neither* by determining that it has no reference, *nor* by looking at its own internal structure, but rather when we abandon any possibility of its belonging to an organized sequence of other signs in a language convention. Saussure, likewise, rejected the notion that words simply reflect ideas by diagnosing two ways in which linguistic signs are arbitrary. First, the particular phonetic shape of a word is arbitrary, and the concept *dog* in English could have been signaled by another combination of phonetic sounds without changing its meaning. But Saussure went on to say that the *concept itself* is an arbitrary creation of a language and does not necessarily exist outside that language. Since the facts of reality are infinitely variable, language must organize and simplify them if it is not to have one word for each new situation. Different languages group, organize, and even interpret such situations in different ways, and there is no possibility of avoiding arbitrariness in this process. Saussure argues that because of this arbitrariness in the conceptual process of language, its concepts are not simple, positive terms but achieve their meaning by the place they take within the system of concepts of the language and, in particular, by their function in differentiating one category of things from another. It is the system of differentiation, therefore, that is the source of meaning.

What then becomes important is the particular set of characteristics that are the causes of the differentiation introduced by the set of concepts.[7] *Warm water* is in one sense not a fact of nature; it represents instead a decision of the English language to cut up the range of temperatures in a particular arbitrary way. There is no concept of *warmness* outside language, and the meaning of that word derives not primarily from its reflecting reality but rather from its place in the system of terms – its differentiating *warm* from *hot*. The fact that *warmness* as a concept is a creation of the English language does *not* mean that warmness has nothing to do with reality or that statements that refer to warmness are only statements about the English language, not about the world. On the contrary, variations in temperature must exist and be perceptible to allow the contrast between *warm* and *hot* to measure anything. It is just as wrong to say that warmth is only a fact of nature as it is to say that warmth is merely a fact about language. An equally wrong conclusion about Saussure's position is that the arbitrariness of the sign makes meaning indeterminate. On the contrary, it is precisely the fact that the conceptual system of English is the common property of its speakers (i.e. that all, in a sense, agree to make the same arbitrary decision) that gives its words any meaning at all. The individual speaker does not have the power to change the meaning of a sign in any way once it has been established in the linguistic community. It does not mean that the meaning of a given *word* is arbitrary, for unless that word has a place in the system of terms, there is no system, no agreement, no meaning, and thus no language and no communication.[8] Derrida uses Saussurean terminology to develop his own ideas; preserving especially Saussure's key terms *difference, signifier*, and *signified*. But Derrida insists that nothing within the system is simply present or absent anywhere, since there are only differences and traces of traces everywhere.[9] In the absence of a center or origin, everything becomes discourse: that is to say, a system in which the central signified, the original or transcendental signified, is never absolutely present outside the system of differences. The absence of the transcendental signified extends the domain and the play of signification infinitely.[10]

For Derrida, meaning is the infinite implication and indefinite referral of signifier and signified.[11] The field is in effect that of play, that is to say, one of infinite substitutions, and the distinction between signified and signifier becomes problematic at its root.[12] Saussure had argued that meaning is not a matter of sounds being linked to concepts existing outside a given language but instead arises from specific contrasts between terms that are differentiated in specific ways. Derrida's move is to introduce the word *play* and substitute it for *contrast*, so that we now have a play of differences as the source of meaning. Play is no longer a matter of specific constraints; it is "limitless," "infinite," and "indefinite," and in this way meaning has also become limitless, infinite, and indefinite. By playing on the two meanings of the French verb *différer* – to differ and to defer – Derrida takes the play of difference to indicate that meaning is not present to us but that it is deferred, i.e. postponed into the future rather than being a presence.[13] Meaning is never present to us, no final act of perceiving may be possible and everything becomes discourse. That is to say, since we are cut off from ultimate referents, there is only language.[14] By introducing the word *play*, Derrida suggests that the mechanism of differentiation is much less controlled and specific than it was in Saussure. This amounts to a very radical change from Saussure's position – and yet Derrida introduces his new terms *play*, *supplement*, and *trace* as if they were merely linguistic flourishes, a matter of style. Ellis points out that if we take Saussure's notion of *differences* and try to combine it with the notion of a limitless, indefinite play, we render it meaningless. If terms could play against all other terms indiscriminately rather than specifically, the result would be no specific contrasts that generate meaning, nothing identifiable or recognizable, and hence no communication and no meaning at all. To see a difference between things is to see specific qualities uniquely contrasted with each other, whereas to see unspecific, indeterminate differences is to see nothing. Derrida has abolished language, not redefined it, for difference and differentiality are inseparable from specific, finite decision making. The notion of infinite and indiscriminate play is impossible in any context that requires distinctiveness.

Ellis emphasizes that the notion that the passage of time is an essential part of a word's achieving its meaning (i.e. deferral of meaning, postponing of meaning, indefinite extending of meaning) rests on a misunderstanding of the process of making choices among words. The problem is that Derrida has confused the process of meaning with the analysis of that process. The meaning of one word does indeed depend on the meaning of many others, but to choose one word from a system is to employ *all* of the systematic contrasts with other words at that very moment – the process of contrasting does not stretch out into the future. When choosing one word, I have done all the work involved in not choosing the other, and my act has all the meaning it can have straight away. The full analysis of all the ways in which a word functions in a language can indeed stretch out into the future, and defining a word may take weeks of careful thought, but the full use of it is achieved immediately upon that use. Analysis of an action may run into a potentially infinite future but the action itself is still made in its entirety at a specific moment in time. Its consequences and ramifications may belong to the future but its character is set once it is made. All words are in a sense present for possible choice, and then all but one are rendered absent by actual choice. That is how language works. This absence is not something that requires a search or a diagnosis of absent meaning. Absence *is* meaning when a systematic choice is being made. Ellis, therefore, concludes that Derrida's ideas on meaning and language do not achieve any real coherence and force. The free play of meaning is an incoherent idea, and the same holds for logocentrism, long since discarded by philosophers of language, for virtually all philosophers of language have understood that the relationship between the vocal sound of "apple" and the idea to which it refers is arbitrary. Saussure's contribution was in something much more interesting and unique: he saw a *second* arbitrariness, the arbitrariness of the structure of the concept "apple" and its relation to physical objects. Yet a confusion between these two ideas, and derivations from it, permeate most deconstructive writings. The point of "difference" in Saussure lies in the differentiation of words from other words and ideas from other ideas – not in the trivial notion that a word is different from a thing.

Derrida's major thrust lies in his attack on the essentialist view of meaning typified in logical positivism and going back all the way to Platonism. The prevailing emphasis on the iconoclast character of deconstruction prevents Derrida from facing the real task at hand: to develop an alternative, not to logocentrism, but to the alternatives that have already been developed to it by thinkers whom he does not consider.[15] As a result, he jumps from one extreme (meaning as a fixed immutable concept) to the other (meaning as indeterminate, infinite play of signs). Derrida fails to establish any coherent view of meaning of the way language functions, yet his opinions have gained considerable attention in literary criticism. His habit of denouncing unexamined assumptions, his vocabulary of "putting in question," "problematizing," and his addiction to provocative statements have proved to be most influential. To deconstruct a discourse is to show how it undermines the philosophy it asserts.[16] Deconstruction performs an operation that is variously described as undermining, subverting, exposing, undoing, transgressing, or demystifying, and it performs this operation on something variously described as traditional ideas, limits, logic, authoritative or privileged readings, illusions of objectivity, mastery or consensus, the referential meaning of a text, or simply what the text asserts or says.[17] In deconstruction, the traditional idea is questioned, subverted, and undermined but then *retained*, so that we can focus on the act of subversion itself – and this does not amount to a final rejection of that idea. Some deconstruction is out to demonstrate that what the text says is the opposite (or is also the opposite) of what it seems to say. Thus, the traditional version is the reference point that deconstruction needs both during and after it has done its work.[18] It is now commonplace that every interpreter learns something about the text from interpretations he rejects, and, in this sense, all language undermines to some extent what it asserts. But if we say that a text *often* works on different levels, we are back in the province of traditional criticism. The radical character of deconstruction requires that there always be a uniquely privileged reading sanctioned by authority and achieved by repression. Deconstruction comes down heavily on the side of discord and discrepancy as the universal result. Whatever the text, it must work with the traditional, literal, authoritative, superficial, referential meaning and cannot exist without it. But there is really no such thing as a single traditional meaning of a literary work. There is no privileged meaning of *Hamlet* or *Moby Dick*: on the contrary, there is an extraordinary diversity of critical schools, and a near chaos of conflicting interpretations.

To anyone who is familiar with the present critical scene, with its countless different methodologies and ideological commitments, its divergent readings that are Marxist or Freudian, semiotic or stylistic, historical or New Critical, biographical or feminist, to anyone who surveys this extraordinary scene, it will be obvious that there is no single privileged reality. Ellis emphasizes that one should not *both* reject a particular theory of language as inadequate *and* also accept it to describe the surface meaning of the text that must then be transcended. There is virtually no such thing as a literal reading of a work of literature, for all readings are abstractive and interpretive to some degree. Questions raised about the adequacy of readings always concern the kind or degree of abstraction: to be sure, a critic will sometimes claim that another's reading of a literary text is too literal. But this really amounts to a demand for a more complex abstraction or perhaps a different one. The critic attacked would hardly be worth discussing had he not already made some sort of abstraction. Deconstruction, on the other hand, requires us to give up our normal practice of differentiating between the various degrees of superficiality or profundity that we experience. Some readings are obvious, while some are not. Yet some of those that are obvious to some writers seem less obvious to others, and some obvious readings seem never to be challenged. The deconstructionist, however, cannot admit any of this without seriously compromising his radical position. He is forced to deny that experience is variable, for he must hold that there is always an obvious reading, which is then shown to be inadequate and subject to undermining and reversal. His problem is that whenever a reasonable program for criticism is described, the deconstructionist must reject it as part of the received opinion, since the word "reasonable" for him is just a label for business as usual. But readings vary enormously in their abstractness and complexity, and in the real world of inquiry, undermining and overturning a traditional view happens because a more defensible one has been set up to replace it. While deconstruction puts its emphasis on debunking the old, it inevitably becomes a victim of the restrictive binary logic that it likes to belittle. Since old views are not allowed to be discussed and replaced, the doctrine that the traditional and obvious must be systematically opposed turns out to be pointless.

There is currently a widespread dissatisfaction with the state of literary studies in the universities, and deconstruction gives both a forum to that dissatisfaction and a sense that it is part of a bold move to sweep aside what is conservative and deadening. But when deconstruction puts such heavy emphasis on undermining the traditional view, it is giving that view a privileged status. It has become popular because it adopts an ironic reading of the text, but since it applies this to all texts indiscriminately, its irony becomes vacuous and pointless. It tends to reduce myriad possibilities of interpretation to only two: the traditional view and its polar opposite. By now the view that all interpretation is misinterpretation, and all reading misreading, has been around for a considerable time, and has been debated and criticized thoroughly. There is by now a long history and an extensive literature on whether clear and certain knowledge is possible, and for some time now, the most common position in the philosophy of science has been that this cannot be the case, and that all knowledge is provisional. The criterion of validity lies not in the psychological conviction of the researcher but in the always pro-visional assent of the community of scientists to the arguments and evidence in favor of an alleged "fact." In the study of literature, likewise, it is the majority view, and in fact commonplace, that certainty is not available. If "all interpretation is misinterpretation" is merely making the point that there are no absolutes and no special claims of unanswerable knowledge in criticism, then this is rather uninteresting. That any assertion or claim to know something is open to later rethinking is obvious enough, and has long been so. It doesn't amount to a new view on interpretation. However, if there are *never* any supportive reasons for any interpretation, the whole process becomes undecidable. Advance in knowledge comes from a search for a specific new view, not from obsession with the categorical inadequacy of old views. "All interpretation is misinterpretation" is not really a theoretical position but a slogan designed to strike an attitude and to intimidate the opposition.

The notion of *textuality* has been introduced to question the assumption that all texts should be interpreted according to the intentions of their authors. The author may not grasp the full impact of his writing, but for that reason a critic may be required. But the notion of textuality turns out to be considerably more radical than this, for by severing the connection with the author, the implication of textuality is that we are denying the very possibility of a statable meaning. The text is now assumed to have a life of its own, an endless series of possible meanings that are no longer subject to control either by the author's intentions or by the rules and conventions of language. Textuality, therefore, links with Derrida's play of signs: the signs that make up the text play infinitely against each other to defeat any possibility of statable meaning. Attention now shifts to the role of the reader, and common to all versions of this point of view is the notion that the critic is far more important than traditional criticism has usually assumed him to be. There is no limit to these meanings since the mind finds in the text whatever it is looking for.[19] The statement that "authors make meaning," thought not of course untrue, is merely a special case of the more universal truth that readers make meaning – the number of possible meanings of a poem is itself infinite.[20] The idea that signs play infinitely and indiscriminately against each other is one that is asserted without any real supportive argument, and it is inherently an impossible one to justify. To be recognizable as anything, a sign must have a distinctive shape and function that recognizably sets it apart from other signs. To postulate a sign that simply plays indefinitely and infinitely against other sings is to imagine one with no distinct character at all, i.e. one not recognizable as having a shape or function of its own. This produces not more and richer meaning, as deconstructionists like to think, but no meaning at all.

Ellis points out that the prevalent error associated with the word *textuality* lies in the failure to see that there are *two* steps, not one, involved in the notion that a text must be liberated from its author to mean whatever it is taken to mean. There is, first of all, liberation from the author; but second, there is liberation from the rules and conventions of the language in which it is written. These are logically separable ideas, requiring separate justifications, whereas the textuality argument always proceeds as if the two were really one, and as if a justification of the first were a complete justification for both. In effect, the argument operates with just two alternatives: either a text means what its author meant, or we have textuality and free play. In doing so it jumps over an enormous middle ground as if it did not exist. It was the argument over the intentional fallacy, as Wimsatt and Beardsley termed it,[21] that first raised doubts about the author's intention as the ultimate appeal in deciding the meaning of a text. But in the forty years since the first appearance of this article, the matter has been discussed at length, and further explained and refined by scores of writers and critics. Ellis points out that the assumption to liberate a text from the author is to liberate it from all constraints is a mistaken one, for it leaps form one extreme to another: total constraint or none at all. Any productive argument should by now have focused on the *kind* of instrument at our disposal and how it operates. There is indeed one obvious constraint that operates on all texts – the language they are written in. Total freedom (and textuality if so understood) is, therefore, an impossible notion.[22] The reader-response argument makes all mental processes arbitrary, so that no mental process has any real connection with the text that provokes it, and it follows that my meaning has no discernible connection to your meaning. But this ignores the obvious fact that we are sharing common assumptions and ways of interpretation due to a common language. Indeed it renders communication literally impossible, for if there are no constraints, we have to abandon meaning altogether.

The most widely held view is that all knowledge is in the nature of a hypothesis, always open to be overturned and modified by later insight. There is no knowledge such that its complete objectivity can be the occasion for an inner conviction in the mind of the knower that he could not possibly be mistaken. The judgment of the community of scholars as to which of several competing views is currently the most plausible one is the test of any hypothesis, and that judgment is always provisional. Knowledge then is neither completely objective, if by that is meant "incontrovertibly true," nor is it a matter of individually arbitrary responses that are not answerable to anything but the individual's current frame of mind. Progress is achieved through a class of different views and conflicting opinions, not by individuals stubbornly clinging to their first thoughts and not talking to others. There is always modification and abandonment of ideas in the process of discussion; some views are pervasive and grow in influence while others are forgotten. The development of knowledge is a social process in which arguments count for a great deal and appeal to a text under discussion may be an important part in such an argument in which we have to distinguish between different degrees of plausibility. Deconstruction's inability to monitor the quality of criticism is, therefore, a serious omission, for we do not simply get a response from the critic; we expect his or her reasoned argument. Reading a critic is not just taking notice of his conclusions; it involves evaluating his reasons and forming a judgment on their cogency. In all fields of inquiry ideas are advanced and argued for, and the arguments are weighted against those of competing positions.[23] Ellis concludes that textuality's infinity of meanings of a text is a pernicious doctrine, for it encourages us to stop discriminating, to cease thinking about interpretations, their strengths and their weaknesses. Deconstruction is right to stress the creativeness of the critic, but it is wrong to take creativity as freedom from constraints or standards. We judge someone to be creative only if he produces an idea that is both original and valuable. To be creative is *not* to let one's imagination run free – it is to use imagination productively. It follows from deconstruction and reader's response theory that we can neither discriminate between qualities of great writers, nor between great and poor writers, nor between good and poor critics – and in this manner intellectual laziness is encouraged.

Deconstruction invariably begins by focusing an the naive, common-sense viewpoint of each particular issue in order to undermine it, to "put it in question," and to "problematize" it. When discussing the issue of certainty in knowledge, deconstruction tends to begin with the naive belief in clear, certain language, even though current philosophy of science has generally abandoned this idea long ago. The extended debate on the intentional fallacy in which the majority view has been that the author's intent does not control the meaning of a literary work is likewise ignored.[24] Ellis emphasizes that whereas the so-called free play is an incoherent notion, deconstruction creates by means of it a sense of intellectual confrontation and the illusion of progress. Formulations are chosen not for their logical and intellectual appropriateness but mainly for their drama and shock. The first step is to focus on the most literal surface meaning of the text, disregarding any of its subtleties, and the second step is to show that there is a larger ironic layer of meaning. Ellis concludes that deconstructive logic is not conductive to productive original thinking, merely to creating the illusion of it. Objections to deconstruction are always assigned the role of the naive believer who has to be denounced, but there is a tendency to resist any attempt to translate the argument into existing forms of scholarship for fear of revealing its unoriginal character. When Culler explains that the shocking claim "all interpretation is misinterpretation" simply means that no interpretation can ever be final, he is giving the game away. Deconstruction makes its appeal not in any genuine logical fashion but by psychological means; it offers its adherents a lot of psychological satisfaction and, essential to its style is the sense of belonging to an intellectual elite.

It is not difficult to see, however, that deconstruction has been part of a larger movement in modern criticism. Whereas in France, deconstruction is part of a revolt against a narrow rationalist tradition, in America it represents only a new way to cling to an old set of attitudes.[25] The prevalent view has been that criticism is not like science because it does not lead to clear and objective results; good criticism is stimulating rather than true, and such stimulation may occur in many different ways. This, in turn, meant that the critic's individual character and personality are an important factor in criticism. The point of good criticism lies not in discovering *the* meaning of a text, for that would be a return to the unitary truths of science. This produces a reluctance to say that one response to a text is right and another simply wrong: instead, there is a tendency to allow that each illustrates different aspects of the work. Criticism comes to be judged less by the logic of its arguments than by the qualities of discriminative imagination it displays, and by the stimulus it provides to the reader's own imagination. With such an approach, attempts to show that a particular piece of criticism does not meet accepted standards of intellectual coherence or relevance to the actual terms and emphases of the text under discussion are usually thought of as being intolerant and dogmatic, especially since certainty is not available in any case. The prevailing critical consensus has long insisted on pluralism; on the value of different critical views, and on criticism lacking the character of science. But if no one defends standards, the quality of particular criticism is likely to decline. The problem is that deconstruction opposes explanation as such,[26] whereas in theoretical discourse, argument is invariably met by argument in a communal process. There is no room in it for individual license, for claims to exception, for appeals to a unique logical status, or for freedom to do as one wishes. The most enduring fault of literary criticism as a field of study has been its readiness to abandon the communal sense of a shared inquiry in which individual perceptions are expected to be sifted and tested by others. A shared inquiry means a commitment to agreement and dialogue, whereas criticism that insist on the value of each individual writer's perspective in effect refuses to make this commitment. The result is apparent novelty that, looked at more closely, consists in resistance to change and, more particularly, to that change that is most urgently needed: the development of some check on and control of the indigestible, chaotic flow of critical writing, through reflecting on what is and what is not, in principle, worthwhile.

Notes

[1] John M. Ellis, *Against Deconstruction,* Princeton, NJ: Princeton University Press, 1989, p. vii.

[2] *Ibid.,* p. 9.

[3] Jacques Derrida, *Of Grammatology*, trans. G.C. Spivak, Baltimore, MD, 1976, p. 14.

[4] Ellis, *Against Deconstruction*, p. 29.

[5] Vincint Leitch, *Deconstructive Criticism,* New York, NY, 1983, pp. 24-25.

[6] Ellis, *Against Deconstructoin,* p. 40.

[7] *Ibid.,* p.46.

[8] *Ibid.,* p. 50.

[9] Jacques Derrida, *Positions*, trans. A. Bass, Chicago, IL, 1981, p. 26.

[10] Jacques Derrida, *Writing and Differnce*, trans. A. Bass, Chicago, IL, 1978, p. 280.

[11] *Ibid.,* p. 25.

[12] Derrida, *Positions*, pp. 19-20.

[13] Jacques Derrida, *Speech and Phenomena*, trans. D. Allison, Evanston, 1973.

[14] Ellis, *Against Deconstruction*, p. 53.

[15] *Ibid.*, p. 66.

[16] Johnathan Culler, *On Deconstruction*, Ithaca, NY, 1982, p. 86.

[17] Ellis, *Against Deconstruction*, p. 69.

[18] *Ibid.*, p. 71.

[19] Steven Rendall, "Mus in Pice: Montaigne and Interpretation," MLN 94 (1979), pp. 1056-71.

[20] Robert Crosman, "Do Readers Make Meaning?" in *The Reader in the Text: Essays on Audience and Interpretaion*, eds. Susan R. Suleiman and Inge Crosman, Princeton, NJ, 1980, pp. 151 and 154.

[21] William K. Wimsatt and Monroe Beardsley, "The Intentional Fallacy," in *The Verbal Icon: Studies in the Meaning of Poetry*, Lexington, KY, 1954.

[22] Ellis, *Against Deconstruction*, p. 120.

[23] *Ibid.*, p. 133.

[24] *Ibid.*, p. 138.

[25] *Ibid.*, p. 154 n1.

[26] *Ibid.*, p. 156 n3.

Chapter Eighteen

Paradoxes of Reflexivity

The central achievement of the sociology of scientific knowledge has been the demonstration that even the most esoteric features of scientific and mathematical knowledge can be understood as social constructs. Scientific facts are not so much reflections of the world as persuasive texts, accomplished within and shaped by a complex of contingencies and circumstances. Ashmore asks what happens when the power and success of the sociology of scientific knowledge is turned upon itself.[1] In this treatment, the deconstruction of deconstruction does not just "cancel things out" but throws doubt upon the notion of an objective world. The grounds for knowledge have come under challenge within a wide range of disciplines – anthropology, psychology, sociology, philosophy – and more recently in a number of intellectual movements that share a concern for the problem of representation and that cut across traditionally defined disciplinary boundaries – poststructuralism, postmodernism, and the theory of literature. Ashmore argues that reflexivity need not be conceived as a "problem;" his strategy is to sustain and explore the paradoxes that arise when we attempt to escape the inescapable, not to attempt their resolution.[2] This perspective in reflexivity is bound to require modifications to expectations about what counts as an adequate ("useful") answer, and what counts as a serious approach to the problem in the first place. The study proceeds to examine the various ways in which practitioners conceive and subsequently manage the reflexivity of their practice. The management strategies identified vary from outright rejection through (in principle) acceptance, to explicit attempts at celebration. Reflexivity is an issue that is relevant to a wide range of intellectual concerns from literature to logic, and from physics to photography. It is an issue for all modes of representational practice. To some it is a threat, while to others it is a crucial tool for use only against opponents, and yet to others, still, it is an opportunity. The interest in exploring the role of reflexivity in the sociology of scientific knowledge is that all these management strategies coexist. The intellectual tradition within which reflexivity and self-reference have been objects of the most intense study is philosophical logic. There have been periods in this extensive tradition when the self-referential and paradoxical have been treated in a positive fashion.[3] But the approach, at least in the Anglo-American world, which has been dominant throughout the modernist era, is that all phenomena are paradigmatically destructive of rationality. The history of reflexivity in the arts and humanities is as extensive as it is in philosophy, the difference is that the phenomenon has been more frequently thought of as liberating than as threatening. Experimentation with self-referential techniques has been a staple of the twentieth century avant gardes in literature, painting, drama, and film.

The sociology of scientific knowledge has potentially the interesting property of being self-exemplifying. It is frequently thought that there is something odd about such a procedure, for it appears to be blatantly circular, and to introduce the specter of infinite regress. To deal with the problem of the *status* of their work and its findings with regard to contemporary debates in philosophy, sociologists of scientific knowledge frequently tend to characterize their research in the standard empiricist manner as providing essential support for those epistemological theories they approve of, such as the Duhem-Quine view on underdetermination of theory by evidence as well as doctrines of the theory-ladenness of observation. Equally, the findings of the sociology of scientific knowledge are deemed to discomfirm less well-liked philosophical schemes, such as Popper's falsificationism and other forms of rationalism and empiricism.[4] If physics can be explained by sociology, this threatens to invert the hierarchy of the sciences. Relativism is a feature of investigation that translates "knowledge" into whatever counts as knowledge in any particular society, culture, period, language, discipline, or group. Not so to translate, say cognitive relativists, is to fall prey to an ethnocentric view; it is to operate under the illusion that one can know which beliefs are *really* true or false. In practice such a stance merely ends up denigrating the beliefs of others, while celebrating one's own. But even among the practitioners of the sociology of scientific knowledge, there is a great diversity of views on the proper role of reflexivity. Some seek to outlaw it, seeing it as a paralyzing influence on their practice, and judge the assimilation between the object and the method of investigation upon which a reflexive stand rests as arbitrary, unnecessary, and undesirable.[5] Others accept reflexivity in principle, usually on grounds of full generality and self-consistency. However, such programmatic advocacy is largely sterile and has little notable effect on the outcome of these practitioners. While centered in the sociology of scientific knowledge, such an approach ranges over general sociology, anthropology, psychology, Marxist studies, philosophy, fiction, and literary studies as well as logic and mathematics. Ashmore wants to show that the negative evaluation that the reflexivity of reflexivity elicits is neither singular nor necessary. His concern throughout is to deconstruct the theory and the practice of level separation, emphasizing the fundamental uncertainty of discourse. He points out that what is meant by a reflexive individual, reflexive interpretive procedures, a reflexive use of knowledge, and reflexive practical accomplishment is by no means clear. This is largely because in most social science, and indeed the majority of discourses of all kinds, this self-referential aspect is latent, in that it has no obvious or immediate consequences. But in metascience, and especially in the sociology of scientific knowledge, the consequences of self-reference are manifest. It is the claim that knowledge is only contingently valid that is likely to be found the most troublesome.

The position of the sociology of scientific knowledge is that science's knowledge is a form of false consciousness, and that science is deceived by its unproblematic realism. One of the things that sociologists of scientific knowledge are becoming very skilled at is suspending taken-for-granted ways of seeing. But a notion that can be so easily applied to everything is not really a criticism of anything. It is also argued that the exclusive concern with writing reflexive texts, that is, texts which display their own modes of construction, reflects a narrow and limited conception of reflexivity. Reflexive fiction, though, is not exclusively a modern phenomenon. Limiting ourselves to the development of the novel, reflexivity was there at its birth in the eighteenth century. Cervantes' *Don Quixote* and Sterne's *The Life and Opinions of Tristram Shandy* are both reflexive, the latter extremely

so. One feature of the general reflexive tenor of recent literary practice
and study is a move toward a blurring of genres with the effect of
deconstructing the distinction between literary practice and literary
study. This blurring of genres is evident, too, in the current interest
across a whole variety of scholarly disciplines in the analysis of their
rhetorics of inquiry. Indeed it seems as if "rhetoric" is taking the place
of epistemology as the all purpose metadiscipline. According to
Gruenberg, any sociology of science has a "critical obstacle" in the
shape of its self-referential aspects. It undermines the capacity of the
sociologist of science to define his subject matter independently of
methodology, because the specification of the methodology
presupposes an understanding of the subject matter, which the
methodology itself is intended to provide.[6] The empirical variety,
which treats science as an unalterable given that yields certified
knowledge, avoids the problem by simply denying its existence.
Interpretive sociology is deemed incapable of making any distinction
between rational and irrational beliefs and practices.[7]

The philosophy of science has gained its ideal of good science
from a particular reading of scientific history.[8] But according to this
paradigm, the construction of the boundary between good and bad
science could not become a topic of investigation, and neither could
the boundary between science and philosophy.[9] Thus, one should
beware of theories that naively assume the truth of one's own
knowledge and the falsehood of everyone else's. One should ignore
theories of knowledge that do not give proper explanation of why we
believe what we believe but merely explain it away.[10] For the new
sociological relativism, the metaphor must be that of the onion, which
has no kernel. We find ourselves rapidly moving from a critique of
others' knowledge toward an escalating reflexivity. The new relativists
speak of a theory and practice based, in the end, on personal
commitment. Examples of metareflexive texts include Derridean
deconstruction, and in metareflexive writing of this sort, the necessary
reflexivity is achieved by applying principles of analysis that are self-
exemplifying.[11] This is done by multiplying genres, by getting on the
side of the known, and by refusing to build a metalanguage.[12]
Ashmore argues, however, that Latour's tale of metareflexivity is a
romance,[13] for findings cannot be regarded as valid until we have
satisfactory methodological theories. These are no different in
principle from other sociological theories in that they need the support
of firm methodological criteria. We appear, consequently, to be caught

in an infinite regression, which effectively prevents us from intellectual advance.[14] Banishment of self-reference was attempted in the domain of language in the logical positivist movement. The stratification of this domain into an object language and various distinct metalanguages succeeded in getting rid of Grelling's and similar self-referential paradoxes – by declaring such formulations "heterological," i.e. meaningless – at the immense cost of outlawing *all* linguistic self-reference whether paradoxical or not. The final irony of the scheme is that all discussions of it are, on their own terms, meaningless because they could not take place on any of the levels of language "internal" to the scheme.[15] Ashmore concludes that the problem lies in the basic assumption of the program that no contradiction can be true, and hence that the meanings which result in the paradoxes must be fallacious. But there is an alternative – accept the adequacy of the reasoning that leads to paradox and embrace *dialetheia:* some things just are both true and false.[16] We should not think of reflexivity as a "problem," since it has no conceivable solution. Yet Ashmore cannot know that a problem has no solution in an a priori fashion either. Beyond truth and falsity there are many fictions, some work and some do not. Ashmore prefers to cultivate this limitlessness as a new pragmatic pluralism – a pluralism that recognizes itself. Some philosophers face reflexivity head on: Nietzsche, Heidegger, and Derrida constantly control the negative paradoxical deconstructive face of reflexivity and, while using it as a weapon against the enterprise of knowledge, attempt to transform the phenomenon into something positive. The move from Nietzsche through Heidegger to Derrida is a move from the subject to the text. The strategies they use for confronting their reflexivity are anarchic assertion, endless postponement, and perpetual unraveling where closure is the enemy.

The psychologist must also face the reflexivity of his practice, for if he is unable or unwilling to do so, he pays the penalty of falling into the paradoxes of self-reference.[17] The suggestion is that the winning side does not posses truth, but rather that it has monopolized plausibility.[18] We constantly make sense of the world and fashion paths leading to one another, convincing people that a particular path is more straightforward than any other. The ridicule of "navel-gazing" expresses an uneasiness with all efforts at self-knowing and self-reflection. All forms of rationalism essentially appeal to the overriding importance of the self-grounded ideal, insisting that the speaker be able to articulate the necessary and sufficient premises for his argument and conclusion. Critiques of this kind tend to be systematically ambiguous with respect to their ideal and authority. To be doing reflexive sociology is to be rendering problematic the central topic of inquiry, that very tradition in whose (unexplicated) terms sociology is understood as what it is.[19] The concrete grasp of the world does not include itself (in the act of grasping) as a topic of inquiry. The *tu quoque* strategy only uses reflexivity *against* the discourses it seeks to attack, and its unmasking of reflexive inconstancy is, finally, only a strategic move played to discredit the target discourse on grounds other than reflexive inconsistency itself. These grounds are, more often than not, skepticism and/or relativism. On the latter ground, the sociology of scientific knowledge is frequently the target for *tu quoque* arguments.[20] But Ashmore concludes that the problem of reflexivity turns out to be the preserver of relativism and not its destroyer.

One redeeming feature of the sociological perspective is that relativizing analysis, in being pushed to its final consequence, leads back upon itself. What follows is *not*, as some of the early sociologists of knowledge found, a total paralysis of thought.[21] Logical positivism demarcates meaningless from meaningful statements by the principle of empirical verification: if a statement cannot (in principle) be empirically verified, it is meaningless; if it can be, it is meaningful. However, a statement of the verification principle cannot *itself* be so verified, and is therefore meaningless.[22] Ashmore rejects the historical myth that suggests that logical positivism simply ceases to be as a result of this inconsistency. As Gellner suggests,

> making an exception on one's own behalf, having difficulty in accounting for oneself, is the professional ailment of philosophers, and is virtually written into the terms of reference under which they work.[23]

The power of the *tu quoque* cannot reside in its logic, however perfect, because logic *in itself* does not compel. Getting beyond the *tu quoque* is not and cannot simply be a matter of using the same form of argument as a counteraccusation or a meta- *tu quoque*. Such self-protective arguments are counterproductive because these researchers implicitly assume that self-contradiction is unavoidable, but that it is also something negative to get rid of. Both the *tu quoque* and its counterargument share the logician's prejudice against paradox grounded in a negative belief, in its evil power. Whereas in chess the fear of being mated belongs to the essence of the game, contradictions in the logic of natural language (but not in mathematics) can be tolerated to some extent. What the limits are depends on context; a language that lacks logic altogether becomes incoherent.

The major relevant features of Kuhn's historiography are that scientific knowledge is non-accumulative across successive paradigms, and that it is, therefore, historically and cognitively limited. However, this insight is generally unavailable to members of scientific communities working at their "puzzle solving," embedded in their "disciplinary matrices," and articulating their particular exemplars. This is because the historical succession of paradigms is made invisible. Each paradigm constitutes a rewriting of scientific history such that previous paradigms appear as mistaken, and yet as historically inevitable– as the necessary path that has been traveled on the way form yesterday's ignorance and error to today's (relative) knowledge and truth. The history of science of paradigm-embedded participants is progressive. Kuhn is at pains to emphasize that this situation of historically false consciousnesses is beneficial and indeed necessary for the very existence of the practice of science as we know it.[24] We can say that each new historiography rewrites the history of historiographies in a progressive fashion, and that the exposition and criticism of the old is an essential part of the new.[25] Kuhn and other writers in the new historiography of science talk of their immediate predecessors' tradition and its way of doing history pejoratively as the practice of "Whig history"[26] which is glossed as the "progressive eradication of error and revelatoin of truth."[27] But the new historiographers and their supporters turn out to be no less Whig historiologists. In analyzing scientific knowledge and scientists, historians tell us that what they see is not visible to the scientist – participants. They implicitly exercise the time honored-privilege of the accredited and competent observer: the ability to look at things in perspective, to take the big picture, to tell the wood from the trees.

Ashmore suggests that Kuhn's insistence on limiting his thesis to physics and similarly "mature" science asks to preserve the boundary between his own practice and the practice he observes. This allows Kuhn to argue that his theory of puzzle solving" constitutes a "less equivocal and more traditional"[28] criticism of demarcation of true science from pseudo-science than Popper's theory of falsification.[29]

Ashmore suggests that there must be something wrong with the Kuhnian scheme: if one is a Kuhn fan, as many social scientists and most sociologists of scientific knowledge seem to be, then this conclusion must seem to be less than welcome. Kuhn's doctrine contains a fair proportion of potential self-destructiveness.[30] Kuhn is caught in his own relativism because the new historiography cannot, on Kuhn's premise, properly claim any special status in relation to other historiographies.[31] The historiographer cannot at the same time be both inside and outside history. The establishment of a connection between document and underlying reality is a back-and-forth process,[32] and thus a circular one. The independence of word and world which is both a basic feature of "mundane reasoning" and the minimal necessity for an adequate rationality, appears to be compromised by ethnomethodolical reflexivity. On this account, the facticity of the world – its out-thereness – is a paradoxical product of reflexive and circular interpretive procedures. What the reflexivity of reflexivity appears to do is to make ethnomethodology just another life-form and its practioners just another group of special pleaders. That these practitioners should find this position so uncomfortable is both interesting and seemly. Puritanism (i.e. distrust of the messiness of ordinary language, and desiring clarity and certainty) is a hallmark of much of ethnomethodological discourse. Thus, such theories are found to be tautological rather than explanatory.[33] Tautology is impossible to avoid, since reflexive circularity is the ground and condition of all forms of sense-making. To find upon analysis that Kuhn reasons in a circle is not, then, very surprising. The price paid for "using common-sense knowledge" is a total surrender to realism.

Ashmore's solution is turning the problem into a topic, and resisting the terminology of fear ("specter," "abyss") by realizing that this abyss is only a paper tiger. Another popular solution is to hold that our knowledge and our epistemology have no absolute grounds and, in fact, do not need them. Although we believe that there is a limit to our inquiries, we will never find out what it is. The most theoretically sophisticated solution strategy is McHoul's proposal for a dual vision in ethnomethodology. The proposal affirms the reflexivity of reflexivity, and recognizes that ethnomethodology can be a topic of investigation for itself. However, in its other model of operation – in its investigative mode – ethnomethodology might usefully rely upon the research heuristic ("myth") that the phenomenon it treats comprises a real order of events, that they are objects in an independently existing world.[34] At this stage, then, McHoul's proposal looks like a pragmatic compromise. The discourse of ethnomethodology is deconstructive even if it doesn't want to be. To show how objectivities *become* objectivities is to show that they are *not* objectivities. Ashmore claims that the initial answer to this question is that self-destructiveness does not entail self-destruction. For self-destruction, in this context, is the willful abandonment of speech on the grounds that clear speech is both highly desirable and completely impossible. Relativists know that the charge of unclarity can be brought against all discourses, especially those whose speech seems clearest, as in logic and the sciences. Every statement incorporates a metastatement that asserts the truth of the statement. Problems of a paradoxical nature arise within universal negative statements, such as "nothing is true." The paradigm of such semantic paradoxes is the paradox of the liar. It is paradigmatic in that it introduces explicitly the notion of lying, that is, it points to the usually implicit element of the metastatement, "It is true that ...," in all statements. There are certain propositional statements that our language does not let us make without contradicting the form in which all such statements must be made. The major class of such nonstable statements are those that are skeptical, relativistic, or agnostic about claims to knowledge, including (paradoxically but necessarily) their own.[35] The argument would suggest that the problem of relativism is basically linguistic: language is not an epiphenomenon that can be ignored or disposed of in favor of more direct approaches to the (more) real. In the world according to relativist discourse, *no* discourse has a firm grounding.[36]

Ashmore wants to persuade us that McHoul's nonprivileging cognitive precariousness is more interesting than the mindless hankering for authority, status, and comfort that animates the *tu quoque*. But in order to do so Ashmore has to deconstruct not just the *tu quoque* but the way in which his own analysis appeals to the authority of the lower level or the metadiscourse. Each move to a higher level produces a domino effect on all levels below, since deconstruction essentially means the subversion of a particular level of self-understanding by a superior analytical level of metaunderstanding. It represents the superior vantage point of the observer or the superior knowledge of the expert. However, people have not always and everywhere experienced the world in this way. Nonscientific cultures (if we believe our historical anthropology) lived *in* the world, not off it. People in such cultures are part of the world in a way that we find hard even to imagine. The world, to these others, was not a dead realm of matter, moved but unmoved, incapable of action; the world of objects is the *result of,* not the *warrant for* science. The old pre-science reality is deconstructed and replaced by a new contrast that to some, has been there all along: the objective world. It is not a deficiency in the personal intellectual capacity of the potential researcher that makes metainquiry so comparatively rare and difficult. It is rather that there is always a comparative paucity of paradigmatic environments (in the Kuhnian sense) with which to undertake the inquiry. This is because metainquiry is pervasive upon its objects: it requires for its existence the prior development of the lower levels. This insight is based on the recognition of the vulnerability of all discourses to metadiscourse deconstruction, and this recognition, in turn, relies on the imagery of the infinite regress for its plausibility. Moreover, an argument that stresses the importance of pragmatic limitations to regress can itself be used for discourse-privileging purposes. Thus, there is indeed a contradiction.[37]

The inside can only speak via the outside. To describe even one's own skills as tacit knowledge is to produce public knowledge. In some versions, only the participants are capable of knowing anything, but insider epistemology has no credibility in (natural) science.[38] Indeed the hallmark of science is its belief in the virtue, and even the necessity, of the outsider stance, which is called objectivity. To study anything scientifically is thus to study it from the outside, whereas to be scientific is to practice science, and to practice science is to be a scientific insider. In the study of science (and knowledge practices generally) the student cannot avoid being inside and outside at the same time. Any particular stopping point will be arbitrary and unjustified, since it is neither a matter of being correct nor a matter of analysis.[39] Rather, it constitutes a denial and a dissolution of its prime assumption, which is at the root of the problem: that inquiry requires, to be inquiry, a realist practice and a realist writing. In the opinion of Ashmore, the way to solve the problem of realist inquiry is to concentrate on textuality and by articulating the practice he calls "wrighting." It is not a matter of solving the problem; rather, it is something to be shown, not to be told.[40] Refutations share the deep ground of that which they refute; the grounds for the *tu quoque* are a design for certainty, straightforwardness, and clarity, a fear of regress, paradox, and the loss of control.[41] The *tu quoque* is preserved with the aim of transcendence. Science, unlike philosophy, is wrapped up in its own way of making things intelligible to the exclusion of all others. Or rather, it applies its criterion unselfconsciously, for to be self-conscious about such matters is to be philosophical.[42] In the standard version, the reproducibility of scientists' findings is seen as a major epistemological guarantee of scientific validity. But since there are no two events that are totally identical, there is always a "space" for negotiation of this sameness/difference. The success or lack of success of any replication claim can never rest, therefore, on the way the world is; rather it must rest on social agreement in the relevant community.[43] In the sciences, the apparent externality of things is reinforced by the notion that anyone could see the same things if they looked at the same place. Realists typically choose to study science only because it is generally counted as the canonical example of knowledge.

But a problem can arise for speakers in accounting for the fact that it took some years before they publicly admitted that they had accepted a newly proposed theory that they believe to be correct. One way they can do so is to explain that the delay in adopting the theory was to allow time for the confirmatory evidence to appear. However, because of the massive, fundamental and irresolvable variability in participants accounts on any given topic, traditional analysis is unable to achieve the objective that it sets itself, that is, to tell it like it is.[44] The majority of researchers, having invested their careers in traditional analysis, talk more often about the essentially interpretive nature of their kind of sociology, and the way in which their studies are, of course, open-ended and revisable. Much of what passes for sociological knowledge of science is merely contingent and incorrect. Scientists do not agree about what constitutes a good argument, and it has become increasingly clear that participants with different perspectives, different interests, and different technical backgrounds interpret formulations differently. The same analyst furnishes quite different versions within a single context, and this provides a major reason for not taking scientists' accounts of theory literally. Ashmore argues that the resolution of paradoxes in Russell's theory of types is simply not desirable. While the theory of types was at least workable when confined to set theory, it was a thoroughly misguided product of a mind obsessed with control. When it was taken over by the wider, logical positivist movement and adopted for natural language, it became not only pernicious but self-destructive in its unintended consequences of ruling out all self-referential formulations however innocent, such as any reference to the first person by that same first person, or any reference to a text or speech in the same text or speech. It would thus fail to account for the very root of intelligence and creativity, which is largely responsible for raising man above the level of beast, namely his capacity to refer to himself and thus to know himself as a speaking subject. It fails to assimilate man's capacity to represent and to imagine, which is manifested throughout art, music, literature, science, mathematics, and logic.

The world we live in is normally experienced as knowable (if not entirely known in common by most of us), and as independent of our accounting practices (except for the microscopic level of physical reality and certain self-fulfilling or negating social phenomena). A construction that refuses to remain content with its own formulations is especially difficult to read "comfortably." When describing "science," one unavoidably participates in traditional distortions, which are embedded in the vernacular discourse. The language is, however, not so fixed as to preclude disclosure through the use of, for example, tortured sentences that turn upon themselves. Any attempt to discount the practical is interpretively problematic, given the wealth of successful interpretations, adequate common-sense, and practical reasoning. As Derrida says of the power of reason, one cannot speak against it except by being for it, and one can protest it only from within, and within its domain.[45] Some sociologists concede that descriptions are essentially flawed, but their explanatory practice treats this point as a mere technical difficulty.[46] Descriptions are acknowledged to be unreliable, but the source of this unreliability is located in the process whereby descriptions are generated. Indeed Woolgar's "radical reading" of the problem treats attempts at reformation as a fool's errand. The unreliability of descriptions is a fundamental feature of discourse, and attempts to improve upon the accuracy of descriptions are doomed. It is important to note that explanatory work inevitably proceeds by ignoring the problem of descriptions. That is, practical explanation has to treat the character of entities as fixed for the practical purposes of explanatory argument.[47] Woolgar attempts to preempt the *tu quoque* response by implicitly claiming a relative immunity from the effect of his practice of conceding that *some* aspect of analysis must always remain unexplicated. Many practitioners in the social study of science make statements suggesting a wish to retain some role for the independent existence of objects in the real world. Dialectical literature strives to do what it cannot do; it attempts to transcend its own limitations as a text while never forgetting that these limitations cannot be transcended. It makes a primary virtue of honesty, yet proves its virtue by means of winning tricks. Like Sisyphus, it goes on trying.[48] That is why Ashmore concludes that the mistake is to seek for some way out.

One cannot get out of history, for as structure it is always there as the system of belief or truth that allows us to understand. Art is as natural an artifice as nature; the truth of fiction is that fact is fantasy, and that the made-up story is a model of the world.[49] The distinction between fiction and nonfiction is illusory since all writing is fiction. Realist writing refuses to recognize its status as writing (fiction). Science's lack of reflexivity is well-known to metascientists, especially in the sociology of scientific knowledge. But the solution to the problem of reflexivity is not a simple matter of not making claims. Rather, according to Ashmore, one has to realize that the subject and the field are one and the same. Among students of reflexivity there is a great diversity of views on its proper role. Perception of similarity and difference seem to be at the root of the construction of all knowledge. But while a perceived difference is always highly visible, its evaluative status is altogether uncertain. If it is possible to deconstruct one's own knowledge claims – or the claims of one's own tradition of scholarly praxis – than that is the truly hard case for a sociology of knowledge. The problem of writing a valid conclusion to this thesis is an exceedingly difficult one, but we would not have come this far if there were nothing to be said.[50]

Notes

[1] Malcom Ashmore, *The Reflexive Thesis, Wrighting Sociology of Scientific Knowledge,* Chicago, IL and London: The University of Chicago Press, 1989, p. xvii.
[2] S. Woolgar, in *The Reflexive Thesis, Wrighting Sociology of Scientific Knowledge,* p. xix.
[3] Steve Fuller, "Making Reflexivity Save for Relativism," Presented at the Society for Social Studies, Pittsburgh, PA, October 1986.

[4] Ashmore, *The Reflexive Thesis*, p. 6.

[5] Harry Collins and Trevor Pinch, *Frames of Meaning: The Social Construction of Extraoridanry Science*, London: Routledge and Kegan Paul, 1982, p. 190.

[6] Barry Gruenberg, "The Problem of Reflexivity on the Social Sciences," *Philosophy of the Social Sciences* 8, 1978, pp. 321-343.

[7] *Ibid.*, p. 336.

[8] Thomas S. Kuhn, "The Relation Between the History and the Philosophy of Science," in *The Essential Tension*, Chicago, IL and London: University of Chicago Press, pp. 3-20.

[9] cf. Joseph Grünfeld, "Science and Philosophy in Popper," in *Science and Values*, Amsterdam: B.R. Grüner Publishing Co., 1973, pp. 21-46.

[10] John Dean. "Empiricism and Relativism – A Reappraisal of Two Key Concepts in the Social Sciences," *Philosophy of the Social Sciences*, 8, 1978, p. 281.

[11] Bruno Latour, "The Politics of Explanation – An Alternative," in *Knowledge and Reflexivity: New Frontiers in the Sociology of Knowledge*, S. Woolgar, Beverly Hills, CA and London, England: Sage, 1988, pp. 155-76.

[12] *Ibid.*, p. 174.

[13] Ashmore, *The Reflexive Thesis*, p. 60.

[14] Michael Mulkay, "Methodology in the Sociology of Science: Some Reflections on the Study of Radio Astronomy," *Social Science Information* 13, 1974, pp. 107-19.

[15] Ashmore, *The Reflexive Thesis*, p. 68.

[16] *Ibid.*, p. 69.

[17] Donald W. Olivier and Alvin W. Landfield, "Reflexivity: An Unfaced Issue in Psychology," *Journal of Individual Psychology*, 18, 1962, p. 122.

[18] Bill Harvey, "Plausibilty and the Evaluation of Knowledge: A Case Study of Experimental Quantum Mechanics," *Social Studies of Science*, 11, 1981, p. 124.

[19] Barry Sandywell, David Silverman, Maurice Roche, Paul Filmer, and Michael Phillipson, *Problems of Reflexivity and Dialectics in Sociological Inquiry: Language Theorizing Difference*, London, England: Routledge and Kegan Paul, 1975, p. 155.

[20] Ashmore, *The Reflexive Thesis*, p. 86.

[21] Peter Berger, *A Rumour of Angles*, Harmondsworth, Middlesex: Penguin Books, 1969, p. 59.

[22] Malcom Ashmore, "A Question of Reflexivity: Wrighting Sociology of Scientific Knowledge," Dphil Dissertation, University of York, 1985, p. 159.

[23] Ernest Gellner, *Legitimation of Belief*, Cambridge: Cambridge University Press, 1974, p. 49.

[24] Ashmore, *The Reflexive Thesis*, p. 89.

[25] Arne Naess, *The Pluralist and Possibilist Aspect of Scientific Enterprise*, London: George Allen and Unwin, 1972, p. 114.

[26] Herbert Butterfield, *The Whig Interpretation of History*, London: Bell, 1931.

[27] David Thomas, *Naturalism and Social Science: A Post-Empiricist Philosophy of Social Science*, Cambridge: Cambridge University Press, 1979, p. 175.

[28] Thomas S. Kuhn, "Logic of Discovery or Psychology of Research?" in *Criticism and the Growth of Knowledge*, eds. Imre Lakatos and Alan Musgrave, Cambridge: Cambridge University Press, 1970, p. 7.

[29] Ashmore, *The Reflexive Thesis*, p. 235 n8.

[30] Naess, *The Pluralist and Possibilist*, p. 114.

[31] *Ibid.*, p. 117.

[32] Steve Woolgar, "Critique and Criticism: Two Readings of Ethnomethodology," *Social Studies of Science* 11, 1981, pp. 504-14.

[33] Ashmore, *The Reflexive Thesis*, p. 95.

[34] Alexander McHoul, *Telling How Texts Talk: Essays on Reading and Ethnomethodology*, London: Routledge and Kegan Paul, 1982, p. 101.

[35] Ashmore, *The Reflexive Thesis*, p. 101.

[36] *Ibid.*, p. 102.

[37] *Ibid.*, p. 105.

[38] *Ibid.*, p. 108.

[39] *Ibid.*, p. 110.

[40] *Ibid.*

[41] *Ibid.*, p. 111.

[42] Peter Winch, *The Idea of a Social Science and Its Relation to Philosophy*, London: Routledge and Kegan Paul, 1958, pp. 102-3.

[43] Ashmore, *The Reflexive Thesis*, p. 115.

[44] Michael Mulkayu and G. Nigel Gilbert, "What Is the Ultimte Question? Some Remarks in Defence of the Analysis of Scientific Discourse," *Social Studies of Science* 12, 1982, p. 310.

[45] Jacques Derrida, *Writing and Difference*, trans. A. Bass, London: Routledge and Kegan Paul, 1978, p. 36.

[46] S. Woolgar, "Critique and Criticism," p. 509.

[47] *Ibid.*, p. 508.

[48] Ashmore, *The Reflexive Thesis*, p. 192.

[49] John Barth *LETTERS*, London: Secker and Warbung, 1979, p. 33.

[50] David Silverman, *Reading Castenada: A Prologue to the Social Sciences*, London: Routledge and Kegan Paul, 1975, p. 111.

Chapter Nineteen

Derrida's Deconstruction

Derrida questions the tradition of philosophy as an autonomous discipline, the pursuit of timeless self-validating truth having nothing to do with either politics or everyday experience.[1] It was the intensive reading of Husserl that led him to perceive certain problems in the way of phenomenal inquiry, problems that had to do with writing, inscription, and what might be called the "literary" aspects of philosophy. Deconstruction, he holds, is not a matter of philosophical content but rather one that focuses on the frames of meaning, institutional structures, and rhetorical and pedagogical norms. "Differance" is a neologism Derrida coined to suggest how meaning is at once "differential" and "deferred," the product of a restless play with language that cannot be fixed or pinned down for the purposes of conceptual definition.[2] It is a cardinal discovery of contemporary structural linguists that signs do not have meaning in and for themselves, but only by virtue of their occupying a distinctive place within the systematic network of contrasts and differences that make up any given language. And this practice is complicated, in Derrida's view, by the fact that meaning is nowhere practically present in language but is always subject to a kind of semantic slippage or deferral, which prevents the sign from ever being completely grasped. Deconstruction is not, Derrida insists, a method, a technique, or a species of critical judgment. Yet its moves do invoke the dismantling of conceptual oppositions, the taking apart of hierarchical systems of thought, which can then be reinscribed within a different order of signification. It is in the margins of the text that he discovers these unsettling forces at work, questioning the assumption that meaning can always be grasped in the form of some proper self-identical concept.

This has the effect of undermining most of what passes for "rigorous" thought in philosophy no less than literary theory. What makes Derrida's work attractive, no doubt, is the implicit invitation to new and more adventurous forms of interpretive criticism. But while he rejects the notion of deconstruction as a kind of anti-philosophy, he characterizes the traditional philosopher as one who habitually forgets that he is writing. He concludes that all attempts to keep philosophy separate from literature – to maintain it as a privileged truth seeking discourse, immune from the vagueness of writing – are bound to fail. That is why he rejects what he takes to be the "logocentric" bias in our thinking about mind, language, and reality. At the same time he holds that deconstruction should not be content to simply *invert* certain cardinal oppositions (speech/writing, philosophy/literature) so as to leave the "inferior" term henceforward firmly established at the top. For this could be nothing more than a notational gesture and, at the end of such a reading, philosophy would stand revealed as nothing more than a particular literary genre. Derrida emphasizes that one should respect the particular demands of philosophical writing,[3] and he implicitly invokes the normative standards of logic, consistency, and noncontradiction to which he denies however any absolute binding force. Yet he suggests that their authority rests on our not perceiving the extent of the disseminating power of certain root metaphors raised into concepts. They bring with them a whole network of articulated theses and assumptions whose meaning anywhere links up with other texts, other genres and topics of discourse. Writing is characterized by Derrida as being altogether intertextual, i.e. connected to other texts, while there is nothing outside the text *pre se*. Norris warns us that this should not be taken as a license for that other kind of wholesale "intertextuality" that rejoices in simply riding roughshod over all such genuine distinctions. For it is precisely this stratified character of language – the fact that it has been endlessly worked over by specific genealogies and logics of science – that demands the effort of a prudent, slow, and differentiated reading. And among these, as Derrida argues, are the various "philosophemes" or ways of thinking, which by now have impressed themselves so deeply on our language that we take them as common-sense truth and forget their specific philosophical prehistory.[4]

In an interview given in 1984, Derrida revealed that he has attempted to find a nonphilosophical site from which to question philosophy, but that this does not amount to an antiphilosophical stance.[5] Yet by his own admission, all such attempts to go "beyond" philosophy inevitably end up only in more philosophy. It is largely because of such self-defeating gestures that Derrida has become suspect to Anglo-American analytic philosophy. While he attempts to "deconstruct" the rationalist philosophical tradition, he at the same time appeals to its critical authority. But what is at work here does not amount to a rigorous logic of exclusion. It is a major point in Derrida's argument that there can be no thinking back to origin and sources, no escaping from the logic of supplementarity that he adopts. It is only in terms of a presence deferred, of a truth that still awaits its fulfillment – much like the character of writing – that Plato can explain the power of dialectics to draw the philosopher endlessly on toward a vanishing point of ultimate wisdom. These are not, Derrida argues, just casual metaphors or accidental phrases. Rather they belong to a whole intricate system of logical and semantic rules and entailments, which must be taken into account by an adequate reading of the text. Derrida emphasizes that there is a politics and an ethics that are bound up with the insistence on speech as a model for the wise and responsible conduct of human affairs. For with such a system, there would always be the ultimate reference back to an authority residing outside and beyond the specific differences of age, class, or political interest. Such is the self-perpetuating logic that guarantees truth and social stability alike. Derrida opposes that tradition by pointing out that certain forces may be absent yet present – inscribed through a different supplementary order of necessity. It then becomes apparent that what we call a word is far from determining the limits of imaginable sense. The freewheeling readings that some of Derrida's American followers have adopted are, therefore, not mere misunderstandings of Derrida, as Norris claims. Derrida is fully aware that any breaking with philosophical language can only be self defeating, since there is simply no alternative ground on which to stand, no language that has not been endlessly worked over by the logical grammar of Platonism. The facile strain in post-structuralist thinking that passes directly from the "arbitrary" nature of the sign (the lack of any natural or determinate link between signifier and signified) does lead to the inescapable conclusion that a text cannot possibly "refer" to any world outside its theoretical domain. Derrida realizes that language is inherently referential or mimetic, and that there is simply no way of breaking its hold by mere deconstructionist fiat.

It is, nevertheless, precisely the correspondence theory of truth that is chiefly under attack by Derrida's deconstruction. He holds that deconstruction is always already at work even in those texts that would seem most expressly committed to a "logocentric" order of assumptions. It is, therefore, impossible for deconstructive readings to escape that ubiquitous system of ideas, impossible to leap outside it and land on some alternative ground. What Derrida is out to resist as far as possible is the Platonizing drift that would restore interpretation to a quest for self-present accuracy and truth. Even interpretation of the kind that literary critics most commonly practice is itself caught up in a structure of assumptions that philosophy continues to dominate. Such is the effect of removing the privilege that allows criticism to decide which terms shall be taken as key words of the text. Derrida thinks that it is pointless to ask who is speaking in any given passage of the text, for there is no last word, no metalanguage or authoritative voice exercising control that could ultimately serve to adjudicate the matter. Writing, he claims, is not a theme in any normal sense, even though it is altogether impossible to conceptualize language without falling back upon writing. Language is consequently not a theme either, but then neither is deconstruction. He admits the *de facto* priority of speech over writing, yet insists that this is not to be confused with the *de jure* argument that would take it as a logical necessity.

Typically Derrida focuses on metaphors, footnotes, passing analogies, or turns of argument, which philosophers would regard as scarcely meriting such attention. His point is that philosophy has maintained its long-standing prerogative by dictating in advance what shall count as worthwhile topics of debate. If the very idea of "literal sense" is merely a metaphor, it follows inevitably that there is nothing that is literally a metaphor either. Metaphorical meaning achieves its effect by subverting the established significance, and similarly deconstruction presupposes a structure to be dismantled. Derrida has consequently nothing resembling a theory or a method with which to work, and all he can do is point to the ultimate undecidability of all such conceptual differences. What is at stake here is not just a generalized sense of metaphorical drift, but the attempt to reveal the few tendencies in the text where writing *resists* this seductive process, where something escapes, exceeds, or perplexes the sovereignty of logocentric reason. Since he is not challenging this massive consensus on grounds of factual or historical accuracy, deconstruction remains of necessity marginal. It is a major precept of contemporary structural linguistics that meaning is not a relation of identity between signifier and signified but a product of the differences, the signifying contrasts and relationships that exist at every level of language. To think logocentrically is to dream of a transcendental signified, and deconstruction defines its project by contrast to this illusion, as a perpetual reminder that meaning is always deferred, and that thought cannot escape this logic of endless supplementarity. In this manner, Derrida claims that writing is always at the origin of language, while at the same time rejecting as illegitimate all references to origin. Since there is no such origin, we need to understand "writing" not in the narrow, familiar sense of graphic inscription or literal marks on a page. But writing for Derrida is not just one metaphor among others,[6] for there can be little doubt that he attaches to it a great deal of literal meaning.

If the sign is indeed an arbitrary relation between signifier and signified, this leaves room for all kinds of secondary elaboration in the spheres of cultural and literal study. For Derrida, "difference" is not a self-possessed concept; it is a fissile term that introduces all manner of disturbing and contradictory effects into theoretical discourse. The "logic of difference" is a non-self-identical logic, one that eludes all the normative constraints that govern classical reason. It is not at all clear, however, what such a logic working with nonidentical concepts can accomplish, for to the degree it becomes incapable of prohibiting inferences as illegitimate, it no longer does what logic has been invented to do. Derrida's language is marked by the absence of positive terms that permit conceptualization, and this inevitably inhibits his ability to explain matters. He wants to grasp language as a system of different yet non-self-identical terms, but it then becomes an easy prey to what Norris considers "arbitrary" practices and interpretations. Written signs have traditionally been thought of as marks of difference, while Derrida's notion of writing extends far beyond the standard intended sense of literal marks on a page. If writing, however, is not treated as a concept, as a word to which corresponds some fixed and definite meaning, the idea of writing cannot be grasped either. Since writing is taken by Derrida as the very condition of knowledge, this renders knowledge as well into a metaphor lacking literal meaning. Contrary to Norris, Derrida is, therefore, incapable of performing a transcendental deduction in the manner of Kant. Thought is said to be deluded if it attempts to comprehend the nature of writing from a standpoint seemingly outside or above it. And it is philosophy that most often falls prey to this illusion, overlooking the fact that history itself is tied to the possibility of writing.[7] Derrida entertains a notion of writing that supposedly precedes and delimits all oral language; yet the claim that speech already belongs to writing[8] is, in effect, counterfactual. That is why Derrida is unable to tell us what writing is.

He rejects Rousseau's philosophy of origins that sets a cardinal opposition between *nature* and *culture* with everything authentic and original belonging to nature, and everything false and degenerative being the result of culture. But no more than Rousseau is he himself able to conceive of knowledge or writing except in terms of language and structure. If there is no such thing as literal meaning, there can be no metaphorical meaning either and, hence, no deconstruction. Derrida is incapable of explaining how writing ever got started; the very distinction between speech and writing cannot be carried through, for along with writing there comes a whole tacit system of meanings and presuppositions that cannot be identified. What he wants to bring out here is a different kind of logic; it turns out, however, that this remains parasitic on our usual ways of talking and reasoning. Such deconstruction by necessity presupposes standard norms of literal meaning and coherence, and hence there remains an unbridgeable gap between what Derrida says and what he means to say. He claims that there is no ultimate truth of psychological, historical, or any other kind of discourse, yet proceeds to make an exception in his own case. If texts do not yield any kind of authoritative truthful reading, this applies *a fortiori* to his own notion of "writing." Something always escapes the reading of a text and, consequently, any commentary that aims to speak the truth of a text will find itself outflanked or outwitted by a supplementary logic. If, however, nothing like a concept can be said to exist, there is, by the same token, no argument Derrida can legitimately make. Writing for him is whatever escapes, unsettles, or complicates the commonplace assumptions – yet this becomes pointless if there is no literal meaning. Derrida rejects the idea of a text that is opposed to the real world existing outside and beyond it. What he is asking us to recognize is the radical instability, the strictly undecidable character of any such metaphysical opposition. He substitutes, however, for the difference between nature and culture his own pivotal contrast between speech and writing.

When he attempts to think about the origin of writing, he is caught up in a shifting exchange of priorities, which resists any form of coherent theoretical grasp. Writing and deconstruction are governed by counterfactual metaphors that defy consistent identification. He realizes that metaphor and metaphorical truth cannot be sustained without literal meaning,[9] yet he somehow manages to forget this when he discusses the role of writing and deconstruction. What is at issue here is the status of explanatory theories, the question of how far or by what conceptual logic reason can exercise its sovereign claims. Claiming only marginality for his own deconstructive tactics, he in effect decides in advance that they are going to fail. Since all such alternative readings have no particular claim on either meaning or truth, they cannot prevail in the long run. Attempting to undermine the totalizing of theories, his own brand of deconstruction is conceived as a total and consistent strategy, but by adopting a logic of chance and of random anomalies, such an approach is no longer critical in the required sense. Having renounced the quest for determinate structure, Derrida lacks an effective defense against what Norris considers an arbitrary misuse of language. Once deconstruction sets itself up as the antithesis of philosophical reason, it becomes self-destructive and pointless. Derrida cannot restrict deconstruction to the questioning of "naive" ideas of reference that assume a straightforward matching up of language and the world "outside." While attempting to resist and deconstruct the antinomies of classical reason, his characterization of "writing" does not escape the metaphysics of the real. This is why Derrida has been read by his Marxist critics as denying any reality outside the text. When there is more than just one way to read a text, the interpreter is more likely to make of it whatever he pleases. No reading, however meticulous or prudent, can serve as an effective limit on metaphorical proliferation once the existence of literal meaning has been denied. When conflicting interpretations are left as undecidable by Derrida, a close textual analysis becomes, in effect, pointless.

Debates like these are misconceived if philosophy is just another kind of writing with no privileged access to knowledge or truth, and deconstruction becomes futile by the same token. Derrida fails to show that it is possible to make sense of any strategy that issues such a radical challenge to prevailing ideas. Contrary to his declared intentions, this amounts to the skeptical claim that we cannot know anything at all. It is largely such self-defeating claims that have made it difficult for philosophers in the Anglo-American analytical tradition to take Derrida seriously. While some loosening of restrictions on interpretation may be beneficial, there is no way of knowing what the consequences are going to be. In the absence of metanarrative norms and criteria, we can only take our bearing from shifting metaphors that make up the currency of deconstruction and leave such questions as beyond hope of a definite answer. Norris, of course, is quite right when he points out that there is no "post-philosophical" realm of pure textuality where truth and falsehood are mere words, and the principle of reason no longer applies.[10] The problem is that the logical bite of such arguments has been lost to undecidabilty, and that such "post-modern" musings no longer amount to either a rational critique or a definite proposal of viable alternatives. Derrida cannot quite make up his mind whether we have entered a "post-modern" era of forms of legitimacy whose reason no longer exerts any general critical force. But there can be little doubt that he lacks any effective defense against the freewheeling American modes of deconstruction that take their inspiration from his work. What Norris calls "thinking through one's own position"[11] becomes altogether futile once logocentrism has been renounced, appealing as it does to an implicit consistency without which deconstruction lacks both target and method. Those who want to adopt a critical stance in these matters cannot set themselves up in opposition to reason or logic without, in effect, demolishing their own case. Derrida regards rationality in its current technological and communicative forms as a specific historical formation that cannot be appealed to as some ultimate ground. But neither can he think the limits of reason without invoking what he denounces as the logocentric tradition. Deconstruction remains wedded to this practice of enlightened rational critique, and that is why Derrida's principle of undecidability constitutes such a serious obstacle to his deconstructive strategies. By suspending the power to decide between different readings of a text, he is left without any real choice in his deconstruction.

Derrida, nevertheless, claims that there is a sense in which deconstruction is fitted to press beyond the present stalemate, the paralysis of reason engendered by nuclear threat. He points out that "deterrence" is a word for which there exists no adequate concept, no place within a system of coherent intelligible theory that would make proper sense of it in a given context. Competence is, therefore, no longer exclusively vested in these experts – whether nuclear scientists or strategic analysis – whose knowledge becomes increasingly obsolete given the extraordinary complexity of the issues involved. Such knowledge is neither coherent nor totalizable[12] but neither, of course, is Derrida's own brand of deconstruction. While strategies of deterrence may not be mere matters of applied expertise and rational prevision, his own analysis fails to provide any alternative strategies either. By focusing on the rhetorical dimension of the conflict, he in effect renders it proof against reasonable resolution. If there is no weakening of the multiple chances of error and misinterpretation that are opened up at each new gambit in the nuclear game, Derrida has to leave everything as it is. The situation, however, is not one of total uncertainty and some strategies are more likely to be effective than others. By treating nuclear reality as an apocalyptic fantasy, he in effect removes it from the scope of rational deliberation and decision. While it may be granted that questions of competence are not merely a matter of technical know-how and strategic expertise, they are not just a matter of literary style either. Derrida may plausibly argue that nuclear confrontation is more complex than the facts of the matter indicate, but by declaring these issues undecidable he becomes himself unable to advocate any specific policy. By treating diplomacy as a predominately rhetorical phenomenon and by stressing its irrational and unpredictable consequences, he in effect reduces the chances for any pragmatic resolution of conflict.

Derrida lacks an effective defense against those modern literary critics who want to turn the table on philosophy and argue that "all concepts are metaphors." In "White Mythology," he emphasizes that all our working definitions of metaphor since Aristotle have been expressed in terms that ultimately derive from the language and the conceptual resources of philosophy.[13] For it is only to the extent that we have inherited certain ways of conceptualizing metaphors – i.e. criteria and techniques for distinguishing between "literal" and "figurative" language – that we can get any kind of argumentative hold on discussing these questions.[14] Rejecting "logocentrism," Derrida cannot effectively refute the claim that it is language and culture that decisively determine the ways in which the world is interpreted. He stresses the philosophical origin of certain key terms and definitions in literary criticism, while denying the legitimacy of all such claims to "origin." He admits that philosophy always reappropriates the discourse that delimits it,[15] yet looks for a place "outside" philosophy to ground his deconstructive strategies.[16] He certainly blurs the distinction between philosophy and literature when he treats philosophy as a textual phenomenon, and thus in effect subjugates reason to rhetoric. What philosophy has failed to think through in his view is the salient fact of its textual condition, its dependence on the figural resources of language that open up strange and unsettling possibilities of sense. In this manner he questions the idea of "context" to the point of denying that it can ever serve as a ground of appeal for deciding what speech acts properly mean in any given situation. Since language is subject to a generalized readiness to be grafted into new and unforseeable contexts, there is no appeal to performative intent that can serve to delimit the range of possible meaning. What Derrida calls into question is the right of philosophy to maintain a wholesale theory of the mind and language on the basis of common-sense notions that work well enough for all practical purposes but take on a different, more doctrinaire aspect when applied as a matter of philosophic principle. He repudiates the idea that philosophy can lay down the rules of procedure by explaining how language should and must work. Thus, he rejects the prevalent notion that there is just one way a text should "properly" be read. He admits that we require at least some presumed general grasp of an author's purpose in order to read the text at all. But he insists what any theory will have to get along in the end without in itself implying either that I fully understand what the other says, writes, means to say or write, or even that any adequate equivalence could obtain between what he consciously intended, what he did, and what I do while reading.[17]

Derrida thus questions the Cartesian ideal of clear and distinct ideas on which the standard speech act theory is founded, and the related notion of a privileged access to self-present meanings and intentions. It is this tradition that sustains the belief in the recoverability of intentions, the power of a text to reveal its true meaning in the presence of an authorized interpreter. Derrida rejects the rationalist presumption that claims to know in advance of reading precisely what standards and criteria a text must obey if it is to count as "serious" philosophy. He concludes that the most a rigorous reflection on the process and limits of textual critique can show is that such matters remain undecidable. The problem is, however, that such "prelogical possibilities of logic" are not amenable to Derrida's deconstruction anymore than to standard analysis. This is also what makes his notion of writing so opaque to rational explanation, since anything Derrida can affirm about it is already part and parcel of the logocentric tradition he rejects. His aim is to expose the habitual presumption that enables philosophers to go (as they think) straight to the conceptual heart of the text without wasting time over matters that are distant or (to them) unnecessary detail. In *La Carte Postale,* he emphasizes that communication is not always what philosophers imagine it to be – an exchange where intentions are never mistaken and where messages always arrive on time and at the appointed place. He stresses the multiplicity of meaning, which prevents any assurance that true communication has in fact taken place. The postcard is a message casually written and promiscuously open to all to read. At the same time, it is a writing that can only make sense to one person (the presumed addressee) whose knowledge of the sender enables him to figure out its otherwise impossibly cryptic message. What Derrida suggests is that we read the great texts of the written tradition as so many messages that circulate without any absolutely authorized source or designation. The particular postcard that so caught Derrida's fancy was one that he found in the Bodleian Library reproduced form the fontpiece of a thirteenth century English fortune telling book.[18] The remarkable thing about this engraving was that it showed Plato standing and apparently dictating his thoughts to a seated Socrates who obediently wrote them down. One can see why this image should have struck Derrida with the force of a revelation. One of his chief arguments or strategies of reading has to do precisely with this mythical relationship between Socrates, Plato, and the writing of philosophy. Thus, Plato is the prototype of all those unfortunate philosophers who must resort to writing in order to communicate their thoughts, but who lay themselves open in the process to all manner of unauthorized reading and interpretation. Norris argues that to envision a Socrates who writes is to open up a counter tradition, however apocryphal, where the old logocentric myth of origins no longer holds exclusive sway. It suggests that writing is in at the source of philosophy, that there is no turning back to an authorized voice that doesn't pass by way of certain images or metaphors derived from writing.[19]

Derrida's point in deploying the postcard is to show how circumstance always and everywhere enters the discourse of philosophical reason. Philosophy is motivated by a natural desire to treat its discoveries as a timeless a priori truth rather than a series of interesting notions thrown up by chance encounter with events and ideas. The problem is that there are no given boundaries on deconstruction once he has localized logic to shifting contexts. That is why he finds himself incapable of abiding by the consequences of his own epistemological skepticism. By rejecting the common sense view that language signifies literal meaning, he is left without strict laws of deductive inference. He stresses the undecidability that attaches to speech acts in general and shows that this has extensive political consequences in the American context where a written constitution enshrines certain supposedly "self-evident" values and principles. These can be interpreted in very different ways by Supreme Court judges with the power to overturn even well-entrenched acts of state legislature. What Derrida objects to in the standard consensus version of speech act theory is the idea that meanings can be simply read off by an authorized interpreter who knows as if by natural right what constitutes true understanding. The presence of a written constitution where principles are left open to all manner of far-reaching juridical review gives a political edge to questions of textual interpretation.

Derrida also discusses the related issue of an author's responsibility for future interpretations of his text. He believes that it is by no means an accident that Nietzsche's writings, for example, took on their bad eminence in the Nazi period. But denying, as Derrida does, all literal meaning and original intent on the part of the author, he inevitably invites such second guessing of his own text. He attacks the Aristotelian tradition that defined metaphor on philosophical terms as a figure of speech whose workings can always be explained by reference to some other, more reliable or epistemologically more privileged use of language. Derrida, however, pursues this critique to the point where any distinction between "concept" and "metaphor" altogether disappears. If all propositions concerning metaphor are undecidable, there is always the possibility of some radical new meaning that could utterly change the way such writings signify. Contrary to Norris, there seems to be little in Derrida's notion of deconstruction that is capable of imposing effective control on interpretative discourse. He holds that thought is deluded if it tries to achieve a standpoint "outside" or "above" the discourse of philosophical reason, and at the same time this is precisely what his deconstrictive strategies are out to accomplish. To speak or to write against reason becomes, in the end, always a self-defeating gesture. It is why deconstruction has been regarded as a species if irrationalism that denies the very possibility of objective meaning and knowledge. It appears, however, that no case can be argued, no proposition stated, no matter how radical its intention, that does not appeal to the conceptual resources of ordinary language. And such language is steeped in all kinds of anthropocentric and metaphysical meanings that determine its intelligibility and logic. Structuralism, therefore, is heir to all the epistemological projects from Plato to Kant and Husserl that have tried to fix limits to the discourse of knowledge and the truth claims of universal reason. And literary criticism since Aristotle has taken over these ambitions, since it has worked with a handful of concepts (*mimesis,* form, metaphorical versus literal meaning) whose line of descent is altogether philosophical. Derrida emphasizes that what structuralism manages to leave out is the excess of meaning over form, the fact that certain elements of force or meaning must always escape its organization. There are many indications in his work identifying closely with the heritage of Jewish religion. What distinguishes such commentary from its orthodox Christian counterpart is precisely the emphasis on writing as an endless productive signifying practice irreducible to some ultimate self-evident truth.[20] To set the Jewish against the Graeco-Christian tradition is implicitly to focus on writing and its place in the economy of knowledge and truth. What is intelligible to the thinkers in the Greek tradition is whatever lends itself to various totaling methods and strategies that thought has devised in order to maintain its grasp on the otherwise recalcitrant real world. For the only kind of knowledge that *counts* philosophically is that which finds its place in the grand dialectical scheme, and thus has a claim on world historical status. This position is attained, however, only at the cost of confining philosophy to its narrowed epistemological mode of inquiry. While Derrida attempts to broaden this scope, he still wants to remain within the tradition of what he regards as the present-day enlightened thought. Yet these two aspirations seem incompatible.

Notes

[1] Christopher Norris, *Derrida,* Cambridge, MA: Harvard University Press, 1987.

[2] Jacques Derrida, *Margins of Philosophy* (1972), trans. Alan Bass, Chicago, IL: Chicago University Press, 1982, pp. 3-27.

[3] *Ibid.,* p. 305.

[4] Norris, *Derrida,* p. 26.

[5] See Derrida's interview with Richard Kearney in *Dialogues with Contemproary Continental Thinkers,* ed. Richard Kearney, Manchester University Press, 1984, p. 100.

[6] Norris, *Derrida,* p. 187.

[7] Jacques Derrida, *Of Grammatology,* (1967), trans. Gayatri Chakravorty Spivak, Baltimore, MD: John Hopkins University Press, 1976, p. 27.

[8] *Ibid.,* p. 55.

[9] Jacques Derrida, *Dissemination* (1972), trans. Barbara Johnson, London: Athlone Press, 1981, p. 258.

[10] Norris, *Derrida,* p. 156.

[11] *Ibid.,* p. 159.

[12] Jacques Derrida, "No Apocalypse, Not Now (full spead ahead, seven missiles, seven missives)," *Diacritics,* vol xv (1984), p. 24.

[13] Derrida, *Margins of Philosophy,* pp. 207-21.

[14] Norris, *Derrida,* p. 170.

[15] Jacques Derrida, "The Supplement of Copula," in *Margins of Philosophy,* p. 177.

[16] Interview with Kearney, p. 98.

[17] Jacques Derrida, "Limited Inc abc (response to John Searle), *Glyph,* vol II, Baltimore, MD: John Hopkins University Press, 1977, p. 199.

[18] Jacques Derrida, *La Carte Postale de Socrate à Freud et au-delà,* Paris: Aubier-Flammarion, 1980, pp. 101-118.

[19] Norris, *Derrida,* p. 187.

[20] *Ibid.,* p. 229.

Chapter Twenty

Derridean Displacement

Although displacement is not explicitly discussed in Derrida's writings, it is central to his de-centering mode of critique. He remains conspicuously modest in his conception of what deconstruction can accomplish, yet the subject of his literary study includes society, culture, sexuality, and the unconscious – all considered as texts. Displacement is above all about writing itself, but it is also about woman, the unconsciousness, and Jewishness, for these are all exemplary instances of the marginal. Derrida's drift remains indeterminable and undecidable, the old organizations are shaken, yet they remain. Even when we think against metaphysical concepts, we do this by means of words that cannot be cleansed from their metaphysical associations. There seems, therefore, no way back to what all right-thinking persons can agree on, based on common sense and the evidence of the senses. Certitude of theory gives way to the characteristic Derridean undecidability, the vertigo that has its analogue in the flutter, oscillation, and trembling of Op Art.[1] For Derrida, ornament and style are not mere embellishment; rather, ornament generates texts and concepts. Thus, the seemingly arbitrary conjunction of *oir* words – *Moira, moiré, grimoire* (medieval book of spells in *La Carte Postale)* turn out to obey a certain (non-Aristotelian) logic: neither pure randomness not pure determinance. Derrida emphasizes that metaphor is never innocent, since it orients research and fixes results,[2] and he constructs an entire philosophical program on the homonym (the homophone, pun, and related devices) providing a non-Aristotelian grammatology that tolerates equivocity. In dissemination, thought is guided not by forms of sight but by the sounds of puns or the distribution of letters. This functions on the assumption that language itself is intelligent, and hence that homophones "know something."

Derrida reveals the power of thought residing in decorative devices[3] through the equivocacy of his terminology, such as the term *différance,* which combines difference and deferment. He takes this as a model of the history of philosophy, which in spite of its insistence on clarity is subject to blurred repetitions, as in the exemplary case of the distinction between platonism and sophistics. These discriminations become so subtle that, in the end, they separate nothing. Derrida's own writing therefore deals only marginally with what it is about. It proceeds by means of contamination, as it were, a discontinuous model of innovation and change, as happens when the analogy is weak. Under such circumstances, analogy may well mislead us, becoming frivolous, as in the blurring of the distinction between discourse and quotation. The unfolding that most interests Derrida is the interlacing of the narrator and the narrative. He challenges the cognitive prejudice against rhetoric as "ornament" by showing that ornamentation itself can prove the methodology of a science: grammatology.[4] There is a "world view" at work in the decorative in which part and whole have a supplementary relationship.[5] Against the logocentrism of Western metaphysics, which takes the style as something added on to thought, Derrida emphasizes that the "center" itself is not a natural or fixed focus. Unlike symbolism and analogy, which tend to assume a basic or literal foundation on which an analogy is based or a symbol is drawn, the concept of transformation assumes no fundamental dimension.[6] Derrida plays with our conceptual habits and displaces the normal line of logic resulting in a conceptual "vertigo," and the liability of his own system is thereby readily admitted. Thus for Conley, Derrida is primarily a writer rather than a philosopher; he includes literary styles in his inquiry and within this "supplemental" view of the craft, the "styles" of philosophy and literature tend to overlap. An apprehension of other, different languages in use allows us to discover the limits of our monocular perspective. Lines of binary logic that had been associated with writing find themselves loosened up by the vagaries of style. Shifting to single words and what attention makes of them brings us to a much broader horizon of discourse, not entirely controlled by grammar. Derrida calls this play of order and disorder "dissemination" in which the so-called free play is not controlled by some godlike context the analyst imposes on it. When Derrida's styles are followed up carefully, there is no way that his thought can be appropriated by a single tongue.[7] Rather than arguing, he constructs a dialogue of several voices that approach, blend, harmonize for a moment, and take leave of each other. The power inherent in the use of language is such that every user marks off a space that he takes to be his own.

Ryan concludes that liberal institutions are not founded on anything that can be called "real," and that natural rights are never fully natural – they are displaceable from the outset. Liberal reason assumes that it is possible and necessary to begin the search for knowledge with a clean slate, and to base knowledge claims on a clear and distinct indubitable, self-evident foundation. The appropriate formal standards for all human knowledge are those of mathematical modes of inquiry, and the key to the progress of human knowledge is the development and pursuit of explicit rules of method. The entire body of valid human knowledge is a unity both in method and in substance, and, thereby, human knowledge can be made accessible to all men. Deconstructive philosophy, on the other hand, questions this normativization of the logos and the natural rights of reason, and it denies the possibility of a clean slate altogether free of historical presuppositions. It also doubts the possibility of a self-evident foundation of complete unambiguous ideas. It questions the absolute certainty of the mathematical model, the validity of formal method abstracted from practical situations as well as the unity of knowledge. It thus denies the possibility of absolute certainty or determinacy, and much of this skepticism has to do with the value and use of the language within which knowledge must necessarily be committed. Deconstruction discredits oppositions within liberal reason, such as those of thought and practice, semantics and syntax, mind and body, oppositions that permit a supposedly natural form of knowledge disassociated from institutions, history, and technology.[8] Displacement is a process in rhetoric that presents one thing to be compared and identified with another by virtue of contingency and analogy. Such contrivances are seen as secondary and degraded from the point of view of the natural light of reason, which prefers self-evident, ideal, or natural foundations.

Liberal social theory is subject to displacement because it is based on two founding metaphors or analogies: the metaphor of nature, which connotes freedom and lack of constraint, and the metaphor of scientific law, which suggests order and harmony between parts subsumed under a whole. Liberalism consists of a number of concepts and institutions that form a coherent system only as long as the initial analogies are accepted. The initial assumptions are that anyone in civil society is equal and free, and that civil society functions according to laws that are analogous to those of natural science. A power is a power to dispose, and the assertion of that power immediately implies the possible threat of its removal. The very assertion of right is always a denial of its naturalness, that is, of its permanence and necessity. Ownership is merely a displacement that is recognized by convention as legitimate, and by its very existence as law; property right testifies to its own nonuniversality and nonuniformity. Its authority rests on the metaphorical analogy to the laws of natural science, which must be uniform and universal. Individual reason may determine rational truth, but it does so on the basis of socio-historical contexts. Individualism and collectivism are undecidably intertwined,[9] yet liberal reason is intolerant of the undecidability (between individual and collective, universal and particular, fact and value, subject and object, etc.) that is in fact the case in our world.

Handelman's point of departure is also the fluidity of boundaries between text and commentary in both the Jewish hermeneutical tradition and in Derrida. Her interpretation of Derrida as "Reb Derissa" treats his writings as a form of heretic hermeneutics within a larger tradition of heresy. Usually translated as "writing," Derrida's *écriture* can also be translated as "Scripture." Most readers of Derrida interpret his displacements as extensions of the Nietzschean-Heideggerian tradition, whereas Handelman argues that they may be read and understood just as much as an extension of the long tradition of rabbinic scriptural hermeneutics. Displacement constitutes the historic Jewish tradition of exile, and Derrida in his essay on the French-Jewish writer Edmond Jabès traces this connection between Jew as exile and writing. For the Jews the central problem is interpretation, and in order to come to grips with it, the rabbis created a system that itself became another equally authoritative canon, another Scripture. Interpretation in Derrida is always already there because the commentator's discourse cannot be really or methodically separated from that of the author, this relation being a contaminating one. The model of interpretation of the rabbis arose out of the tension between continuity and rebellion, attachment to the text and alienation from it. This became particularly acute for the post-Enlightenment Jews who have, like Freud and Derrida, assimilated into Western secular culture. Like Freud, Derrida is obsessed with the need for a revisonary interpretation, and his target is all the fathers of philosophy. His project is to deconstruct the entire Western tradition of "onto-theology," to undo "logocentrism," and to send the word into the exile of writing.[10] Writing is the realm not of presence – to which the word is so intimately related – but of absence, deferment, and difference. Rabbinic thought has always been an alternative metaphysics due to the Biblical doctrine that the world is created, not as in the Greek view, eternally existent. It is a place for the contingent within philosophy, and against the latter's original bias.[11] Rabbinic reason could not be founded on necessary axioms inherent in the nature of things that furnished neat syllogisms and universally true statements. There is also the standard contrast between the Greek emphasis on seeing and the Hebrew emphasis on hearing: seeing is presence, whereas hearing implies absence. When sight is the predominant mode, then the search for identity in knowledge or resemblance will be defined in terms of copy, re-presentation, and thought as speculative, as in specular. And this view of knowledge as *mimesis* is exactly what Derrida and the deconstructionists attack.[12]

The Jewish concept of idolatry was a kind of fetishism, the worship of reified signs devoid of significance. The loss of a stable referent that grounds the "literal" and "proper" meaning of words is a manner of exile. Freedom comes in the characteristically rabbinic mode: through interpretation, a chain in which signifier and signified do not merge. In Derrida there is a *Midrashic* play, which makes his deconstruction so different from Heidegger's or Nietzsche's. Philosophy, Derrida points out, is Greek in the most ethnographic sense. Absence does not equal nonexistence; like otherness, it is one of Derrida's prime terms in a vocabulary that seeks to evade the trap of Being and Nonbeing. Derrida's reality is not Being but Absence, not the One but the Other, not unity buy plurality, dissemination, writing and difference. Much of Derrida is in the spirit of the Kabbalistic interpreters who created baroque mythologies out of the elements of Scripture.[13] He reveals the irrational, daemonic, and mythic secrets at the heart of reason, science, and the hermeneutic tradition. Derrida chooses to stay in exile, to differ infinitely and defer; there is for him no end to exile, but rather a rising of the Jewish condition of exile into the paradigm of existence – to be is to be in exile. That is why there is something sacred about writing (as in Kafka's "writing as a form of prayer"), commentary, and text, even after it has been displaced into the profane fields of psychoanalysis, literature, and philosophy.

Notes

[1] Mark Krupnick, ed., *Displacement, Derrida and After,* Bloomington, IN: Indiana University Press, 1983, p. 22.

[2] Jacques Derrida, *Writing and Difference,* trans. A. Bass, Chicago, IL: University of Chicago Press, 1978, p. 17.

[3] Gregory L. Ulmer, "Op Writing: Derrida's Solicitation of Theoria," in *Displacement, Derrida and After,* p. 41.

[4] Jacques Derrida, "Living On: Border Lines," trans. James Hulbert, *Deconstruction and Criticism,* ed. H. Bloom et al, New York, NY: New York Seabury Press, 1979, pp. 99-100.

[5] Jacques Derrida, *Vérite en pienture,* Paris: Flammarion, 1978, p. 392.

[6] James Ogilvy, *Many Dimensional Man,* New York, Oxford, 1979, pp. 46-7.

[7] Tom Conley, "A Trace of Style," in *Displacement, Derrida and After,* p. 85.

[8] Michael Ryan, "Deconstruction and Social Theory: The Case of Liberalism," in *Displacement, Derrida and After,* p. 155.

[9] *Ibid., p. 166.*

[10] Susan Handelman, "Jacques Derrida and the Heretic Hermeneutic," in *Displacement, Derrida and After,* p. 102.

[11] Hans Jonas, *Philosophical Essays,From Ancient Creed to Technological Man,* Englewood Cliffs, NJ: Prentice Hall, 1973, p. 29.

[12] Handelman. "Jacques Derrida and the Heretic Hermeneutic," p. 105.

[13] Harold Bloom *A Map of Misreadings,* New York, NY: Oxford University Press, 1975, p. 43.

Chapter Twenty-One

Limits of Deconstruction

Deconstruction is the general strategy that exposes the myth of a fixed, essential, timeless, and naturally acceptable structure of an independent reality which can be discovered. Derrida's speculation is a deconstruction in the absence of a given, but lacking literal meaning his metaphors remain inconclusive. He argues that theorizing about human discourse, Saussure turns to construct a more congenial but entirely fictional world of language, which he finally acknowledges to be such, and yet somehow, as he proceeds, he seems to forget that the system of language is but a fiction. The resulting "order" Derrida rejects as "logocentrism." Although Derrida admits that we cannot avoid language and its implicit inconsistencies even when we express its presumptions, he rejects the resulting order. He believes that we are forever subject to the illusion that what we say captures how the would really is, yet his deconstruction is not altogether successful in dispelling this fallacy. Even though he insists that we can never go beyond language, he holds, like Wittgenstein, that by exposing the deformative power of what we say, deconstruction enables us to recover what cannot be said. This, for Derrida, coincides with the puzzle of "writing," which is, of course, not merely the recording of what is uttered, but a reflection of the power of difference underlying the joint process of speech and of written language. We should not expect that by means of deconstruction of conceptual networks we will somehow become more inclusive and accurate, since deconstruction merely reflects the contingent provisional supplement of all such reflexive efforts deprived of their logocentric pretensions. Because for Derrida there is no decipherable alternative structure, deconstruction is the denial of decipherment,[1] but while there is a sense in which a mere notation is arbitrary, the fact that the "graphic sign" represents the linguistic (or phonic) sign presupposes a deeper unanalyzed ability to fix the latter so that it can thus be represented, however arbitrarily. The thing that constitutes language (*l'essentiel de la langue*) is itself unrelated to the phonic character of the linguistic sign, and linguistics is finally only a part of a more general semiology. Derrida emphasizes that Saussure illegitimately assumes that there is an unproblematic cognitive faculty that human beings manifest in using language naturally in their intercourse with the world. What Saussure fails to question, he insists, is the essential possibility of nonintuition,[2] i.e. the profound possibility that there are no recognizable structures of the world independent of our mind.

The theory of deconstruction is only a comment on whatever ability we may have to generate and interpret a text, but which for Derrida essentially remains a mystery. What he offers is not a methodology of interpretation or, what comes to the same thing, a link between interpretive text and the world[3] because deconstruction makes no sense unless some networks of difference are already in place, and since all communication is necessarily modeled in the decoder's way, however provisionally and heuristically. On the deconstructive view, signs are merely traces, and they are traces of nothing. Deconstruction begs to expose the myth that the structure of language and thought is ultimately the structure of reality, but the problem then becomes to show that any one established scheme for analyzing or interpreting familiar phenomena is more adequate than another. While deconstruction opposes the pretensions of totalizing any system of differences imposed on the unending changes in human experience, it fails to show how any such distinction will make a difference. By acknowledging the inescapabilty of conceptual systems, it presupposes literal truth at least as an ideal that all interpretation must tacitly assume. Derrida opposes what he takes to be the delusions of essentialism, foundationalism, correspondence, cognitive privilege, and logocentrism, but all such global arguments against logic must in the end become self-defeating. He recognizes that internal to any conceptual scheme, and relative to it, judgments of comparative value and power are both unavoidable and convincing, yet his rejection of logocentrism is itself radical and global, and it is particularly suspect when applied to mathematics or technology. If logic is relative to a particular language, Derrida fails to have a medium in which logocentrism can convincingly be refuted. On the one hand, he warns us that any conceptual framework remains deconstructable, and at the same time he resists all attempts to deconstruct deconstruction.[4] But of course, this is exactly what his interpreters and critics have been doing all along.

In "White Mythology," Derrida's analysis implies a profound suspicion of the concept of metaphor, and it is indeed not quite clear how metaphoricity can yield a structure that accounts for the difference between the figural and the properly literal. Ricoeur concludes in *The Role of Metaphor* that the entire theory of analogy is no more than a pseudoscience.[5] Only to the extent that being is difference can it be said to be analogical, and it is within such a perspective that this doctrine is taken by both Heidegger and Derrida. In *Being and Time* everything is primarily understood not by focusing on the thing itself but with regard to something else, such as the *what-for* of the thing. Being is dif-ference; it is analogical; it is nothing in itself. But it is the very articulation of its own understanding within which it appears as a multiple of irreducible sense. Already Aristotle had indicated that a certain multiplicity is constitutive of the very variety of being. The movement that is constitutive of metaphor *(epiphora)* is present in all understanding of the *as-what.* In the *Poetics,* Aristotle considered analogy one species of metaphor whereas in his *Rhetoric,* it already had become the paradigm of metaphor. Derrida accepts that metaphor and the movement of *epiphora* are to be thought of in the background and with respect to the more general problem of analogy.[6] Analogy brings together the concept and what is without concept; it serves to think the difference.[7] The hierarchization of logocentric analogy proceeds from the fact that one term within the relation of relations comes to name the relation itself. Language, according to Derrida, is analogy through and through,[8] but language engenders also a negative product: the analogy of the analogy, the useless and vain simulacrum of discourse, prattle, nonsense – in short, the frivolous.[9] The message of such frivolous use of language is that its proper and legitimate use is restricted, but Derrida's theory of language cannot tell us where this line between meaning and nonsense is to be drawn.

Ricoeur claims that philosophical discourse maintains its authority by stripping the mathematical notion of analogy of its conceptual rigor. Derrida, on the other hand, emphasizes that it is from the trope that we learn about the status of the literal proper meaning.[10] He admits in *Dissemination* that since everything becomes metaphorical, there is no longer a literal sense, and hence no longer a metaphor either.[11] It would seem, however, that without the contrast with literal meaning, Derrida's insistence on the metaphorical character of language becomes pointless. Since the "logic" of metaphors is taken to be one of contamination (i.e. lacking discernible structure or method), this leads to an erosion of the very distinction between concept and metaphor. Such figures of speech can no longer define the limits of what is proper and legitimate within language. For Derrida, the metaphor "retreats," as does Being for Heidegger: both are vanishing concepts, as it were, and are no longer capable of being imposed as norms for what is proper and legitimate, or for making the required distinctions and differences. In this manner, Being is also no longer resistant to metaphor as Heidegger claims, because for Heidegger, the being of language resides in the *as-structure* characteristic of *logos,* whereas for Derrida, it coincides with the problematic context of being a metaphor. Derrida emphasizes that Being, the proper, etc., do not escape the claim of making distinctions, and that there is consequently nothing outside the text, no reality that can serve as a touchstone for language. While the concept in its universality may be irreducible to metaphor, figure of speech, or trope, its intelligibility nevertheless hinges on the possibility of lending itself to metaphorization. Such irreducible metaphoricity, which is said to be the origin of sense or meaning, is due to syntax. This self-destruction of metaphor, although similar to the Hegelian "sublation" *(Aufhebung)* in many respects, differs from it in that it lacks a direction or purpose. For Derrida, metaphor always carries its own death within itself.[12] Metaphoricity is said to be quasi transcendental and to reflect the limits of philosophical discourse. Yet like Wittgenstein, Derrida makes a point to philosophize about what cannot be said to have a literal meaning

Paradoxically, it is Husserl who provides Derrida with a paradigm of his deconstructive method. While Husserl emphasizes direct seeing, the things themselves, presence, fulfilled meanings, and the like, Derrida points out that these are all promises that cannot be kept. The perceptual object, contrary to Husserl's repeated claims, is not an unproblematic presence, but precisely a complex interplay of presence and absence. And as Husserl himself admits, there is always more to the intentional object than what is present.[13] What is true of Husserl's analysis of perception is no less true of intersubjectivity. The other is not present in person but is precisely absent, and this absence must be compensated for. Presence is always infiltrated and undermined by absence, and Derrida concludes that while there is a phenomenon, "experience is a dream of presence."[14] It is precisely insofar as the thing itself eludes the aspirations of intuitive consciousness that it is taken to be real. In other words, absence is the indicator, the transcendental clue to reality. The real is what resists the grasp of intuition, and it is just because the object cannot be seized by intuition that it is taken to be real. The irreducibility of the phenomenon to intuitive consciousness in Husserl becomes in Heidegger a playful alternation of mutual concealment and disclosure, and the failure of presence which in Husserl is the clue to the transcendence of the real, becomes in Heidegger the withdrawal of Being. The task of thought is to wait upon and heed the hidden movement of Being, and *Dasein* (existence, presence) is swept away in this receding movement. The response of *Dasein* to the withdrawal (transcendence) of Being is what Heidegger calls *Gelassenheit* (composure), letting go, letting be. It expresses the mystery precisely in its withdrawal, but it is in this movement of *Gelassenheit* that Caputo[15] locates the most important difference between Derrida and Heidegger. Absence for Derrida is not the gentle power of withdrawal but the variety of signs and writings; he moves from the failure of presence not to the transcendence of recessive mystery of things, but into the indefinite play of differential systems of interchangeable interpretations. All such representations are due to the will to subdue things to our purposes and thus are violent; all discourse is caught up within a system of differences, and the matter itself, things, are indefinitely put off, de-ferred. There remains only a network of signs in which all are caught. Derrida's thought lacks piety since it refuses to serve any purpose, but such experience of loss in the end becomes a loss of experience.[16]

This loss of experience inevitably brings about a loss of literal meaning and objectivity. Graeme Nicholson argues that our experience of reality is profoundly linked with our experience of seeing, and with the fact that both are interpretive. His point is that the dynamic conditions of perception should be treated in a parallel way: perception is shaped by projections both practical and linguistic. Projection is at the root of our visual interpretation since there is no seeing without interpretation. What we have to realize, however, is that the interpretations of perception are background renderings. When we just see something, we do not employ a complicated skill or any specialized knowledge like we do in learning how to read and write, but exercise species specific instincts. We hardly ever need to puzzle over identifying an object under ordinary circumstances, while reading a text requires often complex and sophisticated skills. Seeing is precisely the elementary encounter with entities that can be made subject to further interpretation. The factors of visual interpretation are at work only in the background, and that means that we are not at liberty to deconstruct them under normal conditions. We remain largely unaware of the practical interests and conditions that shape our seeing and resist deconstruction. Whenever there is interpretation, there is something seen as requiring explanation, and thus as appealing to some literal sense or concern. Derrida's deconstruction assumes that interpretation is part even of background knowledge,[17] yet what we are unaware of cannot normally be deconstructed. If there is nothing capable of being identified apart from interpretation, the concept of interpretation itself becomes empty. To interpret is to explain, and all explanation presupposes something that is understood and in terms of which the explanation is being accomplished. We are acquainted with interpretations of many different kinds: linguistic, psychological, structuralist, and what not, and we accept such explanations with reference to what we take to be their literal or common-sense meaning. Every such attempt needs to identify a nucleus of meaning to which the broad periphery can be attached,[18] and that is why the alleged metaphorical character of interpretation remains parasitic on literal meaning. Such literal meaning is taken for granted in each specific context and remains consequently much more resistant to deconstruction than are the accompanying versions of interpretation and explanation. Derrida's position that emphasizes the uniform metaphorical nature of *all* discourse turns out to be self-defeating.

Heelan likewise claims that visual perception – and by analogy, all perception – is hermeneutic, i.e. it has the capacity to "read" the appropriate structure imposed on the world. The clues that are "read" perceptually as giving an Euclidean visual space are engineered objects, such as streets and buildings with repetitive architectural elements. Hence, scientific artifacts belong to a family of readable technology central to the phenomenological and hermeneutical analyses of what natural science takes to be real. But Heelan follows Gadamer's hermeneutics that confronts the text or cultural object with an antecedent domain of meaning suggested by clues through the playful interaction of part and whole, text and context. Heidegger also regarded perception in which the world is disclosed and articulated as being hermeneutical. Heelan, however, rightly points out that states of the world are by definition real and public,[19] and that consequently this reality is expressed as the standard for a perceptual judgment formulated in a common descriptive language of a linguistic community. Derrida, on the other hand, denies that there are any such states of the world prior to interpretation. Perceivers "pick up" information about the world, but it is the picking up that *creates* the information, not discovers it. He denies that the information gathered is in some sense "present" in the world prior to the acts of perception. For him, *esse* is *interpretari,* to explain, expound, an agent between two parties, a broker, negotiator, and any isolation of meaning is, therefore, an illusion created by the misuse of language. Yet some meanings are more resistant to deconstruction than others, e.g. perceptual images. The term "information" analogously refers to both the signs that are read and to the visual clues that are automatically picked up by the referent. There is no necessary, unique, one-to-one mapping between seeing and reading, and all such affinities remain problematic.

However, the manner in which an information system is utilized depends on the context chosen for its interpretation. Heidegger observes that eidetic analyses cannot be unique and definite, and while such a determination may be possible for a rule-governed mathematical object, perceptual profiles are never exact. Heelan identifies this inexactness as metaphorical,[20] but the suitability of metaphors is more a matter of aptness than of accurateness. Such cases merely reveal a relativity of perception as something that cannot be precisely identified, a profound ambiguity at the root of all natural language. Nevertheless, and contrary to Derrida, metaphors remain parasitic on literal meaning, for to say that the interpretation of a text is due to unconscious analogy is to leave the alleged metaphorical nature of language unexplained. It inevitably assumes a kind of preunderstanding that identifies the subject in anticipation of interpretation but does not amount itself to explanation in the normal sense. Some marks are identified as a piece of writing, and thereby a text is assumed to exist, but its reading is the result of acculturation and training, as is the reading of a scientific instrument. Moreover, scientific explanation comprises a reality guided by the physical interaction by means of a suitable technology. Since the principal argument in favor of the hermeneutical character of perception is based on the contrast between perceiving and reading. Derrida's declaring the reading of a text to be paradigmatic for all perceiving becomes pointless. Reading and perceiving differ in their hermeneutical preconditions since perceiving is largely intuitive and species specific, while reading is an acquired skill not shared by billions of humans. Any meaning conveyed by a text is open to deconstruction only to the extent that it is not taken to be self-evident, and all such analysis inevitably refers back to meanings that are accepted as unproblematic at least in the given context. A deconstruction that does not amount to such an explanation lacks even the force of an alternative reading. While we are genetically programmed to speak a human language, which language we happen to master depends upon upbringing and skill. What can be deconstructed is only the text, i.e. a set of words in some specific language and explained according to its particular conventions. Scientific instruments are likewise manmade conventional texts in this sense, and their mastery requires apprenticeship and indoctrination; all such interpretation is based on specific conventions that can be questioned in deconstructive analysis. While it is characteristic of hermeneutics that it presents more than just one interpretation, mathematical notation as well as scientific terminology generally have been largely successful in resisting such ambiguity.

Classical metaphysics reads the imperfect from the viewpoint of the perfect, and movement from the standpoint of repose. One of Derrida's major contributions was to find this constructive core of traditional metaphysics – poetic identity and its supplement in logocentric technology – still operative in Edmund Husserl's *Logical Investigations*. Derrida criticizes this entire metaphysical tradition as being fundamentally due to the desire to exclude writing, taken primarily not as "putting words on paper," but as irreducible difference.[21] But deconstruction is, after all, itself a way of reading texts critically. To read is to interpret; it is to articulate one sense rather than another. Derrida insists that when the writing is words on a page, we cannot move outside language and remain in the blissful innocence of animal immediacy. We are forever reading things in terms of this or that or for such and such a purpose. The notion of empirical immediacy, as Derrida says, is a dream that vanishes at daybreak, as soon as language awakens.[22] Reading, *hermeneua* and *logos* name the same thing: the human way of being. Reading is intrinsically metaphysical and ontological, but is nevertheless a referral to no presence. At best we can speak only of a relative priority of open-mindedness over closure in any ongoing movement in which there is no advance or goal, no identity of sense outside of interpretation. One lives and acts in unending plurality, and entities are traces of the movement of reading itself. For that reason Derrida does not use the term "criticism," at least in its standard meaning. In *"Double Séance,"* he says that "criticism," as the term indicates, is linked to the possibility of decision, whereas *"Double Séance"* is precisely a deconstructive critique of the possibility of decidability. To read, to interpret ourselves, to turn *logos* critically back upon itself, is to achieve nothing stable and substantial, but only the very movement of reading itself. Criticism is the retrieval of indecidability right back to the indeterminateness of what makes sense. It is an ongoing subversion of all stability.

The scientific prejudice is a belief in self-evident facts and unconditioned grounds. Derrida, on the other hand, insists that there are no such unproblematic facts and grounds, and that what arises is merely a play of changing conditions that we do not fully understand. Whether existence without interpretation makes any sense cannot be decided because to decide would require that we get around our own perspectives and interpretations. According to Nietzsche, it is the affirmation of chance, of the irrational, that must be faced because reason is no more than unquestioned belief. All is interpretation, and what remains is the indefinite play of life itself, the will to power. Even physics is an interpretation rather than the paradigm of certainty and justification. Scientific discourse is part of the infinite series of translations and interpretations, and truth persists merely as a rigidified effect in this movable array of interpretations.[23] Since we cannot escape our own practices or paradigms, we cannot get around the issue of certainty. Nietzsche's "overcoming" (*Überwindung)* is at the center of thought not only of the later Heidegger and of Derrida, but also of Wittgenstein and Carnap who wanted to "overcome" metaphysics by means of a logical analysis of language. The issue remains undecided, however, once we realize that rationality has no foundations. In the more recent philosophy of science, Kuhn and Feyerabend demonstrated that all scientific judgments remain historically relative.[24] All true thought is open to more than one interpretation,[25] and Derrida, therefore demands that reality should free itself from the timeless categories of the history of philosophy.[26] But Ormiston suggests that one can interpret Derrida in terms of possibilities for reading, writing, and critical inquiry, even though difference operates in and through dissemination, i.e. beyond any discernible methods, and the mark of difference becomes one of self-effacement.[27] In this manner deconstruction finally disintegrates, for by becoming an activity without a purpose, it loses not merely direction but all discoverable meaning. Derrida believes that he can retain relative significance even when there is no absolute or universal truth, yet his rejection of logocentrism is itself comprehensive and radical. Questioning logic, he cannot draw a line between what makes sense and what does not, since he faces no problems that demand a definite solution. Lacking a discoverable philosophical content, he has no identifiable framework to refer to, because, unlike Wittgenstein, there are for him no unproblematic lifeforms to fall back on. Reading for Derrida is to thwart the very desire for analysis, but then there is nothing to be understood, no meaning to be discovered, and no task to be accomplished. Critical reading, for him, does create conflict, but since logic can always be overruled, there is no need to resolve such conflict. If we are asked by Derrida to be mindful of, and attentive to, what is being passed over in silence, the appeal is to some overall implicit consistency whose existence, however, he repeatedly denies. All such quests aim inevitably at some literal and stable truth, for if I speak or belong to a discourse for which no one else has ears, I fail to communicate, and such a discourse that is addressed to no one in particular will not be comprehensible even to myself. If I have no choice but to articulate questions or insights that are culturally relative, there is no philosophical point to what I am doing. Derrida fails to provide a rational justification for our desire to do philosophy.

Thus, while Heidegger, like Hegel before him, announced the "end of philosophy," Derrida leaves this open.[28] What is at stake here is not merely a view of knowledge that aims at ultimate and final truth but the questionable validity of any argument that denies logic. It may plausibly be argued that if philosophy is understood as the search for a permanent neutral matrix, or ultimate foundation, or final framework and vocabulary, skepticism just is the end of philosophy.[29] According to Derrida, there are no solutions to problems called "philosophical," and the history of philosophy is just a failed attempt to define philosophical problems, the failed search for infallible methods, and a series of failed proposed solutions. But if Derrida argues that there are no philosophical problems or solutions, he may rightly be said to be doing philosophy himself. We are urged to give up the view that philosophical problems arise naturally upon reflection, and to pretend that philosophy names no natural kind, no activity intrinsic to our species, but that it is merely a historic, principally Western tradition.[30] This entails giving up the view that there is a fixed permanent philosophical agenda, a set of problems that defines philosophy, a common paradigm that transcends natural languages, frameworks, idioms, definitions, and interests. Deconstructionists are decidedly Kuhnian[31] in their interpretation of science, and at the extreme end they view science as a literary genre. If there is no metahistorical agenda, we are asked to recognize that there are no final solutions to putative philosophical questions. Rather, in philosophy as elsewhere in culture, interests ebb and flow, and topics of conversation change. Since there are no final solutions to philosophical questions, there is no final vocabulary – no ultimate principles, distinctions, insights, and frameworks that define rationality in virtue of its privileged attachment to reality. It is, however, fair to ask what is left once the quest for truth has been given up in this manner. Derrida claims that knowledge is not the kind of thing about which one ought to have a theory, but then goes on to offer just such a thesis denouncing logocentrism. He wants us to give up the visual metaphor that inspires the Platonic picture of knowledge, of a mind seeing things as they really are, but even when he rejects that picture, Derrida remains part of a skeptical tradition that is philosophical to the extent that it makes global and consistent claims. He seems to be saying that whereas there can be explanation and illustration of successful discourse on a case-by-case basis, there can be only a misconceived "theory" of successful discourse – yet even his deconstructivist denial of such a claim amounts to further philosophical argument.

Schrag convincingly argues that the main lesson to be learned from the contemporary flurry of deconstructionist strategy is that no complete deconstruction is possible.[32] Just as, according to Descartes, all contents of experimental and natural truth can be doubted, save the inescapable fact of the doubter, so in deconstruction the very strategy reinvents the subject and assures that no complete deconstruction can ever be accomplished. The Cartesian way fails because the inquiry's standpoint presupposes a center of consciousness, a stale presence that

somehow supports the provisional stream of consciousness. Spoken or written discourse likewise implicate a speaker or author because all discourse displays a world of concerns that go beyond the text and serve as background for its interpretation. Explaining the text renders manifest a specific understanding of human behavior and operates within a network of intentions that the interpreter *brings* to the text by speaking its language and by being familiar with its culture. Such reference is more than just metaphorical since it is not only *about* something but also *by* someone and *for* someone. It is within such a specific context that literal meaning emerges as an epistemological framework, an interiority seeking commerce with an external world. The speaker or writer is implicated by his discourse by means of these specific practices, both verbal and nonverbal. No speaking or writing subject is an isolated island, but functions as a member of a specific linguistic and cultural community. As a subject or agent, he is implicated both in a confined time-space point, as an abstracted here-and-now, and is a decentered co-subject cohabiting the world with other subjects. Responsiveness to cultural conventions and demands on the part of the speaker or writer, no less than explicit discourse, comprises our understanding of the text. What "scientific" means is likewise determined by pregiven disciplines that are considered to be already on the secure path of established knowledge. While it is usually assumed that all such philosophical problems can be solved by means of the new scientific method, the specific understanding of "scientific" that emerges has the consequence that most of the original problems become meaningless since they cannot be formulated in the new language of science.

The history of philosophy teaches us, however, that there have always been skeptical traditions that have questioned its authority. Even a general answer to the question, "What is philosophy?" cannot be provided because the very definition of topics has changed considerably over time as have the methods to solve them. There are no eternal principles or fixed frameworks within which philosophical questions can be answered. While Derrida is part of this philosophical tradition, he resists all attempts at deconstructing deconstruction as frivolous. Like Sextus Empiricus,[33] he maintains that knowledge is not altogether impossible, but an issue that cannot be conclusively settled. The real problem seems to be that all such radical and comprehensive skepticism remains parasitic on philosophical speculation, as have been similar attempts in language analysis to demonstrate the "meaninglessness" of philosophy. It is, therefore, not surprising that these movements have been manifestly unsuccessful at bringing philosophy to an end. Like Wittgenstein, Derrida's deconstruction ultimately leaves everything as it is, largely because its logic is incapable of making its criticism stick. The attempt to "overcome" philosophy in Logical Positivism comes to an end with the recognition that all scientific knowledge is historically relative. This, of course, raises new questions, for history's concern is primarily with the real world, while its narrative record seems always to be contaminated by fiction. What stories and history portray is not physical reality but human activity, and this invariably involves projecting human concerns into events. As Husserl reminds us, all experience involves anticipation and intentionally. We cannot experience anything as happening or as present except as succeeding something else, and as leading to something further. Everything we experience is expressed as expected or as unexpected, as confirming or as disconfirming our anticipations.[34] As Merleau-Ponty has pointed out, sensations are highly abstract products of analysis, and we are always in the midst of something by virtue of the teleological structure of action.

We describe as actions some long-term and extremely complex endeavors: getting an education, conducting a love affair, raising a child, fighting a war. It is true that in a good story we are told only what is necessary to further the plot, and that life differs from stories in that such a selection is not made.[35] Unlike the historian, we are not describing events already completed, but are in the middle of our stories, and cannot be sure how they will end. We must then give up any pretension we might have to anything like being the authors of our own lives, even when we exercise some control over our surroundings. Frank Kermode's intriguing observation is that the very idea of crisis is a way of making a story out of this very lack of ending. Merely by giving it a voice, we provide life with a narrative structure, and it may well be that a life that is not some kind of a story is neither thinkable nor livable.[36] Descombes rightly concludes that the controversy between the positivist and the hermeneutical philosophy cannot be resolved. One cannot abolish the category of fact and keep the category of interpretation, as Derrida proposes, because these words get their meaning in part from the contrast between them. An interpretation is opposed to a fact insofar as it is said to involve the evaluation of that fact. This is because a fact is necessarily beyond dispute. Descombes emphasizes that it is useless to call upon facts in this controversy since facts cannot become arguments without losing the privilege of remaining indisputable. A fact used as an argument will share the fate of opinion or interpretation.[37] There has to be a difference between knowledge and belief.

Notes

[1] Joseph Margolis, "Deconstruction; or, The Mystery of the Mystery of the Text," in *Hermeneutics & Deconstruction,* eds. Hugh J. Silverman and Don Ihde, New York, NY: State University of New York Press, 1985, p. 143.

[2] Jacques Derrida, *Of Grammatology,* trans. Gayatori Chakravorty Spivak, Baltimore, MD: John Hopkins University Press, 1975, p. 148.

[3] Margolis, "Deconstruction," p. 148.

[4] *Ibid.,* p. 151.

[5] Paul Ricoeur, *The Role of Metaphor,* Toronto: University of Toronto Press, 1977, pp. 259-280.

[6] Jacques Derrida, *The Margins of Philosophy,* trans. A. Bass, Chicago, IL: University of Chicago Press, 1982, p. 238.

[7] Jacques Derrida, *La Vérité en peinture,* Paris: Flammarion, 1978, p. 143.

[8] Jacques Derrida, *Speech and Phenomena,* trans. D. B. Allsion, Evanston: Northwestern, 1973, p. 13.

[9] Jacques Derrida, *L'archéologie du frivole,* Paris: Galilée, 1973, p. 83.

[10] Derrida, *Margins of Philosophy,* p. 280.

[11] Jacques Derrida, *Dissemination,* trans. B. Johnson, Chicago, IL: Chicago University Press, 1981, p. 258.

[12] Derrida, *Margins of Philosophy,* p. 271.

[13] Edmund Husserl, *Cartesian Meditations,* trans. Dorian Cairns, The Hague: Martinus Nijhoff, 1960, p. 46.

[14] Derrida, *Of Grammatology,* p. 49.

[15] John D. Caputo, "From the Primordiality of Absence to the Absense of Primordiality," in *Hermeneutics & Deconstruction,* p. 197.

[16] *Ibid.,* p. 200.

[17] Graeme Nicholson, "Seeing and Reading: Aspects of their Conneciton," in *Hermeneutics & Deconstruction,* p. 39.

[18] *Ibid.,* p. 41.

[19] Patrick A. Heelan, "Perception as a Hermeneutical Act," in *Hermeneutics & Deconstruction*, p. 44.

[20] *Ibid.*, p. 47.

[21] Jacques Derrida, *L'Ecriture et la différance*, Paris: Seuil, 1967, p. 293.

[22] *Ibid.*, p. 224.

[23] Friedrich Nietzsche, "On Truth and Lie in an Extra Moral Sense," in *The Portable Nietsche*, trans. Walter Kaufmann, New York, NY: Viking Press, 1954, pp. 46-47.

[24] Joseph Grünfeld, *Changing Rational Stnadards*, Lanham: University Press of America, 1985.

[25] Martin Heidegger, *What is Called Thinking?* trans. J. Glenn Gray, New York, NY: Harper & Row, 1968, p. 71.

[26] Derrida, *Of Grammatology*, p. lxxxix.

[27] Gayle L. Ormiston, "Binding Withdrawal," in *Hermeneutics and Deconstruction*, p. 251.

[28] *Ibid.*, p. x.

[29] Bernd Magnus, "The End of 'The End of Philosophy'" in *Hermeneutics & Deconstructoin*, p. 4.

[30] *Ibid.*, p. 5.

[31] T. Kuhn, *The Strucutre of Scientific Revolutions*, Chicago, IL: University of Chicago Press, 1962, 1970.

[32] Calvin O. Schrag, "Subjectivity and Praxis at the End of Philosophy," in *Hermeneutics & Deconstruction*, p. 25.

[33] Sextus Empricus, *Outlines of Phyrronism*, Loeb, Harvard University Press, 1967, pp. 122-123.

[34] David Carr, "Life and the Narrator's Art," in *Hermeneutics & Deconstructoin*, p. 112.

[35] *Ibid.*, p. 115.

[36] Frank Kermode, *The Sense of an Ending, Studies in the Theory of Fiction*, (London: Oxford University Press, 1966, p. 93ff.

[37] Vincent Descombes, "The Fabric of Subjectivity," in *Hermeneutics & Deconstruction*, p. 58.

Postmodernism

Chapter Twenty-Two

Prerational Power Play

The concept of play, which was initially pushed into the background by the dominant Cartesian tradition of the seventeenth century, finds its way back into metaphysics at the end of the Age of Reason. Then in the wake of Schopenhauer, prerational play itself returns to the philosophical center stage both through Nietzsche and through such twentieth century artist-metaphysicians as Heidegger, Fink, Gadamer, Deleuze, and Derrida. Although prerational play concepts surface in modern science as well, they remain subordinated to rational modes of play. Thus, the play of contemporary scientific discourse, unlike that of contemporary philosophical discourse, remains a predominantly rational one.[1] Spariosu points out that in our methodologically self-conscious age, one can no longer write history from an unbiased, objective, and factual point of view because "positivism" itself is seen as a bias. The history of what we call "play" in the Western tradition is a history of conflict, of competing play concepts that have alternatively become dominant according to changing conditions. We all seem to know what play is and can recognize it, but find ourselves at a loss when confronted with the task of conceptualizing such knowledge. Scholars draw a distinction between play and games, *paidia* and *ludus,* the former remaining indefinite and the latter defined as governed by rules and institutionalized custom. In contemporary philosophy, therefore, play has an ambivalent status, being both phenomenon and subjectivity, or both behavior and intentionality. This double nature of play has been seen as a mixture of reality and nonreality, of truth and illusion, and it is precisely this ambiguous nature of play that accounts for its centrality in contemporary thought. The family of play concepts goes back to ancient Greece and its history reveals that it has been subordinated to the power principle that has dominated Western mentality. Like play, power is all pervasive and, therefore, difficult to define, it is part of tacit knowledge and family resemblances. Indeed, Spariosu is quite incapable of telling us what would not count as power in Western mentality.

The Hellenic idea of play, which originally in the Homeric epic and in Hesiod is linked to the notion of immediate physical power (*agon*), gradually loses this meaning until it becomes *paidia,* a word that initially denotes only the harmless play of children. It then becomes in Plato a philosophical term for the transmission of culture, and a proper understanding of the concepts of power and of play reflect the polarized character of Western mentality that since its origin in ancient Greece, has altered between a prerational and a rational meaning. A prerational mentality conceives of power as something physical, unrestrained, and immediate; authority depends on physical strength or cunning, and it is imposed by violence. Competitive values prevail throughout, and violence or the threat of it are employed as a matter of course in resolving conflict, and that is why a prerational mentality usually creates highly unstable authoritarian and hierarchical forms of government.[2] A prerational mentality is often also a preconscious one. It does not distinguish between speech and action, or between cognition and emotion; its language is concrete and poetic, and structured according to mnemonic rather than visual or logical principles. By contrast, a rational mentality is largely conscious since its prerational part remains suppressed at the subconscious level. Writing emerges and addresses itself to an increasingly broader section of the community, and a rational mentality is also largely a literate one. Since the early Renaissance, most of Western Europe has steadily moved towards a rational mentality, which becomes prominent in the seventeenth century and prevails to the present day. The concept of evolution is itself a product of this mentality and is employed as an ideological weapon against prerational ways of thinking. Rational mentality experiences the transition to mediated forms of power as a loss of presence and a yearning for authority, and that is how the prerational past becomes idealized as a "golden age." Prerational thought, by contrast, conceives of play as a manifestation of power in its innocent form, its sheer delight in emotional release and raw arbitrary violence.

Spariosu points out that the modern notion of play shares this divided character when applied to art. Literature has from the beginning been associated with play and despite its repression by rational philosophy and science, it has proven a powerful antagonist, indeed an indispensable factor in the quest for power and cultural authority. By openly displaying its fictitiousness, it allows science, philosophy, history, ethics, politics, jurisprudence, and religion to be invested with the authority of knowledge and truth. In Romanticism, however, and more recently in Postmodernism, literature reasserts its claim to supreme cultural authority by exposing all such truths as fiction. It resists these claims chiefly through an "as if" mode of knowledge whose origins in play can be traced back to Greek thought. The establishment of aesthetics as a branch of philosophy during the Age of Reason facilitates the introduction into metaphysics of consciously simulative or fictional proceedings that were primarily concerned with the fine arts. Philosophers speak again about conscious illusion and necessary fiction, not only in literature and art but also in metaphysics and even in science. It is Schiller who, for the first time, explicitly calls the heuristic fictions of philosophy "play," and thereafter this idea is frequently adopted by Fichte, Schelling, and Hegel, who ground their metaphysical speculation not only ontologically and ethically but also aesthetically. Like Schiller however, they subordinate aesthetics and play to morality, seriousness, and rationality. Play is gradually stripped of its prerational violent and arbitrary connotation, and becomes a useful instrument in support of the ontological and ethical traditions of philosophy. In Kant, play cannot even be called a concept *(Begriff)*: rather it resists all attempts at conceptualization, and this is what makes the critique of pure reason and of the power of judgment necessary. Like Plato and Aristotle, what Kant dismisses as "mere play" is the irrational ecstatic operation of power whose medium is the senses, emancipated from the control of reason. Only Nietzsche breaks with this Schillerian tradition by going back beyond Plato to the archaic origins of play as a violent, exuberant, and innocent manifestation of power, and thereby introduces the notion of prerartional play into modern philosophy. The notion of art as self-consious illusion becomes prevalent in nineteenth century aesthetics as Coleridge's "willing suspension of disbelief," and such theories of play remain influential even today.

Art is able to carry out the task of reason because of its dual nature as both resemblance and reality, play and seriousness, entertainment and morality. This allows art to mediate between philosophical and scientific discourse on the one hand, and unknowable reality on the other, between the arbitrary and chaotic physical world, and human understanding. Schiller's theory of play and aesthetics provides a crucial link, not only between literature and philosophy but also between art and science generally. With Schopenhauer, there begins a second aesthetic turn in philosophy in which the game of reason is taken over by the arbitrary and violent operation of physical forces or the unmediated play of power.[3] Through his idea of Will as endless striving, Schopenhauer shows power to be the hidden source of Western metaphysics, and this notion is taken up by Nietzsche, Heidegger, and other twentieth century artist-metaphysicians. Like the Presocratics, Nietzsche conceives of the will to power as prerational play, as an overflowing and violent cosmic movement, beyond good and evil. Nietzsche's philosophy can be seen as a return to Hellenic prerational values in the light of which he offers a profound critique of contemporary culture. To a rational mode of thinking, Nietzsche and Heidegger appear paradoxical and confused but, viewed from a prerational perspective they offer a far-reaching analysis of modern values. The aesthetic perspective that Nietzsche has in mind concerns the world of the senses and becoming rather than that of reason and being, and is seen as gaining priority over mere intellectual understanding. Unlike Schiller and Kant, Nietzsche views play as a cosmic, rather than human disinterestedness, beyond human rationality and ethics. Fundamental throughout his philosophy is the idea of power as play that can be traced back to Greek archaic mentality. It is the ancient Sophist doctrine that might is right that was tacitly taken for granted in ancient Greece.

While play is central in this prerational aristocratic mentality, with the advent of a rational democratic mentality it becomes separated from unrestrained power and presents itself as reason, knowledge, morality, and truth. As a consequence, play loses its centrality in culture and becomes tamed and repressed along with other archaic values. Nietzsche defines his Will to Power in terms of prerational play; the world is conceived of as an enormous play of forces, both creative and destructive. Since becoming is eternal and can never resolve itself into either being or nothingness, the world as incessant play of forces repeats itself endlessly, producing the same combinations over an infinite time span. The will to power and its play finally remain undefinable and groundless, or in positive terms constitute their own justification. But while in Nietzsche play and the will to power remain undefinable, they are partly describable in terms of each other: play is an unfolding of power, just as power is a manifestation of play. Spariosu, therefore concludes that both terms should be understood in their archaic sense, as a Dionysian ecstatic and violent play of physical becoming, as aristocratic agon, and as chance-necessity.[4] Since knowledge functions as a tool of power, there are not one but may realities that are the product of the agent's interpretation. For Nietzsche, the world is a process through which the agent (or "player") crates the world as he goes along. He challenges the positivist assumption of the existence of "facts" independent of interpretation.[5] Human existence is governed not by a will to truth but by a will to illusion, which is the foundation not merely of art but also of metaphysics and science. His perspectivism is far from being a modern (e.g. Feyerabend's) pluralism, a benign and tolerant acceptance of other points of view; its context remains antagonistic throughout. For Nietzsche, just as for the ancient Greeks, truth and lie are not moral categories but are used indifferently as long as they further our purposes. Truth is not something to be found or discovered; it is something that must be created and that gives a name to this process of invention. Semblance, illusion, appearance, simulation, the world of the senses, and becoming are valued over being, truth, reality, essence, and the world of the spirit. Violent play, the aesthetic, and art are valued over science, seriousness, and morality. The prerational mentality does not disappear with the advent of the rational one but becomes submerged and repressed, and the artist is replaced by the artist-metaphysician and the artist-tyrant.

Like Nietzsche, Heidegger also stresses the link between power and play as risk taking. He no longer perceives truth as an agreement or conformity of knowledge with fact,[6] but as the Greek *aletheia* (un)concealment. Man is not the measure of all things as in Protagoas; rather as in Plato, he is the toy of Being, and the most he can do is play along (*mitspielen*).[7] Heidegger defines Being itself as play or as the interplay of ground and groundlessness, of sending forth and withdrawal that cannot be rationalized or thought of in terms of particular being: it is a sudden, spontaneous, and arbitrary unfolding.[8] It is pointless to ask why Being plays its game of destiny *(Geschick)* as it would be to ask why a child plays. Heidegger realizes that one cannot overcome metaphysics but only walk away from it, yet in spite of his straying into mysticism, the question remains whether he

ultimately steers clear of the power-oriented mentality of Western
metaphysics, in particular form Nietzsche's "world play" (*Weltspiel*).[9]
Although he no longer thinks of being as will, Heidegger sees it as an
inscrutable and incomprehensible force that overpowers man, playing
with him a dangerous and fearful game[10] whose stake is death. Like
Nietzsche, Heidegger thinks of power in prerational terms as arbitrary,
spontaneous, and violent play. Man is by nature violent, accepting the
challenge of the play of Being and venturing himself in this play.
There is no major religion that has conceived of divinity otherwise
than as power, even if the nature of this power is supposed to be
benevolent.[11] With Kant, Schiller, Nietzsche, and Heidegger, play has
gradually moved into a key position in modern philosophy. But this
makes also for an inherently unstable situation since even when one
group of players seems to have gained dominance, their victory turns
out to be only temporary. Eugen Fink, therefore, proposes a
cosmological interpretation of the "world game," *(Weltspiel)* which is
already implicit in Heidegger, as a "play without players."[12] While
Spariosu adopts Fink's dialectics of power and play, he rejects Fink's
assumption that power is all there is.[13] Spariosu fails to tell us,
however, what would count in metaphysics as not being power-
oriented. While he treats both power and play as metaphors rather
than as concepts, it would nevertheless seem that if everything is both
power and play these designations are quite meaningless. In Nietzsche,
human play, especially the play of the child or the artist, becomes a
cosmic metaphor, a poetic expression beyond all valuation. Indeed, it
is through its "unreality" that play manages to express its essential
relationship to the world of power. But to see human play as a cosmic
metaphor by no means amounts to saying that one can understand the
play of the world on the analogy of human play. The world reflects
itself merely in the unreality of human play and, therefore, can be
perceived only in a broken and fragmentary fashion.[14] The play of the
world must be understood, as in Heidegger, as a play of presence and
absence in which all beings emerge into presence and then disappear
again into the groundless abyss of absence (which equally belongs to
the world). All beings are cosmic toys, and all players are in turn
playthings.

   In Gadamer, play also serves as a metaphor for describing the
way in which the truth of Being occurs through man's hermeneutical
activity. The truth of Being is not something man arrives at through an
objective and rigorous scientific procedure, but rather is something

that happens to him in the course of his history. Kant's high price for establishing the autonomy of art is to give up all its traditional claims to knowledge. In this manner, the artist is being deprived of his traditional place in the community and loses most of his traditional authority. For Gadamer, a work of art is an interplay of subject and object, and the audience is part of this structure. The true being of a work of art is the play of interpretation, and according to Gadamer, this is the model for genuine understanding in all human sciences.[15] For him, man's relation to the world is fundamentally linguistic in nature and hence intelligible,[16] and the symbolic character of all art reflects both its rational and its irrational character. Deleuze also points out that the relationship between being and becoming, between one and many, is to be understood in terms of a game played by an artist, a child, and a god – three embodiments of Dionysus.[17] To affirm chance is to know how to play, but modern man is a bad player because he counts on a great number of throws – on the use of causality and probability to produce the right combination. To be a good player is to recognize that the universe is purposeless, that it has no cause nor goal, and hence to affirm chance in one throw.[18] What we have here, of course, is again the opposition between rational and irrational play when, instead of the labor of opposition, we experience the joy of destruction. The world of becoming is two-rather than three-dimensional, and, therefore, one needs to ignore such traditional logical principles as the excluded middle and the law of contradiction, and one has to redefine the traditional notions of space, time, event, cause, effect, necessity, chance, structure, sense – and play.[19] The so-called real world of economics, morality, and politics is as much a matter of surface events as is the world of thought and of art.

Like Heidegger, Derrida identifies the foundation of Western metaphysics with being, understood as presence *(ousia)*. But unlike Heidegger, he concentrates on "writing" *(l'écriture)* as what has continually been excluded in a metaphysics of presence, and which, therefore, is predominately a metaphysics of the spoken word, or the *logos*. To the reactive structuralist notion of play, Derrida opposes a Nietzschean joyous affirmation of the play of the world and the innocence of becoming – a world of signs without truth, origin, or fault. There is thus a prerational notion of play in Derrida who admits that it is altogether impossible to choose between it and the rational concept of play.[20] Derrida conceives of deconstruction as a violent subversive movement; the play of *différance* is power play, and that of deconstruction a contest for authority, even as it claims to do away with all authority. Spariosu shows how the most influential contemporary artist-metaphysicians favor prerational over rational play. They consider the ancient quarrel between philosophy and poetry part of a larger contest between rational and prerational values in Western culture. Plato challenges Homer and the tragic poets because he sees them as influential spokesmen of a prerational mentality. Such a mentality views the world as a ceaseless arbitrary play of forces (unlimited becoming), whereas philosophy sets itself the task of imposing a spiritual world of order, clarity, permanence, rationality, and morality – the world of Being in the Platonic sense. Spariosu observes how, since the end of the Age of Reason, prerational values have made a gradual comeback in Western philosophy, and how this has brought about a reversal of Platonic and Aristotelian modes of thinking and a return to archaic presocratic speculation.

The history of the play concepts demonstrates a parallel reversal. There is play as a serious object of scientific investigation, and there is the playful aesthetic attitude toward one's object of study or investigation. Spariosu admits, however, that the rational play concepts are likely to continue dominating the prerational ones, despite their being challenged in biology, physics, and the philosophy of science.[21] Thus, the theory of evolution is based on a "struggle for life" metaphor leading to natural selection by an interplay of necessity and choice. The tendency has been to move away from play as imitation (*mimesis*) and emphasize its exploratory and creative character. But while in our postmodern world play is assigned a productive role, its prerational origins remain in force; it is predominately seen as an orderly, rule-governed process that reflects a rational mentality. Spariosu points out, however, that since competition has always been a dominant value in Western mentally, its scientific vindication was bound to be met with general approval. Still, our rational mentality focuses only on certain kinds of competition – those that are nonviolent and rule-governed. Spariosu shows that the concept of natural selection as the interplay of randomness and design has implications that go beyond science. The reason Darwin's ideas caused such an uproar when they were first announced was that they presented the living world as a world of change, determined by natural forces in place of a world determined by a divine plan. Many people find the idea that we are living in a meaningless and fortuitous world frightening and repellent. Order, prediction, and certainty are crucial to science, and chance means uncertainly, unpredictability, and chaos. For most scientists, Darwin's theory of evolution by natural selection is not just another hypothesis but an incontrovertible law of nature.

Society has a vested interest in rational thought as ensuring order, stability, predictability, and facility of communication. Science sees itself, and is seen by others as a neutral and objective pursuit of knowledge and truth, as an enlightened champion of freedom and progress. But like art and religion, science is engaged in a contest for authority and power. While its claims as a principal source of knowledge and truth have been frequently challenged by outsiders, science has been able to resist internal pressures much better than either philosophy or art. Reflecting institutional pressures, this has been accomplished by a neo-Kantian strategy and an "as if" approach to knowledge. While Newton's famous dictum *hypotheses non fingo* (I do not feign hypotheses) implied that the purpose of science is to discover, not to create, the laws of nature, physicists at the beginning of this century maintained just the opposite. They no longer claimed merely to disclose an objective reality but admitted to inventing it as they went along. Much like mathematics, physics has worked with such deliberate fictions as force, the atom, and more recently, subatomic particles.[22] Influential physicists like Planck and Einstein started as Machean positivists but then moved on to a Schillerian neo-Kantianism, which has been largely ignored by contemporary Anglo-American historians and philosophers of science. For Vaihinger, thought processes and constructs are not rational but primarily biological phenomena; many of them are admittedly false assumptions that contradict not only experience, but also each other. They have, however, a practical value in our struggle for survival and dominance,[23] and Vaihinger explains that thought in the course of time has gradually forgotten its original function and has turned theoretical and contemplative. It is now practiced for its own sake. Fictions for Vaihinger are mental strategies forged in the struggle for survival yet, contrary to Nietzsche, he manages to suppress these irrational aspects and to justify them on utilitarian grounds.

The great majority of theoretical physicists likewise stick to rational values. But while Kepler, Newton, and the classical physicists had an unshakable faith in the rational order of the world, for Max Planck[24] faith is at the root of science, as it is at the root of religion. He explicitly links scientific progress to the imagination and the irrational. For Einstein, the "real world" is a creation of a rational God and this makes it possible of us to understand the law according to which God has made the world.[25] Our concepts and conceptual reactions are free creations of the human intellect[26] and, in the manner of Vaihinger, Einstein stresses the purely fictitious character that distinguishes the new physics from the classical one. He objects to the positivist mode of theorizing in science that has, under the influence of Mach, given rise to what Einstein calls a phenomenal, as opposed to a metaphysical physics. Metaphysical physics recognizes the need for a free, constructive, theoretical element that goes beyond a mere ordering of empirical material. He deplores the "fear of metaphysics" of such philosophers of science as Bertrard Russell,[27] arguing that if physical concepts are free mental creations then the imagination, rather than logic and experience, have a decisive role in their production. Imagination is more important than knowledge, and Einstein assumes in the Kantian fashion that there exists an unbridgeable gap between the two. The empirical world forever defies reason, and the fact that the world turns out after all to be comprehensible is nothing less than a miracle.[28] In true neo-Kantian fashion, Einstein considers even such basic scientific categories as time, space, and causality to be of merely limited and relative validity. These constructs are only real in the sense in which a game can be said to be real: its rules are operative only within a "playing space" *(Spielraum)* and the duration of the game. Occam's razor is explained by the fact that a conceptual system, like a game, requires the greatest possible economy and simplicity of rules and concepts to account for the greatest number of situations. Such a demand is an aesthetic one and has been imposed on works of art from Aristotle onwards. It is what philosophers of science even today mean when they talk about the aesthetic criteria of science. Despite his polemic against Mach's positivism, however, Einstein embraces the rational assumptions of science and so does Planck. Einstein adopts the Kantian distinction between the unstructured play of the imagination and the rule-governed operation of the rational faculty that imposes a certain (arbitrary) order on this chaotic world. In attempting to solve this cosmic puzzle, the scientist in a sense plays a divine game, and it is this religions feeling that compels Einstein to oppose some of the theoretical principles of quantum mechanics (indeterminacy, statistical rather than causal laws, etc.) at the risk of becoming a lonely voice in the scientific community. As in the case of Planck, this is not so much a scientific as an ethical and aesthetic choice. It does not seem to affect scientific practice because the religious and the nonreligious scientist remain part of the same community and share the same power-oriented institutional goals and methods. Einstein rejects the prerational view of play as chance that regards the cosmos as being due to an irrational dice game. He takes it to be the creation of a rational God, a puzzle or labyrinth with a complicated but decipherable code.[29] At the same time, however, Einstein admits the fictitious character of his own theoretical concepts.

Schrödinger also views science as a form of play. He emphasizes that the choice between a determinist and an indeterminist interpretation of natural science is a matter of personal taste that cannot be settled by either rational argument or experience. His aesthetic and relativist approach is justified by emphasizing the historical character of all truth claims in science. Science is not an objective and perennial body of truth; on the contrary, not unlike poetry, literature, or music, it is the product of an age and changes with time and culture. Scientific knowledge depends as much on the personality of the researcher and on his specific cultural traditions as on objective and impersonal observations. Even a general consensus of the scientific community is no conclusive evidence for objectivity, since it merely reflects common goals, instruments, and techniques of research. There is a dominant world view and various lines of activity become attractive because they happen to be the fashion of the day, whether in politics, art, or science. Among the fashionable ideas that dominate our own age, Schrödinger emphasizes evolution and our positivist bias to exclude from scientific discussion everything that cannot in principle be subjected to experimental verification. Thus, by adopting a relativist and aesthetic approach, and by viewing science as a specific historical and cultural product, Schrödinger anticipates much of the work of N. R. Hanson, Thomas Kuhn, and Paul Feyerabend. Heisenberg is likewise aware of the prerational origins of modern atomic theory as a ceaseless play of physical forces. But while his ontology is admittedly prerational, his epistemology remains neo-Kantian, not unlike that of Vaihinger. For Heisenberg, the world is fundamentally unknowable; reason is not a mirror of nature but a tool in man's struggle for existence. The scientist is not a purely objective and disinterested observer but an active participant in this process. Quantum theory reveals the arbitrary character of the Cartesian division between subject and object (*res cogitans* and *res extensa*). The

Copenhagen interpretation of quantum mechanics starts from the premise that natural science does not simply describe and explain nature, but is part of the interaction between nature and ourselves; it describes nature as it is exposed to our particular mode of questioning.[30] Heisenberg agrees with Schrödinger that all scientific truth is relative or subjective and that science is a specific human product, the result of particular human interests. He suggests that Einstein and the other determinist scientists are reluctant to accept the Copenhagen interpretation of quantum theory because they still operate under the premise of a Cartesian division, according to which the external world (*res extensa*) "really exists." Actually, however, such an approach is more like an artistic style that invokes specific idealizations essential for human understanding.

But while Heisenberg emphasizes the similarity of epistemic approaches in the arts and sciences, he still stresses their rational quality. Bohr, Heisenberg, and the advocates of the Copenhagen school (no less than Einstein, or for that matter, Derrida) remain in the Western metaphysical tradition precisely because they adhere, openly or tacitly, to the power-oriented mentality of that tradition in either its rational or irrational form.[31] The physicists vacillate between a prerational ontology that focuses on ceaseless becoming, and a rational epistemology that assumes a determinate and orderly nature of reality. They adopt a neo-Kantian "as if" approach to knowledge because it enables them to argue that, within such a flowing totality, constructs like the atomic theory have a place, if only as a simplification or abstraction and valid only within a limited context. David Bohm[32] traces the idea of a flowing totality of being (which bears a remarkable resemblance to Heidegger's "world-game" *(Weltspiel)*) back to Heraclitus and to Eastern holistic modes of thinking. Like Heidegger and the other artist-metaphysicians, Bohm justifies this idea aesthetically, while at the same time holding on to his rationalist assumptions in science. The artist-metaphysicians always attempt to impose Being upon Becoming, and they discover ways to impose law and order upon the ceaseless play of arbitrary physical forces in order to subordinate such play to their own rational aims.

It is Feyerabend who questions science as an essentially rational enterprise. Adapting a playful approach, he proceeds *as if* he shared the values of the rationalists (progress, objective criteria for scientific knowledge, logical consistency, etc.) but only in order to show that these values do not really motivate scientific practice. He replaces his own earlier methodological anarchism by something he calls "Dadaism" in order to emphasize the playful and aesthetic nature of his antitotalitarianism. But in doing so, he represses the prerational and violent aspects of this power play. Feyerabend denies that any rationalist methodology can ever adequately account for scientific practice which, like nature and life itself, is in continuous flux and remains unpredictable. For him, as for Nietzsche, facts do not create a theory; the theory creates the facts. Contrary to the prevalent rationalist beliefs, scientific theories are not different interpretations of the same impersonal data; they create their own data. One cannot, therefore, say that new theories conflict with reality, merely that they run counter to earlier and more established theories that have already produced the empirical support for what is taken to be real. Feyerabend argues that scientific knowledge develops the same way infants acquire their language skills – by playing games with new words and concepts. Since science is essentially historical practice or a fashion of the times, it may succeed even when it employs contradictory and irrational methods. Scientific theories often prevail when they proceed counterinductively (from speculation to fact) and when they ignore consistency. A theory may succeed, not because of its increased empirical content or because it has proved a more satisfactory explanation of the phenomena, but merely because of favorable social and cultural circumstances, or at times, purely by chance.[33] Discovery is largely irrational and is not due to any conscious method; indeed the distinction between science and art or between science and religion ("myth") turns out to be specious. Particularly during times of upheaval, style, elegance of expression, and simplicity of presentation become important features of our knowledge. Like other artist-metaphysicians, Feyerabend operates with aesthetic and relativist figures of speech; he emphasizes that rationalism is only one tradition among several others in Western thought. Knowledge is the product of a ceaseless contrast between interpretations, the accumulation of mutually incompatible and even incommensurable alternatives. Nothing is ever settled in science and what does seem established is due merely to the suppression of opponents. For Feyerabend, Western science is a kind of myth that has defeated and replaced its earlier competitors. Today science reigns supreme because its practitioners are unable to understand and unwilling to condone different ideologies, and because they have the power to enforce their wishes.[34] He demands that no tradition be given an unfair advantage and (unlike Nietzsche) he has faith in the democratic instincts of private citizens to settle such matters. But Spariosu rightly points out that a democratic society will inevitably favor rational values since they tend to make life more predictable and safe. While Feyerabend's pluralism is predominately rational, in an agnostic world balance comes about by an equilibrium of forces, not by a sense of fair play. It is in the very nature of such a world to be unstable, and to move back and forth between anarchy and totalitarianism. Feyerabend is caught between his irrational impulses and his rational upbringing.

Thomas Kuhn[35] is fully aware that what he describes as a scientific revolution is a power mechanism that reflects an "essential tension" between tradition and limited innovation. He justifies this in terms of a neo-Darwinist notion of progress. There is a sense, he believes, in which Copernicus is "better" than Ptolomy and Einstein than Newton. He admits, however, that what finally prevails after such revolutions (whether political or scientific) have taken place is the same unchanged power oriented mentality. While Kuhn's model of scientific practice takes its inspiration from the history of art, he emphasizes that aesthetic turns in science are important only during its rare revolutions, not during normal practice. The process of normalization involves a rejection of aestheticism and of play, that is, a return to a more authoritarian and power-oriented state of affairs. But the kind of aestheticism and play that even extraordinary science favors is that of Kant and Schiller, rather than of Nietzsche and Heidegger. Scientists like Einstein, Schrödinger, and Heisenberg value "beauty" in a new theory, but by this they mean unity, consistency, neatness, symmetry, and simplicity – and these are all rational aesthetic criteria originally imposed by metaphysics on the fine arts. Even those scholars (like Kuhn and Gerald Holton) who recognize the "essential tension" between the rational and the prerational in science never question the need for "law and order" as an essential condition of the scientific enterprise. That is why even during times of upheaval scientific discourse remains essentially rational, and the few dissenting voices are largely ignored. Spariosu points out, however, that the conflict between rational and prerational mentality (and between rational and prerational play) is as fierce today as it has always been.

Notes

[1] Mihai I, Spariosu, *Dionysus Reborn, Play and the Aesthetic Dimension in Modern Philosophy and Scientific Discourse*, Ithaca, NY and London: Cornell University Press, 1989, p. x.

[2] *Ibid.*, p. 7.

[3] *Ibid.*, p. 66.

[4] *Ibid.*, p. 91.

[5] *Ibid.*, p. 92.

[6] Martin Heidegger, "The Origin of the Artwork," (1935-36), in *Poetry, Language, Thought*, trans. A. Hofstadter, New York, NY: 1977, p. 48.

[7] Spariosu, *Dionysus Reborn*, p. 119.

[8] Martin Heidegger, *The Principle of Ground, (Der Satz vom Grund)*, Pfullingen, 1957, p. 187.

[9] Spariosu, *Dionysus Reborn*, p. 120.

[10] Heidegger, *The Principle of Ground*, pp. 60-61.

[11] Spariosu, *Dionysus Reborn*, p. 123 n75.

[12] Eugen Fink, *Spiel als Weltsymbol*, Stuttgart: 1960, pp. 205-206.

[13] Spariosu, *Dionysus Reborn*, p. 128 n 78.

[14] Fink, *Spiel als Weltsymbol*, p. 238.

[15] Spariosu, *Dionysus Reborn*, p. 137.

[16] Hans Georg Gadamer, *Truth and Method*, trans. Garrett Barden and John Cumming, New York, NY: 1975, p. 473

[17] Gilles Deleuze, *Nietzsche and Philosophy*, trans. H. Tomlinson, New York, NY: 1983, p. 25.

[18] Spariosu, *Dionysis Reborn*, p. 146.

[19] *Ibid.*, p. 148.

[20] Jacques Derrida, "Scientific Sign and Play in the Discourse of the Human Sciences," in *Writing and Difference*, Chicago, IL: 1978, p. 293.

[21] Spariosu, *Dionysis Reborn*, p. 166.

[22] *Ibid.*, p. 245.

[23] *Ibid.*, p. 247.

[24] Max Planck, *The Philsophy of Physics*, New York, NY: 1936, p. 78.

[25] David Bohm, *Physics in My Generation*, London: 1956, p. 205.

[26] Albert Einstein, "On the Method of Theoretical Physics," in *Ideas and Opinions*, trans. S. Bargmann, London: 1954, p. 272.

[27] Albert Einstein, "Remarks on Russell," in *Ideas and Opinions*, p. 24.

[28] Albert Einstein, "Physics and Reality," in *Ideas and Opinions*, p. 292.

[29] Spariosu, *Dionysis Reborn,* p. 272.

[30] Werner Heisenberg, *Physics and Philosophy,* New York, NY: 1958, p. 80.

[31] Spariosu, *Dionysis Reborn,* p 285 n76.

[32] David Bohm, *Wholeness and the Implicate Order,* London: 1980.

[33] Spariosu, *Dionysis Reborn,* p. 296.

[34] Paul Feyerabend, *Against Method,* London: 1975, p. 299.

[35] Thomas Kuhn, *The Structure of Scientific Revolutions,* Chicago, IL: 1962, 1970.

Chapter Twenty-Three

Postmodernist Discoveries

Megill shows how under modern conditions Nietzsche's will to power becomes self-defeating. His approach to Nietzsche, Heidegger, and Foucault is a product of his reading of Derrida.[1] It is with Nietzsche that the "failure" of the Enlightenment becomes manifest, and we are reduced to seeing "art" or "language" or "discourse" or "text" as constituting the primary realm of human experience. The work of art creates its own reality, and so does language/discourse. Each makes a world that ostensibly only it represents.[2] The intellectual problems that the Enlightenment project to construct a science of society modeled after natural science gave rise to are most clearly reflected in the writings of Kant who separated the theoretical, the practical, and the aesthetic from each other. In Germany, Romanticism started as an aesthetic movement but soon turned into a comprehensive and explicit world view. Yet whereas the Romantics entertained a great deal of hope for the future, Nietzsche and his successors did not. Nietzsche sees the world in which we live as a work of art created by ourselves. He became the originator of the aesthetic metacritique of truth wherein the "work of art" or "the text" or "language" is seen as establishing the ground for truth's possibility.[3] At the same time, however, he considers art not as a vehicle of truth but of illusion. He extends the notion of art as illusion to the whole conceptual world, and views metaphysics, religion, morality, and science as products of an underlying aesthetic will to falsification.[4] In Nietzsche's view, men cannot bear the full burden of realty, and only in illusion does culture flourish or even survive.

In the realm of the aesthetic, we engage in the willing suspension of disbelief. There is a distrust of conceptual knowledge, a feeling that it is a defect of concepts that they do not give us contact with the immediacy of things themselves, and a related tendency to view concepts as subjective projections upon nature. Concepts are seen as bare schemata that rob reality of its multiplicity, and human experience of its original richness and vitality. Man's much vaulted abstractions turn out to be metaphors in disguise, and his language, far from embodying logical truth, reflects rather his innate talent for aesthetic creation.[5] Truth tells us nothing about reality but only about man's aesthetic appreciation of reality. Whereas the Kantian categories are derived from the human mind and are conceived as being the same for all men, in Nietzsche the process of "constructing" reality is portrayed as an individual and even arbitrary matter. Thus, Nietzsche tells us that "truth" is essentially the creation of the language we employ. The linguists realm in question is an aesthetic one, language itself being a product of man's predilection for the making of metaphors. Theoretical man believes that he can correct the world by means of knowledge, while Nietzsche points out that the sphere of solvable problems is a narrow one. Instead of living by a common creative myth that would give our culture a firm foundation and protect it from the dissolving effects of the historical process, we try to live by a passive optimism and by faith in knowledge.[6] Nietzsche thus tends to the view that there is no correct interpretation, and that all interpretations are ultimately aesthetic. Language is a prison from which escape is utterly impossible, even though language is nothing other than a system of interpretations or a set of illusions. In *Twilight of Idols,* Nietzsche tells us, "I fear that we are not getting rid of God because we still believe in grammar."[7] Myth, for Nietzsche, is an aesthetic illusion to which we submit while still knowing it to be an illusion. All ground is lost, and we are left with a free-floating, aesthetic universe. This, however, is incapable of either proof or disproof, and it, therefore, becomes a free decision whether to accept Nietzsche's perspective or to reject it.

Heidegger's philosophy is in many respects a radicalization of Nietzsche and, in Heidegger, the anti-analytical spirit is given free play. Megill argues that one is able to regard the later Heidegger as mistaken, and still hold that he opens up important perspectives.

Whereas in Anglo-American philosophy the dominant orientation has been empirical and analytic, Nietzsche and Heidegger provide us with an intellectual articulation of the assumptions underlying modernism and postmodernism.[8] There are connections with the work of Kuhn[9] and Feyerabend,[10] but they are rarely allowed to breach the dominant notions of method in natural science.[11] Heidegger, on the other hand, is concerned not with knowledge and cognition but with the art of thinking itself. His thinking is always "under way," and he constantly wants to go back, to go home to some earlier, less articulate, more authentic state or condition. He moves ambiguously between the realm of thought and specific, German, social and political conditions at the time of writing. Technology is conceived by him as an anonymous force that is gaining ever more control over our lives. Man projects a conceptual grid upon the world and attends only to what can fit the grid. Megill points out that, for those who have difficulty in seeing why anyone could take Heidegger seriously, much of the answer is to be found in the fact that his nostalgia and idealistic technological catastrophism, do seem in many of its aspects to accord with our twentieth century experience. The Holocaust, nuclear weapons, the growing technologization and bureaucratization of modern life – all these realities seem to confirm Heidegger's text, or at least can be convincingly interpreted on his terms.[12]

Heidegger sees art as a counterforce to the manipulative forces of technology. The Greeks kept themselves open to the experience of art, and Heidegger envisages a return to this openness.[13] Our own relation to art, by contrast, has been turned into "aesthetics," that is, into yet another post-Cartesian science. The redemption will come (if it comes) through an integration of technology and art. Though Heidegger rejects such a designation, what we have here is a thinking that is essentially aesthetic. The notion of truth in art comes as close as anything to being the central theme of Heidegger's later thought. Art serves to sensitize us to realities of which we might not otherwise be aware. It is language/thought that brings the whole human world into existence, and the aesthetic implications of this view become even clearer when one notes how persistently Heidegger attempts to identify language with poetry.[14] Since he treats fiction as if it were truth, it attains the same exemption from conventional logical criticism that a consistent religious fideism has. But like fideism, Heidegger makes statements regarding his own enterprise and the world that an "ordinary" perspective is forced to reject. He is satisfied to counsel "composure" (*Gelassenheit*) with regard to whatever forces happen to dominate the human scene. It is entirely in the spirit of this response that he declares in a *Der Spiegel* interview of 1966 (published in 1976, after his death) that only a God can save us. Megill rightly points out that those who think that the forces of technology are utterly beyond human control are likely to find that this is indeed the case.[15] While Heidegger is a poor guide to those who want to understand how the ordinary world operates, much of what he says can, nevertheless, plausibly be considered true.

Whereas Heidegger's quest ends in pietism, Foucault is a radical activist who engages in a relentless struggle with the world. He is a revolutionary who frequently denied even being a philosopher, and whose friends in the late 1940s and early 1950s were mostly painters, writers, and musicians. Foucault denies that there is any ultimate philosophical or social truth, or that there can be a final end to oppression. There is no such thing as a historical past "as is really happened" and, as Ranke wanted to rediscover, and in general, no such thing as "objective knowledge." Foucault rejects all forms of generalized discourse as misleading, and puts forward no vision of happiness or liberation of his own. His vision of structuralism is an attack on the Cartesian *cognito* and its contemporary successor, the phenomenological subject. Viewed in this way, Foucault can be seen as continuing the later Heidegger's attack on the whole tradition of Western science and technology. There are no facts, only interpretations.[16] Megill emphasizes that, until the advent of postmodernism, it was customary to read Nietzsche, Marx, and Freud on the model of "depth" interpretation – that is, on the model of a search for "deep structures." It was customary to read these thinkers as engaging in an attempt to find the will to power underlying the moral ideal, the social force underlying the ideological fetish, the latent wish underlying the manifest dream. But this is not the way Foucault reads them. Interpretation does not illuminate some "thing" that passively allows itself to be expounded. Rather it seizes upon a "meaning" already in place and, consequently, "depth" itself is shown to be deceptive. The task of interpretation, which would otherwise have ended in the discovery of a foundation, becomes an infinite task of self-reflection.[17] Postmodernism teaches us to look at a work of art not in order to discern a meaning that lies "beneath" it, but rather to enjoy it for what it is with nothing concealed, no intention to be discovered, only the ultimate play of words itself. Foucault is viewing the world as if it were discourse, and holds that every science is an ideology, not in the strict sense of its being a reflection of the interests of some particular class, but in the broader sense of its being immediately caught up with reflections of power. Such "power," however, like everything else in this rhetoric, remains an ungraspable entity. Whereas Nietzsche had considered the will to power to be a universal principle to which even the search for truth is subject, his own project claims to be an articulation of truth. A similar objection applies to Foucault who tells us that there is no such thing as a "genuine" rhetoric, but does so in discourse that by this very argument cannot be genuine.

Megill concludes, therefore, that such writings are intended to be provocative rather than instructive. It was Derrida who in a 1967 interview had stated that he takes the risk of not wishing to say (or to mean) anything.[18] It is no accident that at crucial points he moves into interrogative or suppositional modes, thus distancing himself from the text and destroying the apparently declarative force of what he is saying. Whereas Nietzsche, Heidegger, and Foucault reject the extant world but admire ideal (nostalgic or imaginative) alternatives, Derrida seems to reject the alternatives as well. The "play of ironic seriousness" we find in Derrida renders explicit a prevalent attitude in modernist and postmodernist art, and it can help us to come to grips with certain assumptions pervasive in works of art in our time.[19] Derrida has become a central figure in a storm of controversy concerned with the question of how literary texts ought to be interpreted. Inevitably, however, it is also concerned with how we ought to live our lives. Derrida attacks the distinction between the aesthetic and the nonaesthetic domain that is crucial in the work of such mondernist writers as Yeats, Pound, and Eliot. Postmodernism has consistently called in question the distinction between "art" and "reality." Works of art in the postmodernist mode demonstrate an ontological concern, continually asking what it is to be a sculpture, a play, a novel, or a painting. Already Nietzsche had used the notion of art both in its narrow and in its wide sense; there are artists of art, and there are also artists of politics, science, and religion. The usual distinction between "art" and "reality" is inadequate because the reality within which we live is itself partly the product of art/interpretation/language. This is how reading and writing become "originating" operatives in Derrida: they involve not the discovery of truth but its invention. Derrida's writings are putative; none comes to a disclosure of truth. The task of writing is not to say something, to make a point and be done with it. On the contrary, writing is its own justification.

Derrida's philosophical investigations, like Wittgenstein's, are a crisscrossing of territory, the expedition of a mapmaker or land surveyor, not of a traveler from one place to another. One is also reminded of Heidegger's *Holzwege* and that side of Freud that makes analysis interminable.[20] All contexts are constructed; none is simply given, and there is no single thing that we can designate as, say, "French intellectual life." Instead one finds a multiplicity of disorganized competing strands, and how we decide to organize them depends on what we are interested in. As with Heidegger and Foucault, an initial engagement with Phenomenology appears almost a precondition for the aestheticist move. Derrida no longer takes seriously the distinction between scientific and nonscientific discourse, or between the literal truth of science and the metaphorical truth of art. For him criticism and creation are not separate, and he creates a literary/philosophical collage that one must read as a work of art. What is left is the writing of dreams, a fiction without either truth or falsity. Derrida here describes a literature that refuses to "represent" reality. His own thesis is that, in the course of Western history, writing has been "abased" in favor of speech.[21] Speech stands for immediacy, or more precisely, for intelligibility, for the possibility of contact with truth, with the "transcendentally signified." Writing stands for a particular kind of secondariness – but one that recognizes that secondariness is all we have. Derrida's grammatological thesis seems a shorthand version of condemning the Western tradition for its commitment to the ultimate possibilities of literal truth. Derrida sees the Socratic rejection of writing[22] as dominating the entire subsequent history of the West. Speech is presence, writing is the dismissal of presence, and Socrates' dismissive view of writing parallels his equally dismissive view of art. Derrida concludes that reading cannot legitimately transgress the text towards something other than itself, toward a referent (a realty that is metaphysical, historical, psychological, etc.), or toward a signified outside the text whose context would take place outside language.[23] He rejects the Kantian notion that aesthetic function is something separable from the serious truth of science.

There is the question of interpretation – the whole process of writing that, in view of the inaccessibility of any ultimate interpretation becomes an end in itself. Writing and interpretation come to be valued not because they can reveal to us the light of truth, but because they are themselves truth. Thus, they have a "purposiveness without purpose" analogous to that which Kant found in aesthetic objectivity. Derrida's move beyond Kant is to argue that "purposiveness without purpose" pervades all we do. His move beyond Hegel and Heidegger is to substitute an explicit theory for their conviction that in one way or another art gives us access to the truth of being.[24] If God is dead, then we all live in secondariness, and the essence of such secondariness is writing. Derrida (who was born into a Sephardic Jewish family living in El Biar, a suburb or Algiers) finds a model of such writing in Judaism, and especially in Lureanic Kabbalism, which could make a given text mean whatever the believer wanted it to mean. In this manner, the prioirty of text over interpretation is eliminated, and the text really becomes a pretext. In his own "method" of dealing with texts, Derrida stands as a successor to Kabbalah, with one crucially important difference. For whereas the Kabbalist sought an interpretation of words and letters (*Gematria*) in order to find a way to God, Derrida takes the manipulation of words and letters as something close to an end in itself. For Derrida there is nothing beyond the letter, no final voice speaking a long-concealed truth. Interpretation becomes "literature," an end in itself. It is easy to see why Derrida should find Freud's enterprise congenial. As Rief[25] observes, Freud places us in an incredible world, a world in which events that never occurred control those that do. Derrida makes clear how hard it is to find in Freud's various analytical endeavors a reality prior to its own interpretation. The frame turns out to be crucial to being a work of art, for it is the frame that separates art from what is not art. Exposing the arbitrary division between what is art and what is not art, by focusing on the frame or paradigm, calls into question the whole tradition of aesthetics as it has been developed by Kant and Hegel.

Discourse creates its own reality, but Megill warns us not to take these aestheticist theses too literally. One way of avoiding these difficulties is by the simple expedient of ceasing to speak of the "truth" of art altogether, and this is indeed what both Foucault and Derrida seem to suggest. We should be equally suspicious of the notion of the "creative lie," for if one adopts in a cavalier fashion the view that everything is discourse or text or fiction, then the realities are trivialized. Real people who really died in the gas chambers of

Auschwitz become so much discourse. With this in mind. Megill suggest that we ought to read these "prophets of extremity" not as guides, but ironically as opponents. We ought to view the work of the artist as existing in a state of tension with the given. There is, however, something important to be learned from these philosophers of paradox, for in attacking the primacy of literal truth, they are denying that there is "one true way." Nietzsche and his followers call certainty into question, and return us to a situation when there is no longer one, single, literal truth, one privileged meaning. We ought to look with suspicion at the notion of a single, privileged truth and the corresponding distinction between the possessors of such truth – the chosen – and those who are not chosen. Such exclusion becomes unbearable when each community has the power to destroy the other as becomes increasingly the case.

Notes

[1] Allan Megill, *Prophets of Extremity, Nietzsche, Heidegger, Foucault, Derrida,* Berkeley, Los Angeles, CA, London: Univeristy of California Press, 1985, p. xi.

[2] *Ibid.,* p. 3.

[3] *Ibid.,* p. 33.

[4] Walter Kaufman, ed., *The Will to Power,* trans. Walter Kaufman and R.J. Hollingsdale, New York, NY: Random House, 1967.

[5] Megill, *Prophets of Extremity,* p. 50.

[6] *Ibid.,* p. 75.

[7] Friedrich Nietzsche, *Twighlight of the Idols,* trans. R. J. Hollingdale, Harmondsworth, England: Penguin Books 1961, sec. 5.

[8] Megill, *The Will to Power,* p. 109.

[9] Thomas S. Kuhn, *The Structure of Scientific Revolutoins,* Chicago, IL: Chicago University Press, 1970, p. 111.

[10] Paul Feyerabend, *Against Method: Outline of an Anarchistic Theory of Knowledge,* London: NLB, 1975, p. 295.

[11] Joseph Grünfeld, *Changing Rational Standards,* Lanham, NY, London: University Press of America, 1985.

[12] Megill, *The Will to Power,* p. 140.

[13] *Ibid.,* p. 144.

[14] Martin Heidegger, *On the Way to Language,* trans. Peter D. Hertz, New York, NY: Harper & Row, 1971, p. 59.

[15] Megill, *The Will to Power,* p. 180.

[16] Michel Foucault, *L'archéologie du savoir,* Paris: Gallimard, 1969, p. 65. English trans. Alan Sheridan under the title *The Archeology of Knowledge,* New York, NY: Random House, Pantheon Books, 1972, p. 47.

[17] Megill, *The Will to Power,* p. 224.

[18] Jacques Derrida, *Positions,* Paris: Minuit, 1972, p. 24. English trans. by Alan Bass under the title *Positions,* Chicago, IL: University of Chicago Press, 1981, p. 14.

[19] Megill, *The Will to Power,* p. 272.

[20] *Ibid.,* p. 272.

[21] Derrida, *Positions,* p. 72, trans. P. 53.

[22] Phaedrus 274c - 276e.

[23] Jacques Derrida, *De la grammatologie,* Paris: Minuit, 1974, p. 27. English trans. by Gayatri Spivak under the title *Of Grammatology,* Baltimore, MD: John Hopkins University Press, 1976, p. 28.

[24] Megill, *The Will to Power,* p. 305.

[25] Philip Rief, *The Mind of the Moralist,* Garden City, NY: Doubleday Anchor, 1961.

Chapter Twenty-Four

The Crisis of Modernity

The seventeenth century anticipation of unimpaired progress and the early universal confidence of modernity are long-gone. Decades of revolution in art, music, and literature have promulgated widely divergent views of what art is, have denied the validity of representation, and have left the uncritical public entirely at sea. The advances in scientific understanding of the chemical, neural, and behavioral determinants of human experience and conduct, despite their benefits, make belief in the freedom, responsibility, and rationality of the human individual harder and harder to maintain. It is now for an individual in the modernized world difficult to understand, let alone control, the manifold moral, social, and economic conditions that determine his or her life. The West is plagued by seemingly unsurmountable social problems, such as crime, drug abuse, alcoholism, and teenage pregnancy that repeatedly raise in the public mind the question of how free the individual is or should be. Despite the great power and seeming stability of some of the Western democracies, anti-humanist solutions are always tempting and increasingly so. Globally, of course, humanism is the exception and not the rule, but Cahoone argues that the modern world is caught in a dilemma, and that modernity is eroding its own cultural foundations. Philosophy has been declared dead, most noticeably by the philosophers themselves. People outside philosophy find it increasingly meaningless and irrelevant to their own social and intellectual concerns. Those within philosophy seek new ways to reduce philosophy to literary criticism or conceptual therapy, to deconstruct, analyze and generally define their own discipline out of existence.[1] Contemporary philosophy's sense that it is cut off from its past, that pre-twentieth century philosophy is out of date, naive, and irrelevant to present concerns, mirrors the indifference to history that is characteristic of modern culture in general. There has been a progressive self-undermining of a problematic but important strain of modern culture, and this has brought about the emergence of an anti-culture, a delegitimization or undermining of the value of knowledge, communication, and the sense of significance of human acts and artifacts.

In the ongoing debate over the nature of modernity, the choice of the starting points tends to depend on which principles are taken to be constitutive of *recent* modernity, that is, of late nineteenth century culture. The concept of modernity is based on the conviction that we are heirs to a relatively coherent, modern, Western heritage of ideas. It assumes that the technological mastery over nature, democracy, the supremacy of the natural state, modern science, secularism, and humanism all cohere in some way, despite their differences and alleged contradictions.[2] Cahoone assumes that the new artistic, literary, and philosophical movements are within the orbit of modernity, but that they represent the critical response of late against early modernity. He follows Adorno and Horkheimer's[3] dialectical theory of modernity as negating its own fundamental principles when apprehending the seeming paradoxes of the late-modern world. It is by no means clear that our arts have become more creative or profound, or that democratic nations are more capable of conducting their affairs. Neither is it self-evident that technology and the military might have made the West more secure. For American conservatives, the earlier or classical phase of modernity culminating in nineteenth century culture is the sole foundation for democracy, science, the rule of law, individual freedom, and personal as well as social morality. They consider the cultural and social developments of late or twentieth century modernity – the welfare state, the erosion of the patriarchal family, the assault on Western world leadership, non-representational and avant-garde movements in art, the rejection of communal moral absolutes, changes in sexual mores, and the popular adoption of a hedonistic ethic, as a tragic turning away from the foundation of the modern.[4] Liberals, on the other hand, view the recent movements towards greater individual choice and freedom in lifestyle, public control of private property, the liberation of racial minorities from the white majority, women from men, and third-world nations from Western influence, the philosophic and artistic rejection of traditional concepts of truth and beauty, the loss of religious authority, all as a fulfillment of early modernity. Cahoone points out that when liberals approve of the avant-garde culture of late modernity as a culture of free expression, they fail to see that much of this culture ideologically undermines the positive conceptions of human nature and political society, which alone prove a possible intellectual basis for such freedom. Many liberals reject religious values and the belief in a universal morality, but fail to recognize that the commitment to radical freedom, which is one of the cornerstones of early-modernity, itself implies something like a faith in a universal morality. The point is that from early to late modernity, the concept of the human individual changes in such a way that the notion of universal freedom becomes altogether problematic. In particular, it becomes difficult to conceive of a community of free individuals.[5]

A philosophy must begin with certain questions rather than others. The choice of topic – the subject matter is at least as important as the choice of basic premises, and makes a philosophy even more the product of individual decision and personal insight. Philosophies are accepted or rejected on the basis of whether they address and offer fruitful and valuable interpretation of what the community of relevant listeners feels most needs to be addressed. Each philosopher's work is one piece of a constantly shifting mosaic that is the culture of a period and a place. A philosophy that is found to be valuable by a community provides ideas that guide action, thereby shaping the development of community life. Cahoone emphasizes that the great figures of the dominant, philosophical tradition (Descartes, Locke, Kant) share a mind-body dualism and as a result an emphasis on epistemology. Cahoone identifies this ultimately self-negating strain with a subjectivism that he thinks we must overcome. He realizes, at the same time, that subjectivism runs deep in late-modern culture, and that subjectivist categories are manifest in twentieth century philosophers as different as A.J. Ayer and Martin Heidegger. Subjectivism takes individual consciousness to be the distinctive feature of reality in spite of its respective multiple meanings. This pervasiveness of the subjectivist dichotomy and its massive influence on our thinking often goes unnoticed. To deny subjectivism means to regard the subject-object dichotomy as no more fundamental than the distinction between appearance and reality, the finite and the infinite, or matter and form. The conception of mind and matter as metaphysically antithetical is not particularly modern, but the identification of mind, *nous,* or *psyche* with subjectivity or personal consciousness is characteristically post-Cartesian. This view severely restricts the kind of interaction that can be asserted to exist between the mental-subjective and anything else we wish to talk about.[6] Cahoone believes that, within the subjectivist framework it is more or less inevitable that nature and physical reality have no inherent value, or at least that subjectivity is taken as preserving greater inherent or moral value than nature, and that the consciousness taken as a primary realm of evidence is fundamentally private. From Descartes to Ayer, modern rationalism and empiricism, however much they are opposed, agree that analysis and human knowledge of the world must begin with an understanding of the contents of the individual human mind or consciousness. Descartes fails to question the integrity of his own self or mind; he questions only the mind's opinions, sensations, and their sources of referents, external existences. The upshoot of the Cartesian viewpoint is to move one particular aspect of human being – consciousness or subjectivity – to center stage. Cahoone, on the other hand, prefers the Aristotelian tradition, according to which the knower and the known exhibit an internal relation.

He realizes, however, that subjectivism cleared the metaphysical and epistemological ground for the development of modern science by separating science from religion, and by making possible the simultaneous retention of religion and the pursuit of science. It was also conceivably compatible with the Christian belief regarding the nature of the soul, especially in the Protestant versions. Its answer was strictly to separate the spiritual and the material, giving the spiritual domination.[7] The decline of aristocracy, the growth of the middle class, democracy, and progressively widening suffrage, all served to erode the power of super-individual structures in determining the life of the individual. Society became more and more a community of politically and legally equal individuals or citizens. Economic position, class status, and career increasingly came to be interpreted as purely a matter of extrinsic conditions. As thinking subjects, individuals were understood to be equal and free, and religion came to be regarded as a private and personal, hence subjective, matter. This equally applied to aesthetics, some ethical questions, and sexual habits. The problem, however, was that God alone could make the subjectivist world hang together, and that without God, or some equally transcendent concept, the modern notion of a thinking subject tended to lose the grounds of its relation to the rest of reality. Nature became mere stuff, devoid of spiritual qualities or value. In this manner, not only natural qualities but also social and economic conditions were seen to be contingent, and thus subject to human manipulation. In a liberal democracy, people are regarded predominately as private individuals whose beliefs and thoughts are their own, and who confront a non-subjective, non-religious, mechanical, and material world. This is how modern society developed in ways that made the subjective viewpoint more and more legitimate, pervasive, and obvious. But what conforms to subjectivist dualism tends at the same time to deligitimize the transcencental doctrines and images associated with it. During the early-modern period, the transcendental abilities of the human mind were taken to be those intellectual capacities of the subject that were able to bridge the subjectivist dichotomy, that is, capable of grasping the truth about the world itself. Chief among these faculties was transcendental reason – the notion that human understanding functions not only in mathematics and logic but that it is also able to perceive what is real and necessary beyond the individual mind. As a result of the radicalization of such views during the late nineteenth and twentieth centuries, such transcendental capacities of the subject were interpreted as either purely subjective, the product of wishes, illusions, perspectival limitations, or as the effect of objective determinations, the product of environment, conditioning, and biological factors.

Cahoone insists that the groundlessness of metaphysical claims is by no means obvious, and that the fact that it may appear obvious is merely an indication of the thoroughness with which such a viewpoint has been accepted. He points out that it is the perspective that determines doubt, not vice versa, and that the "critical" rejection of transcendental notions is frequently determined by a prior commitment to subjectivist categories.[8] Moreover, this gradual fading of the transcendental initiated a profound change in the subjectivist categories themselves. These categories now lacked any transcendental mediation, any overarching context in which to limit and to harmonize their respective applicability and scope. Transcendental reason was an essential component of liberalism and its politics, jurisprudence, and economic theory. The notion that every individual mind is capable of perceiving both reality and universal "self-evident" truth, and capable of rational discourse, was written into the American Constitution as well as Kant's *Critique of Pure Reason*. Without a moral "light of reason," all that could be of value to the subject can only be conceived as purely personal, and thus not subject to rational discussion, organization, or criticism.[9] The so-called demystification of nature and the destruction of metaphysics and religious belief were understood, on the subjectivist model, as steps towards human liberation. The unintended result, however, was that the progressive denial of the referent value of anything outside the subject left it with noting of value except materiality since, under subjectivism, any other proposed value can be understood only as a private wish or fantasy. Other disciplines do not need philosophy in order to have validity, but they do need philosophy to be understood beyond the context of their own perspective in relation to other human activities, intellectual and otherwise. Philosophers, of course, have always responded to non-philosophical concerns, but subjectivist theories are remarkably indifferent to common-sense realities. Subjectivist philosophers deprive reality of depth; they accept the Cartesian principle that it is impossible to question the existence of appearances as appearances. The result is an oscillation between the abstract subject and the abstract world, and both these terms lack what we would call reality. For Husserl, the problem of how transcendental subjectivity can constitute within itself other subjectivites becomes the crucial issue of transcendental phenomenology.[10] The problem arises within the fundamental phenomenological method of distinguishing between the realm of natural existence and the realm of subjectivity, and of "bracketing" the former. It becomes harder to say what is subject and what is object, and this leaves us in the end with no ego or subject at all, if these words are to have any legitimate meaning. Subjectivity or consciousness has no nature, no content, no structure that determines events or leaves its mark on the world it creates.[11] While Heidegger is opposed to Husserl's "egology," he takes over Husserlian phenomenology as the basis for his own method. The world into which *Dasein* has been thrown is essentially a subjective world – a world that has no independent existence, and behind whose phenomena there is essentially nothing else. Heidegger does not give us an answer to what *Dasein* is, but for him a human being is absolutely distinct form all nature and all natural entities, as it is in Descartes, Kant, and Husserl, and this is the most fundamental fact in subjectivism. What is claimed to exist must appear to the subject, yet the subject never appears.

Cahoone admits that the reason why philosophical subjectivism has been so influential since the seventeenth century is that it expressed a general cultural and social movement. The evolving cultural perspective was the conviction that the individual human subject, considered as a thinking, perceiving, valuing mind, is the ultimate locus of all judgments of truth, value, and political authority. This perspective was implicit in the methodology of the new seventeenth century science, which rejected Scriptural authority in favor of the conceptually analyzed perceptions of individual researchers. It was also implied by the economic individualism of the growing capitalist class, and it originated in the distinction between the individual's inner faith and the outer forms of worship and ritual. It formed the basis for liberal, republican ideology, and thus of political and social reforms that eventually came to define much of modern Western life.[12] But important strains within modern culture have been undermined by delegitimizing the context within which they had functioned. In early modernity, the view that these cultural processes are intrinsically valuable and meaningful provided the context by which subjectivity could be conceived as related instead as isolated and disparate. But the subjectivist categories proved too strong, and the loss of context and mediation changed the meaning of the categories themselves. There is a continuing erosion of the felt value of communication, and a profound effect on intellectual, economic, political, and personal life.

Nearly everyone admits that modernity – the related economic, social, scientific, political, and cultural programs of the Western world since the Renaissance – had its costs as well as its benefits. The achievements of modernity, such as mobility, often cause undesired outcomes such as a limited sense of family and community. But admitting that modernity involves a trade-off of some values against others does not necessarily mean that the very achievements of modernity undermine and negate themselves. Cahoone somehow concludes that the attempts to rationalize life necessarily end in greater irrationality and that the goal of personal freedom leads to collective compulsion. He follows Adorno and Horkheimer in holding that mastery over nature, and the organization of social and sexual life in civilized society requires ever greater instinctual renunciations as Freud has pointed out in *Civilization and Its Discontents.*[13] As a consequence, previous demystification of the power of fate, the divine right of kings, the sanctity of the hierarchic social order, belief in God and religious values now questions natural reason, metaphysics, a universal moral conscience, and the very idea of human nature. Reality comes to be regarded as devoid of inherent meaning, as a mere manipulable substance, and the enlightened self views as illusory any projects and hopes other than knowledge and manipulation of the given. Adorno and Horkheimer had argued that this reversal, which is most virulently demonstrated in fascism, can also be said to be present in various doctrines of positivism and in institutions of mass culture. The banishing of metaphysics and value from the domain of rational thought leads to a worship of facts, and to a rejection of all non-factual questions as meaningless. This, in turn, brings about a weakening of liberal, enlightened, bourgeois culture in which all realty external to the individual subject comes to be regarded as inherently value-neutral, as manipulable commodities. Thus, there is little left for the individual to value, and he remains subject to a natural world, which at a deeper level he does not value. The subject becomes a mere manipulator of this world lacking any other source of interest, concern, value, or belief.[14] Christopher Lasch[15] suggests that the radical effacement of aesthetic conventions or even of the concept of art itself reveals not a greater imaginative and creative freedom, but rather an unwillingness or inability to place oneself within the universe of the artwork and to take its truths seriously. This, not surprisingly, also impairs the ability to encounter reality because such cultural conventions do not limit and obscure the truth, rather they are truth's only vehicle, they are the way human beings know and understand. The attempts to "get outside" of culture and contact reality, as it were, independently of everything humanly created is nonsensical, for reality, insofar as it is available to human beings, is formed within culture.[16]

Cahoone emphasizes that no culture is monolithic since it comprises indefinitely complex and conflicting meanings. From such a weakly consistent concept of culture, however, very little may be legitimately excluded. It is thus by no means obvious that culture becomes meaningless when its artifacts or symbols are taken as psychologically, economically, or politically determined. Neither does this necessarily amount to what Cahoone calls anti-culture, a culture that is hostile to itself. The economic life of the nation can be understood as the sum of contractual agreements between free individuals as envisioned by early modernity and before the radical self-negating tendencies of late modernity have set it. Cahoone claims, however, that these conditions of modern society could not prevail were it not for the presumption that all free individuals share certain guiding principles, such as enlightened self-interest or "natural reason." Early modernism was characterized by the prevalence of such beliefs, and it was a significant theme in early modern culture that economic activity had religious and cultural meaning, and had implications for the moral character of the individual. Later when these transcendental mediating themes lost their hold, all meaning and value were reduced to the intentions of individual subjects, and the objects of these intentions were taken to be merely instrumental. Religious convictions came to be regarded as a subjective matter, not appropriate to the determination of public life. The claim that a particular religious belief is true of reality and ought to determine communal behavior (something that would have been considered obvious during the two thousand preceding years) would today be unacceptable to all but a small minority in the West. But the decay of the *res-publica* undermines the integrity of the self as well, and anti-culture reduces culture to merely economic, administrative or private significance. Within philosophy, thinkers as diverse as Wittgenstein and Heidegger have written philosophical works maintaining that philosophy has or should "come to an end." Post-structuralism regards theoretical culture as largely exhausted, and art is widely regarded as mere entertainment or business. Politics is taken as the impersonal preservation of the status quo or as the expression of personal greed or fanatical impulses of a few individuals. Noneconomic and nontechnical discussions are widely considered to be mere matters of taste, personal opinion, or subjective preference. The exposure to massive advertising reduces the encounter with a large portion of daily experience to something nonmeaningful. But the subjectivist anti-culture fails to understand that human beings create, and become individual and independent only within a context of meaningful relations to other human and non-human beings.

Each philosophy is designed to address a limited set of problems and it becomes a part of the public tradition of philosophical thought. Cahoone realizes that subjectivism had a degree of adequacy and fruitfulness in its application to the reconciliation of competing claims of scientific materialism and Christian spiritualism – issues that made it the dominant force in modern philosophy and culture. Consciousness seemed to be that in which all evidence must appear in order to be evidence at all. Cahoone, on the other hand, insists that it is only through culture that human individuals attain personality. He rejects the prevalent view that culture is actually an obstacle to some of the most fundamental projects of modernity. For such philosophers, culture obscures reality by providing a context of implicit beliefs and interpretive models imbibed by the individual since infancy. Philosophy, since Descartes and until recently has clung to various epistemological fantasies criticized by Quine and Rorty. Quine questioned the myth of the "given," the distinction between the order of thought or higher truth and the order of receptivity or empirical truth, whereas Rorty rejected the metaphor of the mind as a mirror of nature. Such ideas reveal the persistent dream that if only the inquirer could get outside the totality of human interests, beliefs, institutions, interpretations, inherited traditions dictated by birth, family, status, religion, social role, history, and personal idiosyncrasies, the individual would come to know reality as it really is, independently of human bias and limitation. It is this dream that Rorty in his *Philosophy and the Mirror of Nature*[17] attacks. This fantasy assumes that the highest form of human knowledge is that of a mere register, a passive mirror of the given. Cahoone accordingly concludes that culture does not hide truth, for culture is truth's only vehicle.

Early modern philosophy tended to view Reason itself as providing the basis for truth and knowledge, and to regard philosophy's task as one of showing what reason implies. Kant presumes the truth of Newtonian science; he believes that he is exposing, systematizing, and interpreting the nature and limits of that truth. It is only since the late nineteenth century that philosophy conceives of itself as providing the basis for truth. Husserl and Heidegger are at pains to point out that the natural and social sciences are epistemologically groundless, and that they require a phenomenological philosophy to provide them with a foundation. The logicist project of early twentieth century analytic philosophy, which attempted to base the truth of mathematics – and thus of modern science – on logic, is another example of this tendency.[18] It is impossible for Husserl and Heidegger to conceive of community, communication, and cultural processes as a primary source of meaning and value, and as the vehicle for truth and understanding. In the positivist view, likewise, values are part of the cultural process, and cultural artifacts as well as communicative events cannot be value-neutral. The positivists denied that values and meanings have any nonsubjective existence, that the empirical could be meaningful and valuable, or that values could be anything but emotions. Indeed, many contemporary philosophers write as if the whole history of human culture has no truth to tell. Positivism considered the rational discussion of political values to be nonsensical, whereas phenomenology renders the physical constitution of the universe irrelevant. Philosophy becomes a nonempirical, value-neutral metacritique, primarily concerned with problems of language, logic and signification. Philosophy's goal is not to enhance our understanding of the world, nature, art, or human existence, but to improve our knowledge of the tools of understanding (i.e. language, logic, text). Such a view divorces philosophy from the rest of culture, and renders philosophy irrelevant to whatever nonphilosophical human beings do, say, or think.[19] The subordination of society and culture to economics could justifiably be considered one of the hallmarks of modernity in both its capitalist and Marxist versions. This stands in sharp contrast to the approach of traditional, premodern societies that Cahoone favors.

He maintains that subjectivism has been so dominant and pervasive within modernity that many philosophers cannot distinguish between subjectivism and philosophy. Cahoone believes that, whereas subjectivist modernity has exhausted itself, modernity was never synonymous with subjectivism and that it still has more cards to play.[20] Many philosophers, even those who consider their work politically relevant, accept Wittgenstein's prescription on the function of philosophy that philosophers may reveal the problematic nature of any pronouncement on human affairs, but that in response to the question of how then we ought to understand reality and human affairs, and what we should do about them, philosophers must remain silent.[21] The postmodernists, who call for a radical rejection of modernity, tend to forget that we have a stake in the preservation of some aspects of modernity; a stake that is not merely philosophical but has implications for humanism and democracy as well. Cahoone wants us to hold together two thoughts that are often treated as antithetical or incompatible: that existing things are both individual integrities, and that they are essentially related to other things.[22] The problem is that from such an inconsistent ontology any epistemological conclusion may be derived. The tradition in Western philosophy that finds internal relations beneath and behind every case of individual integrity begins with Heraclitus, has been radicalized by Hume, and more recently by structuralists and poststructuralists. This tradition emphasizes that each individual entity is what it is only because of its relations with other entities, processes, and factors. The more one looks for such relations, the more one finds them, of course, and ultimately it will appear that each individual is nothing but a nexus of relations. Hume reduces entities to collections of sense impressions, and there is no underlying substance supporting these impressions. This analysis applies to human beings, to mind, or self no less than to the nonhuman substance. The "self" is a collection of impressions and ideas.[23] At the end of his *Inquiry*, however, Hume admits that life dictates that we must act as if we know what philosophical inquiry tells us we can never know. Life forces us to live beyond what we can know in a rational philosophical sense. When we engage in philosophical inquiry, we must have at least an implicit sense of the goal of what we are doing. Much in philosophical argument turns on this fundament question, which is one of its goals and hence, a value commitment.[24]

Cahoone rejects the idea that culture is a third, a mediator between subjectivity and objectivity in the manner of Popper's "third world,"[25] but unlike Popper, his notion of culture is essentially precritical and Aristotelian. Much of culture is inherited, and the inheritance provides a context of cultural activities, events, artifacts, and meanings that serve as an interpretive reservoir on which each individual draws. Since language is itself part of this cultural inheritance, it is clear that communication virtually could not exist without culture.[26] But there are, of course, biological and genetic elements in human communication as well, and language is no more reducible to culture than vice versa. Cahoone regards culture as the matrix of both community and individual since the individual cannot develop without culture, communication, and community. Even the extreme individualist, the revolutionary, and the iconoclast, all use the cultural materials of their community, interpreting some strains and rejecting others. Cahoone concludes that communication, community, and the inheritance of a culture have little to do with agreement and shared belief, but that they have to do with a shared language.[27] He sees culture not as a monolithic, but as an ever-changing, plurality of activities, events, and artifacts that are continuously being interpreted and reconstructed. Cahoone explains that, despite the seeming defeat of Cartesianism within philosophy, the dualistic and subjectivistic approach remain dominant.[28] He insists, however, that the most fundamental and deepest level of experience remains beyond the subjectivist distinction. The process of experiencing, assimilating, interpreting, and creating meaningful things is a specifically human activity. Humans happen to be the kind of beings for whom sound waves, ink marks on paper, the movement of facial muscles, the facade of a building, the color of a sunset have elaborate meaning and value.

Culture connects human beings not only with things, but also with each other and with past generations whose products are interpreted and reinvested with meaning by the living.[29] The problem of knowledge, which has been the primary concern of much of philosophy since the seventeenth century, has been strongly influenced by subjectivist categories. The dichotomy produced a distinction between the empirical order of things and the order of spontaneous thought insulated from direct contact with things, and thus incapable of organization and analysis, i.e. a formal, logical, and analytical order. Some influential twentieth century philosophers whom Cahoone follows have refused to accept the belief in an order of receptivity or observation that is independent of perspective, historical traditions, interpretive paradigms, and theoretical commitments. They recognized that the strict distinction between interpretation and perception, which had been inherited from early modern thought and applied in more extreme terms by language positivism, could not be maintained.[30] But what Cahoone really proposes is a return to premodern lines of thought, as he himself realizes,[31] a precritical Aristotelian position according to which the mind has an "internal" relation to the things themselves. What he seems to forget is that Aristotelianism was defeated by modern science – and by subjectivism, which made modern science possible – for good reasons. Since Galileo and Descartes, modern science and modern philosophy have consistently attempted to interpret nature in quantitative, material, and until recently, mechanistic terms. Postcartesian science conceives culture as subjective, free, and ideal, and nature as material, determinate, and value-neutral, and this is what makes the two incompatible. What Cahoone is, in effect, proposing is a return to an Aristotelian concept of reality: the doctrine that all material entities contain a principle of movement or change, and that their internal being is determined by an innate teleology. He himself realizes that Aristotle's doctrine of substantial forms and his teleological conception of nature are untenable today. Modern Western thought was founded on the autonomy of the thinking, doubting individual and on the aesthetic reaction that expressed his uniqueness. The achievements of modernity in science, medicine and technology, democracy and economic well-being are a consequence of this dichotomy into subject and object. Modern humanism is the belief that the ultimate arbiter of truth, and the ultimate source of value and political authority is the human individual. Such humanism, of course, cannot be proven, for it is itself a choice, a philosophical conviction whose legitimacy can only be established by its achievements and failures. It is generally agreed that the achievements of humanism have been substantial, and that it would be virtually impossible to conceive of modern science, Western standards of living, the diversity of modern intellectual and artistic culture, democracy, and civil liberation without the persuasiveness of humanism in contemporary Western culture. Like humanism, democracy is a process that is inherently self-threatening, and there is a widespread conviction that the public realm is impersonal, uncontrollable, and dangerous, and that one is free only in privacy. A similar conviction prevailed during the late stages of the Roman empire, and this conviction has generally been identified with a culture's decline. Since one of the definitions of modernity is the self-conscious break with the past, it is a largely antihistorical movement. There is indeed an implicit tension between modernity and traditional culture quite apart from any reference to humanism.

Notes

[1] Lawrence E. Cahoone, *The Delimma of Modernity, Philosophy, Culture and Anti-Culture*, New York, NY: State University of New York Press, 1988, p. xiv.

[2] *Ibid.*, p. 1.

[3] Theodor Adorno and Max Horkheimer, *Dialectic of Enlightenment*, trans. John Cumming, New York, NY: Seabury, 1972.

[4] Cahoone, *The Delimma of Modernity*, p. 5.

[5] *Ibid., p. 6.*

[6] *Ibid., p. 23.*

[7] *Ibid.*, p. 68.

[8] *Ibid.*, p. 72.

[9] *Ibid.*, p. 75.

[10] *Ibid.*, p. 111.

[11] *Ibid.,* p. 133.

[12] *Ibid.,* p. 178.

[13] 1930, trans. James Strachey, New York, Ny: Norton, 1961.

[14] Cahoone, *The Delimma of Modernity,* p. 186.

[15] Christopher Lasch, *The Culture of Narcissism,* New York, NY: Norton, 1979.

[16] Cahoone, *The Delimma of Modernity,* p. 187.

[17] Princeton University Press, 1979.

[18] Cahoone, *The Delima of Modernity, p. 223.*

[19] *Ibid.,* p. 226.

[20] *Ibid.,* p. 228.

[21] *Ibid.,* p. 231.

[22] *Ibid.,* p. 236.

[23] David Hume, *Treastise of Human Nature,* Oxford: Claredon, 1955, p. 251ff.

[24] Cahoone, *The Delimma of Modernity,* p. 306 n10.

[25] Karl Popper, John Eccles, *The Self and Its Brain,* New York, NY: Springer International, 1977, p. 38.

[26] Cahoone, *The Delimma of Modernity,* p. 248.

[27] *Ibid.*

[28] *Ibid.,* p. 250.

[29] *Ibid.,* p. 254.

[30] *Ibid.,* p. 255.

[31] *Ibid.,* p. 258.

Chapter Twenty-Five

Postmodernist Dimensions

The lines of demarcation between modernism and postmodernism are not well-defined. To be modern is to break with tradition and to search for new self-conscious, expressive forms, whereas the postmodern artist has no such privileged status.[1] It was Nietzsche who used the idea of self-overcoming to describe developments and transformations in Western thought, and we find that this process of self-overcoming also characterizes the development of his own thinking. While he had impulses for underlying truth, his thinking does not primarily present itself within the metaphysical formulations of truth and goodness. Self-overcoming and the manner in which Nietzsche's discourse puts itself in question have exerted significant influence both consciously and unconsciously on twentieth century style and thought. It prevents us from thinking with Nietzsche and through him, and at the same time from making his work either a model or a true and sufficient evaluation of Western culture. When self-overcoming controls the discourse, there is no transcendence of the discourse to explain it and to justify its own processes. Nietzsche is a countermetaphysics metaphysician; for him falseness of judgment is becoming less of a concern, and the issue is whether a group of evaluations is life promoting and life preserving.[2] This thinking does not have an overriding interest in certainty, literal truth, or speculative coherence; and permanence, in contrast to change, is taken to be more a function of grammar than of reality. The self-overcoming that occurs in this discourse sets in motion ways of speaking and thinking that bring about alertness to their own logical and moral way of being.

Kuspit thus concludes that the contradictory character of post-modernism is unresolvable, and that this reflects the inflated and contradictory character of our society and culture. The existence of seemingly unresolvable contradictions undermines our critical capacity, and to counteract such frustration, the meaning of the term "post-modernism" is kept open, even if it is thereby reduced to preserving only marginal significance. Indeed, it implies the collapse of an established critical sense; postmodernism is an artistic phenomenon of sorts, for it gets harder to distinguish the things aesthetic from their cognitive aspects, and its very analysis becomes a form of narrative. Nevertheless, the theory of postmodernism is the latest attempt to reinforce the credibility of critical thinking, even when it turns out to be without teeth, so to speak.[3] While postmodernism implies the contradiction of the modern, it lacks any transcendence of it, for while it is usually critical of the past, the past also represents lost integrity – the "home" the subject no longer inhabits but still yearns for. Postmodern historians of art make the past contemporary by using it to satisfy living needs symbolically, and in this sense postmodernism represents an extended range of the possibilities of the past. The contention that there is nothing outside of language is unacceptable largely because it is ourselves who are outside of language to begin with. Having reduced language and history to our own uses, we are as unaware of our own place among their shifting signifiers. In such context everything becomes surface, and objectivity and authority are lost, and without them even grammar falls apart. Such a culture collapses contrasts, combines sentimentalism with indifference, exploitation, and emancipation, recalling suffering only through the rosy glasses of nostalgia. Men are no longer sure of their knowledge, and are unable to legitimize the master narrative of truth and justice.

It was no accident that Kant chose the figure or schema of architectonics, sure of its apparent connection with the geometric method. But Kant was also the first to realize the failure of this attempt to reconcile the principles of mechanics with the spontaneity and freedom that characterize both the basis of responsibility in the human sphere, and in human creativity, the free play of imagination in the arts. What the division in Kant's text foretells is precisely the failure of modernism. He realizes that one cannot simply choose either one or the other; hence the failure of modernism, it could be said, is a matter of not seeing the difference between things intellectual and things sensible, imaginary, and aesthetic. It led to the delusion that the formal might itself dictate a style, that style could become objective, instead of the symbolic, indirect presentation, or figurative expression of the conceptual. What the modern lacked was the recognition of the problem of interpretation – the recognition that there is a kind of abyss between the formal and the figurative that demands a certain translation. The search for a single algorithm for decision has to be foregone; it becomes a question concerning the right thing to do at the right time in the right way. It is a situation where nothing can be decided by proofs,[4] but it is all the same a problem of art, as Kant defines it. Beyond the canons of science, the problem of interpretation remains, and summons the figural as an extension of the rational. Kant and Hegel open up a space for other logics and other grammars, even though for most viewers, the object of attention is always people. Thus an art without sentimental attachment leaves them without a clue to what it is about. The work of art is no longer a sign, a means to think about some other reality and to make it present; rather it is itself made the object and aim of thought.[5] It is a displacement that disrupts our ordinary ties with the world, so that knowing is transformed into a study of openness.[6] Derrida explains that the painting serves such a reference, and in this way the work of art is open to anyone's interpretive understanding. However, no one understanding can ever claim possession of it; there is no idiomatic reality to painting since detachment always leaves the work open to the unconscious of the other.[7] Wendy Steiner notes that prose stresses the already established signifying system whereas painting focuses on the work of art as a thing. Structuralism has made language the model of understanding all cultural phenomena.[8]

Magritte "names" his paintings in a manner that brings into question the act of naming, undermining the obvious relation between the title and the work, the name and the thing. This represents the subject-predicate relation projected by language onto things, and leads us to question presence and time as they have imposed themselves upon the work of art. One can no longer affirm that "this" painting, word, or image is not a pipe because similitude, insofar as it is neither subject-predicate nor ontological, renders identify and its difference meaningless. The simulacrum, always reversible, ranges across the surface, eliminating the original and forcing a reorientation of thought. What must be made clear is the hold that language has over what it describes – the pictorial image – over the vast realm of the unthought. In the postmodern world, it seems that history no longer provides identity or autonomy, but is another commodity served up in tel-evision reruns, nostalgia, and endless repetition.[9] Signs no longer refer to either a subjective or an objective realty, but to themselves, because there is no "reality" left to represent. Reality is constructed by the codes of society, by the already written, by the received languages and conventions that assume the subject's place.[10] On video and television everything is infinitely repeatable, and Gilles Deleuze suggests that we consider a metaphysics that is not a metaphysics of substance but a metaphysics of the event. An event is without substance, and this is why we must be alert to the surface of the domain of intelligible (non-spatial and nontemporal) objects. The photograph repeats mechan-ically what could never actually be reproduced.

Some modernist writing lets go of the foundations of discourse; *Finnegan's Wake,* for example, turns us against interpretation and onto the path of surrealist analysis, where the end of reading is no lon-ger to determine the meaning of anything but rather to lay open to view the deep structure of production that makes meaning possible. The question posed is not "what does it mean?" but "how does it work?" *Finnegan's Wake* works like a dream and requires something like a Freudian model of analysis. The text is not something that we "read through" but, like a dream, is something to be reconstructed on another level. Husserlian language seeks total intelligibility, whereas Joycean language turns itself loose in this manner. So there is no pre-Babel relationship between word and thing; there is no deep structure as in Husserl or in the analytic tradition, merely a textual mosaic lacking any overall logical form. Analysis is not taking us deeper into an inner world of preconscious grammar; on the contrary, the deeper we go, the more open things get.[11] For Heidegger, likewise, poetry and thinking are not containable within unitary language; the point is that words are not something under control. Language speaks but not in the strucutralist sense that, whatever the surface variability of our speech, meaning remains the product of deep structure (grammar and ideology). For Heidegger, our linguistic competence consists less in the neological ability to produce intelligible sentences than in the ear's ability to pick up all the punning that is always going on in language. Language speaks, but not in the structuralist sense that we are con-strained by its rules and can say only what it allows us to say.

Contrary to the philosophical tradition, in Heidegger the infeli-cities of words are not repressed; on the contrary, they are what poetry and thinking must remain open to. This is why Heidegger's way with words is more Joyce-like than Husserlian. The upshot of Heidegger's listening is that it has more to do with receptivity or openness than with meaning. To think is, above all, to listen, to let the Saying happen to us, and not to ask questions.[12] This seems roughly the idea of Heidegger's *Gelassenheit,* letting be or letting go; renunciation, Heidegger says, means giving up language as logos, i.e. as the power of framing representations. It means giving up signs as names that "rule over things."[13] Renunciation is the way with words of the poet who must relinquish the claim to the assurance that he will on demand be supplied with a name for what he as posited as what truly is. Poetry does not connect up with things in a way of worldmaking but simply lets them be, treating them like a work of art in their otherness or strangeness. Heideggerian things are more events than objects; his "listening" is not a form of exegesis, or a listing of meaning. In a similar vein, Artaud attacks the theater in which the author functions like an absent God, controlling the process from a distance, providing the illusion of a closure with meaning for both the author and the audience.[14] In place of plot and developed action, we have stasis lacking both meaning and possibility in which the audience is confronted with the defeat of all its traditional expectations of meaning. The theater of representation is thus an illusion, and in the language of deconstruction, truth is undecidable, for there is nothing to refer to, only more language.

For Benjamin, the photographic image (or simulacrum) entails the dissolution of the aesthetic aura and inaugurates the political use of the image. As such, catharsis can no longer be understood according to a personalist psychological model but must be grasped in accordance with a political, revolutionary paradigm. Discussing the relation between mechanical reproduction and mass movements, he points out that their most powerful agent is the film. Benjamin regards the final transformation of catharsis as an apocalyptic political upheaval, and this new reign of photographic and cinematic simulacra entails a radical epistemological break. Metaphysics is not overcome by deconstruction, rather it is presented as a particular discursive possibility in which rationality, dialectics, and "master-narrative" are rejected.[15] Writing about the differences between modernism and postmodernism, Craig Owens explains:

> Postmodernism neither brackets nor suspends the referent but tends instead to problematize the activity of reference. When the

postmodernist work speaks of itself, it is no longer to proclaim its
authority, self-sufficiency, or transcendence; rather it is to narrate
its own contingency, insufficiency and lack of transcendence.[16]

Perhaps the most profound implication entailed by the postmodern
condition is that it is no longer possible to determine unequivocally
whether any given enunciation of image is a statement or a metastatement, while no enunciation (especially the metaphysical one) may be
deemed devoid of narrative content. Significance is subject to a radical
questioning in which both authorship and spectatorship become rhetorical (grammatical) constructs; every signified is nothing but another
signifier, literacy another trope, depth a play of surfaces and the
person a role of acting.

David Levin traces modernist aesthetics back to its origin in the
Kantian revolution, and shows that in modernist art the defining conditions of the work finally become the sole subject of presentation. Because of their essentially constitutive function, however, these conditions cannot be made present as the subject of traditional techniques of
representation; they can only be made present indirectly and obliquely.
They become manifest in the play of their deconstruction. Modernist
works of art defy the structural law of identity; they are what they are
not, and they are not what they are. They are implicitly subversive, not
innovative or original in the traditional sense. In modernist art, the
"substance" of the work, which used to be called "content," has become an implicitly upsetting process of self-reflection and self-
disclosure. Jacques Derrida, Richard Rorty, Michael Foucault, and
Paul Feyerabend are presumably postmodern writers and their postmodernist philosophy is a family of deconstructive strategies, questions,
and suspicion instigating playful procedures that challenge our prevailing logocentrism because it suppresses feeling and imagination.
These postmodern philosophies question the traditional binary opposites insofar as they constitute fixed, independent, reciprocally exclusive positions. Instead, postmodern thinning embraces relativities,
conflicts, and complications in interpretation, ruptures and discontinuities, the proliferation of differences, multiplicites, ambiguities, and
complexities. It acknowledges contingencies and accidents, accepts the
unfinished, the open, the fragmentary; it appreciates spontaneity, and
gives ready attention to the local, the regional, the specific, and the
unique, and it recognizes the existence of microprocesses.[17] Thus
while modernist aesthetics continued essentialism, the postmodern

approach rejected it. Contrary to modernism, it proclaims itself open to meaning, but in it the various media are mixed together: idioms of the vernacular, and elements taken from mass culture. There is no longer any privileged standpoint either expressing or interpreting the work.

Of all the commodities, the fashion object appears to be the most superfluous, transitory, and trivial – infinitely distanced from its historical origins in the magic and mystique of ceremonial costume or bodily adornment. Faurschou argues, however, that it is not despite, but precisely because, fashion has this ephemeral volatile existence that it becomes the exemplary site for exploring the deviant tendencies and contradictions of our late, capitalist, consumer, or postmodern society. Fashion discloses a pervasive and enveloping logic, since production is compelled to drive production to ever new extremes of insatiability. Fashion becomes the propelling momentum, the dominant role of consumption itself, and understood this way, it can be seen to exceed all other cultural logics. Commodities are now marketed first and foremost as "symbolic goods," and only secondarily as utilitarian objects.[18] Advertising has become a multibillion dollar industry denying the instrumentality of all social relations. While the markets of late capitalism present immense selections of differentiated commodities that appear to compete on the basis of ever more minute distinctions, in fact, the more effective strategy to increase consumption (an imperative to the survival of late capitalism) is to create even more elaborate and expensive categories of signs that can be consumed systematically and, just as systematically, rendered obsolete at an increasingly accelerated pace. The greater the integration of consumer universes, and the more quickly they are rendered obsolete, the more fashion asserts itself as the totaling logic of commodity consumption in late capitalism.[19] Baudrillard's main polemic is the oversimplified critique of consumption as manipulation, as the creation of false needs that prevent the satisfaction of "natural" or truly human desires. Such a critique fails to consider that the power and selection of consumption lies in the degree to which it establishes itself as the only form of collective activity in which the atomized individual of bourgeois society can participate. But to the extent that the system of objects is gaining coherence, its imposing strategy is also growing more complex and, as a consequence, such integration never becomes permanent or substantive.

Fashion is one of the more inexplicable phenomena; its compulsion to innovative signs is apparently arbitrary. It is now an overriding stylistic code in which the novel is a quality independent of the use of the commodity. In it the representation of the ever "new" erases the record of growth, maturation, and decay that history inscribes on material objects and bodies. Fashion collapses the coordinates of space and time into a variety of marketable environments. No longer occupied with the latest styles in clothing and hair, fashion magazines provide us with up-to-date recommendations on what, where, and with whom it is fashionable to be eating, working, living, traveling, etc. This produces the effect of flatness or depthlessness, a new kind of superficiality in the most literal sense, which Frederick Jameson has described as "perhaps the most supreme formal feature of postmodernism."[20] Even the theorist's critical capacity becomes paralyzed, since the late capitalist market has developed strategies that allow it to remain as rigorous as ever in spite of the internal contradictions on which it operates, and to resist outside challenges.

One of the patterns distinguishing the televised and the untelevised is the traditional metaphysical line between the true (reality) and the false (television), which refuses to recognize the productive power of TV. Another path, a distinctively postmodern one, is advanced by Baudrillard who proclaims the coming of a "hyperreality" constituted by the collapse of all real distinctions.[21] Seitz argues that the truth must be different from either of these polar positions, something in between. He emphasizes the inseparability of the televised and the untelevised, and claims that, if TV is a system of communication at all, it is one that radically transforms what communication is. While the power of television has been likened to the power of speech or immediate presence (as opposed to writing), it should also be seen that television is not speech – it is audio-visual, which is not the same as oral – and that the power of televised speech is an effect or dimension of the power of this complex electronic system of "writing" or markmaking. Television not only repeats, but also generates, powerful mythologies of our times; it does not only express, but creates, stories ("realities").[22] Even a quite average person can sound smart reading a prepared speech on television, and a persuasive actor can shape public opinion in this manner. Thus, television is a new decisive element the likes of which has never existed until just now.[23] It becomes a medium by means of which political and economic power are exercised. The real untelevised is restricted to the few who know the whole story since television is used effectively to deceive and manipulate the public in a variety of ways. At the same time, television is a medium, a form of adhesive, a binding agent that holds our culture together; it is a basic dimension of what and who we are. In the process, politics has become more of a show, but this does not mean that the world outside television turns into a separate entity or is sealed off from it.

Those who present TV as a network of nothing more than appearances reduce it to the level of mere image, a deviation from Reality that is considered fundamental. The danger here is a reliance on a conception of reality as ultimately self-evident, and a refusal to recognize television's productive capacities. It lies in misunderstanding the powerful way in which the televised informs and contributes to what the untelevised is. TV makes reality; it does not only reflect it. The traditional metaphysical viewing of television will necessarily miss the power of this point and will thus miss the power of television, reducing it to laziness, ignorance, and stupidity on the part of the viewers.[24] But an equally hazardous reading is Baudrillard's nihilism because here all distinctions vanish, and television "is" reality. The police have not disappeared, they have simply developed more sophisticated techniques of regulation and control, which produce less need for coercion. Not that coercion has disappeared either,[25] and we may reasonably doubt that Baudrillard's views are very popular with the victims of police power. If "power is dead,"[26] it is at least less dead than the academic theory that announces its demise, for it deals with real people, not just actors on a stage. While not altogether separate, the televised and the untelevised are different from each other, and certainly not interchangeable. By privileging reality, traditional metaphysics underestimates the productive capacities of television and misses its power as the generating and binding agent, and by privileging TV, Baudrillard loses the world that has not just turned into a simulacrum. Television is not merely a communications technology that presents itself as a choice, as just one more human activity. It contributes to the formation of the untelevised, and we are the first generation to live with its indefinite but disturbing co-presence. The relationship between the televised and the untelevised is not simple polarized metaphysical differences between appearances and Reality, rather the difference between the televised and the untelevised remains unresolved.

Wurzer and Silverman expose filming as a nonlogocentric, postmodern interplay between thinking and imagining.[27] In modern metaphysics we encounter the beginning of this kind of thinking in Kant's *Critique of Judgment*, in Nietzsche's *Birth of Tragedy,* and more recently, in Heidegger's philosophy. Traditional philosophy from Plato to Spinoza has consistently suppressed the notion of image and reduced its limited significance to a logocentric view of reason. In Heidegger's discourse, on the other hand, philosophy is a thinking that can be either metaphysics or science, and according to Wurzer and Silverman, filming is just such a thinking. Filming may be conceived as the postmodern displacement of metaphysics, suggesting an "imagistic" mode of thinking that is not prerational or irrational. It is rather a kind of reflection *(Besinnug)* that has the courage to question the truth of its own presuppositions as well as recognize the diverse direction of interests.[28] According to Kant, the aesthetic idea occasions the imaginative spreading over a host of related representations,[29] and is not restrained by the usual spatial and temporal intuitions. Indeed in a vaguely postmodern sense, Kant describes the aesthetic idea as that representation of the imagination which reduces such a wealth of thought that would never admit comprehension in a definite concept.[30] Kant's attempts to formulate a "discontinuous" relation between thinking and the imagination in the sublime lacks definite form, transcends the boundaries of imagination, and emerges as the self *(Gemüt)* participating in imagination's play of presence and absence. Neither presence nor absence can ever be fully attained conceptually, or – and this may be the demise of Kant's *Critique of Judgment* – by means of taste or reflection. The categories of the transcendental analytic become fluid in filming, and thus are made free for imagination's transition to the aesthetic zone of reason's play. The realm of invention is then no longer conceived in terms of a logocentric operation of objects of knowledge, but rather in terms of a postontological, genealogical, and epistemologically more disruptive terrain of difference.

When Heidegger separates the world from the metaphysical concept of idea towards a play of images, he makes it possible for us to introduce filming as a reflection of the power of imagination.[31] Filming in Heidegger's sense of *Besinnung* distinguishes images of being form the hermeneutic power of establishing a new presence. This interaction may be conceived as subjective and objective representation of images wherein neither subject nor object are readily discernible. Discussing the postmodern aspect of his work, Heidegger remarks that what withdraws may concern and claim man more essentially than anything present that strikes and touches him.[32] "True sublimity," Kant writes, "must be sought only in the mind of the subject, not in the natural object."[33] Filming is a paradox; thus in the postmodern era, the relation of thinking and filming may be considered as a gathering of images that is not wedded to a representational experience *(Erlebnis)* of imagination's identity. In filming, an activity occurs that designates the space in which alternative readings multiply and coexist, for filming is that ontological activity and space which has no identity of its own. It is neither transcendental nor empirical, neither subjective nor objective, neither a reality nor an appearance, neither a thought nor a thing. For Heidegger, the tendency to separate the self as subject and the world as object has come to an end in the modern age, and this "world-picture" is neither of the world nor of the subject. Filming does not render determinate what is multiple and indeterminate; it is not a specification of what is broad, disparate, and nonspecific. The filming language has no place in the world except as a commodity, as expression of viewpoints, and as a representation of reality. The only frame that filming produces is the frame of the modern age, and the indeterminacy of what is post-modern is due to the fact that it has no style. The perplexity about postmodernism is that, like filming, it has no definite shape, no determinate form or context. Filming as such offers no content, style, or form of its own; what it offers is a content-style, or a form of modernism and, thereby, modernism within its own frame.

Notes

[1] Hugh J. Silverman, "The Philosophjy of Postmodernism," in *Postmodernism – Philosphy and the Arts,* ed. H. J. Silverman, Routledge, NY and London: 1990, p. 3.

[2] F. Nietzsche, *Beyond Good and Evil,* trans. Walter Kaufmann, New York, NY: Random House, 1966, vol. I, p. 4.

[3] Donald Kuspit, "The Contradictory Character of Postmoderism," in *Postmodernism – Philosphy and the Arts,* p. 57.

[4] Immnanuel Kant, *The Critique of Judgement,* trans. J. H. Bernard, New York, NY: Hafner, 1968, p. 183.

[5] Ortega Y Gasset, *The Dehumanization of Art and Other Essays in Art, Culture, Literature,* trans. Helene Weyl, Princeton, NJ: Princeton University Press, 1968, pp. 18-19.

[6] Martin Heidegger, "The Origin of the Work of Art," in *Poetry, Language, Thought,* trans. Albert Hofstadter, New York, NY: Harper & Row, 1971, p. 67.

[7] Jacques Derrida, *La vérité en peinture,* Paris: Flammarion, 1978, p. 435.

[8] Wendy Steiner, *The Colors of Rhetoric,* Chicago, IL: University of Chicago Press, 1982, p. 123.

[9] Thomas Lawson, "Generation in Vitro," *Artforum,* September 1984, p. 99.

[10] Kate Linker, "From Imitation to Copy to Just Effect: On Reading Jean Baudrillard," *ArtForum,I 1984,* p. 46.

[11] Gerald L. Bruns, "The Otherness of Words: Joynce, Bakhtin, Heidegger," in *Postmodernism – Philosphy and the Arts,* p. 76.

[12] M. Heidegger, *On the Way to Language,* trans. P.D. Hertz, New York, NY: Harper & Row, 1971, p. 76.

[13] *Ibid.,* p. 144.

[14] Antonin Artaud, *The Theater and its Double,* trans. M.C. Richards, New York, NY: Grove Press, 1958, p. 75.

[15] Allen S. Weiss, "Lucid Intervals: Postmodernism and Photography," in *Postmodernism – Philosphy and the Arts,* p. 160.

[16] Craig Owens, "The Allegorical Impulse: Towards a Thoery of Postmodernism," (part 2) *October* 13, (Sumnmer 1980), p. 80.

[17] David Michael Levin, "Postmodernism in Dance; Dance, Discourse, Democracy," in *Postmodernism – Philosphy and the Arts,* p. 224.

[18] Gail Faurschou, "Obsolescence and Desire: Fashion and the Commodity Form," in *Postmodernism – Philosphy and the Arts,* p. 238.

[19] *Ibid.,* p. 241.

[20] Frederic Jameson, "Postmodernism and the Cultural Logic of Late Capitalism," *New Left Reveiw,* Fall 1985, p. 60.

[21] Brian Seitz, "The Televised and the Untelevised: Keeping an Eye On/Off the Tube," in *Postmodernism – Philosphy and the Arts,* p. 187.

[22] *Ibid.,* p. 191.

[23] *Ibid.,* p. 192.

[24] *Ibid.,* p. 202.

[25] *Ibid.,* p. 292 n33.

[26] Jean Baudrillard and Sylvère Lotringer, "Forget Baudrillard," trans. Phil Beitchman, Lee Hildreth and Mark Polizzotti, in Jean Baudrillard, *Forget Foucault,* New York, NY: Semiotext(e), 1987, p. 173.

[27] Wilhelm S. Wurzer and Hugh J. Silverman, "Filming: Inscriptions of *Denken,"* in *Postmodernism – Philosophy and the Arts,* p. 173.

[28] Martin Heidegger, "The Age of the World Picture," in *The Question Concerning Technolgoy,* trans. William Lovitt, New York, NY: Harper & Row, 1977, p. 183.

[29] Immanuel Kant, *Kritik der Urteilskraft,* Stuttgart: Philip Reclam, 1976, p. 146.

[30] *Ibid.,* p. 147.

[31] Heidegger, "Age of the World Picture," p. 140.

[32] M. Heidegger, "What Calls for Thinking?" in *Basic Writings,* trans. D.F. Krell, New York, NY: Harper & Row, 1977, p. 350.

[33] Kant, *Kritik der Urteilskraft,* p. 135.

Chapter Twenty-Six

Postmodern Aesthetics

The project of modernity was formulated in the 18th century by the philosophers of the enlightenment in their efforts to develop objective science, universal morality, and autonomous art. But the 20th century shattered this optimism; there is now a prevalent view that the project of modernity is deeply problematic.[1] The fiction of the creative subject gives way to a frank confiscation, quotation, excerption, accumulation, and repetition of already existing images. Lately we have come to regard this condition as postmodern – decentered, allegorical, schizophrenic. However we choose to diagnose its symptoms, postmodernism is usually treated by its protagonists and antagonists alike as a crisis in the cultural authority vested in Western European institutions. Suddenly it becomes possible that we are just others, that we ourselves are an "other" among others.[2] What is at stake in this kind of pluralism is our sense of identity as a culture. In the modern period, the claim of work of art to represent some vision of the world was based on the universality of modern aesthetics, on something like Kant's dream that the judgment of taste is universal. Not only does the postmodern at work claim no such authority, it actually seeks to undermine all such claims, and hence its deconstructive thrust. Postmodern thought is no longer binary, and what we must learn to conceive is difference without opposition.[3] For Jameson, the loss of narrative is equivalent to the loss of our ability to locate ourselves historically, hence his diagnosis of postmodernism as "schizophrenia", i.e. meaning that is characterized by its collapsed sense of temporality. The great recitals of modernity are all parables of mastery over nature;

nonillusionistic objects presented a new and original source of interplay between artistic expressions and the experience of the everyday world. "Collage" is the transfer of materials from one context to another, and "montage" is the dissemination of these borrowings through the new settings. Photography is a collage machine (perfected in television) producing simulacra of the life-world. Photography selects and transforms a fragment of the visual continuum into a new frame. The photographic image signifies itself and something else, for in it the real is viewed as an element of discourse (as pointed out by Sergei Eisenstein), montage does not reproduce the real but intervenes in the world – not to reflect but to change reality.[9]

Barthes concludes that the categories of literature and criticism can no longer be kept apart, that now there are only writers. Authors and critics both face the same material; the critic's text is an analogy with a distorted perspective, which in post-criticism is given expression by means of collage or montage.[10] Derrida has consequently pointed out that what critical vangardism cannot bear is for anyone to tamper with language. Even vangard criticism can accept more readily the most apparently revolutionary positions if only they do not affect language and all the juridical an political assumptions they imply.[11] It is not a question of "rejecting" these notions, Derrida writes; they are necessary. And, at least at present, nothing is conceivable for us without them. Since these concepts are indispensable for unsettling the heritage to which they belong, we should be even less prone to renounce them.[12] Derrida's alternative to "mimetologism", then, does not abandon or deny reference, but rethinks reference in another way. As Aristotle provides a theory of tragedy (*mimesis*) and a method (formal analysis) for the study of all literary modes, Derrida in a text such as *Glas* (identified as the "exemplary" text of post-structuralism) offers a theory of montage (grammatology) and a method (deconstruction) for working with any mode of writing.[13] Whether in spoken or in written discourse, no element can function as a sign without referring to another element that itself is not simply present. Indeed nothing, either among the elements or within the system, is anywhere ever simple present or absent. Everywhere there are differences and traces of traces.[14] Collage's heterogeneity produces a signification that can be neither univocal nor stable; each cited element breaks the continuity or the hierarchy of discourse, and leads necessarily to a double reading: that of the fragment as incorporated into a new whole, a different totality.

Thus, the art of collage proves to be one of the most effective strategies of representation.[15]

Such an undecidable reading effect, oscillating between presence and absence, is just what Derrida tries to achieve in his publishing of two books under one cover.[16] The tendency of Western philosophy throughout its history has been to attempt to pin down and fix a specific signified to a given signifier (logocentrism), but this violates, according to grammatology, the nature of language, which functions, not in terms of matched pairs (signifier/signified) but of couplers and couplings. Every sign, linguistic or nonlinguistic, spoken or written, in a small or large unit, can be cited, put between quotation marks, and in so doing can break with every given context, engendering an infinity of new contexts in a manner that is altogether illimitable.[17] In criticism as in literature, collage takes the form of citation, grammatology being the theory of writing as citation.[18] Derrida's discussion of montage writing as "grafting" in *Dissemination* is itself couched in the collage style (it does what it says). Collage writing is a kind of theft which violates "property" in every sense – intellectual property protected by copyright as well as the properties of a given concept. Writing, in short, is a simulacrum of "true sense", but true sense from Plato to positivism, is what post-criticism puts into question. There is no simple reference, and it becomes apparent that representation without reference is the description of the way film or tape functions as a "language". The temporal oscillation generated in this play between presence and absence is what Derrida terms *difference*. Contrary to Heidegger, who claimed that art "speaks", Derrida insists on its capacity to work without concepts and without conclusions. Deconstruction proves without showing, without entailing anything, without an available thesis; it transforms itself in this process rather than advancing a signifiable object of discourse. It constitutes a hybrid of literature and criticism, art and science, demonstrating that knowledge of an object of study may be obtained without conceptualization or explanation. Post-criticism functions with an epistemology of performance – knowing as making, producing, doing, acting – similar to Wittgenstein's account of knowing as the mastery of a technique.

Whereas modernist theory presupposes that the art object can be substituted metaphorically for its referent, postmodernism neither brackets nor suspends the referent but instead works to problematize the activity of reference.[19] Describing one theory under the image of another, traditional criticism "suspends" the surface of the text, applying a terminology of levels and of hidden meanings. Post-critics, by contrast, write with the discourse of others (the already written) as proposed by Walter Benjamin, who was the principal precursor of such post-critical use of collage-allegory. Montage became for him the active form of allegory, the ability to connect dissimilars in such a way as to "shock" people into new recognitions and understandings.[20] Revealing the conventional academic book as an outdated mediation between two different filing systems,[21] Benjamin wanted to write a book made up entirely of quotations in order to purge all subjectivity and allow the self to be the vehicle for the expression of "objective" cultural tendencies.[22] The "truth" that Benjamin had discovered was that allegory is not an arbitrary representation of the idea that it portrays; it is instead the concrete expression of this idea's material foundation.[23] Benjamin's procedure was to collect and reproduce in quotation the contradictions of the present without resolution. The collage strategy was itself the image of the breakup, the disintegration of civilization in the modern world and, once articulated, the material could be rearranged in order to render intelligible its "truth". The thinker reflects on the sensuous, nonidentical reality, not in order to eliminate it, nor to butcher it to fit the Procrustean bed of mental categories, or to liquidate its particularity by making it disappear under abstract concepts. Instead, the thinker, like the artist, proceeds mimetically and, in the process of imitating matter, transforms it so it can be read as a nonanalogical expression of social truth. In philosophy no less than in artwork, form is not indifferent to context. But it is important to realize that this object-become-thing in montage/allegory functions in terms of a representation that is neither allegorical nor symbolic in the traditional sense. The interest is in the concrete particular, with what since Plato has been dismissed as transitory and insignificant, and which Hegel called "foul existence".[24]

J. Hillis Miller points out that a deconstructive reading of a given work is not simply parasitical on the obvious univocal reading:[25] the selection of texts is not itself random, but a major part of the critical statement. For Derrida, deconstruction is a process of decomposition at work within the very root metaphors – the philosophemes – of Western thought. In other words, what those who attack post-modernism as parasitical have not realized is that montage-allegory provides the very technique of popularization, for communicating the knowledge of the cultural disciplines to a general public. Postmodernism, however, is not widely accepted or even understood nowadays. Most post-modernisms constitute specific reactions against established forms of modernism that have become prevalent in universities, museums, art-galleries, and foundations. There is an effacement and erosion in postmodernism of the older distinction between high culture and so-called mass or popular culture. The immense fragmentation and privatization of modern literature – its disintegration into a host of distinct styles and mannerisms – foreshadows deeper and more general tendencies in social life. Each group comes to speak its private language, each profession develops its private code or idiom and, finally each individual becomes a linguistic island, separated from anyone else. But in that case, the very possibility of linguistic norms in terms of which one could articulate such languages and styles vanishes, and we would have nothing but stylistic diversity and heterogeneity.[26] It thus becomes apparent that this kind of extreme individualism is largely ideological, creating an aesthetic dilemma for contemporary artists and writers. That is one reason why postmodern art is increasingly about art itself, for there has been a tendency in postmodernism to argue that reference is a myth, and that one can no longer talk about the "real" as external or objectively given. The tendency in structuralism has been to dispel the old conception of language as naming, which involves a one-to-one correspondence between signifier and signified. We do not translate the individual signifier or words that make up a sentence back into their signifieds; rather, we read the whole sentence, and it is from the relationship of its words or signifieds that a more global meaning is derived. For Lacan, the experience of temporality is also an effect of language. The schizophrenic has a far more intense experience of any given present of the world than we do because our own present is always part of some larger set of projects that force us selectively to focus our perceptions. We do not globally receive the outside world as an undifferentiated vision, but are always engaged in using it, in attending to this or that object or person within it. The signifier in isolation becomes ever more material or literal, ever more vivid in sensory ways, whether the new experience is attractive or terrifying. In normal speech we try to see through the materiality of words, (their strange sounds and printed appearance, voice timbre, peculiar accent, and the like) towards their meaning. But as meaning is lost, the materiality of the words becomes obsessive, as when children repeat a word over and over until its sense is lost and it becomes an incomprehensible incantation. A signifier that has lost its signified has thereby become transformed into an image.[27]

Modernism was originally oppositionist; it posed as a scandalous and offensive art attempting to shock the middle-class public by being ugly, dissonant, bohemian, and sexually offensive. It was an outrage to good taste and to common sense, a provocative challenge to the reigning reality and performance principles of early 20th-century, middle-class society. But not only are Joyce and Picasso no longer considered weird and repulsive; they have themselves become classics, and now look rather realistic to us. Indeed, there is little in either the form or the content of postmodern art that contemporary society finds intolerable or scandalous. The most offensive forms of this art are all taken in stride by society, and they are even commercially successful unlike the productions of early modernism. Commodity production – our clothing, furniture, buildings and other artifacts is intimately tied up with changes in style, and are due to artistic experimentation. Our advertising is fed by postmodernism in the arts and would be inconceivable without it. By the early 1960s, modernism had emerged as the dominant aesthetics and, consequently, it was felt to have become part of the academic tradition on the part of a whole new generation of poets, painters and musicians.[28] There is the prevalent awareness that at some point following World War II a new kind of society began to emerge variously described as postindustrial, multinational, capitalistic, consumer, media, and the like. New types of consumption, planned obsolescence, an ever more rapid rhythm of fashion and style changes, the penetration of advertising and television throughout society, universal standardization, a net of superhighways, and the arrival of automobile culture – these are some of the features that would seem to mark a radical break with that older prewar society in which modernism was still an underground movement.[29] Jameson emphasizes that the emergence of postmodernism is closely related to this moment of late, consumer, or multinational capitalism, and the disappearance of a sense of history due to a perpetual change that obliterates traditions.

Baudrillard points out that the television image is the ultimate and perfect object for this new era for it reflects a regulated system, control, and global management of the ensemble. What used to be taken as metaphor as mental or metaphorical sense, is henceforth projected into a reality that is also that of simulation.[30] Advertising invades everything, and there is an omnipresent visibility of enterprises, brands, and social interlocutors, whereas the traditional public spaces of the street and market-place disappear. Not surprisingly, this loss of public space brings about a loss of private space as well, since the one is no longer a spectacle and the other no longer a secret. Unlike the object that never completely gives up its secret, the commodity remains always accessible and readable. The promiscuous communication networks may fascinate us, but such attraction remains superficial as real passion disappears. Baudrillard argues that we now live in a new form of schizophrenia, at too great a proximity to everything. What characterizes the schizophrenic is not loss of the real, the pathos of distance and radical separation, as is commonly believed, but very much the opposite, the absolute proximity and impossibility of retreating from things, which induces a feeling of defenselessness. This results in a loss of interiority and intimacy. Said is also convinced that the cult of expertise and professionalism has so restricted our scope of vision that a positive doctrine of noninterference has set in. According to this doctrine, most crucial policy questions affecting human existence are best left to "experts" who supposedly know how things really work. Critics read each other and care about little else.[31] The trouble with such interpretation is that it tends to homogenize evidence since it aspires to be accepted at almost any cost. We suffer from an arbitrary notion of history as a canon of classics that was developed by professors of literature. By elevating the subject beyond his or her time and society, an exaggerated respect for single individuals is produced. An almost invariable rule is that very little of the circumstances making interpreting activity possible is allowed to be considered. If the study of literature is only about literary representation, then it must be the case that writing, reading, and producing humanities, the arts and letters are essentially ornamental. Literary studies are taken to be not about society but about masterpieces in need of periodic adulation and appreciation. The particular mission of the humanities is, in the aggregate, to represent noninterference in the affairs of the everyday world. There is the mystification of science through the promotion of formalized decision methodologies, the restoration of the authority of expertise, and the use of science as legitimization for social policy. Said concludes that we need to break out of the disciplinary ghettos in which, as intellectuals, we have been confined.

Notes

[1] Hal Foster, "Postmodernism: A Preference," in *The Anti-Aesthetic, Essays on Postmodern Culture,* ed. Hal Foster, Port Townsend, WA: Bay Press, 1983, p. ix.

[2] Paul Ricoeur, "Universal Civilization and National Cultures," (1961) in *History and Truth,* trans. Chas. A. Kelbley, Evanston: Northwestern University Press, 1965, p. 278.

[3] Craig Owens, "The Discourse of Others: Feminists and Postmodernists," in *The Anti-Aesthetic,* p. 62.

[4] M. Heidegger, *Die Zeit des Weltbildes* 1938, published 1953.

[5] Owens, "The Discourse of Others," p. 70.

[6] Gregory L. Ulmer, "The Object of Postcriticism," in *The Anti-Aesthetic,* p. 83.

[7] Richard Kostelanetz, ed., *Esthetics Contemporary,* Buffalo, NY: Prometheus, 1978.

[8] Edward Fry, *Cubism,* New York, NY: McGraw Hill, n.d., p. 27.

[9] Ulmer, "The Object of Postcriticism," p. 86.

[10] Roland Barthes, *Critique et verité,* Paris: Seuil, 1966, pp 68-9.

[11] Jacques Derrida, "Living On: Borderlines," in *Deconstruction and Criticism,* New York, NYU: Seabury, 1979, pp. 94-5.

[12] Jacques Derrida, *Of Grammatology,* trans. Gayatari Spivak, Baltimore, MD: John Hopkins University Press, 1976, pp. 14-15.

[13] Ulmer, "The Object of Postcriticism," p. 87

[14] Jacques Derrida, *Positions,* trans. A. Bass, Chicago, IL: University of Chicago Press, 1981, p. 26.

[15] Group *Mu* eds. *Collages,* Paris: Union Générale, 1978, pp. 34-5.

[16] Ulmer, "The Object of Postcriticsim," p. 88.

[17] Jacques Derrida, "Signature Event Context," in *Glyph* (1977), p. 185.

[18] cf *Collages,* p. 301.

[19] Craig Owens, "The Allegorical Impulse: Toward a Theory of Postmodernism," *October* 12 (1980), p. 84.

[20] Stanley Mitchell, "Introduction" to Walter Benjamin's *Understanding Brecht,* trans. Anna Bostock, London: New Left Books, 1977, p. xiii.

[21] Walter Benjamin, *One-Way Street and Other Writings,* trans. E. Jephcott and K. Sharper, London: New Left Books, 1977, p. 62.

[22] Ulmer, "The Object of Postcriticism," p. 97.

[23] Susan Buck Morss, *The Origin of Negative Dialectics,* London: Macmillan, 1977, p. 56.

[24] *Ibid.,* p. 69.

[25] J. Hillis Miller, "The Critic as Host," *Critical Inquiry* 3 (1977), p. 439.

[26] Frederic Jameson, "Postmodernism and Consumer Society," in *The Anti-Aesthetic,* p. 114.

[27] *Ibid.,* p. 120.

[28] *Ibid.,* p. 124.

[29] *Ibid.,* p. 125.

[30] Jean Baudrillard, "The Ecstasy of Communication," in *The Anti-Aesthetic,* p. 128.

[31] Edward W. Said, "Opponents, Audiences, Constituencies and Community," in *The Anti-Aesthetic,* p. 140.

Aesthetics

Chapter Twenty-Seven

Gadamer's Aesthetics

Gadamer is concerned with the sense we might speak of as the truth in a work of art. His point is that we gain access through the arts to an irresistible truth that the dogmatic application of scientific truth tends to overlook. His reader is left in no doubt that concentration on method can conceal much that art and history have to teach us.[1] Modern writers and artists may frequently have understood themselves as being in revolt against previous forms of art, but their real target was often no more than the aesthetic definition of art developed in the late eighteenth and nineteenth centuries. In Gadamer's account, modern art does not so much break with tradition but extends the awareness of our heritage as pointed out be Hegel. When Hegel spoke of art as a thing of the past, he meant that art was no longer understood as a presentation of the divine in the unproblematic way in which it had been understood in the Greek world. Hegel's real thesis was that while for the Greeks the divine was principally and properly revealed in their own aesthetic forms of expression, this kind of reverence became impossible with the arrival of Christianity. The truth of Christianity with its more profound insight into the transcendence of God could no longer be adequately expressed within the visual language of art or the imagery of poetic language. In the nineteenth century, every artist lived with the knowledge that he could no longer take for granted the former unproblematic communication between himself and those among whom he lived and for whom he created. A new challenge arose in the second half of the twentieth century by the breakdown of the status of linear perspective, which was one of the fundamental presuppositions of the visual arts as practiced in recent centuries.[2] Linear perspective is not a self-evident fact of aesthetic vision and expression, since it did not exist at all during the Christian Middle Ages. It was during the Renaissance, a time of enthusiasm for scientific and mathematical constructions, that linear perspective became the norm for painting as an achievement of artistic as well as scientific progress. Its rejection anticipated even more far-reaching developments in modern art, as the destruction of traditional form in cubism from about 1908 led to the total elimination of reference to any external object in aesthetic creation, We can no longer take in a cubist painting at a glance, but are asked to make an active contribution of our own if we want to make sense of it.

While modern art is opposed to traditional art, it is also the case that it has been stimulated and nourished by it. The real question now is how to distinguish "art" from mechanical production. The artwork has no real use, and it is part of our natural sense of the beautiful that we cannot ask why it pleases us. In the Platonic tradition, the ontological function of the beautiful was to bridge the chasm between the ideal and the real. Gadamer's appeal to ancient thought makes him realize that in art and the beautiful we encounter a significance that transcends all conceptual thought. The truth that is encountered in the beautiful, and can come to be shared, is not the sort of understanding that is the result of conceptual analysis. Kant's presumption that everyone should agree with my aesthetic judgment[3] does not imply that I could convince him by argument, for it does not come about by producing good reasons or conclusive proofs for one's taste. In so-called classical art, we often are talking about the production of works that were not originally taken as art, but were encountered as religious or secular ornaments, objects of worship, the representation of a ruler, and the like. The aesthetic revolution of modern times led to the emancipation of art from all such traditional subject matters, and it began when art insisted on being art and noting else. Kant emphasized that art is the creation of something exemplary that is not simply produced by following rules. A work of art allows us "to go on to think much that cannot be said."[4] Kant means that the concept functions as a kind of sounding board, capable of articulating the free play of the imagination. Culture is quite inconceivable without an element of play, as J. Huizinga[5] has shown, play here appears as self-movement that does not pursue any particular end or purpose. One of the prevailing impulses of modern art has been the desire to eliminate the distance separating the audience from a word of art. A genuine experience of a work of art can exist only for someone who participates actively himself. Its identity consists precisely in there being something to "understand," as the work issues a challenge that it expects to be met. The participants belong to the play, for every work of art leaves the person who responds to it some leeway, a space to be filled out by him. There is always some reflective or intellectual accomplishment involved, whether I deal with traditional forms of art handed down to us, or whether I am challenged by modern forms. Reading is not just scrutinizing or taking one word after another; it means performing a constant hermeneutic movement guided by the anticipation of the work.

Gadamer follows Heidegger in holding that the symbolic in general, and the symbolic in art in particular, rest upon an intricate interplay of showing and concealing. Heidegger emphasized that the Greek concept of *aletheia* (concealment) only represents one side of man's fundamental experience of the world.[6] The work of art does not refer to something else but signifies an increase in being, and this is what distinguishes it from all technological achievement. Against Hegel, Heidegger argued that truth in art can only insufficiently be represented in philosophy, and that this is precisely why we need art. Art is only encountered in a form that resists pure conceptualization. Thus, the sense of the symbolic lies in the fact that it is not located in an ultimate meaning that could be recovered in intellectual terms. All art, whether traditional or contemporary, demands constructive activity on our part.[7] It is not allegory in the sense that it says one thing and gives us to understand something else; rather there is a fundamental similarity between the objective vision with which we orient ourselves in the world, and the claim art makes upon us. We should remember that we learn to read pictures, and that one picture may not become accessible to us as quickly as another. The longer we allow ourselves to dwell upon a work of art, the more it displays its manifold riches to us. Recognition means knowing something as that with which we are already acquainted, and it is the proper function of the symbolic, and the symbolic content of the language of art, to accomplish this. As finite beings we always already find ourselves within certain traditions irrespective of whether we are aware of them or whether we deceive ourselves into believing that we can start from scratch. Indeed our attitude does very little to diminish the power that tradition has over us. Art, like any festive celebration, is meaningful only for those who actually take part in it.

Gadamer emphasizes that we only interpret something when its meaning is not clearly stated or when it is ambiguous. Classical examples of things that require interpretation are the flight of birds, oracles, dreams, pictorial images, and enigmatic writings. We have only to interpret that which has a multiplicity of meanings.[8] Art demands interpretation because of its inexhaustible ambiguity, and because it cannot be satisfactorily translated into terms of conceptual knowledge. This applies no less to poetry, for words are not merely complexes of sounds; they are meaning gestures that point away from themselves. Interpretation is already part of all composition.[9] The ambiguity of poetic language answers to the ambiguity of human life as a whole and therein lies its unique value. What poetry interprets for us and point to is not, of course, the same as what the poet intends, for what the poet intends is in no way superior to what anyone else intends – poetry does not consist in intending something else. Whenever we find ourselves in the presence of real poetry, it always transcends both poet and interpreter. The poet's own self-conception or conscious situation is guided by many different possibilities of reflective self-understanding, and is quite different from what he actually accomplishes if the poem is a success. The truth of poetry is not subject to the distinction of true and false as it was understood by hostile philosophers who claimed that "poets tell many lies."[10] Gadamer explains that it is precisely the dearth of the symbol that characterizes contemporary art in all its forms. All symbols facilitate recognition, and the dearth of the symbol that is characteristic of our times reflects the growing unfamiliarity and impersonality of the world around us. In painting, we encounter these signs as the surface elements of point, line, and color, yet the meaning ascribed to such signs remains intangible, ineffable, and incommensurable with anything else we have ever experienced. Nevertheless, a dynamic interplay has been captured and in this manner a solution has been found, for there is a meaning in all these forms of modern art, even though it is a meaning that cannot be rendered explicit. Since the time of the Baroque and Christian-humanistic expressions associated with it, there is no longer a unified symbolic language capable of gaining our acceptance.

Hegel understood "substance" as something that supports us, although it does not emerge into thought of reflective consciousness. It is something that can never be fully articulated, even though it is absolutely necessary for the attainment of clarity, consciousness, expression, and communication. Hegel invoked the idea of substance to grasp the nature of the spirit of a people or the spirit of an age – the all-pervasive reality that supports us, but does not become fully conscious in any one particular individual. We are always other and much more than we know ourselves to be, and what exceeds our knowledge is precisely our real being.[11] When we are at a loss for words, what we want to say is something for which we have to seek new words. In European painting, such speechlessness began with the still-life and the landscape, for when we encounter such subjects in a painting, they clearly do not require the same degree of interpretation as did the depiction's of gods and men in classical art. Here it seems that the sensible world around us finds expression in a language that needs no words.[12] The still-life enjoys a unique freedom in the arrangement of its subject matter because the "objects of composition are things that we can move around: fruit, flowers, everyday objects – anything, in fact, that we choose to display. Compositional freedom thus begins with the subject matter itself, and to that extent the still-life anticipates the compositional freedom of modern art. It was a truly momentous event when, at the beginning of this century, the unity of our pictorial experience began to dissolve and splinter into a great variety of possible forms. We live in a world of play, design, assembly, technical competition, delivery, and sale, a world that is dominated by advertising techniques that strive to render the finished product obsolete once it has become an article of consumption, and supplant it by something new and different. There are still many skeptics who consider abstract painting to be nothing more than a fashion, and consider the art business to be ultimately responsible for its success. Gadamer emphasizes that if the visual artist could express what he has to say in words, he need not create images to being with.

The truly momentous invention of alphabetic script has enabled us to capture human experience by means of a combination of abstract individual signs in an orthographic system. In part this has already influenced the way in which we perceive images; we no longer see these paintings as copies of a reality that presents a unified view with an instantly recognizable meaning. Gadamer is well within the Aristotelian tradition according to which all art is a form of recognition that serves to deepen our knowledge of ourselves, and thus our familiarity with the world as well.[13] He points out that poetic language has a particular and unique relationship to truth, for every poem worthy of the name is quite different from all forms of motivated speech. What the poet intends and what motivates him to say this or that are not the issue. When we grow up in a language, the world is brought close to us, and comes to acquire a certain stability. Language always furnishes the traditional articulations that guide our understanding of the world because when something is recognized, it has liberated itself from the uniqueness and contingency of the circumstances in which it was encountered. Gadamer follows the Aristotelian tradition according to which poetry participates in the truth of the universal.[14] But he points out that unconscious factors, compulsive devises, and interests not only determine our behavior but our consciousness as well.[15] We discover forms of play in the most serious kinds of human activity: in ritual, in the administration of justice, and in various forms of social behavior generally. Human productivity exhibits an enormous variety of ways of trying things out, rejecting them, succeeding, and failing. Art "intends" something, and yet it is not what it intends. The work of art has something of the "as if" character that we recognize as an essential feature of play. There has always been the tendency to link the experience of art with the notion of play. Art as imitation enables us to see more than so-called reality because in it play and seriousness interact.

Notes

[1] Robert Bernasconi in Hans-Georg Gadamer, *The Relevance of the Beautiful and Other Essays,* Cambridge: Cambridge University Press, 1986, p. xii.

[2] *Ibid.,* p. 7.

[3] I. Kant, *Critique of Judgment,* trans. J. H. Bernard, New York, NY: Hafner, 1951, sec. 22, p. 76.

[4] Ibid., p. 160.

[5] Johann Huizinga, *Homo Ludens,* London: Paladin, 1970.

[6] Martin Heidegger, "The Origin of the Work of Art," trans. A. Hofstadter, in *Poetry Language Play,* New York, NY: Harper & Row, 1971, pp. 58-72.

[7] Gadamer, *The Relevance of the Beautiful and Other Essays,* p. 37.

[8] *Ibid.,* p. 69

[9] *Ibid.*, p. 70.
[10] *Ibid.*, p. 73.
[11] *Ibid.*, p, 78.
[12] *Ibid.*, p. 84.
[13] *Ibid.*, p. 100.
[14] *Ibid.*, p. 120.
[15] *Ibid.*, p. 123.

Chapter Twenty-Eight

Virtue and Taste

One consequence of the dramatic turn in philosophy during the seventeenth century towards an examination of our experience was a fixing of attention on the phenomenon of taste. This focus upon our experience of beauty extended into the study of our subjective, psychological responses to the natural world and resulted in a clarification of these responses, which is still of interest. Schier argues that Hume was wrong to assimilate moral judgments to aesthetic judgments.[1] Rationality requires us to tailor our ends to our abilities; while pragmatists tell us to restrain our ambitions, romantics want them to run free. We should aim at the stars, not to achieve more on earth, but to have our sights on what is noblest in itself.[2] While pragmatists want our beliefs constrained by evidence, romantics tell us to soar beyond evidence. The romantic view has many literary expressions, but the best illustration of romanticism is Don Quixote: inspired by the chivalry that no longer fits his world, Quixote pursues beautiful goals that cannot be realized. As nineteenth century psychology has revealed, we humans have deep-seated tendencies to inner conflict that can be hard to acknowledge, let alone overcome. Whatever our personal tendencies to irrationality, our modern society contains many institutions that reinforce them, such as advertising. People whose goals conflict often oscillate between them. The possession of taste is something we value highly, for it would seem that its possession makes its possessor a better person. Good taste requires aesthetic sensitivity. Whereas aesthetic and moral sensitivity are different, there is at least a widespread belief that developed aesthetic taste should have a beneficial effect upon moral character. Basically, aestheticism is allowing aesthetic principles to overrule moral principles. One reason why people may be alert to matters of taste is that lapses of taste may provide insights into character that are not so easily obtained otherwise. Similarities of attitude and outlook smooth the path of friendship and affection between people. We value intelligence in itself, and not just because it is a help in the attainment of wisdom and the performance of good works. Good taste, Brooks argues, is a perfection of our emotional nature.[3] It has a tendency to improve us morally and make us wiser. It can be a guide to character but, beyond these instrumental merits it is a good in itself. In order to appreciate it, one needs to possess it in some measure oneself. Mill, in open defiance of the Benthamite belief that pushpin is as good as poetry, says that no intelligent person could consent to be a fool, even though he should be persuaded that the fool, the dunce, or the rascal is better satisfied with their lot that he is with his.[4] These higher and lower grades of existence are associated with enjoying or not enjoying the higher pleasures – in short, with taste. Moreover, taste is closely associated with social class. For the snob, people with taste form a sort of natural kind; they have a distinctive character. Possession of taste is manifested not only in aesthetic choice, but in qualities like urbanity and imaginativeness. By and large, the higher the social class, the better the taste, but good taste is exercised differently in different cultures. Those who hold important positions and function adequately in them are likely to be educated and appreciators of Mill's higher virtues. Those without these advantages are less likely to function so adequately.

There are obvious advantages to be able to tell at a glance whether food is fresh, and an animal or plant is healthy. Our ancestors have had good reason to be aware of, and to be attracted by, what is healthy and well-proportioned. If in multiple photography male and female human beings are superimposed to form composite male or female faces, the result, it seems, is a pair of surprisingly beautiful faces, and not the characterless features we might have expected. People are beautiful in so far as they approximate to the human norm, the evolutionary explanation of our having such tastes is that what is beautiful is also socially engineered. This may also serve to explain Hermann Weyl's apparently shocking claim that he had always tried to unite the true with the beautiful, but that when he had to choose one over the other, he usually chose the beautiful.[5] A great scientist's educated sensibility is sometimes more reliable than what can – at the time – be demonstrated by less subtle wits.[6] The philistine wishes us to believe that efficiency is all that matters to us, but efficiency is essentially instrumentalist. Things can only be efficient for definite ends. The philistine transforms all things into tools, but leaves himself no goal in terms of which such instrumental efficiency can be calculated except sensual pleasure or the feeling of power over others. Modern subjectivists are difficult to convince – partly, no doubt, because they admit no objective rational obligation to be convinced by anything. Natural selection has produced many ways of solving social and personal problems, but the creatures concerned cannot usually be supposed to have it in mind to solve these problems. What attracts them in the direction they must go is not the thought of a solution. They do things because, at the time, they want to, and what they want to do is usually what they need to do if their kind of creature is to survive. Animals do not court and mate in order to have offspring whereas we, who can conceive of having offspring and of acting towards that goal, can also take steps to mate and not have offspring.[7] Our goals are not determined by our biology; what we choose to value need not be what has guided natural selection, nor need it be what natural selection has caused us to desire. The virtuous do not act in order to win the game and are not much troubled if they sometimes lose: that is why they win.[8] We can expect that virtue will prevail in the sense that too great a departure from the human norm in any popuiation is likely to eliminate itself over the long run. Most human beings, accident and illness and corrupt manners permitting, will be fairly healthy and fairly virtuous.

Natural goods are those things that people will, by and large, desire: honor, wealth, and bodily strength; friendship and good fortune. Such things, by and large, will assist their fond possessor to survive and to reproduce his kind. Fashions of physical beauty change. Our morality is founded on our biology, in one sense, just as our science is founded on our biology; creatures of other imaginable biological natures would have very different ways of perceiving the world, and (for all we know) quite different ways of experiencing it. The world apart from value is a theoretical construct devised for political purposes quite as much as for "scientific" ones, and not obviously the only really real world. Clark's conclusion is that the beautiful is indeed a constraint on what can happen. The idea of higher and lower pleasures (which is, of course, an idea that goes back to the Greeks) is in a nutshell the idea that some types of pleasures are better than others, and that the person whose pleasure is in question is not necessarily the best judge of its quality. The assumption is also that intellectual aesthetic and moral pleasures are of higher quality than physical pleasure, and that when there is a choice one should prefer the higher pleasures. Even if we accept that we should try to behave in ways characteristic of our species, we might argue that our species has a dual nature; we are rational animals, not angels, and it is as appropriate to human beings to enjoy animal pleasures as it is to enjoy intellectual pleasures. The ordinary person would be reluctant to exchange his mixed style with its discontents, both mental and physical, for a purely intellectual life as for a purely physical one.[9] The language of aesthetics is designed to shield the initiate, disarm the critic, and exclude the vulgar. It follows that taste cannot be reasoned about, cannot be taught or learned, and cannot be communicated. It is something you just "have" if you belong to the elite, and you get it largely by claiming to have it. Functionalism simply begs the question; the functionalist, like the utilitarian, is forced to value all human needs on the same scale, and it is no wonder if he thus misconstrues, or simply fails to recognize, the more profound.[10] At any rate, let no one presume to say that such things are only a question of taste.[11]

Our aesthetic judgment about something cannot be made in abstraction from what sort of thing it is. Different things are beautiful in different ways, and to say something is beautiful does not provide the slightest indication about its appearance.[12] When Kant says that something is "purposive without purpose," all he means is that the object in question serves some function in our spiritual economy; it is rewarding or salutary for us in one way or another. Being caught up in fictional worlds and at the same time recognizing their fictionality involves a delicate balance – even a tension – which accounts for much of the pleasure and value of imaginary works of art.[13] In the game of make-believe associated with fiction, readers and viewers can speak about, refer to, reflect on, and form attitudes towards characters and events in much the same way as their otherworldly companions can do to one another.[14] But it would be wrong to suppose that the internal perspective is characterized by special *semantic* features. Rather, sentences reflected or thoughts entertained from the internal perspective are subject, not to linguistic constraints, but to rules of make-believe. Few philosophers are comfortable with simply admitting fictitious entities into the class of things that can be referred to or can be the subject of these predictions. Lamarque believes that a more promising line is simply to take the idea of "character" at face value. Internally, the problem is epistemological; there are certain facts we just don't know, but that doesn't disturb our imaginings because ignorance about people is familiar to us in the actual world. What we know, we know as much by description as by acquaintance, just as our thoughts are as often general as singular. Here there are further reasons why fictitious and real things seem so intimately connected.[15]

In the pursuit of knowledge, we naturally strive to an objective perspective transcending both our individual and subjective points of view, but also those of our species and world: the attempt is made to view the world not from a place within it, or from the vantage point of a special type of life and awareness, but from nowhere in particular.[16] From the internal perspective, I am immersed in my projects, desires, and achievements, and take them seriously, but from a more detached external point of view, my petty strivings can come to seem pointless or without justification, making my life seem objectively insignificant. I am, nevertheless, unable to extricate myself from an unqualified commitment to it, and the sense of the absurd is the result of this juxtaposition.[17] The value of adapting an internal perspective to an imaginary world is that it allows us to adopt a point of view that is not our own. One difference between fantasy and art is that the former is self-centered, literally self-indulgent, while the latter seeks more detachment, a transcending of self-interest. The imaginary worlds of works of art provide an excellent example of the simultaneous non-conflicting occurrence of the subjective and objective points of view.[18] When we adopt the viewpoint of and participate in an imaginary world, we can do so with varying degrees of self-consciousness. In one familiar view of art, great art is "timeless" or "universal" in the sense that it transcends the circumstances of its production, whether personal or historical. But however the artist strives to cover his tracks, in order to portray universal truths timelessly, there is no escaping the historical rootedness of art. To appreciate these worlds, we need both an external awareness of their artifice and an internal involvement with their content. Some readers will insist that fictional characters be viewed and judged as real people, while for others, characters should be seen for what they are. No doubt different genres of writing encourage an emphasis one way or another. But the simple conclusion must be that imaginative involvement and awareness of artifice are both indispensable in an appropriate response to imaginative works of art.[19] Perhaps one reason why we accept artistic fictions so readily is that the tension between these two attitudes so closely mirrors that more familiar tension that Nagel notices between our self-absorbed involvement in our own lives, and our predisposition to stand back and view ourselves as mere players in a game.[20]

The distinctive mark of a picture is that it represents its subject by virtue of looking like what it depicts. But Budd points out that this naive idea is inadequate as it stands. Perhaps its most important deficiency is that it operates with the concept of one thing's looking like another, and that this is a notion too loose to bear such weight. It is indeed the vagueness of this concept that renders the analysis of depiction based on it vulnerable to counterexamples and, at the same time allows it further life when a different aspect of the concept is turned to face the objection. If there is one thing that the most impressive, recent, philosophical theories of depicting are in agreement about, it is precisely the negation of the idea that depiction should be elucidated in terms of one thing's looking like another. A black and white line drawing does not thereby depict its subject as lacking color, and a spectator who understands it does not see it as depicting a colorless state of affairs.[21] The artist's intuition is not to depict a black and white state of affairs, or a colored state of affairs as being black and white; it is to depict only the spatial structure of a state of affairs and the comparative brightness of its parts. The extraction of pictorial content by pictorial perception should not be thought of in a simplistic way as an instantaneous occurrence. There is no such thing as *the* visual appearance of an object or scene. The (murky) intuition that depiction is based on a natural, rather than a purely conventional, relation, can easily be preserved in the face of the obvious fact that, even given constancy of point of view and prevailing conditions, there are indefinitely many ways or styles of depicting a particular kind of thing.

A philosophically more modest way of calling attention to the cognitive virtues of art is to claim for it the power not so much to represent things as they are in themselves, as to represent how they appear to observers stationed at certain points of view. But internalized canons of taste are necessarily unstable. The idea that a painter might try to paint human perception will strike the philosophical mind as a bit odd, for it will appear that in order to paint something one must know what it looks like. However, even if a painting cannot depict perception, it can allude to or intimate facts about perception, in rather the way that a metaphor like Shakespeare's "Juliet is the sun" alludes to, but does not state or represent facts about, human love. The idea is that the power of art consists in giving us truth about how things look and feel to human beings.[22] Works of art do not have a purely visual interest for us, and their formal power is not independent of the various thematic uses the artist makes of the form. It might look as though the doctrine of the radical autonomy of art, or art's unconditional value, must collapse from the start, for we cannot help but speak of art in aesthetic terms, or in terms of the intelligence of the work, and these aesthetic and artistic terms immediately impart values from the outside into the art world. We must understand such modernists as Eliot and Greenberg as proposing that the standards of aesthetic excellence are specific to each art, and are not to be incorporated under standards that cover domains other than that particular artistic enterprise. If the value of art is thus radically incommensurable with, or unconnected to, our other values, how do we ever come to be sensitive to the value of art? Sometimes the most excellent agency can be displayed in the pursuit of ends that are, in themselves, rather trivial seeming. The last move in a chess game has no significance apart from the fact that its motive is the result of worthwhile play. Sometimes these intuitions are summed up in the thought that what matters is not the product but the process. Art is a unique kind of value, but we can explain it as emerging out of a particular structure consisting of other values, perfectionist and aesthetic values, that exist independently of the art world.

Notes

[1] Flint Schier, "Hume and the Aesthetic Agency," *Proceedings of the Aristotelian Society* 7 1986-7, p. 131.

[2] Thomas Hurka, "Excellence: Trying, Deserving, Succeeding," in Dudley Knowles and John Skorupski, *Virtue and Taste,* Oxford, England and Cambridge, MA: Blackwell, 1993.

[3] David Brooks, Taste, Virtue and Class," in *Virtue and Taste*, p. 66.

[4] J.S. Mill, *Utilitarianism,* chp. 2.

[5] S. Chandrasekhar, *Truth and Beauty,* Chicago, IL: University of Chicago Press, 1987, p. 52.

[6] Stephen R.L. Clark, "Natural Goods and Moral Beauty," in *Virtue and Taste,* p. 86.

[7] *Ibid.,* p. 90.

[8] *Ibid.,* p. 91.

[9] Elizabeth Telfer, "The Pleasures of Eating and Drinking," in *Virtue and Taste,* p. 108.

[10] R.A.D. Grant, "Home Truths: Charles Rennie Mackintosh and the House," in *Virtue and Taste,* p. 118.

[11] *Ibid.,* p. 122.

[12] Anthony Savile, "Architecture, Formalism and the Sense of Self," in *Virtue and Taste,* p. 136.

[13] Peter Lamarque, "In and Out of Imaginary Worlds," in *Virtue and Taste,* p. 144.

[14] *Ibid.,* p. 145.

[15] *Ibid.,* p. 147.

[16] Thomas Nagel, *Moral Questions,* Cambridge University Press, 1978, p. 208.

[17] Thomas Nagel, *The View from Nowhere,* Oxford University Press, 1986, p. 218.

[18] Lamarque, "In and Out of Imaginary Worlds," p. 149.

[19] *Ibid.,* p. 151.

[20] *Ibid.*

[21] Malcolm Budd, "How Pictures Look," in *Virtue and Taste,* p. 164.

[22] Flint Schier, "Van Gogh's Boots: The Claims of Representation," in *Virtue and Taste,* p. 185.

Chapter Twenty-Nine

Acquiring Taste

Traditionally, theories of taste have stressed the close connection between aesthetic appreciation and the feeling of pleasure.[1] We think that a person has taste when he makes appreciative remarks that are intelligent, interesting, suitable, show discrimination, and are not banal, trivial, or boringly obvious. But we think that he has taste only if we believe that what he says arises from his own experience, and is not parroted or feigned. Schaper points out that, on the one hand, we believe that taste is bound up with the immediacy of feeling, and that taste judgments, therefore, cannot be derived from principles or canons. On the other hand, we hold that taste can be cultivated and educated, and that taste judgments are reasoned appraisal. To have taste is more like having learned how to read than it is like having a taste for curry. But while feelings are sometimes not justified by our reasons, it does not follow that feelings never have reasons. We do not feel obliged to defend our culinary preferences, whereas aesthetic preferences can be refuted. Taste judgments are not merely capricious or idiosyncratic, and giving reasons is legitimate for them. While it is possible to maintain that the felt delight is primary, and that there is no reason why feelings should be consistent, Schaper agrees with Burke that aesthetic preferences are rational in a way culinary ones are not. A preference for which no reason *could* be given – like preferring wine to cider – is not aesthetic. However, finding reasons may modify our responses, for it alters what we see in the object, and that in turn affects what we feel towards it. But there are no criteria for determining judgments of taste as false, as there are for empirical judgments. Consensus, even if there were one in these matters, would not amount to a means of assessing the objective validity of individual judgments.

This does not mean, however, that failing such standards, the only alternative is to fall back on a simple subjectivism, considering taste judgments merely as statements of likes and dislikes about which dispute would be futile. We may not believe in rules of taste, but neither do we think that in matters of taste anything goes. There is a way to be found for speaking of errors and lapses of taste, and for the cultivation and education of taste.[2] Taste judgments must be based on the individual response of the person making them, that is, on the felt pleasure in or repugnance to, something. Part of what it is for a person to have taste is to have, among other qualities, those of sensitivity and discrimination. This, Schaper believes, does more justice to our intuitions about how tenuous our grip on our emotions often is. There is always reason for uncertainty, not whether one feels pleasure but why. Yet individual taste judgments are not on that account corrigible. What is corrigible is a person's attitude to his feelings. I appeal to all persons of taste, to those who know its pleasures. They form a community in which communication is possible, even though not always easy. So the appeal implicit in the taste judgment that I can share with the members of a privileged community of taste is not that others should agree with my particular appraisals but that everyone should come to see that such appraisals are possible. Such an aesthetics owes much to Kant and the view that without conceptualization, no communication would be possible. There would be nothing to communicate, for there would be nothing that was believed or known. Falk points out that what is a candidate for communicability is knowledge of feelings, not the feelings themselves.[3] To find anything beautiful, Kant insists, is not something one can be argued into; it is to have a feeling. It is something that happens to one. Yet, the subject who experiences "that is beautiful" refers to the object, not to a state of oneself. It is not, Kant says, a judgment about a psychological fact. To judge an object beautiful is *not* to subsume it under concepts. That this does not happen is the proper reason for saying that we are dealing with a feeling here, not a knowing. However, feeling something beautiful, the feelings I have, result not from contingent features in my own personality, but from a part of human nature that is common to all. Having an interest (and therefore in suitable circumstances, a feeling) is not a communicable state. It does not arise out of my following any correct procedures or out of a nature that I share with all other men. The mere noticing of an aspect, as opposed to thinking that it is important, is something that neither requires nor can receive justification. The crucial question, Falk suggests, is what we can suppose ourselves to be sensitive to. The meaningfulness of presenting a sad sequence of events is not something that can have an external source. The artist manipulates the material of the world and provides an object that will only seem nonarbitrary to one who finds in his own feelings what will make sense of it – that justifies its exclusions, and the specific connections it makes.

The concept of pleasure has played a double role in the philosophy of art. It has been thought to be the reason for cultivating art, since pleasure has been thought to require no justification. At the same time, pleasure has been considered to be the criterion that enables us to distinguish between good art and bad art. Sharpe[4] rejects both these views based on the assumption that the art connoisseurs cultivate art that gives us pleasure. He points out that a great deal of art is uncomfortable, upsetting, even horrifying, and is not valued any the less on that account. Tragedy provides the paradigm example of art that is not pleasing, and the minimum claim we can make of art is merely that it should not be boring, as T.S. Eliot has emphasized. But as long as we rely on the consensus of connoisseurs, our understanding of beauty has to explicate the idea in terms of some experimental response. In the mid-eighteenth century, it was taken for granted that the response in question was that of pleasure. Both Kant and Schiller explained art in terms of a certain kind of fit between the imagination and understanding, The spectator cannot appreciate the beauty of art if his response of fit is not based upon the discovery of what the artist's endeavor is, and what the relevant aesthetic canons are according to which his statement of fit must be guided.[5] Because objects of similar configuration can be devised in answer to different projects and in different styles, the very same material features of one work that make it beautiful may well condemn another to be a dismal and ugly feature. Savile suggests that given the way beauty characterizing fit has been designed – simply as fit of work to project – it is hard to understand why it should deeply engage our affections. While there can be beauty that is nonattaching, unless it were sometimes found attaching, we should not be able to say that a man had an aesthetic experience at all. We should not be able to see a work of art exhibit sufficient richness of style to generate those constraints that make a sharp experience of fit possible.

The world is represented as coherent under the values of style in point, and the artist's work is only judged to be beautiful insofar as it is experienced under these values as compelling and making sense. We cannot make a correct judgment unless in so doing we make the experimental judgment of coherence or sense. This suggests that the beauty of nature is parasitic on that of art. Unless we extended the perception of beauty beyond the self, it is hard to see how its norm could be something that is sufficiently common to form the basis of a public institution. Cohen[6] explains this by focusing on the functional similarities between works of art and jokes. Failing to be amused by a good joke is like lack of taste. In failing to make the proper response, one is not so much wrong as different, and it is a difference that leaves one outside a vital community. But one cannot will oneself *in* anymore than one can will oneself *out*. The point of telling a joke is the attainment of community, and likewise the artform induces particular expectations and forms of attention. We are all virtually agreed that no description or explanation of an artwork will do in place of the work. The explanation of a joke will inevitably be discursive; it will give the solution discretely, and that will prevent the magical all-at-once kick. But although exegesis won't be a substitute in either artwork or joke, it can augment appreciation of artwork while it seems to destroy the joke altogether. Cohen points out that when your special background is called into play, your sensibility is galvanized. The appreciative audience discovers that it can supply what is needed, and in doing this it collaborates in the success of jokes and artworks – by creating intimacy. Our capacity to entertain a thought without accepting it, to make believe without believing, and to imagine what we know has not happened are all instrumental in this. It is not necessary for a reader to share the beliefs of the author to enjoy a work of fiction or poetry.

We take a lot as intelligible and imaginable that to men of other times and places would seem queer and nonsensical. We have thus to accept the essentially perception-relative nature of aesthetic descriptions and their perceptual elusiveness. Pettit emphasizes that you have to "see" that something is graceful, sad, or charming, and that no argument can show that it is so. Whether a picture represents this or that person or scene would seem to depend on factors other than its color properties. In particular, it would seem to depend on the painter's intentions. But the proper interpretation of artistic characterizations may have truth value only in a weak sense. To agree to an aesthetic description is to "see the point," and to justify it is to justify merely an experience and not a belief.[7] Just as one must be amused before one is fully entitled to describe a joke as funny, so one must be moved in some non cognitive fashion before one has a full title to endorse an aesthetic characterization.[8] In aesthetics you have to see for yourself precisely because what you have to "see" is not a property. Aesthetic characterizations are perceptually elusive, and what this means is that visual scrutiny of a picture, necessary though it might be for aesthetic knowledge, is not always sufficient to guarantee it. One may look and look and not see its elegance, economy, or sadness. There is no exercise that is guaranteed to bring the perceptually elusive into view. Since a picture has many aesthetic properties, it is posited at once in many different reference classes. Each of these classes can be seen as a dimension, and the concept of a multidimensional aesthetic space offers a useful way of thinking about what happens when a picture assumes an overall aesthetic character for an observer.

Pictures display themselves as suitable objects for a given aesthetic characterization only insofar as they are cast in appropriate contrast. Thus, it is not surprising that some observers will look and look at a picture, and yet fail to come to a point where they can sincerely assent, on the basis of what they see, to an aesthetic characterization.[9] Pettit argues that a given position will be illegitimate, if it means that we cannot make unified sense of the picture as a whole, that is, if it gives raise to a certain incoherence, or if it allows to make sense of only part of the picture.[10] But he has to admit that such holistic constraints need not be taken very seriously, since the standards of what is a perceptual or aesthetic unity have been dramatically altered in modern art. It is natural to wonder whether the idea of transcending special points of view really make sense in aesthetics.

In David Hume's essay "Of the Standard of Taste," which he published in 1757, he makes the point that, although common sense agrees with the "skeptical philosophy" in holding it fruitless to dispute about matters of taste, common sense also dismisses certain critical judgments as not merely false, but absurd and ridiculous. This is the paradox of taste. He tries to show that although the judgment of taste depends not on reason but on "sentiment," nonetheless, some critics have better judgment than others. It is a sort of "soft" logic that makes it possible for them to identify not only what constitutes art but also what makes it beautiful or significant. While today we no longer believe that there is a universal standard of taste, we do discover that in art there is invariably something to be learned and to become acquainted with. Artists and philosophers – unlike scientists – have been largely unable to convince each other in their disputes, and one reason for this is that they accept different standards of relevance in their arguments. The model of mathematical logic has misled philosophers since Plato, and made them insist on standards of decidabilty and finality, which in practice they cannot attain. Even skeptics (like Hume) accepted this ideal while declaring it unat-tainable. The "logic" of context and relevance to which they appealed proved incapable of becoming fully verbalized, let alone adequate for settling their disputes. It tolerates some ambiguity and even contra-dictions (like Hume's paradox), but at the same time any such interpretation takes it for granted that not anything goes. Such soft logic is different from fuzzy logic in that in fuzzy logic we have a *range* of correspondences that can be determined, whereas soft logic remains usually unquantifiable, as in the interpretation of a text. To judge that something is relevant is to judge it by analogy, and there is more than just one way to do this.

Notes

[1] Eva Schaper, "The Pleasures of Taste," in *Pleasure, Preference and Value, Studies in Philosophical Aesthetics*, ed. Eva Schaper, Cambridge University Press, 1983, p. 39.
[2] *Ibid.*, p. 47.
[3] Barrie Falk, "The Communicability of Feeling," in *Pleasure, Preference and Value*, p. 58.
[4] R.A. Sharpe, "Solid Joys or Fading Pleasures," in *Pleasure, Preference and Value*, p. 86f.
[5] Anthony Savile, "Beauty and Attachment," in *Pleasure, Preference and Value*, p. 103.
[6] Ted Cohen, "Jokes," in *Pleasure, Preference and Value*, p. 120f.
[7] Roger Scruton, *Art and Imagination*, London: Methuen, 1974, p. 49.

[8] Philip Pettit, "The Possibility of Aesthetic Realism," in *Pleasure, Preference and Value,* p. 26.

[9] *Ibid.,* p. 34.

[10] *Ibid.,* p. 35.

Chapter Thirty

Scharfstein's Aesthetic Universal

Scharfstein argues in favor of an aesthetic universal rooted in human biology. Art, of course, is so varied that anyone can discover artists with whom he is in sympathy, but this pluralism makes it more difficult to appreciate the artists whom art historians and critics have praised.[1] History teaches us that there is every reason to believe that our own evaluations of artists will be subjected to extensive re-evaluations.[2] Not surprisingly, the prevalence of a given fashion influences the choice of exemplary works from the past. Both short-term and long-term fashions change, and the always victorious present leaves disturbing inconsistencies. But rejection of the past is also much harder to accomplish than it might seem at first, for something always remains in one's conscious or unconscious memory. Even the song of a bird develops in a given sequence, a development that is not unlike the speech of a child. The observed trends may be the outcome of chance, which resists scientific explanation much as our own human history does. The often complicated animal reactions that we think of as automatic or instinctive are not well-understood. Though parrots do naturally well with a vocabulary of sounds, and apes with one of gestures, we find it difficult to fathom the intelligence of nonhumans because we identify intelligence with our own anatomical structures, needs, and values. This applies even more to our sense of beauty and to human art.

Scharfstein argues that even if animals or birds were never either intelligent or conscious, the likeness of their song and display to our own would still be convincing. This is because art, too, has biological grounds.[3] The song of birds and of humans has similar uses: to establish intimacy, to court, claim, warn, and fight. But he has to admit that no one really knows why certain species of birds have such an ability to imitate sounds, including those of human speech. He speculates that birdsong, like human art, creates a pattern of challenge and response. Like the bird that sings at large to attract a still unknown listener, an artist tries to attract someone as yet, and perhaps forever, unknown. Dialects make those who use them more intimately responsive to one another; they make them more a family, clan, tribe, or nation. The dialects also make strangers of those who do not use them. The apes, and particularly chimpanzees, give facial and bodily expression to sadness, anger, resentment, satisfaction, reassurance, friendship, and love, much as we do. Whether or not apes can learn syntactic structure, they have imagination enough to deceive on purpose, for example, by pointing in the wrong direction to mislead a human searching for food they want to keep for themselves. Imagination is also implicit in the ability of apes to recognize pictures for what they are. An ape experienced with pictures can ask for something by pointing to its picture. Apes can also recognize photographs of themselves and their own mirror images. A young chimpanzee brought up with a child scribbled pencil marks on paper just as the child did. But, of course, painting by an ape is possible only because of the human material and the human example. What Scharfstein calls the "art" of an ape is really a simian response to human curiosity – the human attempt to see how an ape might fit into the human tradition.

As long as we consider only informal abstraction, the painting of an ape cannot be distinguished from that of a human. However, human art presupposes a cultural context, a web of associations, words, and memories, which give art its specific significance. Scharfstein himself realizes that what looks exactly like art in animals may well be something altogether different,[4] so that, strictly speaking, there is no such thing as proto-art or an aesthetic universal. In early infancy, there may be signs of preference for music over noise or the mother's voice over that of another woman, but it is certainly an oversimplification to reduce the cultural complexities of art to such elementary reactions. An infant's art naturally expresses his observation of the world, and his pleasure in recording and imagining it after his own fashion, yet artists who cultivate simplicity or sincerity do not become children thereby. To survive, animals learn a traditional fidelity to type of food, potential enemies, prey, territories, feeding grounds, courting, shelter, and migratory routes, but most of this fidelity is genetic, built into their nervous system. Scharfstein believes that art and play are invented to unite populations by creating a local dialect and way of living, so that the function of the aesthetic is mainly to create a sense of familiarity and mutual support. It means that whoever wants to appreciate art fully, can do so only by becoming acquainted with the local tradition – and this leaves little room for the aesthetic universal.

Scharfstein stresses spontaneity and lack of constraint in art, the appeasement of elementary interests in serving our sensuality. But there is more to art than the pleasure of manipulating materials and instruments, as there is in sport. Identifying spontaneity with the art of children, he comes to look upon art as a mental aberration, a product of "crazy" Taoists, Romantics, Dadaists, and Surrealists. He sides with those who identify with the nonmoral whole of order-in-chaos, or even with chaos itself, and he interprets the belief in genius as a rejection of imitation and of academic study. But most artists prefer to believe that inspiration and intellect, or imagination and the skills of crafts-manship, can still be joined in a civilized harmony. Scharfstein is convinced that anything done for its own sake is suspect because (by definition) there is no reason for it. Thus, he refuses to believe that inspired creation may become an end in itself rather than the means of life.

It cannot be denied that many writers and artists have shown evident signs of suffering and mental disturbance, and that in many cases this has entered deeply into the fabric of their art. Against the strong human need for tradition, there is an equally intense desire on the part of some creative individuals to remain stubbornly individual. By learning to shed his inhibitions, the artist discovers that as good as such spontaneity may be for his art, it is otherwise unpleasant or even pathological, and likely to frighten him into self-punishment, silence, and suicide.[5] It seems also that a usual condition for aesthetic creation is loneliness experienced and overcome by means of one's imagination, a use by which one turns to oneself for the company that is missing. Scharfstein believes that there is a great deal of truth in the stereotyped picture, already in Vasari, of the artist as someone with-drawn, introspective, independent, imaginative, unpredictable, and alienated from community expectations. His work requires the artist to be sensitive to his inner states and to that extent narcissistic, and many artists feel alienated from their work and are not satisfied with it.

Pride, shame, depression, and a degree of obsessiveness characterize artists of all sorts and, even if they regard themselves free individuals, they usually remain subject to the vagaries of the marketplace. Whereas Scharfstein believes that the insistence on context is no more than a refuge from analysis, his own aesthetic universal is said to be not only biological and psychological but metaphysical, i.e. beyond all context. The "objective" character of art is supposed to result from the biological and psychological likeness between individuals, and from the similar methods by which all communities have tried to preserve their unity. The function of art is reduced by Scharfstein to that of uniting individuals who make up a community as well as to distinguish communities from each other. He emphasizes that sensation and perception, no less than preference and emotions, are the same in all human beings. That is why different cultures proceed by means of similar modes of response in what he calls "aesthetic overlap." He realizes that out of context a work of art must lose its subtlety, and at the same time he maintains that it retains its proto-or pancultural values – it is the attempt to remain individual while merging with what is beyond the individual. The desire to fuse is also evident in what the artist feels to be inspiration and which links him to something beyond himself. Hume and those who claimed that beauty lies in the eyes of the beholder retained the belief in inspiration. This belief that art, or good art, must be inspired, remains as widespread as ever.[6] Taking the aesthetic to be some sort of absolute universal, Scharfstein links it to *Einfühlung* or empathy, but any such preestablished harmony between the intentions of the artist and what the artwork comes to mean to his audience remains highly problematic.

Notes

[1] Ben-Ami Scharfstein, *Of Birds, Beasts, and Other Artists, An Essay on the Universality of Art,* New York, NY: New York University Press, 1988, p. 12.

[2] *Ibid.,* p. 21.

[3] *Ibid.,* p. 47.

[4] *Ibid.,* p. 63.

[5] *Ibid.*, p. 166.
[6] *Ibid.*, p. 209.

Art

Chapter Thirty-One

Defining Art

In most traditional theories of art, it is generally assumed that the art theorist should provide a definition that enables us to distinguish art from nonart. Historically such definitions have been "essentialist," that is, they presuppose that there is a complete set of necessary and sufficient conditions for something to be a work of art. It is clear, however, that traditional theories of art differ radically in just what the necessary and sufficient conditions of art may be. Until the nineteenth century, everyone understood what counted as a work of art. What such a work as *Ulysses* or Duchamp's *Fountain* might be trying to do or say could not have been taken into consideration by the pre-twentieth century artworld. These works would have been rejected as art simply because they did not conform to what was expected as a proper art medium, a proper formal structure, or a proper subject matter.[1] The idea was that if art is a unique cultural activity, then all kinds of art, e.g. painting, music, and literature, must have similar shared characteristics that are not exhibited by other phenomena. These essential characteristics have been alternatively defined as mimesis, beauty, expressiveness, symbolism, or significant form. The history of aesthetics is, in part, a running dispute about what qualities best define and apply most uniquely to art. But the claim that art is a unique cultural activity becomes questionable when literally everything is so called. Thus, in our century the relatively simple distinctions between art and other artifacts have broken down, and traditional concepts for evaluating works of art have been challenged.

For Kennick and many early "analytic aestheticians," such theories as Croce's and Collingwood's are fundamentally flawed by their reliance on an underlying assumption that it is possible and useful to attempt to answer a question as broad as the one Croce attempts – namely "What is Art?" It is to hold that for the term *art* to apply to any work there must be a common nature that applies to all works of art and to nothing else. This is the essentialist fallacy of supposing that the meaning of every common noun must designate a feature shared by every object denoted by that word. Philosophers analyzing the meaning of the word should, therefore, pay attention to the variety of uses of the word *art,* and not, like Croce, look for some nonexistent essence shared by all artworks.[2] We ought to be able to look at the various works of art and *see* what art is – yet we fail to do so. We are, therefore, inclined to think that its essence must be something hidden, something that only the aesthetician can see.

But Kennick points out that no amount of looking and scrutinizing gives us what we want. The word "art" has complicated variety of uses, which is nowadays called a complex "logic." It is neither a word coined in the laboratory or studio to name something that is hitherto escaped our attention, nor is it a relatively simple term of common parlance like star or tree which names something with which we are all quite familiar. It is the complicated concepts like space, time, reality, change, art, knowledge, and many more like them that give us trouble. Dictionaries and their definitions are of use in answering questions of the form "What is x?" only in relatively simple and comparatively trivial cases. Kennick concludes that we are able to separate the objects that are works of art from those that are not because we know English; that is, we know how to correctly use the word "art" and to apply the phrase "work of art." "Correctly" and "properly" here have nothing to do with any "common nature" or "common denominator" of all works of art; they have merely to do with the rules that govern the actual and commonly accepted usage of the word.[3] Admittedly, there are occasions on which we are not sure whether something is a work of art or not. But this merely reflects the systematic vagueness of the concept in question, an "open texture," which the definitions of the aestheticians do nothing at all to remove. On such occasions we can indeed tighten the texture, remove some of the vagueness by making a decision, drawing a line; and this is what curators and purchasing committees of art museums are sometimes forced for practical reasons to do. But in doing so, they and we are not discovering anything about art.[4] It is the compulsion to reduce the complexity of aesthetic concepts to simplicity, neatness, and order that moves the aesthetician to make his first mistake, to ask "What is Art" and so to expect to find an answer that can be given to "What is helium?"[5] There is no such thing as the aesthetic experience, since different sorts of experiences are properly referred to as aesthetic. There is, however, a fruitful and enlightening search for similarities and resemblances in art, which the search for a common denominator sometimes furthers – the search for family resemblances. One of the prime reasons for the aesthetician's search for definition of art, beauty, and the rest, is his supposition that unless we know what art or beauty is, we cannot say what good art or beautiful art is. Traditional aesthetics mistakenly assumes that responsible criticism is impossible without standards or criteria universally applicable to all works of art. Kennick points out, however, that we can and do praise art for a variety of reasons, and not always the same variety. Since "art" and "beauty" do not name one and only one substance and attribute respectively, it is no wonder we cannot find the thing they name, nor to render intelligible the felt discovery that they name one thing.

Art has no function or purpose in the sense in which knives or telescopes have functions. There is no one thing we do with all works of art: some we hang, some we play, some we perform, some we read, some we look at, some we listen to, some we analyze, some we contemplate. There is no special aesthetic use for works of art. In the arts we are not as a rule interested in uniformity, and those critics and aestheticians who are interested in uniformity issue their alleged definitions as slogans of reform. Kennick emphasizes that criticism has in no way been hampered by the absence of generally applicable canons or norms; different works of art, are,or may be, praiseworthy or blameworthy for different reasons. Realism in art, for example, is not always a virtue, but this does not mean that it is not sometimes a virtue. A work of art is not essentially the answer to a question or the solution to a particular problem.[6] Not all artists are doing the same thing – solving the same problem, answering the same question, playing the same game. Yet contrary to Kennick,[7] it would seem that we do have an interest in the uniformity of taste for quite similar reasons that we have an interest in the uniformity of moral norms. People who have deep differences in taste are less likely to live side by side in peace and amity. We may not always be consistent in our aesthetic and artistic demands (anymore than we are in our moral demands), but we do require *some* consistency in both, for we offer arguments for our preferences in aesthetics no less than we do in ethics. Weitz argues that it is futile to attempt to state the conditions that are necessary and sufficient for an object to be a work of art; the concept of art must be treated as an open concept. But he admits that theory has been central in aesthetics and that it is still the preoccupation of the philosophy of art. Like Kennick, Weitz pleads for the rejection of this problem; both are convinced that theory – in the requisite classical sense – is *never* forthcoming in aesthetics. The inadequacies of these theories are not primarily due to any legitimate difficulty such as the vast complexity of art, which may be sorted out by further probing and research. Art, as the logic of the concept shows, has no set of necessary and sufficient properties, hence a theory is logically impossible and not merely factually difficult. Like in Wittgenstein's "games," what we find are not necessary and sufficient properties, only a complicated network of similarities overlapping and crisscrossing. Knowing what a game is is not knowing some real definition or theory, but being able to recognize and explain games, and decide which among imaginary and new examples would or would not be called "games."[8] Knowing what art is not apprehending some manifest or latent essence, but being able to recognize, describe, and explain those things we call "art" in virtue of these similarities. In elucidating the term, certain paradigm cases can be given about which there can be no question as to their being correctly described as "art" or "game," but no exhaustive set of cases can be given. Unforseeable or novel conditions are always forthcoming or envisageable. If necessary and sufficient conditions for the application of a concept can be given, the concept is a closed one. But this can happen only in classical logic or mathematics where concepts are constructed and completely defined. It cannot occur with empirically descriptive and normative concepts unless we arbitrarily close them by stipulating the ranges of their uses.[9]

What is at issue is not factual analysis concerning necessary and sufficient properties but a decision as to whether a work under construction is similar in certain respects to other works already called for example, "novel," and which, therefore, warrants the extension of the term to cover the new case. "Is N a novel?" is not a factual but rather a decision problem, where the verdict turns on whether or not we enlarge our set of conditions for applying the concept.[10] "Art" itself is an open concept, for new conditions and cases have certainly arisen and will undoubtedly arise – new art forms, movements that will demand decisions on the part of those interested, usually professional critics, as to whether the concept should be extended or not. Weitz argues that the very expressive and adventurous character of art, its ever-present changes and novel conditions, make it logically impossible to ensure any set of defining properties. As we actually use the concept, "art" is both descriptive and evaluative. There are not necessary and sufficient conditions but there are strands of similarities, i.e. bundles of properties, some of which are criteria of recognition of works of art. Statements like "X is a work of art" and "was made by no one," or "was made by accident when he spilled paint on the canvas," in each case of which a normal condition is denied; are also sensible and capable of being true in certain circumstances. None of these criteria is a defining one, either necessary or sufficient, because we can sometimes assert of something that is a work of art and then go on to deny any one of these conditions, even the one that has traditionally been taken to be basic, namely that of being an artifact. For many theorists, "This is a work of art" does more than describe; it also praises. Its conditions of utterance, therefore include certain preferred properties or characteristics. What makes these honorific definitions valuable is not their disguised linguistic recommendations; rather it is the debates over the reasons for changing the criteria of the concept of art that are built into the definitions. If we take the aesthetic theories literally, they all fail, but if we reconstrue them in terms of their function and point as being serious, and argued for recommendations to concentrate on certain criteria of excellence in art, we shall see that aesthetic theory is far from worthless. It teaches us what to look for in art and how to look for it.

Weitz emphasizes that many, perhaps most, fundamental problems of aesthetics are conceptual, not empirical, and that some of the concepts of aesthetics are especially relevant to logic in its indigenous quest for the limits and scope of valid argument. Aesthetics invites logic to consider, if not ultimately to accommodate, certain irreducibly open concepts that do not simply dissolve into the traditional notions of ambiguity and vagueness.[11] The history of philosophy of the arts is, in large part, a history of successive competing affirmative answers to the question of whether there is a true theory of art, whereas Kennick and Weitz deny this. The problem, they insist, is not factual but conceptual. The concept of art, as its use reveals, is open, whereas a theory of art presupposes or entails the false claim that the concept of art is closed, governed by necessary and sufficient criteria. Weitz argues that "art" and it subconcepts, such as "novel," "drama," "music," "tragedy," "painting," and so forth, are employed either the describe or to evaluate certain objects, and that though this description or evaluation is dependent on certain criteria, these criteria are neither necessary nor sufficient. All, therefore, are open in the sense that they perform their descriptive and appraising jobs on the overall condition that new cases with their new properties can be accommodated by the addition of new criteria for those terms. The concept of art reflects this origination of the new which, until it occurs, is unpredictable. Since aesthetic concepts are also, and more radically, open in the sense that they must allow for the possibility of the rejection of any of the prevailing criteria as well, "This is a work of art" can be joined with "and it was made by no one," "and it is not an artifact," "and it was created by accident." With the help of Wittgenstein's talk about games, Weitz claims that we do not need a theory in order to argue intelligently about art. The doctrine, then, is one about the logical grammar of certain words or concepts, not about the less-than-essential ontology of things. But Tilghman argues that despite the considerable increase in debate, those who are skeptical about the role of theories in aesthetics have clearly been in the minority. The prevailing opinion seems to be that theories are not only possible but are essential to the philosophical enterprise of thinking about art and aesthetics.[12] In none of these contexts does the theory carry with it a high level of generality, and we can understand the theory only in particular contexts. Thus, we have to reject the assumption that behind our practices there is a latent essence that will make everything clear once it is brought to light, and no theory can help us to pick out works of art from things that are not works of art.

Soon after the second World War, Anglo-American aestheticians gave their field a dismal review and progress report: aesthetic theory was dismissed as being logically incapable of playing the roles in which it traditionally had been cast. In his 1964 essay, "The Artworld," Arthur Danto turned the tide for aesthetic theory by arguing that a decisive factor in determining whether any object counts as art is whether the history of the artworld has rendered the art public ready to accept the object as art. To see anything as art requires something the eye cannot descry – an atmosphere of artistic theory, a knowledge of the history of art; an artworld.[13] Likewise, the answer usually given to what it is to be creative, is that there is a "creative process," and most writers on creativity have taken their task to be a description of the kind of activity that takes place when one is acting creatively. Glickman, on the other hand, argues that one must attend to the aesthetic product rather than to the process.[14] To say an idea is an inspiration is to say that it is a good idea or the right idea, for if the idea is a poor one, it is not called an inspiration. But then there can be no characterization of inspiration in terms of the agent's feelings. It is likely that an artist might think he is creative when he is not. It is precisely because we do not call an activity creative unless the product is new and valuable that no characterization of reality simply in terms of the artist's actions, thoughts, and feelings can be adequate, for such a characterization cannot distinguish activity that results in a valuable new product from that which does not. Creating is not an insoluble activity; to know whether someone has created, we have to see (or be told about) the results of his work. We say that an activity such as painting, writing, or composing is creative if it achieves new and valuable results. In saying that the agent is creative, one is praising him for what he has accomplished, not for having gone through a special process in accomplishing it. "Creative" is a term of praise, but there is no specific sort of activity necessary or sufficient for producing things of value.[15] No one can tell at a glance which of two paintings or poems is the more creative. To tell this, one must be acquainted with comparable works of art and be able to appreciate the aesthetic significance of any artistic innovation, see how it enlarges the range of viable artistic alternatives.[16] There are creative painters, creative teachers, creative businessmen, creative mathematicians, and ascription of creativity implicitly compares what has been created to other things of similar kind and provenance. The driftwood case is illuminating because it shows that, although in Danto's view anything might become a work of art, this doesn't mean *anything goes;* rational argument has a place in formulating and assessing the theory that would extend the concept of art to some new kind of object.[17]

Margolis emphasizes that we individuate works of art in unusual ways. When an artist creates "beach art," he creates a type particular. Works of art are products of culturally informed labor, whereas objects are not. Thus, works of art are culturally emergent entities; their properties are what might be characterized as functional or intentional properties that include design, expressiveness, symbolism, representation, meaning, style, and the like.[18] Dickie insists that the descriptive use of "work of art" is used to indicate that a thing belongs to a certain category of artifacts. Nothing is said about actual appreciation, and this leaves open the possibility of works of art that, for whatever reason, are not appreciated. But many artifacts that are obviously not works of art are appreciated. Danto shows that there is more to being a work of art than what is visually apparent; it is a web of relations within which an object is enmeshed that makes it art, and the visually indistinguishable object that is not a work of art lacks these relations. We have to deal with a context that is rich, structured, and historical. Traditional theorists, in the view of Dickie, do not exploit the cultural and historical background from which art emerges; they proceed as if art is the result of individual initiative unrelated in any essential way to its cultural background.[19] Dickie concludes that the context or framework of art is institutional, a cultural practice that consists of a variety of roles of persons behaving in certain established ways. The artworld is not a formally organized body of some kind; rather it is a broad informal cultural practice. The various artworld activities, like painting, are rule-governed, but art *making* is not the only facet of the artworld. Ziff and Weitz conceived of the members of the class of artworks as having no common nature of any theoretical significance: the members of the class of works of art are created only by means of similarities. According to this view, an object becomes a work of art by sufficiently resembling a prior established work of art.[20] The reason that the traditional theories are easy prey for counterexamples is that the frameworks composed by these theories are too narrowly focused on the artist. Each of the traditional theories purports to describe an established practice. And in each case, the artists is seen as the creator of an artifact with a property such as being appreciative, being symbolic, or being an expression. What an artist understands and does when he creates an artwork far exceeds the simple understanding and doing entailed by the traditional theories.[21] The notion of a public always hovers at the background, and there are as many different publics as there are different arts. The knowledge required from one public is different from that required from another public. There are innumerable conventions involved in the creation and presentation of art but there is not one primary convention to which all the other conventions are secondary. The theater, painting, sculpture, and the like, are not ways of doing something that could be done in another way. What is primary is the understanding shared by all involved that they are engaged in an established practice within which there is a variety of roles: artist roles, critic roles, public roles, and so on. Our artworld consists of the totality of such roles, and these roles are subject to change. What the definitions of art reveal is that artmaking involves an intricate correlative structure, which cannot be described in a straightforward linear fashion envisaged by the ideal of non-circular definition. The inflected nature of art is also reflected by the way we learn about art, by being taught how to be an artist – how to draw pictures that can be displayed as well as how to be a member of the artworld public. Both approaches teach us about artists, works, and publics all at the same time, for these notions are not independent of one another.

Stecker criticizes Dickie mainly for failing to distinguish works of art from any other artifacts. He thinks that Dickie's new account turns out to be closer to the approach of those who claim that art cannot be defined than to Dickie's own later approach. Dickie fails to show that existing in an institutional framework is a necessary condition for being art.[22] Dickie acknowledges the circularity of the set of definitions, yet denies that this poses a problem. But unless artworld systems can be distinguished from nonart artifacts presentation systems, the framework Dickie gives us tells us no more than that art resembles many other kinds of artifacts. What has to be accepted is the arbitrariness of being an artwork system.[23] This is an admission to Stecker that there simply is no such thing as the nature of art – at least nothing that is sufficient for being art. Stecker argues that these definitions are unilluminating, since we cannot doubt that Duchamp's *Fountain* is an artifact but can doubt that it is a work of art. Dickie claims that institutional facts about art reveal a sufficient condition for being art, while at the same time admitting that the institution of art cannot be distinguished from other systems in an informative noncircular, nonarbitrary way. Stecker concludes that although Dickie does not acknowledge it, he is best construed as holding a position similar to the one he once opposed, vis., that the project of defining art is misconceived.[24] The concept of art that emerges from Dickie's account resembles Weitz's concept: what things turn out to be art is a function of practice, not a function of statable conditions for arthood.[25] It does have to be admitted that the concept of art in Dickie's view is not as *wide* open as is Weitz's. Part of our common understanding of art is that works of art are objects of value. The problem is that no one has ever succeeded in defining art in terms of the valuable qualities it has. Art is not a natural kind; it is a cultural kind. And it is often a feature of our cultural phenomena that are our collective conventions that they exhibit arbitrariness. Ted Cohen points out that if part of what makes a thing a work of art issues from an "institution" or "social practice," we need to be told something of the details of the institution. Art and its institutions are inbred and self-justifying in ways that are hard to disentangle. Dickie seems to believe that we are all, or nearly all, in the artworld, and that in the artworld everyone is empowered to make art. But Cohen insists that there must be a boundary, however hard to chart, between making art, and trying but failing to make art, and Dickie cannot account for this.[26] Blisek also emphasizes that it will be very difficult to determine what objects in the world are works of art if *everyone* who sees himself a member of the artworld can transform any object into a work of art simply by treating it as a candidate for appreciation. We merely would not know whether most of the objects we encounter had been so treated. Works of art would become a matter of private rather than public concern and the role of art in the culture would certainly be diminished. If membership in the artworld is extended to everyone who "sees himself as a member," there is no need to introduce a special institution (the artworld); the customary practice is likely to be diffuse, and the institution it defines ambiguous.[27] Dickie wants a clearly defined institution (in which case art is recognizable and public) and an open door for creativity. It appears however, that moving towards one aspect of this theory means moving away from the other. The artistic activity, according to Dickie, is equivalent to conferring status, but there is nothing in this theory by which to distinguish between appreciation in one art and appreciation in general. The more narrowly the artworld is defined, the more likely it is that the range of art will be limited.

Notes

[1] Patricia H. Werhane, ed., *Philosophical Issues in Art,* Englewood Cliffs, NJ: Prentice Hall, 1984, p. 436.

[2] John W. Bender, H. Gene Blocker, eds., *Contemporary Philosophy of Art,* Englewood Cliffs, NJ: Prentice Hall, 1993, p. 124.

[3] William E. Kennick, "Does Traditional Aesthetics Rest on a Mistake?" in *Contemporary Philosophy of Art,* p. 137a.

[4] *Ibid.*

[5] *Ibid.,* p. 137b.

[6] Stuart Hampshire, "Logic and Appreciation," in *Aesthetics and Language*, ed. W. Elton, Oxford: 1954, p. 162.

[7] Kennick, "Does Traditional Aesthetics Rest on a Mistake?" p. 143a.

[8] Morris Weitz, "The Role of Theory in Aesthetics," in *Philosophical Issues in Art*, p, 450.

[9] *Ibid.*

[10] *Ibid.*, p. 451.

[11] Morris Weitz, "Art as an Open Concept," in *Aesthetics*, eds. G. Dickie, R. Sclafani, and R. Roblin, St. Martins, NY: 1989, p. 152.

[12] Benjamin R. Tilghman, "Reflections on Aesthetic Theory," in *Aesthetics*, p. 160.

[13] Arthur Danto, "The Artworld," *The Journal of Philosophy*, vol. 61 (1964), pp. 571-584.

[14] Jack Glickman, "Creativity in the Arts," in *Philosophy Looks at the Arts*, ed. J. Margolis, Philadelphia, PA: Temple University Press, 1987, p. 168.

[15] *Ibid.*, p. 174.

[16] W.E. Kennick, "Creative Arts," in *Art and Philosophy*, New York, NY: 1964, p. 225.

[17] Glickman, "Creativity in the Arts," p. 182.

[18] Joseph Margoplis, "The Ontological Peculiarity of Works of Art," in *Contemporary Philosophy of Art*, p. 321b.

[19] George Dickie, "The Return of Art Theory," in *Philosophical Issues in Art*, p. 471.

[20] George Dickie, "The New Institutional Theory of Art," in *Aesthetics*, p. 197.

[21] *Ibid.*, p. 201.

[22] Robert Stecker, "The End of an Institutional Definition of Art," in *Aesthetics*, p. 206.

[23] George Dickie, *The Art Circle*, New York, NY: 1984, p. 77.

[24] Stecker, "The End of an Institutional Definition of Art," p. 209.

[25] *Ibid.*, p. 210.

[26] Ted Cohen, "The Possibility of Art," in *Philosophical Issues in Art*, p. 487.

[27] William L. Blizek, "An Institutional Theory of Art," *Contemporary Philosophy of Art*, p. 220a.

Chapter Thirty-Two

Art and Progress

Roberts argues that the emergence of the aesthetic in the second half of the eighteenth century signaled a new stage in the historical self-reflection of modern art. It announces the crisis and the end of art in Hegel, and at the same time denies that art itself has become theoretical. The second critical turn arises in the first decades of the twentieth century, signaled by the collapse of perspective in painting and tonality in music. But modernism is a term that has become increasingly indeterminate.[1] Art since the first World War has brought to an end the preceding five hundred years of ordered sequential change. We have now entered a period characterized not by a linear cumulative development of a single style, but the coexistence of a multiplicity of quite different styles in a fluctuating and dynamic steady state.[2] Functionalism and historicism are both responses to the revolutionary break that reduced the European tradition to freely disposable material, open to recombination as rational organization or parodistic quotation. The radical impulse of modernism and its critical dominance had to succumb to its own contradictions. The multiplicity of styles and tendencies renders aesthetic theory as we know it from Kant to Adorno no longer possible, for what comes after post-avant-garde art defies aesthetic theory. Hegel's verdict on the end of art does not mean that art ceases to be produced, but that it can no longer claim or retain our highest interest.[3] This explains, according to Roberts, why Hegel may justly be considered the godfather of postmodernism. Atonal music and abstract painting register in our time unmistakably the end of the European tradition. It is expressed in the unique development of music from *ars nova* to Gustav Mahler, and of painting from Giotto to Cézanne. These are significantly European arts, and have no parallel elsewhere. The abandonment of tonality corresponded to that of philosophical idealism, for the crisis of the new music is at the same time a crisis of theory.[4] The prospect of unending progress revealed, however, the cunning of reason as the cunning of the devil. Progress ends for Adorno's philosophy of music in the "satanic parody" of nihilism. The self-understanding of the modern age as movement from the physics of the seventeenth century to the historical materialism of the nineteenth century is thus driven to absurdity in Adorno's view. Art falls victim to the terminal logic of the enlightenment.[5] Leonard Meyer argues that the end of the Western paradigm of art history, dominant since the seventeenth century, is tied up with the demise of the idea of progress. The end point of this dialectic is *indifference* the avant-garde is an end that is no end. What we might call the crisis of art in Hegel's theory becomes the crisis of theory itself in Lukács and Adorno. And yet for Hegel, Adorno, and Bürger, the postmodern situation of art is the outcome of progress, of enlightenment. The predicament of contingency in modern art signals the need for a change of paradigm. Art becomes its own metatheory since aesthetic theory can no longer claim a vantage point beyond art.

The new music is, for Adorno, aesthetic philosophy: music and dialectic belong together.[6] Music, no less than architecture, mathematics, bureaucratic organization, systematic theology, or economic calculation is for Max Weber part of the history of occidental reason, a process of development unique to Europe. The pluralization of value spheres and the consequent multiplication of partial conditions simultaneously disenchant the world and create an irrational polytheistic universe. Since the middle of the nineteenth century all consensus of taste has disappeared, and the new music exists in a social vacuum. Development – that is, the subjective reflection of the theme – becomes the justifying impulse and center of dynamic form, whose potentiality unfolds in the dialectic of identity (theme) and nonidentity (variation). Progress comes to self-knowledge in philosophy, and what is left is the fragmentary work. The dialectic of enlightenment drives Adorno on to negation as the sole expression of freedom. Progress and reaction converge into the indifference of time and space. *Aesthetic Theory*[7] is Adorno's Endgame, since nothing significant can happen anymore. Unconcerned with development as it is commonly understood, Beckett views his task in an infinitely small space, ultimately an one-dimensional point. It is also transdynamic in that it "marks time," shuffling its feet and, thereby, confessing to the uselessness of dynamics. Since the potential for freedom is scuttled by social conditions, it cannot come to the fore in art either. All history becomes the record of the fall, whereas progress has been the concept that expresses the self-understanding of the bourgeois age. It enabled Hegel to view the philosophy of history as the progress to freedom. By contrast, for both Lukács and Adorno, modernity (the postmodern) lies beyond progress, reason, and history. The dialectic of the rational/ irrational ends in the indifference of Adorno's and Hochheimer's "universal system of delusion" in which it is no longer possible to distinguish between reason and myth. It had originated in the understanding of form as an inner-directed, self-evolving system, in which each part is respectively means and end, "purposedness without purpose," (Kant), the expression of "inner truth and necessity" (Goethe), that is the source of both Adorno's and Lukács's conception of a work of art. Adorno has no place for the new versions of "mechanical" order – the aggregations of *montage* in which the organizing primacy of the whole is surrendered to the parts.[8]

The contemporary rejection of the ideal of progress had started with Spengler's thesis on the decline of Western culture as an inescapable fate. It is in explicit opposition to the Enlightenment idea of universal history as the self-understanding of the modern age. To Spengler's macrocosm of a culture corresponds Adorno's microcosm of a work of art. Just as for Lukács history comes to self-knowledge in the proletariat, so for Adorno musical history realizes its own nature in the twelve-tone music of Schoenberg. Adorno, however, destroys dialectical reason; his negative dialectics detaches itself completely from history to circle endlessly in the iron cage of timeless modernity. In Adorno's negative dialectics, abstract form confronts totally opaque content. Progress is Adorno's immanent absolute, the logic of historical necessity, which completes and destroys history. It is thus a retrospective category: Adorno's model of progress is tied to the end of tradition, which in turn becomes the endless crisis of tradition, as European progress ended in World War. Adorno's adoption of the bourgeois principle of individuation forces him to condemn modern art with few exceptions. For him, neoclassicism and surrealism are complementary aspects of the arbitrary association of the incongruous. Unlike any previous school of painting or music, they are defined not by style but by the alienation from content (the pregiven model or materials). Roberts points out that if Stravinsky epitomizes for Adorno the abdication of music to painting, Kandinsky, by contrast, was strongly inspired by Schoenberg and thought of painting as music.[9] Like Schoenberg, Stravinsky, too, is in search of order, that is, an obligatory style that would make composition possible again. But Roberts points out that the final result of this play with the past adds up to no more than a gigantic quotation.[10] Boulez would like to explain the fascination that the "world of quotation" exerted over the most brilliant minds in the twentieth century. Fear of regression is an eminently modern phenomenon, a reaction to the advancing rationalization progress. Already Hegel predicted a free disposition over forms and objects after the "end of art," and this process becomes cogent when there is no longer a generally binding system of symbols.[11] As ever in art, theory lags behind practice; the postmodernist debates of the last twenty years in aesthetic theory are a belated recognition of what twentieth century art has been demonstrating for some seventy years. The division between "modernism" and "postmodernism" is artificial in that both are themselves reflections of the postmodern situation. Although we can distinguish "modernist" and "postmodernist" positions in contemporary critical *discussions,* it does not follow that we can identify recent *art* as "postmodernist." There is no agreement on what would constitute postmodernism in contemporary painting, music, or literature. The familiar argument that anything and everything goes is impossible to sustain in practice.

The emergence of an autonomous aesthetic sphere in the eighteenth century sets in train a system-immanent process of differentiation (rationalization), which progressively eliminates content and whose endpoint is the doctrine and practice of art for art's sake. The development of art in bourgeois society can be grasped from the vantage point of the avant-garde, but not the other way round. Music remains the clearest example of rationalization, just as painting can be taken as the most obvious specimen for the disappearance of content. Without the assumption that postmodernism is a new, systematic, cultural norm, we fall back into the view of present history as sheer heterogeneity, random difference, a coexistence of a host of distinct forces whose efficiency is undecideable.[12] Progress as viewed from this final perspective allows Jameson simultaneously to assert progress and catastrophe (the end of difference). Whereas the idea of a ruling class was once the dominant ideology of bourgeois society, the advanced capitalist conventions today are a field of stylistic and discursive heterogeneity.[13] Roberts concludes that the norm of postmodernism is no norm. There is the poststrucrualist dissolution of depth models of hermeneutics, the dialectical model of essence and appearance, the psychoanalytical model of the latent and the manifest, and the existentialist model of authenticity and inauthenticity. All of these enter into combination with the schema of progress and decline. If we cannot distinguish essence and appearance, the appearance becomes essence; and similarly with the latent and the manifest, and the authentic and the inauthentic. Pastiche represents a world transformed into sheer images of itself; it is the world of surface, spectacle, pseudo-event, simulacrum. But where there is no depth, there can be no signifying surface either, and parody becomes a quixotic gain. "Progress" from metaphysical depth to blank surface transforms modernist art into identity without mystery or the scandal of modernism.

In *The Postmodern Condition,*[14] Jean François Lyotard argues that the postmodern condition is defined by the recognition of an irreducible plurality of language games, the consequence of exhaustion of the grand narratives of modernity and its epistemologies of representation. By *modern* Lyotard understands any sense that legitimizes itself by reference to some metanarrative, whether it be the dialectics of the spirit, the emancipation of the subject, the hermeneutics of meaning, or even their negation, as in the negative dialectics of Adorno. Such nihilism means the collapse of all criteria for judging a musical work, the breakdown of the traditional limits that insured the standards that separated the authentic and the inauthentic. It is a non-Hegelian dialectic because the totality is missing, and because there is no overarching good to reconcile; it thus becomes a "satanic" work in the opinion of Lyotard. The irrational limit is the sign of the self-destruction of the dialectical model, the completion of the grand narrative of the European modern age. Postmodernism is not the immanent critique of modernism but its indifferent parody. And yet "postmodernity" in art is for Hegel, Adorno, and Bürger the product of the progress of enlightenment. This rupture is both the historical and the logical ground for paradigm change. Indifference is the vanishing point of aesthetic progress; this failure of dialogue is the result of contingency conceptualized negatively as indifference. That is why Roberts returns to Hegel and German romanticism in order to reopen the dialogue terminated by Adorno, that is, the model of literature rather than music. Roberts proposes an alternative reconstruction of the enlightenment in which the vanishing point of indifference becomes the ground for paradigm change – the emancipation of contingency. It is the recognition of the historically contingent nature of social structures, institutions, and systems, which may be considered a general condition of modernity. The freedom of modernity dissolves into a split between subject and object, the inner world of reflection and the external world of objects. What Hegel already registered as the problematic condition of art in modern times becomes evident in the crisis of modern tradition at the beginning of the twentieth century. In postmodern music and painting, the collapse of the progressive paradigm of art history becomes manifest. The freedom of the artist is no longer limited by tradition; rather it has become the problematic consciousness of potentially unlimited, experimental alternatives. It gives us a new indeterminate paradigm in which the work of art is no longer conceived as essence but as virtuality.

Thus, the social function of modern literature is to present and explore alternatives to the given order of society through the multi-plication of imaginary models of reality, of possible experiences and actions. Reality is pluralized in the form of critical, utopian, dystopian, or fantastic alternatives. The freedom of literature – the fictionalization (or rendering contingent) of its truth-claims enables it to demonstrate the contingency of something without, thereby, calling society in question.[15] The emancipation of literature from social control is a slow process; it covers the long period of transition from hierarchically stratified to functionally organized society. Roberts opposes Hegel's and Adorno's terminal dialectic of enlightenment, an open-ended model that takes us from a determinate to an indeterminate realm of art. To literature's pluralization of reality corresponds the pluralization of perception in painting, which multiplies the possible worlds of vision, and the pluralization of audition in music, which multiplies the possible worlds of sound. The crisis of tradition in painting and music is related to the "age of mechanical reproduction" – Benjamin's version of the "death of art" – but is also the medium of Malraux's concept of world art.[16] The progress of art requires latency and destroys latency; all that is secret and mysterious (i.e. unilluminated, blind to itself, unconscious) is brought to self-consciousness and leads to the self-critique of art. All structures represent selections that exclude other possibilities since certain things must remain unconscious to persons and institutions if they are to function. Structures incorporate contingency by recognizing the equivalence of alternative problem situations. The emergence of radical critique in the eighteenth century (the search for radical social order) and the radical practice in the nineteenth century (revolutionary social change) must, therefore, be seen in its relation to the problem of latency and progress. As Luhmann expresses it, echoing Brecht, "If something does not work, something else will."[17]

It is not surprising that idealist aesthetics, which privileges the autonomy of the artwork, has remained indifferent or hostile to the practice of parody as a critique of "authenticity" and aura. In traditional stratified society, parody expresses the possibility of reversal. In *Don Quixote,* the ironic ambiguities of enchantment and disenchantment, lament and liberation, govern the emerging world of prose. The rise of the novel, which accompanies the decline of the classical genres (the verse epic, tragedy), is above all a result of the openness and indeterminacy of its form, which makes it the typical medium of social contingency, the chronicle of the vicissitudes of the individual facing an increasingly alien and problematic reality. It also leads to the self-thematization of the progressively autonomous system of literature, literature motivated by literature, literature criticized by literature.[18] Irony plunges the artwork into endless ambiguities of interpretation, and parody is transformed from oppositional criticism from below into internalized self-critique. In the modern age, even the Devil is coopted by progress: the principle of negation (Goethe's Mephisto) is made to serve higher ends, but the unconscious-made-conscious brings progress to an end. Freedom is now the recognition of contingency, and this is the question of postmodern art.[19] Forms as well as contents of all previous art are now freely and indifferently available. If freedom has become the recognition of contingency, it transposes the dialectic of freedom and necessity into the problematic of indeterminism, in other words, the change from a determinate to an indeterminate system.[20] Schoenberg's technique of composing with twelve tones is Adorno's example for the pure rationalism that seeks to overcome the threat of contingency. Other examples are the renewal of painting through the spirit of geometry (Mondrian, Schlemmer), the search for pure sculptural forms or, more generally, abstract painting as the emancipation of pure surface or color, the insistence on the total self-reference of the artwork. The other main response Roberts calls *impure irrationalism.* Here the recognition of contingency takes the form not of a rationally posited order but as the chance of disorder, as a source of new latentness. We find it in the widespread recourse to primitivism and the archaic, the fascination with the darkness of mystery and madness, the prerational. The surrealists adopted Freud's "logic" of the unconscious in their work, the arbitrary connections (free associations, dream images), the mysterious power of coincidence. Surrealist combination techniques appear in collage and montage, which explore the possibilities of the assembly of materials. They are the source of the paradoxes of postmodern art. The deconstruction of appearance produces the paradox of an open system in which apparently anything can be art and everyone an artist. John Cage's "Four minutes and thirty three seconds of silence," or Beckett's "Breathing" are gestures of challenge. The question, art/nonart, cannot be decided as long as order remains indeterminate. A juxtaposition of discrete contingent chains of events, the acceleration or slowing down of time, the simultaneity of multiple personalities that we find in montage, register the relativities and multiple interferences of the diverse artistic media. Montage is based on technology, not nature; the montage work reflects and responds to the transformation of industrial society to the age of mass production and reproduction that have destroyed the ideology of the bourgeois personality and the unique work.[21] Facing an increasingly complex world, montage becomes the organizing principle that permits the assimilation of heterogeneity in the form of the indeterminate work, and that dissolves the form/content dialectic into the relation of its elements. The dehumanization multiplicity of dimensions and materials signals the end of teleological integration.

Robert's example for the change of traditions is the work of Brecht who was convinced that bourgeois society was bankrupt and that its tradition had been exhausted. The problem art/nonart becomes critical once the boundaries of tradition collapse. Science alone for Brecht transcends the limits of bourgeois consciousness by overcoming the illusory viewpoint of individuation. The presumed knowledge of the laws of society, the dynamics of social movement and motivation is intended to eliminate the prescientific dichotomy between individual freedom and social determinism, exchange and law. The laws of society form the deep structure of social being, which must be brought to consciousness through estrangement in order to reveal the historicity (contingency) of all social formation. This puts all action and speech within quotation marks. It subverts not only the naive illusion of representation but, equally, the separate identity of art and life. Only by treating reality as "literature," by quoting it, can its otherness, its contingency, be demonstrated.[22] This assault on all hierarchies and boundaries opens the era of postmodern art. Henceforth, art enters into an alienating relation to tradition, cut off, as in montage, from its origins, context and "intrinsic" meaning – the wealth of tradition has become freely convertible.[23] The primacy of method means that everything can be adapted, translated, retooled. The image-become-simulacrum signifies for Baudrillard the triumph of appearance (surface) and the disappearance of the illusion of depth. We have learned that meaning is unstable, and that the reign of enlightenment was ephemeral. What the enlightenment sought to dissipate – appearances – that alone is immortal.[24] But Roberts points out that Baudrillard's version of enlightenment is itself a myth due to the logic of indifference. The simulacrum is the truth of the trans-political in which all that is latent must surrender its secrets in the glare and publicity of communication.[25] That is why the image and the pseudo-events of public relations cannot be deconstructed or parodied. And this is also the reason why the visual media are so fascinated by the spontaneous, the naive, the private. Politics is now openly part of the spectacle, treated cynically by both actors and spectators. The "deceptions" of the political system are endlessly discussed and dissected in terms of the all too familiar criteria of credibility. It is a system that takes a sophisticated and cynical audience for granted.

Benjamin in his "Theses on the Philosophy of History" adopts a historical materialism that rejects both legacies of the nineteenth century; progress and historicism. We wait in vain for the messianic-revolutionary redemption of mankind. The discovery of the past was the achievement of the modern age; it was subsumed, however, under the progressive perspective of universal history. Benjamin proposes two contradictory versions of emancipation of the past: secularization and redemption. Reproduction emancipates for the first time in world history the code of the artist from its parasitic existence in and as ritual, whose final expression was the theology of art for art's sake. In this progression from depth to surface, the whole function of art is revolutionized. Mass reproduction together with the new techniques of reproduction in film, brings art close to the masses. Beethoven is more our contemporary than he was for the Vienna of his time. It is the move from European to world culture that has brought with it an enormous expansion of horizons and a corresponding openness and indeterminacy of the boundaries of art. Picasso did not see African masks with the same eyes as those for whom they were intended.[26] Meyer argues that art since the First World War has brought to an end the preceding five hundred years of ordered sequential change. We have entered a period of stylistic statis, a period characterized not by the linear development of a single fundamental style, but the coexistence of a multiplicity of quite different styles. Past and present are chronologically separate but epistemologically equal.[27] The pluralism of styles reflects the diversity of perception and taste, the loss of a cohesive audience for serious painting, music, and literature since 1914. Danto's starting point is also the collapse in the first decade of this century of what he calls the progressive model of art history, most evident in painting and sculpture.[28] Since then, art has been characterized by a history of discontinuities in which each new movement presupposes some sort of theoretical understanding. The crisis of tradition − the collapse of the progressive paradigm of art history − opens for Danto the posthistorical stage of art. Once the question of the philosophical nature of art has been posed from within art − Danto's key example is Duchamp's ready-makes − art becomes philosophy. There is no further place to go; having reached the point where art can be anything at all, art has exhausted its conceptual mission. Endless reflection on the end of tradition is thus the critical condition of aesthetic modernity.[29] Roberts concludes that the vanishing point of progress is equally the vanishing point of theory. What this "endgame" of enlightenment leaves behind is not only the suicide of aesthetic art but also the endless paradoxes of Adorno's negative aesthetics, or what Baudrillard has described as the position of objective irony − the vanishing point of discourse itself.

Notes

[1] David Roberts, *Art and Enlightenment, Aesthetic Theory after Adorno*, Lincoln, NE: University of Nebraska, 1991, p. 3.

[2] Leonard Meyer, *Music, the Arts, and Ideas: Patterns and Predictions in Twentieth Century Culture*, Chicago, IL: University of Chicago Press, 1967, p. 98.

[3] Georg Wilhelm Friedrich Hegel, *The Philosophy of Fine Art*, trans. F. Osmaston, 4 vols, New York, NY: Hacker Fine Art, vol. 1, pp. 125-44.

[4] Roberts, *Art and Enlightenment*, p. 14.

[5] *Ibid.*, p. 16.

[6] Theodor Adorno, *Philosophy of Modern Music*, trans. Anne G. Mitchell and Wesley V. Blomster, New York, NY: Seabury Press, 1973.

[7] Theodor Adorno, *Aesthetic Theory*, trans. C. Lenhardt, London: Routledge and Kegan Paul, 1984.

[8] *Ibid.*, p. 232.

[9] Roberts, *Art and Enlightenment*, p. 119.

[10] *Ibid.*, p. 121.

[11] Peter Bürger, "The Decline of the Modern Age," *Telos* 62, (1984-85), p. 129.

[12] Frederic Jameson, "Postmodernism, or the Cultural Logic of Late Capitalism," *New Left Review* 146 (July/August 1984), p. 57.

[13] *Ibid.*, p. 65.

[14] Jean Francois Lyotard, *The Postmodern Condition: A Report on Knowledge*, trans. Geoff Bennington and Brian Massumi, University of Minnesota Press, 1984.

[15] Siegfried J. Schmidt, *Die Selbstorganisation des Sozialsystems Literatur im 18 Jarhundert*, Frankfort, Germany: Suhrkamp, 1989, pp. 21-22.

[16] Roberts, *Art and Enlightenment*, p. 116.

[17] Niklas Luhman, *Soziale Systeme, Grundriss einer allgemeinen Theorie*, Frankfort, Germany: Suhrkamp, 1985, pp. 21-22.

[18] Roberts, *Art and Enlightenment*, p. 168.

[19] *Ibid.*, p. 174.

[20] *Ibid.*, p. 175.

[21] *Ibid.*, p. 183.

[22] *Ibid.*, p. 190.

[23] *Ibid.*, p. 191.

[24] Jean Baudrillard, *Simulacres et simulation*, Paris, France: Galilée, 1981, p. 236.

[25] Roberts, *Art and Enlightenment*, p. 202.

[26] André Malraux, *Museum without Walls*, trans. Stuart Gilbert and Francis Price, London: Secker and Warburg, 1967, pp. 208-9.

[27] Meyer, *Music, the Arts, and Ideas*, p. 151.

[28] Arthur C. Danto, *The Philosophical Disenfranchisement of Art*, New York, NY: Columbia University Press, 1986, p. 90.

[29] Roberts, *Art and Enlightenment*, p. 226.

Chapter Thirty-Three

Art and Alienation

McEvilley argues that religious reverence for aura was presupposed by both the great artworks and the great critical writings of the modernist period. The intense reverence of the original masterpiece was based on it. But under the influence of Walter Benjamin, Theodor Adorno, and other European thinkers in the Marxist tradition, artists began to point to the socioeconomic set surrounding the canvas as well as to the rest of aesthetic forces operating within it. Artists themselves began to take over the critical function, for dogmas were seen as support of the ruling groups, as the expression of the will to power, seeking to enforce conceptual closure. The history of Western culture is marked by the continuing struggle between the forces of dogma supporting claims for authority, and criticism undermining them.[1] From the Earl of Shaftesubry to Clement Greenberg, the worship of the faculty of taste is the disguised form of Platonic doctrine of unchanging soul, which the rational and scientific culture of the Enlightenment had relegated to the periphery of practical affairs, that is, to the realm of art. Rejections of change function as buttresses of existing power structures. Greenberg maintained that visual art should confine itself exclusively to what is given in the visual experience and make no reference to anything given in other orders of experience.[2] Content, to be believed, must become strictly optical and be dissolved completely into form.[3] The impossible idea of pure form (form without content) quickly became an absolute. This project is rooted in the Romantic tradition and in Neoplatonism, which yearned to see the artwork as transcendentally far beyond the web of conditionally. Spurred on by a desire for a sacred in a secular age, the enterprise took a quasi-religious aura. Artworks were to be granted a self-validating status, but McEvilley points out that the claim for freedom from any plane of content whatever is a contradiction in terms. The claim is unprecisely and incompletely made because the formalists take a much too narrow view of what can constitute "content." What is not representational in the sense of recognizable objects, persons, and places may well be representational in other senses. It may be bound to the surrounding world by its reflection of structures of thought, political tensions, psychological attitudes, and so forth.[4]

Jackson Pollock is one of Greenberg's prime examples of the artist whose work is supposedly "pure," and without semantic function. J. Campbell, however, reads Action Rhythm as a cosmological diagram of flux and indeterminacy, as at times Pollock himself seems to have done.[5] Piet Mondrian was Greenberg's foremost example of an artist whose work is set over against the extra-pictorial references of old-time illusionist art. But McEvilley emphasizes that Mondrian was not the first to demonstrate that art can survive without representing recognizable objets, persons, and places. He was preceded by the abstract artists of the Paleolithic, Neolithic, and Bronze ages, and by later Tantric and Islamic artists who eliminated this type of representation in favor of abstract quadrature, heraldic symmetry, monochromy, and so forth. In fact, abstract painting is a practice that precedes our species; for the earliest known examples are Neanderthal finger paintings. In these older traditions, content was read comfortably from abstract form, and the ideas produced by these premodern abstract artists are widely interpreted as representing ideas about reality.[6] While nonrepresentational in terms of physical objects, these works have clear metaphysical or ontological content.[7] McEvilley argues that, in much the same way, Mondrian's mature paintings can be read as presenting a model of the real: they suggest a geometrically ordered universe made up of a flow of unchanging and universal elements which shifts their arrangements to create the impression of changing particulars. Pollock models reality as indefinite and in perpetual flux, whereas Yves Klein presents a counterview of reality as unified and fundamentally static. Marxist critics have insisted that any act (including any art act) is saturated with political meaning; each act is grounded in a subtext of implied assumptions about the nature of reality. This hypothesis that a work of art is a proposal about what is real might explain why art that people don't like makes them so angry.[8]

When Harold Rosenberg wrote that "paintings are today apprehended with the ears,"[9] he was revising Greenberg's entirely-through-the-eyes approach, and pointing to the plain fact that verbal supplements are of universal importance in relating to art. Much interpretation masquerades as description, and much avowedly formalist criticism contains hidden references that cannot escape content. This is most obvious in the widespread cult slogan of "art for art's sake." It is very doubtful that any cultural object, being a product of human consciousness, can exist except in a web of intentions and meanings.[10] The relationship between form and content is one of universal concomitance, that is, neither of them ever appears without the other. The same relationship exists between any paired terms, such as cause and effect, up and down, right and left, and does not in the least mean that we cannot distinguish one from the other, but rather that the existence of the one always implies the existence of the other. Ultimately, the idea that reference and associations are to be excluded from the art experience is naive. Obviously art experience is conditioned by what one knows, by what one has learned to expect, and by what one likes. The experience of a work of art depends not only on the natural sensitivity and visual training of the spectator, but also on his cultural equipment. Language seems to provide a background stratum against which every mental and perceptual event takes place. If that is the case, then it is impossible that we could ever achieve a "purely optical" experience of a work of art. In several ways it is clearly impossible to exclude the artist's intentions from the critical process. The critic should at least know the approximate date of the work, and this information is, of course, biographical and intentionalistic. Even more basic is our awareness of the genre of the work: we are asking really whether the artist intended it as a painting, or a poem, or whatever.[11] If the form/content relationship is unmotivated, a limitless number of possible interpretations exists, none more firmly bound to the artwork than any other. But texts impose constraints and limits upon their interpretation. Of course, not every viewer will experience the work with the same feeling-tone and the same associations, yet within these variable limits some connections will be widely recognized as appropriate and others not. There are thus limits to interpretation, even though the artists can sometimes willfully override this correlation, thereby introducing levels of tension into his work.

McEvilley concludes that once we recognize that artworks exist in the world and are of it, we are driven to a multimodel approach to criticism. Such an approach recognizes the work as a complex in which different semantic realities coexist and interpenetrate without interfering with one another. Criticism is not a metalanguage above art, but just another game on the same level with similar motives and satisfactions. Like art, it operates on constantly shifting foundations, peaking in flashes of special insight. Ultimately the workshop of form as an absolute is a distant resonance of the Pythagorean/Platonic doctrine of the music of the spheres. McEvilley points out that the doctrine of the soul has always been an argument for unchanging totalitarianism – from the Old Kingdom in Egypt to the aristocratic Plato to the divine right of kings in eighteenth century Europe. But soulism did not simply disappear, it crept into art and hid there. From the Cambridge Platonists to Shaftesbury, Kant and Clement Greenberg, it would now be called the faculty of taste. This soulism in art was soon joined by an equally myth-based view of history that became the foundation of art: that history is driving toward this or that end, and that past events could only have happened as they did. Spirit expressed itself through art, which was, as Hegel said, "the sensuous appearance of the absolute."

We tend to feel that representation works by a recognizable element of objective resemblance, but it seems more accurate to say that what we experience as representation is, like aesthetic taste, a culturally conditioned habit-response not involving objective resemblance. The resemblance we seem to see between pictures and nature does not result from the fact that art imitates nature, but from the fact that our perception of nature imitates our perception of art. Just as it seems that we cannot think anything that our language cannot formulate, so it seems that we cannot see anything that our pictorial tradition does not include or imply.[12] The fact that Greenberg used Pollock's work as proof of the idea of contentless painting is now part of the content of these paintings.[13] A Pollock drip painting asserts flux and indefiniteness of identity as qualities that can be found in the world. Thus, abstract art, far from being nonrepresentational, is in effect a representation of concepts; it is based on a process like that of metaphor, and overlaps somewhat with both iconography and representation.[14] Conflict between all these levels can occur, and the artwork thereby gains yet another level involving paradox, inner struggle, tension, and the negation of meaning processes. By contrast, works that exhibit a high degree of harmony or mutual confirmation among the various levels of content tacitly model the real as integrated, whole, and rich in meaning, somewhat in the manner of the traditional masterpiece.[15] What is essential, according to McEvilley, is that we begin to appreciate the complexity of what we do when we relate to an artwork. Far from being a "purely optical" and unmediated reflex, the art event is an infinitely complex semiotic bead game involving many different levels and directions of meaning. One of the great achievements of antiformalist periods of twentieth century Western art is precisely their deliberate foregrounding of categories of content that had been working on us unnoticed for so long.[16]

The recent history of content may be described (on one level) as expressing a constantly intensified attention to the question of representation. So-called abstract art challenged the (discredited) inherited canon of representation and explored new ones that, since they differed from the established type of representation, were not recognized as representation at all. Kant asserted that these three human faculties (aesthetic, cognitive, and practical) were independent of one another. This meant that no verbal (i.e. cognitive) formulation could ever approach the aesthetic experience. Largley under the influence of this doctrine, formalist critics from Benedetto Croce to Clement Greenberg denied the appropriateness of any acknowledgment of content whatever. But in written supplements in the form of titles, interviews, essays, and catalogue statements, artists like Kandinsky, Rothko, and Mondrian rejected in effect the pure form analysis of their work and specified the contents they intended it to carry. This is why critics in the heyday of formalism insisted that one should never listen to artists. John Dewey stressed that with reason, pragmatism, and good will, communication can identify and solve human problems. History, in this view, is regarded as a process of problem solving driven by an inner imperative towards progress. This ideology arose under Greek influence in the eighteenth century, and gained momentum in the nineteenth century from an uncritical extension of Darwinism from biological to cultural affairs and processes. But such appreciation has flourished mainly in democracies, and the opposite stance – an attempt to make change appear taboo or unnatural – has characterized cultures with hereditary rulers or self-perpetuating ruling cliques. Modernism arose in the context of a positivistic democracy carried away by a sense of its ability to solve all social and cultural problems. Traditions that developed over centuries were discarded almost casually on the historicist assumption that something better would inevitably replace them. The intellectual origin of this approach is to be found in the sophists who were the first to state publicly that convention is not a binding law. A period in which traditions are destroyed is apt to be followed by a period of nostalgic longing for them, and by attempts to reconstruct them. The guilt of having destroyed them is allayed by incorporating them into the very context of their destruction.

McEvilley admits that postmodernism amounts to a failure of nerve, but he still rejects as a superstition the idea that cultural history is inherently progressive. The flaw in modernism was precisely its conviction that it was not quoting and varying but creating. Quoting is an inevitable component of all acts of communication; it is what makes communication possible. Communication operates upon a foundation of habits, that is, codes shared between the senders and the receivers of these messages. Every message is a quotation or allusion to a mass of past messages in the same code that have established the habits of recognition. Communication not based on quoting is a mythic ideal, like the innocent eye; both are part of the myth of Eden, an ahistorical condition in which everything happens for the first time. In most acts of communication, the quoting is in the background; it functions almost invisibly, the better to foreground the specific present message. Such an experience teaches one the relativity of one's own values or produces a xenophobic reaction designed to avoid that realization. Roland Barthes likened the impersonality of semiotic transmission to the "death of the author:" it is not an individual who speaks, but language that speaks through the individual.[17] In the same sense, it is not the individual who makes images, but the vast reservoir of world culture that imagines itself forth through the individual. To that extent, art based on quoting postulates the artist as a channel as much as a source, and negates or diminishes the idea of Romantic creativity. If we feel a conscientious resistance to quoting, it may be because we cherish an essentialist prejudice about what art should be. Our ability to see things as they are is affronted by quoting, as is the ultimately myth-based conviction of a historical inevitability.

Modern American culture has inherited the Platonic-Christian concept of an eternal soul as its most common presupposition about the self; the idea of the unique value of the individual and his or her moral or aesthetic decisions is a somewhat secularized version of it.[18]

The same soul concept that opposed Darwinism opposes artificial intelligence for similar reasons. The traditional Western idea of the self as an underlying essence feels threatened by all these critiques. The soul is removed from the process of evolution, and defends itself by declaring it irrelevant. Language, the collective unconscious, the historical dialectic, natural selection, the double helix, all have acquired something of a metaphysical status. For the self, which transpires through the melting and merging of intricate transpersonal patterings, the idea of freedom becomes ambiguous or even ironic. Modern thought has evolved a composite view of the self as a shifting ripple in the Heraclitean river, a view that has much in common with Buddhist psychology.[19] But one person's enlightenment is another's dehumanization.[20] McEvilley believes that it is precisely the authoritarian claims of the soul that have rendered Christianity and Islam among the most violent and repressive traditions in history. The goal is to rearrange one's relation to language so that the metaphor of selfhood is not constantly presupposed in one's thinking. Fascination with the unique object is another disguised Edenic myth; questions of originality and authenticity of the creative artwork depend on the belief in the integrity and creative freedom of the self that produced it as a trace of the soul.

The Graeco-Roman tradition has been on the whole positivistic and critical, emphasizing doubt over faith and empirical investigation over inspiration. The Judeo-Christian tradition, on the other hand, has been generally transcendentalist and faith-oriented, with a tendency to denigrate reason and investigation in favor of feeling and intuition. The failure of transcendentalist feeling was compensated in the Romantic period by the widespread belief in the transcendental power of poetry and art, which were reinvested with traces of their archaic magical uses in order, as Matthew Arnold pointed out, to buffer the shock of the dechristianization of Europe.[21] Postmodernism, seen in this broad perspective, is a renewed codification of the Graeco-Roman aspect of our inheritance. Not long after Seneca, the idea of progress acquired a hidden religious meaning by its merging with the Judeo-Christian idea of the millennium. Progress became the reverse of the myth of the Golden Age, heralding the end of history and the restoration of Eden on earth. It was, in effect, a disguised form of providence. This sort of belief invites abuse in the form of claims, however disguised, either that a certain state of society is the end condition, toward which all history has been striving, or that a certain leader or party (or art critic, for that matter) knows the direction that things must inevitably take. The conviction, originally religious, that progress is a working out of the will of God – that art is, in other words, a sacred history – was the basis of transcendentalist modernism. This became the standard means of writing history in the West, including art history. Transcendental modernism was definitely formulated in the work of Hegel: history was to be seen as a story of the progressive self-realization or self-remembrance of the transcendental spirit. The progress would culminate at the end of history in the absorption of nature entirely into spirit. Auguste Comte based his theory of history on what he called the law of progress, implying that progress is a natural law, like the law of gravity: as gravity always pulls things down, so progress always pulls history forward and upward. Darwinism was received as scientific proof of the idea that progress is inherent in nature itself. Herbert Spencer generalized Darwinism to apply to culture, and, during the industrial revolution and its inherited belief in unlimited technical advance, this seemed eminently plausible and self-evident. Progress was simply in the nature of things. But this myth concealed the fact that history had shown not only periods of progress but also equally massive regression. Because of this, contemporary biologists do not view evolution as a progressive force but as a neutral flow that has no value quality at all.

Following Plotinus,[22] Hegel regarded art as a series of intimations of the absolute-foretastes, as it were, of the ultimate reality towards which all history, under Western leadership, was said to be striving. Along with religion and philosophy, art was a channel to the beyond, the reality of the transcendent spirit. Because of its connection with the absolute, aesthetic form was regarded as freed from reference to changing circumstance. Artistic development, in other words, is not dependent upon changes in society or religion or anything else outside of its own formal means. The idea of progress in art in terms of the spiritual advancement of humanity motivates the works of Kasimir Malevich, Wassily Kandinsky, Piet Mondrian, Mark Rothko, and many other modern artists. All of them spoke of their work in exalted religious terms that go back to the age of Hegel – the ability of the art-work to embody the infinite in finite form, its purity and separation from the here and now, its ability to lift the veil that lies before the realm of the Platonic pure form. Many of them actually suspected that their works were the last physical artifices that immediately preceded the absorption of matter into spirit. The idea of progress in art history implied some transcendent and unchanging criteria of quality. Changes in different styles and periods were all regarded as expressions of a single overriding essence, ultimately of spirit itself. Artists have tended to favor spiritual terms, whereas writers and historians have usually preferred the terminology of cognitive achievement, but these are variants of the same myth. [23] The overall myth of Western art history maintains that with the renaissance of perspective an objective rendering of outer reality became possible, and that, over the following five centuries, representation was developed in more and more perfect terms until mid-nineteenth century realism and early impressionism. At that time, art, having perfected representation, was ready to transcend it by its own inner directive or law of progress, and proceed from the mastery of nature to the mastery of the sublime and the absolute. The stage, in other words, was set for abstract art, which in the minds of such as Malevich and Modrian, was a final or very advanced stage in the self-realization of the spirit. The belief that biological evolution exhibits progress parallel to that projected into Western culture, had the effect of cultivating nature, making it seem on our side. But from a postmodern point of view, history no longer seems to have a shape, nor does it seem to be going any place in particular. The elimination of the human figure from representational spaces expresses a loss of direction of selfhood, an uncertainty of what it should, or could, or will, perform. The enmeshedness of the self in the general causal web leads to the rejection of the traditional dichotomies of abstract/representational and figure/ground. The art that moves us from modernism to postmodernism expresses a return of history into time and the dissolving of the self into the welter of spaces. In its attempt to break down the balance that separates nature from culture it claims the transcendent criteria of quality. The point is now not one of formal originality but one of response to the ambient world moment. Every age has certain things that it needs to have said. Postmodernism is an opportunity to adjust our inherited myths into a frame of mind in which we may begin to embrace traditions other than ours on something like equal terms.[24]

Evolutionary change happens not steadily and gradually but in unpredictable bursts following long periods of comparative statis. McEvilley proposes that the idea of history be redefined: the modernist period was dominated by Hegel's view that history had an internal direction and goal, and that progress was, in effect, a law of nature.

Entranced by this faith. The Western nations felt that history was on their side, that it was taking them where they wanted to go – to the vaguely conceived spiritual culmination that Hegel had proclaimed. Alongside the Hegelian myth of history, the second guiding principle of the modernist period was the Kantian judgment of quality. The apprehension of value, according to Kant's *Critique of Judgment,* was supposedly a self-justifying and primarily simple act of aesthetic conception made without the intervention of cognitive, ethical, or social awareness. But lately a more complex and conciliatory idea of quality has been emerging, an idea that involves the fusion of cognitive and social attitudes with the aesthetic presence. The postmodern counterproposal operates by relativizations instead of puritanical rejections and reductions. In a similar sense, something like metaphysics still plays a role, but without reference to an "otherworldly beyond," so much as an to an indefinability or unknowableness within the world of experience. From a classical, positivistic point of view, the unknowable has not been considered a real topic, since it insisted that a question without the possibility of an answer is not a real question. But today this seems less clear; art now makes approaches towards the unknowable as it is found in incommensurabilities between culture and nature or between different aspects of culture. The act of focusing attention on specific areas of unknowability assumed that something can be derived from the experience despite the fact that the unknown object of attention will remain unknown. It would seem, however, that, contrary to McEvilley, art and criticism are not in the same position in that respect.[25] The artist may work with the unknowable, but the critic inevitably demands some sort of understanding of it. Thus, the artist may make unverifiable hypotheses or intuitive proposals about the unknown, whereas the critic deals with a network of their open implications. These two activities drive one another forward, and together they comprise an investigative tool that does not duplicate the model of science, but rather follows those of scholarship and philosophy.

Modernism postulated a pure essential reality in which each self maintained its identity. Yet self cannot be known without the other to establish its boundaries; so otherness becomes a necessary correlate of self, something that self is never encountered without. Socially this idea appears in Hegel, in his assertion of the integral selfhood or distinctive character of each culture, a doctrine that seems to make significant cultural mixing impossible. The affirmation of change, on the other hand, gives rise to insecurity, since with selves in flux, there can be no real identifications. McEvilley proposes a view of history redeemed from Eurocentric perspective in which culture seeks a global framework of imperfect meaning constructed by the balanced interplay of sameness and difference. In a culture founded on essence, and hence terrified of the other, there are deep frustrations and a longing to go back. A hybrid object attempts to incorporate into itself its own counterweight or critique – its other. Thus, the postmodern/post-historical/postcolonialist/postaesthetic moment involves pastiche, or meltdown of elements from manifestly different matrices. With a little time, the grotesque no longer looks grotesque – it becomes a new norm,[26] and meanwhile a new criterion of quality will arise. McEvilley points out that, while seeming to emphasize universality or sameness, art in the West became a force for divisiveness and exclusion.[27] To correct the fit, a fundamental shift in Western modes of cognition seems to be called for. During the modernist period, Western anthropologists, despite all attempts at objectivity, tended to represent the rest of the world through Western conventions, as if they were normative and given. Western culture, taking its paradigm from science, was regarded as the universal self. The idea of taking an anthropological approach towards one's own culture – treating one's own culture as the other – would have seemed subversive. Nowadays, however, many Western anthropologists have come to see their goal as one of shedding light on their own culture as much as on others. To this end they recognize the need to listen to voices previously excluded.

The mainstream tradition in Western philosophy – what Richard Rorty has called the Plato-Kant axis – has argued for universal and unchanging criteria of quality that are supposedly valid for all times and places. Absolute values, in this view, are inborn in all humans identically in what Plato called the eye of the soul, and what Kant called the faculty of judgment, or taste. Some people can apprehend these inborn ideas clearly, and some cannot, because of a variety of obscuring factors.[28] Even if they do not articulate this, the most outspoken proponents of the priority of quality over all other issues in art today still take this theoretical assumption for granted. McEvilley, by contrast, emphasizes that the very notions of what makes a work of art good have been observed to change from age to age.[29] He, therefore, questions the modernist belief in progress, the idea that all past ages were essentially striving to become what we now are. The classic modernist position, which was characteristic of the colonialist era, was essentially to say that every culture but our own was wrong. Only relatively recently have we come to admit that quality changes from culture to culture, as it does from age to age, and that no idea of quality can claim universal validity. By recognizing fluctuations in quality, we are not giving up such discourse altogether; rather we are setting merely its limits. People of the same culture, with the same education and class background, may well have similar ideas of quality. The history of connoisseurship suggests that quality judgments do have a degree of stability within limited contexts of time and space. The conditioning situation does not bring about that all members of the same culture will agree, like identically programmed robots, but merely that the set of options available within a given culture, though, complex, is still limited. A society's prevailing value system is in part a hidden ideological tool, and it is to the advantage of the controlling groups to posit its own criteria as eternal and universal.[30] McEvilley is not advocating that we dispense with the value judgment; he wants us, however, to become more self-conscious in our exercise of it. Value judgments serve to define and bond groups – communities of taste – in ways that are often useful, and always dangerous because, by bonding some individuals, they inevitably exclude others.

Art's primary function is to define the communal self, and to redefine it when the community is changing. From the inspection of the artworks of any culture it may be inferred what that culture has tried to think of itself at any moment. Normally this confirms a class's or clique's belief that its point of view is "natural." One's community's hegemony of taste always works to the advantage of some and to the disadvantage of others – those who see things differently.[31] By mutual identification with the body of images regarded as its own, the group's interest and its sense of their natural rightness are reinforced. Mainstream modernist art has an array of disguised fetish objects and hidden propositions. Thus, Jackson Pollock's drip paintings are cosmograms of the idea of metaphysical flux, the process by which entities arise and fall without intermediate periods of fixed definitions. And these propositions bring with them others about human values and social reality. McEvilley regards modern art as a single massive icon representing the international primacy of the wealthy and educated class who appreciated, collected, and exhibited these modernist fetishes.[32] The artspace is cut off from any contagion of change, from the context of society as a set of shifting circumstances rather than an internally structured order. As early as the seventeenth century, the idea was common in Europe that colonial conquests had demonstrated the superiority of Western civilization. This view was confirmed in nineteenth century curio rooms and early ethnographic museums, where "captured" tribal objects represented booty brought home from dark skinned people much as in the triumphal processions displayed in ancient Rome. Captured tribal objects came to be called art by Western commentators in the early twentieth century, and began to be shifted from ethnological to art museums. It still assumes that the makers of these objects did not understand their own intentions, that it took the allegedly superior eye of the Western connoisseur to tell what these objects really were for. Modernism, relying on a system of progress and scientific method, saw itself as a global or transcendent viewpoint. But lately it has come to be seen as a tribal view itself, that of Western Christendom since the Renaissance. The sense of community of nations as a global village has caused Western attitudes to be criticized from within.

The view that one's culture is not a standard by which all others are to be measured, but merely one stance among many, is the essence of the reversal that is called postmodernism, which relativizes all communities of taste. This does not mean the end of quality, but its limitation to a conditioned group within a community of similarly conditioned people. Consensual standards of quality define and bond, and are within the limits of that consensus, valid. Within another community, however, or within the same community at another time, completely different standards may obtain. They offer their group a field of self-reflection, a mirror in which to glimpse the meanings of its changes and developments, as well as its relatively unchanging foundational assumptions.[33] A postmodern exhibition strategy begins with the realization that categories and criteria have no innate validity – only the validity that is projected upon them – and thus that their transgression can be an opening to freedom. The postmodern exhibition does not compete in the conflict of different ideas of quality, priority, or historical centrality. It allows different intentions, definitions, and standards of quality to stand side by side without giving one of them dominance or authority over the others. The postmodern exhibition involves the difficult ideal of letting things be what they are before being appropriated into categories not their own. It posits no unifying idea of quality, but many pluralistic relativized ideas of it, and no classified hierarchy. The community of modern art,

especially of modernist abstraction, was in part a cultic attempt to
regain a sense of wholeness and unity that the society around no
longer provided with sufficient intensity. It ratified a certain community of taste, and with it, at a somewhat hidden level, a community
of shared spiritual and social ambitions.[34] The artworks speak only to
the initiates, keeping their secrets safe from interlopers.[35] Modernism
involved a cultic belief in progress and a messianic belief in a Western
avant garde that would make it happen. While modernism was
universalist in its championing of a certain idea of quality, postmodernism might recognize the appropriateness of different ideas of
quality to different cultural situations.

McEvilley argues that at the heart of modernism was a myth of
history designed to justify colonialism through an idea of progress.
Thus, he interprets postmodernism in the visual arts as part of the
global project of cultural decolonization. It involves (among other
things) an attempt on the part of Western people to get beyond strictly
European ideas of aesthetics and its history. The European colonial
myth was evident in the claim that the conquered people were outside
of history. When one culture regards the objects of another, these
objects are constantly incorporated into an alien mental framework.
Similarly, to see an object in another place than that in which and for
which it was made is to see it surrounded with questions. Power
relationships govern these (as other) feelings. There is the myth of
cultural purity, that humans were once psychologically and socially
whole, and that it is the mixing of cultures that destroys this wholeness
and creates monsters. This attitude assumes something like the
Hegelian idea that each culture has a nature or essence. On the basis of
Kant's epistemology, Western philosophers developed a feeling that
their cognitions were the best that could be attained with human
faculties. The Western judgment of art was said to be exclusively
aesthetic when properly exercised, with no clouding of social and
cognitive concerns. This view of the inadequacy of the perceptions and
cognitions of the non-Western peoples was akin to the Christian view
of their soullessness, and to Hegel's view that oriental cultures are "for
the most part really unhistorical."[36] Part of epistemological im-
perialism was the conviction that Western modes of regimentation,
whether visual or otherwise, were superior – that is, more objective or
true to nature than those of non-Western cultures. One of the common
social functions of art has been its role of shaping and sustaining the
sense of identity (hence, of changing it). Art represents communically

generated and received objects that invite a bonding of communal identification around a shared understanding of their meaning. Yet as an instrument of persuasion, art has the ability to sever no less than to bond. The advent of postmodernism in the West has been expressed prominently as a crisis in our representations.[37]

All art is derived from sources, and most culture is made up in large part of elements diffused from elsewhere. Quotational art in Europe and America contains elements of homage, but usually the dominant force has been one of criticism of art historical notions of originality, style, and, especially, progress. By holding up for mental inspection the aesthetic or representational canons of the past, out of context and stripped of their aura, the artist is often asking us to perceive the limits of these canons. The formalist or aesthetic attitude contained with it a little regarded contradiction: it features the idea of change, but puts no value on it for its own sake, imagining it instead as a movement toward some kind of end or culmination of history. What was not realized was that, if no such conclusion was forthcoming, these endless changes would inevitably become trivializing. If an aesthetic innovation is going to last only for a few years or months, what really is the value of it? The loss of faith in the advance of formalist movements reflected a deeper loss of faith in the similarly discredited march of technological progress, which had been the underpinning of the modernist faith in progress. It reflects the general loss of faith in the importance of art and a suspicion that what happens in art history has no real importance for anything except the market. But McEvilley emphasizes that the visual arts have a global social importance that is quite independent of formalist notions of aesthetic presence. A culture's visual tradition embodies the image it has of itself, and it has not become evident that in the emerging global scenario no one culture will be paramount, as he confidently predicts.[38] Western culture seems to be dominating the global village by its technology, mass entertainment, music, and instant communication.

Modernism was an age when a single model of history seemed adequate to the experience of white Westerners, and this model was basically the model of progress so influentially articulated by Hegel. But the vast undeveloped spaces can no longer be regarded as an ahistorical limbo, nor will their inhabitants any longer accept a view of history that they understandingly feel has victimized them.[39] History has seemed to be taking us some place we do not want to go. But

McEvilley admits that no new view has definitely established itself yet. Because revolutions never begin with a clean slate, it is inevitable that even the most genuinely multicultural approach contains residual elements of Hegelianism. Thus, McEvilley's own dialectics of self and other is no less Hegelian than the end of history he rejects. Moreover, it is not at all obvious that cultures are going to reach some stable interaction. McEvilley himself realizes that multiculturalism cannot be the end of history, since it contains countless unresolved themes and issues. We are living in a period when every ethnic group or community is writing and rewriting its own fragment of history in very conflicting versions.

Notes

[1] Thomas McEvilley, *Art and Discontent, Theory at the Millennium*, New York, NY: McPherson, 1991, p. 18.

[2] Clement Greenberg, "Modernist Painting," in *The New Art*, ed. Gregory Battock, E. P. Dalton, 1973, p. 74.

[3] Clement Greenberg, *Art and Culture*, Boston, MA: Beacon Press, 1961, p. 6.

[4] McEvilley, *Art and Discontent*, p. 29.

[5] Joseph Campbell, *The Mythic Image*, Princeton, NJ: Princeton University Press, 1974.

[6] William S. Wilson III, "Art, Energy and Attention," in *The New Art*, p. 247.

[7] McEvilley, *Art and Discontent*, p. 31.

[8] Wilson, "Art, Energy and Attention," p. 251.

[9] Harold Rosenberg, "Art and Words," in *Idea Art*, ed. Gregory Battock, New York, NY: Dutton, 1973, p. 153.

[10] McEvilley, *Art and Discontent*, p. 41.

[11] *Ibid.*, p. 47.

[12] *Ibid.*, p. 75.

[13] *Ibid.*, p. 79.

[14] *Ibid.*, p. 81.

[15] *Ibid.*, p. 86.

[16] *Ibid.*, p. 89.

[17] Roland Barthes, "Death of the Author," in *Image, Music, Text*, trans. Stephen Health, New York, NY: Hill and Wang, 1977, p. 145.

[18] McEvilley, *Art and Discontent*, p. 109.

[19] *Ibid.,* p. 115.

[20] *Ibid.,* p. 118.

[21] *Ibid.,* p. 135.

[22] Plutonis, *Enneads,* trans. S. Mackenna, London: Faber, 1956, 5.8.1.

[23] McEvilley, *Art and Discontent,* p. 164.

[24] *Ibid.,* p. 164.

[25] *Ibid.,* p. 173.

[26] *Ibid.,* p. 177.

[27] Thomas McEvilley, *Art and Otherness, Crisis in Cultural Identity,* New York, NY: McPherson, 1992, p. 9.

[28] *Ibid.,* p. 17.

[29] *Ibid.,* p. 18.

[30] *Ibid.,* p. 22.

[31] *Ibid.,* p. 60.

[32] *Ibid.,* p. 62.

[33] *Ibid.,* p. 67.

[34] *Ibid.,* p. 75.

[35] *Ibid.,* p. 76.

[36] G.F.W. Hegel, *The Philosophy of History,* New York, NY: Dover, 1956, p. 106.

[37] McEvilley, *Art and Otherness,* p. 105.

[38] *Ibid.,* p. 132.

[39] *Ibid.,* p. 135.

Chapter Thirty-Four

Understanding Art

Following Wittgenstein, Best emphasizes the dependence of language and the arts on prelinguistic behavior. He points out that unless there was something that humans just do, an innate instinctive response, there would be nothing to which learning could appeal, nothing on which reason could get a grip.[1] The relevant responses are learned, not as a result of explicit teaching, but by growing up in and emulating the practices of a social environment. Examples are learning to wave good-bye, smiling as a greeting, nodding in agreement and approval, and various other gestures and facial expressions that a child associates as the norms of behavior. Best argues that such nonrational ways of behaving and responding are the roots of the concept of art, and that they give sense to the reasons used in the discussions of the arts. He rejects the foundationalist picture, that is, the notion that our concepts need, or can coherently have, underlying justification. Instead, he asks us to focus on the ways in which concept formation is a development from instinctive behavior and purpose, as well as a result of being brought up in the ways of behaving of a particular community.[2] There are various loosely related sets of human activities, and one should look not for an underlying justification of each, but rather at what *counts* as justification *within* each. A child grows up in an environment where there are responses to the arts in which he learns to join. It makes no sense to speak of "reasons" at this level because a precondition of being able to engage in rational discourse is to have grasped, without rational justification, what counts as rationality.[3] Thus, understanding art presupposes roots in nonrational feelings, responses, and attitudes.

But this does not imply that there are no criteria for appropriateness of responses to particular works of art. Some people are said to have "a feeling for" the subject, and part of what this means is that they make what are often fruitful, conjectural leaps ahead of the evidence and reasoning. Without such intuitive leaps, no progress could be made – the scientist, for instance, could have no idea in what direction his search for evidence should proceed. Thus, no explanation of such a principle would be comprehensible to anyone who had not already some experience of responding to the arts. Artistic meaning and responses are not derived from an underlying rational principle; on the contrary, if any principle could be formulated, it would have to be answerable to the ways in which people respond to the arts. But while agreeing with the subjectivist that feeling is natural in the arts, Best insists that aesthetic appreciation is *not* unreasoned, a matter of irrational or nonrational feelings and attitudes. The question of whether reason has a place in the arts is the question of whether it is intelligible to speak of knowledge in the arts. The subjectivist is in the odd position of denying that some works and performances are better than others. Best emphasizes that the very sense of "interpretation" requires limits, and that only within these limits is there scope for agreement and discussion of whether a particular interpretation is valid or invalid. Thus, although there are different traditions and concepts of art, this does not imply that we could choose which one to adopt.[4] In stressing, however, the rootedness of the arts in one's own culture, Best faces the problem of explaining how we are, after all, able to acquire a knowledge of alien languages and forms of art.

Like Wittgenstein, Best believes that the contribution of the arts and other activities to conceptual understanding cannot be coherently distinguished from that of language. Thus, he denies that the notion of a reality independent of language makes any sense. Rather, the concepts implicit in language and the arts determine what counts as truth and falsity. On the other hand, it would be misleading to imply that different conceptual schemes are all equally available to us for, in that case, reality would be what one chooses it to be. This, of course, is precisely the argument of the realist that Best, somewhat surprisingly, adopts. He holds that it is not a matter of choosing to see reality in a certain manner, but rather of learning a language, and the natural responses and activities which give sense to it. The conceptual network embodied in language presents reality to us in its terms. It is not that one sees reality according to one's interests and purposes, but that, to a very large extent, the concepts one has acquired in learning a language determine the interests and purposes it is possible to have. The initial limits of intelligibility given with language can be developed and extended according to people's interests and purposes.[5] The network of concepts, which one acquires in learning a language and the arts, constitute the limit of intelligibility of reasons, values, and knowledge. The notion of interpretation, however, requires agreement about what is being interpreted, and it follows from the meaning of "interpretation" that disagreement is possible. One can disagree only if there is something to disagree about, and if one can recognize contradictory reasons as reasons. In Best's opinion, this does not imply understanding being irrevocably confined to the conceptual limits that one has acquired in growing up in a certain culture. Other conceptions are available to the extent that one can learn other languages, arts, attitudes, and ways of acting and responding. But he fails to explain how this is really possible.

Best's picture of aesthetic appreciation allows for an indefinite, though not unlimited, possibility of interpretation, and for a corresponding extension of concepts that give sense to interpretation and judgment. He rightly points out that, on a strictly subjectivist basis, a disagreement would amount merely to personal likes and dislikes passing each other by. Rational differences of opinion are possible only if there can be an exchange of reasons for one's judgments;[6] however, such exchange may turn out to be inconclusive. To be able to recognize something as very different art, dance, drama, or music in another culture, *some* overlapping with our own concepts would seem to be required. But this, of course, will provide only partial understanding since we can operate only with the concepts we have. The point is that we are asked to extend the limits of intelligibility beyond what is provided for in our own culture. It may indeed be rare for someone in another culture to develop the complete grasp that is possible for the native, but learning to understand foreign languages and artforms is an everyday occurrence nevertheless. If one were consistently to respond in a way, or to reveal an attitude, that was completely at variance with the norms, it would constitute good grounds for saying that one did not understand the art form at all. Best insists that it makes no sense to suppose that the facts or reality give us our picture of the world. Rather, it is our ways of behaving and responding that determine what counts as a fact and reality. The same applies to objectivity and to what can count as a valid reason. Since there are different grounds, and grounds may change, what counts as rational and objective in one culture or era may also be different and change.[7] Rationality and objectivity in one sphere are relative to the grounds of natural action and response that give them sense, and that may be quite different in different cultures and at different times. Best admits that such conceptual differences cannot always be resolved or even understood.[8]

The possibility of being able to understand a very different concept, and thus to extend one's own notion of what is intelligible, depends upon connections with these concepts that already constitute the grounds of one's present understanding. The more tenuous the connection, or the farther the innovation has moved from the grounds that give them sense, the more the innovator is likely to be regarded as a fool or lunatic,[9] or alternatively, a creative genius. The onus is on the innovators or their apologists to provide connections. Convincing someone of the validity and value of conceptual innovation requires not proof but persuasion, and Best has a hard time convincing the skeptic that what purports to be rational discourse of critical appreciation in the arts, is really no more than a thinly disguised attempt to justify subjective preferences. The fact is that even within the same culture and concept of art, there remain irreconcilable differences of opinion. By mastering the discipline of correct language usage the child learns to see the world in terms of that language. On the other hand, any account of creativity in the arts has to recognize that there is necessarily something inexplicable about it. Even those who are most creative are at a loss to explain creativity or to say where their ideas come from. The point is that one may use language creatively or recognize something as creative even though one is unable to state the criteria for creativity. Best insists that to recognize something as creative is to employ objective criteria,[10] but differences of opinion as to whether something is creative can only be settled by hindsight. Originality is given its sense by a background of the traditional, and the creative genius is thus always involved in conceptual change. He is, to some extent, changing the criteria for what counts as art and as good art. Best points out that any aesthetic innovation, to be understood as an innovation, necessarily employs many of the criteria of the concepts it is changing.[11] Thus, creativity depends upon cultural traditions, and the criteria for innovation cannot be purely private but require public manifestation.

Best concludes that an image is not sufficient for meaning, and that what is required for knowing the meaning of a term is the ability to use it correctly in various linguistic and aesthetic contexts. Two people watching a game of chess, one of whom understands it and one of whom knows nothing of chess or any similar game, may have the same sensory experience. The difference between them is that only one has the conceptual grasp.[12] In the discussion of feeling and knowledge in the arts, this conceptual difference is likewise crucial. We cannot look outside language for an understanding of what it is to possess concepts expressible in it anymore than we can look outside chess to understand the chess moves. Language cannot coherently be regarded as isolated from the natural ways of acting and responding that surround it and give sense to the utterance of words. These natural forms of behavior, not images, are the roots of language and the arts.[13] Like Wittgenstein, Best conceives of art as a way of behavior and an associated manner of speaking and reasoning. The possibility even of raising questions depends upon the existence of concepts or a vocabulary in which they can be formulated. He rejects the positivist doctrine according to which the only things that really exist are physical entities. This, he thinks, is like asking "How can what is really no more than a carved piece of wood be a king in chess?" For those who know what chess is, it is not normally seen as a piece of wood but as a chess piece. In a similar fashion, a written word or a portrait are not mere physical marks on paper or canvas, but are given sense and identity by their respective language or artform. Thus, while a physical object is not the kind of thing that can express feeling, a work of art is. It is, however, questionable whether, as Best maintains, only by having a language can a human being come to know that, e.g. sobbing is a criterion of sadness.[14] Focusing on the language dependence of concepts, he tends to underestimate the shared roots of all cultural responding.

Since he believes that a social practice like painting does not admit further justification, he cannot explain why some responses are more "natural" than others. He fails to distinguish between what is innate and what is acquired in the learning of language and the arts. Since, in his view, what is rational is merely the function of a changing context, aesthetic arguments unavoidably remain inconclusive; they constitute no more than a set of loosely connected language games. What it means to say that an artform is a language is thus precisely at issue. Contrary to Best, intention or feeling can be "private" in ways their concepts are not, and that is how we may be mistaken about our own intentions. Neither is it incoherent to say that an intention may precede or be separate from what is done, since some intentions fail to be realized, such as the sincere intention to stop smoking. What a person does or fails to do is not the *only* criterion for what his real intentions are in either the arts or ordinary affairs. The grammar and vocabulary of a language set limits, although not rigid or timeless limits, to what words can mean. But whether there are corresponding limits to what we can appropriately feel in responding to art is much less clear. We may, for instance, be equally bored by a novel or symphony because we fail to understand them or because we find them trite. Thus, Best's explanation of aesthetic feeling as a "mode of understanding"[15] is largely metaphorical. There are no readily identifiable rules for the appropriateness of feeling as there are for language use, and that is indeed one reason why in the arts we are frequently unable to say coherently what it is that we understand. Inconclusive reasoning may be the paradigm case in the arts; it is not in ordinary discourse, and Best's identification of artform with language fails to address this crucial difference. The problem with such inconclusive reasoning is that it tends to become pointless. While there are synonyms in language, each work of art is essentially unique. It is a failure in understanding the nature of art to suppose that the aesthetic meaning of one artwork could be expressed by another. Understanding art is far less "natural" than is understanding language.

Best realizes that when one is engaged in artistic appreciation, one is not concerned how others respond to it,[16] while this is crucial in the understanding of language. He claims an understanding of art that is not exhausted by whatever discursive intelligence manages to render explicit, and at the same time insists that there can be no feeling prior to or apart from language. But even if we did know a priori what is appropriate in the arts (and this is far from obvious), this does not help us to decide between competing interpretations of a work. One interpretation of a text may be refuted by pointing out internal contradictions or overlooked evidence, but deciding what response is "natural" to a given work of art cannot usually be settled in this fashion. Even if we grant Best that not everything goes in art, this will not provide us with valid criteria for judging specific responses as appropriate. While understanding art is impossible without being familiar with the relevant social practice, it is misleading to say that an artform is a language in the literal sense. To understand art is to be familiar with a social context, but in the case of modern art, for example, this may fail to provide us with relevant criteria. Unlike chess, the rules that govern art are largely insufficient for settling disputes. The learning experience that art is said to provide by Best is an emotional one, the "casting a new light on the object," and such an experience tends to remain private and indeed unstatable. Such an "understanding" is *not* to do something specific and identifiable, like the learning of facts or the meaning of words; it is merely a change of feeling that may remain private and nonconceptual.

Notes

[1] David Best, *Feeling and Reason in the Arts,* London: George Allen & Unwin, 1985, p. 4.

[2] *Ibid.,* p. 5.

[3] *Ibid.,* p. 7.

[4] *Ibid.,* p. 20.

[5] *Ibid.,* p. 22.

[6] *Ibid.,* p. 43.

[7] Joseph Grünfeld, *Changing Rational Standards,* Lanham: University Press of America, 1985.

[8] Best, *Feeling and Reason in the Arts,* p. 58.

[9] L. Wittgenstein, *On Certainty,* Oxford: Blackwell, 1969, para. 611.

[10] Best, *Feeling and Reason in the Arts,* p. 78.

[11] *Ibid.,* p. 80.

[12] *Ibid.,* p. 100.

[13] *Ibid.,* p. 104.

[14] *Ibid.,* p. 110.

[15] *Ibid.,* p. 137.

[16] *Ibid.,* p. 126.

Chapter Thirty-Five

Understanding The World Through Art

We value art for a great variety of reasons. It yields much pleasure, exercises our perceptual and imaginative faculties, expands our emotional and reflective capacities, and reflects individuals' and cultures' images of themselves. The focus is upon a certain kind of objectivity.[1] Unless we are ready to accept the propositional truth model as a paradigm for all knowledge, the dismissal of these other claims to be knowledge seems dogmatic, sweeping, and far too simple. Knowledge of other persons, of moral values, of art, cannot be reduced to empirical statements "that something is the case." In the experience-knowledge of works of art, feeling and knowing are inseparable. The content of our cognitive feeling for art can never be translated adequately into words and symbols other than those of art itself.[2] Everyday language is not a model of consistency; there is, more often than not, a range of indeterminacy, a penumbra of uncertainty. The assumption that the object to be interpreted has, or should have, a single meaning in relation to which the interpretation is correct or incorrect, no longer holds in these contexts. It is generally believed nowadays that works of art, including poems and literary art in general, contain a multiplicity of varied but not always compatible meanings that become apparent only in course of time, and not all of which are consciously known to the artist or intended by him. It is not assumed that there is only one "true" interpretation, and it is regarded as a merit, not a defect, in a work of art if it is replete with an abundance of meanings that are thus gradually discovered.[3] A portrait

438   *Soft Logic*

is more than an accurately depicted assembly of individual features. Language is meager in words with which to express and discriminate finer shades of aesthetic flavor or emotional complexion. Such qualities of things can be brought to attention only through art, and by art alone can people be helped to a richer and more sensitive experience of their world. When works of art are representational, neither exactness nor completeness of correspondence are criteria of their excellence. By inventing fictional, even impossible situations, the arts widen man's experience, engendering new and more sensitive attitudes with which to face these realities. The arts bring back into life the richness and variety that scientific understanding has abstracted from the world.

Goodman emphasizes that truth by itself matters very little even in science. We can generate volumes of dependable truths at will, as long as we are not concerned with their importance: the multiplication tables are inexhaustible, and empirical truths abound. Scientific hypotheses, however true, are worthless unless they meet minimal demands of scope and specifity imposed by our inquiry, unless they raise or answer significant questions. Minor discrepancies are over-ridden in the interest of breadth or power or simplicity and, given an assemblage of evidence, countless alternative hypotheses conform to it: we judge them by such features as their simplicity and strength. Truth of a hypothesis is a matter of fit – fit with the body of theory, and fit of hypotheses and theory to the data at hand and the facts to be encountered. But such fitness, such aptness in conforming to and reforming our knowledge and our world, is equally relevant for the aesthetic symbol. A persistent tradition pictures the aesthetic attitude as passive contemplation of the immediately given, direct appreciation of that which is presented uncontaminated by any conceptualization. Goodman rejects this view and likens it to holding that the appropriate aesthetic attitude towards a poem amounts to gazing at the printed page without reading it.[4] He emphasizes, on the contrary, that we have to read a painting no less than a poem, and that this involves making deliberate discriminations and discovering subtle relationships, identifying symbolic systems and characters within these systems, and determining what these characters denote and exemplify. The aesthetic attitude is restless, searching, testing: it is less attitude than action, creation, and recreation. The aesthetic is directed to no practical end. Disinterested inquiry embraces both scientific and aesthetic exper-ience,[5] and that a picture or poem provides more pleasure than does a proof is by no means clear. Goodman rejects the dominating dichotomy between the cognitive and the emotive; he maintains that syntactic density is characteristic of nonlinguistic systems. "Ineffability," upon analysis, turns into density rather than mystery.

Attempts to assimilate aesthetics into epistemology are often dismissed out of hand. But Elgin points out that, because of its narrow focus on the conditions of knowledge, contemporary epistemology cannot say what makes insights interesting and important; thus cannot say what sort of knowledge is worth seeking and having. Not being constrained to facts, understanding is more comprehensive than knowledge ever hoped to be. Understanding need not be couched in sentences; it might equally be located in apt terminology, insightful questions, or effective nonverbal symbols. Even a scientist's understanding of his subject typically outstrips his words. It is realized in his framing of problems, his design and execution of experiments, his response to research failures and successes. Understanding physics involves a feel for the subject, a capacity to operate successfully within the constraints the discipline dictates or to challenge these constraints effectively. Understanding a particular fact or finding, concept or value, technique or law, is largely a matter of knowing where it fits and how it functions in the matrix of commitments that constitute a science. Neither knowing where nor knowing how reduces to the knowing that traditional epistemology explicates.[6] Aesthetic understanding, likewise, is not primarily a matter of knowing truths about art or truth that art describes, but of using art effectively as a vehicle for exploration and discovery. Examples, samples, experiments, and abstract painting then all serve as symbols. Exemplification is selective; thus, an experiment can metaphorically exemplify properties like power, elegance, and promise and a painting properties like balance, movement, and depth.[7] New categories often reconfigure a domain, connecting previously isolated features to form patterns focusing on factors hitherto considered unworthy of attention. The features a symbol exemplifies depend on their functions, and a symbol often performs a family of functions. Functions, moreover, vary with context. The intention of its producer does not determine an exemplar's interpretation, for its producer has neither privileged access to nor a monopoly on a symbol's function. Many symbols admit multiple, right interpretations, and whether such multiplicity was originally intended makes no difference.[8] Exemplars operate against a constellation of background assumptions, and an interpreter ignorant of these assumptions may be incapable of interpreting or even recognizing symbols. These assumptions need not be articulate, they need not presuppose their truth or adequacy. Not all background assumptions are propositional; what we cannot quite put into words is often captured in equations or harmonies or diagrams or designs.[9] Interpretation is rarely a matter of routine application of fixed rules, for exemplars are largely sensitive to context, function, and background assumptions, and these admit enormous variation. Nevertheless, interpretation is neither arbitrary nor hopelessly difficult; traditions, accepted rules of thumb, interpretive practices and precedents guide us, though they provide no recipes. What a symbol exemplifies or denotes may permanently elude us, or remain forever in dispute. Works of art often bring out hitherto unnoticed or poorly differentiated features. Fiction feeds back on fact, but justification in the sense of argument from accepted premises is out of place – nor is truth crucial. Effectiveness sometimes depends on nonsemantic features such as syntax, style, reflection, or emphasis. The disciplines complement one another, each contributing to the achievement of understanding.

Putnam considers it wrong either to say that novels give knowledge about man as to say categorically that they do not. No matter how profound the psychological insights of a novelist may be, they cannot be called knowledge if they have not been tested. What a novel provides us with is knowledge of a possibility, i.e. conceptual knowledge.[10] Thinking of a hypothesis that one has not considered before is conceptual discovery; it is not empirical discovery, although it may result in empirical discovery if the hypothesis turns out to be correct. There are both empirical and conceptual elements in the knowledge we gain from literature, since imagination and sensibility are essential constraints on practical reasoning of this kind. Anglo-American philosophers of this century continue, for the most part, to speak of the growth of knowledge only in the context of scientific inquiry. But Putnam believes that this tendency has not only hampered the epistemological enterprise, but has encouraged many to ignore the products of fanciful imagination, and especially works of art, as a potential source of knowledge. Indeed, attentive readers who respond to fiction frequently claim that they have acquired knowledge of the real world. It helps us to understand, and to come to terms with, what otherwise would be baffling. It is also possible to acquire certain values or attitudes from fictional works, and a good deal of what we learn from fiction is practical and attitudinal. Fiction may impart conceptual or cognitive skills that offer radically new ways of thinking about or perceiving aspects of our environment. Usually our imaginings are guided and contrasted by what we actually know; they will be used as a foundation on which we base our understanding of, and our action in, the situation. Fiction often explores, teases, and tests our moral standards and attitudes. Bender concludes that art in general functions in a multiplicity of cognitive, perceptual, and expressive ways, and sometimes this includes the conveyance of propositional knowledge.[11]

Some philosophers have argued that a successful account of pictorial representation must give a central place to the notion of aspect-seeing. Wilkerson argues that interpreting pictures is a special case of seeing aspects. In a portrait, I may see anger and disgust or fear. Others can guide and assist my efforts by drawing my attention to crucial parts of the figure, or by obscuring elements, by turning the figure around, or by offering verbal encouragement. There is a clear contrast here with ordinary seeing: I cannot try to believe that Napoleon is in front of my eyes, but I can attempt to see a Napoleon aspect.[12] Aspects may suddenly dawn as, after effort, I detect the sense of a knotty passage in a foreign language. The "look" of a figure is not a simple nonrelational property; it is a focusing of attention that pulls everything together. Aspect-seeing is an exercise of the imagination; indeed, in many respects this is the most important feature of aspect-seeing. Some aspects demand a selective connection and organization of detail. It is no good to distinguish "purely optical" aspects from "purely intellectual" ones because the perception of aspects, like the perception of everything else, requires the cooperation of sense and intellect. I must both perceive the object in front of me and bring it under concepts, classifying it as belonging to a kind or kinds. So no perception is purely intellectual, as Kant remarked; thoughts without content are empty, and intuition without concepts are blind. What is often forgotten, however, is that understanding, on Kant's view, is assisted by the imagination in its work of organization and com- bination. Knowledge requires thought not merely about actualities but also about possibilities. If I am to identify a chair or a chimpanzee, I must have views about its *possible* behavior, about how it might and might not behave, how it can and cannot change. I need to think about all kinds of counterfactual possibilities, for I am implicitly connecting actual representations with possible representations. Indeed, if I could not think about possible representations, I could not think about actual ones.[13] In normal perception, the role of the imagination is necessary, but subordinate to the roles of sense and intellect. Yet, in the perception of aspects the imagination dominates, and sense and intellect are both in a subordinate role. My comprehension of the actual (e.g. the figure in front of my eyes) is subordinated to my thoughts about what is possible. The imagination takes over, and I concentrate entirely on what might be the case, or on what could be the case, given the limited sensory information available. I use the sensory information, not in an effort to form beliefs, but in an effort to explore possibilities. Developing possibilities and pondering counterfactuals is consistent with believing that they are only possibilities, and indeed counterfactual.[14] Imagination is required to see new applications to old rules and formulas; to develop original solutions to knotty problems; to make connections between apparently disparate things; to display a sensitivity to, and a talent for, metaphor; to develop a sense of humor and a feeling for the incongruous, the ridiculous, the ironic, the ambiguous. Aspect-seeing is a special kind of imagining.[15]

Kivy points out that the language of aesthetics is used in the writings of men of science. It is in aesthetic value that the justification of a scientific theory is to be found, and with it the justification of scientific method. Yet the line seems to be sharply drawn between "aesthetics" on the one hand and truth on the other. Roger Fry is expressing no more than what "common sense" will allow when he argues that if aesthetic value is *the* measure, or even an important measure, of scientific value, than a false but beautiful theory must be preferred over a true but homely one. Aesthetic evaluation and appreciation meant for Fry, as for many, paradigmatically the evaluation and perception of art *qua* art. But since for Fry the foremost aesthetic appreciation was solely estimation of formal properties, to read that science is evaluated primarily on aesthetic grounds means that it is appreciated for its formal properties, in which case truth is irrelevant. People who are able to understand scientific theories at the highest level sometimes describe their enjoyment as "aesthetic." The criteria that scientists customarily cite in support of their apparent aesthetic judgments are symmetry, order, unity, coherence, elegance, and harmony – to name the most representable. Kivy emphasizes, however, that all these criteria are what we might call "classical" ones. No one ever heard of a scientist gushing over a theory because of its wild sublime disorder, its intriguing obscurity and ambiguity, or its gothic complexity. A historian of science, or even a working scientist, might well enjoy aesthetically the Baroque complexity of the Ptolemaic astronomy with its profligate multiplication of epicycles to save the appearances. What such an example suggests is that Baroque and Romantic features of theories are objects of appreciation only after the theories have ceased to be in the running; when, that is, the question of truth has ceased to matter because a verdict of "false" has been declared by scientific consensus.[16] When scientific theories are, however, established doctrine, or at the cutting edge in the process of confirmation or computation, it would appear that the classical aesthetic criteria exclusively prevail. When I appreciate the elegance of a theory, I do not have to choose between its elegance aesthetically and appreciating it epistemologically, for in doing the one I am doing the other, and vice versa.[17] On first blush, it would seem difficult to follow Sullivan in his stronger claim that aesthetics is the only motivating force in theoretical science.[18] But when one is asking the grand questions of theoretical physics or cosmology, or evolutionary biology, it is difficult not to see the quest as aesthetically motivated and the answers as aesthetically satisfying. One cannot solve problems of such a theoretical kind whiteout fulfilling, at least in part, the requirements of theoretical harmony, unity, elegance, simplicity, and the like, that excite the scientist's aesthetic emotions. One cannot intelligibly ask whether aesthetic criteria are ever decisive in themselves in deciding for the truth of a scientific theory, unless one has severed the aesthetic from the true in a formalist fashion.[19] But the beauty of a theory can be compelling enough to keep it alive, even if believed to be false long enough to be ultimately vindicated.

Kraut defends a critical pluralism, which contrasts with critical monism (There is one single, correct complete interpretation of an artwork") and with critical anarchism ("All interpretations of an artwork are equally acceptable"). Critical pluralism entails that two artifices could lay equal claims to understanding the same aesthetic phenomenon despite serious disagreements with one another. It presupposes rival interpretations, equally correct, and genuinely incompatible. But it is not clear how artistic understanding relates to other varieties of understanding, for example, to the varieties of understanding at work when a native speaker (or translator) understands a grammatical sentence, or when a scientist understands the data, or when a person understands another person's actions or natural states. Quine claims that natural language meaning is indeterminate:

for a given language L, it is possible in principle to construct acceptable translations of L ("rival translation manuals"), all of which are equally correct.[20] The critical pluralist might attempt to appropriate Quine's arguments for the indeterminacy of translation and urge their applicability to the artworld. That some ways might seem more natural than others is due to our parochial sense of what counts as a natural kind; it does not point toward the incorrectness of the apparently bizarre translation schemes.[21] The linguist begins with the capacity to use his own language (this is the "preunderstanding" that is derived from the interpreter's initial situation). He asks about the conditions under which his sentences are true, and this involves idealizations, approximations, counterfactual hypotheses, appeals to normalcy, and *ceteris paribus* conditions, as well as other aspects of theory construction.[22] Two interpreters immersed in quite distinct initial situations have different interests and explanatory goals, different senses of what is or what is not important, different ideological commitments. But no argument has been provided that these interpretations are in any interesting sense incompatible, or rival interpretations, or that, if they are, they have an equal claim to correctness. Artworks are artifacts; they cannot be understood in isolation from the communal norms that spawn and sustain them. There are many such artworlds, just as there are many distinct natural languages. Locating an artist's work within a style or genre and, thereby, determining what is or what is not important in the work is often difficult, not because we do not know enough but because the facts resist classification. Often – perhaps usually – we cannot say where one community of interest groups ends and the next begins. A critical pluralist rejects the specification of a privileged community, but ambiguity is not indeterminacy, and it is not pluralism. No population enjoys privileges over any other in fixing the artistic facts constitutive of the "proper interpretation" of an artwork. And this spells doom to strict analogies between linguistic and artistic meaning.[23] The incompatibility of rival interpretations is not a truth-fictional matter consisting of disagreement about the facts; it is more like the incompatibility between a "boo" stance and a "hooray" stance taken toward the same state of affairs. The discourse of aesthetic interpretation seems remarkably similar to the discourse of psychological interpretation, linguistic interpretation, and semantic content description generally. So the monist and pluralist are, on this construal of their dispute, not in disagreement about some matter of fact; rather they have clashing sentiments about how art should be approached, about what sort of considerations should constrain one's aesthetic experiences.[24] There is more to incompatibility than logical inconsistency.

Notes

[1] Louis Arnaud Reid, "Art and Knowledge," *The British Journal of Aesthetcis,* 25 (1985), reprinted in John W. Bender and H. Gene Blocker, *Contemporary Philosophy of Art,* Englewood Cliffs, NJ: Princeton Hall, 1993, p. 563.

[2] *Ibid.,* p. 566.

[3] Harold Osborne, "Interpretation in Science and Art," *The British Journal of Aesthetics,* 23 (1983) reprinted in *Contemporary Philosophy of Art,* p. 572.

[4] Nelson Goodman, "The Activity of Aesthetic Experience," in *Languages of Art,* Indianapolis, IN: The Bobbs-Merrill Co. 1968, reprinted in *Contemporary Philosophy of Art,* p. 397.

[5] *Ibid.*

[6] Catherine Z. Elgin, "Understanding: Art and Science," *Midwest Studies in Philosophy, Volume XVI, Philosophy and the Arts,* Notre Dame, IN: University of Notre Dame Press, 1991, p. 197.

[7] *Ibid.,* p. 198.

[8] *Ibid.,* p. 201.

[9] *Ibid.*

[10] Hilary Putnam, "Literature, Science, and Reflection," in *Meaning and the Moral Sciences,* Boston, MA: Routledge and Kegan Paul, 1978, reprinted in *Contemporary Philosophy of Art,* p. 583.

[11] John W. Bender, "Art as a Source of Knowledge: Linking Analytic Aesthetics and Epistemology," in *Contemporary Philosophy of Art,* p. 594.

[12] E.E. Wilkerson, "Pictorial Representation: A Defense of the Aspect Theory," in *Midwest Studies in Philosophy, Volume XVI,* p. 154.

[13] *Ibid.,* p. 158.

[14] *Ibid.*

[15] *Ibid.,* p. 159.

[16] Peter Kivy, "Science and Aesthetic Appreciation," in *Midwest Studies in Philosophy, Volume XVI, p. 186.*

[17] *Ibid.*

[18] J.W.N. Sullivan, "The Place of Science," *Athenaeum,* April 11, 1919, p. 76, reprinted in *Aspects of Science,* New York and London: 1927, p. 14.

[19] Kivy, "Science and Aesthetic Appreciation," p. 190.

[20] W.V. Quine, *Word and Object,* Cambridge, MA: 1960, p. 27.

[21] Robert Kraut, "On Pluralism and Indeterminacy," *Midwest Studies in Philosophy, Volume XVI,* p. 211.

[22] *Ibid.,* p. 212.

[23] *Ibid.,* p. 219.

[24] *Ibid.,* p. 223.

Chapter Thirty-Six

Knowledge Through Art

Berleant argues that engagement is not only an explicit factor in the work of any innovative artist but that it becomes the principle key for making the various regions of aesthetic experience intelligible. We face an array of dualisms, especially that of subject and object, that are widely accepted as fundamental truths. Despite Hegel and the succeeding efforts of Bergson, Dewey, and Merleau-Ponty, among others, these dualisms still remain primarily philosophical tenets for most philosophers. And they join with other basic convictions, such as the cognitive primacy of science, the universality and exclusiveness of truth, the objectivity of knowledge, and the hierarchical order of being, to form the foundation of modern intellectual culture.[1] Aesthetic engagement challenges this tradition; it claims continuity rather than separation, contextual relevance rather than subjectivity, historical pluralism rather than certainty, ontological parity rather than priority. The natural world does not stand apart from human presence and action, and an impressive impulse compels people toward the aesthetic and the artistic. Not only are these experiences distinctive and valuable; they cannot be excluded from any consideration of human culture. As an empirically grounded discipline, aesthetics must establish itself in the evidence of artistic activities and artistic experience, but what we select as identifiable and relevant is guided by the conceptual frame we employ. Aesthetic theory has not only often failed to reflect aesthetic practice and artistic experience, it has presumed at times to decide them. From the earliest times art has been an integral part of human culture. The classical age centered on art as an activity that is at once cosmic, social, and individual – an activity that brings understanding of a sort. Since the eighteenth century, however, this has changed, and now at the end of the twentieth century, we have finally recognized that the human factor in every kind of awareness and knowledge is structurally unavoidable. Art has become both a symptom of the change and a standard for grasping it.[2] The scope of our claims has narrowed, and while the human place has become less cosmic, it is more pervasive and personal. Theories of beauty have given way to doctrines of emotion, meaning, communication, with even symbols being taken as the embodiment of feeling.

Berleant challenges the traditional theory that art consists primarily of objects, that these objects possess a special status, and that they must be regarded in a unique way. Disinterestedness began to emerge as the mark of a new and distinctive mode of experience called "aesthetic," a kind of awareness distinct from more commonly recognized alternative modes, such as historical, cognitive, moral, and religious experience.[3] It was in the work of Kant that the concept of aesthetic disinterestedness became fixed, and assumed a distinct and integral place in aesthetic thinking. By making taste disinterested, Kant provided the theoretical impetus for isolating art from commerce with the world of human activity, and setting it in its own region beyond the command of practical affairs. From this formative period in the history of modern aesthetics, there emerged an identification of the art object as separate and distinct from what surrounds it, isolated from what surrounds it, and isolated from the rest of life. One can read the history of the philosophy of art as a reflection of the powerful impact of this contemplative ideal, which was continued to the present day in the attempt to identify art with language, symbol, and symbol systems.[4] For Berleant, on the other hand, experience is the critical term in aesthetics and all that we can say about art and the aesthetic is in some way an elaboration of this notion. In attempting to describe experience, it is essential to escape the prevalent tendency to regard it as a purely subjective event, a tendency that emerges in phenomenology as strongly as in traditional empiricism. To the Western philosophical mind, *experience* connotes sense experience, and the appeal to sensation as the source of knowledge, or *empiricism,* as this is known, suggests the major tradition in British philosophy. What we have inherited from that tradition (it, too, like aesthetics, a product of the seventeenth and eighteenth centuries) is a view of experience as the composite product of separate, discrete sensations. Yet this dualistic tradition of separating consciousness from the external world, so deeply ingrained in modern thought, cannot be assumed as given. For it presumes a structure of experience that, for all its initial plausibility, rests upon a particular historical and cultural tradition not shared in other times and places.[5] But this pattern of separation continues to prevail in the way the arts are explained and treated. Our Western involvement with science and technology, where the automatic pattern of experience seems so effective, may in fact have provided us with a misleading paradigm. The contemporary arts, in particular, frequently insist on experiences of engagement by provoking us into movement or action, or by forcing us to adjust our vision and imagination. A clear alternative to the dualistic claims of the empiricist tradition lies in the claim for a continuity of experience, joining perceiver with the world in complex patterns of reciprocity. One must enter into the work in an intimate fashion, active, not as a pure spectator, but as an involved viewer.[6] Berleant concludes that the arts of this century demand a transformation of theory,[7] since the evolution of the arts in the twentieth century has often been described as experimental, controversial, even chaotic. Yet contemporary art exhibits more than an expression of styles, materials, and techniques, for technical innovations do not stand alone; they reflect the manner in which we engage with and appreciate art. Artists have altered our very ability to identify what art is and our capacities for expressing it. By modifying what we accept as art, and by reordering the conditions and character of our experience of it, these developments have, at the same time, undermined the customary beliefs through which people have appreciated, understood, and esteemed art.

Berleant argues that it is presumptuous for the theories of the arts to decree what qualifies as art and aesthetic. The converse is more appropriate: aesthetic theory must examine aesthetic practice carefully, and consider how best to respond to this alteration and enlargement of the traditional station and experience of the arts. During the last century, the art object has become less important in the aesthetic situation, and at times has vanished altogether. Impressionist painting began the process; it dissolved the substantiality of things into atmospheric appearances, from the pointillism of Seurat to Monet's multiple versions of haystacks, suggesting a painterly exemplification of Berkeley's dictum of the previous century, "To be is to be perceived."[8] Analytical cubism flattened out the thickness of things by delivering a multiplicity of perspectives simultaneously. The perspectival process took a psychological form in the work of the Expressionists where subjects were transfigured in their emotive significance. In Surrealism, the painter's oneiric world dominated the visual one, and painting relied more on a metaphorical than a literal image. Just as Newton proved in 1666 that color was not a property of matter but rather of light as it interacts with objects, artists in this century seem to be showing us that art is not a property of objects but emerges from the perception of human beings in interaction with objects or elements.[9] The tragic hero becomes a nondescript unsuccessful salesman; the dramatic situation is described in the transcript of a trial; the poetry of language is sacrificed to the dullmindedness of common speech. Action, furthermore, is nonexistent, and the force of a situation emerges from the intimations that rise out of a seemingly pointless reiteration of banalities, and perhaps even more, from the silences that interrupt them.[10]

The experience of art is indeed distinctive, and the doctrine of disinterestedness attempted to promote this by putting a frame of sorts around art, thereby isolating it from the rest of the human objects and activities, and placing it in a special realm different from practical demands. This frame is primarily a psychological one, a shift in attitude that leads the appreciator to attend to the qualities of the art object without concern for the usual meanings and uses it may have in ordinary experience, therefore, disinterestedness no longer identifies what is distinctive in the aesthetic situation and, in the past century artists have been producing work that denies the isolation of art from the active involvements of daily life. Aesthetic experience thus becomes an emphasis on intrinsic qualities and lived experience rather than a shift in attitude. Such engagement emphasizes connections and continuities, and it leads ultimately to the aesthetization of the human world. Active discernment is a demand of all painting, from recent color field and minimalist art to traditional landscape and portrait painting. Innovations in theater have also appeared that disrupt dramatically the conventional projection of distance. The modernist novel, along with some notable precursors, makes the reader a collaborator in the fictional process. In place of a plot developed in a more or less direct manner, situations, events, and perceptions are described, which the reader is compelled to fit together in order for the novel to become coherent.[11] The lines between what happens and what is imagined are indiscernible, according to Berleant, he rejects the philosophical doctrine that has dominated both understanding and appreciation of art for some two centuries largely because it has shaped an aesthetics of separation, isolation, contemplation, and distance. Instead, Berleant emphasizes that both theory and appreciation must rest on what happens in art. The artistic developments of the past century are part of a transformation in perception and understanding that compels us toward a different aesthetics. New materials, objects, and techniques that arise out of technology of industrial production have entered into the art world, and profoundly influenced the vocabulary and the practice of artists. At the same time, fundamental social changes in the modern world have reshaped our perceptual activities in the arts into new and different forms. Art is one of the powerful elements in human culture, and its evolution has significance not only for its own future but for understanding the larger society as well. For the arts, both popular and high, pervade modern societies in unprecedented variety and scope. Industrial techniques have transfigured the art object just as it has transformed other objects of human making, and our relationship with them. This undermined the sharp distinction between people's practical activities, which demanded an unqualified commitment to utility, and artistic activities of aesthetic enjoyment, which were cut off from practical affairs and regarded for their own intrinsic worth. The emancipation of the arts from subservience to historical accuracy and devotional purpose has encouraged their propensity to abstraction. At the same time, their integration into the traffic of daily life has replaced the isolated object of art with one absorbed through its function into the course of ordinary human activity. Science and technology have continued to exercise a profound influence on artistic production. Technological tools like the computer and the music synthesizer are now commonplace, and recording on magnetic tape has both assisted performers and replaced them. The music no longer lives and grows as a freshly recreative act; it is constructed like a machine product.[12] While traditional theater has continued to function, a new technology has produced a new art in which the actual movement and discourse of people is replaced by the presence of images fixed on celluloid strip, and shown in rapid succession so as to create the illusion of movement. In portraying movement in time and space, the film approaches the directness and randomness of life. The distancing logic of the plot has receded, and in its place appear the ordinary details of life that we never trouble to notice: dramatic shape is replaced by the mystery of the mundane.

As art is not eternal, neither are the modes of perception and consciousness with which we experience them. The interpretive richness of good art leads us beyond the qualities inherent in the object alone and makes art relevant to new conditions. Art can thus outlive the theories in which it has been explained, and gain in force through a more inclusive aesthetic. Berleant believes that contemporary theories impede the full force of art, and misdirect our understanding of how art and the aesthetic actually function. Social, historical, and cultural factors influence the kind of work artists do and the uses that are made of their art; aesthetic experience is part of the entire spectrum of human experience. In art, as in modern society, traditional rules have blurred; the psychology of perception has joined philosophical psychology in undermining the common division of sense experience into separate channels of sensation, each governed by its dominant sense. As human beings we are cultural creatures, unable to sense without the presence of associations and meanings. The very process of sensory development is, in fact, a process of acculturation through which ideas and beliefs become embodied in our direct experience. The meanings and attitudes are not merely intellectual constituents or internal accomplishments of sensation, but are subtly infused into our sensory experience. New ideas mean new perceptions, and this involvement occurs in many different orders of activity – sensory, conscious, physical, and social – but it is most pronounced in aesthetic experience. Art does not consist of objects but of situations in which experiences occur. Art objects are not inherently different from other objects but they express features that make them effective in the aesthetic situation in which they become art.

Paintings are the typical referent of the term art, and the painter is taken as the prototypical artist. Painting seems to accord completely with the tradition of aesthetic theory for which disinterested contemplation is the appropriate mode of appreciation. Space is often used to exemplify the traditional attitude of pictorial appreciation, for disinterestedness is commonly expressed by the spatial metaphor of distance. Yet there have been major changes in both our scientific and philosophical understanding of space, and these changes hold implications for aesthetic perception. The usual treatment of space in painting assumes the classical model of Newtonian physics; it is a conception that Newton developed by extending the system of Cartesian coordinates into a universal order. In this system both space and time are absolute; space is a medium that is abstract, universal and impersonal – a medium in which discrete objects are placed and in which they can be located clearly and irrefragably.[13] Despite the radically different orientation of modern relativity physics, common sense continues to struggle along under the Newtonian conception. We still tend to see ourselves as inhabitants of a Euclidean universe, preserving the functions of simultaneity and absoluteness of space and time. We persist in the Cartesian illusion that we can stand apart from things, regard them from some remove, and remain unimplicated in their processes. Not yet having accommodated ourselves perceptually to the vastly altered world of Einsteinian physics and quantum mechanics, we continue unwittingly to apply the repudiated spatial orientation to pictorial as well as ordinary experience.[14] Distance develops not only as a space that separates perceiver and object but as a division between them as well. The perceiver becomes primarily a visual awareness who adopts a contemplative attitude toward an isolated object. We learn from the history of art that pictorial space was absent in the visual art of Egypt, Crete, and India; that it was limited and idealized in Greek and Roman art; and that it began to emerge as an important component in the West during the Middle Ages. Space first appeared in paintings in the form of imaginative landscapes constructed as settings for mythological and religious figures and events. Distance was neglected, the size of figures rather than their spatial distribution designating their importance. Joined to the interest in physical space and the emergence of the landscape was the development of pictorial techniques for reading depth accurately. Linear perspective is a carefully studied technique that rests on the visual perception of distance, and while the perceiver is a necessary factor in the perceptual array, he functions only as a distant observer.[15] The theory of linear perspective was developed with such mastery that it has continued to the present time as the model for the realistic appointment of pictorial space. It solidified in graphic form the primacy of vision as the preeminent sensory modality, a status that reflected its superiority, and the long-standing metaphorical identification of sight with the cognitive process.

Our visual understanding of space continues to reflect the same scientific and artistic traditions and to share similar premise. We still understand an account of spatial perception in common experience largley in Euclidean terms, taking space as independent of the perceiver within fixed and unchanging orthological coordinates, and within which separate objects are located. The changes that modern relativity physics has made in perception of space, however, are well-known. Space and time are now understood as a continuum that is curved in the presence of a gravitational field in which time and position of events can be fixed only relatively to the location of the observer. Thus, the perceiver's placement is critical: one's location not only makes a difference in the knowledge of events, it makes a contribution to what they are. We can, therefore, no longer speak of things as if they occurred independently in absolute spatial and temporal frames, and any specification of occurrences depends on the presence and position of a perceiver.[16] Recent approaches to the psychology of perception, such as those of the Gestalt and trans-actional schools, provide additional reasons for recognizing the human contributions to the world we perceive. The space of appearance is far different from the space of Euclidean geometry.[17] Perception is not entirely a sensory phenomenon, and recent interest in hermeneutics has made us realize how meaning never stands alone, and how the knower contributes through the interpretive process to the very nature of what is known. Interpretation is ubiquitous, and this is as true of the physical spatial world as it is of the social and cultural one, of fact and perception as it is of texts. Facts are themselves hermeneutical; like all forms of meaning they are human constructions. Thus the impartial objective knowledge, to which we have been accustomed to ascribe the results of scientific inquiry, appears to be going the way of the absoluteness and objectivity of space and time. The individual is no longer a spectator, distinctly removed from objects and events, and viewing them with uninvolved objectivity. The spectator has been transformed into an actor, wholly implicated in the space continuum in which everyone else is involved. We have now come to recognize our contribution to the world we inhabit through action, perception, and consciousness, whether involving scholarly research, scientific inquiry, and knowledge or aesthetic experience. How the world is known makes a difference in what is actually there as well as how it is perceived. The implication of the knower in what is known is a major claim in this century, supported scientifically by relativity theory, quantum mechanics, and the psychology of perception as well as interpretively by phenomenology, pragmatism, deconstructionism, hermeneutics, and feminism, among current intellectual movements. Thus a blurring takes place between the seeing and the seen; both our understanding and our perception of space have changed and become fused. From being thought of as an absolute and independent medium known in itself alone, space has been transformed into a condition that includes the perceiver as a constituent. This works to reshape not just physical space and our awareness of it, but all spatial perception, transforming our encounter with pictorial space as well. Euclidean-Newtonian space and Einsteinian-phenomenological space lead to dissimilar ways of ordering the world and thus experiencing it. Their influence on the arts can be traced in many directions; the panoramic landscape vividly expresses Newtonian space. Such paintings exhibit pictorial tendencies that present an objectified space and encourage a disinterested attitude. Yet, Berleant emphasizes that it is possible to set aside Newtonian objectivity and turn to the capacities most landscapes have for perceptual engagement. Perspective does not require a precise and immobile spectator but is remarkably able to accommodate a whole range of viewing positions. We now understand space differently, and this change enables us to experience it more freely and more personally. Berleant concludes that the history of aesthetics has long labored under a rationalistic burden.[18] Art does not legislate experience it invites it. The participating landscape requires a new way of seeing, a new way of perceiving pictorial space as continuous with the viewer instead as opposed to him. It is undoubtedly true, as Goethe maintained, that people see what they know, the task, then, is to enlarge our knowledge so as to expand our vision.

The objects of our ordinary world often impose themselves forcibly on our thought and actions, and our involvement with them is likely to be active as well as reciprocal. Environmental experiences are not only sensory, the environment can no longer be regarded as an internal location but must be considered a physico-historical condition of engagement, a dynamic field of forces continuous with human life.[19] Yet, the active patterns in which the human world takes shape display forms of grasping the environment that are far more varied than those that conventional usage has made orthodox. In constituting their habitat, people have created different kinds of environmental order that reflect the contrast in attitude and experience between disinterested contemplation and aesthetic engagement. Urban design is replete with examples of the contemplative visual approach to space. The eye becomes the reflective organ of space, since starting from the seventeenth century, it has been the metaphorical origin of thought.[20] It is becoming increasingly clear that environment, far from being a contemplative object, collaborates in human perception and action. The eye is but one factor in our perception of space, an awareness that we grasp through multiple sensory channels. The recent sources of this approach are in the American pragmatic tradition and the continental experimental phenomenological philosophy, but the origin of the active approach goes back to identification of practical modes of knowing, and the development of craft technology in the West. This sense of environment considers people to be embedded in their world, implicated in their constant processes of action and response. A physical interaction of body and setting, a psychological interconnection of consciousness and culture, a dynamic harmony of sensory awareness – all make the person inseparable from his environmental situation. Traditional dualisms, such as those separating idea and object, self and others, mere consciousness and external world, dissolve in the integration of person and place.[21] What is common to the various expressions of the active model is the recognition that the objective world of classical science is not the experiential world of the human perceiver. Environment is not outside us to be experienced in consciousness and feeling, nor can it even be construed as surroundings. As actors in the world, we are inseparable from it and fully implicated in its dynamic processes.[22] Philosophical attempts to articulate this conception have become increasingly influential. Human perception is not purely visual but rather semantic; for Merleau-Ponty perception starts with the body, and thus leads to grasping the perceived object not as a discrete material thing, but in relation to the space of the perceiver. The world is all around me, not in front of me.[23] Extending Merleu-Ponty's spatial concept, O.F. Bollnow uses the notion of *lived space,* in which space becomes the medium of action.[24] The environment has become the stage on which the beholder has metamorphosed into the actor.[25] Not only is it impossible to objectify environment, we also cannot take it simply as a reflection of the perceiver or as the ground on which people carry out their activities. The visual tactic of removal and distance is unavailable, since the environment becomes our very world. Although not usually formulated theoretically, such a sense of environmental participation often appears in research areas such as the ecological sciences and cognitive science, in applied fields like urban planning and agriculture, and in activities such as hiking, camping, small boat cruising, and wilderness travel. The fundamental participating character of such experience is being understood by people following many routes: phenomenological, hermeneutic, psychological, religious, environmental, aesthetic.

The participating environment develops a spatial continuity with the view, and there is a concrete manipulation of space in which all senses collaborate. This phenomenological aesthetic of space defines a world vastly different from the traditional scientific ideal of physics. Space has no precise boundaries; it is not quantitative and mathematically measurable, for it is not universal and homogeneous. It is not objective, distinct, and separate from the person inhabiting it. Personal space is instead qualitative, not uniformly measurable, but with fluid, fuzzy boundaries. Space is perceived as identical with the events occurring in them, and time is recognized only in relation to movement and spaces. Space, then, is human space, personal space, relative to the perceiver, and it is as heterogeneous as the infinitely varied terms and conditions of human life. We can regard space as a rarefied or liquid means, a medium through which we move much as fish swim through water. Objects are not solids opposed to empty space; they are part of that space, concentrations of it, so to speak. To understand how this happens requires us to enter the environment as participants, and not just to regard it as observers. Yet this is difficult to talk about, in part because we have few concepts and techniques in our tradition to assist us. Environment is not foreign territory surrounding the self; rather understanding the environment involves recognizing that human life is lived as an integral part of a physical and cultural medium. There is no inside and outside, human being and external world – even in the final reckoning – no discrete self and separate other. The conscious body moving as part of the spatio-temporal environment medium becomes the domain of human experience, the ground of human reality within which and from which discriminations and distinctions are made. The human environment is always historico-cultural, and certain places exemplify such an aesthetic. We must, then, dispense with the notion of space and consider place instead, for it is through dwelling, belonging to a place, that the human relation appears.

Berleant emphasizes that a text requires a cohort of critics and readers, a literary public, a linguistic system, all surrounded by a larger society with its conventions and beliefs, and all placed within an ordered historical perspective to be interpreted and understood. Edges blur and domains merge in the different efforts of formalists to locate and comprehend literature. For Ferdinand de Saussure, who established the study of structural linguistics early in this century, words have no meaning in themselves, nor do they refer directly to things themselves. Only within the objective structure of its system does a sign possess meaning, and the system, moreover, is entirely conventional. Words do not "refer" to things themselves; rather they have meaning as parts within the entire system that is a language.[26] Both sign and referent carry a certain arbitrariness. Together they acquire an identity, fluid but cohesive; yet, the closed system of signs is essentially incomplete. Words in themselves do not refer; people use words to refer, and it is the user who creates the bond between sign and referent. We must escape from the system of signs into the larger conditions of their use.[27] The study of language in literature directs us beyond the written word, even beyond its author, to the reader who actualizes language at any given moment. It is the reader who reinvents the sign, locates the referent, and joins them into a unity by the act of reading, and the referent, too, never stands alone but is selected and focused by the reader.[28] Reading transforms literature from an object into an event, and an event cannot be objectified, grasped, and held at arm's length. It is something more elusive, more intangible; moreover, it assumes a life of its own. Different texts imply different kinds of readers. Literature is no independent body of special texts culled from the vast ocean of print by standard canons of normative judgment. The reader does not discern the meaning hidden in the text, for apart from the reader, the text has none. We do not first read a text and then proceed to interpret it; interpretation strategies shape our reading, deciding not only *how* we read but *what* we are reading. But placing the weight of literature so heavily on its reader does not necessarily rest it on the soft ground of subjectivity. Even though there are no "true" objective meanings embedded in literature, there is the obvious fact that readers agree widely on meanings, formal units, and even interpretations and judgments. As readers we are never independent but members all of interpretive communities who will agree with others in the same group. Fiction does not rest on opposition to reality but has an obvious connection with it. Actually fiction tells us something about reality. An interaction occurs between familiar experiences and new ones, and the reader's response to the text develops out of this interplay.

But in spite of the radical transfer of attention from the text to its reader, the content of criticism has remained virtually unchanged. Recent criticism continues to occupy itself with interpretation, and thus centers the discussion of literature around questions of meaning. Berleant emphasizes that it is crucial to recognize the difference between the experience of literature, and the analysis and theory of that experience. For literature is more than a vehicle for embodying and transmitting meanings. It has sensuous dimensions; it requires semantic involvement; it stimulates psychological processes of imagination and association. Our engagement with literature comes first, and how we interpret it or otherwise explain that experience is, in the final analysis, derivative. Confounding theory with experience is the great danger of the scholarly process, and Berleant questions the essentialist assumption that literature possesses a fundamental function. Literature may be a socializing force, acquainting the reader with the belief system, convictions, attitudes, values, and traditions of a culture. Literature may have psychotherapic value, offering opportunities for wish fulfillment, sublimation, or projection; it may provide occasion for daydreaming, reverie, oneiric activity.[29] Restricting criticism's function exclusively to interpretation rests on the narrow assumption that the cognitive role of language is the only legitimate one, all others being dismissed as intellectually unacceptable. It is exceedingly hard to evade the pervasive dualisms of Western culture, and thus to move beyond the dualism of text and reader in dealing with the literary experience seems to leave us without a vocabulary to describe it.[30] We face the difficulty of describing the language of experience by the language *about* experience, and this is the primary underlying problem of all criticism. The novel has the ability to make a world present, to become the means whereby readers immerse themselves in human experiences. The means are as varied as the modalities, techniques, and styles of that art; for each style, each period in literature, invents its own ways of creating its world. Thus, a writer's style is not a peculiarity of skill but rather a mirror of that individual's sense of reality. The adoption of stylistic devices and other technical features is the power of the vital image and the metaphor. The force of the metaphor does not lie principally with what it means but with what it does. Images alone in vivid construction or in metaphor and symbol impose a demand on the reader for participation. The poem does not *tell* us the truth; it confronts us with it. Language cannot *hold* meaning; it can lead us to *encounter* meaning, and nowhere more effectively than in literature. The relation of the reader to the text, like the more general philosophical problem of the relation of words to things, is a scholar's problem for those who use language and experience literature. In our customary use of language we observe no real division between word and thing, and this identity is especially marked in ritual, as well as in literature, where language occurs in conjunction with overt dramatic devices, objects, and symbols.[31] Without a reader, a text has no meaning; in various ways the reader and the text interact and interpenetrate, each making contribution of equal substance.

In music, as in the other arts, the work is not a construction from elements but a growth toward an integral unity. Thus, melodies have a kind of logic in their fulfillment, although works like *logic* or *necessity* have connotations too rational to convey the dynamic qualities of sound that the composer shapes intuitively. Every original work is newly made, not by building up a structure but by the process of germination and growth. A musical work is not a container within which sounds are situated or a framework inside which they are arranged. There is relatedness and cohesion to musical sounds; improvisation reflects the generative characteristics of musical material, and offers a first approximation of where it might go. Improvisation embodies the creative quality central to the experience of music; meaning becomes an aura of awareness, while improvisation evolves the unfolding life of musical ideas. We need logic and rhetoric both in philosophy and in art, since a true metaphor may be more eloquent than a valid argument.[32] Within dance, object, artist, and audience join in a bond of extraordinary intimacy, directness, and force. Movement becomes art when it is removed from purposive action and is placed in an imaginary virtual realm.[33] Such powers do not separate into traditional dualistic regions of illusion and reality. Dance creates a realm of powers, of forces at work, and the appearance of dancers in a performance space changes that space. Dance makes explicit an essential constituent of the aesthetic field – the dynamic presence of the human body in its immediacy and its possibilities. Dance establishes a world through the moving presence of the body. Movement always occurs in context, and in a world without movement we would have no sense either of time or space. Like the tortoise, we produce our accompanying place – no material shell, but a perceptual realm that we inhabit and with which we are continuous. The aware body is thus the center of our personal world, and as it moves, it generates that world. Space becomes not something exterior and objective but something I live inside.[34] Space in this sense is alive; a dance performance is not a display of object moving in empty space but an array of conscious human bodies moving in a field of forces, forces that they create and to which they respond. Through their movement, dancers generate the perceptual space of their dance. Like space, time arises out of motion, and time stops with the cessation of motion. This is lived time, time generated and brought to awareness through the vital movement of the body. From its source in such movement derive all special forces of temporal understanding devised for such specific purposes as comparison, measurement, abstraction, calculation, and even imagination. As the body moves, so does time, and in some sense, time, like space, is transcendental, as Kant held. It lies at the basis of experience; a condition without which perceptional experience would not occur.[35] Time is inherent in the very condition of experience, and experience must be extended to include the transition of thoughts, of perceptions, and of bodily actions and sensations. The awareness of their movement engenders our consciousness of temporality.[36] Both the impulse to move and our awareness of the power inherent in motion have their sources in our body consciousness. Nowhere is the function of the conscious human body revealed more directly.[37]

Film is the mass art of our day. In this modern equivalent of crystal gazing, everyone becomes able to see beyond the ordinary limits of time and place to the farthest distances of artistic imagination. Film is the composite of magic carpet and time machine, capable of transposing us instantly to any place in the world and any moment in history. More than any other art, film can order the pure dimensions of experience directly and without any apparent physical intermediary to create a convincing and absolute reality of its own. Filmmakers manipulate time the way composers order sound; it is experimental time, the time of perceptual awareness. Stopping the camera freezes time, and temporality becomes multidimensional, as we move along different chronologies without regard to their historical sequence. Through montage the filmmaker transcends the linearity of time moving horizontally to achieve simultaneity, or doubling back to repeat or reenact events. The flashback allows sequences depicting past and present to be exchanged and rearranged in any order. Berleant argues that we engage in this process of temporal reordering not only in waking and sleeping, but also in the deliberate activities of remembering and planning. By means of the editing process, the film artist fashions a temporal mosaic that pleases the creative purpose and standards of regularity, uniformity, and objectivity are disregarded in this process. Since temporal sequences can now be arranged at will in any order whatsoever, they all become "timeless" segments of an extended present.[38] Time in film is inseparable from the space in which the action moves; the cinematic space is not the space of physical action but of perceptual experience; the fixed dimensions of the so-called objective world dissolve into the changing horizon of human action. Like the space of dreams, cinema space is fluid and its periphery mobile, and it can be manipulated and ordered in whatever way the director desires. Space in film becomes place, the place of human habitation, action, and meaning. Unlike the so called physical space, the absolute space of Newtonian physics, cinema space is not homogeneous. It is associated with human feeling, human endeavor. Space is the place in which life is lived and assumes the qualities of the characters who inhabit it. Proximity and remoteness lose their visual meanings; distances are under the director's control and can be bent in multiple ways. Like the space of a map, cinema space is elastic and can be made to expand or contract. A history of perception would show that spatial awareness is different under different geographical and cultural conditions. Cinematic space is the paradigm of the modern world because it projects the experience of a relativism and malleable quantum universe, the space of satellite communication, and instantaneous electronic transmission and transformation.[39] The distinction between the real and the verbal disappears; they are continuos and they embrace in art as they do in life. The situation resembles dreams for, from the standpoint of living experience, no reality has precedence over any other. Films do not mirror empirical reality but structure a *sui generis* technological reality.[40] In film we often find ourselves shifting from one world to another, or inhabiting two or more different realities concurrently. We are accustomed to seeking frequent transitions in ordinary waking life, shifting from the immediate present to the projected future, and returning in the next instant to the various strands of the present that jostle for attention in our memory. Like the film, human reality is often multiple.[41] The boundaries of the ordinary world fade away, and the cinematic sphere is so comprehensive, so pervasive, and so powerful that it easily displaces the apparent reality of everyday life.

Implicit in any mode of perception are presuppositions about what experience is, what it means, and what it entails. So it may be that the history of the arts is more than anything else a history of changes in the way we experience and comprehend our world. This diverges from the empiricist tradition in philosophy, which has continually narrowed the purview of experience until for some it has been reduced to pure, isolated elements of sensation. Berleant uses the aesthetic as a corrective to this abridgment of experience; although its foundation lies in sense perception, the scope of aesthetic experience leads us to extend the domain of perception to include the rich regions of imagination, fantasy, memory, and dream. In fact, all this tampering with the range of perception and experience leads one to wonder about the truth of the usual boundaries between the real and the unreal.[42] We begin to realize that aesthetic theory is bound to epistemology, since perception and consciousness is never empty and unconditional. The aesthetic web is multidimensional.[43] Every art dwells in its own sphere of experience, and yet it transcends that domain with connections tenuous or strong to other regions in the world: of personal action, of ordinary objects, of "real" people and places. We come to realize that each art shapes a distinctive world of its own condition of being. One can identify different orders of experience, such as the religious, erotic, social, playful, and humorous, each of which can claim its own authenticity, and yet may, at the same time, enter into reciprocity with the aesthetic. Object, perception, and meaning coalesce in aesthetic engagement.[44] To speak of art as an illusion ascribes to it a defective character; even Coleridge's "willing suspension of disbelief" implies the underlying falsity of art. The tendency to confine art to the realm of the unreal is so deep-rooted and well-established as to seem unchallengable. But Berleant points out that this order is not fixed in advance; rather it emerges from the activities, conditions, and requirements of the situation, and that it can always be redefined. When we enter the world of literature, we tend to take ordinary experience as our standard of reality and regard everything that diverges from that standard as less than real. But novels do not imitate reality; they create it. Imagination and reality are not opposite poles but are so essentially interdependent that they become equal and inseparable.[45] For the world of men is not merely a world of things; it is a world of symbols where the distinction between reality and make-believe is itself unreal.[46]

It is easy to dismiss the belief in the magical power of art as a fanciful exaggeration, but Berleant rejects this as a condescending response to a more serious intent.[47] It is a curious border, this line between the real and the illusory. Not only does art claim its own reality, it refuses to remain apart from the "real" (read ordinary) world and stay in its own place. An editing process comparable to the cinematic one occurs in the ways we shape and experience the daily environment. As the film editor cuts and chooses his materials, we pursue our conscious lives through our choice of activities, selective attention, fantasizing, dreaming, and other imaginative constructions. And as the viewer cannot remain aloof and removed, so we cannot avoid participating in some fashion in daily life.[48] As with film and the other arts, the environment is the result of the same actions by which we fabricate every reality. What is central to them all is the human domain. This ambiguity of the real inhabits all the modes and forms of art, and it links in various ways the world that lies both within and beyond art. Nor is the realm of art less real than any other by not being objective, absolute, and eternal. Such an impersonal and independent status we now recognize as both unnecessary and impossible in any human enterprise – scientific, practical, or social as well as aesthetic. Aesthetic engagement is the very condition of art and aesthetic reality its ultimate achievement.[49] Aesthetic theory is not intellectually derivative or subsumed under philosophical disciplines mistakenly considered more basic. Like the fundamental axioms of a metaphysical system, the basic concepts of aesthetics do not lend themselves to logical deconstruction. In the directness and immediacy of aesthetic experience, art precedes reflective judgment and so forestalls the difficulties and indeterminacies of philosophy and science. Indeed, as a model of engaged experience, perhaps the most effective one, the aesthetic may well serve as a model for science.[50] The story of aesthetics reaffirms human participation in the natural and cultural world.

Notes

[1] Arnold Berleant, *Art and Engagement*, Philadelphia, PA: Temple University Press, 1991, p. xiii.

[2] *Ibid.*, p. 10.

[3] *Ibid.*, p. 12.

[4] *Ibid.*, p. 13.

[5] *Ibid.*, p. 14.

[6] Mikel Dufrenne, *The Phenomenology of Aesthetic Experience*, trans. E. Casey et al, Evanston, IL: Northwestern University Press, 1973, p. 55.

[7] Berleant, *Art and Engagement*, p. 18.

[8] *Ibid.*, p. 21.

[9] *Ibid.*, p. 24.

[10] *Ibid.*

[11] *Ibid.*, p. 29.

[12] *Ibid.*, p. 36.

[13] *Ibid.*, p. 55.

[14] *Ibid.*, p. 56.

[15] *Ibid.*, p. 57.

[16] *Ibid.*, p. 58.

[17] *Ibid.*, p. 59.

[18] *Ibid.*, p. 73.

[19] *Ibid.*, p. 77.

[20] *Ibid.*, p. 84.

[21] *Ibid.*, p. 85.

[22] *Ibid.*, p. 86.

[23] Maurice Merleau-Ponty, *Philosophy of Perception*, trans. Colin Smith, London: Routledge & Kegan Paul, 1962, p. 234.

[24] O.F. Bollnow, "Lived Space," *Philosophy Today* 5 (1961), pp. 31-39.

[25] Berleant, *Art and Engagement*, p. 88.

[26] Saussure quoted in *Saussure*, Jonathan Culler, Glasgow, Fontana: Collins, 1976, p. 50.

[27] Berleant, *Art and Engagement*, p. 108.

[28] *Ibid.*, p. 109.

[29] *Ibid.*, p. 120.

[30] *Ibid.*, p. 122.

[31] *Ibid.*, p. 129.

[32] *Ibid.*, p. 150.

[33] Suzanne K. Langer, *Feeling and Form*, New York Scriberner's, 1953, p. 184.

[34] M. Merleau-Ponty, *The Primacy of Perception*, Evanston, IL: Northwestern University Press, 1964, p. 16.

[35] I. Kant, *Critique of Pure Reason*, trans. N. Kemp Smith, London: Macmillan, 1956, I First Part, pp. 65-91.

[36] Berleant, *Art and Engagement*, p. 165.

[37] *Ibid.*, p. 168.

[38] *Ibid.*, p. 178.

[39] *Ibid.*, p. 181.

[40] Pierre Rouve, "Reel to Real: The Cinema as Technological Co-Reality," in *Art and Technology*, eds. René Beger and Lloyd Eby, New York, NY: Paragon House, 1986, p. 96.

[41] Berleant, *Art and Engagement*, p. 187.

[42] *Ibid.,* p. 192.

[43] *Ibid.,* p. 193.

[44] *Ibid.,* p. 194.

[45] Wallace Stevens, "The Noble Rider and the Sound of Words," in *Modern Poetics,* ed. James Scully, New York, NY: McGraw Hill, 1965, p. 139.

[46] E.H. Gombrich, *Art and Illusion,* 2nd ed., New York, NY: Pantheon, 1961, p. 99.

[47] Berleant, *Art and Engagement,* p. 202.

[48] *Ibid.,* p. 206.

[49] *Ibid.,* p. 208.

[50] *Ibid.,* p. 213.

Chapter Thirty-Seven

Art, Interpretation, and Reality

Hermerén argues that aesthetics is, and should be, relevant to the production, understanding, and enjoyment of art. The problem is analogous in some ways to the one between metaethics and ethics, or between ethics and moral action. But experience shows that when an aesthetician tries to tell an artist what to do, the result is usually bad art. On the whole, Anglo-American aestheticians do not seem concerned about the relevance of aesthetics to art, nor would they regard it a failure if their work did not have such relevance. Language has been their primary concern, and it is assumed that conceptual clarification and analysis is practically and normatively neutral, has no practical or normative consequences, and does not tell us what works of art are beautiful.[1] But this alleged neutrality of conceptual analysis has been questioned. Theories of art are crucial for the identification of possible works of art and their interpretation. Such theorizing serves several functions: descriptive, prescriptive, and predictive. Claims of relevance can be given several different interpretations.[2] Still, even if there are no obvious direct relations between aesthetics and art, there might be indirect ones. It would be difficult to exclude on a priori grounds the possibility that an artist might be positively or negatively influenced by aesthetic doctrines, and even more so the possibility that new trends in art will confront aestheticians with altogether different sets of problems. At least prima facie it would seen as if aesthetic doctrines have a pragmatic relevance to art. Hermerén concludes that aesthetic doctrines of certain kinds may help us to see works of art in a fresh way, to notice things that we might otherwise have missed. Each generation takes over, often without too much reflection, cultural habits and traditions of the past. Aesthetic theorists can liberate us from the prejudices of earlier generations, and from their ways of seeing. Artistic problems are hard to state verbally, and most of them are dealt with intuitively, yet our standard vocabulary is not quite equal to this purpose. Aesthetic considerations also play a role in science, as do the often discussed beauty of mathematical proofs. Theoretical considerations of parsimony, fruitfulness, scope and generality play a role in aesthetic theorizing. But the variety of aesthetic theories is only too conspicuous, and the difficulty of maintaining a sharp distinction between form and content in art is well-known.[3]

Drawing on Peirce's elaborate taxonomy of various species of signification, a picture was described as an iconic sign, one which signifies by virtue of the natural relation of resemblance. Goodman, however, argues that resemblance is neither sufficient nor necessary for depiction. The way we see and depict depends upon and varies with experience, practice, interests, and attitudes.[4] The painter's eye, like any other, does not so much mirror as take and make.[5] There is no doubt that what we are accustomed to seeing and saying tends to color our judgment, affect our memory, and influence the pictorial records that we make of visible things. What we choose to call the "appearance" of an object, and what we are content to acknowledge as a significant measure of visible similarity will depend upon what predicates we are accustomed to employing when describing our visible environment. The visible qualities that we require a painting to possess in order to qualify as reproducing the appearance of an object will vary correspondingly. Inductive validity depends not only on what is presented, but also on how it is organized. Yet the organization to which we point is influenced by the use of language, and is not attributable to anything inevitable or immutable in the nature of human cognition.[6] Repetition, Goodman has convinced us, is relative to organization. A world may be unmanageably heterogeneous or unbearably monotonous according to how events are sorted into kinds.[7] Goodman's proposal is that the manufacture of a picture, like the use of language, is a symbolic activity governed by a complex array of semantic and syntactic rules. Different pictorial stages are different schemes, and we are inclined to say that some styles are more naturalistic than others. But if Goodman's argument is sound, then it would certainly be absurd to suggest that a style is naturalistic according to the degree to which paintings in that style resemble what they depict. Instead, he maintains, it is the familiarity of the style in which the picture is painted, rather than optical correspondence between the painting and its subject, that leads us to regard it as more naturalistic than another. Realism is relative, determined by the system of representation standard for a given culture or person at a given time. Newer or older or alien systems are accounted artificial or unskilled.[8] Goodman's theory reflects a radical rejection of the view associated with the academic tradition that originated with the Renaissance writers on art. They maintained, or so it was believed, that painters, unlike poets, really do hold a mirror up to nature.

Margolis agrees with Beardsley that description and interpretation do not form distinct species of a common genus. There is, therefore, no reason for denying that interpretations may also be descriptions. Margolis takes the intentional to be identical with the cultural. Once we grasp that reference is inherently informal and context-bound, we must see that reidentification of a particular similarity depends on society's combined practices. Margolis construes texts as lacking "nature" in the sense of their also being "natural kinds" – kinds, that is, whose properties and change of property can be expressed in terms of physical laws, or physical or biological essentialisms. He agrees with Goodman that reidentification is always a function of the range of tolerance and remembered sense of coherence of a society's persistent practice. Contrary to Brentano and Husserl, Margolis insists that the "intentional" mind need not be confined to the mental; instead he identifies it with the cultural – that is, the collective features of a society's "form of life" along linguistic and other semiotic lines. The "aboutness" of pictorial studies is taken to be an intrinsic attribute of these texts because the texts themselves are identifiable as interpretable in the space of a given society's consensual pertinent practices. Margolis takes the world to be nontransparent; there is no privileged disjunction between the structure and the "brute" world independent of the categories of our understanding. Thinking has a history, the concepts by which cognizing agents make truth claims about the world are artifacts, subject to conditions of the changing consensual history of diverse societies. The "nature" we impute to ourselves is a function of our having internalized the "forms of life" of our native culture. Texts are evolving histories; they are not strictly ordered objects, as physical and natural objects are said to be. Intentional properties belong to the space of historical cultures and cannot be more determinate than they are. There is, therefore, no principled difference between a text and the interpretation of a text. We need not subscribe to any of those particular models, for there is always a form of historized change capable of overtaking even the most powerfully entrenched tradition. The distinction of the "same" and "different" are artifacts of that same interpretive picture. Consensually valid interpretations may, nevertheless, be incompatible among themselves on the usual bivalent model of truth. A tolerance of such diversity is a function of limits in interest, coherence, and effective accommodation that a society is willing and able to support. The result is an explicit relativism: given the openendness of history and the constructed nature of selves and texts, we may claim that if there are valid interpretation of a text, then, in principle, there may be infinitely many valid interpretations being synchronically and diachronically incongruent.

Fishelov criticizes Margolis's radical historicism, pointing out that the problems of interpretation are not unique to the literary or artistic world. Interpretations are based on metadescriptions and these descriptions are in their turn intimately related to certain interpretive schemata. The difference between interpretation and description does not lie in the fact that interpretations take different kinds of predicates or are attached to certain kinds of objects, but in the relative position of a statement within the framework of a means-ends model. Descriptions are those statements holding the "means" position, and interpretations the "end" position.[9] Sometimes the same statement can be labeled both, depending on its relation to the concomitant statements. Texts do not have stable descriptions upon which different interpretations are imposed. Providing a rational and economic interpretation is the foundation of our interpreting activity applied to art as well as to human actions and artifacts in general. By overemphasizing the importance of the interpreter's ideological worldview in the act of interpretation, a literary or artistic work is diminished to the status of a Rorschach inkblot into which the interpreter reads his own preoccupations. Fishelov denies that an interpretation is historically *bounded,* i.e. that its validity can be measured only with respect to a specified historical phase and worldview.[10] Our responses and interpretations should primarily be directed at and contrasted with the work's structure, and not by our historical, ideological, and other private preoccupations. Brinker also questions whether several of the new approaches to interpretation are compatible with our full interpretive practices. Such new approaches include analytical philosophy when it speaks of "radical interpretation," and the absurdity of the very idea of different conceptual schemes that order the same world, experience, or sense data. There are the interpreter's "horizon" of which Gadamer speaks, the "episteme" of Foucault and, with some adjustments, the "home language" of Quine, and the interpreter's "light" to which Davidson appeals in his discussion of "radical interpretation."[11] When a Western anthropologist faces the task of understanding another culture, what hope do we have for a full and complete fusion of horizons? Brinker concludes that intuitive understanding (*Verstehen*) is an indispensable part of any research in the humanities. A total denial of presence or a total rejection of commensurability reduces the richness that some interpretations do have. Such richness is due to the ability to subjugate the text simultaneously to two types of understanding or episteme: that of the object of study and that of the student.[12] Brinker admits, however, to having no transcendental argument for the superiority of the kinds of interpretation he prefers.

Krausz also wants to continue to do ontology while adopting a nonfoundational approach. Thus, for musical interpretation based on traditional musical scores, there is no single right musical interpretation. Neither is there a metastandard in virtue of which literature or artistic merit can be conclusively ranked. For Margolis, to use the same predicate does not commit one to an invariant order, but to principles, rules, genres, or laws are abstractions from within some life form or practice. Discourse cannot foundationally or algorithmically be separated from its communicative context. Yet Margolis's program is avowedly progressive; it allows for truth accommodation of basic ideas like objectivity, truth, and rationality in a reconstructed light.[13] Margolis emphasizes that the intelligible world as articulated under certain conditions of history is itself a function of a historically emergent inquiry. Such a view allows for laws of nature, and whatever else is needed for doing science. But he emphasizes that the cognizing subject and the cognized world are symbiotically related in one unanalyzable unity. The concepts under which we understand the world are themselves historical. Thus, the knowing subject has no fixed structure, but is a center of cognitive activity that is open to change over time.[14] Margolis insists that we cannot escape from the historical condition, and there is correspondingly no changeless understanding. Human beings have no essential or fixed nature; rather they transform and make themselves. The distinction between ontology and epistemology is not given independently of a theoretical context, and such a context may be construed in different ways. While he allows that our survival depends on our being in touch with the real world, the specific details of that world are always under historical construction. This kind of realism does not inhibit distinguishing the reality of the cultural from the reality of the physical. In a culture, as opposed to the physical world, humans are both the subject and the object of discourse. Along Wittgensteinian lines, Margolis holds that it does not make sense to suppose that in a massive way human beings do not understand the form of life they manifest in their lives. What we take to be the real structure of the world is systematically connected with the descriptions and explanations we take to be central.[15] It is impossible to speak about discourse, as such, in terms that resemble how we speak about claims within the discourse. We cannot speak about discourse from the outside, as it were, for any supposedly successful attempt to do so will but expand the discourse, and so will have failed to speak from its "outside." But we are not left dumb at this stage, for there are nontruth valued-ways of speaking about myth or the context of all contexts. That is, we may speak of one's being more or less amenable to certain ways of thinking and acting, or more or less perspicuous, apt, illuminating, or useful for one or another theoretical purpose.[16] Language has a discursive function concerned with truth claims, and it has a mythic function beyond truth claims. While we need evidence for discursive claims, we do not need evidence, at least in some ways, for mythic theorizing. In the latter, aptness, perspicuity, amenability, at-homeness, and related aesthetic notions enter into consideration. Being part of our background, they remain unfathomed at any particular moment in the emergence of inquiry. To change absolute presuppositions is to change one's inquiry, and this choice cannot entirely be rational, for the grounds of rationality are historically tied to the nature of a systematic inquiry to begin with. One's own guiding myths may, at any stage of theorizing, remain clouded, inchoate, and incomplete to oneself. But this does not mean that they may not, in principle, be articulated from another historical perspective.

Zemach holds aesthetic properties to be supervening on nonaesthetic ones; the former are observed, when the latter are seen through a special medium of desire. Since the phenomenal properties we perceive depend on our biological and psychological structures as humans, it seems that aesthetic properties cannot be properties of things themselves. Aesthetic predicates are primitive. The statement that x is coarse is not synonymous with any sort of nonaesthetic predicate; neither is the relation of aesthetic to nonaesthetic properties a Humean "causal," i.e. constant, conjunction. A conscious mind that has no interests can discern nonaesthetic phenomenal properties (e.g. it can see x as blue), but it cannot see things aesthetically, that is, encoded in aesthetic properties. A thing looks lovely only if we desire to have it in some way, whereas relative to another system of desires the noble will look vain or pompous. The aesthetic merit of a thing depends on the degree to which it satisfies our desire to make sense of the world, to organize it perceptually or conceptually in a form that is appropriate to our cognitive faculties. What is too much for us to digest, what has too many items that we find impossible to integrate, is noisy and chaotic. If, on the other hand, the information delivered is too meager relative the capacity of our cognitive system, if it has too much order and too little innovation, the subject is boring. We see beauty when the ratio of richness or order in the object examined is optimal for us to grasp. Zemach rejects realism as naive: to believe that our parochial phenomenal distinctions, determined as they are by human-specific organs and interests, are properties of things themselves, is chauvinistic if not downright silly. He emphasizes, however, that aesthetic properties, too, are essential to and inelimin-able from any adequate theory of reality as it is in itself. Indeed, our acceptance or rejection of theories, worldviews, and purported facts depends on their aesthetic properties. To be accepted as genuine, a purported fact must cohere with other facts, preferably explain them, and be explained by them. For theories, it is unity and simplicity, generality and depth, elegance and power (their ability to predict phenomena) that makes them worthy of our belief. Zemach reverts to the ancient Greek tradition that declared the identity of truth and beauty, and that was taken up by romantic poets like Keats. But Zemach offers a philosophical argument that he himself does not take quite seriously: he accepts Duhem's thesis that our science is but one of infinitely many theories that can account for exactly the same data. Even the predictive power of our science is not an argument in its favor, since each one of these infinity of other theories would have had the same rate of success. Zemach concludes that alternative Duhemian systems may be no less successful than our science, but they are not as pretty.[17] Pragmatism to the contrary, our thinking is not the one that works best, but the fairest of those which work.

Lyotard points out that artists have always expected and will always expect the philosopher to make intelligible what they have made. What art gives us is not "the given," but the generalization of a gesture, a movement and passage of colors, lines, volumes, and sounds. Lyotard concludes that we must rid our discourse of the referential, cognitive, and objectifying function that philosophy, like other intellectual disciplines, naively and consciously confers upon words and their arrangement, even if it does this in a different way than the other disciplines. The philosophers who are summoned in this way must thus begin to talk about thought itself as a work of art, and no longer simply as argument. This results in a profound change in the modus of their discourse, a modus that, as a result, leaves the province of the philosophical community.[18] Speculative and romantic thought resorted to the principle that there is an organic continuity between plastic, sonorous, or theatrical gestures on the one hand, and the discourse bearing on these gestures on the other. As Valéry has already shown, explications of the work of art that have been borrowed from psychology, psychoanalysis, sociology, history, semiotics, or linguistics, all have in common that they treat the real as a definite object. The question of what is art is usually understood as inquiry about the nature of the object that has been qualified as artistic. But this question can also be read as seeking to put an end to every attempt to "read" the gestures – to put an end to every kind of conceptual operation on the work. Morawski emphasizes that there is no fixed order within social reality. The regularities discovered by scholars are only circumstantial, i.e., they hinge on changing conjectures. The postmodern artist despises or merely ignores all theorizing in art.[19] Unlike his modernist predecessors who were constantly theorizing about their aesthetic productions, he is anti-intellectual. But theorizing goes on all the same by means of pastiche and parody, which are the most suitable vehicles for exploring the confusions, permissiveness, and eclecticism in our culture. Postmodernism entails a disbelief in art's meaning and dignity. There is no masterplan and no established order of things, and we look in vain for such foundations. Nevertheless, a yearning for a history that makes sense cannot be denied, even if there is no Hegelian final tribunal of appeal. Lacking philosophical constraints, art criticism and aesthetics come to be expressed in a profusion of attitudes that accept aporias as unresolvable. The critic today is a kind of artist, for one and the same logic governs all these arguments, which results in the not surprising suggestion to abandon philosophy altogether. Mooij points out that art in modern culture has powerful irrational features.[20] But while many of the relevant decisions may depend on taste, preference, political attitude, or even mere folly, other claims are certainly based on rational expectation, calculation, and argument. In "applied" art, the part of rationality is even more evident, for the role of practical, even technical, constraints demands rational deliberation. Reasons can be given why some means are better or worse than others. While science yields the most important paradigm of strict rationality, there remains a legitimate role for weaker versions of logic. Scientific attitudes and strategies can be criticized in the name of rationality, and the alleged logic can be understood and explained in different ways. The paradigmatic role of scientific intelligence is connected with the place science and scientific technology play in modern society. Alleged superrational forces are viewed with suspicion and irony.

According to I.A. Richards, the value of literature in the modern period is based on its capacity to bring about a complex temporary balance and harmony between otherwise divergent and incompatible emotive reactions. Richards argues that when religion disappears, literature is essential to the mental health of individuals and of society as the emotive counterpart of the rational and cognitive aspect of the sciences.[21] This is made possible by the capacity of literature to suspend or cross the border between the rational and the irrational. It often plays with strange or "unbelievable" notions, and it might suggest profound insights by making connections that are illusive from a scientific or even commonsensical point of view. Poetry, and literature in general, order the world in a way different from the rational ordering of the sciences. It subjects phenomena to the needs of the human mind, and it appropriates insights and powers that are contrary to rational expectation and technical control.[22] One might even say that it puts forth a resemblance of magic in a world that is increasingly dominated by the scientific attitude. Poets, consciously or unconsciously, playfully or seriously, are inspired by magical beliefs. The universe of poetry, and of literature in general, is still a universe of meaning, even though science teaches us not to believe this anymore. Owing to the vitality of its magic, modern culture is richer and more complex than it would be otherwise. The aesthetic view of magic supplants the classical scientific world view and the common-sense attitude with fascinating glimpses of other ways of interpreting the world. Moreover, the boundary between quasi-magical sophistication and crude obscurantism, or between intelligent symbolism and sentimental self-projection is by no means sharp or definite. Science, also, has its own region of fantasy and marvel in the ever-changing set of riddles and speculation correlated to its teachings. Literature and art can make us aware of how things are, what a certain type of reality is like, and what is really at issue in a specific situation.[23] It can bring unknown or half-known areas of experience home to us. Such speculation may have only a weak link with the observable facts, for not only the boundaries between science and philosophy, but also those between science and art turn out to be indeterminate. It has become evident that the differences between scientific and artistic creativity are not at all easy to define. One should realize that fact and fancy inevitably interfere with one another.

Notes

[1] Göran Hermerén, "The Relevance of Aesthetics to Art," *Iyyun, The Jerusalem Philosophical Quarterly*, vol 42 (January 1993), p. 75.

[2] *Ibid.*, p. 80.

[3] *Ibid.*, p. 98.

[4] N. Goodman, *Languages of Art*, Brighton: Harvester, 1981, p. 8.

[5] *Ibid.*, p. 10.

[6] N. Goodman, *Fact, Fiction and Forecast*, 3rd. Ed., Indianapolis, IN: Bobbs-Merrill, 1973, pp. 96-7.

[7] N. Goodman, *Ways of Worldmaking*, Hassocks: Harvester, 1978, p. 9.

[8] Goodman, *Languages of Art*, p. 37.

[9] David Fishelov, "Interpretation and Historicism," in *Iyyun*, p. 20.

[10] *Ibid.*, p. 26.

[11] Menachem Brinker, "Interpretation and Otherness," in *Iyyun*, p. 31.

[12] *Ibid.*, p. 35.

[13] Michael Krausz, "Culture and the Ontology of Music," in *Iyyun*, p. 172.

[14] *Ibid.*, p. 173.

[15] *Ibid.*, p. 175.

[16] *Ibid.*, p. 176.

[17] Eddy M. Zemach, "The Ontology of Aesthetic Properties," in *Iyyun*, p. 65.

[18] Jean-Francois Lyotard, "Gesture and Commentary," in *Iyyun*, p. 43.
[19] Stefan Morawski, "Art, Philosophy and Art Criticism," in *Iyyun*, p. 128.
[20] J.J. A. Mooij, "Art and Rationality," in *Iyyun*, p. 105.
[21] I.A. Richards, *Poetry and the Sciences*, London: Routledge & Kegan Paul, 1970.
[22] Mooij, "Art and Rationality," p. 115.
[23] *Ibid.*, p. 120.

Chapter Thirty-Eight

The Philosophical Disenfranchisement of Art

Danto adopts the Hegelian view that regards history as the drive to break through to the consciousness of itself.[1] But while Hegel believed this to have been attained in his own philosophy, Danto does not accept that the history of philosophy came to a final end with Hegel. He does, however, adopt an eschatological view of art, maintaining that art has reached the stage where it no longer has a history, and all that remains is a philosophy of art. Unlike Hegel, Danto is not content to understand the present situation of art but goes on to predict its future. He claims that progress in the visual arts has come to an end at the turn of the twentieth century with the invention of modern motion picture technology. At this stage, further progress could be achieved only in this new medium which was able to show movement directly, and which could, in this way, tell a story previously unknown to the audience – something painting and sculpture could never hope to do. Traditional painters and sculptors had to assume that viewers were already familiar with the biblical, classical, or whatever stories they were depicting, whereas the cinema need not presume any such knowledge on the part of the audience. While movies were understood by a largley passive audience, the visual arts demanded considerable cooperation from the viewers. Danto explains how this state of affairs led to abstract art and a formalist aesthetics that have remained a central feature of modernism. It led to the belief that how the artist orders the world is very much up to him, and to a pluralism that characterizes, not only artmaking, but postmodern culture generally in its morality, politics, theories of history, and even philosophies of science. Danto's point is that such a pluralism becomes self-defeating once it loses control over what is permissible. Having reached a stage when art can be anything at all, it has exhausted its historical mission. He maintains that it would be inconsistent with such an approach to believe in any future history of art, and cites Hegel to the effect that any further step is philosophy's to take because philosophy, unlike art, has no post-historical phase. Once the truth has been found, there is nothing further to be done, and history comes to an end.

Danto fails to explain, however, what there is to philosophize about once art no longer matters. He himself treats the history of art, not just as the record of a (Hegelian) "form of thought," but also as one that reflects an account of its long and persistent suppression. Thus, for Danto, art is not only the tale of the spirit's progress towards self-consciousness, it is also the record of something perceived to be dark and dangerous. He believes, on the one hand, that persecution constitutes an essential part of the history of art going back all the way to Plato and, on the other hand, that this view is philosophically mistaken. He dismisses the near unanimous belief among philosophers that art makes nothing happen, while explaining that modern art has reached the stage of historical insignificance where it no longer needs to be suppressed because it no longer matters. But his explanation is inadequate largely because contemporary philosophy considers itself to be no less problematic than does modern art. For Wittgenstein, philosophy begins when language goes on a holiday and, since philosophy leaves everything as it is, its future is to disappear and become some sort of linguistic therapy. Danto realizes that if art makes nothing happen, and if art is but a disguised form of philosophy, then philosophy makes its appearance only when it is too late for anything but understanding. When Duchamp, therefore, calls his urinal *Fountain* and declares it a work of art, Danto regards this not as a logical definition or philosophical classification, but strictly as a matter of power politics. It is not surprising that under such circumstances contemporary criticism and philosophy of art are unable to reach agreed-upon resolutions of conflicting interpretations. A modern artwork is taken as a mirror that reflects only a particular viewer and, as such, is incommensurable with what other viewers perceive it to be. While Danto prefers an interpretation that coincides most closely with the artist's own interpretation, what may be at work here is a Hegelian "cunning of reason" that renders the artist unaware of the true historical significance of his own work.

Hegelian reason may act to achieve ends that come about even though the secondary agents of historical realization are totally unaware of the grand scheme in which they figure. Since Danto considers Hegel's "absolute knowledge fatally flawed,"[2] he lacks a convincing argument for the "end of history," or for deciding which events are not part of history. His philosophy of art is likewise incapable of providing a plausible explanation for the transformation of an ordinary object into a work of art and that is how this becomes a matter of sheer power politics. Contrary to Hegel, for Danto *all* interpretation is contextually relative, but since he rejects the meaning-conferring context of the Fregean sentence, he can provide nothing approaching the rules of syntax and grammar for the interpretation of a text. The contextual links he does provide exhibit only a network-like structure that is unable to prevent conflicting interpretations. These interpretations are not rule-governed in the required manner, and fail therefore to yield logical calculi or convincing arguments. The "contextual logic" Danto proposes is said to cut across the traditional boundaries between the pictorial and the verbal, but there is little he is able to say about such a logic. What the required skills of interpretation are that turn an ordinary object into a work of art is consequently also obscure. Danto defines as "transformation" the process whereby quite commonplace objects are raised to the level of art, yet his coherence criteria leave such a metamorphosis incomprehensible. Since relevance for him is merely a matter of context and not of reference, the artwork remains a semi-opaque object that resists his kind of analysis. He focuses on the historical domain every artwork is said to display in consequence of the interaction between its content and mode of representation, and in this manner "style" reflects aesthetic responses that combine interpretation with appreciation. But Danto has to concede that we hardly have any idea what sort of under-standing this involves. He is unable to render explicit the criteria for judgment of taste that are essential for his kind of analysis.

Thus, Danto starts, not only with what he takes to be the "present dismal state of the artworld," but goes on to proclaim this sorry state of affairs to be irreversible. While he realizes that nothing belongs so much to its own time as to an age's glimpses of the future, he all the same insists that there is not going to be a future in which art matters. Predicting that art has no future involves anticipating complex social

and economic conditions of society as a whole, yet Danto's
eschatological vision is not an extrapolation of existing trends. Hegel
saw the task of philosophy as one of understanding present reality,
whereas Danto regards the contemporary proliferation of styles as an
indication that there is no future in which art is going to matter. Even
though periods of anarchy are as much part of history as are ages of
stability, Danto rejects the present pluralism of styles as "cultural
entropy" because this does not meet Hegel's rational criteria for
progress. But since he himself fails to adhere to Hegel's absolute
standards for what is rational and real, he has no way of knowing
whether what comes next is going to matter. What is at issue here is
not the mere survival of art but its historical role, yet Danto's notion of
evolution owes much more to Darwin than it does to Hegel. He accepts
that "our present institutions of art – museums, galleries, collectors,
and art journals – all share the assumption of a significant and even
brilliant future,"[3] and at the same time insists that the concept of art is
"internally exhausted." It is a well-known fact, however, that even the
great philosophers were notoriously bad at predicting the future.
Aristotle was altogether unaware that the Greek city state he was
setting up as a model for civilized government was about to disappear
in consequence of Alexander's conquests. Kant, likewise, was
convinced that after Aristotle, there was nothing of consequence to be
discovered in the science of reasoning, and that logic, therefore, had
no future. While we know by hindsight how wrong they both were,
predicting the future is an urge few philosophers are able to resist.

When at the beginning of this century the basic cinematic
strategies had been discovered, painters began asking themselves what
was left for them to do. Given the manner progress was perceived, they
could justify their work only be redefining art in ways that were bound
to be shocking to those who continued to judge painting by the
traditional standards. In subsequent art, progress was no longer
specified in terms of the artist's mastery of illusionist techniques, but
was conceived as consisting in his ability to give expression to his
feelings and move an audience. Danto rightly points out, however, that
this is always a delicate matter, and one for which we lack clear-cut
criteria. Interpretation of expressionist work, therefore, lacks the
developmental sequence we take for granted in mimetic interpretation.
The point is that modern art has a history, even though it cannot be
said to make progress in the Hegelian sense, Hegel believed that
history ends with the advent of self-knowledge; for Danto, however,

such self-knowledge is no longer unique, yet he still wants it to be final. Given the philosophical nature of historical knowledge, it becomes inevitable that the termination of art's history brings about an end to its philosophy. If there ever comes a time when art no longer matters, there will be, by the same token, nothing of importance to philosophize about.

Indeed philosophy after Hegel has been no less a record of discontinuities than is modern art. Analytic philosophy failed in its attempt to gain for itself scientific status, and what passes today as philosophy is by no means an easily defined subject matter. In spite of such lack of identifiable uniformity, however, Danto insists that post-Hegelian philosophy has a history while he denies one to modern art. Since contemporary philosophy cannot answer the question of its own identity any better than does modern art, the history of neither can nowadays be told as a novel of self-education (*Bildungsroman*) in the Hegelian manner. Danto concedes that even future artists will continue to do whatever they are doing in their historical insignificance. For Hegel, art was free only when it had established itself in the sphere it shared with religion and philosophy, becoming, thereby, an additional form of thought through which spiritual truth is brought to consciousness. Since Danto realizes that decoration, self-expression, and entertainment are abiding human needs, he fails to explain why they should not have a history, like fashion and cooking have histories. The traditional boundaries between the arts are no longer in place – as collage, assemblage, mobile sculpture, and concrete poetry demonstrate – but this only partly accounts for why contemporary philosophy of art isn't what it used to be. Indeed, Danto's dilemma is not so much due to recent changes in the arts as to the very problematic status of contemporary philosophy. In trying to reconcile Hegel's view with that of Nietzsche, he attempts to understand art both as a stage in the development of the spirit, and as something dark and dangerous. While he considers this latter view to be philosophically mistaken, he nevertheless believes that there is extensive historical evidence for the suppression of art and the persecution of artists. He does adopt Nietzsche's conjecture that classical tragedy is a development out of the Dionysian rites, and that it reflects the insertion of a certain distance between the audiences – itself an evolution out of celebrants – and what happens on the stage. Greek tragedy reenacted this at the level of art rather than religious practice, and this brought about a separation of images from reality in the particular way modern theories of the image take for granted. The god is merely represented by the actor, and the actor is no longer believed to be possessed by the god as he was in the Dionysian rites. Danto finds support for this view in Aristotle's doctrine of *catharsis* designed to explain why, in going to the theater, something profound happens to the audience. The audience is mystically purged as the original Dionysiast must have been by the climax of the enactment. Danto explains that even modern audiences come to the theater for something like this to happen, not merely to enjoy a spectacle and have a good time. As a Hegelian, however, he is bound to mistrust the revival of such magical elements in art as "going against the historical grain."[4] Danto's claim that "art is dead" owes more to Nietzsche than it does to Hegel; it is Nietzsche's "death of god" rather than Hegel's "end of history" that provides Danto with a paradigm for his philosophy of art.

Because of such inconsistencies, Danto's Hegelianism amounts to an inadequate refutation of the positivist and deconstructivist attacks that view philosophy itself as an artform or metaphor. By reducing philosophy to literature, Carnap and Derrida question its claim to objective knowledge, and Danto in effect admits that Plato's theory of ideas expresses the feelings of the philosopher – his fear of poetry and of the magical qualities that are latent in art. Plato is thus regarded by Danto as an artist who was frightened by the destruction spells he perceived to be lurking in artistic make-believe. Following Nietzsche, he in the end agrees with Carnap and Derrida that philosophers use the appearance of scientific discourse to create the illusion of objective meaning, when it is in fact the philosopher's feelings that are being expressed, and for which the conventions of literature would be much more suitable and less misleading. Since Danto's half-hearted Hegelianism is unable to substantiate the intellectual claims of philosophy, his argument that denies a historical role to all future art also becomes self-defeating.

Notes

[1] Arthur C. Danto, *The Philosophical Disenfranchisement of Art*, New York, NY: Columbia University Press, 1986.

[2] *Ibid.*, p. 113.

[3] *Ibid.*, p. 85.

⁴ *Ibid.*, p. 133.

Chapter Thirty-Nine

Danto on the End of Art

Danto discusses the history of contemporary art from the perspective of what has happened during the last two decades in the New York artworld. As a philosopher and art critic, he is concerned with the very possibilities of art criticism for anyone who is sensitive to the discontinuities between the artistic present and the conceptually comfortable past.[1] If Duchamp's *Fountain* is an artwork, there must be an answer to the question of why other urinals are not, even if the resemblances are perfect. When the Medici Tomb or the Cathedral of Beauvais were made, no one could have imagined there could be works like those of Duchamp and Warhol. Duchamp's great philosophical achievement was to demonstrate that "work of art" is not an expression we can learn to apply on the basis of perceptual criteria. Danto's point is that this could not have been shown until history made it possible, that is, by hindsight. When the question about the identity of art became possible, it also became evident that the beautiful and the sublime did not belong to the essence of art. Danto's outlook in all this is one of an art critic writing reviews on upcoming exhibitions for some of the leading New York museums and galleries. He is disappointed by what he sees and draws from this far-reaching philosophical conclusions on the nature and history of art in general. He believes that art, as it has been historically understood, has come to an end, and he concludes that this is a crisis not only for the philosophy of art, but also for art education and for art making in general. And it is, of course, a crisis for art criticism itself; how does one judge what are the appropriate responses, where are the standards, and how can we evaluate? There is no longer any validity to the critical charge that something is not art because if fails to meet some standard of aesthetic purity.

The mystery of art has to do with the way it attaches us to images – to the showing of things rather than the things shown. But the fact is that the bulk of our experience with works of art comes from reproductions, and there is no question that the reproduction is an image that never attaches us to itself but only to the object – the painting or the statue in question. Discussing Sienese painting, Danto argues that modernism began when the surface became something to look at rather than look through, and artists no longer sought illusion because painting had become an object in its own right rather than a transparent opening into an ulterior reality. Yet even with abstract art, the distinction between looking and looking through and, hence between subject and surface remained. The moment the work became all surface, it collapsed into decoration. In order to remain art accordingly, illusory or pictorial space had to be retained; so artists may just as well have remained realists for all the good the revolutions did them. The window-paradigm co-opts those who undertake to overthrow it.[2] The relationship between the viewer and the event is essentially perceptual and cognitive. Because the viewer has no access to the scene depicted other than visually, he becomes reduced to a disembodied eye, a geometric point. Internal and external illusory space are repudiated, and paintings are made supervisually to stifle the possibility of illusion, as if the work consists only of its own surface.[3] There is also the sense in which Western civilization has lost the belief of being at the apex of progress as it came to accept the view that progress had been bought at too great a cost. "Primitive" art, which until then had been dismissed as a mere anthropological curiosity or as evidence of the inferiority of the cultures that produced it, became instead an inspiration. Until Picasso began work on *Les Demoiselles d'Avignon* in 1907, the carvings and assemblages of Africa and Oceania had been viewed chiefly as ethnographic data for the science of man that addressed primitive cultures primarily as yielding analogical insights into stages through which our own culture must long have since passed. But primitive artworks had been ripped from a context in which they functioned as something much more important to its makers than museum pieces. In its native provinces, the sculpture was vested with powers of which Western art has not been capable for centuries, except for those special cases where a certain Madonna or some sacred bambino is believed miraculous and is worshipped for its powers.[4] Modernist sensibility opened our eyes to the polished surfaces, the rhythmic ornamentation, and the clean forms of African carving. In their original context, most of what we class as a primitive art was not intended to be responded to aesthetically, even if aesthetic excellence was acknowledged as an index that deep and important powers had been captured. In Africa, even today, works of art are concealed form alien eyes and are believed to hold powers that must be understood as preconditions for responding to the work in the intended way. The ancient Egyptian figure was a configuration of prototypical body parts whose obviousness and familiarity were the criteria of representation. In a similar manner, cubism analyzes into prototypical aspects objects of the most commonplace order. When Japanese prints impinged upon European artwork in the late nineteenth century, a whole order of representation opened up for artists. It was out of this encounter that Van Gogh, Gauguin, Bonnard, and Matisse began what became modern art, in which the eye as an optical system was disenfranchised in favor of something altogether more cerebral.

It was as though beneath the visual appearances of the familiar world there was another system of reality altogether, covert and disguised, but that stands to the surface world as the unconsciousness stands to conscious rational processes. Freud saw in dreams, jokes, and free associations the aperture into primary processes of the unconscious, which the surrealists treated as the creative substratum of the mind. The image is endowed with magical possibilities, and if the surreal world has some "logic," it would record the magic to which rationality is blind. The surrealists used the premise of optical exactitude to demonstrate the fantastic exterior of the ordinary world. But often they achieved this only by flagrant manipulations and montages, or by using as motifs things they found rich in their own particular meanings. Now the moral transformation of the viewer is an ancient and respected goal of art; it underlies the phenomenon of *catharsis* in Aristotle, and it defined the priorities of censorship in Plato's political aesthetics. But the term "aesthetics," with its notions of disinterestedness and deletion, was very much an eighteenth-century invention and, except for the period of the Impressionists and Cezanne, art has always been part of the arsenal of moral education. Danto concludes that you cannot fuse propositions about reeducation in painting and injunctions into a coherent concept to better one's moral condition. He fails to recognize, however, the role of technology as one of the major sources of modernity – photography, the movies, and television on the one hand, and the capacity for rapid and continuos movement on the part of the viewer, on the other. Such movement is not an extra property that can be added or subtracted, leaving all other properties as they are, as in the way a change of color leaves shape unaffected. Rather, the perception of movement affects the way we perceive everything else.

Some modern painters want us to look at a painting as if it were merely a flat surface, yet it is not obvious that an image is the kind of entity that exhausts its essence by being pure surface either. At a certain moment in the history of painting, flatness, which one might have supposed could be taken for granted, served an almost impossible goal. Its being a goal was connected with the struggle against illusion, in which abstraction was a strategy. The problem with abstraction is that the moment one makes a mark on the canvas, it seems immediately to assume a position in an illusory pictorial space. Another mark will be seen as behind it or in front of it, and neither of them seems really to be staying at the surface. If flatness could be achieved, the painter would no longer be engaged in representing reality but in creating it. There would be no hidden depths because there are no depths, and it should be a world in which the only problems are aesthetic problems. But it also illustrates the fact that what we see depends on how we feel and on what we believe. There are those who maintain that our perception of the visible world is so laden with perception that, in science as in common life, there is no sharp line to be drawn between observation and theory "To draw" brings to light some of the primitive beliefs about aesthetic power that could explain some of the magic association with art, and some of the reasons ancient writers found it dangerous and fearful.[5] Portraiture must have evoked an even more mysterious achievement, the drawing forth, as it were, of the inner self or soul. In the archaic form of representation the picture is a copy, and the subject is really present in his or her picture, since the spirit was believed to be literally present in the icon that was made holy and potent for just the same reasons that a relic was holy and potent. It also explains why iconoclasm was so powerful and influential a movement in Byzantine and Protestant theology and politics. It offered us a theory of the artist as magician and even Wittgenstein believed that the human body is the best picture of the human soul since nothing is intelligibly interior that lacks an external criterion.

Danto argues that the relationship between museum and big business is our society's version of the symbiosis of church and state. Today artworks have sunk to the level of commodities, and investing in art futures has become the "truth" of contemporary art. The corporate presence dominates the museum and, while insisting on the ideology of disinterestedness, art has become transformed into a showroom of classy investments. At some point it was recognized that the demand for appreciable artworks was seriously exceeding the supply. There are only so many Manets around, only so many Seurats, and the response to this in the 1980s was to augment the supply by according a spiritual status to a number of artworks on condition that they look important. The museums are needed to certify the investments, yet the idea of the masterpiece has come itself under attack. It came from the artmakers who understood that a period had been entered in which the rules and practices that made the master-piece a possibility and an ideal no longer defined the making of art. The second attack came from the direction of politics and was motivated by a new generation of art makers who felt themselves disenfranchised by the institutions and attitudes embodied by the masterpiece, construed as the symbol of everything eliticist, exclusion-ary, and oppressive in the world of art. The task of art is no longer to produce masterpiece but to use the making and showing of art in the service of more socially urgent endeavor. In this manner the museum, like the university, has become an arena of political conflict, and masterpiece turned into a charged concept. Part of what we mean in calling a work of art a masterpiece is that it is of "museum quality," yet the museum itself is a deeply contested idea in the artworld today.[6] The possession of art was the symbol of authority, and this power was symbolically transferred to the people from their rulers when their art was seized in the name of the Revolution. It is also as the emblem of power that the museum enters modern consciousness, and not simply as a place to see aesthetically impressive works, or to study the masters. The idea of an aggregation of masterpieces having in common only their museum quality has been the dominant component in the concepts of museum and works of art ever since Napoleon, and the masterpiece has come to play a role that is at once political and con-ceptual. The museum did not exist merely for pleasure or the development of taste, but for the moral education of the citizens.

Today the masterpiece is an essentially contested concept, no less than the museum or the work of genius that define it.

Danto takes his model of the history of art from Vasari, a history of stages that come to an end when no further breakthroughs were thinkable. Danto construes the history of contemporary art as the collective investigation by artists into the philosophical nature of art. Pop violated every component of theory and somehow remained art. It was Warhol who revealed as merely accidental most of the things his predecessors supposed essential to art, and who carried the discussion as far as it would go without passing into pure philosophy. In the opinion of Danto, he brought the history of art to an end by demonstrating that no visual criterion could serve the purpose of defining art. Warhol achieved this with the celebrated Brillo boxes he exhibited in 1964 in New York.[7] What was most striking about them was that they looked sufficiently like their counterparts in the supermarket stockrooms that the difference between them could hardly be of a kind to explain why they were art and their counterparts merely cheap containers of scouring pads. Warhol did not himself make these boxes nor did he paint them, but when they were displayed, the question was inevitable: why were these boxes art when their originals were just boxes? Danto believes that just by asking this question, no less than a century of deflected philosophical investigation came to an end. Artifacts were liberated to enter the postphilosophical phase of modernism, free from the obligation of self scrutiny.[8] This in spite of his contention that art has come to an end and that philosophy has taken over art. Part of what makes Danto think that we have reached the end of art is the near consensus in the artworld today that we are living through bad aesthetic times. There is a lot of style, but there doesn't seem to be much substance. The irony is that these feelings arise against a background in which, in every other way, the times are very good for art. There are more art magazines, more interest than ever before in what artists are doing, more galleries and museums, incredible prices at auctions even for living artists, more art schools turning out more artists who see art as a viable profession like dentistry or accounting, more money all around. And yet, while the engines of the artworld turn furiously, the output has been aesthetically stalled for two decades, and if there is a direction to speak of it is that of bad aesthetics. Disturbatory art exploits aesthetic means to achieve social and moral change; it is not meant to be beautiful, symmetrical, composed, tasteful, pretty, elegant, or perfect. But it often fails and collapses into something merely embarrassing, boring, silly, and awful. From this, Danto senses that the charge is to end one form of history and to begin another. Viewing the history of art from his narrow New York vantage point, he concludes that further breakthroughs are unthinkable. But breakthroughs always come as a surprise, and the notion of history coming to an end is one with which he is not himself quite comfortable.

Notes

[1] Arthur C. Danto, *Encounters and Reflections, Art in the Historical Present*, New York, NY: Farrer Straus Giroux, 1990, p. 5.

[2] *Ibid.*, p. 265.

[3] *Ibid.*, p. 186.

[4] *Ibid.*, p. 166.

[5] *Ibid.*, p. 63.

[6] *Ibid.*, p. 317.

[7] *Ibid.*, p. 288.

[8] *Ibid.*

Chapter Forty

Iconology

In a series of historical essays Mitchell connects theories of art, language, and the mind with conceptions of social, cultural, and political value.[1] Central to his theory is an explanation of the fear of images, and the struggle between iconoclasm and idolatry. He shows that icons have not lost their power over us, and that we still do not seem to understand their nature. But language and imagery are no longer presumed perfect and transparent media; instead they are seen to be in need of analysis and justification. At the same time, discussions of imagery often proceed on the questionable assumption that there are kinds of images, such as photographs or mirror images that provide a direct unmediated copy of what they represent. Mitchell emphasizes, however, that the meaning of a picture does not declare itself by simple direct reference to the object it depicts. Following the later Wittgenstein, he conceives of knowledge as a matter of social practices, disputes, and arguments, not as a copy or image of reality imprinted in the mind. But contrary to Wittgenstein, Mitchell concludes that it is futile to attempt to purge the world of images. Instead, he offers a historical explanation of how the notion of image as transparent picture has dominated our ideas of the mind and of language. Aided by the political and economic ascendance of Western Europe, artificial perspective conquered the world of representation under the banner of science and objectivity. No amount of counter-demonstration by artists that there are other ways of picturing what we really see has been able to shake the conviction that these pictures have a kind of identity with natural human vision and objective external space. The invention of the camera build to produce this sort of image has only reinforced the conviction that this is a natural mode of representation. Mitchell insists that there is no objective and independent visible world out there to match things against, no unmediated "facts" about what or how we see.

He argues that the category of realistic or naturalistic image has become the focus of modern secular idolatry, linked with the ideology of Western science and rationalism. Indeed, he largely identifies with the iconoclastic reaction that the hegemony of these images has generated. Rejecting G. E. Lessing's separation of painting from poetry, he justifies the crossing of such lines as inevitable. Moreover, he conceives the relation between words and images in political terms, as a contest of rival ideologies. While we create much of our world out of the dialogue between verbal and pictorial representation. We have not been able to provide a unified theory of verbal and pictorial signs. Thus, we are inclined to think that to compare poetry with painting is to make a metaphor, whereas to differentiate poetry from painting is to state the literal truth. These are powerful distinctions that reflect the ways the arts are understood and practiced. Mitchell criticizes Gombrich's linguistic approach to imagery who holds that vision, picturing, and plain seeing are activities much like reading and writing. He likewise questions Nelson Goodman's contention that language provides the model for all symbol systems including the pictorial. Mitchell emphasizes that the sign type that has proved most difficult to assimilate into semiotics has been the *icon*, the traditional contrary to the verbal sign. The major reason for this is that similarity is such a capacious relationship, that everything in the world is similar to everything else in some aspects, if we look hard enough. Signs are everywhere, and there is nothing that is not potentially or actually a sign. Mitchell agrees with Goodman that the test of fidelity is never simply "the real world" but some standard construction of the world. People who have never seen photographs have to learn how to see them, that is, how to read what is depicted. But Goodman deliberately avoids questions of value and offers no canons for criticism; he proceeds on the assumption that art is simply a universal category that can be described from a neutral analytic perspective. Mitchell points out, however, that in spite of Goodman's proclaimed relativism, his work has been devoted to the problem of how to tell right versions from wrong versions in art.

Gombrich also regards the naturalness of perspective painting as a literal truth. Perspective is not merely one conventional procedure for interpreting the visible world but occupies a privileged position that Gombrich sees represented in the objective nonconventional element of a photograph. Mitchell points out, however, that the nature implicit in Gombrich's theory of the image is far from universal; rather it is a particular historical formation, an ideology associated with the rise of modern science and the emergence of capitalist economics. Mitchell argues that the notion of image as a "natural sign" is the fetish or idol of Western culture. This Western idolatry disguises its own nature under the cover of ritual iconoclasm, the claim that our own images, unlike "theirs," are constructed by a principle of effective self-criticism. But since all signs, whether words or images, work by custom and convention, the mistake is to think that we can know the truth about things by knowing their right names, signs, or interpretations. The other mistake is to believe that we can know anything without names, images, or representations. Mitchell concludes that because signs and images are all we have to work with, we have to learn to use them dialectically, as a starting point for a dialogue or conversation. He discusses the visual-verbal relationship in the arts as a dialectical struggle in which the opposed terms take on different ideological roles at different moments in history. Exclusive preferences become improper because they are abstracted form one another as independent antithetical categories that define the nature of art. Lessing's "laws of genre," which were said to be imposed by the nature of the subject, turn out to be artificial and historical conventions. Lessing merely rationalized a fear of imagery that dominates Western philosophy in the works of Bacon, Kant, and Wittgenstein. Mitchell follows the nineteenth century German art historian Alois Riegl who pointed out that vision has a history. Our ideas of what vision is and of what is worth looking at are all deeply embedded in social and cultural history.

Since the time of Locke, our theory of the mind has rested on the conception of consciousness as a recorder and reflector of images. Later on, a confusion of sensory aesthetic symbols of the natural order of gender, social class, and symbolic modes became the basis for Burke's rejection of the French Revolution. Mitchell emphasizes that both sides were caught up in a rhetoric of iconoclasm, and the imputation of idolatry to the other. It is only when we come to understand the text-image relationship as a historical one, characterized by all the complexities and conflicts that plague the relationships of individuals, groups, nations, classes, genders, and cultures that our study might be freed from the craving for unity, analogy, harmony, and universality. Such a shortcoming Mitchell discovers in Marx's treatment of ideology, which is dominated by the image of the *camera obscura*. The *camera obscura* is thought to produce highly realistic images, exact replicas of the outside world. It is constructed in accordance with of a scientific understanding of optics, whereas the fetish serves as the antithesis of the scientific image, epitomizing irrationality in both its crudity of representational means and its use in superstitious ritual. Mitchell claims that there is a tendency in Marx to treat ideology and commodity as refined and separate abstractions instead of dialectical images. Ideology, which begins historically as an iconoclastic "science of ideas" designed to overturn "idols of the mind," winds up being characterized itself as a new form of idolatry. For Marx, ideology is primarily the false consciousness of the Young Hegelians who thought that revolutions could occur at the level of consciousness, ideas, and philosophy without a material revolution in social life.

Mitchell emphasizes that the problem with the facts and mental images of the empiricists is not that they are false, but that they are static and dead. There is no such thing as an ideology apart from particular social and historical tendencies, and the critique of ideology is possible only because of its localization and particularity. The iconoclast sees himself working from a more "advanced" or "developed" stage in the human evolution and, therefore, in a position to provide a historical interpretation of the myths taken literally by the idolater. While iconoclasm has a history almost as old as idolatry, it prefers to appear as a relatively recent revolutionary breakthrough overturning some previously established cult of image worship. The iconoclast chooses to believe that he worships no images of any sort, or at least that his own images are purer or truer than those of the idolater. The problem is that all this applies to Mitchell's "iconology" as well. While his historical analysis does provide some illuminating and intriguing insights and perspectives, it proclaims a relativism that must become self-defeating. His own critique of iconoclasm requires that we relativize and particularize our scope of investigation, and this inevitably defeats his purpose of providing a general theory of icons. He is thus unable to show that his dialectics can eliminate error and imperfection in images.

Notes

[1] W.J.T. Mitchell, *Iconology: Image, Text, Ideology,* Chicago, IL: University of Chicago Press, 1986.

Philosophy

Chapter Forty-One

Rorty's Pragmatism

Rorty believes that the attempt to explain the success of astrophysics and the failure of astrology is bound to be merely an empty complaint unless we can attain what Putnam calls a God's-eye standpoint – one that has somehow broken out of our language and our beliefs, and tested them against something known without their aid.[1] Rorty's pragmatism is thus unable to account for the success of astrophysics and the failure of astrology. Reducing objectivity to cultural solidarity, he aims to eliminate both ontology and epistemology. But to argue that we need not argue is still to argue; even if moved by the desire for solidarity he prefers the images of the Romantics in praise of poets to those used by the Greeks to praise mathematicians.[2] We talk of poets and painters as using some faculty other than "reason" in their work because, by their own confession they are not sure what they want to do before they have done it. If to be rational means to lay down criteria in advance, then it is plausible to take natural science as the paradigm of rationality.[3] But Rorty believes that it is characteristic of democratic and pluralistic societies to continually redefine their goals and, if to be rational means to satisfy criteria, then such a process of redefinition really is irrational. He sees himself as a proponent of what Clark Glymour calls the "new fuzziness," since he supports the attempt to blur the distinction between fact and value that the critical conception of rationality (i.e. of Hume and Kant) have introduced. To take Rorty's "unforced argument" as primitive is to ignore complex psychological, social, and economic factors that cause us to change our mind.

Rorty adopts the Davidsonian position that the term "true" should not be analyzed or defined. Combining this with what he calls "ethnocentrism," he maintains that our present beliefs are inevitably the ones we use to decide how to apply the term "true." In this manner he trivializes the term "true,"[4] making it relative to upbringing and culture, while insisting at the same time that there is nothing special about prediction and control.[5] The problem is that a pragmatism that renounces prediction and control will have a hard time distinguishing what works and what doesn't. While there may not be a "best" explanation for anything, we still need some sort of criteria to prefer one explanation to another. An explanation which merely suits the purposes of the explainer will not be able to convince anybody not already in agreement with his aims to begin with. Rorty denies that there is a general view about the nature of inquiry or a universal method of fixing belief, but what counts as "persuasion" and what as "force" is by no means easy to decide. It is not obvious when persuasion turns into brainwashing, and at what point the power to starve people into submission is to count as violence. Even if Rorty is right that "serious" politics is always reformist, these issues should not simply be ignored. Since "truth," for Rorty, is ultimately what gives us comfort, his notion of philosophy is not anymore likely to produce definite results than is literary criticism. He picks favorite philosophers by consonance with his desirata, realizing all the while that to make comparisons between different philosophers in this fashion is to discriminate unfairly.[6] Declaring his pragmatism to be "without method," he intends to render it immune to attack, but what cannot be attacked in this manner cannot be defended effectively either. He offers an analysis of science that construes the reputed hardship of facts merely as an artifact produced by our choice of language. Facts, for Rorty, are hybrid entities, that is to say, the causes of assertability of sentences include both physical stimuli and our antecedent choice of response to such stimuli.

Rorty would prefer to do away altogether with the notion of an ideal language and an ideal experience, but describing language as a "tool" or a "set of tools" is in the end no less metaphorical than had been taking it as a "veil" between ourselves and reality. All he can do is tell us a story about his favorite metaphor, realizing that he is unable to convince us, since he considers diverse language-games as incommensurable. As he is unable to distinguish between more and less useful language-games, he lacks convincing arguments for excluding any of them. Thus for Rorty, the views of idiosyncratic nature mystics are on a par with the views of professors of chemistry. The only objectivity he allows is agreement whether a particular set of desirata has been satisfied.[7] But the gap that is said to exist between language and reality is not automatically bridged when we say what we want. Rorty follows Dewey in holding that not all questions can be answered in terms of the alternatives that the questions themselves present. Progress is said to occur through the sheer abandonment of questions together with the alternatives they assume – we do not solve them, we get around them. But whereas Dewey still takes some sort of realism for granted, for Rorty there is no such thing as an intrinsically privileged context. The only kind of entities he admits are individual beliefs because he accepts them as equivalent to individual sentential attitudes.[8] He believes that whereas a sentence cannot correspond to anything real, it does correspond to a given belief or desire. But he also holds that a belief is what it is by virtue of its position in a web of other beliefs. He insists that there are objects that are causally independent of human beliefs and desires,[9] yet he never really gets outside his own head.

Rorty rightly realizes that interpretation is an exciting notion only as long as it contrasts with something harder, firmer, less controversial – something like "explanation" or "natural science."[10] When we are told that a certain activity should be viewed as *interpretive,* it is implied that we should not, contrary to our expectations, expect this activity to produce either knock-down arguments or a consensus among the experts. We should neither expect to have a natural starting point nor a method. But advising us to settle for such fuzziness is interesting only insofar as we have reason to think that other people, in other disciplines, manage to be less fuzzy than this. What constitutes a useful contrast is one of the crucial issues for Rorty's pragmatism. He denies categorically that there is *any* area of culture in which the essentialist has a point, but it is hard to see how such a "mistake" could have survived for so long and in so many diverse cultures. There seems to be at least a *prima facie* case for this doctrine, which enables us to simplify our environment and helps us to discover what it is that we really want.

Rorty questions Quine's distinction between areas of culture in which there are "facts of the matter" (roughly the physical sciences) and those in which there are not.[11] When these patterns of behavior differ widely, instead of saying that we have different world-views, cultures, or theories, Rorty prefers to say merely that communication becomes harder and translation less helpful. While talking about "essentialist instincts," he insists that they have no biological or social significance. At the same time, he speaks of objects as something we find useful to talk about in order to cope with the stimulations to which our bodies are subjected. Since these stimulations tend to cluster in certain typical ways, philosophers since Aristotle have explained them by means of essences. But Rorty wants to modulate philosophical debate from the methodological-ontological to the ethical-political key,[12] in this manner turning liberal democracy into a privileged context. Rejecting essentialism, he realizes, nevertheless, that it is virtually impossible to show that a language-game that has been played for some time is in fact dispensable. After five hundred years of experience with the language of secular culture, we are still not done with theological terminology in our moral and political deliberations. Even Rorty believes that we shall very likely continue to talk about mental entities – beliefs and desires – and that what he calls folk psychology will remain the best way of predicting what our friends and acquaintances will do next. But this is just to assume the "human nature" that Rorty supposedly rejects. His strategy to avoid these difficulties by giving up introspection altogether[13] ignores the fact that our ordinary talk about beliefs and desires takes introspection very much for granted. What the individual human being identifies as "himself" or "herself" is, for the most part, his or her beliefs and desires. Rorty admits that the picture of a network, which is not rewoven by an agent but reweaves itself, as it were, in responses to stimuli such as new beliefs acquired, is hard to reconcile with common speech, according to which the "I" is distinct from its beliefs and desires, picks and chooses among them, and the like. His pragmatism fails to give an account of why some metaphors are successful in the sense that we find them compelling, and make them candidates for belief and for literal truth.[14]

Rorty counts Davidson and Quine as belonging to the American pragmatist tradition,[15] even though Davidson denies this.[16] Whereas Rorty thinks of pragmatism as an "identification of truth with assertability under ideal conditions" – that is a privileged context, after all – Davidson does not want to see truth identified with anything at all. What Rorty calls "pragmatism" is largely a disinclination to talk in certain ways, in particular to deal with certain philosophical problems that originated in Kant's theory of knowledge. But deciding to take "true" as primitive in this manner, in effect, begs the question of assertability in an ideal context. "True" is said by Rorty to have no explanatory use, merely an endorsing one; thus, his pragmatism is no longer a philosophical doctrine in the usual sense to be argued about and defended. It amounts to stopping the playing of certain language-games without being able to give reasons for such a decision. For holists, like Rorty, truth is always evidence-transcendent,[17] so pragmatism isn't true either. That such sweeping pictures of the nature of language and reality are not called for is precisely one of the major points of a more traditional pragmatism. Rejecting the Enlightenment idea of "reason," Rorty denies that free and open discussion will produce one right answer. The effect of giving up this theory is to break the link between truth and justifiability,[18] including, it would seem, a pragmatic justification. He wants us to "bracket" philosophical inquiry, and put aside such topics as an ahistorical human nature by treating them as irrelevant to politics, as Jefferson thought questions about the Trinity and transubstantiation.[19] Rorty admits, however, that the question how we should determine what issues to discuss on political or on "theoretical" (for example, theological or philosophical) grounds remains unanswered.[20] There is no a priori way to decide what vocabularies and modes of discourse are going to be appropriate or useless. Preaching an "end to ideology," his own plea for pluralism and tolerance is no less ideological than is a neo-Darwinist "survival of the fittest." Rorty fails to discuss the crucial issue of how to defeat a free society against those who attempt to overthrow it by violence. Thinking of enemies of liberal democracy like Loyola and Nietzsche as "mad," Rorty is likely to *increase* the likelihood of violence in settling such disputes. He wants democracy to take precedence over philosophy,[21] but by declaring argument in favor of tolerance and representative government pointless, he reduces them to mere custom or arbitrary choice. He hopes that "light-mindedness" will make it unnecessary to offer such arguments because it will render these issues to be no longer threatening or indeed important. But it is only for a tiny privileged minority in the West that politics seems a "game" they can afford to ignore.

Rorty realizes that American society's self-image is bound up with the Kantian vocabulary of "inalienable rights" and human dignity, and that American society has traditionally asked to be based on something more than mere solidarity. For Rorty, by contrast, the principal backup for historiography is not philosophy but the arts, which serve to develop and modify a group's self-image by apotheosizing its heroes and diabolizing its enemies.[22] Moral dilemmas, in his view, are due to the fact that we identify with different communities and are reluctant to marginalize ourselves in relation to any of them.[23] But it would seem that the notion of "progress" in either rationality or morality is an instance of metaphorical metadiscourse that Rorty is reluctant to give up. Renouncing standards that are merely local, he concludes that there are people not worth understanding, and that those who disagree with us on fundamentals are to be treated as crazy, stupid, base, or sinful. This in turn is not likely to increase tolerance or make violence less likely in settling disputes on fundamental issues. To be part of society, in his sense, is to be taken as a possible conversational partner but, since we cannot escape our merely contingent spatio-temporal affiliations, Rorty really lacks any criteria for progress in either rationality or morality. He cannot know that the ideals of human equality and procedural justice are the best hope for our species, as he claims.[24] Rejecting the ahistorical ideal of a world polity whose citizens share common aspirations, he has a hard time reconciling private narcissism with public pragmatism. It is by no means obvious that Cartesian clarity and critical thinking are politically pernicious by preventing the solidarity Rorty aspires to achieve. Preferring the welfare state, he simply ignores the libertarian arguments that it diminishes human freedom and personal responsibility. His contrast between force and persuasion certainly demands more than an anecdotal treatment. He rejects the Kantian idea that we think of inquiry on the model of juridical proceedings, suggesting that we consider rationality not as the appreciation of criteria (as in a tribunal) but as the achievement of consensus.[25] This suggestion is in accord with Wittgenstein's idea that we think of linguistic competence, not as theoretical knowledge, but as the ability to get along with other players of the language-game, a game played without referees. So when we say that Aristotle and Galileo, or Holbein and Matisse, did not speak the same language, we should not mean that they had different semantical rules with which to organize their experience. Rather, we should say merely that there would have been no simple, easy, quick way for either to convince the other in a common project.

Davidson's point is that it is misleading to interpret the expression "the metaphorical use of language" as implying that lots of "metaphorical meanings" in addition to "literal meanings" are already present in our language. Metaphor does not expand logical space, for to learn the language is already to have learned all the possibilities for metaphor as well as all the possibilities for fact. No theory of metaphorical meaning or metaphorical truth can help explain how metaphors work. What distinguishes metaphor is not meaning but use – in this it is like assertion, hinting, lying, promising, and criticizing.[26] Davidson likens metaphors to pictures, and holds that words are the wrong currency to exchange for a picture. Another way of putting this is to say that the "irrational" is essential for intellectual progress. The irrational intrusions of belief that "make no sense" (i.e. cannot be justified by exhibiting their coherence with the rest of what we believe) are just these events that intellectual historians look back upon as "conceptual revolutions." Rorty adopts Davidson's theory of metaphor and concludes that things will get better for everybody if only new metaphor is given a hearing. The task of intellectuals in democratic societies is precisely to help their fellow citizens with the idea that we do not have an adequate language. Whereas the analytical tradition regards metaphor as a distraction from Reality, Rorty sees metaphor as a way of escaping the illusion that there is such a reality. He is, however, somewhat ambivalent about this, for he too would like his work to be continuos not only with fictitious literature, but also with politics, which is for him as close to reality as we are ever likely to get.

The only thing we can be certain about, in Rorty's view, is that we know what we want.[27] Liberal democracy, however, proceeds on the assumption that we know what we want only by hindsight; all our answers remain incomplete, and this is something that even most realists do not dispute. Rorty wants to recapture our sense of contingency by rejecting the philosophical tradition that what counts is literary truth, not the choice of words or metaphors. So, like Heidegger, he defends the poets against the philosophers by insisting that philosophical reflection is historical through and through and that no language is fated or necessitated. Forgetting this, we Westerners tend to think of poets as referring to the same old things under fuzzy new metaphorical descriptions, instead of thinking of poetic acts as the original opening up of the world.[28] Heidegger, however, was never able to shake off the philosophy professor's conviction that politics and art stand to philosophy as superstructure to base. So when he decided that Western philosophy had exhausted its possibilities, he concluded that the West had reached the end of its tether. Rorty, by contrast, predicts that things will turn out well in the end, even though his sense of contingency reduces this to a mere hope. Thus, his pragmatism turns out to be too honest to survive – since we cannot distance ourselves from time and chance by anything we may do, progress in rationality or morality becomes as problematic as is knowledge of any other alleged kind of reality.

Rorty wants us to give up the notion of "the limits of language," and thus Wittgenstein's early doctrine that there are things that can be shown but cannot be said. But he also wants philosophy to be more than therapeutic, even after he has asked us to resist the taste for theory as opposed to narrative. He claims the privileges of a novelist but his pragmatism remains a theory of human behavior, not just some sort of fiction. Like the rest of philosophers, Rorty sees himself as engaged in something more than a mere private project. Since no alternative can be shown to be superior to any other, neither can this be done for pluralism and tolerance. Blurring the literature-philosophy distinction, Rorty would like to eliminate philosophy altogether. Of course, as long as people agree on what is wanted and on how to achieve it, philosophical concerns will be at a minimum. But when ultimate goals are questioned, the appropriateness and relevance of vocabularies and ways of expression inevitably do become an issue. Philosophical problems arise when people take up alternatives that have not been envisaged before and thereby question a common-sensical belief that they had previously had no reason to doubt. Rorty wants us to give up the philosophical dream of finding the one true metaphor, offering us pluralism and ambiguity instead. But his criticism of Derrida applies no less to himself: when he forgets about philosophy, Rorty's own writing loses focus and point. His "soft" pragmatism offers us the metaphor of "reweaving a vocabulary," yet this never adds up to a conclusive argument because not enough premises are shared across competing language-games. Revolutionary philosophers, like physicists or even politicians, have always taken words and given them new meanings – but not to the point of terminating their own language-game. Rorty, therefore, doesn't succeed in leaving philosophy behind him; his hope that philosophy will "wither away" is not more realistic than was the Marxist prediction that the state will wither away. His ethnocentrism shows most clearly in the assumptions that the majority of contemporary intellectuals will self-consciously renounce ontology and essences, or that they are content to give up rigor and objectivity. To argue that rationality consists in the continuos adaption of our language in an expanding world or to investigate what metaphor can or cannot do, is to make a philosophical argument.

Rorty believes that the premise philosophy is pervasive seems plausible only if one identifies "the discourse of philosophy" with any and all binary oppositions. But his strategy of evasion merely turns philosophy enigmatic; it does not amount to an argument capable of convincing opponents. He tells us that he doesn't believe in philosophical argument because the only thing that can displace one intellectual world-view is another intellectual world-view rather than an argument.[29] He fails, however, to present us with a world-view that can take the place of philosophy; all he can do is to advise us to "forget" about certain philosophical issues. It is one thing to point out that philosophical arguments are often not rigorous, and quite another to deny their legitimacy altogether. The way in which we are supposed to "forget" our philosophical convictions remains obscure, and why certain language-games go out of fashion is something Rorty never explains. He certainly is not providing us with criteria to decide what is and what is not "pointless." If there is no preexisting logical space shared by such philosophical alternatives, there can be no rules or techniques for choosing between them either. Argumentation requires that the same vocabulary be used in premises and conclusions – that both be part of the same language-game. What Rorty wants us to do, on the other hand, is to use different vocabularies for different purposes without bothering about their relation to each other. He reduces language to human beings using marks and noises to get what they want,[30] as if this were not just another metaphor. We do not know what we want anymore reliably or definitely than we know what is real, nor is it any easier to decide this. Rorty would like to argue that there is no such thing as "language" but for the fact that this would make his own "interweaving" metaphor inapplicable. No language-game starts from scratch; it always arises form the modification of a previous language-game. Every metaphor presupposes a literal meaning in an idiom that is taken for granted, and that is why we never literally live in a "different world" after a conceptual revolution or paradigm shift has occurred.

Rorty wants us to discard the fallacy of unmediated expression, and to get rid of the metaphors of transparency and identity by accepting Saussure's claim that language is a play of differences. Signs have meaning by virtue of their relations to other signs – relations of similarity and dissimilarity rather than by their coincidence with something mental. Rorty further insists that all thought is in language, so that thoughts, too, have meaning only by virtue of other thoughts. Once one drops the essentialist idea that things have both intrinsic and relational properties – properties that they have "in themselves" and properties that they have merely in relation to, for example, human desires and interests – then a Saussurian notion of language and a Davidsonian account of knowledge follow naturally. Rorty generalizes Wittgenstein's and Quine's points by saying that the significance of a sentence like that of a belief or desire is its place in the web of all sentences, beliefs, and desires. He emphasizes the context-sensitivity not only of signs but also of thoughts by treating them not as quasi-things but as nodes in a web of relations. He prefers the metaphor of seeing ourselves as a centerless web to those of centrality and depth because he considers them to be more in accord with democratic politics. Thus, he concludes that the spirit of tolerance which is a condition for the working of constitutional democracies precludes our holding strong convictions of any kind. This, however, is likely to weaken the senses of personal and social responsibility, which liberal democracies require no less. Moreover, it renders Rorty powerless to change the *status quo* – political, economic, or philosophical – in any effective manner. He has very little to say about how power "corrupts," i.e. is likely to change our convictions and, therefore, to modify what we think we want. Denying that the *status quo* needs justification; Rorty in effect renders suspect any attack on it.

He denies that humanity is a natural kind or that it has a center; rather we are more like machines, and it is up to us to invent a use for ourselves.[31] The world of living creatures is as pointless as Newtonian mechanics has rendered cosmology, and the world in which we live no longer teaches us anything about how we should live. We, therefore, speak one language for Baconian purposes of prediction and control, and quite a different language for purposes of moral attention. Thus, contrary to his romantic leanings, Rorty is among those who have given up on the possibility of radical political engagement. His principal technique of self-enlargement (even if there is supposedly no "self") is the enrichment of language, the acquisition of new vocabularies for moral reflection. Since philosophy is incapable of contributing to such an enrichment, Rorty turns this task over to poets, novelists, and dramatists. His enthusiasm for mechanization and decentering is challenged by those who, like Heidegger, see the mechanization of culture a prelude to barbarism. Rorty thinks that his suggestion that our stories about ourselves as centerless mechanisms will seem to strip us of human dignity only to the degree that we believe we need *reasons* to live romantically, to treat others decently, or to be treated decently ourselves.[32] Somewhat naively he concludes that we will have fewer bully boys to cope with if people had more education, leisure, and money.[33] But being suspicious of all metadiscourses, Rorty is nevertheless incapable of giving them up. It is only in a formalized language like mathematics that one can legitimately speak of a metalanguage, whereas in ordinary discourse – and, therefore, in philosophy – this is only a manner of speaking. Like Feyerabend, Rorty sees scientific and political discourse as continuous; science is something that a certain group of people invented, in the same sense in which they can be said to have invented Protestantism, parliamentary government, and Romantic poetry. He, therefore, resists attempts to reduce all discourse to either science, politics (as did Lenin), or aesthetics (as did Baudelaire and Nietzsche). The trouble is that, on his own terms, Rorty cannot know *in advance* whether a certain language-game is to be avoided. He accepts with equanimity the fact that truth and power are inseparable, yet opposes violence under all conditions. He wants us to stick to the concrete, even though the concrete-abstract opposition is no less problematic than the one between theory and narrative. Rorty asks that intellectuals give up their traditional function of going beyond the limits, and use words that are not part of everyone's language-game,[34] even if that means giving up their innovative function in society. He wants to bring the philosophical tradition to an end, but he also believes in emancipation and progress. It isn't clear, however, how we are supposed to work for progress and rational change if we cannot even make a good argument for them. Rorty is a philosopher who claims a novelist's privileges, yet isn't content to offer his pragmatism as mere fiction.

514   *Soft Logic*

Notes

[1] Richard Rorty, *Objectivity, Relativism, and Truth, Philosophical Papers*, vol. I, Cambridge University Press, 1991, p. 6.

[2] *Ibid.*, p. 28.

[3] *Ibid.*, p. 36.

[4] *Ibid.*, p. 50.

[5] *Ibid.*, p. 58.

[6] *Ibid.*, p. 79.

[7] *Ibid.*, p. 90.

[8] *Ibid.*, p. 95.

[9] *Ibid.*, p. 101.

[10] *Ibid.*, p. 102.

[11] *Ibid.*, p. 103.

[12] *Ibid.*, p. 110.

[13] *Ibid.*, p. 120.

[14] *Ibid.*, p. 124.

[15] *Ibid.*, p. 126.

[16] Donald Davidson, *Inquiry into Truth and Interpretation*, Oxford University Press, 1984, p. xviii.

[17] Rorty, *Objectivity, Relativism, and Truth*, p. 147.

[18] *Ibid.*, p. 176.

[19] *Ibid.*, p. 180.

[20] *Ibid.*, p. 182 n15.

[21] *Ibid.*, p. 192.

[22] *Ibid.*, p. 200.

[23] *Ibid.*, p. 201.

[24] *Ibid.*, p. 208.

[25] *Ibid.*, p. 217.

[26] Davidson, *Inquiry into Truth and Interpretation*, p. 259.

[27] Richard Rorty, *Essays on Heidegger and Others, Philosophical Papers*, vol. II, Cambridge University Press, 1991, p. 29.

[28] *Ibid.*, p. 46.

[29] *Ibid.*, p. 121.

[30] *Ibid.*, p. 127.

[31] *Ibid.*, p. 144.

[32] *Ibid.*, p. 162.

[33] *Ibid.*, p. 162 n31.

[34] *Ibid.*, p. 176.

Chapter Forty-Two

Limits of Philosophy

Woods argues that much of what we think of as clarity and distinctness in our philosophical ideas rests on topological hygiene, mending fences, and defining boundaries.[1] Since Kant's day, the legacy of Euclid and Newton has faded and we are much more inclined to understand the transcendental more realistically either in terms of mathematical or physical models of experience or language. What consequently opens up are more complex topological possibilities that radically unsettle any simple assignation of inside and outside, and hence of limits. Contemporary philosophers are increasingly impressed by the impact of language on experience. If there is one thing Nietzsche, Wittgenstein, Heidegger, Foucault, and Derrida have each taught us, it is that traditional epistemologically oriented demarcation of the subject's relation to the world, in which perceptual knowledge provides a guiding thread, is fatefully undercut by the linguistic character of our being. Language understood in this way cannot be assigned a place within the traditional topological scheme of regions and linear limits. Wood emphasizes that our whole way of thinking about limits and whether or not they can be overcome is mistakenly visual. The most obvious meaning of "limit" is that of a boundary that marks off whatever is on one side from whatever is on the other. Much of the difficulty arises from the attempt to visualize limits using notions, pictures, and schemes drawn from geography, geometry, or real estate. "Being able to be talked about" does not seem to be a property in any ordinary sense, and there is a strong and important sense in which the idea of there being something that cannot be said is itself an effect of language. Language just is not the same as experience, but it intensifies experience by forcing certain ambiguities to resolve themselves and raising the particular to the level of the concept, as Hegel would say, for experience and language cannot be separated in a way necessary for experience to constitute a limit to language. Experience, in this view, is not a silent movie but a great Babel of voices interwoven with concepts and perceptual schemata, with much of the internal structure derived from language.

Any language, or particular conceptual framework, rests on prescriptions that cannot be made explicit within that language. Foucault and Gadamer agree that it is only through time (i.e. history) that the presuppositions of the present become visible and so discussible.[2] Whereas the early Wittgenstein and Heidegger agree that there are things that cannot be said ever, Foucault, Gadamer, and Kuhn hold that every overarching conceptual scheme rests on certain tacit assumptions that cannot be stated within that scheme but that the subsequent course of intellectual history reveals. We cannot, Wittgenstein declares, use language to describe the conditions of the possibility of language. But these remarks, and indeed the whole of the *Tractatus,* are the very sort of observations that Wittgenstein has claimed are not descriptive. And yet description is the essence of his account of language. While the limits of the sayable in the *Tractatus* are taken to be rigid, in his *Philosophical Investigations,* they become soft, a function of the various language-games we play. What cannot be said within one language-game may well be expressible in another, since there are no a priori limits to what can be said. Even in the *Tractatus,* Wittgenstein emphasizes that what we cannot say in language can nonetheless be shown, thus the wonder of existence cannot be expressed in a logically appropriate form, yet poets have been expressing the wonder of existence for ages. From a logical point of view one is "saying nothing," but what is shown or pointed at is of enormous importance.[3] Thus, Heidegger's questioning reveals a significantly richer understanding of language than is offered by the early Wittgenstein, and this leads to a different understanding of the limits of language as well. For Heidegger, it is language that makes it possible to think of possibilities, relations, complex times, and moods. To use language in a nonobjectifying way is to show what cannot just be stated, to point to something without directly describing it, to allow something to appear without slapping a label on it.[4] What Heidegger tries to do is to handle language in such a way that the uttering of descriptive propositions occurs as one possibility among others. What is unspoken is what cannot revealingly be stated in a propositional form, or cannot be stated without producing an essential distortion.

The rise of twentieth century positivism, logical atomism, and the linguistic philosophy were seen as the virtual eclipse of historical perspective within influential philosophical circles. The interpretation of history was often regarded as something of an intellectual swamp in which anyone with any ambition would soon catch the fever of "metaphysics." One of the obvious problems in a philosophical treatment of the history of ideas is that one is dealing with a succession of thinkers who were convinced that what they said was true quite independently of the time at which they said it. And yet the frames of reference they adopted (their conceptual schemes, their theories, their basic assumptions about the shape of knowledge) – things which seemed so self-evident to them that they often were not even visible as assumptions – these change from epoch to epoch. Foucault and Gadamer agree that our most basic assumptions about the nature of knowledge, the relation between language and the world, the division between madness and reason, always constitute a layer that is structurally invisible, and that we cannot make explicit at the time. In each case we have a limit to what can be said, thought, understood, communicated, even noticed. It is a limit of language, if language here is understood as the totality of available procedures for observation, interpretation, description, and explanation. What each of these accounts recognizes is that there have been enormous and characteristic shifts in these webs of comprehension. The question of the limits of language does not only depend on one's theory of language but, when one is dealing with these forms of structural invisibility, it depends crucially on the level at which the "framework," or whatever one wants to call it, is conceived.[5] Heidegger rightly points out that we cannot separate our "world" or our "existence" from the manifold linguistic practices in which we engage. When we think of language as essentially descriptive and as a means of everyday information, we distort our understanding of the "world" and our "existence" in it. It was Kierkegaard who emphasized that subjectivity cannot be communicated directly. He contrasts indirect communication using metaphor, parables, irony, and the like in which subjectivity is evident but not stated with ordinary direct communication in which, he claims, one is not really giving anything of oneself, and so it is not truly communicating. The sense and significance of there being something that cannot be said is itself an effect of language. We usually treat description as the paradigm of language use, and what seems closed or constant to description takes on a value that has often been thought of as transcendent, as beyond our ken. It is not that language cannot handle the transcendent; rather, the transcendent is the name we give to the discovery of the limits of descriptive language, tacitly but erroneously supposing that it names a realm that cannot be described. Wood argues that if we expand our understanding of the functions of language, our sense of there being such a realm will disappear.

Philosophy is said to have taken a "linguistic turn," but this is not a single-strained phenomenon. The reassessment of the relationship between philosophy and metaphor in the English-speaking world was precipitated by the demise of the logocentric view of language, language thought of as (literally) picturing reality, the breakdown of procedures for deciding on the metaphorical/literal claims made during periods of philosophical/theoretical transition from one frame of reference to another.[6] Metaphor, then, becomes part of a way of understanding language without a real job to do after the displacement of the locentric model. This way of understanding language takes for granted a rigid distinction between literal and figurative uses of language. With the disappearance of the belief that language pictures the world or directly represents it, the merely derivative status of metaphor is threatened. It is no longer at all obvious that metaphorical claims are to be treated either as literally false, or more charitably , as disguised forms of literal utterance, into which they should be retranslated. There is the recognition that at least some claims about the proper relationship between concepts (such as Ryle's claim that some statements are "category mistakes") are not eternal truths, but rather prescriptive reflections of the constitutive semantic order of certain language-games. Once we recognize that these games can change, there will be transitional periods (in science, but also in ordinary discourse) in which it will often be unclear whether an utterance is to be taken metaphorically or literally because no clear categorical structure is available.

After Aristotle, philosophers have often taken it for granted that there are different categories of stuff in the world, different kinds of being. A philosophical discourse that recognized this would be governed by an understanding of which words are proper to what things. It would not, for example, make sense to take thoughts as being located in space. Metaphor feeds on and exploits just such categorical confusion; it brings together things that should be kept apart. Metaphor, in short, is a threat to categorical order and hence to philosophy, for it endangers the Cartesian clarity and distinctness of our ideas. Metaphorical expressions, taken literally, are false, and when we probe them more deeply, we discover indeterminacy and vagueness. Metaphors work on similarity, and in some sense everything is similar to everything else, whereas philosophy requires identity and sameness, not merely the empirical relation of similarity. Figurative language has meaning only in so far as it can be given a literal translation, and it is more usually responsible for those misuses of language that generate philosophical error. The meaningful core of metaphor is discovered by translating it back into its literal origins, but already Nietzsche shows that the most primitive contact through sensations we have with the world reveals things to be of infinitely complexity. We pick them out in language only by means of certain particular features they have, and only in this manner do we get classes and categories of things to which we apply general words. In picking out these features of things and grasping them linguistically, Nietzsche's concept of truth (understood, as it generally is, as representation) is a kind of compounding of an original metaphor.[7] What this really suggests is that in philosophy the claim of truth is underpinned by a whole system of concepts and values, not just a single concept of truth in the abstract. One thinks of the foundation model in terms of "conceptual geography" or "logical space," and the spatial rhetoric of structuralist thought – of limits, discontinuities, thresholds, and the like.[8] Thus, the same metaphysicians who want to escape the world of appearance are destined to live perpetually in allegory and metaphor. Philosophers cannot acknowledge the metaphorical nature of abstraction, but neither can they escape it.

Metaphysics, for Heidegger, is philosophical thought alienated form the question of being, and as such it includes all philosophy since Plato. What Heidegger attempts in his later writings is not to go beyond metaphysics but to do something different, and this requires a new relation to language. Heidegger's later writings remain highly metaphorical, however, even though he claims that the very distinction between the metaphorical and the literal is one that makes sense only within a metaphysical framework.[9] Metaphor is traditionally based on the distinction between these predicates that belong to a certain subject

and those that do not belong. Wittgenstein was presumably drawing on
such a distinction when he talked about philosophical problems arising
when "language goes on holiday." However, in *On the Way to
Language,* Heidegger tells us that, in thinking, the important thing is
not to get anywhere else but to get where one is already, i.e. to
transform one's being, and in particular one's relation to language.
The same issue is taken up by Derrida when he discusses the nature of
writing, which might be called "parametaphorical." Derrida understands language, not via some relation to being (as does Heidegger),
but as the play of differences. The distinction between words and their
meaning is "in play" because the notion of metaphor presupposes a
level of semantic stability that Derrida has long since given up.
Derrida explains that he has to "borrow from metaphor" even to talk
about it, just as it is impossible in principle to step outside metaphysics. Deconstruction works from within, or on the boundaries of
abandoning or eliminating metaphor precisely because of its links to
metaphysics.[10] Derrida agrees with Heidegger that we are inside
language, but whereas for Heidegger this "inside" is a kind of
dwelling, Derrida emphasizes that we remain always on the move.
Heidegger may have released us from a naive acceptance of the
metaphor/literal distinction, but he still ascribes to language a special
sacredness, as it were. For Derrida, on the other hand, the very distinction between reality and writing is something difficult to make. His
philosophical methods are a self-conscious, transformative rewriting,
since he denies the implicit reference to a proper literal meaning that
this would imply.

Deconstruction is not reductionist in any simple way; rather it is
a critique that operates on the blind side of philosophical practice.[11] It
performs on philosophy an operation that philosophy traditionally
applies to the world. Philosophers do all sorts of things – explain,
analyze, argue, construct, criticize, etc. but the operation that seems
quite central is one of defamiliarzation, or distancing oneself form the
taken-for-granted. Deconstruction involves some sort of contradiction,
making use of standards such as rational accountability, which it itself
puts in question. The features of a philosophical text deconstruction
picks on are not logical inconsistencies, weak arguments, and unlikely
premises, but the features that seem philosophically most acceptable.
To say that all philosophy is writing is to claim that it is never a
transparent expression of thought. A philosophical text chases what
Derrida calls presence – self-sufficient accessible points of reference,

unequivocal terms, and the like – and it does so intermittently and always without success. Wood stresses the similarities between deconstruction and Wittgenstein's therapeutic model of philosophy. While for Kant, the general error of speculation lay in employing empirical concepts beyond their proper sphere, Wittgenstein's therapeutic approach to philosophy sees perplexity arising when language is disengaged from its proper everyday context of use. Once the perplexity vanishes, the philosophical problem has been solved, even if it is necessary to understand how it came about in the first place. But this need not be statable and need not apply to other philosophical perplexities. Not only is there no need for such a philosophy to institutionalize itself in a more systematic form, it arguably cannot do so because it is just such rigid formulations; such attempts to make language behave in artificial ways that generate philosophical problems. Wittgenstein not only abandoned theoretical truth as a goal in philosophy, but his practice resembles deconstruction in forging a counter-philosophical strategy.[12] His strategy involves a privileging of normal standard use over philosophical use and, hence we are supposed to need determinate context, settings in which language thrives in natural health.[13] But there is no therapeutic intent in deconstruction, since from a theoretical perspective the practice of deconstruction is self-defeating. Where Wittgenstein talks about language-games, Derrida refers to "play" and, contrary to Wittgenstein, deconstruction does not leave everything as it is. Derrida questions the distinction between relations of meaning and relations of association, and reading him brings about a more acute sensitivity to the figural and metaphorical dimensions of philosophical writing. "Metaphor" comes to be seen not just as one philosophical topic among others, but as playing a pervasive role in the construction of philosophical arguments. Metaphor and other forms of equivocation, ambiguity, figurative meaning, and semantic indeterminacy cannot be eliminated from philosophy. A complacent falling back to a therapeutic grasp of the philosopher's activity is likewise not possible because of the aporias latent in the goals of therapy itself.

History has witnessed considerable changes in what counts as philosophy, and there is no consensus. But there is a recognition of the weaknesses of a linguistic philosophy that is almost entirely concerned with ordinary language. English-speaking philosophers have been stressing the importance of clarity, yet Wood considers this insistence on clarity to be problematic: mere coherence is superficial, and it takes little account of the depth of a text. Philosophical terms and concepts are to be understood not just "in context," but in the way their meaning actively informs and structures a text, and this may occur at a number of different levels. Wood follows Hegel in arguing that formal thought destroys the natural movement of thinking, ignoring the self-modifying character of speculative judgment. That is why we are unable to give a formally adequate representation of dialectics. But following Derrida, Wood interprets dialectics as writing, for writing, unlike speech, renders time explicit. Philosophical truth is not a relation between a set of propositions and some real world; rather it is the reflexive structure of a text.[14] Examples of this are Nietzsche's multiple styles and Kierkegaard's insistence that true communication is always indirect. Nietzsche's basic insight denies that there are necessary connections in the world, that the world as such exhibits logical relations. He denies this also to language as a whole and claims that what we read off as the structures of language are no more than internal grammatical properties of a particular language. The referential and communicative success a language may have is the result of the implicit agreement to see the world the way a particular language depicts it. This is a product of needs and desires, not an appeal to an independent and neutral truth. Language is at base, he claims, a lie, but there is, nevertheless, a joyous affirmation of language's rhetorical and metaphorical functions. It amounts to the claim that the original relationship of language to the world is both negatively misrepresentation, and positively metaphorical and rhetorical play. No nonmetaphorical or unrhetorical natural language exists that could serve as a point of reference.

In *Beyond Good and Evil*, Nietzsche observes how unfailingly the most diverse philosophers always fill in a definite fundamental scheme of possible philosophies. Under an invisible spell, they always revolve once more in the same orbit prescribed by the unconscious domination and guidance of similar grammatical functions.[15] This bewitchment by language appears, he suggests, in metaphysical projections of the subject-predicate structure of grammar. It appears in the way the matrix of philosophical possibilities is set up by a collection of oppositions – reason and emotion, matter and form, subject and object, man and woman, good and evil. These oppositions supply us with analytical tools but also serve as invisible straightjackets for our thought, unconscious limits of which we are largely unaware. Nietzsche's point is that philosophy is seen to have come full circle, and to have exhausted itself. Heidegger's judgment on Nietzsche was that the will to power – the position from which he diagnosed the limits of all previous philosophy – was itself caught up in the circle of metaphysics, and this makes Nietzsche "the last metaphysician." The product is a philosophy that contests its own possibility, while at the same time never quite destroying it. Derrida points out that Nietzsche's text is marked by a strategy of writing, a multiplicity of styles, which not only renders its meaning radically undecidable, but which promotes the cause of undecidability. This started with Kierkegaard's account of individuality from the point of view of the thinker who reflects on his own existence from within. For Kierkegaard, subjective existence is no mere aspect of philosophy but the basis on which philosophical problems matter at all. When Kierkegaard turns the table on Hegel and claims that subjectivity is truth, what he means is that the essence of being human is one's "ethical" existence, one's commitments, one's relation to limit situations. The subjective thinker is significantly aware that it is he who is thinking his thoughts, and presumably what they mean to him in his particular state of existence. By "inwardness" he means that any thinking is both an activity not adequately reflected in a summing up of results, and ultimately something that concerns me and as such cannot just be said.[16] What he wants to express is not a fact about himself, not a state, but a striving, plagued by doubts, the risk of failure, and the need for constant reaffirmation. That is why all communication is in some sense indirect, and why there are limits to what we can communicate that are specific to one particular language, but that can be overcome by a change of style.

Derrida demonstrates the persuasiveness of metaphor in philosophy, yet at the same time he rejects the suggestion that we reduce philosophy to the status of metaphorical discourse. The idea of metaphor is historically linked to the notion of a proper meaning, or a proper application of a word, in which metaphor could be a replacement. The concept of metaphor is bound up with certain philosophical commitments for a privileged proper object for a name. In order for one's textual performance to have philosophical value, it must convince the reader that it demonstrates a general truth rather than an idiosyncratic one. Direct communication is unfit to express the subject's engagement with his own thought, the fact that his thought is a process, a thinking, and never done with, and that it is all this precisely to the extent that it is not given outward expression. Straightforward, declarative, descriptive language only nourishes the old philosophical illusion of the representational adequacy of language. But it is not the natural function of language to represent the world nor is language capable of doing so. Representation is just a philosopher's dream, perhaps the dream of philosophy. Nietzsche recommends that philosophers give up seriousness and recognize language for what it is, an expression of the will to power, and governed by aesthetic rather than epistemological values. Philosophy is essentially repetition, and its sharpest analytical tools rest on linguistic and philosophical conditions open neither to inspection nor reflection.[17] Even Heidegger came to realize that he cannot treat existence as a privileged source of primordial experience untouched by history. One specific change at which Heidegger aims and Derrida endorses (in "The *retrait* of metaphor") is an end to treating language as an instrument, a transparent vehicle of thought that could, in principle, be formulated in some independent fashion. Derrida's version is that the history of philosophy is one of presence, the belief in privileged points of reference. He opts for an obsessive, self-conscious and reflexive writing, for the traditional values of philosophy (truth, objectivity, reality) are none of them simple unities independent of language but always formulated in a syntax of truth/function, literal/metaphorical, objectivity/subjectivity, and the like. So when a philosopher appeals to truth, or even to subjectivity, as Kierkegaard does, he is making a move within writing.[18] Language is not an instrument of epistemology, and the ideal of a philosophical text that would demystify or enlighten us in the name of truth is no longer credible. The breakthrough to a philosophical "beyond" is a mirage.

Notes

[1] David Wood, *Philosophy at the Limit,* London, Boston, Sidney, Wellington: Unwin Hyman, 1990, p. xvi.
[2] *Ibid.,* p. 10.
[3] *Ibid.,* p. 13.
[4] *Ibid.,* p. 15.
[5] *Ibid.,* p. 20.
[6] *Ibid.,* p. 27.
[7] *Ibid.,* p. 31.

[8] *Ibid.*

[9] *Ibid.,* p. 35.

[10] *Ibid.,* p. 38.

[11] *Ibid.,* p. 42.

[12] *Ibid.,* p. 55.

[13] *Ibid.,* p. 56.

[14] *Ibid.,* p. 87.

[15] F. Nietzsche, *Beyond Good and Evil,* trans. Helen Zimmern, Edinburgh: Foulis, 1908, Section 20, p. 28.

[16] Wood, *Philosophy at the Limit,* p. 109.

[17] *Ibid.,* p. 142.

[18] *Ibid.,* p. 146.

Chapter Forty-Three

Philosophy's Future

Nielsen follows Rorty in arguing that there is no coherent knowledge claim that can be constructed as if we at last found nature's own language.[1] The philosophical illusion is that we can gain foundation knowledge of what is "real," and working from this, assess the soundness of various knowledge-claims in art, science, morals, religion, and politics. While he is convinced that philosophy cannot coherently go on in its traditional manner (including that of analytical philosophy), he still wants a philosophy that (in Wilfrid Sellar's phrase) is the attempt to see "how things, in the broadest possible sense of the term, hang together, in the broadest possible sense of the term." Although many philosophers – J.S. Mill, Spinoza, Plato, Bertrand Russell – have been philosophers in this sense, many people who are not in any technical sense philosophers – Fyodor Dostoyevsky, Heinrich Heine, Thucydides, George Eliot – have also been philosophers. Rorty construes philosophy as something that includes, but is broader than, the Descartes-Kant epistemology-based conception of philosophy. Nielsen considers Wittgenstein's *Tractatus* to be as metaphysical as the works of Aristotle, Scotus, or Leibniz.[2] Only with Dewey and the later Wittgenstein, he believes, do we get a firm break with the metaphysical tradition. Where Wittgenstein remained ambivalent and alienated, Rorty is quite at home in what he considers a post-philosophical culture. But contrary to Rorty, Nielsen believes that philosophical problems emerge naturally and repeatedly out of the natural and social sciences, literature, art, and out of life itself. Rorty's account undermines any confidence we might have in the powers of conceptual analysis to resolve or dissolve "conceptual confusions" emerging out of the sciences and everyday life. Philosophers frequently suffer from the self-deception that they have a mastery over "conceptual questions" that others lack, and that this gives them a certain expertise in the articulation and critique of culture. We should renounce the idea that we have access to some super-concepts that are the concepts of no particular historical epoch, and no particular profession, position, or culture. All that the argumentative abilities of a philosopher will enable him to do (that is, what is implicit in the stylistic variety of his work) is what a sophist or a good lawyer is adept at doing – namely to provide an argument for whatever our client has decided to do, to make the chosen cause appear the better.[3] We do not know what it would be like, Rorty argues, to have a set of critical concepts or categories that could in some nonarbitary way serve to order and assess the validity of various practices, language-games, and forms of life.

It is, therefore, not clear to Nielsen how, or even that, philosophy helps us to understand ourselves. He argues that the Kantian distinction between the analytic and the syntethic implies that there is some clear line of demarcation between philosophy and something else – a line that a philosopher must not cross if he wants to do philosophy. Professionalism with its drawing of boundary lines and its invocation of sanctions against those who cross them, its conception of what is central to "the discipline" and what is marginal, is the inevitable accompaniment of bureaucratization. Whether philosophy can in any coherent way have an overseer role is what is at issue.[4] McIntyre argues that demarcating astronomy from astrology (thus, distinguishing good science from bad science) is something philosophy cannot do.[5] Nielsen likewise believes that whereas physicists and chemists know something first-order, philosophers of science, with their second-order talk about the natural sciences, know something very modest comparable to what grammarians know about how language works. Logic, he believes, is a discipline of its own akin to mathematics, and there are the logicians (including analytical philosophers of science) and the lotus eaters, and nothing else in between. When we give up the Cartesian "mental turn," we give up the quest for certainty.[6] Nielsen suspects that there may be an unconscious nostalgia for the Absolute even among those philosophers who have consciously given it up. Like Rorty, he holds that we are plagued by irrational religious hang-ups, but contrary to Rorty he thinks it reasonable that reflective and intelligent human beings should want some standards of rationality and adequacy to assess the conditions of our social life. Rorty puts the very possibility of such a critical narrative in doubt, believing that even science must cease to be inquiry and become conversation.[7] He insists that we cannot break out of the web of language into some brute state of affairs, some fact that is nonlinguistically specifiable for a sentence to correspond to. Rorty is making the familiar point that scientists do not bring a naked eye to nature, and that the propositions of science are not simple transcriptions of what is present to the senses.[8] In saying that speech is not representational, Rorty is making the point that any specification of a referent is going to be in some vocabulary and thus one can only compare two descriptions of a thing, rather than a description with the thing itself. There is no privileged standpoint that can just give us the state of affairs as it is in itself.

Put in the older epistemological idiom, the principal task of philosophy is to ascertain how we can assess knowledge claims, i.e. determine what genuine knowledge is. The rationale for this is evident enough, for a sound epistemology would enable philosophy to set itself up as an arbiter of culture. On that self-image, philosophy is to determine when genuine knowledge claims in art, morality, religion, the sciences (both natural and social) and politics are made and what they are. According to this Cartesian-Kantian view, implicitly shared by positivists with their claim of having a criterion of cognitive significance, philosophy is "foundational" in respect to the rest of culture because culture is the assemblage of claims to knowledge, and philosophy adjudicates such claims.[9] There is no way of providing an indubitable foundation for knowledge, but there can be claims that do not claim certainty. Instead, we take the various activities – not only in science, but in art, morality, literature, law, politics, and religion – and investigate what knowledge in these domains comes to and the styles of reasoning involved in these practices. Contrary to Rorty, it seems that this means that we can say what is and what is not knowledge, and what it makes sense to say in a given context by representing what has already been certified as knowledge or as being coherent in some particular domain.[10] Nielsen insists that there is no epistemology that is purely descriptive, for what we are describing is knowledge *claims*. To display what mathematical knowledge claims and styles of reasoning look like is to play a somewhat weaker variation of traditional epistemology. To argue that epistemology cannot be normative is to make the very reductionist and critical moves that Rorty and Nielsen claim cannot be made. There is no radically different way of playing the epistemological language-game or of doing philosophy in a radically different manner. That there are forms of knowledge of which we are unaware of is certainly part of the philosophical tradition Nielsen says he rejects. There can be no coherent claim to knowledge in a particular domain if we a priori reject that we can ever understand what knowledge is.

The very doing of philosophy became problematic with Wittgenstein, but Wittgenstein plainly would have had no sympathy with Nielsen's attempt to show how the whole of reality hangs together. Wittgenstein stresses the plurality and diversity of language-games, practices, and forms of life, and how they set the very conditions of intelligibility. It is Nielsen who claims that, in spite of their diversity, such language-games and practices hang together, albeit loosely. At the same time, he maintains that our practices may well make coherent sense without its being the case that we can have a synthetic picture of how the whole of reality (as if we knew what that means) fits together. Doubts, to be intelligible, need grounds, must be specific, and presuppose the making of a language-game; whereas doubt about a whole language-game, form of life, world-picture, system of principles, or deeply embedded convictions is impossible, according to Wittgenstein. The concept of knowledge does not apply to the propositions that stand fast come what may, that are bedrock in a knowledge situation, background beliefs for the very possibility of our being able to make knowledge claims at all.[11] This certainty is less in our thought than in our practice of judging and acting;[12] these are not esoteric beliefs but part of our mundane commerce with the world. The difficulty is to realize the groundlessness of our believing.[13] Nielsen accepts the view that the system of framework beliefs is a kind of "preknowledge" (*Vorwissen*) that we cannot state as a set of axioms or be enumerated once and for all. In that respect, as in many others, our language is not at all like a calculus. This *Vorwissen*, however, hangs loosely together in something like a cluster, a network of interwoven properties. Such a "world-picture" (*Weltbild*) is the common ground we share with others in our culture; it comprises those deeply embedded elements that make communication, understanding, action, and a common life possible within a culture. Our quest for justification comes to an end, not in "self-evident" knowledge or necessary truths but in action. We must say in the end "this is what we do," this is the way we act and respond, and we cannot think, act, and respond otherwise. And this practice is not a more or less arbitrary and doubtful point of departure for all our arguments – rather it belongs to the essence of what we call an argument.[14] If you are not certain of any fact, you cannot be certain of the meaning of your words either.[15] We cannot discuss the totality of our system of convictions or render a unified perspicuous display of its structure. But we can describe certain parts of our "preknowledge," recognize how they are bits of the bedrock of *our* system, and how they relate to each other. We have no idea what the totality of our background beliefs is, and thus we cannot state this totality.[16] At any given time we operate with some cluster of groundless beliefs we accept and do not justify, and it is through the certainties of my way of believing and understanding that I gain my most fundamental understanding.[17]

The system of bedrock convictions constituting our "world-picture" has no fixed boundaries, for the concept of knowing is coupled with that of the language-game.[18] A language-game is a distinctive doing of things with words, as when we negotiate or claim to know or assent or question or pray or complain. Language-games are no more rigidly ordered than is an ancient city, and our *Weltbild* – the system of such convictions – is neither true nor false.[19] Resolving disputes can only take place within a system and about considerations internal to a framework, because a form of life is a loose system of primitive convictions, and a language-embedded mode of action. We would say of a person rejecting his own world-picture that he was mentally deranged, though he is not in error. Wittgenstein maintains that no argument or justification is in order here, though there can be persuasion leading to conversion.[20] Some things stand unshakably fast not because they are intrinsically obvious or convincing but because of what is around them.[21] We live and act and think within systems we simply are socialized into, systems we passively imbibe and learn to take on trust, and we do not know how to think outside that system. In the interaction of this network some beliefs will come into conflict or at least will not fit well together, and there will come to be anomalous situations. Certain beliefs, including sometimes rather central beliefs, will come to be questioned, but too much of what we understand being human, for example, is tied up with our having a head to make a headless existence coherently thinkable. Skepticism here is senseless.[22] Most of what we know or think we know of history and science rests largely on trust, and we have utterly firm primitive certainties that we cannot but take on trust. Wittgenstein maintains that gaining that kind of understanding, which would enable us to break with the tradition, will give us no guidance at all. Nielsen, following Rorty, on the contrary, believes that it will enable us to live and flourish without a philosophical culture as traditionally conceived. In that way – taking the fly out of the fly bottle – this understanding will help to emancipate us from the tyranny of philosophical obsessions.[23] Wittgenstein denied that he articulated philosophical themes, but this is a posture, a self-deception, for there are philosophical themes galore in his work. Wittgenstein gives, however, no encouragement at all to the idea that we may one day come to see things together as a whole, as Nielsen demands. Somehow Nielsen believes that there is no logical connection between Wittgenstein's *Lebensphilosophie* – his attitudes towards life, culture, and religion – and his characteristically philosophical stances as set out in the *Philosophical Investigations* and *On Certainty*.

Nielsen maintains that if we want to know what the basic features of the world are, we should go to physics and its allied sciences. Traditional philosophy, in his view, is essentially a quest for certainty, which is unattainable; however he wants to retain philosophy as a quest for meaning. It would certainly seem that those who are bored with philosophy or treat it with irony are not its most competent judges. The kind of fallibilism Nielsen defends is, when all is said and done, an epistemological theory, well within the skeptical tradition. Arguing that there are not and cannot be epistemological theories, he is playing a traditional language-game. Like Putnam, Goodman, and the pragmatists, Nielsen believes that justification is social and heterogeneous. Justification consists in giving reasons in accordance with certain norms embedded in social practices within historically determinate communities. Yet, this may not be any more decidable than what is basic or irrational. The traditional epistemologists' penchant for fastening on rather brute conceptual knowledge obscures its social nature and renders it prone to the solitary cognizer model. Even if there is no God's eye view of knowledge available to us, this does not make all knowledge claims ethnocentric, for coherence, suitably understood, is not at all implausible as a test, or a partial test, for truth. Nielsen, however, rejects coherence as a weaker form of foundationalism. The underlying common-sense assumption of realism is that there are truths about the world to be discovered in a verification process. Nielsen, on the other hand, insists that the correspondence theory of truth is incoherent, for the world does not consist of factlike entities of the sort that would correspond exactly to properties and sentences. He makes the by now familiar claim that objects and kinds do not exist independently of conceptual schemes. He follows Putnam in claiming that we cut up the world into objects when we introduce one or another scheme of description.[24] There are no self-identifying objects, rather it is we, conceptualizing in our varying ways, who sort the world into kinds. Traditional correspondence theories use the metaphor of mirroring, which Rorty and Nielsen reject, taking it, however, literally. Yet the mirror metaphor is only one possible version for characterizing knowledge as fittingness, and there may be structural similarity, as Wittgenstein suggests in the *Tractatus* or a weak kind of coherence. All Rorty and Nielsen can do is chose one metaphor rather than another.

Thus, the sense in which clothes fit the body is said by Alvin Goldman to correspond to the statement creating ability of the speaker. At the same time, it captures the basic realist intuition that what makes a statement true is the way the world is.[25] Custom and sartorial ingenuity decide what parts of the body to cover, what types of garment should cover what parts, whether garments should be loose fitting or snug, and the like. It is people with their interests, preferences, and inventiveness who devise standards for proper fittingness. Conventions determine the conditions of fittingnness for a given type of garment, but it remains the case that whether any given sentence, thought system, or proposition is true depends on something extra-human, namely, the actual world itself.[26] The conditions of truth are set by human convention and devising that, in many cases, answer to various human interests. Nielsen argues against Goldman that since there is no unique word-world relation that can be identified with truth, the correspondence notion of truth is untenable. Reference relations are always indeterminate, and this, according to Putnam, has key implications for truth.[27] There is no determining what is the correct reading independently of societal conventions or determinate uses of terms in certain language-games built into the linguistic practices of a given society. There is no truth to be had here that is independent of conceptualizing things in accordance with some conceptual framework. But there is nothing in the world that forces us to accept that or any other conceptual framework; there are no conceptual considerations of a pragmatic sort that may reasonably induce us to accept one framework rather than another. People and particularly different peoples, have various visions and versions of the world. To some extent, at least, it is a matter of consent how we individuate and count objects.

Davidson has denied that it makes sense to speak of alternative realities, each with its own truth untranslatable into another way of thinking.[28] We come to comprehend the language of others, including people from very different cultures with very different languages, in basically the same way we come to understand our own language, namely, by systematically grasping the truth conditions of the sentences in the languages in question. If I am a field linguist and I profess to understand the language of another society, in gaining such an understanding, I match its sentences with our own truth conditions. Davidson concludes that we cannot attribute a *wholly* alien scheme of thought to an articulate people. He argues that all of our beliefs cannot be false together, and that if we understand what belief is, we will come to appreciate that most of our beliefs are true, and that it is impossible that anyone could be mostly wrong about how things are. C. B. Martin[29] claims, however, that the skeptic is neither refuted nor do we have any proof that his concerns can be legitimately set aside. Everything here depends on the power of Davidson's a priori argument to show that the majority of our beliefs *must* be true. While Davidson calls our attention to a number of natural and reasonable enough assumptions, he does not give us a sound a priori proof or demonstration that they must be so. Consequently, he does not with his transcendental argument refute global skepticism or even properly set it aside. Davidson, in Martin's view, in typical philosophical fashion (the rationalist in us dies hard) tries to refute global skepticism and predictably fails. But Nielsen believes that if we communicate, and communicate across cultures, then it must be the case that most of our beliefs are true. It is more reasonable to believe that the skeptic's argument has gone wrong somewhere than to believe that there is no communication across cultures, and that field linguists and anthropologists always fail in constructing translation manuals.

As different as people are in various culturally specific ways, it is perfectly obvious (Michel Foucault to the contrary, notwithstanding) that there is at a certain level of abstraction a common human nature. All people have beliefs and desires and a language they use; moreover some of these beliefs and desires are very much alike, and the languages we use all find ways of expressing them. Given all this, we are perfectly justified in attributing to people in other tribes a massive number of mundane beliefs and concerns that run together with ours. We could not even identify an alien scheme of thought as an alien language if all or even the great mass of the utterances were "translated" in ways that made no sense to us or did not run together with a considerable portion of our common-sense beliefs. To have an understanding of different cultures, we must have such background beliefs, and they must be reasonably extensive. But it remains impossible for Nielsen to demonstrate that there are no untranslatable languages, nor can he really know that philosophy has no future. He believes that what makes us go wrong here is the deeply embedded basically Kantian conception that has its hold on both Goldman and Putnam as well as on Goodman – namely, what Davidson calls the dogma of scheme and reality.[30] This picture, Davidson thinks, is incoherent, as if there are various human schemes for perspicuously displaying this reality by categorizing it in different ways. But in the wide-ranging Kantian picture of scheme and content, there is no possibility of standing outside one or another of these conceptual schemes, and identifying the reality we are talking about. The kind of objectivity we achieve is not of a foundationalist sort, but a way of seeing how the sentences of a natural language hang together as part of a web of belief, and where truth conditions are in a parallel way mutually dependent. When another language of an alien belief system is in question, we have good reason to say that we have correctly interpreted it when we have got the sentences, devices, and feelings into a coherent set.

Justification is clearly something that admits of degrees. The problem is that Nielsen denies that truth is coherence or is what is maximally coherent. He could very well take "truth" as primitive, as Derrida does, were it not for his conviction that we need not try to state or search for any set of foundational beliefs or basic propositions that must be true in a correspondence sense (weak or otherwise).[31] Nielsen remains skeptical of Davidson's grand holism, given the multiplicity and complexity of social practices and that of related language-games, and the seemingly different styles of reasoning that go with them. But by the same token, Nielsen cannot a priori know that epistemology is not a viable enterprise either, or that there is no point in engaging in metaphysical inquiry, for that is precisely what he is doing himself, when all is said and done. His own supposedly holistic and empirically grounded account of knowledge is well within the philosophical tradition going back to Locke, on the one hand, and to Montaigne and the ancient skeptics on the other. Whether epistemology based philosophy has a future is not something he can a priori know or decide, since it is made up of precisely the kind of metahistorical statements he supposedly rejects. To find out systematically how things hang together is what the historical tradition has been concerned with all along; the idea being that this will give us the kind of certainty of which we are capable. The trouble is that Rorty and Nielsen ignore the historical impact of the philosophical tradition in Western civilization, in science, the arts, morality, and politics. Indeed that philosophy has no future was already argued against Socrates and has been a major philosophical theme in the twentieth century. Nietzsche believed that philosophy had come to an end, and so did the early Wittgenstein and Carnap, yet there has been no letup in either the quantity or the quality of philosophizing. To predict that philosophy (or even theology) has no future is to take precisely that God's eye view of the possibility of human knowledge that Rorty and Nielsen supposedly reject. Being skeptical of the philosophical tradition, they nevertheless remain part of it. To claim that all truth is historical is to do metaphysics, and is not, in the end, more coherent than other "realist" statements. Nielsen cannot help being what he calls "ontologically serious," and neither is he, of course, willing to stop doing philosophy or turn to other things.

Nielsen somehow believes that there is progress in intellectual history because human intellectual resources have expanded and developed in the course of time. At the same time he denies, however, that philosophy has progressed[32] because, in his opinion, "philosophy" does not name a natural kind – it has denoted various things in the course of its history. In the earlier periods philosophy was not clearly distinct from other activities, including science, whereas in the modern era, in the West, philosophy became an epistemologically based activity, claiming a disciplinary matrix that would make it cultural overseer or adjucator. Nielsen insists that we do not have anything that counts as a distinctly philosophical knowledge. All justification, it is necessary to recognize, is context-bound and inescapably involves reference to existent social practices. Since such practices not infrequently conflict, Nielsen denies that philosophy, even properly reconstructed, can play a critical or constructive role. In this manner, Dewey's instrumentalism conflicts sharply with Rorty's and Nielsen's aesthetic pragmatism. But against Rorty, Nielsen argues that even if one rejects foundationalism, and "timeless" questions and answers, there can be sound historically determinate arguments for resolving at least some of these questions. Like Rorty, Nielsen is convinced that epistemologically based speculation has no future, while advocating at the same time a philosophy focusing on how things hang together in a theoretic and systematic, that is, timeless fashion. He fails to explain how a piecemeal solving of problems is going to give us anything like a comprehensive vision.

Without a firm distinction between theory and ideology, we have no basis for the hope of making rational criticism of our social institutions. While there are no context-independent criteria of rationality and validity, we are nevertheless able, Rorty maintains, to solve such problems even thought our criteria of rationality and validity are only implicit and determined by our diverse language-games. It would be better, Rorty tells us, to be frankly ethnocentric here. To establish that our social practices of justification are more than just local has been philosophy's traditional interest in reason. What we should avoid, Rorty follows Lyotard in claiming, are metanarratives, i.e. narratives that describe and predict such activities as the noumenal self or the Absolute Spirit or the Proletariat.[33] They are bits of ideological mythmaking that distort our knowledge of ourselves and the societies in which we live. There is no supercommunity such as humanity itself with whom we can identify.[34] But in arguments against nuclear war or for preserving the global environment such overriding nonethnocentric considerations would seem to play a crucial role. Like Hume and Burke before him, Rorty takes humanity to be a biological rather than a moral entity; "there is," he claims, "no human dignity that is not derivable from the dignity of some specific community."[35] Liberal society, under the influence of the Kantians, has tried to ground liberal institutions on something more than mere solidarity. But that is a myth, for one cannot give an account of "rationality" or "morality" in transcendental and ahistorical terms.[36] At the same time, however, Rorty realizes that relativism is self-refuting, i.e. that he cannot simply accept the notion that every community is as good as any other. He believes that solidarity with one's tribe is a sufficient (and indeed the only) basis for solidarity. But sticking with that solidarity will bring the liberal into conflict with the Afrikaner, though it will give him no rational basis for criticizing the Afrikaner. What made liberalism attractive in the first place is that it seemed to have a place for humanistic values that could take one beyond ethnocentrism and tribalism. Rorty's democratic liberalism, by contrast, rests on an accident of cultural history. These views, Rorty is in effect saying, just happen to be the views that got socialized into him as he grew up in North America rather than the significantly different circumstances of Saudi Arabia, Nazi Germany, or the Orange Free State.

From a reading of *Philosophy and the Mirror of Nature* it is easy to get the impression that Rorty is telling us we should go from epistemology to hermeneutics, from systematic philosophy to edifying philosophy, giving us a new kind of philosophical theory. Edifying philosophy, with its hermeneutical turn, sees philosophy not as a rational inquiry but as conversation that can be civilized, illuminating, intelligent, revealing, exciting.[37] We move from a scientific style to something like a literary style, and philosophy is no longer to be viewed as an inquiry into truth or an attempted discovery of foundations. Yet, considerations of truth do not simply drop out; rather they enter, along with many other elements, into the conversation. Bernstein believes that Dewey[38] sees deeper and further than does Rorty or Wittgenstein as to what a reconstructed philosophy would look like. These issues cannot be resolved by appealing to existing social practices, for the heart of the controversy is the conflict of competing social practices.[39] Nielsen likewise appeals to a kind of *phronesis,* a type of practical reasoning that doesn't appeal to cultural foundations, eternal standards, or algorithms. The rationality available to us within this contextual fallibilism is always a form of persuasion that can never attain a definite ahistorical closure. Rorty rejects not only talk about conceptual foundations but also talk about methodology: methodological issues, however, remain all the same part of his argument. In reacting against scientism, Rorty, like Wittgenstein, is too ready to view science as just one language-game among others. He generalizes Kuhn's incommensurability thesis to apply beyond different scientific paradigms or disciplinary matrices to different political and economic arrangements, aesthetic stances, conceptions of philosophy, and religious world views. Levi rightly points out, however, that in no case are we just struck with incommensurabilites. Against Feyerabend, Levi argues that it is silly to give a serious hearing to every fool proposal that comes along.[40]

Nielsen concludes that it is plainly not the case in predicting what will lead to progress that anything goes, but he admits that he is unable to explain why this is so. One plausible explanation might well be that he ignores the epistemological role coherence plays, i.e. the notion of conceptual relevance[41] or of "soft" logic in determining what renders a context relevant. In attempting to solve real life problems of people (when language is not idling), and when faced with seemingly intractable conflict, we only need to keep reasoned argument alive and not block inquiry to be able to move to a point of view neutral to the issues under scrutiny. We do not have to be able to move to a point of view neutral for all controversies,[42] and we need not therefore assume that there are situations in which our intellects cannot give us guidance and discussions must turn irrational. Nielsen's rejection of the decision metaphor in favor of a pragmatic one begs the question of rationality, since the choice of model largely decides what "inquiry" is. If we are thorough antifoundationalist coherentists, we will not postulate incommensurable conceptual frameworks, or assume a sharp distinction between issues concerning conceptual frameworks. That seems to go with the rejection of a sharp, nonrelativized distinction between analytic and synthetic propositions. Following Kuhn, Rorty argues that controversies in the sciences do not differ in kind from controversies in politics and morals. When we look at various belief systems in different cultures and historical epochs, we are not confronted with unorganizable, distant world views. Morals, the arts, politics, and science may well be different life-forms with different ends and distinct rationalities, but they are all in important respects goal-oriented and, because of this, they share common norms of rational inquiry, and thus are not incommensurable. We may not be able to rely without supplementation on these general standards of rationality and scientific method for resolving all, or even most, of our problems. But in spite of his antifoundationalism, Nielsen admits that an underlying, commonly required method with common standards of rationality undercuts incommensurability claims and extreme forms of relativism.[43]

Rorty argues that he no more appeals to standards of objectivity and rationality than novelists appeal to standards of good novel writing, or that Newton appeals to standards of scientific inquiry. Typically a new history or a new theory or a new novel succeeds by striking its readers as "just what is needed." The opposition between rational argument and irrational persuasion is too coarse to describe what happens in intellectual history.[44] Against Rorty, Nielsen argues that sometimes the practices correct the standards, and sometimes the standards are used to correct the practices. We shuttle back and forth until we gain what for a time is an equilibrium. Recent developments in the philosophy of science, Rorty contends, show that we cannot hold theory and evidence apart in the relatively sharp way that E. G. Nagel requires.[45] There is no theory-independent objective given that we just take the evidence to confirm or disconfirm competing theories. Rather, Rorty argues, we should take pragmatism in Quine's way, as a holistic and syncretic theory. We must come to realize that appealing to the evidence is not a very useful notion when trying to decide what one thinks of the world as a whole.[46] We need instead, and in all kinds of different ways, to make adjustments from time to time in our intricate web of belief. Nielsen likewise argues that this nostalgia for the Absolute, this begging for some ultimate final context in which our deepest hopes will be met and our perplexity resolved is something pragmatists have long since overcome. But he believes that even with the demise of the tradition, philosophy as social critique would still be much to the point in setting out answers to such problems. Nielsen concludes that Rorty's "Pragmatism Without Method" fails to see that there is all the same in science a loose family of networks that constrain and help define scientific activity, and distinguish it from uncontrolled speculation and various a priori and intuitive methods. Rorty ignores the natural role scientific method (construed broadly) plays in our understanding of the world, and tends to treat science as just one language-game among others. There is indeed no such thing as nature's own language or a particular privileged vocabulary in which the world demands to be described. Rorty seems to assume that there is no progress in science and this is very counterintuitive; his "pragmatism without method" heuristically enmeshes us in a web of words from which Nielsen is unable to extricate us. Nielsen's problem is that he cannot carry out an effective critique of ideology on his own terms.

Notes

[1] Kai Nielsen, *After the Demise of the Tradition, Rorty, Critical Theory and the Fate of Philosophy,* Boulder, CO, San Francisco, CA, Oxford: Westview Press, 1991, p. 4.

[2] *Ibid.,* p. 9.

[3] Richard Rorty, *The Consequences of Pragmatism,* Minneapolis, MN: University of Minnesota Press, 1982, p. 222.

[4] Nielsen, *After the Demise of the Tradition,* p. 36.

[5] Alasdair MacIntrye, "Philosophy and Its History," *Analyse & Kritik* I no. 1 (October 1982), p. 108.

[6] Nielsen, *After the Demise of the Tradition*, p. 42.

[7] Jaegwon Kim, "Rorty and the Possibility of Philosophy," *Journal of Philosophy*, lxxvii no. 10 (October 1980), p. 579.

[8] Rorty, *The Consequence of Pragmatism*, p. 142.

[9] Richard Rorty, *Philosophy and the Mirror of Nature*, Princeton, NJ: L Princeton University Press, 1979, p. 45.

[10] Nielsen, *After the Demise of the Tradition*, p. 53.

[11] *Ibid.*, p. 95.

[12] L. Wittgenstein, *On Certainty*, Oxford: Basil Blackwell, 1969, pp. 24, 33.

[13] *Ibid.*, #209, #262.

[14] Wittgenstein, *On Certainty*, p. 105.

[15] *Ibid.*, p. 17.

[16] Nielsen, *After the Demise of the Tradition*, p. 100.

[17] *Ibid.*, p. 101.

[18] Wittgenstein, *On Certainty*, #560.

[19] *Ibid.*, p. 205.

[20] *Ibid.*, p. 471.

[21] *Ibid.*, p. 144.

[22] Nielsen, *After the Demise of the Tradition*, p. 110.

[23] *Ibid.*, p. 114.

[24] H. Putnam, *Reason, Truth and History*, New York, NY: Cambridge University Press, 1981, p. 152.

[25] Alvin Goldman, *Epistemology and Cognition*, Cambridge, MA: Harvard University Press, 1986, p. 152.

[26] *Ibid.*, p. 153.

[27] Nielsen, *After the Demise of the Tradition*, p. 78.

[28] Donald Davidson, *Inquiries into Truth and Interpretation*, Oxford: Claredon, 1984, pp. 183-241.

[29] C. B. Martin, "The New Cartesianism," *Pacific Philosophical Quarterly*, 65 (1984), pp. 236-58.

[30] Davidson, *Inquiries into Truth and Interpretation*, pp. 193-98.

[31] Nielsen, *After the Demise of the Tradition*, p. 88.

[32] *Ibid.*, p. 125.

[33] Rorty, "Postmodernist Bourgeois Liberalism," *Journal of Philosophy*, lxxx n 10, (October 1983), pp. 585, 587.

[34] Nielsen, *After the Demise of the Tradition*, p. 150.

[35] Rorty, "Postmodernist Bourgeois Liberalism," p. 583.

[36] Nielsen, *After the Demise of the Tradition*, p. 151.

[37] Richard Bernstein, "Philosophy and the Conversation of Mankind," *Review of Metaphysics,* xxxiii n 4 (1980), p. 765.

[38] J. Dewey, *Reconstruction in Philosophy,* Boston, MA: Beacon Press, 1957.

[39] Bernstein, "Philosophy and the Conversation of Mankind," p. 771.

[40] Isaac Levi, "Escape from Boredom: Edification according to Rorty," *Canadian Journal of Philosophy* xi n 4 (1981), p. 591.

[41] Joseph Grünfeld, *Conceptual Relevance,* Amsterdam: B.R. Grüner Publishing Co., 1989.

[42] Levi, "Escape from Boredom," p. 591.

[43] Nielsen, *After the Demise of the Tradition,* p. 175.

[44] Rorty, "A Reply to Six Critics," *Analyse & Kritik,* 6 n 1 (1984), p. 86.

[45] Ernest Nagel, *Teleology Revisited,* New York, NY: Columbia University Press, 1979, pp. 29-48.

[46] Rorty, *Pragmatism Without Method,* pp. 262-3.

INDEX

Ashmore, M. xvi, 235, 237-245, 247, 247n, 248n, 249n
astronomy 36, 41, 43, 47, 53, 443, 528
Augustine, St 181, 183n
Ayer, A. J. 317-18

background 79, 92, 114, 125, 135, 148-49, 161, 167-68, 176, 193, 198, 205-206, 245, 273, 276, 282, 289, 374, 394, 413, 416, 422, 432, 439-40, 472, 492, 530, 531, 535
Bacon, F. 55, 63, 147, 181, 497, 512
Barth, J. 249n
Barthes, R. 346, 352n, 416, 427n
Baudelaire, C. 513
Baudrillard, J. 337-39, 343n, 350, 352n, 407, 408, 409n
Beardsley, M. 229, 233n, 469
beauty 15, 40, 302, 442, 448, 467-68, 473, 492
Beckett, S. 400, 406
Beethoven, L. V. 407
behavior 7-8, 15, 21, 30, 32-35, 39, 42-44, 47, 92, 121-24, 127-28, 135, 153-55, 282, 289, 315, 323, 360, 366, 429, 432-33, 441, 506, 510, 521
being 68-69, 71, 82, 103-104, 114, 133, 137, 147, 153, 196, 269, 273-75, 293-96, 300, 357, 447, 463, 488, 518, 520
belief xiv, 24, 80, 104, 105, 108, 109, 119, 124-25, 127, 147-48, 151-53, 155, 157, 161, 166-69, 174, 177, 203-204, 207-208, 211, 220-22, 230-31, 237-38, 241, 244, 247, 260, 279, 284, 291, 301, 306, 311, 315, 318-19, 323-

24, 326, 357, 363-66, 371-72, 374, 376, 379, 381, 382, 411, 417-19, 422, 424, 441-42, 449, 452, 457, 459, 463, 469, 373, 475, 479, 487-88, 490, 503-506, 511-13, 518, 524, 529, 530, 531, 532, 534-36, 540
Bellarmino, R. 139
Bender, J. W. 441, 445n
Benjamin, W. 335, 348, 352n, 404, 407, 411
Bentham, J. 364
Berger, P. 248n
Bergson, H. 447
Berkeley, G. 449
Berleant, A. xxi, 447-49, 451-52, 455, 459, 463, 464n, 465n, 466n
Bernasconi, R. 80, 85n, 360
Bernstein, R. 106, 108, 110n, 538, 542n
Best, D. xix, 429-435, 435n
biology xii, xix, 32-34, 39, 41-43, 47, 57, 59, 63-64, 105, 116, 154-55, 207, 296-97, 319, 326, 365, 379, 380, 382, 415, 418-19, 443, 439, 473, 506, 537
bivalence 13-21
Black, M. 26n, 179n 203n 208n, 213n 216n
Blisek, W. L. 396, 397n
Bloom, H. 207n
Bohm, D. 300, 303n, 304n
Bohr, N. 150, 300
Bollnow, O. F. 456, 465n
Boltzmann, L. 139
Bonnard, P. 489
Boyle, R. 53
brain xiii, 9, 14, 16, 23, 25, 29, 46, 64
Braque, G. 345
Brecht, B. 405-406
Brentano, F. 125, 469

564 *Soft Logic*

319-20, 323, 331-32, 336,
340-41, 355, 358, 367, 375,
411, 417-19, 423, 461, 471,
507, 515, 518, 537
translation x, xiv, 47, 62, 80, 93,
99, 101-105, 122-24, 126,
128, 140, 142, 182, 216,
231, 236, 268, 333, 349,
358, 407, 437, 444, 506,
518, 519, 534-35
truth x, xi, xii, xv, xvi, xvii, xvii,
xxi, 4, 6, 13-15, 17, 19, 21,
22-23, 25, 56-57, 59, 67,
58, 70-71, 73-74, 76-77, 81,
82-83, 87, 90, 92, 96, 99,
100, 104-109, 119-121,
126-28, 131, 133-34, 136,
141, 148-50, 152-53, 155-
56, 158, 163, 165-69, 185-
199, 202, 207, 214-15, 221,
228, 231, 237, 239, 241,
243, 247, 251-54, 256-58,
261-63, 268-69, 272, 275,
279-82, 289, 291-95, 297,
299-300, 305-312, 319,
321-25, 331-32, 335, 338,
340, 347-48, 355-58, 361,
364, 367, 369, 375, 391,
400, 404, 407, 430, 437,
438, 440, 442-44, 447, 459,
463, 469-70, 472-73, 480,
481, 491, 496-97, 504, 506,
509, 513, 518-19, 521-24,
530, 532-35, 538
Turing, A. 8

Ullman, S. 118
Ulmer, G. L. 270n, 351n
understanding xiv, xv, xvii, xviii,
xx, 8-9, 17, 31-32, 36, 39,
42, 46-47, 67-69, 71-72, 74,
75-79, 81-83, 87-93, 95-
111, 113-114, 117, 120,
124, 126-28, 135, 141, 143,
148-49, 152-55, 157, 161,

165-69, 178-81, 185-86,
188, 190-99, 201-208, 211,
212, 215-216, 229, 235,
238, 240, 243, 247, 255,
260, 262, 268, 273, 276,
277, 279-82, 290, 294-95,
298, 300-301, 308, 315,
318, 320, 322, 323, 324,
325, 333, 335, 339, 348,
355-57, 358, 360, 368-69,
373, 379, 387, 392, 394-95,
401, 403, 408, 420, 425-26,
428-35, 437-45, 448, 454,
455-57, 461, 467, 469, 471,
472, 474, 479-83, 487, 489,
497-98, 508, 515-522, 530,
531, 562, 534-35
Urban, W. 114
utility 37, 61, 82, 120, 126, 133,
162-63, 188, 201, 277, 291,
297, 337, 366, 380, 401,
422, 472, 506

vague 8, 13-14, 19, 22-24, 69,
119, 120, 122, 124, 126,
127, 154, 180-81, 252, 368,
288, 391, 519
Vaihinger, H. 297-99
Valéry P. 474
value xviii, xxi, 14, 24, 40, 54,
56, 61, 87, 99, 120, 126,
132, 135, 137, 139, 142,
148, 155, 177, 180, 185-87,
191, 197-98, 230, 232, 262,
267-68, 272, 290, 292, 294,
296-97, 300-302, 311, 317,
318-19, 321-22, 324-28,
345, 358, 363-67, 369, 373,
374-75, 379, 382, 387, 393,
395, 400, 416, 418, 421-22,
431, 432, 437, 440, 442,
447, 459, 475, 495-96, 503,
518-19, 523-24
Vasari, G. 381, 492